Romeo and Juliet

Texts and Contexts

>‹

WILLIAM SHAKESPEARE

Romeo and Juliet

Texts and Contexts

—>‹‹—

Edited by

DYMPNA CALLAGHAN

Syracuse University

Bedford / St. Martin's   BOSTON ◆ NEW YORK

For Bedford/St. Martin's

Developmental Editor: Jennifer Blanksteen
Senior Production Supervisor: Dennis J. Conroy
Production Associate: Christie Gross
Marketing Manager: Jenna Bookin Barry
Text Design: Claire Seng-Niemoeller
Project Management: Stratford Publishing Services, Inc.
Cover Design: Mark McKie
Cover Art: (Top) Lorenzo Lotto, *Marsilio and His Wife*, 1523. © Francis G. Mayer / CORBIS; (Bottom) "The Gentleman. Lusty, or Sad: Thou Must Be Had," from Richard Day, *A Book of Christian Prayers* (1590); "Medlars, or Open Arses," *The Great Herbal* (1529); "The Bones of the Dead Shall Appear above the Sepulchers" and "The Mayde. Fresh, Gallant, and Gay: All Must with Me Away," from Richard Day, *A Book of Christian Prayers* (1590). Reprinted by permission of the Folger Shakespeare Library.
Composition: Stratford Publishing Services, Inc.
Printing and Binding: Haddon Craftsmen, an RR Donnelley & Sons Company

President: Joan E. Feinberg
Editorial Director: Denise B. Wydra
Editor in Chief: Karen S. Henry
Director of Marketing: Karen R. Melton
Director of Editing, Design, and Production: Marcia Cohen
Manager, Publishing Services: Emily Berleth

Library of Congress Control Number: 2002112227

For information, write: Bedford/St. Martin's, 75 Arlington Street, Boston, MA 02116 (617-399-4000)

ISBN-10: 0-312-19192-8
ISBN-13: 978-0-312-19192-4

Acknowledgments and copyrights are continued at the back of the book on pages 458–59, which constitute an extension of the copyright page.

Published and distributed outside North America by

PALGRAVE MACMILLAN
Houndmills, Basingstoke, Hampshire RG21 2XS and London
Companies and representatives throughout the world.

ISBN: 0-333-94713-4

A catalogue record for this book is available from the British Library.

For Chris R. Kyle

About the Series

Shakespeare wrote his plays in a culture unlike, though related to, the culture of the emerging twenty-first century. The Bedford Shakespeare Series resituates Shakespeare within the sometimes alien context of the sixteenth and seventeenth centuries while inviting students to explore ways in which Shakespeare, as text and as cultural icon, continues to be part of contemporary life. Each volume frames a Shakespearean play with a wide range of written and visual material from the early modern period, such as homilies, polemical literature, emblem books, facsimiles of early modern documents, maps, woodcut prints, court records, other plays, medical tracts, ballads, chronicle histories, and travel narratives. Selected to reveal the many ways in which Shakespeare's plays were connected to the events, discourses, and social structures of his time, these documents and illustrations also show the contradictions and the social divisions in Shakespeare's culture and in the plays he wrote. Engaging critical introductions and headnotes to the primary materials help students identify some of the issues they can explore by reading these texts with and against one another, setting up a two-way traffic between the Shakespearean text and the social world these documents help to construct.

Jean E. Howard
Columbia University
Series Editor

About This Volume

***

Contrary to popular opinion, Shakespeare's plays bear no resemblance either to mathematical problems requiring a solution (the meaning of the play) or to Sphinx-like riddles whose enigmas must eternally haunt us (the mystery of the play). The premise of this volume is that plays are dynamic works of art that give pleasure even as they press us to reflect on moral and social issues as well as on the aesthetic principles that inform them.

But if, as an art form, drama is a particularly open-ended dialog that engages with the specific circumstances of its performance, what are we to make of the big "unknowns" of Shakespeare's plays, all the questions that the dramatist raises but does not resolve for us? It is my contention in this volume that contextual materials enable us to transform speculative questions — about unrequited love, arranged marriage, parental consent, or the role of astrological predestination in human affairs, to name but a few — into historical and literary ones. In doing so, this edition pays particular attention to the ways in which the lyricism of *Romeo and Juliet* is expressed in relation to some of the period's most pressing social themes, especially freely chosen love versus enforced marriage. This is partly because in Shakespeare's day, the events and practices we now characterize as "social" or "political," were not regarded as the antitheses of poetic and other literary practices. Instead, they were understood to be profoundly intertwined with the aesthetic dimensions of Elizabethan culture. Looking at the play's contexts enables us to examine afresh the relation that ranges from mirror-image to antithesis — between life and art; between literary and non-literary writing; between the social and the aesthetic.

ACKNOWLEDGMENTS

I am enormously grateful to Bedford/St. Martin's editor Karen Henry for her extraordinary patience and kindness during the course of this book's production. I am also grateful to the editorial staff, in particular to Emily Berleth, Jennifer Blanksteen, Caroline Thompson, and Christine Turnier-Vallecillo at Bedford/St. Martin's, and Linda DeMasi and Kate Cohen at Stratford Publishing Services. Jean Howard, the series editor, whose intellectual generosity informed this project at every step, has my deepest gratitude. Without Fran Dolan's brilliant suggestions and unfailing encouragement, this volume would not have been possible. Her own book in the series sets the bar very high and provides a wonderful model and inspiration. I owe a particularly heavy debt of gratitude to Laurie Maguire and Lukas Erne, who helped me sort out the knotty business of textual scholarship for an undergraduate readership. As always, J. W. Binns gave unstintingly both of his friendship and his breathtaking knowledge of Latin in early modern England. Anonymous readers for the press offered sage and sound advice, for which they have my most heartfelt thanks. Georgianna Ziegler and Heather Wolfe answered several impossible queries along the way with their usual speed and erudition. Jay Halio generously shared his own work with me prior to its publication. I especially want to thank my students at Syracuse University and at the Cambridge University Summer School, who not only helped me shape and refine this project but also provided the incentive for undertaking it in the first place.

None of the research for this book could have been done without short-term fellowships from the Huntington and Folger libraries. In both places, the library staff was unfailingly helpful and gracious. Certainly, I could not have tied up the final threads of the book without the superb assistance of LuEllen DeHaven and Betsy Walsh.

My biggest debt of gratitude is to my historian husband, Chris R. Kyle, of whose prodigious knowledge of early modern England I availed myself at every opportunity. My labors are dedicated to him.

Dympna Callaghan
Syracuse University

Contents

—>‹—

Illustrations

Romeo and Juliet

Texts and Contexts

Introduction

><

Romeo and Juliet is both the preeminent document of love in the West and the most insistently and exquisitely lyrical of Shakespeare's plays. For precisely this reason, it is tempting to read the play as evidence of the capacity of love and Shakespeare to transcend time rather than as a work immersed in the dominant rhetorical and lyrical tropes of the 1590s. To suggest that this literary rendition of love is a product of its own historical moment denies neither its enduring appeal nor its capacity to speak powerfully to us today. For *Romeo and Juliet* addresses us more fully and more meaningfully in the present when we see the degree to which it is embedded in the past — the present of the 1590s. That is, the play is both of its time and of ours, but the emphasis of this edition is on the former.

Understood in its historical context, *Romeo and Juliet* challenges the notion of an absolute difference between the literary and the socio-historical. A love story is never just a fact of social history, a record in the parish register, or a matrimonial dispute at the church court, but is always bound up in the aspirations, fantasies, and desires of which the historical document about a marriage or an elopement is but a trace. In other words, love participates in those phenomena for which the literary text rather than the historical record is the privileged site.

Falling in love is a powerful experience, the description and consequences of which it is the special task of literature to extrapolate. More than anything else, literature takes as its subject matter erotic (especially heterosexually motivated) love, particularly at its most heightened moments, namely those at the beginning of a relationship and during courtship leading up to marriage. A country and western song about how disillusionment with brief sexual encounters provokes a longing for the depth of romantic attachment epitomized by Shakespeare's lovers, for instance, demonstrates the way the play stands as an ideal of erotic love:

> I get the feeling that he's never read *Romeo and Juliet*
> I'm getting tired of these one night stands,
> But if you wanna make a real romance
> I'm that kind of girl.
> — Patti Lovelace

Romeo and Juliet's relationship, then, stands as a cultural ideal that shapes our social understanding about what love should be. Since none of us hopes, consciously at least, for a bloody and tragic conclusion to our erotic relationships, why, we might ask, is *Romeo and Juliet* held up as the consummate ideal? Why do we believe that their love, which is ultimately suicidal after all, is both "natural" and perfect? The point of such questions is not that we should be more cynical. Rather, the point is to help us recognize that our received ideas about *Romeo and Juliet* can sometimes impede our understanding of the text itself.

The play, or at least the values the play has come to represent in the centuries since Shakespeare wrote it, in some quite profound sense also structures and contours hetero-normative desire, that is, the dominant, heterosexual paradigm of love in our culture. There is probably no expression of love, public or private, that is not in someway indebted, albeit unknowingly, to the ideas of love promulgated by *Romeo and Juliet*. Our individual psycho-sexual histories, whatever they may be, heterosexual, homosexual, or even those which from the normative perspective are categorized as culturally aberrant, are in part shaped by literary convention. This is because we experience desire only through the history of desire, both real and imagined, that has preceded us. Whether we accept the cultural ideal, as the singer above does, ignore it as does her boyfriend, or reject it altogether, we are always enmeshed in the normative force of this literary legend of love as a part of the cultural foundation for our desires and identities. Although we probably feel that we are at our most authentic when we fall in love, it may well be that we are at our most conventional, following social scripts and codes of which we are almost totally unaware. From "crush" (love at first sight) to full-scale infatuation, to the allegedly "mature" love that is less driven by burning psycho-sexual desperation to possess the beloved, we are almost living a literary genre. We feel compelled to arrive at the socially appropriate "next stage," however that is defined (the date, the kiss, the engagement are some of the usual heterosexual markers of the teleology of courtship). Love is rather like literary narrative in that, not content with where we are in the present moment, we feel a compulsion to press ahead, to find out how things will turn out. However, this "conventional" aspect of love should not be cynically dismissed as ungenuine. This becomes clearer if we understand "conventions" in the literary sense as ideational structures, which can enable beautifully poetic and poignant expressions of feelings without the connotation of calcified social convention, stifled emotions and dulled sensibility. Indeed, there is no essential contradiction between convention and desire because, as Catherine Belsey points out: "There is no unmediated experience located entirely outside the existing semiotic repertoire" (Belsey 53).

So profound is literature's treatment of the experience of falling in love, then, that we ourselves cannot easily fall in love outside its conventions. Those conventions have a specifically literary and more broadly cultural history, which it is the primary purpose of this edition to explore.

Love at First Sight

Falling in love is so compelling because fundamentally it is not, as many writers on marriage in the Renaissance recognized, an act of will, or a conscious choice of any kind. It appears to be instigated by something beyond and outside the self, namely by the (first) sight of the beloved. As one Renaissance proverb had it, "Love comes by looking in at the eyes" (Charney 9) or as Shakespeare puts it, quoting Marlowe's Hero and Leander in As You Like It, "Whoever lov'd that lov'd not at first sight" (3.5.83). Love at first sight is itself partly a literary convention and in Shakespeare's time derived most immediately from the Italian poet Francesco Petrarch (1304–1374). Petrarch recorded the exact time, date, and place he met his beloved Laura, Good Friday, April 6, 1327: "It was the day the sun's rays had turned pale / with pity for the suffering of his Maker" (Petrarch 3.1–2; see below, p. 298). This is a fateful day for Petrarch personally, and, because it is the day commemorating Christ's crucifixion, it is also the day of what Petrarch calls "universal woe." This inauspicious beginning marks the moment when the poet's life was changed forever; the beginning not of personal happiness but rather of complete emotional collapse. In his account of this fateful first meeting, Petrarch describes being fatally wounded with Cupid's[1] arrow: "Love found me all disarmed and saw the way / was clear to reach my heart down through the eyes, which have become the halls and doors of tears" (3.9–11). Aware that the poet is vulnerable in the eyes, love has found the direct passageway to his heart, and because this is in essence a tragic encounter, his eyes subsequently become the avenue for his heart's grief, the path of his tears. From this moment on, the poet is never the same. He has lost his former self because Cupid has opened his soul and given it to Laura. He can recover and regain the integrity of his identity only through union with Laura. This would require that she return his love, but she never will.

The convention of love at first sight is so compelling in part because it draws upon a perceived truth about the nature of desire. In the *Symposium*, the Greek philosopher Plato (428–327 B.C.E.), tells Aristophanes' story that all human beings were once quadrupeds, male and female conjoined in one creature, who were split in half when they incurred the wrath of the gods. From that time on, humans were destined to search and long for the lost part of themselves. According to Platonic theory, the striking moment of recognition often described as love at first sight is the apparent recovery of a perceived loss, and is, in some sense, a reenactment of the original, founding moment of our identity in the ecstatic merging of the lover's identity with that of the beloved (Joyce 38–67). In contemporary psychoanalytic theory, especially that of the French post-Freudian theorist Jaques Lacan, falling in love is thought to be a recapitulation of what is known as "the mirror stage," the phase of infancy when we are first able to recognize ourselves in the mirror. This moment is something of an epiphany, "Aha, that's me!" In an important sense, however, this moment is one not of recognition but of *misrecognition*. Because the image is not of ourselves, but merely a reflection, we have made a fundamental error. Nonetheless, from then on, we are all condemned to lives of longing for a figure who mirrors us. We aspire to a phantasmic state of primordial unity (the "me" *before* the mirror incident) of which we have no conscious recollection. It is important to remember that Lacan is describing the *unconscious* (unknown to ourselves) operations of desire rather than anything willed, intended, or conscious.

According to Lacan, we reenact this moment of misrecognition by falling in love, "Aha, that's my soul mate," and because this reiterates the earlier, more fundamental error that founded our identity, there is a level at which when we fall in love, we are always making a mistake about iden-

---

[1] **Cupid:** the child-god of love, son of Venus.

tity. If we hope to find the self we lost, paradoxically in the very same moment we recognized it outside ourselves, we are, like Petrarch, doomed to failure. In the play, this occurs at the most literal level when Romeo and Juliet discover that they have fallen in love with their enemies. Romeo's shocked interrogative "Is she a Capulet?" bespeaks his horror on discovering his mistake: "O dear account! My life is my foe's debt" (1.5.114–15). Similarly, upon discovering that the man she has just fallen in love with is "Romeo, and a Montague, / The only son of your great enemy" (1.5.133–34), Juliet declares:

> My only love sprung from my only hate!
> Too early seen unknown, and known too late!
> Prodigious birth of love it is to me
> That I must love a loathèd enemy.   (1.5.135–38)

Here Juliet metaphorically envisages the ominous progeny of this new love, which results from the coupling of incompatible entities, namely love and hate. The offspring of this ill-fated union is what was called in the Renaissance a "monstrous birth," the deformed issue of some inappropriate sexual union. (For instance, popular belief held that deformed children were the result of the copulation between humans and animals.) Notably, this image prefigures references to sight at the end of the play: "Pitiful sight" (5.3.174); "This sight of death is as a bell / That warns my old age to a sepulcher" (5.3.206–7). When Juliet's premonition comes true, death is represented as an horrific birth from the "womb" of the Capulet monument, which the Prince refers to with an image that connotes a sort of birth canal of death, "the mouth of outrage," and asks about the cause of the tragic events in terms of lineage and parentage:

> Seal up the mouth of outrage for a while,
> Till we can clear these ambiguities
> And know their spring, their head, their true descent;   (5.3.216–18)

Juliet sees early on in the play that this love is doomed from its moment of conception, and while this is a response to the very specific position of the lovers as the son and daughter of feuding parents, there is a level at which hers is an archetypal recognition. After all, is love ever what we thought it would be when we fall in love at first sight? And would it be a good thing if it were?

Of course, in the social reality of early modern England, people quite often married someone they had met only once before the wedding ceremony. As Ann Jenalie Cook points out, "The literary tradition of love at first sight may have received reinforcement in those social ranks where introduction to one's future spouse was sometimes restricted to a single visit" (Cook 152). Even this is a luxury not afforded Juliet when she is ordered to marry Paris: "I wonder at this haste, that I must wed / Ere he that should be husband comes to woo" (3.5.118–19).

What happens after love at first sight is, ideally, a love more consciously chosen than the unconscious rapture of romantic passion. When Friar Laurence discovers that Romeo has given over his love of Rosaline for Juliet, he quips: "Young men's love then lies / Not truly in their hearts, but in their eyes" (2.3.67–68). What are we to make, indeed, of Romeo's abrupt change of love object from one woman to another? Benvolio urges him to go to the Capulet feast and "with unattainted eye" (1.2.85) compare Rosaline's beauty with those of the other young women of Verona, and Romeo swears that he will be true to his first love:

> ROMEO: When the devout religion of mine eye
>   Maintains such falsehood, then turn tears to fires;
>   And these who, often drowned, could never die,
>   Transparent heretics, be burnt for liars!
>   One fairer than my love? The all-seeing sun
>   Ne'er saw her match since first the world begun.
> BENVOLIO: Tut, you saw her fair, none else being by,
>   Herself poised with herself in either eye;
>   But in that crystal scales let there be weighed
>   Your lady's love against some other maid
>   That I will show you shining at this feast,
>   And she shall scant show well that now seems best.   (1.2.88–89)

At this point in the play, before he has met Juliet, Romeo swears that his love for Rosaline is like a religion, the one true Church, and that turning from it is tantamount to heresy. We should remember that in early modern England, this is not just a metaphor. In the second half of the sixteenth century, in the aftermath of huge religious upheaval, hundreds of so-called heretics were burnt at the stake for their failure to espouse the state religion. We will take up the matter of religion in due course, but for now it is important simply to emphasize that Romeo takes love as his religion, and regards forswearing his first love as the conversion to a false and alien faith. Love based on sight then can be fickle. We should also note that even if Romeo becomes a heretic in love (a common Petrarchan trope) he will only exchange love's tears for the fires of a heretic on the pyre. Romeo never entertains the possibility of a happy conclusion, only the exchange of one pain for an even worse one.

Young Love

Several of the predominant characteristics of eros (sexual love) are worth emphasizing, partly because they are so familiar to us that they have become almost invisible. First, falling in love is a specifically erotic experience — we do not "fall in love" with our parents (or we do, in psychoanalytic terms, but we repress the memory of it), or with our children. In fact, falling in love typically constitutes a compulsion to move *beyond,* just as in the Lacanian drama of the mirror stage the spark of that desire that founds our identity involves a movement outward from our experience of the familiar, the infant "self" or proto-self, to the image beyond. Typically, in erotic love, we move outside our kin, clan, and immediate blood relatives in order make a connection with someone beyond this circle. So, incest and other endogamous relations (that is those within our own "network" or kinship group) do not comport with the normative understanding of the necessary ingredients of that heady experience of falling in love. Of course, this does not mean that there is no such thing as incestuous desire or that incest was never deliberately practiced to preserve property and power, especially among sovereigns and the aristocracy. However, incest does not follow the predominant cultural pattern, and there were numerous prohibitions against incest in early modern England, far more than there are now. Tables of consanguinity, the various degrees of blood relation, hung at the back of every parish church, and their violation contravened canon law and could prohibit a marriage, or invalidate it if the information came to light only after the wedding. The Capulet household condemns what it reads as Juliet's quasi-incestuous, excessive grief for her cousin Tybalt. Juliet declares the desire "To wreak the love I bore my cousin / Upon his body that hath slaughtered him!" (3.5.101–02). In this profoundly erotic statement, Juliet articulates the wish to transfer her love from her cousin, a love object within the family, to "the enemy," that is, someone outside it, namely Romeo. Of course, Juliet's parents interpret this as a desire to transform the love for her cousin into an act of vengeance on his killer. There is a deliberate ambivalence at the heart of this utterance, and as readers we can only assess its complexity rather than resolve the statement into a single meaning.

Typically the experience of falling in love is temporary — either the love is unrequited (as in Petrarch's love for Laura or Romeo's love for Rosaline), or the relationship matures from that first burst of psycho-sexually charged emotion. *Romeo and Juliet,* as we have noted, presents an exacerbated friction between the literary and the social, that is, between amatory eloquence and the familial, governmental, economic, and other forces that nonetheless shape and condition it. So it is that the conventions of lyric poetry are

Shakespeare's famous love tragedy *Romeo and Juliet* was probably written in 1595 and is roughly contemporary with his equally famous comedy, *A Midsummer Night's Dream*. In addition to the problem of dating the play's composition, there are three printed versions of the text. Although the complex

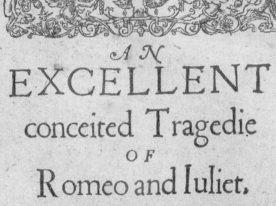

AN EXCELLENT conceited Tragedie OF Romeo and Iuliet,

As it hath been often (with great applause) plaid publiquely, by the right Honourable the L. of *Hunfdon* his Seruants.

LONDON,
Printed by Iohn Dancer.
1597

FIGURE I *Frontispiece for Q1*

textual history of *Romeo and Juliet* deserves more room than I can give it here, the basic outlines are as follows: The first Quarto (that is, a book made up of sheets of paper folded twice to form four leaves) of *Romeo and Juliet* was published in 1597 and is sometimes referred to as the "bad Quarto." Until recently, scholars believed it was based not on an authoritative manuscript but

(continued)

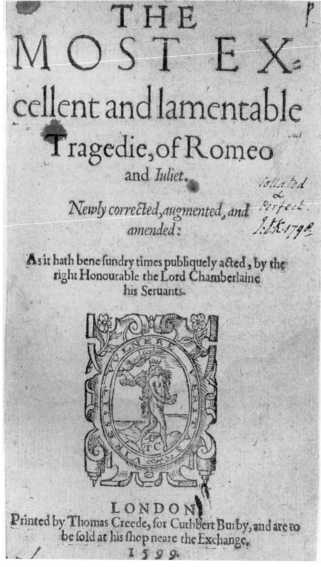

FIGURE 2 *Frontispiece for Q2*

Q1 AND Q2 (continued)

on an unauthorized version of the play, possibly one inaccurately recalled by a former member of the cast. (See Hoppe.) However, scholars have increasingly questioned the condemnation of the first Quarto, and critics such as Laurie Maguire have demonstrated that this version of the play could not be a memorial reconstruction. Recently too, scholars have argued that the "bad" 1597 first Quarto (Q1) may in fact represent a version of the play closer to the original performance than the amalgamated versions we now read. This is because in Q1 there are often fuller stage directions and superior phrasing (Watts 4). Critics espouse various theories of origin: Q1 is a Shakespearean draft or a longer version cut down for performance; Q2 represents that longer Shakespearean original or is an expanded and revised version of the draft of Q1 (Urkowitz; Halio, *Handy Dandy*; Goldberg, *Desired Texts*). Jay Halio explains that Shakespeare probably first wrote a full draft of his play. Since this was too long, the company subsequently made a shorter draft presumably with Shakespeare's approval. This revised draft became the acting version of the play and was printed in 1597 as the first Quarto (Halio, *Handy Dandy*). Q2 was printed in 1599, is 800 lines longer than Q1 and is on the whole of superior quality to Q1. Many scholars believe that this version of the play was printed from Shakespeare's first (and, obviously, handwritten) draft, usually known as his "foul papers" (Farley-Hills 27–44). There were subsequent Quarto texts published, but all of these are thought to derive from Q2.

To complicate matters, we have a third variant text, namely that included in the posthumously published First Folio (a much bigger book than the Quarto because the paper is folded only once to form two leaves). This is Shakespeare's collected dramatic works whose publication was overseen by his friends and fellow actors, John Heminges and Henry Condell in 1623 (Shakespeare died in 1616). This version probably also derives from Q2, but it is significantly variant in having no Prologue. The best thing to do, one might think, is to reproduce Q2, but alas this version also has its own flaws: like Q1 it has no act and scene divisions; duplicate speeches (a speech given to Romeo is also given to the Friar); and it has some very garbled lines, which may indicate its closeness to Shakespeare's unrevised thoughts. Modern editors rely heavily on Q2, which is thought to be closer to the Shakespearean manuscript while incorporating elements of Q1, which is thought to be closer to the play as performed.

---

pressured by the enormously controversial matter of children's autonomy in the choice of a marriage partner; but the influence may well go both ways. Young lovers in the 1590s who saw Shakespeare's play may have left the theater with new expectations about love, which may in turn have provided fresh ammunition in the battle with parents over the choice of a spouse. Even in our own time, expectations about falling in love and choosing a marriage partner are shaped largely by our culture's literary and cinematic renditions of love. In Shakespeare's major tragedies, the prognosis for more fully developed love relationships, especially marriages, is not very promising. For example, everything goes awry for Othello and Desdemona during the honeymoon period of their marriage in war-torn Cyprus. Similarly, the Macbeths seem to have achieved marital felicity, and we are given some intimation that the marriage has been a fruitful one, that Lady Macbeth has had children. Yet, the result of this conjugal harmony, and of what might be regarded as Macbeth's uxuriousness, is regicide and tyranny.

Indeed, it is a problem of genre that there is no such thing as a romantic narrative after marriage; somehow or other the story seems to end. *Romeo and Juliet* is probably such a famous love story because, instead of ending because the desire palls, their love is brought to an abrupt conclusion because of events outside themselves, thus giving the impression that the integrity of their love is never violated despite the tragic ending.

Love Poetry

What lends *Romeo and Juliet* its enduring appeal is perhaps that the fidelity and commitment of marriage are compressed into a heady and passionate one-night stand. The play challenges readers and audiences to reconcile stereotypes of romantic and literary love with social reality and lived experience, but it also demonstrates that even in real life, love is "always already" fashioned in the crucible of lyrical convention. *Romeo and Juliet* bears important stylistic affinities with Shakespeare's sonnets and was written at the height of the sonnet vogue. In the 1590s, the sonnet in particular, rather than plays, odes, epics, or any other literary genre, was the primary arena for the lyrical expression of love. The sonnet at its best is a metrically and rhythmically honed verse formation of pure love in a succinct fourteen lines. When the Scotsman William Drummond bought a copy of the 1599 version of *Romeo and Juliet* in 1606, he over-scored lines and phrases, especially passages of intense lyricism. He read the play, not just for the story, but for the language, selecting what were known in the Renaissance as "flowers," the choicest examples of poetic expression, the parts that were adorned or elaborated with poetic figures.

The model for the play's poetry, as we have noted, was Petrarch. His influence among English writers reached its zenith at the end of the sixteenth century. Petrarch was writing at the very beginning of the Renaissance, the rebirth of classical learning and the effloration of art and culture that attended it, a movement that came slowly from Italy into Northern Europe. Although he was a humanist scholar who did much work in Latin, the revered language of intellectual culture at the time, Petrarch became famous because of his work in the vernacular. Writing poetry in the actual Italian spoken by his contemporaries, Petrarch offered a model of stylistic elegance for all vernacular languages. In Italy, Pietro Bembo's prose *Della Volgar Lingua* (*Of Vernacular Language*) (1552) established Petrarch's use of the native tongue (rather than the other possible candidates, Dante and Boccaccio) as the model for vernacular eloquence (Kennedy x). The new heights Petrarch had scaled in the Italian lyric now represented a great new possibility for English poetry. The opportunity presented by a vernacular model was seized upon because English simply did not fit the metrical and syntactic model of Latin or Greek, the languages in which the vast majority of the West's great poetry had been written until that point in history. The great medieval poet Geoffrey Chaucer had appropriated Petrarch's sonnet 132 for the *Canticus Troili* in *Troilus and Cresseide*, but imitating Petrarch's great poetic achievement in English only began in earnest early in the sixteenth century. Thomas Wyatt (1503–1542) translated some of Petrarch's sonnets into English after visiting Italy in the king's service in 1527, and Henry Howard, earl of Surrey (1517–1547), used Petrarch to develop English metrical formations. Taking Chaucer as his model, Edmund Spenser expressed the explicitly nationalistic hope that "we might have a kingdom of our own language" (Kennedy 195). While many early English experiments in Petrarchanism met with only partial success — the verse sounded contrived and awkward, out of rhythm — by the 1580s, the English were hitting their stride, and increasingly managing to avoid the stylistic infelicities of the earlier phase. In the 1580s, when Sir Philip Sidney wrote *Astrophil and Stella*, a Petrarchan sonnet sequence about his passion for his unrelenting beloved, Stella (alias Penelope Rich), it became possible to conceive that, one day, a poet writing in English might rival Petrarch.[2] That day came, of course, with Shakespeare's sonnets, written largely during the course of the 1590s and published together with a longer poem called *A Lover's Complaint* in 1609.[3]

Though a famous humanist scholar in his lifetime, Petrarch is known to posterity for his unrequited passion for a woman called Laura, especially in his lyric poetry, the *Canzoniere* (literally "songs"), also known as the *Rime Sparse* (*Scattered Rhyme*). In fact, Laura was someone with whom Petrarch was probably only slightly (if at all) acquainted, but for whom he bore a love

---

[2] *Astrophil and Stella* was published posthumously in 1591.
[3] Some of Shakespeare's sonnets were published much earlier. See Duncan-Jones 1–28; Wall 188.

that ostensibly transcended the limits of an actual relationship. The influence of Petrarch was such that, as Gary Waller has observed, "it was impossible to locate oneself within the discourse of writing sexuality into poetry (or court society) outside the complex and inclusive code of Petrarchanism" (Waller 77). This code was constituted by a series of rhetorical conventions that took erotic desire as their subject. The beloved is a very distant object in the *Canzoniere*, giving the besotted lover only a chilly reception for his pains while he in turn is caught in a malaise, both tortured by his obsessive desires and convinced of their hopelessness. As a result, the Petrarchan lover is a melancholy, lovesick young man frustrated by his passions, while his unapproachable and unyielding lady conforms to a very rigid set of physical specifications: she has diamantine black eyes, hair like gold wire, cheeks of roses, teeth like pearls. That the *Canzoniere* was finished a full twenty years after Laura died indicates the formal, highly stylized nature of the love relations depicted there. Whether Petrarch's love for Laura was genuine or part of a prolonged exercise in stylistic eloquence, its metaphors and conceits became so absorbed into the culture that they changed forever the expression of love in the Western world (Musa xiii). Thus, it was not just the shape poetry took that was influenced by Petrarch, but even the rhetorical and emotional contours of love itself.

Before we first see Romeo, he is described to the audience as the stereotypically languishing lover and the description itself is rendered in idealized, poetic language. The love of Romeo for Rosaline is the embodiment of the Petrarchan cliché, full of exaggerated and empty poetic rhetoric with all the ingredients of grand infatuation. Little wonder that critics have remarked that in terms of psychological representation, Romeo is less mature than Juliet, as we see from Benvolio's description of this romantic anguish:[4]

> BENVOLIO: an hour before the worshiped sun
> Peered forth the golden window of the east,
> A troubled mind drave me to walk abroad,
> Where, underneath the grove of sycamore
> That westward rooteth from this city's side,
> So early walking did I see your son.
> Towards him I made, but he was ware of me
> And stole into the covert of the wood.
> I, measuring his affections by my own,

---

[4] "Juliet is strikingly similar to the heroines of Shakespeare's comedies. She leads the love game. While Romeo is frantic with grief in act 3, scene 3 and acting in a distracted, grotesque way, Juliet is always trying to cope with the difficulties of her position. She seems to grow up in the course of the action, to become more mature and self-directed, a development that is not equally true of Romeo" (Charney 84).

> Which then most sought where most might not be found,
> Being one too many by my weary self,
> Pursued my humor, not pursuing his,
> And gladly shunned who gladly fled from me.
> MONTAGUE: Many a morning hath he there been seen,
> With tears augmenting the fresh morning's dew,
> Adding to clouds more clouds with his deep sighs;   (1.1.105–20)

Romeo and Benvolio here follow Petrarch, who succeeded in wallowing in melancholic resignation and in nursing the sting of rejection for more than thirty years. Petrarchanism as a literary form is ostensibly dedicated to extolling female beauty, but in fact uses that beauty as an excuse for exalting a densely aestheticized, tormented masculinity. Denis De Rougement defines this "passion love" as "a historical fact" (De Rougement 7), which is not, of course, to suggest that love was invented at a particular historical moment. Rather, as De Rougement explains:

> At all times and in all places the *natural* growth of what I call passionate love has been visible. But alike in Greece and Rome and in the East the frenzy of passion was treated simply as a frenzy and nothing more. Not till the twelfth century . . . in Western Europe did the natural seeds of passion, instead of being destroyed, suddenly begin to be cultivated. The love frenzy was raised to the level of a religious wisdom. It was given a symbolical expression that made it acceptable, a dignified form, and a rhetoric that endowed it with standing. Unfortunate love was admitted to be beautiful and good to the extent that it was woeful.
>
> (De Rougement 7)

So, for example, a writer like the Roman poet Ovid (c. 43 B.C.E.–18 C.E.) gleefully celebrated the tribulations of adulterous love and seduction in the most mellifluous Latin, but he did not translate such exuberant eroticism into excruciating and indefinite deferral of physical passion. Ovid's lovers have far too much bounce and brio to forgo consummation, forever prolonging the pains of desire.

While Petrarch's poetry constitutes an enormous poetic achievement, the passion it describes disguises (or perhaps uncovers) a longing for death (De Rougement 21):

> Away from light steals home my heavy son
> And private in his chamber pens himself,
> Shuts up his windows, locks fair daylight out,
> And makes himself an artificial night.   (1.1.124–27)

Inherent in the Petrarchan form and extrapolated and dramatized in the play, is the sense that love is not all sweetness and light, but rather it also brings to the surface some of the darker, violent, and obsessive aspects of psychological need and sexual desire. The dark melancholy that is intrinsic to Romeo's character does not simply evaporate in the sun of Juliet's love but is played out as tragedy, as suicide in a charnel house. The approach of death intensifies eroticism and aggravates desire, as Maurice Charney points out: "[T]he death of the lovers — the *Liebestod* — is a fullfillment and consummation of their passion. Their deaths celebrate the strength and intensity of their devotion to each other" (80).

Passion of this Petrarchan type involves masochistic suffering and focuses not on the beloved, whose existence is really quite incidental to the self-involved torment in which the lover takes pleasure. This "passion" as in Christ's passion and death on the cross rather than simply inordinate sexual desire, is now infused with erotic intensity, which derives precisely and perversely from pain and suffering: "Passionate love, the longing for what sears us and annihilates us in its triumph" (De Rougement 61).

In relation to such a passion, the woman who is ostensibly the object of the poet's longing is entirely the product of the discourse in which she is placed, and her primary function is to offer an opportunity for the poet-lover to rehearse the turmoil and anguish of his own eloquence. Rosaline, Romeo's first love, has all the qualifications of a Petrarchan beloved: She has taken a vow of chastity and has absolutely no interest in Romeo. That she is never actually seen in the play may allow her to conform more fully to the stereotype of the cold, chaste, distant, and unobtainable Petrarchan lady. What then is the place of the female love object, the Petrarchan lady, in this passion? The rhetoric of courtship incorporated the idea that the woman had the power of a goddess because, at least according to the male poet, she holds his life in her hands. She alone has the power to save him from his torment, and if she spurns the lover, he is lost forever. That the Petrarchan sonnet was the dominant literary language of love in the 1590s is undoubtedly accounted for in part by the political reality that Elizabeth I encouraged her courtiers in rhetoric and behavior that was virtually indistinguishable from romantic courtship. In court circles, the frustrated desires of the lover and the wounds he suffers at the hands of his capricious lady served as a coded language of both political aspiration and profound discontent about the sometimes literal rather than figurative tyranny of the female sovereign.

The biological accident of a female ruler, a woman "on top," posed an enormous conceptual and practical problem for a patriarchal society that proposed sovereignty and femininity as mutually exclusive. One way of negotiating the inherent problem of female sovereignty was to adopt the ideas and rhetoric of the few anomalous spheres in which female figures did — at least symbolically if not actually — have some power. Such areas were myth (Elizabeth was likened to Diana, chaste goddess of the moon; Astrea, the goddess of justice; and Gloriana, queen of Edmund Spenser's Faerieland) and, of course, Petrarchanism. In his monumental study of European Petrarchanism, *The Icy Fire*, Leonard Forster has argued that these poetic conventions

> form the great international system of conventional love, between the chivalric love of the middle ages and the romantic love of the eighteenth and nineteenth centuries. Some of them are not dead yet. They rest . . . on one basic convention which sets the woman on a pedestal, and we are introduced to a world in which women dominate, seen through the eyes of men who languish and adore. This convention itself was a literary fiction to compensate for a real state of affairs in which it was a man's world and a violent one at that. (2)

The Petrarchan trope, then, contains a compelling male fantasy of female power and it does so in the service of the glorification of tormented masculinity.

The fantasy of female power, however, needs to be carefully and clearly distinguished from female agency. In some sense, women were always in the enemy camp. The Petrarchan beloved is potentially the poet's salvation, but since within the convention she refuses this role, she becomes the poet's adversary: she causes him pain, suffering, and torment, and because she will not relent and return his love, she constitutes the Petrarchan paradox, the "dear enemy." Forster points out that the enmity of Montague and Capulet makes the "dear enemy" into a concrete predicament; "the whole drama is devoted to bringing this cliché to life" (51). As we noted at the beginning, upon meeting, Romeo and Juliet discover that they were enemies before they even met. But more than that, love itself is figured as a process of ultimately fatal wounding — leading either to death itself, or, in the bawdy puns of the period, to the little death, the *petit mort*, of orgasm. Crucially, even in the latter case, love cannot be uncoupled from its intrinsic conjunction with death. In the Petrarchan precedent the wounding is one-sided so that the poet is grievously wounded by Cupid's arrow while the lady remains untouched:

> It seems to me it did him [Cupid] little honor
> to wound me with his arrow in my [unarmed, undefended] state
> and to you, armed, not show his bow at all. (*Canzoniere* 3.12–14)

Mercutio recapitulates this trope of one-sided wounding when he reports that Romeo is "already dead, stabbed with a white wench's black eye" (2.4.13–14). Romeo, in contrast, reports to Friar Laurence: "Where on a sudden one hath wounded me / That's by me wounded" (2.3.50–51).

Shakespeare, however, also runs against convention and has Juliet reverse the Petrachan paradox, "My only love sprung from my only hate!" (1.5.135) and iterate it in the conventional form after she hears that Romeo has killed Tybalt: "Beautiful tyrant! Fiend angelical!" (3.2.75). Even the play's physical violence, especially the focus on swordsmanship, is deeply implicated in this rhetorical structure. Jill Levenson remarks: "As a constant theme, violence in *Romeo and Juliet* complements the political implications of the sonnet idiom, the play's literary code: mastery in each demanded skill and had as its purpose establishment of social position" (92). Other critics have argued that the Petrarchan mode is in itself a form of coercive violence because it superimposes the subjectivity of the scripted speaker onto the reader: We experience the emotional world of the sonnet entirely from the viewpoint of the poem's androcentric, egotistic "I" (see Greene). It is this viewpoint Mercutio ridicules when he says that Romeo is without his "roe." That is, he is reduced to the self-pitying Petrarchan refrain on which the second part of his name is a pun: ME-OH!

Another rhetorical practice associated with Petrarch, though in fact only fully developed in the separate French Petrarchan tradition, especially the *Blaison Anatomique du Corps Feminin* (1536), was the *blazon,* the poetic inventory of the beloved's physical attributes (eyes like diamonds, teeth like pearls, and so on). Nancy Vickers has argued that the *blazon* as a list of the beloved's physically ideal attributes is a potentially violent dismembering of the female body. For Vickers, the female love object is the poet's victim, eloquently dissected in a quasi-pornographic rhetorical version of the anatomy lesson. She argues that as an itemized list of body parts and physical attributes, the woman is reduced to the very stuff of matter itself, to pieces — albeit valuable ones — of metal and stone. This discourse of the beloved lady as precious object is echoed in Romeo's elaboration of Juliet's beauty: "she hangs upon the cheek of night / As a rich jewel in an Ethiop's ear" (1.5.42–43) (Vickers 96; Greene 6).

The *blazon* was typically economastic, praising the lady as mute ideal, but it could also be satiric, and at least potentially, misogynist. It is in this parodic vein that Shakespeare writes sonnet 130, "My mistress' eyes are nothing like the sun," and that Mercutio teases Romeo:

> I conjure thee by Rosaline's bright eyes,
> By her high forehead and her scarlet lip,

By her fine foot, straight leg, and quivering thigh,
And the demenses that there adjacent lie   (2.1.18–21)

To conjure means to *raise* the spirit and is a joke about Romeo getting an erection, while "demenses" refers to property directly possessed and occupied by the owner and not leased out. Thus, in this mock *blazon*, Mercutio's witty obscenity includes the part of the female body that was not conventionally open to idealization, namely the pudenda, and he does so using a legal term that explicitly renders sexual possession as analogous to the ownership of property. Mercutio's subsequent bawdy and fairly derisive reference to female genitalia, as "fish" — "how art thou fishified" (2.4.32–33) — relates to the opposition between fish and "flesh" (the male member) with which the play and the quarrel between the houses of Montague and Capulet began:

SAMSON: 'tis known I am a pretty piece of flesh.
GREGORY: 'Tis well thou art not fish . . .   (1.1.23–25)

We are reminded several times in the play that discourse about women and sexuality, whether elevated and poetic or gross and bawdy, is intensely homosocial (and in the case of Mercutio, as we shall discover later in this volume, profoundly homoerotic) — that is, it speaks a language of tropes and jests that are primarily exchanged between men and only secondarily, if at all, directed at women. In this, such language parallels especially the manuscript circulation of sonnets themselves, which was primarily a literary exchange among men.

Whatever its subsequent satiric or misogynist renderings, in orthodox Petrarchanism, then, women are adored on a pedestal — honored, but also immobilized. It is precisely this paradigm, especially evident in Romeo's early love for Rosaline, that the play later contradicts. For what is most notable about the love of Romeo and Juliet is that it is a profoundly reciprocal passion and that Juliet exercises considerable agency — not simply the Petrarchan fantasy of female power — in achieving the mutually desired end of their love, namely marriage. Shakespeare places particular emphasis on Juliet's desires and on *her* history from cradle to the grave. Through her, the play marks all the major elements in the life cycle. From bridal to burial, we see her through (almost) two weddings and two funerals, and, through the Nurse, we know her intimately from infancy and adolescence in a way that we never come to know Romeo.

When Romeo woos Juliet with the religious, and (for the Protestant English audience for which Shakespeare was writing), dubiously Catholic and heretical language of saints and pilgrims, Juliet asserts herself as something other than a plaster saint or a woman on a pedestal, the cool Petrarchan lady. The lovers co-author a sonnet (although strictly speaking, if we take the sonnet to end not after the first kiss but after Juliet's response to the second one, it exceeds fourteen lines) in a sort of amorous duet registering both their voices and desires within a rhetorical convention that typically records only the inner turmoil of the male poet:

> ROMEO: [*To Juliet*]   If I profane with my unworthiest hand
> This holy shrine, the gentle sin is this:
> My lips, two blushing pilgrims, ready stand
> To smooth that rough touch with a tender kiss.
> JULIET: Good pilgrim, you do wrong your hand too much,
> Which mannerly devotion shows in this;
> For saints have hands that pilgrims' hands do touch,
> And palm to palm is holy palmers' kiss.
> ROMEO: Have not saints lips, and holy palmers too?
> JULIET: Ay, pilgrim, lips that they must use in prayer.
> ROMEO: O, then, dear saint, let lips do what hands do.
> They pray; grant thou, lest faith turn to despair.
> JULIET: Saints do not move, though grant for prayers' sake.
> ROMEO: Then move not, while my prayer's effect I take.
>
> [*He kisses her.*]
>
> Thus from my lips, by thine, my sin is purged.
> JULIET: Then have my lips the sin that they have took.
> ROMEO: Sin from my lips? O trespass sweetly urged!
> Give me my sin again. [*He kisses her.*]
> JULIET: You kiss by th' book.   (1.5.90–107)

"What makes this sonnet as distinct from others in the play (most obviously the choral prologue to acts 1 and 2 . . .)," writes Diana Henderson, "is its bantering dialogue after the ritualized octet, capped by a shared split-line finale to a protracted quatrain" (Henderson 1–7). This is a formal and highly stylized, though dynamic exchange, which lends gravity to the budding of this new relationship (Stilling, Ch. 5). Indeed, *Romeo and Juliet* in its entirety might be said to dramatize a sonnet sequence, and in doing so female desire manifests itself in concert with male attraction in a way that is simply impossible within the confines of orthodox Petrarchanism.[5] In

---

[5] Alan Hager has brilliantly suggested that the whole play is like an Elizabethan sonnet: "[W]hereas Petrarch's stanzas of eight lines followed by six lines (or, less often, six followed by eight) allow for a leisurely call and answer, the Elizabethan sonnet has three quatrains (four-line stanzas) crashing up like a tidal wave against a tiny couplet that tries to sum up or answer the twelve preceding lines. Complex ideas are answered in a few words that may resemble an

this limited sense, the play resembles Edmund Spenser's famous sonnet sequence the *Amoretti* (1595), written to woo his future wife, Elizabeth Boyle, because from the outset of this sequence, it is clear that the end of love is not frustrated male desire, but chaste, conjugal consummation. Even here, however, Spenser accords the male poet the controlling voice, whereas Shakespeare emphasizes mutuality.[6] Romeo and Juliet's "sonnet" consists of dialogue, exchange, and relationship rather than the adulation, frustration, and final victory that characterizes the *Amoretti*.

During the course of the play, events move from the social, represented by the prose speeches of the Capulet servants Samson and Gregory, to the romantic, represented by the play's extraordinary lyricism. At the end of the play, we are returned to the political world of Veronese society. The final movement is in part a return to the prosaic doggerel of the metrically flat-footed "For never was a story of more woe / Than this of Juliet and her Romeo" (5.3.309–10). But this is also in part a sacred transformation, known in Greek as *metanoia*, change of heart, a moment when ancient enmity becomes present love. We are no longer in the realm of lyricism and romantic love but in that of civic accord, the social bonds of amity that are underpinned by the innate capacity of eros to propel and extend itself from the lover to the beloved, and from the lovers to the wider social order.

Love as a Social Science

It is important, then, to recognize the specifically rhetorical, quasi-ritual conventions through which love is depicted in the play's lyrical and especially Petrarchan dimensions even as we acknowledge the important social ramifications of these ideas. In Shakespeare's time, ideas about romantic love, sexual relationships, and the organization of the family were undergoing drastic changes. As Protestantism emphasized the importance of marriage over celibacy and forged the ideological connection between the government of the family and of the state, the married couple as an auton-

---

aphorism, proverb, or jingle. . . . What happens if one reads the whole of Shakespeare's *Romeo and Juliet* as a celebration — and criticism — of the Elizabethan sonnet's form and content? One can see the sonnet used in significant scenes throughout the play, and its abrupt ending couplet reflected in the sudden, unexpected events at the play's end" (84).

[6] William Kennedy has described the *Amoretti* as being "unique in the canon of Petrarchan amatory poetry because it tries to resolve its social and sexual tensions in an approved Christian marriage, a resolution conservative in its outcome but revolutionary in its address to a readership familiar with the cautionary moralism of the Elizabethan sonnet craze" (Kennedy xi).

omous unit came to ideological prominence as never before (Callaghan, *Woman and Gender* 15–27). If the conjugal pair had new priority, then what was to become of the parental contribution to the choice of marriage partner? The struggle to answer this question resulted in increasing tension between parents and children over the matter of choosing a spouse. While in the medieval period daughters in the upper echelons of the social order suffered enforced marriage, the problem now manifested itself at all levels of the social hierarchy.

At the same time, there was greater vigilance about determining the legitimacy of marriage, in part to ensure that the wedding service was appropriately Protestant, but also to clarify in both legal and ecclesiastical terms precisely what constituted irreversible conjugal commitment. Getting married was far from being the single, incontrovertible act it has become since. Although certain property rights were contingent on a church wedding, and although marriage was widely understood to be a formal public act that took place in church, there were aspects of what was known as "the law of spousals" that led to conjugal irregularities. Such marriages included secret or clandestine nuptials, weddings without parental consent, Catholic marriages, and marriages that involved only the private exchange of vows between a couple instead of a church ceremony. Juliet explicitly rejects a private contract: "I have no joy of this contract tonight. / It is too rash, too unadvised, too sudden" (2.2.117–18) and urges the fully solemnized exchange of vows. Even so, the marriage of Romeo and Juliet might have looked far less certain to an early modern audience than it does to us today, at least until (though possibly beyond) its consummation in act 3. Solemnized irregular marriages were also prosecuted. For example, in 1598 Sir Edward Coke (1552–1634) made what was to be an immensely unhappy clandestine match with Lady Elizabeth Hatton. Ironically enough, the bride's father had only the previous year headed a large and vigorous committee in Parliament for reforms of abuses against marital regulations, which had attracted the interest of the queen herself (Dean 185). Upon learning of Coke's marriage, the archbishop of Canterbury, John Whitgift, immediately issued a decree against all such private marriages. The archbishop threatened the couple and the parson who married them with "the greater excommunication," the penalty for which potentially included forfeiture of goods and perpetual imprisonment (Warburton 28–29; Bowen 125). Only after careful negotiation were the culprits exculpated.

Whereas medieval society had neither the will nor the wherewithal to scrutinize its subjects, in Elizabethan England there developed a complex administrative apparatus — a tremendous increase in numbers of justices of the peace and other officials who monitored births, marriages, deaths, vagrancy, bastardy, criminal activity, and recusancy (failure to conform to the religious practices of the Church of England). The endeavor to determine exactly what constituted Protestant marriage (and in England, of course, no other form was valid) was part of this administrative expansion. Consolidation of the nuclear family, the little commonwealth, the microcosm of the social order, required formal, legal sanctification of marriage in an indisputable way. Even in the midst of their struggle to arrive at this state of affairs, authorities were obliged to uphold informal contracts as well as the legal and moral ambiguity that inevitably ensued from unregulated unions. A marriage ceremony was regarded as clandestine, argues Martin Ingram, when it neglected one or more of the canonical regulations governing the solemnization of matrimony. After 1604 this meant a marriage without three public announcements of the banns ("banns" refers to the notice in church of an intended marriage, issued thrice in order to allow time for objections) or the issue of a valid license, a ceremony conducted outside the diocese in which the couple dwelt, or a marriage performed during certain prohibited seasons or outside certain set hours, or in any circumstances save within a lawful church or chapel and in the presence of a properly constituted minister of the Church of England (Ingram 213). In the mid-1590s, when *Romeo and Juliet* was first performed, controversy over this issue must have been at a pitch, especially because only a few years later the canons, that is the ecclesiastical regulations, of 1604 (which were never ratified by Parliament) also insisted on parental consent for couples under twenty-one, although it could not actually invalidate marriages without such consent (Gowing, *Domestic* 157).

At every social level, all manner of people from the crown to a couple's parents or masters might have a vested interest in the marriage of those associated or related to them. What is beyond the shadow of a doubt is that many young people did not control their own marriages and could wrest only a partial degree of autonomy from social and family networks on whom they necessarily still relied when they were married. For most people, freedom of choice in marriage was severely circumscribed by social pressures, which intensified towards the top of the class hierarchy. The play's characters represent powerful Veronese families of the rank that in England would be expected to practice arranged and enforced marriage.

In England, at the top of the social order, Queen Elizabeth I certainly controlled the marriages of her nobles as a matter of personal idiosyncrasy and usually took umbrage when dashing young courtiers had the temerity to enter into the married state without her consent. In July 1592, for example, she had Walter Raleigh put to the Tower for marrying Elizabeth Throckmorton. The crown as an institution further sought to regulate marriages among its subjects for political and fiscal reasons. One of its means of exercising this control was the court of wards, an institution that essentially sold fatherless heirs into marriage and did so even while their mothers and other close relatives were still alive. Like the long-lived feud between the Montagues and Capulets, which weighs so heavily on the lives of the next generation, wardship was similarly a vestige of the defunct feudal system, an ancient practice reinvigorated by Elizabeth's chief minister, Lord Burghley. Whereas, theoretically, feudalism posited all wealth and property (land tenure), and therefore all transactions related to it, including marriage, as ultimately belonging to and deriving from the Crown, in practice the system was incapable of efficiently controlling and collecting on economic and social relations. Not so the Elizabethan government. "The crown established more firmly, and openly proclaimed, its control over the main items of its feudal revenue and stood ready to tap these sources more effectively than it had done for generations," argues Joel Hurstfield. "In so doing it would make . . . marriage pay a dividend greater than ever before in its long history" (17). Comparing Shakespeare's Escalus, the Prince of Verona, with Burghley is instructive here, since neither of them is so much the champion of free choice in marriage as the instrument of centralized social control. As modern readers, then, we would be wrong to assume that the Prince represents the rights of children over parents. To an early modern audience, he might well represent the rights of the crown over wealthy young people above and beyond those of their own families. When Burghley's own ward, Henry Wriothesley, the earl of Southampton (Shakespeare's patron and arguably the young man of his sonnets) refused to marry Lady Elizabeth Vere in 1591, he was fined the then enormous sum of £5000 (Akrigg, *Shakespeare* 31–33; 228–39; see also Hurstfield). At least this young man could afford to resist coercion, but those with fewer resources were not so lucky. Some children were bartered into wealthy marriages before they were even old enough to object. Although the average early modern Englishwoman was in her mid-twenties when she married, there were exceptions such as Lucy Hastings, daughter of attorney general for Ireland, Sir John Davies, and the marvelously eccentric writer and prophetess, Lady Eleanor Audley. With a dowry of £6500, Lucy was married to Ferdinando Hastings, earl of Huntington, in 1623 when she was only ten years old (Cope, 26). Because she was not of legal age for marriage, however, she had to be married without a license (Roy Porter 52).

In the meeting between Capulet and Paris (1.2), we are given the impression that their current conversation is but one of many that have gone on before, and therefore that while Paris may not have received much encouragement, he has not been dismissed outright:

> PARIS: ... [W]hat say you to my suit?
> CAPULET: But saying o'er what I have said before:
> My child is yet a stranger in the world; (1.2.6–8)

Yet when we next see Capulet with Paris after Tybalt's death, he tells Paris that he has not had time to persuade Juliet to the match, "Things have fallen out, sir, so unluckily / That we have had no time to move our daughter" (3.4.1–2). At this point in the dialogue, it seems that Juliet's consent is still necessary to the making of the match. Then, however, Capulet shifts abruptly into making a unilateral decision that Juliet will be married:

> PARIS: Madam, good night. Commend me to your daughter.
> WIFE: I will, and know her mind early tomorrow.
> Tonight she's mewed up to her heaviness.
> CAPULET: Sir Paris, I will make a desperate tender
> Of my child's love. I think she will be ruled
> In all respects by me; nay, more, I doubt it not.
> Wife, go you to her ere you go to bed,
> . . . .
> O' Thursday, tell her,
> She shall be married to this noble earl. (3.4.9–21 ff)

At this point in the play, consideration of Juliet's desires has been eliminated from the marriage negotiations. Further, the rash decision, the "desperate tender" of his daughter, marks a point in the play where Shakespeare departs from his primary source, Arthur Brooke's narrative poem, where it is Lady Capulet, and not Juliet's father who suggests the marriage (Evans 144). Its suddenness is further emphasized in Q1, the 1597 version of the play, where the stage direction reads: "Paris offers to go in, and Capulet calls him in again." How are we to understand this brief scene? How might Juliet's mother have reacted on stage to the news of her daughter's imminent nuptial? Performance choices here will certainly direct the audience's interpretation of the scene, and the direction from Q1 may give some indication of how the scene was played in its original performance. Even without that information, it is clear that Capulet does not trouble to discuss matters further with his wife, even though she is with him at the time of his decision. Rather, she is the person to whom he conveys his orders, not the helpmeet who shares his decision-making processes.

In early modern England, such decisions caused tension not only between parents and children, but also between the parents themselves. Sir Edward

Coke (he of the clandestine marriage cited earlier and sometime attorney general of England) tried in 1617 to marry Frances, his fourteen year-old daughter, to Sir John Villiers, the brother of King James I's rising favorite. Out of office at the time, Coke's motivations for the marriage were wholly political. Sir John protested that Frances was so pretty he would take her penniless, "in her smock." However, this assertion was probably disingenuous since it was reported by the Jacobean newsletter writer John Chamberlain that he had in fact been offered a £20,000 dowry, 2,000 marks yearly maintenance (a mark was a monetary denomination of 13 shillings and fourpence), and £2,000 worth of land on Coke's decease (Chamberlain 182). Like Capulet, whose final agreement with Paris does not involve consultation with his wife, Coke entered into negotiations without the consent of either his daughter or her mother, causing them to flee, pursued by a furious Coke who broke down doors in the recovery his daughter. Frances was coerced, not just by her father, but by both her parents in different directions. In the end, Coke's will prevailed, and, with the assistance of the Privy Council, Frances was married off to Villiers. Connubial bliss was rarely, if ever, the outcome of enforced marriage, and predictably perhaps, this couple did not succeed in living together happily ever after.[7] Frances may have finally asserted her autonomy, however, when she absconded with her lover, Sir Robert Howard (Bowen 531).

No matter how deeply enmeshed in the emotional turmoil of marriage and family dynamics, the financial and economic dimensions of nuptial arrangements are the most crucial elements of early modern marriage. This is certainly a facet of the play that modern readers are inclined to miss, reading, for example, "The earth hath swallowed all my hopes but she; / She's the hopeful lady of my earth" (1.2.14–15) as a purely poetic expression of Capulet's interest in his daughter's future. The passage is usually taken to mean merely that Juliet is Capulet's only surviving child. But the lines connote too that Juliet is her father's only heir. "Hopeful" may also indicate wealth and worldly possessions while "earth" includes his property and lands. These are the more fully material dimensions of Capulet's posterity. Clearly, even though Shakespeare took the trouble to include a scene devoted to marriage negotiations, the inclusion of the financial details of the match is somewhat problematic in a play of such lyricism. Indeed, these lines have

---

[7] The most notorious instance in this period of a terrible conclusion to an arranged marriage and the events that followed it, was when Frances Howard was married at the age of 13 to the 16-year-old earl of Essex in 1606. In 1613, in order to marry Robert Carr, earl of Somerset, she sought an annulment, claiming that Essex was impotent. Subsequently, it emerged that in the process of securing this second marriage, Howard had conspired in the murder of Thomas Overbury, who had tried to interfere. See p. 415.

proven a problem for editors and readers. For instance, Samuel Johnson of the famous eighteenth-century dictionary found them "not very intelligible" (Gibbons 95). The line is metrically irregular, and in a passage of regular rhyming couplets it is the odd line out. Further, the repetition of "earth" seems redundant, at least from the point of view of the poetry. On these grounds, and because they are absent from Q1, some editors omit lines 14 and 15 from the text (Gibbons 95). Could Shakespeare have decided to omit these lines from the final version of his text, or did he mean to include them in a way that showed Capulet's awkwardness about bartering his daughter on the marriage market?

Financial considerations reached far beyond the couple themselves and beyond any consideration of what we would regard as private life. Voluminous multiple transcriptions of legal documentation for aristocratic marriages are testament to this effect. They record, sometimes on heavily ornamented parchment, paper, and vellum (very fine parchment usually made from calfskin), complete with beribboned seals, the property and cash transactions that constituted the nuptial exchange, not so much between the couple as between their families. Long before the xerox machine, marriage documents represent dozens if not hundreds of hours of labor and signal the importance of the financial transaction over the personal commitment involved in marriage. These documents employ a specific lexicon of nuptial agreement. The "dowry" or "portion" came from the bride's family and might consist of a combination of property and other valuables such as jewels or plate (gold, silver, or pewterware). The groom's family agreed to the jointure belonging to the bride in the event that she was widowed (Cook 121; Erickson 119–22). This was usually a parcel of land that would revert to the wife as a means of independent income if her husband died before she did; typically the ratio of dowry to jointure was about 5 to 1 (Erickson 119). All parties in the negotiation stood to gain in well-arranged marriage agreements, not just the recipient of the bride's dowry. Indeed, at the end of *Romeo and Juliet*, there is a posthumous marital negotiation between Montague and Capulet: "O brother Montague, give me thy hand. / This is my daughter's jointure, for no more / Can I demand" (5.3.296–98). This would have been understood by an early modern audience as more than a rhetorical flourish, as part of the exchanges and demands that constituted prenuptial fiscal settlements. Montague of course seals (and trumps) the negotiations: "But I can give thee more, / For I will raise her statue in pure gold" (5.3.298–99).

We in modern Western societies tend to regard the fact that most young people in early modern England were given in marriage ("bestowed") to someone their parents had chosen for them as an astonishing abrogation of personal freedom. We might do well to remember that, statistically at least, our own free choice in marriage often leads directly from the altar (or civil ceremony) to the divorce court. Often, young people in Elizabethan England were happy enough to be directed by their parents. Those, like Frances Coke, compelled to marry against their will, were known as cases of "enforced marriage." At any rate, debate about the wishes of parents in this matter and the choices of their children raged throughout the period. However, gender often determined the degree to which candidates for marriage could resist parental coercion. As Ann Jenalie Cook points out, "For most men, marriage was an option they could choose or refuse, depending on their personal inclinations and income. But for most women, wedlock was inescapable" (Cook 5). An unmarried woman was far from being a free agent; she was permanently dependent on her father, her kin, or, if she was a servant, upon her master (8).

Romeo and Juliet initially contract themselves *per verba de futuro,* promising to marry in the future: such a promise was soluble unless it was sealed by sexual intercourse (see Gowing, *Domestic* 143). As Laura Gowing points out "In a set of courtship rituals which depended on men's initiative and women's response, women's mastery of the rules could be crucial" (Gowing, *Domestic* 144). She recounts the instance of Ann Frier who in 1579 was sued by two men who claimed a contract with her (a fate that could easily have befallen Juliet if not for the Friar's sleeping potion):

> Ann had already contracted herself to one man, Richard Robinson, when her father sent him away and tried to persuade her to make a contract with another, Peter Richardson. Ann attended her betrothal dinner but, at the moment of contracting offered Peter her left hand instead of the customary right: she explained to the court that she had already betrothed herself with her right hand to her first suitor, and so could not do so again. Ann's grandmother, however, proved just as observant of this possible loophole and made sure her granddaughter gave the right hand to her prospective husband, though Ann continued her evasions by saying, as she pointed out, "'I take Peter,' not, 'I take him as my husband.'"
>
> (Gowing, *Domestic* 144)

Natalie Zemon Davis has suggested women's identity in early modern society was constituted in part by the sense of "being given away," and that "the time when they answered marriage proposals and 'gave themselves away' could constitute a special moment of self-definition" (quoted in Gowing, *Domestic* 141). So it was that a child like Sage Poovey, almost exactly of an age with Juliet, might decide, "I am past twice 7 years old and therefore will make my choice where I shall like," while Ellen Shawcock said, "My father and my mother may think me to be a lewd girl but I am to make my choice myself" (quoted in Gowing, *Domestic* 137). Thus, despite the sometimes overwhelming restrictions on women's freedom to choose a husband, many girls insisted on exercising whatever agency they could — by simply manipulating the codes of courtship as did Ann Frier, or by rejecting outright parental control, as did Sage and Ellen. Juliet, pressured by the exigent circumstances of the feud, adopts the former approach rather than the direct defiance of her father. Indeed, unlike Sage and Ellen, she has no principled objection to marrying in accordance with her father's will in advance of meeting Romeo: "I'll look to like, if looking liking move, / But no more deep will I endart mine eye / Than your consent gives strength to make it fly" (1.3.98–100). However, once betrothed to two suitors, Juliet is ready to exercise agency in terms of the most drastic action. What is fascinating here is that however melodramatic Juliet's situation may be, many girls of her age found themselves in situations not vastly dissimilar in early modern England.

Paradoxically, despite the incoherencies of legal and ecclesiastical regulation and the coercion of parents, what defined marriage in this period was the mutual consent of the couple — solemnized or not. There was a tradition of freedom of consent, regardless of the wishes of parents or the dynastic ambitions of families. The problem, particularly of women's autonomy in selecting a marriage partner, was a trans-European phenomenon, and in England there had been an attempt to address it in the reign of Edward VI in what is known as the *Reformatio legum*. If this had been enacted, it would have rendered invalid all marriages that took place without the consent of parents or "governors." The issue was discussed again at the clerical convocation of 1597, but it failed to pass despite strong minority support. In the demise of this proposal there was a reassertion of the principle of mutual agreement: "Consent in marriage is the matter specially to be regarded, and credit of kindred, honor, wealth, contentment and pleasure of friends be rather matters of conveniency than necessity in matrimony" (quoted in Ingram 135). The problem of family interests remained, however, and family pressure versus individual choice in marriage was the cause of litigation in more than half the spousal cases brought before the ecclesiastical courts, and was especially the case where wealth and property were involved (Ingram 200–01).

It must be emphasized that in the heated debates about freedom of choice in marriage in this period, there was a widespread belief that familial consent was necessary if not to the legality of the marriage, at least to its social acceptability and viability. The defiance of children over parents in choice of marriage partner met with strong disapproval. Note, too, that this controversy at times manifested itself not as a matter of parental control over fully adult offspring, but as a contest between a concerned family opposing the will of an infatuated adolescent.

Families often objected particularly to marriages where there was a class discrepancy between the two parties, not the case of Romeo and Juliet, who appear to have equal status. Indeed, we never discover why Capulet's opposition to Juliet's free choice cannot be overcome in the manner of comedy, whose structure the play so closely resembles and in which the *senex iratus* figure (the difficult old man) is finally won over. Except for a rather non-specific ancient enmity about whose possible parallels in the period one can only speculate (religion would be a prominent candidate), we never discover any substantive rationale for the opposition to the match.

Religion

The source of the Montague-Capulet feud, their "ancient enmity," is never revealed to us. In this, Shakespeare captures one of the most significant characteristics of hatred: It always exceeds the specific circumstances used to rationalize its continuation. One crucial historical connotation for the division between the families is religious division, the schism within English Christianity. These religious differences, which were a matter of both ideology and practice, manifested themselves with staggering violence. As we noted in the earlier discussion of Romeo's reference to "heretics," we should not underestimate the degree of state-imposed violence that was necessary to enforce and maintain these abrupt shifts in religious ideology. The Anglican Church was still a very new phenomenon after the English Reformation, established by law but strongly opposed by both Catholics and more radical Protestants. In 1581, William Allen observed:

> In one man's memory . . . we have had to our prince, a man, who abolished the pope's authority by his laws and yet in other points kept the faith of his fathers; we have had a child, who by his like laws abolished together with the papacy the whole ancient religion; we have had a woman who restored both again and sharply punished Protestants; and lastly her majesty that now is, who by the like laws hath long since abolished both again and now severely punisheth Catholics as the other did Protestants; and all these strange differences within the compass of about thirty years.   (Quoted in Lake 57)

After the Reformation of the 1530s under Henry VIII, England was essentially Catholic in terms of theology but freed from papal interference in spiritual affairs. Henry's primary motivation in separating the English Church from the Church of Rome was not a religious one: He wanted to divorce Catherine of Aragon with the papacy's blessing and get on with the necessary business of producing a male heir. Only when the pope refused permission did Henry decide he would expedite matters by becoming head of the Church himself. Henry was succeeded by his son Edward VI (b. 1537, reigned 1547–53), a child king certainly prey to the more intensively Protestant views of his advisors, but also a devout Protestant in his own right in his early teenage years. An about-face in religious thinking swiftly followed Edward's brief reign (he died at sixteen), with the accession in 1553 of his virulently Catholic half-sister, Mary Tudor (referred to by later Protestant regimes as "bloody Mary" because of the number of heretics she had burned at the stake), who was married to Philp II, king of Spain, the greatest Catholic power in Europe. Then, upon the accession of Mary's half-sister, Elizabeth, in 1558, English Protestantism steadily became an irreversible phenomenon and quite probably a kind of church never envisaged during the reign of her father.

Scholars increasingly resist the view that Shakespeare was England's national and therefore Protestant poet. As Peter Milward points out, it was long assumed that Shakespeare was

> dutifully conformed to the official religion, or else that he was loftily unconcerned with the topic of most concern to the majority of his contemporaries. He is hailed as the national poet of the Golden Age of Queen Elizabeth, riding upon the tide of England's victory over the Spanish Armada. He thus takes his place in the Elizabethan myth which emphasizes the superficial glitter of the period. (11)

Recent and important discoveries made by E. A. J. Honigmann about Shakespeare's so-called lost years (after he left school but before he appeared in London as an actor and playwright) show that, whatever his subsequent religious affiliation, Shakespeare was probably brought up as a Catholic and may have gone to work as a schoolmaster and player for a wealthy Catholic landowner at Houghton Hall, Lancashire.

Whatever Shakespeare's religious identity and affiliation, by virtue of being set in Verona, *Romeo and Juliet* creates an inescapably Catholic world of saints, friar's cells, and Catholic sacraments (especially confession). However, the objects and practices that informed Catholic belief and practice were as ubiquitous in early modern and ostensibly Protestant England as they were in Catholic Verona. They were also imagined to be a threat. As Frances E. Dolan points out:

Catholics were not, then, as socially marginal or as powerless as other demonized groups: consequently, examining how they were represented reveals that even this widely used, helpful formulation — that those who were demonized in the early modern period were socially marginal yet symbolically central — cannot account for Catholics. The position of Catholics was unique. (*Whores of Babylon* 8)

There is a more pressing reason, however, why the unspecified animosity of the play's feud should be considered within the context of Reformation polemics. The Montagues were a leading recusant family in Shakespeare's England — that is, they refused to comply with the regulations governing attendance at religious services mandated by the Church of England. Moreover, Shakespeare was himself distantly related to them (Bowden 66, 107). Unquestionably, audiences would have recognized the name and associated it with Catholicism. The Wriothesleys, the family of Shakespeare's patron, the third earl of Southampton, had profited immensely from the dissolution of the monasteries in 1537 under Henry VIII, the first earl acquiring the lands and priceless artifacts that had belonged to the religious houses. For all that, the earl's wife was a devout Roman Catholic who had the second earl of Southampton (the father of Shakespeare's patron) brought up in the Catholic faith (Akrigg, *Shakespeare* 6–7). Confusions and divisions generated by religious differences existed not just between families, but within them, and were in fact exacerbated by the very marriage practices that were simultaneously causing such political and domestic strife. The second earl at nineteen married a thirteen-year-old called Mary, the daughter of Catholic Anthony Browne, first viscount Montague. He did so without the full consent of his Catholic mother, who seems to have had substantial reservations about the match "solemnized at London in my Lord Montague's house by his advice without the consent of my Lady, his [the young earl's] mother" (Akrigg, *Shakespeare* 7). The marriage was an unhappy one, and when Southampton suspected his wife of adultery with a commoner called Donesame, the two separated. The quarrel, however, was not confined to the couple themselves but was taken up by their respective families. G. P. V. Akrigg points out:

> An entry in the register of the Privy Council indicates that, as with the Montagues and Capulets, so with the Montagues and Wriothesleys, the servants took up the family quarrel: "xxiii February, 1579 This day Edmund Prety, servant to the Earl of Southampton was, for certain misdemeanors by him used against Mr. Anthony Browne, the eldest son of the Lord Montague . . . committed to the Marshalsea [a London prison]."
> (*Shakespeare* 13)

One of the foremost Jesuits in England at the time, Father Parsons, claimed that the quarrels among the leading English Catholics had weakened their position: "One thing also increased the difficulties of the Catholics at this time, which was the falling out between the Earl of Southampton and the Lord Montague about the Earl's wife, which was daughter to the Lord, and put away by the Earl, as suspected of incontinency [infidelity]" (Akrigg, *Shakespeare* 15). Interestingly, this quarrel was not grounded on religious difference but was a rancor that developed between families who practiced the same dissenting faith.

Given the existence of such complexity, we should not read the feud between the Montagues and the Capulets, or for that matter any other aspect of Shakespeare's play, as an allegory of real historical events. Nor should any of the documents included in this edition be read as a key to the play, or as a means of deciphering a kind of literary code. Dramatic poetry is not a puzzle to be solved and done with, but a complex, imaginative vision of the social world, and the tensions of the culture of which it is a part.

Thus, when Mercutio upon receiving his fatal wound cries repeatedly, "A plague o' both your houses" (3.1.80, 87–88, 93), his disgust may speak to any number of possible reasons for social discord. Mercutio's point is surely that such "differences," though fun to fight about, are not worth dying for. In early modern England, however, many people felt that their religion was certainly worth killing for; fewer — though a still significant number of Protestant and Catholic martyrs — thought it worth dying for.

Documents

The documents in this edition come from the late sixteenth and early seventeenth centuries. I have tried to give a sense of the specific and often quite distinct context of the 1590s (this is especially true of the literary materials), but since the documents are neither sources nor analogues to the play, I have not shirked at including some later material. After all, many people's lives, including Shakespeare's own, straddled the centuries.

The documents that follow are arranged around two broadly central yet inseparable organizing ideas: love and death. Every chapter in some way addresses both these themes.

The first chapter on Italy suggests the quasi-erotic fantasy of a place that is associated with sexual, religious, and political intrigue. Many of the storylines of Elizabethan literature originate in Italy, and it is the object of both fear and desire for the period's English Protestants.

Chapter 2 examines alliances and antagonisms between men in London and in Verona. Somewhat surprisingly from a present-day perspective, the homoerotic aspect of male bonding co-existed fairly easily with the system of heterosexual alliances. Potentially sexualized bonds between men in this play, the friendship between Romeo and Mercutio specifically and the culture of male friendship and violence more generally, do not threaten marriage. Certainly, in early modern culture there was nothing approaching the moral outrage evident in some responses to homosexuality in our own day. Nor did anyone at the time think to comment on the fact that patently homosexual declarations necessarily precluded marital attachment. Whereas in our own day, sleeping with someone of the same sex is taken to mean that a declaration of identity — coming out — is required, in the Renaissance, homoerotic practice was never seen as a crisis or as a sign of a transformation of identity. In other words, for early moderns, the gender of your sexual partner did not define who you were.

Sexual contact between men may not have rent the social fabric either in the play or in urban society, but violence between them did. Like unauthorized heteroerotic attachment such as that between Romeo and Juliet, violence, both at the level of orchestrated social unrest, and at that of "spontaneous" personal antagonism, was understood to constitute a threat to the order of the city and the realm. Time and again, edicts, proclamations, and decrees prohibited weapons, affrays, and riots, and called for a return to order. Their very iteration indicated the narrow limits of their success. Much violence in London was undoubtedly the result of class antagonism. There were many conflicts between young gentlemen and the youthful apprentices who were their lower class counterparts. Confrontations among socially privileged men, which resemble the volatile energies of the gentry that spell ruin for the city of Verona, were primarily the product of the sophisticated arts of violence cultivated in the fencing schools.

Romeo and Juliet may represent a dramatic, drastic scenario, an exaggerated depiction of the potentially destructive energies early modern society invested in controlling the marriages of its youth, but if anything, the role of violence at all levels of the social order is underplayed. For instance, Samson and Gregory, the servants of the Capulet household, are relatively harmless buffoons, not the angry menials and apprentices who regularly attacked theaters, brothels, and the Inns of Court in the early modern city. In real life London, the lower orders were restrained from destroying the fabric of social hierarchy only by dint of constant vigilance and bloody reprisals against miscreants.

Chapter 4, "Family Life," examines the diurnal round of mating, reproducing, nurturing children, feasting, and mourning. Thus, alongside the essentially political struggle to maintain order are the natural cycles of life, birth and death, the struggle to maintain life, to feed infants, to survive pestilence. Since we have already addressed the issues of courtship and enforced marriage, covered in Chapters 3 and 4, all that needs to be added here is that the letters from the Bagot papers in Chapter 4 are not from print sources but have been transcribed from the manuscript archive at the Folger Library. For this reason, unlike all the other documents in the volume (with the exception of the excerpt from Spenser in Chapter 5, on the grounds that Spenser wrote in deliberately contiquoted English), these letters are not modernized. Like all early modern texts, whether in print or in manuscript, these letters were written without any concept of standardized orthography (spelling), a phenomenon only developed in the eighteenth century. A wonderful instance of this is that one of the very few examples of Shakespeare's handwriting we know to be his own, namely the signatures on his will, are not spelled "Shakespeare" as we would expect, but "Shakspere" in two places and "Shakspeare" in a third. In other words, "Shakespeare" is our standardization, not his. While all this sounds odd to us, and even though it is difficult for us to read, early modern orthography conveys the enormous richness of the language as it was then used.

The documents in Chapters 5 and 6 "Friars," and "Death and the Stars" respectively, touch upon the violence of post-Reformation religious discourse. In the seismic wake of the Reformation, religion was about partisanship, and yet religious identities were assumed on all sides in complex and contradictory ways that at times reflect profound spiritual practice, and sometimes utter moral corruption. Across the religious spectrum, from the radical Protestants to the Jesuits, early moderns struggled to discern (and juggle) the relation between the spiritual and the material at the very historical moment when the priority of the former was in sharp decline. Furthermore, religious objects and practices were taking on new and contested meanings. For example, a funeral monument, like the statues at the end of *Romeo and Juliet*, a far more lavish affair than its medieval antecedent, could signify any (or all) of the following possible meanings: a memorial to the dead; the triumph of bourgeois taste over death — in other words, a monument to the living; an idol, a latter day golden calf, the triumph of mammon (money or wealth and prestige) over God; or a reminder to the living of their ultimate fate. Similarly, the religious rituals, prohibited by law from being portrayed on stage — the wedding, the funeral — had also undergone remarkable transformation in the Reformed church. Although they are absent from the play itself, these were in Shakespeare's England the most dramatic rituals of real life.

.   .   .

The documents included here do not simply show a grittier world than the play, one consumed with practical details, but rather reveal elaborate and intricate systems of discourse and social practice. Within this framework, Shakespeare's play becomes a complex object in an intricate setting, sometimes starkly separate from what surrounds it, and at other moments seamlessly continuous with its so-called background. The task of critical reading and interpretation, then, consists of determining, in any given instance, the precise relation between the literary object and the cultural horizon, which both frames and produces it. In terms of these contexts, there is nothing resembling "finality" about the play. Rather, these cultural documents compel us to reconsider some of our critical certainties about dramatic tragedy.

In the final chapter of this volume, the cosmic issues of death and destiny addressed here are appropriately analogous to the entire process of contextualization with which we are engaged in this book. We can move out, almost endlessly from the text, but we must always return to it, re-evaluate and move out again, hopefully, broadening and deepening our knowledge both of Shakespeare's language and of Elizabethan culture as we go. The aim of this book has been to open-up rather than to fix the meaning of *Romeo and Juliet*. I like to think that this was Shakespeare's goal as well.

PART ONE

>-<

WILLIAM SHAKESPEARE
Romeo and Juliet

Edited by David Bevington

Romeo and Juliet

><-

[Dramatis Personae

CHORUS

ESCALUS, *Prince of Verona*
MERCUTIO, *the Prince's kinsman and Romeo's friend*
PARIS, *a young count and kinsman of the Prince*
PAGE *to Count Paris*

MONTAGUE
MONTAGUE'S WIFE
ROMEO, *son of the Montagues*
BENVOLIO, *Montague's nephew and Romeo's friend*
ABRAHAM, *a servant of the Montague household*
BALTHASAR, *a servant of the Montague household attending Romeo*

CAPULET
CAPULET'S WIFE
JULIET, *daughter of the Capulets*
NURSE
TYBALT, *nephew of Capulet's Wife*
PETRUCHIO, *Capulet's kinsman*
SECOND CAPULET, *an old man, Capulet's kinsman*
PETER, *a servant of the Capulet household attending the Nurse*
SAMSON,
GREGORY,
ANTHONY,   } *servants of the Capulet household*
POTPAN,
CLOWN *or* SERVANT,
Other SERVANTS,

FRIAR LAURENCE, } *Franciscan friars*
FRIAR JOHN,

APOTHECARY
Three MUSICIANS (*Simon Catling, Hugh Rebeck, and James Soundpost*)
Three WATCHMEN
Citizens, Maskers, Torchbearers, Guards, Servants, and Attendants

SCENE: *Verona; Mantua*]

39

THE PROLOGUE

[*Enter Chorus.*]

CHORUS:
 Two households, both alike in dignity,°
   In fair Verona, where we lay our scene,
 From ancient grudge break to new mutiny,°
   Where civil blood makes civil° hands unclean.
 From forth the fatal loins of these two foes   5
   A pair of star-crossed° lovers take their life;
 Whose misadventured° piteous overthrows
   Doth with their death bury their parents' strife.
 The fearful passage° of their death-marked love,
   And the continuance of their parents' rage   10
 Which, but their children's end, naught could remove,
   Is now the two hours' traffic° of our stage;
 The which if you with patient ears attend,
 What here shall miss,° our toil° shall strive to mend.

[*Exit.*]

ACT 1, SCENE 1°

Enter Samson and Gregory, with swords and bucklers,° of the house of Capulet.

SAMSON: Gregory, on my word, we'll not carry coals.°
GREGORY: No, for then we should be colliers.°
SAMSON: I mean, an° we be in choler,° we'll draw.°
GREGORY: Ay, while you live, draw your neck out of collar.°
SAMSON: I strike quickly, being moved.°   5
GREGORY: But thou art not quickly moved to strike.
SAMSON: A dog of the house of Montague moves° me.
GREGORY: To move is to stir, and to be valiant is to stand.° Therefore, if
 thou art moved, thou runn'st away.

PROLOGUE. 1. **dignity:** rank, status. 3. **mutiny:** strife, discord. 4. **civil . . . civil:** of civil strife . . . citizens' (with a suggestion of "civility"). 6. **star-crossed:** thwarted by destiny, by adverse stars. 7. **misadventured:** unlucky. 9. **passage:** progress. 12. **traffic:** business. 14. **miss:** i.e., miss the mark (in this performance). **our toil:** the actors' efforts. ACT 1, SCENE 1. **Location:** Verona. A public place. **s.d.** *bucklers:* small shields. 1. **carry coals:** i.e., endure insults. 2. **colliers:** (Coal carriers were regarded as dirty and of evil repute.) 3. **an:** if. **choler:** anger (produced by one of the four humors). **draw:** draw swords. 4. **collar:** i.e., hangman's noose (with pun on *colliers* and *choler*). 5. **moved:** i.e., to anger (with pun in next line). 7. **moves:** incites. 8. **stand:** i.e., stand one's ground.

SAMSON: A dog of that house shall move me to stand. I will take the wall°   10
of any man or maid of Montagues.

GREGORY: That shows thee a weak slave, for the weakest goes to the wall.°

SAMSON: 'Tis true, and therefore women, being the weaker vessels, are
ever thrust to the wall.° Therefore I will push Montague's men from the
wall and thrust his maids to the wall.   15

GREGORY: The quarrel is between our masters and us their men.°

SAMSON: 'Tis all one.° I will show myself a tyrant: when I have fought
with the men, I will be civil with the maids — I will cut off their heads.

GREGORY: The heads of the maids?

SAMSON: Ay, the heads of the maids, or their maiden heads. Take it in   20
what sense° thou wilt.

GREGORY: They must take it in sense that feel it.°

SAMSON: Me they shall feel while I am able to stand,° and 'tis known I am
a pretty piece of flesh.

GREGORY: 'Tis well thou art not fish;° if thou hadst, thou hadst been Poor   25
John.° Draw thy tool. Here comes of° the house of Montagues.

Enter two other servingmen [Abraham and another].

SAMSON: My naked weapon is out. Quarrel. I will back thee.

GREGORY: How, turn thy back and run?

SAMSON: Fear° me not.

GREGORY: No, marry. I fear thee!   30

SAMSON: Let us take the law of° our sides. Let them begin.

GREGORY: I will frown as I pass by, and let them take it as they list.°

SAMSON: Nay, as they dare. I will bite my thumb° at them, which is disgrace to them if they bear it.   [*Samson makes taunting gestures.*]

ABRAHAM: Do you bite your thumb at us, sir?   35

SAMSON: I do bite my thumb, sir.

---

10. **take the wall:** i.e., take the cleaner side of the walk nearest the wall, thus forcing others out into the gutter.   12. **the weakest . . . wall:** (A proverb expressing the idea that the weakest are always forced to give way.)   14. **thrust to the wall:** (With bawdy suggestion.)   16. **between . . . men:** i.e., between the males of one household and the males of the other household; the women would not fight.   17. **one:** the same.   21. **what sense:** whatever meaning.   22. **They . . . feel it:** i.e., it is the maids who must receive by way of physical sensation (*sense*) what I have to offer, because they are the ones who can feel it.   23. **stand:** (With bawdy suggestion, continued in the next few lines in *draw thy tool* and *my naked weapon is out.*)   24–25. **flesh . . . fish:** (Refers to the proverbial phrase, "neither fish nor flesh.")   25–26. **Poor John:** hake salted and dried — a poor Lenten kind of food (probably with a bawdy suggestion of sexual insufficiency).   26. **comes of:** i.e., come members of.   29. **Fear:** mistrust. (But Gregory deliberately misunderstands in the next line, saying in effect, No indeed, do you think I'd be afraid of you?)   31. **take the law of:** have the law on.   32. **list:** please.   33. **bite my thumb:** i.e., make an insulting gesture.

ABRAHAM: Do you bite your thumb at us, sir?

SAMSON: [*Aside to Gregory*] Is the law of our side if I say ay?

GREGORY: [*Aside to Samson*] No.

SAMSON: [*To Abraham*] No, sir, I do not bite my thumb at you, sir, but I bite   40
my thumb, sir.

GREGORY: Do you quarrel, sir?

ABRAHAM: Quarrel, sir? No, sir.

SAMSON: But if you do, sir, I am for you. I serve as good a man as you.

ABRAHAM: No better.   45

SAMSON: Well, sir.

Enter Benvolio.

GREGORY: [*To Samson*] Say "better." Here comes one of my master's kinsmen.

SAMSON: [*To Abraham*] Yes, better, sir.

ABRAHAM: You lie.

SAMSON: Draw, if you be men. Gregory, remember thy washing° blow.   50
They fight.

BENVOLIO: Part, fools!
Put up your swords. You know not what you do.

Enter Tybalt [with sword drawn].

TYBALT:
What, art thou drawn among these heartless hinds?°
Turn thee, Benvolio, Look upon thy death.

BENVOLIO:
I do but keep the peace. Put up thy sword,   55
Or manage° it to part these men with me.

TYBALT:
What, drawn and talk of peace? I hate the word
As I hate hell, all Montagues, and thee.
Have at thee,° coward!   [*They fight.*]

Enter three or four Citizens with clubs or partisans.

CITIZENS:
Clubs,° bills,° and partisans!° Strike! Beat them down!   60
Down with the Capulets! Down with the Montagues!

---

50. **washing:** slashing with great force.   53. **heartless hinds:** cowardly menials.   56. **manage:** use.   59. **Have at thee:** i.e., on guard, here I come.   60. **Clubs:** rallying cry, summoning apprentices with their clubs.   **bills:** long-handled spears with hooked blades.   **partisans:** long-handled spears.

Enter old Capulet in his gown,° and his Wife.

CAPULET:
What noise is this? Give me my long sword,° ho!

CAPULET'S WIFE:
A crutch, a crutch! Why call you for a sword?

CAPULET:
My sword, I say! Old Montague is come
And flourishes his blade in spite° of me.   65

Enter old Montague and his Wife.

MONTAGUE:
Thou villain Capulet! — Hold me not; let me go.

MONTAGUE'S WIFE:
Thou shalt not stir one foot to seek a foe.

Enter Prince Escalus, with his train.

PRINCE:
Rebellious subjects, enemies to peace,
Profaners of this neighbor-stainèd steel° —
Will they not hear? What, ho! You men, you beasts,   70
That quench the fire of your pernicious rage
With purple° fountains issuing from your veins,
On pain of torture, from those bloody hands
Throw your mistempered° weapons to the ground
And hear the sentence of your movèd° prince.   75
Three civil brawls, bred of an airy° word,
By thee, old Capulet, and Montague,
Have thrice disturbed the quiet of our streets
And made Verona's ancient citizens
Cast by their grave-beseeming ornaments°   80
To wield old partisans, in hands as old,
Cankered with peace, to part your cankered° hate.
If ever you disturb our streets again

---

61. s.d. *gown:* nightgown, dressing gown.   **62. long sword:** heavy, old-fashioned sword.
65. spite: defiance, despite.   **69. Profaners ... steel:** i.e., you who profane your weapons by
staining them with neighbors' blood.   **72. purple:** i.e., bloody, dark red.   **74. mistempered:**
(1) having been tempered, or hardened, to a wrong use (2) malignant, angry.   **75. movèd:**
angry.   **76. airy:** i.e., merely a breath, trivial.   **80. grave-beseeming ornaments:** i.e., staffs
and other appurtenances suited to wise old age.   **82. Cankered ... cankered:** corroded ...
malignant.

Your lives shall pay the forfeit of the peace.°
For this time all the rest depart away.   85
You, Capulet, shall go along with me,
And, Montague, come you this afternoon,
To know our farther pleasure in this case,
To old Freetown,° our common° judgment-place.
Once more, on pain of death, all men depart.   90

Exeunt [all but Montague, Montague's Wife, and Benvolio].

MONTAGUE:
Who set this ancient quarrel new abroach?°
Speak, nephew, were you by° when it began?

BENVOLIO:
Here were the servants of your adversary,
And yours, close fighting ere I did approach.
I drew to part them. In the instant came   95
The fiery Tybalt with his sword prepared,°
Which, as he breathed defiance to my ears,
He swung about his head and cut the winds
Who, nothing° hurt withal,° hissed° him in scorn.
While we were interchanging thrusts and blows,   100
Came more and more, and fought on part and part°
Till the Prince came, who parted either part.°

MONTAGUE'S WIFE:
O, where is Romeo? Saw you him today?
Right glad I am he was not at this fray.

BENVOLIO:
Madam, an hour before the worshiped sun   105
Peered forth° the golden window of the east,
A troubled mind drave° me to walk abroad,°
Where, underneath the grove of sycamore
That westward rooteth from this city's side,°
So early walking did I see your son.   110
Towards him I made,° but he was ware° of me
And stole into the covert° of the wood.

---

84. Your . . . peace: i.e., death will be the penalty for breaking the peace. **89. Freetown:** (Brooke's translation, in his poem *Romeus and Juliet*, of *Villa Franca*, as found in the Italian story.) **common:** public. **91. set . . . abroach:** reopened this old quarrel, set it flowing. **92. by:** near. **96. prepared:** drawn, ready. **99. Who, nothing:** which not at all. **withal:** therewith. **hissed:** hissed at. **101. on part and part:** on one side and the other. **102. either part:** both parties. **106. forth:** from forth. **107. drave:** drove. **abroad:** outside. **109. That . . . side:** that grows on the west side of this city. **111. made:** moved. **ware:** wary, aware. **112. covert:** cover, hiding place.

I, measuring his affections° by my own,
Which then most sought where most might not be found,°
Being one too many by my weary self,   115
Pursued my humor,° not pursuing his,
And gladly shunned who° gladly fled from me.
MONTAGUE:
Many a morning hath he there been seen,
With tears augmenting the fresh morning's dew,
Adding to clouds more clouds with his deep sighs;   120
But all so soon as the all-cheering sun
Should in the farthest east begin to draw
The shady curtains from Aurora's° bed,
Away from light steals home my heavy° son°
And private in his chamber pens himself,   125
Shuts up his windows, locks fair daylight out,
And makes himself an artificial night.
Black and portentous must this humor prove
Unless good counsel may the cause remove.
BENVOLIO:
My noble uncle, do you know the cause?   130
MONTAGUE:
I neither know it nor can learn of him.
BENVOLIO:
Have you importuned him by any means?
MONTAGUE:
Both by myself and many other friends.
But he, his own affections' counselor,
Is to himself — I will not say how true,°   135
But to himself so secret and so close,°
So far from sounding° and discovery,
As is the bud bit with an envious° worm
Ere he can spread his sweet leaves to the air
Or dedicate his beauty to the sun.   140
Could we but learn from whence his sorrows grow,
We would as willingly give cure as know.

---

113. **affections:** wishes, inclination.   114. **Which . . . found:** i.e., I who then chiefly desired a place where I might be alone.   116. **humor:** mood, whim.   117. **who:** him who.   123. **Aurora:** goddess of dawn.   124. **heavy:** (1) sad (2) the opposite of *light*.   **son:** (punning on *sun*, l. 121).   135. **true:** trustworthy.   136. **close:** concealed.   137. **sounding:** being fathomed (to discover deep or inner secrets).   138. **envious:** malicious.

Enter Romeo.

BENVOLIO:
See where he comes. So please you,° step aside.
I'll know his grievance or be much denied.

MONTAGUE:
I would thou wert so happy° by thy stay   145
To hear true shrift.° Come, madam, let's away.

Exeunt [Montague and his Wife].

BENVOLIO:
Good morrow, cousin.°

ROMEO: Is the day so young?

BENVOLIO:
But new struck nine.

ROMEO: Ay me! Sad hours seem long.
Was that my father that went hence so fast?

BENVOLIO:
It was. What sadness lengthens Romeo's hours?   150

ROMEO:
Not having that which, having, makes them short.

BENVOLIO: In love?

ROMEO: Out —

BENVOLIO: Of love?

ROMEO:
Out of her favor where I am in love.   155

BENVOLIO:
Alas, that Love, so gentle in his view,°
Should be so tyrannous and rough in proof!°

ROMEO:
Alas, that Love, whose view is muffled still,°
Should without eyes see pathways to his will!°
Where shall we dine? — O me! What fray was here?   160
Yet tell me not, for I have heard it all.
Here's much to do with hate, but more with love.
Why, then, O brawling love, O loving hate,
O anything of nothing first create,°
O heavy lightness, serious vanity,   165

---

143. **So please you:** if you please.   145. **happy:** fortunate, successful.   146. **shrift:** confession.
147. **cousin:** kinsman.   156. **his view:** its appearance.   157. **in proof:** in reality, in experience.
158. **view . . . still:** sight is blindfolded always.   159. **to his will:** to what he wants.   164. **create:** created.

Misshapen chaos of well-seeming forms,
Feather of lead, bright smoke, cold fire, sick health,
Still-waking° sleep, that is not what it is!
This love feel I, that feel no love in this.
Dost thou not laugh?

BENVOLIO: No, coz,° I rather weep. 170

ROMEO:
Good heart, at what?

BENVOLIO: At thy good heart's oppression.

ROMEO:
Why, such is love's transgression.
Griefs of mine own lie heavy in my breast,
Which thou wilt propagate, to have it pressed
With more of thine.° This love that thou hast shown 175
Doth add more grief to too much of mine own.
Love is a smoke made with the fume of sighs;
Being purged,° a fire sparkling in lovers' eyes;
Being vexed, a sea nourished with lovers' tears.
What is it else? A madness most discreet,° 180
A choking gall, and a preserving sweet.
Farewell, my coz.

BENVOLIO: Soft!° I will go along.
An if° you leave me so, you do me wrong.

ROMEO:
Tut, I have lost myself. I am not here.
This is not Romeo; he's some other where. 185

BENVOLIO:
Tell me in sadness,° who is that° you love?

ROMEO: What, shall I groan and tell thee?

BENVOLIO:
Groan? Why, no, but sadly° tell me who.

ROMEO:
Bid a sick man in sadness make his will —
A word° ill urged to one that is so ill! 190
In sadness, cousin, I do love a woman.

---

168. Still-waking: continually awake. **170. coz:** cousin, kinsman. **174–175. propagate . . . thine:** increase by having it, i.e., my own grief, oppressed or made still heavier with your grief on my account. **178. purged:** i.e., of smoke. **180. discreet:** judicious, prudent. **182. Soft:** i.e., wait a moment. **183. An if:** if. **186. sadness:** seriousness. **is that:** is it whom. **188. sadly:** seriously. (But Romeo plays on the word, and on *in sadness,* in the sense of "sorrowfully.") **190. A word:** i.e., *sadly* or *in sadness* — too sad a word, says Romeo, for a melancholy lover.

BENVOLIO:
I aimed so near when I supposed you loved.

ROMEO:
A right good markman! And she's fair° I love.

BENVOLIO:
A right fair mark,° fair coz, is soonest hit.

ROMEO:
Well, in that hit you miss. She'll not be hit   195
With Cupid's arrow. She hath Dian's° wit,
And, in strong proof° of chastity well armed,
From love's weak childish bow she lives unharmed.
She will not stay° the siege of loving terms,
Nor bide° th' encounter of assailing eyes,   200
Nor ope her lap to saint-seducing gold.
O, she is rich in beauty, only poor
That when she dies, with beauty dies her store.°

BENVOLIO:
Then she hath sworn that she will still° live chaste?

ROMEO:
She hath, and in that sparing° makes huge waste,   205
For beauty starved with° her severity
Cuts beauty off from all posterity.
She is too fair, too wise, wisely too fair,
To merit bliss by making me despair.°
She hath forsworn to° love, and in that vow   210
Do I live dead that live to tell it now.

BENVOLIO:
Be ruled by me. Forget to think of her.

ROMEO:
O, teach me how I should forget to think!

BENVOLIO:
By giving liberty unto thine eyes:
Examine other beauties.

ROMEO: 'Tis the way   215

---

193. **fair:** beautiful.   194. **fair mark:** clear, distinct target.   196. **Dian:** Diana, huntress and goddess of chastity.   197. **proof:** armor.   199. **stay:** submit to.   200. **bide:** abide, endure. 203. **store:** wealth. (She will die without children and therefore her beauty will die with her.) 204. **still:** always.   205. **sparing:** miserliness.   206. **starved with:** killed by.   209. **To . . . despair:** i.e., earning her own salvation through chaste living while driving me to the spiritually dangerous state of despair.   210. **forsworn to:** renounced, repudiated.

To call hers, exquisite, in question more.°
These happy masks that kiss fair ladies' brows,
Being black, puts us in mind they hide the fair.
He that is strucken blind cannot forget
The precious treasure of his eyesight lost.
Show me a mistress that is passing° fair: 220
What doth her beauty serve but as a note
Where I may read who passed° that passing fair?
Farewell. Thou canst not teach me to forget.

BENVOLIO:
I'll pay that doctrine,° or else die in debt.° *Exeunt.* 225

ACT I, SCENE 2°

Enter Capulet, County° Paris, and the Clown [a Servingman].

CAPULET:
But Montague is bound° as well as I,
In penalty alike, and 'tis not hard, I think,
For men so old as we to keep the peace.

PARIS:
Of honorable reckoning° are you both,
And pity 'tis you lived at odds so long.
But now, my lord, what say you to my suit? 5

CAPULET:
But saying o'er° what I have said before:
My child is yet a stranger in the world;
She hath not seen the change of fourteen years.
Let two more summers wither in their pride
Ere we may think her ripe to be a bride. 10

PARIS:
Younger than she are happy mothers made.

CAPULET:
And too soon marred are those so early made.
The earth hath swallowed all my hopes but she;
She's the hopeful lady of my earth.° 15

216. in question more: even more keenly to mind, into consideration.   221. passing: surpass-
ingly.   223. passed: surpassed.   225. pay that doctrine: i.e., give that instruction.   die in debt:
i.e., feel I've failed as a friend.   Act i, Scene 2. Location: Verona. A street.   s.d. *County:*
Count.   1. bound: legally obligated (to keep the peace).   4. reckoning: estimation, repute.
7. o'er: again.   15. the hopeful . . . earth: i.e., my heir and hope for posterity. (*Earth* includes
property and lands.)

But woo her, gentle Paris, get her heart;
My will to her consent is but a part;
And, she° agreed, within her scope of choice
Lies my consent and fair according° voice.
This night I hold an old accustomed° feast,   20
Whereto I have invited many a guest
Such as I love; and you among the store,°
One more, most welcome, makes my number more.
At my poor house look to behold this night
Earth-treading stars that make dark heaven light.   25
Such comfort as do lusty° young men feel
When well-appareled° April on the heel
Of limping winter treads, even such delight
Among fresh fennel° buds shall you this night
Inherit° at my house. Hear all, all see,   30
And like her most whose merit most shall be;
Which on more view of many, mine, being one,
May stand in number, though in reckoning none.°
Come, go with me.   [*To the Servingman, giving a paper.*]
    Go, sirrah,° trudge about
Through fair Verona; find those persons out   35
Whose names are written there, and to them say,
My house and welcome on their pleasure stay.°   *Exit [with Paris].*
SERVINGMAN: Find them out whose names are written here! It is written
that the shoemaker should meddle° with his yard and the tailor with his
last, the fisher with his pencil, and the painter with his nets;° but I am   40
sent to find those persons whose names are here writ, and can never find°
what names the writing person hath here writ. I must to the learned. —
In good time!°

---

18. **she:** if she be.   19. **according:** agreeing.   20. **old accustomed:** traditional.   22. **store:** group.   26. **lusty:** lively.   27. **well-appareled:** newly clothed in green.   29. **fennel:** flowering herb thought to have the power of awakening passion.   30. **Inherit:** possess.   32–33. **Which . . . none:** i.e., when you have looked over many ladies, my daughter, being one of them, may be numerically counted among the lot but will count for little in your *reckoning* or estimation. (Capulet puns on *reckoning* in the sense of arithmetical calculating, and also on the proverbial saying "one is no number.")   34. **sirrah:** (Customary form of address to servants.)   37. **on . . . stay:** wait to serve their pleasure.   39. **meddle:** (The bawdy suggestion of sexual activity is continued in *yard* and *pencil*, slang terms for the male sexual organ.)   39–40. **yard, last, pencil, nets:** (The servingman humorously assigns these tools of a trade to the wrong person, to suggest how useless it is for him, an illiterate servant, to be given a written instruction.)   **yard:** yardstick.   **last:** a shoemaker's form.   **pencil:** paint brush.   41. **find . . . find:** locate . . . learn.   43. **In good time:** i.e., here comes help.

Enter Benvolio and Romeo.

BENVOLIO:

 Tut, man, one fire burns out another's burning,
  One pain is lessened by another's anguish;°
 Turn giddy, and be holp° by backward° turning;   45
  One desperate grief cures with another's languish.°
 Take thou some new infection to thy eye,
 And the rank° poison of the old will die.

ROMEO:

 Your° plantain leaf° is excellent for that.   50

BENVOLIO:

 For what, I pray thee?

ROMEO: For your broken shin.

BENVOLIO: Why, Romeo, art thou mad?

ROMEO:

 Not mad, but bound° more than a madman is;
 Shut up in prison, kept without my food,
 Whipped and tormented and — Good e'en,° good fellow. 55

SERVINGMAN: God gi'° good e'en. I pray, sir, can you read?

ROMEO:

 Ay, mine own fortune in my misery.

SERVINGMAN: Perhaps you have learned it without book.° But, I pray, can
you read anything you see?

ROMEO:

 Ay, if I know the letters and the language.   60

SERVINGMAN: Ye say honestly. Rest you merry!°   *[Going.]*

ROMEO: Stay, fellow, I can read.   *He reads the letter.*

 "Signor Martino and his wife and daughters,
 County Anselme and his beauteous sisters,
 The lady widow of Vitruvio,   65
 Signor Placentio and his lovely nieces,
 Mercutio and his brother Valentine,

---

45. another's anguish: the anguish of another pain. **46. holp:** helped. **backward:** i.e., reverse. **47. cures . . . languish:** is cured by the suffering of a second *grief* or pain. **49. rank:** foul. **50. Your:** "the" or "a"; common in this kind of expression of popular wisdom. **plantain leaf:** herb used for cuts and abrasions, such as a *broken* or bleeding shin. (Romeo undercuts Benvolio's sententiousness by taking his medical metaphor literally, as if curing love were like curing a minor cut.) **53. bound:** (The usual treatment for madness.) **55. Good e'en:** good evening. (Used after noon.) **56. gi':** give you. **58. without book:** by memory. (The servingman takes Romeo's flowery response to his simple question as though it were the title of a literary work; his comment also suggests that one can learn misery without knowing how to read.) **61. Rest you merry:** i.e., farewell. (The servingman can see he is getting nowhere.)

Mine uncle Capulet, his wife, and daughters,
My fair niece Rosaline, and Livia,
Signor Valentio and his cousin Tybalt,   70
Lucio and the lively Helena."
A fair assembly. Whither° should they come?
SERVINGMAN: Up.
ROMEO: Whither? To supper?
SERVINGMAN: To our house.   75
ROMEO: Whose house?
SERVINGMAN: My master's.
ROMEO:
Indeed, I should have asked thee that before.
SERVINGMAN: Now I'll tell you without asking. My master is the great rich
Capulet; and if you be not of the house of Montagues, I pray, come and   80
crush° a cup of wine. Rest you merry!   [*Exit.*]
BENVOLIO:
At this same ancient° feast of Capulet's
Sups the fair Rosaline whom thou so loves,
With all the admirèd beauties of Verona.
Go thither, and with unattainted° eye   85
Compare her face with some that I shall show,
And I will make thee think thy swan a crow.
ROMEO:
When the devout religion of mine eye
    Maintains° such falsehood, then turn tears to fires;
And these° who, often drowned,° could never die,   90
    Transparent° heretics, be burnt for liars!
One fairer than my love? The all-seeing sun
Ne'er saw her match since first the world begun.
BENVOLIO:
Tut, you saw her fair, none else being by,
Herself poised° with herself in either eye;   95
But in that crystal scales° let there be weighed
Your lady's love against some other maid
That I will show you shining at this feast,
And she shall scant° show well that now seems best.

---

72. Whither: where. **81. crush:** i.e., drink. **82. ancient:** customary. **85. unattainted:**
unbiased. **89. Maintains:** upholds. **90. these:** i.e., these my eyes. **drowned:** i.e., in tears.
91. Transparent: (1) self-evident (2) clear. **95. poised:** weighed, balanced. **96. crystal
scales:** i.e., Romeo's eyes, in which the ladies are to be balanced and compared. **99. scant:**
scarcely.

ROMEO:

I'll go along, no such sight to be shown,   100
But to rejoice in splendor of mine own.°   [*Exeunt.*]

ACT I, SCENE 3°

Enter Capulet's Wife and Nurse.

WIFE:

Nurse, where's my daughter? Call her forth to me.

NURSE:

Now, by my maidenhead at twelve year old,
I bade her come. What,° lamb! What, ladybird!°
God forbid. Where's this girl? What, Juliet!

Enter Juliet.

JULIET: How now? Who calls?   5

NURSE: Your mother.

JULIET:

Madam, I am here. What is your will?

WIFE:

This is the matter. — Nurse, give leave° awhile,
We must talk in secret. — Nurse, come back again;
I have remembered me, thou's° hear our counsel.   10
Thou knowest my daughter's of a pretty age.

NURSE:

Faith, I can tell her age unto an hour.

WIFE:

She's not fourteen.

NURSE: I'll lay fourteen of my teeth —
And yet, to my teen° be it spoken, I have but four —
She's not fourteen. How long is it now   15
To Lammastide?°

WIFE: A fortnight and odd days.

NURSE:

Even or odd, of all days in the year,

---

101. **mine own:** i.e., the sight of my own Rosaline.   **ACT I, SCENE 3. Location:** Verona.
Capulet's house.   3. **What:** (An expression of impatience.)   **ladybird:** i.e., sweetheart; also,
loose woman (used endearingly, though perhaps also with the immediate apology, "God for-
bid").   8. **give leave:** leave us.   10. **thou's:** thou shalt.   14. **teen:** sorrow (playing on *teen* and
four in *fourteen*).   16. **Lammastide:** the days near August 1.

Come Lammas Eve at night shall she be fourteen.
Susan° and she — God rest all Christian souls! —
Were of an age. Well, Susan is with God;   20
She was too good for me. But, as I said,
On Lammas Eve at night shall she be fourteen,
That shall she, marry,° I remember it well.
'Tis since the earthquake now eleven years,
And she was weaned — I never shall forget it —   25
Of all the days of the year, upon that day;
For I had then laid wormwood° to my dug,
Sitting in the sun under the dovehouse wall.
My lord and you were then at Mantua —
Nay, I do bear a brain!° But, as I said,   30
When it did taste the wormwood on the nipple
Of my dug and felt it bitter, pretty fool,°
To see it tetchy° and fall out wi' th' dug!
"Shake," quoth the dovehouse.° 'Twas no need, I trow,°
To bid me trudge!°   35
And since that time it is eleven years,
For then she could stand high-lone;° nay, by the rood,°
She could have run and waddled all about.
For even the day before, she broke her brow,°
And then my husband — God be with his soul!   40
'A° was a merry man — took up the child.
"Yea," quoth he, "dost thou fall upon thy face?
Thou wilt fall backward when thou hast more wit,°
Wilt thou not, Jule?" and, by my halidom,°
The pretty wretch left crying and said "Ay."   45
To see now how a jest shall come about!°
I warrant, an I should live a thousand years,
I never should forget it. "Wilt thou not, Jule?" quoth he,
And, pretty fool, it stinted° and said "Ay."
WIFE:
Enough of this. I pray thee, hold thy peace.   50

---

19. **Susan:** i.e., the Nurse's own child who has evidently died. 23. **marry:** i.e., by the Virgin Mary. (A mild oath.) 27. **wormwood:** (A bitter-tasting plant used to wean the child from the *dug* or teat.) 30. **bear a brain:** maintain a keen memory. 32. **fool:** (A term of endearment here.) 33. **tetchy:** fretful. 34. **"Shake" . . . dovehouse:** i.e., the dovehouse shook. **trow:** believe, assure you. 35. **trudge:** i.e., be off quickly. 37. **high-lone:** on her feet, without help. **rood:** cross. 39. **broke her brow:** bruised her forehead (by falling). 41. **'A:** he. 43. **wit:** understanding. 44. **halidom:** a relic or holy thing. 46. **come about:** come true. 49. **stinted:** ceased.

NURSE:

Yes, madam. Yet I cannot choose but laugh
To think it should leave crying and say "Ay."
And yet, I warrant, it had upon its brow
A bump as big as a young cockerel's stone° —
A perilous knock — and it cried bitterly. 55
"Yea," quoth my husband. "Fall'st upon thy face?
Thou wilt fall backward when thou comest to age,
Wilt thou not, Jule?" It stinted and said "Ay."

JULIET:

And stint thou too, I pray thee, Nurse, say I.°

NURSE:

Peace, I have done. God mark thee to his grace! 60
Thou wast the prettiest babe that e'er I nursed.
An I might live to see thee married once,°
I have my wish.

WIFE:

Marry, that "marry" is the very theme
I came to talk of. Tell me, daughter Juliet, 65
How stands your disposition° to be married?

JULIET:

It is an honor that I dream not of.

NURSE:

An honor? Were not I thine only nurse,
I would say thou hadst sucked wisdom from thy teat.°

WIFE:

Well, think of marriage now. Younger than you 70
Here in Verona, ladies of esteem°
Are made already mothers. By my count
I was your mother much upon these years°
That you are now a maid. Thus then in brief:
The valiant Paris seeks you for his love. 75

NURSE:

A man, young lady! Lady, such a man
As all the world — why, he's a man of wax.°

---

54. **cockerel's stone:** young rooster's testicle.   59. **say I:** (with a pun on *said* "*Ay*" of previous line).   62. **once:** someday.   66. **disposition:** inclination.   69. **thy teat:** i.e., the teat that nourished you.   71. **esteem:** worth, nobility.   73. **much . . . years:** at much the same age.   77. **a man of wax:** such as one would picture in wax, i.e., handsome.

WIFE:
Verona's summer hath not such a flower.
NURSE:
Nay,° he's a flower, in faith, a very flower.
WIFE:
What say you? Can you love the gentleman?   80
This night you shall behold him at our feast.
Read o'er the volume of young Paris' face
And find delight writ there with beauty's pen;
Examine every married° lineament°
And see how one another lends content,°   85
And what obscured in this fair volume lies
Find written in the margent° of his eyes.
This precious book of love, this unbound° lover,
To beautify him, only lacks a cover.°
The fish lives in the sea, and 'tis much pride   90
For fair without the fair within to hide.°
That book in many's eyes doth share the glory
That in gold clasps° locks in the golden story;°
So shall you share all that he doth possess,
By having him, making yourself no less.   95
NURSE:
No less? Nay, bigger.° Women grow by men.
WIFE:
Speak briefly: can you like of° Paris' love?
JULIET:
I'll look to like, if looking liking move,°
But no more deep will I endart mine eye°
Than your consent gives strength to make it fly.   100

Enter Servingman.

---

79. **Nay:** i.e., indeed.   84. **married:** harmonized.   **lineament:** facial feature.   85. **content:** (1) satisfaction (2) substance.   87. **margent:** commentary or marginal gloss.   88. **unbound:** i.e., because not bound in marriage (with a double meaning in the continuing metaphor of an unbound book).   89. **a cover:** i.e., marriage, a wife.   90–91. **The fish . . . hide:** i.e., the fish has its own suitable environment, and similarly in marriage the fair Juliet (here imagined as a beautiful book cover "binding" Paris) would suitably embrace Paris's worth.   93. **clasps:** (1) book fastenings (2) embraces.   92–93. **That book . . . story:** i.e., in many persons' eyes a good story is all the more admirable for being handsomely bound.   96. **bigger:** i.e., by pregnancy.   97. **like of:** be pleased with.   98. **liking move:** may provoke affection.   99. **endart mine eye:** i.e., let my eyes shoot Love's darts.

SERVINGMAN: Madam, the guests are come, supper served up, you called,
my young lady asked for, the Nurse cursed° in the pantry, and everything
in extremity. I must hence to wait. I beseech you, follow straight.°

WIFE:

We follow thee. [*Exit Servingman.*] Juliet, the County stays.°

NURSE:

Go, girl, seek happy nights to happy days.   *Exeunt.*   105

ACT I, SCENE 4°

Enter Romeo, Mercutio, Benvolio, with five or six other maskers; torchbearers.

ROMEO:

What, shall this speech° be spoke for our excuse?
Or shall we on° without apology?

BENVOLIO:

The date is out of such prolixity.°
We'll have no Cupid° hoodwinked° with a scarf,
Bearing a Tartar's painted bow° of lath,°   5
Scaring the ladies like a crowkeeper;°
Nor no without-book° prologue, faintly spoke
After the prompter, for our entrance;
But, let them measure us by what they will,
We'll measure them a measure,° and be gone.   10

ROMEO:

Give me a torch. I am not for this ambling.
Being but heavy,° I will bear the light.

MERCUTIO:

Nay, gentle Romeo, we must have you dance.

ROMEO:

Not I, believe me. You have dancing shoes

---

102. **cursed:** i.e., for not helping with the preparations.   103. **straight:** at once.   104. **County stays:** Count (Paris) waits for you.   **ACT I, SCENE 4. Location:** Verona. A street in the vicinity of Capulet's house.   1. **speech:** (Maskers were customarily preceded by a messenger or "presenter" with a set speech of compliment.)   2. **on:** go on, approach.   3. **The date . . . prolixity:** such windy rhetoric is out of fashion. (Directors sometimes assign this speech to Mercutio.)   4. **Cupid:** i.e., messenger or "presenter," probably a boy, disguised as Cupid. **hoodwinked:** blindfolded.   5. **Tartar's . . . bow:** (Tartar's bows, shorter and more curved than the English longbow, were thought to have resembled the old Roman bow with which Cupid was pictured.) **lath:** flimsy wood.   6. **crowkeeper:** scarecrow.   7. **without-book:** memorized.   10. **measure . . . measure:** perform for them a dance.   12. **heavy:** (1) sad (2) the opposite of *light* (as at 1.1.124).

With nimble soles; I have a soul of lead 15
So stakes me to the ground I cannot move.

MERCUTIO:
You are a lover; borrow Cupid's wings
And soar with them above a common° bound°

ROMEO:
I am too sore° enpiercèd with his shaft
To soar with his light featurers, and so bound° 20
I cannot bound a pitch° above dull woe.
Under love's heavy burden do I sink.

MERCUTIO:
And, to sink in it, should you burden love° —
Too great oppression for a tender thing.

ROMEO:
Is love a tender thing? It is too rough, 25
Too rude, too boisterous, and it pricks like thorn.

MERCUTIO:
If love be rough with you, be rough with love;
Prick love for pricking, and you beat love down.°
Give me a case° to put my visage in.   [*He puts on a mask.*]
A visor for a visor!° What care I 30
What curious eye doth quote° deformities
Here are the beetle brows shall blush for me.

BENVOLIO:
Come knock and enter, and no sooner in
But every man betake him to his legs.°

ROMEO:
A torch for me. Let wantons light of heart 35
Tickle the senseless° rushes° with their heels,
For I am proverbed with a grandsire phrase:°
I'll be a candle holder° and look on.

18. **common:** ordinary.   **bound:** (1) leap in the dance (2) limit.   19. **sore:** sorely (with pun on *soar;* see also pun on *soles* and *soul* in l. 15).   20. **bound:** confined (with play in l. 21 on the sense of "leap").   21. **pitch:** height. (A term from falconry for the highest point of a hawk's flight.)   23. **to sink . . . love:** i.e., if you should sink in love, you would prove a burden to it.   28. **Prick . . . down:** i.e., if love gets rough, fight back (but with bawdy suggestion of *pricking* as a way to satisfy desire and cause it to subside).   29. **case:** mask.   30. **A visor . . . visor:** i.e., a mask for an ugly masklike face.   31. **quote:** take notice of.   34. **to his legs:** i.e., to dancing.   36. **senseless:** lacking sensation.   **rushes:** (used for floor covering).   37. **proverbed . . . phrase:** furnished with an old proverb.   38. **candle holder:** i.e., onlooker. (Alludes to the proverb, "A good candle holder is a good gamester," i.e., he who merely looks on can't get in trouble.)

The game was ne'er so fair, and I am done.°

MERCUTIO:

Tut, dun's the mouse,° the constable's own word.°   40

If thou art dun, we'll draw thee from the mire

Of — save your reverence° — love, wherein thou stickets

Up to the ears. Come, we burn daylight,° ho!

ROMEO:

Nay, that's not so.

MERCUTIO: I mean, sir, in delay

We waste our lights in vain, like lamps by day.   45

Take our good meaning, for our judgment sits

Five times in that ere once in our five wits.°

ROMEO:

And we mean well in going to this masque,

But 'tis no wit° to go.

MERCUTIO: Why, may one ask?

ROMEO:

I dreamt a dream tonight.°

MERCUTIO: And so did I.   50

ROMEO:

Well, what was yours?

MERCUTIO: That dreamers often lie.

ROMEO:

In bed asleep, while they do dream things true.

MERCUTIO:

O, then, I see Queen Mab° hath been with you.

She is the fairies' midwife, and she comes

In shape no bigger than an agate stone°   55

On the forefinger of an alderman,°

---

39. The game . . . done: (Another proverbial notion, that it is wisest to quit when the gambling is at its best.)   **40. dun's the mouse:** (A common phrase usually taken to mean "keep still." *Dun,* gray-brown color, plays on *done,* done for. *Dun* also alludes to a Christmas game, "Dun [the gray-brown horse] is in the mire," in which a heavy log representing a horse was hauled out of an imaginary mire by the players.)   **constable's own word:** (A constable might caution one to keep still; Mercutio mocks Romeo's caution as lovesickness.)   **42. save your reverence:** (An apology for an improper expression, which Mercutio supposes "love" to be.)   **43. burn daylight:** i.e., waste time. (But Romeo quibbles, protesting that it is not literally daytime.)   **46–47. Take . . . wits:** i.e., try to understand what I intend to say, relying on common sense rather than on the exercise of wit. (The five "wits" or faculties were common sense, imagination, fantasy, judgment, and reason.)   **49. wit:** wisdom (playing on *wits* in l. 47; *mean* in l. 48 plays on *meaning* in l. 46).   **50. tonight:** last night.   **53. Queen Mab:** (Possibly a name of Celtic origin for the Fairy Queen.)   **55. agate stone:** (Precious stone often carved with diminutive figures and set in a ring.)   **56. alderman:** member of the municipal council.

Drawn with a team of little atomi°
Over men's noses as they lie asleep.
Her chariot is an empty hazelnut,
Made by the joiner° squirrel or old grub,°   60
Time out o' mind the fairies' coachmakers.
Her wagon spokes made of long spinners'° legs,
The cover of the wings of grasshoppers,
Her traces of the smallest spider web,
Her collars of the moonshine's watery beams,   65
Her whip of cricket's bone, the lash of film,°
Her wagoner° a small gray-coated gnat,
Not half so big as a round little worm°
Pricked from the lazy finger of a maid.
And in this state° she gallops night by night   70
Through lovers' brains, and then they dream of love;
O'er courtiers' knees, that dream on curtsies° straight;°
O'er lawyers' fingers, who straight dream on fees;
O'er ladies' lips, who straight on kisses dream,
Which oft the angry Mab with blisters plagues   75
Because their breaths with sweetmeats° tainted are.
Sometimes she gallops o'er a courtier's nose,
And then dreams he of smelling out a suit.°
And sometimes comes she with a tithe-pig's° tail
Tickling a parson's nose as 'a lies asleep;   80
Then dreams he of another benefice.°
Sometimes she driveth o'er a soldier's neck,
And then dreams he of cutting foreign throats,
Of breaches,° ambuscadoes,° Spanish blades,°
Of healths° five fathom deep,° and then anon   85
Drums in his ear, at which he starts and wakes,
And being thus frighted swears a prayer or two

---

57. **atomi:** tiny creatures (atoms).   60. **joiner:** furniture maker.   **grub:** insect larva (which bores holes in nuts).   62. **spinners':** spiders'.   66. **film:** gossamer thread.   67. **wagoner:** chariot driver.   68. **worm:** (Alludes to an ancient superstition that "worms breed in the fingers of the idle.")   70. **state:** pomp, dignity.   72. **curtsies:** i.e., bows, obeisances.   **straight:** immediately.   76. **sweetmeats:** candies or candied preserves.   78. **smelling . . . suit:** i.e., finding a petitioner who will pay for the use of his influence at court.   79. **tithe-pig:** pig given to the parson in lieu of money as the parishioner's tithing, or granting of a tenth.   81. **benefice:** ecclesiastical living.   84. **breaches:** opening of gaps in fortifications.   **ambuscadoes:** ambushes.   **Spanish blades:** i.e., swords from Toledo, where the best swords were made. 85. **healths:** toasts.   **five fathom deep:** a very deep or tall drink.

And sleeps again. This is that very Mab
That plats the manes of horses° in the night,
And bakes the elflocks° in foul sluttish hairs,   90
Which once untangled much misfortune bodes.
This is the hag, when maids lie on their backs,
That presses them and learns° them first to bear,
Making them women of good carriage.°
This is she —
ROMEO: Peace, peace, Mercutio, peace!   95
Thou talk'st of nothing.
MERCUTIO: True, I talk of dreams,
Which are the children of an idle brain,
Begot of nothing but vain fantasy,°
Which is as thin of substance as the air,
And more inconstant than the wind, who woos   100
Even now the frozen bosom of the north,
And being angered, puffs away from thence,
Turning his side to the dew-dropping south.
BENVOLIO:
This wind you talk of blows us from ourselves.°
Supper is done, and we shall come too late.   105
ROMEO:
I fear, too early; for my mind misgives°
Some consequence yet hanging in the stars
Shall bitterly begin his fearful date°
With this night's revels, and expire° the term
Of a despisèd life closed in my breast   110
By some vile forfeit of untimely death.
But He that hath the steerage of my course
Direct my suit! On, lusty° gentleman.
BENVOLIO: Strike, drum.°   *They march about the stage,*
                                              and [retire to one side].

---

89. **plats . . . horses:** (Alludes to the familiar superstition of "witches' stirrups," tangles in the manes of horses.)   90. **elflocks:** tangles. (Thought superstitiously to be the work of elves, who would seek revenge if the elflocks were untangled.)   93. **learns:** teaches.   94. **good carriage:** (1) commendable deportment (2) skill in bearing the weight of men in sexual intercourse (3) able subsequently to carry a child.   98. **vain fantasy:** empty imagination.   104. **from ourselves:** i.e., from our plans.   106. **misgives:** fears.   108. **date:** appointed time.   109. **expire:** bring to an end.   113. **lusty:** lively.   114. **drum:** drummer.

ACT 1, SCENE 5°

Servingmen come forth with napkins.

FIRST SERVINGMAN: Where's Potpan, that he helps not to take away?° He shift a trencher?° He scrape a trencher?

SECOND SERVINGMAN: When good manners shall lie all in one or two men's hands, and they unwashed too, 'tis a foul thing.

FIRST SERVINGMAN: Away with the joint stools,° remove the court cup-   5
board,° look to the plate.° Good thou, save me a piece of marchpane,° and, as thou loves me, let the porter let in Susan Grindstone and Nell. [*Exit Second Servingman.*] Anthony and Potpan!

[*Enter two more Servingmen.*]

THIRD SERVINGMAN: Ay, boy, ready.

FIRST SERVINGMAN: You are looked for and called for, asked for and   10
sought for, in the great chamber.

FOURTH SERVINGMAN: We cannot be here and there too. Cheerly, boys! Be brisk awhile, and the longer liver take all.°   *Exeunt.*

Enter [*Capulet and family and*] *all the guests and gentlewomen to the maskers.*

CAPULET: [*To the maskers*]
Welcome, gentleman! Ladies that have their toes
Unplagued with corns will walk a bout° with you.   15
Ah, my mistresses, which of you all
Will now deny to dance? She that makes dainty,°
She, I'll swear, hath corns. Am I come near ye now?°
Welcome, gentlemen! I have seen the day
That I have worn a visor and could tell   20
A whispering tale in a fair lady's ear
Such as would please. 'Tis gone, 'tis gone, 'tis gone.
You are welcome, gentlemen! Come, musicians, play.
                            Music plays, and they dance.
A hall,° a hall! Give room! And foot it, girls.

ACT 1, SCENE 5. **Location:** The action, continuous from the previous scene, is now imaginatively transferred to a hall in Capulet's house. **1. take away:** clear the table. **2. trencher:** wooden dish or plate. **5. joint stools:** stools with joined corners made by a joiner or furniture maker. **5–6. court cupboard:** sideboard. **6. plate** silverware. **marchpane:** cake made from sugar and almonds, marzipan. **13. the longer . . . all:** (A proverb, "the survivor takes all," here used to advocate seizing the moment of pleasure.) **15. walk a bout:** dance a turn. **17. makes dainty:** seems coyly reluctant (to dance). **18. Am . . . now:** i.e., have I hit a sensitive point, struck home. **24. A hall:** i.e., clear the hall for dancing.

[*To Servingmen.*] More light, you knaves, and turn the tables up,° 25
And quench the fire; the room is grown too hot.
[*To his cousin.*] Ah, sirrah, this unlooked-for sport° comes well.
Nay, sit, nay, sit, good cousin° Capulet,
For you and I are past our dancing days.
How long is 't now since last yourself and I 30
Were in a mask?
SECOND CAPULET: By 'r Lady, thirty years.
CAPULET:
What, man? 'Tis not so much, 'tis not so much;
'Tis since the nuptial of Lucentio,
Come Pentecost° as quickly as it will,
Some five-and-twenty years, and then we masked. 35
SECOND CAPULET:
'Tis more, 'tis more. His son is elder, sir;
His son is thirty.
CAPULET: Will you tell me that?
His son was but a ward° two years ago.
ROMEO: [*To a Servingman*]
What lady's that which doth enrich the hand
Of yonder knight?
SERVINGMAN: I know not, sir. 40
ROMEO:
O, she doth teach the torches to burn bright!
It seems she hangs upon the cheek of night
As a rich jewel in an Ethiop's ear —
Beauty too rich for use, for earth too dear!°
So shows° a snowy dove trooping with crows 45
As yonder lady o'er her fellows shows.
The measure done,° I'll watch her place of stand,°
And, touching hers,° make blessèd my rude° hand.
Did my heart love till now? Forswear it,° sight!
For I ne'er saw true beauty till this night. 50

---

25. **turn the tables up:** (Tables were probably made of hinged leaves and placed on trestles. They were put aside for dancing.)   27. **unlooked-for sport:** i.e., arrival of the maskers, making a dance possible.   28. **cousin:** kinsman.   34. **Pentecost:** seventh Sunday after Easter (and never as late as mid-July, two weeks before Lammas or August 1 when, according to 1.3.16, the play takes place; a seeming inconsistency).   38. **a ward:** a minor under guardianship. 44. **dear:** precious.   45. **shows:** appears.   47. **The measure done:** when this dance is over. **her place of stand:** where she stands.   48. **hers:** i.e., her hand. **rude:** rough.   49. **Forswear it:** deny any previous oath.

TYBALT:
    This, by his voice, should be a Montague.
    Fetch me my rapier, boy. What° dares the slave
    Come hither, covered with an antic face,°
    To fleer° and scorn at our solemnity?°
    Now, by the stock and honor of my kin,   55
    To strike him dead I hold it not a sin.

CAPULET:
    Why, how now, kinsman? Wherefore storm you so?

TYBALT:
    Uncle, this is a Montague, our foe,
    A villain that is hither come in spite°
    To scorn at our solemnity this night.   60

CAPULET:
    Young Romeo is it?

TYBALT: 'Tis he, that villain Romeo.

CAPULET:
    Content thee, gentle coz, let him alone.
    'A bears him like a portly° gentleman,
    And, to say truth, Verona brags of him
    To be a virtuous and well governed youth.   65
    I would not for the wealth of all this town
    Here in my house do him disparagement.
    Therefore be patient; take no note of him.
    It is my will, the which if thou respect,
    Show a fair presence and put off these frowns,   70
    An ill-beseeming semblance° for a feast.

TYBALT:
    It fits when such a villain is a guest.
    I'll not endure him.

CAPULET: He shall be endured.
    What, goodman boy?° I say he shall. Go to!°
    Am I the master here, or you? Go to.   75
    You'll not endure him! God shall mend my soul,
    You'll make a mutiny° among my guests!

---

52. **What:** how.   53. **antic face:** grotesque mask.   54. **fleer:** look mockingly.   **solemnity:** time-honored festivity.   59. **spite:** malice.   63. **portly:** of good deportment.   71. **semblance:** facial expression.   74. **goodman boy:** (A belittling term for Tybalt; "Goodman" applied to one below the rank of gentleman, but still of some substance, like a wealthy farmer.) **Go to:** (An expression of irritation.)   77. **mutiny:** disturbance.

You will set cock-a-hoop!° You'll be the man!°
TYBALT:
Why, uncle, 'tis a shame.
CAPULET: Go to, go to,
You are a saucy boy. Is 't so, indeed?   80
This trick may chance to scathe° you. I know what.°
You must contrary° me! Marry, 'tis time.° —
Well said,° my hearts! — You are a princox,° go.
Be quiet, or — More light, more light! — For shame!
I'll make you quiet, what! — Cheerly, my hearts!   85
TYBALT:
Patience perforce° with willful choler° meeting
Makes my flesh tremble in their different greeting.°
I will withdraw. But this intrusion shall,
Now seeming sweet, convert to bitterest gall.   *Exit.*
ROMEO: [*To Juliet*]
If I profane with my unworthiest hand   90
  This holy shrine,° the gentle sin is this:
My lips, two blushing pilgrims, ready stand
  To smooth that rough touch with a tender kiss.
JULIET:
Good pilgrim, you do wrong your hand too much,
  Which mannerly° devotion shows in this;   95
For saints have hands that pilgrims' hands do touch,
  And palm to palm is holy palmers'° kiss.
ROMEO:
Have not saints lips, and holy palmers too?
JULIET:
Ay, pilgrim, lips that they must use in prayer.
ROMEO:
O, then, dear saint, let lips do what hands do.   100
  They pray; grant thou,° lest faith turn to despair.

---

78. **You . . . cock-a-hoop:** i.e., you will behave recklessly, abandon all restraint.   **be the man:**
play the big man.   81. **scathe:** harm.   **what:** what I'm doing, or what I'll do.   82. **contrary:**
oppose, thwart.   **'tis time:** i.e., it's time you were taught a lesson.   83. **Well said:** well done.
(Said to the dancers.)   **princox:** saucy boy.   86. **Patience perforce:** patience upon compulsion.   **willful choler:** i.e., passionate anger.   87. **different greeting:** antagonistic opposition.
91. **shrine:** i.e., Juliet's hand.   95. **mannerly:** proper.   97. **palmers:** pilgrims who have been
to the Holy Land and brought back a palm (with a pun on the palm of the hand).   101. **grant
thou:** i.e., you must answer their prayers.

JULIET:
Saints do not move,° though grant° for prayers' sake.

ROMEO:
Then move° not, while my prayer's effect I take.   [*He kisses her.*]
Thus from my lips, by thine, my sin is purged.

JULIET:
Then have my lips the sin that they have took.   105

ROMEO:
Sin from my lips? O trespass sweetly urged!
Give me my sin again.°   [*He kisses her.*]

JULIET: You kiss by th' book.°

NURSE: [*Approaching*]
Madam, your mother craves a word with you.   [*Juliet retires.*]

ROMEO:
What° is her mother?

NURSE: Marry,° bachelor,°
Her mother is the lady of the house,   110
And a good lady, and a wise and virtuous.
I nursed her daughter that you talked withal.°
I tell you, he that can lay hold of her
Shall have the chinks.°

ROMEO: Is she a Capulet?
O dear account!° My life is my foe's debt.°   115

BENVOLIO: [*Approaching*]
Away, begone! The sport is at the best.°

ROMEO:
Ay, so I fear; the more is my unrest.   [*The maskers prepare to leave.*]

CAPULET:
Nay, gentlemen, prepare not to be gone.
We have a trifling foolish banquet towards.°   [*One whispers in his ear.*]
Is it e'en so? Why, then, I thank you all.   120
I thank you, honest° gentlemen. Good night.
More torches here! Come on then, let's to bed.

---

102. **move:** take the initiative.   **grant:** they grant (through intercession with God).   103. **move:** (Romeo quibbles on Juliet's word in the common sense of "change place or position.") 90–103. (These lines are in the form of a Shakespearean sonnet; they are followed by a quatrain.)   107. **again:** back again.   **by th' book:** i.e., by the rule, expertly.   109. **What:** who. **Marry:** i.e., by the Virgin Mary.   **bachelor:** young man.   112. **withal:** with.   114. **the chinks:** i.e., plenty of money.   115. **dear account:** heavy reckoning.   **my foe's debt:** due to my foe, at his mercy.   116. **The sport . . . best:** i.e., it is time to leave. (Refers to the proverb, "When play is at the best, it is time to leave," as at 1.4.39.)   119. **foolish banquet towards:** insignificant light refreshment in preparation.   121. **honest:** honorable.

[*To his cousin.*] Ah, sirrah, by my fay,° it waxes late.
I'll to my rest.   [*All proceed to leave but Juliet and the Nurse.*]

JULIET:
Come hither, Nurse. What is yond gentleman?   125

NURSE:
The son and heir of old Tiberio.

JULIET:
What's he that now is going out of door?

NURSE:
Marry, that, I think, be young Petruchio.

JULIET:
What's he that follows here, that would not dance?

NURSE: I know not.   130

JULIET:
Go ask his name. [*The Nurse goes.*] If he be marrièd,
My grave is like° to be my wedding bed.

NURSE: [*Returning*]
His name is Romeo, and a Montague,
The only son of your great enemy.

JULIET:
My only love sprung from my only hate!   135
Too early seen unknown, and known too late!
Prodigious° birth of love it is to me
That I must love a loathèd enemy.

NURSE:
What's tis?° What's tis?

JULIET: A rhyme I learned even now
Of one I danced withal.   *One calls within* "Juliet."

NURSE: Anon,° anon!   140
Come, let's away. The strangers all are gone.   *Exeunt.*

Act 2°

[*Enter*] *Chorus.*

CHORUS:
Now old desire doth in his deathbed lie,
    And young affection gapes° to be his heir;

---

123. **fay:** faith.   132. **like:** likely.   137. **Prodigious:** ominous.   139. **tis:** this. (Dialect pronunciation.)   140. **Anon:** i.e., we're coming.   ACT 2. **Chorus.**   2. **gapes:** yearns, clamors.

That fair° for which love groaned for and would die,
   With tender Juliet matched,° is now not fair.
Now Romeo is beloved and loves again,   5
   Alike° bewitchèd by the charm of looks;
But to his foe supposed° he must complain,°
   And she steal love's sweet bait from fearful hooks.
Being held a foe, he may not have access
   To breathe such vows as lovers use° to swear;   10
And she as much in love, her means much less
   To meet her new-belovèd anywhere.
But passion lends them power, time means,° to meet,
Tempering extremities° with extreme sweet.°   [*Exit.*]

Act 2, Scene 1°

Enter Romeo alone.

ROMEO:
   Can I go forward° when my heart is here?
   Turn back, dull earth,° and find thy center° out.   [*Romeo retires.*]

Enter Benvolio with Mercutio.

BENVOLIO:
   Romeo! My cousin Romeo! Romeo!
MERCUTIO: He is wise
   And, on my life, hath stolen him home to bed.   5
BENVOLIO:
   He ran this way and leapt this orchard wall.
   Call, good Mercutio.
MERCUTIO: Nay, I'll conjure° too.
   Romeo! Humors!° Madman! Passion! Lover!
   Appear thou in the likeness of a sigh.
   Speak but one rhyme, and I am satisfied;
   Cry but "Ay me!" Pronounce but "love" and "dove."   10

---

3. **fair:** beauty, i.e., Rosaline.   4. **matched:** compared.   6. **Alike:** i.e., equally with Juliet.
7. **foe supposed:** i.e., Juliet, a Capulet; also, his opposite number in the war of love.   **complain:**
offer his love plaint.   10. **use:** are accustomed.   13. **time means:** time lends them means.
14. **Tempering extremities:** reducing the hardships.   **sweet:** sweetness, pleasure.   **Act 2,
Scene 1. Location:** Verona. Outside of Capulet's walled orchard.   1. **forward:** i.e., away.
2. **dull earth:** i.e., Romeo's body.   **center:** i.e., Juliet. (The figure of speech is that of
humankind as a microcosm or little world.)   7. **conjure:** raise him with magical incantation.
8. **Humors:** moods.

Speak to my gossip° Venus one fair word,
One nickname for her purblind° son and heir,
Young Abraham° Cupid, he that shot so trim
When King Cophetua° loved the beggar maid. —   15
He heareth not, he stirreth not, he moveth not;
The ape° is dead, and I must conjure him. —
I conjure thee by Rosaline's bright eyes,
By her high forehead and her scarlet lip,
By her fine foot, straight leg, and quivering thigh,   20
And the demesnes° that there adjacent lie,
That in thy likeness thou appear to us!

BENVOLIO:
An if° he hear thee, thou wilt anger him.

MERCUTIO:
This cannot anger him. 'Twould anger him
To raise a spirit in his mistress' circle°   25
Of some strange° nature, letting it there stand
Till she had laid it° and conjured it down;
That were° some spite.° My invocation
Is fair and honest; in his mistress' name
I conjure only but to raise up him.   30

BENVOLIO:
Come, he hath hid himself among these trees
To be consorted° with the humorous° night.
Blind is his love, and best befits the dark.

MERCUTIO:
If love be blind, love cannot hit the mark.
Now will he sit under a medlar° tree   35
And wish his mistress were that kind of fruit

---

12. **gossip:** crony. 13. **purblind:** dim-sighted. 14. **Young Abraham:** i.e., one who is young and yet old, like the Biblical Abraham; Cupid was paradoxically the youngest and oldest of the gods. 15. **King Cophetua:** (In an old ballad, the King falls in love with a beggar maid and makes her his queen.) 17. **ape:** (Used as a term of endearment.) 21. **demesnes:** regions (with bawdy suggestion as to what is adjacent to the thighs; bawdy puns on terms of conjuration continue in *raise, spirit,* i.e., phallus or semen, *circle, stand, laid it, raise up*). 23. **An if:** if. 25. **circle:** (1) conjuring circle (2) vagina. 26. **strange:** belonging to another person (with suggestion of a rival possessing Rosaline sexually). 27. **laid it:** (1) laid the spirit to rest (2) provided sexual satisfaction leading to cessation of erection. 28. **were:** would be. **spite:** injury, vexation. 32. **consorted:** associated. **humorous:** moist; also, influenced by humor or mood. 35, 39. **medlar, poppering:** (Fruits used as slang terms for the sexual organs, female and male respectively. The medlar was edible only when partly decayed; the poppering pear, taking its name from *Poperinghe* in Flanders, had a phallic shape; the sound of its name is also suggestive.)

As maids call medlars when they laugh alone.
O, Romeo, that she were, O, that she were
An open-arse,° and thou a poppering° pear!
Romeo, good night. I'll to my truckle bed;°   40
This field bed is too cold for me to sleep.
Come, shall we go?
BENVOLIO: Go, then, for 'tis in vain
To seek him here that means not to be found.   *Exit* [*with Mercutio*].

ACT 2, SCENE 2°

ROMEO: [*Coming forward*]
He jests at scars that never felt a wound.
        [*A light appears° above, as at Juliet's window.*]
But soft, what light through yonder window breaks?
It is the east, and Juliet is the sun.
Arise, fair sun, and kill the envious moon,
Who is already sick and pale with grief   5
That thou her maid° art far more fair than she.
Be not her maid, since she is envious;
Her vestal livery° is but sick and green°
And none but fools do wear it. Cast it off.   [*Juliet is visible at her window.*]
It is my lady, O, it is my love!   10
O, that she knew she were!
She speaks, yet she says nothing. What of that?
Her eye discourses; I will answer it.
I am too bold. 'Tis not to me she speaks.
Two of the fairest stars in all the heaven,   15
Having some business, do entreat her eyes
To twinkle in their spheres° till they return.
What if her eyes were there, they in her head?

---

39. open-arse: (A name for the *medlar* making explicit the sexual metaphor.)   **40. truckle bed:** a bed on casters to be rolled under a standing bed.   **ACT 2, SCENE 2. Location:** The action, continuous from the previous scene, is now imaginatively transferred to inside Capulet's orchard. A rhymed couplet links the two scenes. Romeo has been hiding from his friends as though concealed by the orchard wall. He speaks at once, then turns to observe Juliet's window, which is probably in the gallery above, rearstage.   **1. s.d. *A light appears:*** (Some editors assume that Juliet is visible at l. 1.)   **6. maid:** i.e., votary of Diana, goddess of the moon and patroness of virgins.   **8. Her vestal livery:** the uniform of Diana's chaste votaries.   **sick and green:** (Suggesting the pallor of moonlight as well as anemia or *greensickness* [see 3.5.156] to which teenage girls were susceptible.)   **17. spheres:** transparent concentric shells supported to carry the heavenly bodies with them in their revolution around the earth.

The brightness of her cheek would shame those stars
As daylight doth a lamp; her eyes in heaven   20
Would through the airy region stream° so bright
That birds would sing and think it were not night.
See how she leans her cheek upon her hand!
O, that I were a glove upon that hand,
That I might touch that cheek!
JULIET: Ay me!
ROMEO: She speaks!   25
O, speak again, bright angel, for thou art
As glorious to this night, being o'er my head,
As is a wingèd messenger of heaven
Unto the white-upturnèd° wondering eyes
Of mortals that fall back to gaze on him   30
When he bestrides the lazy puffing clouds
And sails upon the bosom of the air.
JULIET:
O Romeo, Romeo, wherefore° art thou Romeo?
Deny thy father and refuse thy name!
Or, if thou wilt not, be but sworn my love,
And I'll no longer be a Capulet.   35
ROMEO: [*Aside*]
Shall I hear more, or shall I speak at this?
JULIET:
'Tis but thy name that is my enemy;
Thou art thyself, though not a Montague.°
What's Montague? It is nor hand,° nor foot,   40
Nor arm, nor face, nor any other part
Belonging to a man. O, be some other name!
What's in a name? That which we call a rose
By any other word would smell as sweet;
So Romeo would, were he not Romeo called,   45
Retain that dear perfection which he owes°
Without that title. Romeo, doff° thy name,
And for° thy name, which is no part of thee,
Take all myself.
ROMEO: I take thee at thy word!

21. **stream**: shine.   29. **white-upturnèd**: looking upward so that the whites of the eyes are visible.   33. **wherefore**: why.   39. **though not a Montague**: i.e., even if you were not a Montague.   40. **nor hand**: neither hand.   46. **owes**: owns.   47. **doff**: cast off.   48. **for**: in exchange for.

Call me but love, and I'll be new baptized;   50
Henceforth I never will be Romeo.

JULIET:
What man art thou that, thus bescreened° in night,
So stumblest on my counsel?°

ROMEO: By a name
I know not how to tell thee who I am.
My name, dear saint, is hateful to myself,   55
Because it is an enemy to thee;
Had I it written, I would tear the word.

JULIET:
My ears have not yet drunk a hundred words
Of thy tongue's uttering, yet I know the sound:
Art thou not Romeo and a Montague?   60

ROMEO:
Neither, fair maid, if either thee dislike.°

JULIET:
How camest thou hither, tell me, and wherefore?
The orchard walls are high and hard to climb,
And the place death, considering who thou art,
If any of my kinsmen find thee here.   65

ROMEO:
With love's light wings did I o'erperch° these walls,
For stony limits cannot hold love out,
And what love can do, that dares love attempt;
Therefore thy kinsmen are no stop to me.

JULIET:
If they do see thee, they will murder thee.   70

ROMEO:
Alack, there lies more peril in thine eyes
Than twenty of their swords. Look thou but sweet,
And I am proof° against their enmity.

JULIET:
I would not for the world they saw thee here.

ROMEO:
I have night's cloak to hide me from their eyes;   75
And but° thou love me, let them find me here.

---

52. **bescreened:** concealed.   53. **counsel:** secret thought.   61. **thee dislike:** displease you.
66. **o'erperch:** fly over.   73. **proof:** protected.   76. **but:** unless.

My life were better ended by their hate
Than death prorogued,° wanting of° thy love.

JULIET:

By whose direction foundst thou out this place?

ROMEO:

By love, that first did prompt me to inquire.   80
He lent me counsel, and I lent him eyes.
I am no pilot; yet, wert thou as far
As that vast shore washed with the farthest sea,
I should adventure for such merchandise.

JULIET:

Thou knowest the mask of night is on my face,   85
Else would a maiden blush bepaint my cheek
For that which thou hast heard me speak tonight.
Fain° would I dwell on form° — fain, fain deny
What I have spoke; but farewell compliment!°
Dost thou love me? I know thou wilt say "Ay,"   90
And I will take thy word. Yet if thou swear'st
Thou mayst prove false. At lovers' perjuries,
They say, Jove laughs. O gentle Romeo,
If thou dost love, pronounce it faithfully.
Or if thou thinkest I am too quickly won,   95
I'll frown and be perverse and say thee nay,
So° thou wilt woo, but else° not for the world.
In truth, fair Montague, I am too fond,°
And therefore thou mayst think my havior light.°
But trust me, gentleman, I'll prove more true   100
Than those that have more coying° to be strange.°
I should have been more strange, I must confess,
But that thou overheardst, ere I was ware,°
My true-love passion. Therefore pardon me,
And not impute this yielding to light love,   105
Which° the dark night hath so discoverèd.°

ROMEO:

Lady, by yonder blessèd moon I vow,
That tips with silver all these fruit-tree tops —

---

78. **proroguèd:** postponed. **wanting of:** lacking. 88. **Fain:** gladly. **dwell on form:** preserve
the proper formalities. 89. **compliment:** etiquette, convention. 97. **So:** as long as, if only.
else: otherwise. 98. **fond:** infatuated. 99. **havior light:** behavior frivolous. 101. **coying:**
coyness. **strange:** reserved, aloof, modest. 103. **ware:** aware. 106. **Which:** i.e., which
yielding. **discoverèd:** revealed.

JULIET:
  O, swear not by the moon, th' inconstant moon,
  That monthly changes in her circled orb,°   110
  Lest that thy love prove likewise variable.

ROMEO:
  What shall I swear by?

JULIET: Do not swear at all;
  Or, if thou wilt, swear by thy gracious self,
  Which is the god of my idolatry,
  And I'll believe thee.

ROMEO: If my heart's dear love —   115

JULIET:
  Well, do not swear. Although I joy in thee,
  I have no joy of this contract° tonight.
  It is too rash, too unadvised,° too sudden,
  Too like the lightning, which doth cease to be
  Ere one can say "It lightens." Sweet, good night!   120
  This bud of love, by summer's ripening breath,
  May prove a beauteous flower when next we meet.
  Good night, good night! As° sweet repose and rest
  Come to thy heart as that within my breast!

ROMEO:
  O, wilt thou leave me so unsatisfied?   125

JULIET:
  What satisfaction canst thou have tonight?

ROMEO:
  Th' exchange of thy love's faithful vow for mine.

JULIET:
  I gave thee mine before thou didst request it;
  And yet I would it were° to give again.

ROMEO:
  Wouldst thou withdraw it? For what purpose, love?   130

JULIET:
  But to be frank° and give it thee again.
  And yet I wish but for the thing I have.
  My bounty is as boundless as the sea,
  My love as deep; the more I give to thee,
  The more I have, for both are infinite.   [*The Nurse calls within.*]   135

---

110. **orb:** i.e., sphere; see above, l. 17.   117. **contract:** exchanging of vows.   118. **unadvised:** unconsidered.   123. **As:** may just as.   129. **were:** were available.   131. **frank:** liberal, bounteous.

I hear some noise within; dear love, adieu! —
Anon, good Nurse! — Sweet Montague, be true.
Stay but a little, I will come again.   [*Exit, above.*]
ROMEO:
O blessèd, blessèd night! I am afeard,
Being in night, all this is but a dream,   140
Too flattering-sweet to be substantial.

[*Enter Juliet, above.*]

JULIET:
Three words, dear Romeo, and good night indeed.
If that thy bent° of love be honorable,
Thy purpose marriage, send me word tomorrow,
By one that I'll procure to come to thee,   145
Where and what time thou wilt perform the rite;
And all my fortunes at thy foot I'll lay
And follow thee my lord throughout the world.
NURSE: [*Within*]   Madam!
JULIET:
I come, anon. — But if thou meanest not well,   150
I do beseech thee —
NURSE: [*Within*]   Madam!
JULIET: By and by,° I come —
To cease thy strife° and leave me to my grief.
Tomorrow will I send.
ROMEO:
So thrive my soul —
JULIET:
A thousand times good night!   [*Exit, above.*]   155
ROMEO:
A thousand times the worse, to want thy light.
Love goes toward love as schoolboys from their books,
But love from love, toward school with heavy looks.   [*He starts to leave.*]

Enter Juliet [*above*] *again.*

JULIET:
Hist! Romeo, hist! O, for a falconer's voice,
To lure this tassel-gentle° back again!   160

___

143. **bent:** purpose.   151. **By and by:** immediately.   152. **strife:** striving.   160. **tassel-gentle:** tercel gentle, the male of the goshawk.

Bondage is hoarse° and may not speak aloud,
Else would I tear° the cave where Echo° lies
And make her airy tongue more hoarse than mine
With repetition of "My Romeo!"

ROMEO:

It is my soul that calls upon my name.   165
How silver-sweet sound lovers' tongues by night,
Like softest music to attending ears!

JULIET:

Romeo!

ROMEO: My nyas?°

JULIET: What o'clock tomorrow
Shall I send to thee?

ROMEO: By the hour of nine.

JULIET:

I will not fail. 'Tis twenty years till then. —   170
I have forgot why I did call thee back.

ROMEO:

Let me stand here till thou remember it.

JULIET:

I shall forget, to have thee still° stand there,
Remembering how I love thy company.

ROMEO:

And I'll still stay, to have thee still forget,   175
Forgetting any other home but this.

JULIET:

'Tis almost morning. I would have thee gone —
And yet no farther than a wanton's° bird,
That lets it hop a little from his hand,
Like a poor prisoner in his twisted gyves,°   180
And with a silken thread plucks it back again,
So loving-jealous of his° liberty.

ROMEO:

I would I were thy bird.

JULIET: Sweet, so would I.
Yet I should kill thee with much cherishing.

---

161. **Bondage is hoarse:** i.e., in confinement one can speak only in a loud whisper.   162. **tear:** pierce (with noise).   **Echo:** (In Book 3 of Ovid's *Metamorphoses,* Echo, rejected by Narcissus, pines away in lonely caves until only her voice is left.)   168. **nyas:** eyas, fledgling.   173. **still:** always.   178. **wanton's:** spoiled child's.   180. **gyves:** fetters.   182. **his:** its.

Good night, good night! Parting is such sweet sorrow   185
That I shall say good night till it be morrow.   [*Exit, above.*]

ROMEO:

Sleep dwell upon thine eyes, peace in thy breast!
Would I were sleep and peace, so sweet to rest!
Hence will I to my ghostly° friar's close° cell,
His help to crave, and my dear hap° to tell.   *Exit.*   190

ACT 2, SCENE 3°

Enter Friar [Laurence] alone, with a basket.

FRIAR LAURENCE:

The gray-eyed morn smiles on the frowning night,
Check'ring the eastern clouds with streaks of light,
And fleckled° darkness like a drunkard reels
From forth° day's path and Titan's° fiery wheels.
Now, ere the sun advance° his burning eye,   5
The day to cheer and night's dank dew to dry,
I must up-fill this osier cage° of ours
With baleful° weeds and precious-juicèd flowers.
The earth that's nature's mother is her tomb;
What is her burying grave, that is her womb;   10
And from her womb children of divers kind
We sucking on her natural bosom find,
Many for many virtues excellent,
None but for some,° and yet all different.
O, mickle° is the powerful grace° that lies   15
In plants, herbs, stones, and their true° qualities.
For naught so vile° that on the earth doth live
But to the earth some special good doth give;
Nor aught so good but, strained° from that fair use,
Revolts from true birth, stumbling on abuse.   20
Virtue itself turns vice, being misapplied,
And vice sometime's by action dignified.

---

189. **ghostly:** spiritual.   **close:** narrow.   190. **dear hap:** good fortune.   ACT 2, SCENE 3.
Location: Verona. Near Friar Laurence's cell, perhaps in the monastery garden.   3. **fleckled:**
dappled.   4. **From forth:** out of the way of.   **Titan's:** (Helios, the sun god, was a descendant
of the race of Titans.)   5. **advance:** raise.   7. **osier cage:** willow basket.   8. **baleful:** harmful.
14. **None but for some:** there are none that are not useful for something.   15. **mickle:** great.
grace: beneficent virtue.   16. **true:** proper, inherent.   17. **For naught so vile:** for there is
nothing so vile.   19. **strained:** forced, perverted.

Enter Romeo.

Within the infant rind of this weak flower
Poison hath residence and medicine power:
For this, being smelt, with that part° cheers each part;   25
Being tasted, stays° all senses with the heart.
Two such opposèd kings encamp them still°
In man as well as herbs — grace and rude will;
And where the worser is predominant,
Full soon the canker° death eats up that plant.   30

ROMEO:
Good morrow, Father.

FRIAR LAURENCE: Benedicite!°
What early tongue so sweet saluteth me?
Young son, it argues° a distempered° head
So soon to bid good morrow to thy bed.
Care keeps his watch in every old man's eye,   35
And where care lodges sleep will never lie;
But where unbruisèd youth with unstuffed° brain
Doth couch his limbs, there golden sleep doth reign.
Therefore thy earliness doth me assure
Thou art uproused with some distemp'rature;   40
Or if not so, then here I hit it right:
Our Romeo hath not been in bed tonight.

ROMEO:
That last is true. The sweeter rest was mine.

FRIAR LAURENCE:
God pardon sin! Wast thou with Rosaline?

ROMEO:
With Rosaline, my ghostly father? No.   45
I have forgot that name, and that name's woe.

FRIAR LAURENCE:
That's my good son. But where hast thou been, then?

ROMEO:
I'll tell thee ere thou ask it me again.
I have been feasting with mine enemy,
Where on a sudden one hath wounded me   50

---

25. **that part:** i.e., the odor.   26. **stays:** halts.   27. **still:** always.   30. **canker:** cankerworm.
31. **Benedicite:** a blessing on you.   33. **argues:** demonstrates, provides evidence of.   **distempered:** disturbed, disordered.   37. **unstuffed:** not overcharged, carefree.

That's by me wounded. Both our remedies°
Within thy help and holy physic° lies.
I bear no hatred, blessèd man, for, lo,
My intercession° likewise steads° my foe.

FRIAR LAURENCE:

Be plain, good son, and homely° in thy drift.   55
Riddling confession finds but riddling shrift.°

ROMEO:

Then plainly know my heart's dear love is set
On the fair daughter of rich Capulet.
As mine on hers, so hers is set on mine,
And all combined, save what thou must combine   60
By holy marriage. When and where and how
We met, we wooed, and made exchange of vow
I'll tell thee as we pass; but this I pray,
That thou consent to marry us today.

FRIAR LAURENCE:

Holy Saint Francis, what a change is here!   65
Is Rosaline, that thou didst love so dear,
So soon forsaken? Young men's love then lies
Not truly in their hearts, but in their eyes.
Jesu Maria, what a deal of brine
Hath washed thy sallow° cheeks for Rosaline!   70
How much salt water thrown away in waste
To season love, that of it doth not taste!
The sun not yet thy sighs from heaven clears,
Thy old groans yet ringing in mine ancient ears.
Lo, here upon thy cheek the stain doth sit   75
Of an old tear that is not washed off yet.
If e'er thou wast thyself° and these woes thine,
Thou and these woes were all for Rosaline.
And art thou changed? Pronounce this sentence° then:
Women may fall, when there's no strength in men.   80

ROMEO:

Thou chidst° me oft for loving Rosaline.

---

51. **Both our remedies:** i.e., the remedy for both of us.   52. **physic:** medicine, healing property.   54. **intercession:** petition. **steads:** helps.   55. **homely:** simple.   56. **shrift:** absolution.   70. **sallow:** sickly yellow.   77. **wast thyself:** i.e., were sincere.   79. **sentence:** sententious conclusion.   81. **chidst:** rebuked.

FRIAR LAURENCE:
　For doting, not for loving, pupil mine.

ROMEO:
　And badst° me bury love.

FRIAR LAURENCE:　　　　　Not in a grave
　To lay one in, another out to have.

ROMEO:
　I pray thee, chide not. She whom I love now　　　　　85
　Doth grace° for grace and love for love allow.
　The other did not so.

FRIAR LAURENCE:　　　O, she knew well
　Thy love did read by rote,° that could not spell.
　But come, young waverer, come, go with me.
　In one respect° I'll thy assistant be;　　　　　90
　For this alliance may so happy prove
　To° turn your households' rancor to pure love.

ROMEO:
　O, let us hence! I stand on° sudden haste.

FRIAR LAURENCE:
　Wisely and slow. They stumble that run fast.　　　*Exeunt.*

ACT 2, SCENE 4°

Enter Benvolio and Mercutio.

MERCUTIO:
　Where the devil should° this Romeo be?
　Came he not home tonight?°

BENVOLIO:
　Not to his father's. I spoke with his man.

MERCUTIO:
　Why, that same pale hardhearted wench, that Rosaline,
　Torments him so that he will sure run mad.　　　　　5

BENVOLIO:
　Tybalt, the kinsman to old Capulet,
　Hath sent a letter to his father's house.

MERCUTIO:　　A challenge, on my life.

83. **badst:** bade.　86. **grace:** favor, graciousness.　88. **did read by rote:** i.e., repeated conventional expressions without understanding them.　90. **In one respect:** for one reason (at least). 92. **To:** as to.　93. **stand on:** am in need of, insist on. ACT 2, SCENE 4. Location: Verona. A street.　1. **should:** can.　2. **tonight:** last night.

BENVOLIO: Romeo will answer it.°

MERCUTIO: Any man that can write may answer a letter.   10

BENVOLIO: Nay, he will answer the letter's master, how he dares, being
dared.

MERCUTIO: Alas poor Romeo! He is already dead, stabbed with a white
wench's black eye, run through the ear with a love song, the very pin° of
his heart cleft with the blind bow-boy's butt shaft.° And is he a man to   15
encounter Tybalt?

BENVOLIO: Why, what is Tybalt?

MERCUTIO: More than prince of cats.° O, he's the courageous captain of
compliments.° He fights as you sing prick song,° keeps time, distance,
and proportion;° he rests his minim rests,° one, two, and the third in your   20
bosom. The very butcher of a silk button,° a duellist, a duellist, a gentleman of the very first house,° of the first and second cause.° Ah, the
immortal *passado!*° The *punto reverso!*° The *hay!*°

BENVOLIO: The what?

MERCUTIO: The pox of° such antic,° lisping, affecting phantasimes,° these   25
new tuners of accent!° "By Jesu, a very good blade! A new tall° man! A
very good whore!" Why, is not this a lamentable thing, grandsire,° that
we should be thus afflicted with these strange flies,° these fashion-
mongers, these pardon-me's,° who stand° so much on the new form that
they cannot sit at ease on the old bench?° O, their bones,° their bones!   30

Enter Romeo.

BENVOLIO: Here comes Romeo, here comes Romeo.

MERCUTIO: Without his roe,° like a dried herring. O flesh, flesh, how art

---

9. **answer it:** accept the challenge.   14. **pin:** peg in the center of a target.   15. **butt shaft:**
unbarbed arrow, allotted to children and thus to Cupid.   18. **prince of cats:** (The name of the
king of cats in *Reynard the Fox* was Tybalt or Tybert.)   18–19. **captain of compliments:** master
of ceremony and dueling etiquette.   19. **prick song:** music written out.   20. **proportion:**
rhythm.   **minim rests:** short rests in musical notation.   21. **butcher . . . button:** i.e., one able
to strike a specific button on his adversary's person.   22. **first house:** best school of fencing.
first and second cause: causes according to the code of dueling that would oblige one to seek
the satisfaction of one's honor.   23. *passado:* forward thrust.   *punto reverso:* backhanded
stroke.   *hay:* thrust through. (From the Italian *hai* meaning "you have [it].")   25. **The pox of:**
plague take.   **antic:** grotesque.   **phantasimes:** coxcombs, fantastically dressed or mannered.
26. **new tuners of accent:** those who introduce new foreign words and slang phrases into their
speech.   **tall:** valiant.   27. **grandsire:** i.e., one who disapproves the new fashion and prefers
old custom.   28. **flies:** parasites.   29. **pardon-me's:** i.e., those who affect overly polite manners.   **stand:** (1) insist (2) the opposite of *sit,* l. 30.   29–30. **form . . . bench:** (*Form* means
both "fashion" or "code of manners" and "bench.")   30. **bones:** French *bon,* good (with play on
English *bone*).   32. **Without his roe:** i.e., looking thin and emaciated, sexually spent. (With a
pun on the first syllable of Romeo's name; the remaining syllables, *me-oh,* sound like the
expression of a melancholy lover. *Roe* also suggests a female deer or "dear.")

thou fishified! Now is he for the numbers° that Petrarch flowed in. Laura° to his lady was but a kitchen wench — marry, she had a better love to° berhyme her — Dido a dowdy,° Cleopatra a gypsy,° Helen and Hero hildings° and harlots, Thisbe a gray eye or so, but not° to the purpose. Signor Romeo, *bonjour!* There's a French salutation to your French slop.° You gave us the counterfeit fairly° last night. 35

ROMEO: Good morrow to you both. What counterfeit did I give you?

MERCUTIO: The slip,° sir, the slip. Can you not conceive?° 40

ROMEO: Pardon, good Mercutio, my business was great, and in such a case° as mine a man may strain courtesy.

MERCUTIO: That's as much as to say, such a case as yours constrains a man to bow in the hams.°

ROMEO: Meaning, to curtsy.° 45

MERCUTIO: Thou hast most kindly° hit it.

ROMEO: A most courteous exposition.

MERCUTIO: Nay, I am the very pink of courtesy.

ROMEO: Pink for flower.

MERCUTIO: Right. 50

ROMEO: Why then is my pump° well flowered.°

MERCUTIO: Sure wit, follow me this jest now till thou hast worn out thy pump, that when the single sole of it is worn, the jest may remain, after the wearing, solely singular.°

ROMEO: O single-soled° jest, solely singular for the singleness!° 55

MERCUTIO: Come between us, good Benvolio. My wits faints.

ROMEO: Switch and spurs,° switch and spurs! Or I'll cry a match.°

MERCUTIO: Nay, if our wits run the wild-goose chase,° I am done, for thou hast more of the wild goose in one of thy wits than, I am sure, I have in my whole five. Was I with you there for the goose?° 60

---

33. **numbers:** verses. **Laura:** the lady to whom the Italian Renaissance poet Petrarch addressed his love poems. (Other romantic heroines are named in the following passage: Dido, Queen of Carthage; Cleopatra; Helen of Troy; Hero, beloved of Leander; and Thisbe, beloved of Pyramus.) 34. **to:** in comparison to. 35. **dowdy:** homely woman. **gypsy:** Egyptian; whore. 36. **hildings:** good-for-nothings. **not:** i.e., that is not. 37. **French slop:** loose trousers of French fashion. 38. **fairly:** handsomely, effectively. 40. **slip:** (Counterfeit coins were called "slips.") **conceive:** i.e., get the joke. 42. **case:** (1) situation (2) physical condition. (Mercutio also bawdily suggests that Romeo has been in a *case,* i.e., the female genitalia.) 44. **bow in the hams:** (1) kneel, curtsy (2) show the effects of venereal disease. 45. **curtsy:** make obeisance. 46. **kindly:** naturally; politely. 51. **pump:** shoe. **well flowered:** expertly pinked or perforated in ornamental figures. 54. **solely singular:** unique. 55. **single-soled:** i.e., thin, contemptible. **singleness:** feebleness. 57. **Switch and spurs:** i.e., keep up the rapid pace of the hunt (in the game of wits). **cry a match:** claim the victory. 58. **wild-goose chase:** a horse race in which the leading rider dares his competitors to follow him wherever he goes. 60. **Was . . . goose:** did I score a point in calling you a goose.

ROMEO: Thou wast never with me for anything when thou wast not there for the goose.°

MERCUTIO: I will bite thee by the ear° for that jest.

ROMEO: Nay, good goose, bite not.

MERCUTIO: Thy wit is a very bitter sweeting;° it is a most sharp sauce.°   65

ROMEO: And is it not, then, well served in to a sweet goose?

MERCUTIO: O, here's a wit of cheveril,° that stretches from an inch narrow to an ell° broad!

ROMEO: I stretch it out for that word "broad," which, added to the goose, proves thee far and wide a broad° goose.   70

MERCUTIO: Why, is not this better now than groaning for love? Now art thou sociable, now art thou Romeo; now art thou what thou art, by art as well as by nature. For this driveling love is like a great natural° that runs lolling° up and down to hide his bauble° in a hole.

BENVOLIO: Stop there, stop there.   75

MERCUTIO: Thou desirest me to stop in my tale against the hair.°

BENVOLIO: Thou wouldst else have made thy tale large.

MERCUTIO: O, thou art deceived; I would have made it short, for I was come to the whole depth of my tale and meant indeed to occupy the argument no longer.   80

ROMEO: Here's a goodly gear!°

Enter Nurse and her man [Peter].

A sail, a sail!

MERCUTIO: Two, two: a shirt and a smock.°

NURSE: Peter!

PETER: Anon!   85

NURSE: My fan, Peter.

MERCUTIO: Good Peter, to hide her face, for her fan's the fairer face.

NURSE: God gi' good morrow, gentlemen.

MERCUTIO: God gi' good e'en, fair gentlewoman.

NURSE: Is it good e'en?°   90

---

62. for the goose: (1) behaving like a goose (2) looking for a prostitute.   **63. bite . . . ear:** i.e., give you an affectionate nibble on the ear. (Said ironically, however, and Romeo parries.) **65. sweeting:** sweet-flavored variety of apple.   **sharp sauce:** (1) "biting" retort (2) tart sauce, of the sort that should be served with cooked goose (as Romeo points out).   **67. cheveril:** kid leather, easily stretched.   **68. ell:** (forty-five inches).   **70. broad:** large, complete; perhaps also wanton.   **73. natural:** idiot.   **74. lolling:** with his tongue (or bauble) hanging out. **bauble:** (1) jester's wand (2) phallus.   **76. against the hair:** against the grain, against my wish (with a bawdy play on *tale, tail;* continued with *large, short, depth, occupy,* etc.).   **81. gear:** substance, stuff (with sexual innuendo).   **83. a shirt . . . smock:** i.e., a man and a woman.   **90. Is it good e'en:** is it afternoon already.

MERCUTIO: 'Tis no less, I tell ye, for the bawdy hand of the dial is now upon the prick° of noon.

NURSE: Out upon you!° What° a man are you?

ROMEO: One, gentlewoman, that God hath made for himself to mar.°

NURSE: By my troth,° it is well said. "For himself to mar," quoth 'a?° Gentle-   95
men, can any of you tell me where I may find the young Romeo?

ROMEO: I can tell you; but young Romeo will be older when you have found him than he was when you sought him. I am the youngest of that name, for fault° of a worse.

NURSE: You say well.   100

MERCUTIO: Yea, is the worst well? Very well took,° i' faith, wisely, wisely.

NURSE: If you be he, sir, I desire some confidence° with you.

BENVOLIO: She will indite° him to some supper.

MERCUTIO: A bawd, a bawd, a bawd! So ho!°

ROMEO: What hast thou found?   105

MERCUTIO: No hare,° sir, unless a hare, sir, in a lenten pie,° that is something stale and hoar° ere it be spent.°   [*He sings.*]

    An old hare hoar,
    And an old hare hoar,
  Is very good meat in Lent.   110
    But a hare that is hoar
    Is too much for a score,°
  When it hoars ere it be spent.

Romeo, will you come to your father's? We'll to dinner thither.

ROMEO: I will follow you.   115

MERCUTIO: Farewell, ancient lady. Farewell, [*Singing*] "Lady, lady, lady,"°

Exeunt [*Mercutio and Benvolio*].

NURSE: I pray you, sir, what saucy merchant° was this that was so full of his ropery?°

ROMEO: A gentleman, Nurse, that loves to hear himself talk, and will speak more in a minute than he will stand to° in a month.   120

---

92. **prick:** point on the dial of a clock (with bawdy suggestion).   93. **Out upon you:** (Expression of indignation.)   **What:** what kind of.   94. **mar:** i.e., disfigure morally through sin. (Man, made in God's image, mars that image sinfully.)   95. **troth:** faith.   **quoth 'a:** said he. (A sarcastic interjection, meaning "forsooth" or "indeed.")   99. **fault:** lack.   101. **took:** understood.   102. **confidence:** (The Nurse's mistake for *conference*.)   103. **indite:** (Benvolio's deliberate malapropism for *invite*.)   104. **So ho:** (Cry of hunter sighting game.)   106. **hare:** (Slang word for "prostitute"; similarly with *stale* and *meat* in the following lines.)   **a lenten pie:** a pie that should contain no meat, in observance of Lent.   107. **hoar:** moldy (with pun on *whore*).   **spent:** consumed.   112. **for a score:** for a reckoning, to pay good money for.   116. **"Lady, lady, lady":** (Refrain from the ballad *Chaste Susanna*.)   117. **merchant:** i.e., fellow.   118. **ropery:** vulgar humor, knavery.   120. **stand to:** perform, abide by.

NURSE: An 'a speak anything against me, I'll take him down,° an 'a were lustier than he is, and twenty such Jacks;° and if I cannot, I'll find those that shall. Scurvy knave! I am none of his flirt-gills.° I am none of his skains-mates.° [*To Peter.*] And thou must stand by, too, and suffer every knave to use me at his pleasure!   125

PETER: I saw no man use you at his pleasure. If I had, my weapon° should quickly have been out; I warrant you, I dare draw as soon as another man, if I see occasion in a good quarrel, and the law on my side.

NURSE: Now, afore God, I am so vexed that every part about me quivers.° Scurvy knave! Pray you, sir, a word; and as I told you, my young lady bid   130 me inquire you out. What she bid me say, I will keep to myself. But first let me tell ye, if ye should lead her in a fool's paradise, as they say, it were a very gross kind of behavior, as they say. For the gentlewoman is young; and therefore if you should deal double with her, truly it were an ill thing to be offered to any gentlewoman, and very weak° dealing.   135

ROMEO: Nurse, commend me to thy lady and mistress. I protest° unto thee —

NURSE: Good heart, and i' faith I will tell her as much. Lord, Lord, she will be a joyful woman.

ROMEO: What wilt thou tell her, Nurse? Thou dost not mark° me.   140

NURSE: I will tell her, sir, that you do protest, which, as I take it, is a gentlemanlike offer.

ROMEO: Bid her devise
Some means to come to shrift° this afternoon,
And there she shall at Friar Laurence' cell   145
Be shrived° and married. Here is for thy pains.   [*He offers money.*]

NURSE: No, truly, sir, not a penny.

ROMEO: Go to, I say you shall.

NURSE:
This afternoon, sir? Well, she shall be there.

ROMEO:
And stay, good Nurse, behind the abbey wall.   150

---

121. **take him down:** i.e., cut him down to size (with unintended bawdy suggestion).   122. **Jacks:** (used as a term of disparagement).   123. **flirt-gills:** loose women.   124. **skains-mates:** (Perhaps daggermates, outlaws, or gangster molls.)   126. **weapon:** (with bawdy suggestion, perhaps unrecognized by the speaker, as also in *at his pleasure*).   129. **every part . . . quivers:** (More bawdy suggestion, unrecognized by the Nurse.)   135. **weak:** contemptible.   136. **protest:** vow. (Romeo may intend only to protest his good intentions, but the Nurse seemingly takes the word to signify a *gentlemanlike offer* [l. 141] of marriage that would ensure against Juliet's being led into a *fool's paradise* [l. 132] — i.e., being seduced.)   140. **mark:** attend to.   144. **shrift:** confession and absolution.   146. **shrived:** absolved.

Within this hour my man shall be with thee
And bring thee cords made like a tackled stair,°
Which to the high topgallant° of my joy
Must be my convoy° in the secret night.
Farewell. Be trusty, and I'll quit° thy pains.   155
Farewell. Commend me to thy mistress.   [*Romeo starts to leave.*]

NURSE:
Now God in heaven bless thee! Hark you, sir.

ROMEO: What sayst thou, my dear Nurse?

NURSE:
Is your man secret?° Did you ne'er hear say,
"Two may keep counsel,° putting one away"?   160

ROMEO:
'Warrant thee, my man's as true as steel.

NURSE: Well, sir, my mistress is the sweetest lady — Lord, Lord! When
'twas a little prating thing — O, there is a nobleman in town, one Paris,
that would fain° lay knife aboard;° but she, good soul, had as lief° see a
toad, a very toad, as see him. I anger her sometimes and tell her that Paris   165
is the properer° man, but I'll warrant you, when I say so, she looks as pale
as any clout° in the versal° world. Doth not rosemary and Romeo begin
both with a letter?°

ROMEO: Ay, Nurse, what of that? Both with an R.

NURSE: Ah, mocker! That's the dog's name;° R is for the — No; I know it   170
begins with some other letter;° and she hath the prettiest sententious° of
it, of you and rosemary, that it would do you good to hear it.

ROMEO: Commend me to thy lady.

NURSE: Ay, a thousand times. [*Exit Romeo.*] Peter!

PETER: Anon!   175

NURSE: Before, and apace.°   *Exeunt.*

---

152. tackled stair: rope ladder.   **153. topgallant:** highest mast and sail of a ship, the summit.
154. convoy: conveyance, means of passage.   **155. quit:** reward, requite.   **159. secret:** trustworthy.   **160. keep counsel:** keep a secret.   **164. fain:** gladly.   **lay knife aboard:** i.e., assert
his claim (just as a guest did by bringing his knife to the dinner table; with sexual suggestion
also).   **lief:** willingly.   **166. properer:** handsomer.   **167. clout:** rag, cloth.   **versal:** universal.
168. a letter: one and the same letter.   **170. the dog's name:** (The letter *R* was thought to
resemble the dog's growl.)   **170–71. No . . . other letter:** (The Nurse perhaps thinks that the
letter means "arse" and repudiates the association.)   **171. sententious:** (The Nurse probably
means *sentences,* pithy sayings.)   **176. Before, and apace:** go before me quickly.

ACT 2, SCENE 5°

Enter Juliet.

JULIET:

The clock struck nine when I did send the Nurse;
In half an hour she promised to return.
Perchance she cannot meet him. That's not so.
O, she is lame! Love's heralds should be thoughts,
Which ten times faster glide than the sun's beams   5
Driving back shadows over louring° hills.
Therefore do nimble-pinioned doves draw Love,°
And therefore hath the wind-swift Cupid wings.
Now is the sun upon the highmost hill
Of this day's journey, and from nine till twelve   10
Is three long hours, yet she is not come.
Had she affections and warm youthful blood,
She would be as swift in motion as a ball;
My words would bandy° her to my sweet love,
And his to me.   15
But old folks, many feign as° they were dead —
Unwieldy, slow, heavy, and pale as lead.

Enter Nurse [and Peter].

O God, she comes! — O honey Nurse, what news?
Hast thou met with him? Send thy man away.

NURSE: Peter, stay at the gate.   *[Exit Peter.]*   20

JULIET:

Now, good sweet Nurse — O Lord, why lookest thou sad?
Though news be sad, yet tell them merrily;
If good, thou shamest the music of sweet news
By playing it to me with so sour a face.

NURSE:

I am aweary. Give me leave° awhile.
Fie, how my bones ache! What a jaunce° have I had!   25

ACT 2, SCENE 5. **Location:** Verona. Outside Capulet's house, perhaps in the orchard or garden. **6. louring:** threatening. **7. Love:** i.e., Venus, whose chariot was drawn by swift-winged doves. **14. bandy:** toss to and fro, as in tennis. **16. feign as:** act as though. **25. Give me leave:** let me alone. **26. jaunce:** jouncing, jolting.

JULIET:

    I would thou hadst my bones, and I thy news.

    Nay, come, I pray thee, speak. Good, good Nurse, speak.

NURSE:

    Jesu, what haste! Can you not stay° awhile?

    Do you not see that I am out of breath?   30

JULIET:

    How art thou out of breath, when thou hast breath

    To say to me that thou art out of breath?

    The excuse that thou dost make in this delay

    Is longer than the tale thou dost excuse.

    Is thy news good or bad? Answer to that;   35

    Say either, and I'll stay the circumstance.°

    Let me be satisfied; is 't good or bad?

NURSE: Well, you have made a simple° choice. You know not how to choose a man. Romeo? No, not he. Though his face be better than any man's, yet his leg excels all men's; and for a hand, and a foot, and a body,   40 though they be not to be talked on,° yet they are past compare. He is not the flower of courtesy, but, I'll warrant him, as gentle as a lamb. Go thy ways, wench. Serve God. What, have you dined at home?

JULIET:

    No, no; but all this did I know before.

    What says he of our marriage? What of that?   45

NURSE:

    Lord, how my head aches! What a head have I!

    It beats as it would fall in twenty pieces.

    My back o' t'other° side — ah, my back, my back!

    Beshrew° your heart for sending me about

    To catch my death with jauncing up and down!   50

JULIET:

    I' faith, I am sorry that thou art not well.

    Sweet, sweet, sweet Nurse, tell me, what says my love?

NURSE:

    Your love says, like an honest gentleman,

    And a courteous, and a kind, and a handsome,

    And, I warrant, a virtuous — Where is your mother?   55

---

29. **stay:** wait.   36. **stay the circumstance:** await the details.   38. **simple:** foolish.   41. **be not to be talked on:** are not worth discussing (perhaps with a suggestion of being unmentionable in refined ladylike company).   48. **o' t'other:** on the other.   49. **Beshrew:** a curse on (used as a mild oath).

JULIET:

Where is my mother? Why, she is within,
Where should she be? How oddly thou repliest!
"Your love says, like an honest gentleman,
'Where is your mother?'"

NURSE: O God's Lady dear!
Are you so hot?° Marry, come up,° I trow.   60
Is this the poultice for my aching bones?
Henceforward do your messages yourself.

JULIET:

Here's such a coil!° Come, what says Romeo?

NURSE:

Have you got leave to go to shrift today?

JULIET: I have.   65

NURSE:

Then hie° you hence to Friar Laurence' cell;
There stays a husband to make you a wife.
Now comes the wanton blood up in your cheeks;
They'll be in scarlet straight° at any news.
Hie you to church. I must another way,   70
To fetch a ladder, by the which your love
Must climb a bird's nest° soon when it is dark.
I am the drudge, and toil in your delight,
But you shall bear the burden soon at night.
Go. I'll to dinner. Hie you to the cell.   75

JULIET:

Hie to high fortune! Honest Nurse, farewell.   *Exeunt [separately].*

ACT 2, SCENE 6°

Enter Friar [Laurence] and Romeo.

FRIAR LAURENCE:

So smile the heavens° upon this holy act
That after-hours with sorrow chide us not!

---

60. **hot:** impatient.   **Marry, come up:** (An expression of impatient reproof.)   63. **coil:** turmoil, fuss.   66. **hie:** hasten.   69. **in scarlet straight:** i.e., blushing immediately.   72. **bird's nest:** i.e., Juliet's room (with suggestion of pubic hair; the bawdry is continued in *bear the burden* two lines later).   **ACT 2, SCENE 6.** Location: Verona. Friar Laurence's cell.   1. **So . . . heavens:** may the heavens so smile.

ROMEO:

    Amen, amen! But come what sorrow can,
    It cannot countervail° the exchange of joy
    That one short minute gives me in her sight.   5
    Do thou but close° our hands with holy words,
    Then love-devouring death do what he dare;
    It is enough I may but call her mine.

FRIAR LAURENCE:

    These violent delights have violent ends
    And in their triumph die, like fire and powder,°   10
    Which as they kiss consume. The sweetest honey
    Is loathsome in his° own deliciousness,
    And in the taste confounds° the appetite.
    Therefore love moderately. Long love doth so;
    Too swift arrives as tardy as too slow.   15

Enter Juliet.

    Here comes the lady. O, so light a foot
    Will ne'er wear out the everlasting flint.
    A lover may bestride the gossamer°
    That idles in the wanton° summer air,
    And yet not fall; so light is vanity.°   20

JULIET:

    Good even to my ghostly° confessor.

FRIAR LAURENCE:

    Romeo shall thank thee,° daughter, for us both.

JULIET:

    As much to him, else is his thanks too much.°

ROMEO:

    Ah, Juliet, if the measure of thy joy
    Be heaped like mine, and that° thy skill be more   25
    To blazon° it, then sweeten with thy breath
    This neighbor air, and let rich music's tongue
    Unfold° the imagined° happiness that both
    Receive in either° by this dear encounter.

---

4. **countervail:** outweigh, counterbalance. 6. **close:** join. 10. **powder:** gunpowder. 12. **his:** its. 13. **confounds:** destroys. 18. **gossamer:** spider's thread. 19. **wanton:** playful. 20. **vanity:** transitory human love. 21. **ghostly:** spiritual. 22. **thank thee:** i.e., give a kiss in thanks for your greeting. 23. **As . . . much:** i.e., then I greet him with a kiss in repayment, lest I be overpaid. 25. **that:** if. 26. **blazon:** describe, set forth. (A heraldic term.) 28. **Unfold:** make known. **imagined:** i.e., unexpressed. 29. **in either:** from each other.

JULIET:

    Conceit, more rich in matter than in words,   30

    Brags of his substance, not of ornament.°

    They are but beggars that can count their worth.

    But my true love is grown to such excess

    I cannot sum up sum° of half my wealth.

FRIAR LAURENCE:

    Come, come with me, and we will make short work;   35

    For, by your leaves, you shall not stay alone

    Till Holy Church incorporate two in one.   *[Exeunt.]*

ACT 3, SCENE 1°

Enter Mercutio, Benvolio, and men.

BENVOLIO:

    I pray thee, good Mercutio, let's retire.

    The day is hot, the Capels° are abroad,

    And if we meet we shall not scape a brawl,

    For now, these hot days, is the mad blood stirring.

MERCUTIO: Thou art like one of these fellows that when he enters the   5
confines of a tavern, claps me his sword upon the table and says, "God
send me no need of thee!" and by the operation of the second cup draws
him on the drawer,° when indeed there is no need.°

BENVOLIO: Am I like such a fellow?

MERCUTIO: Come, come, thou art as hot a Jack° in thy mood as any in   10
Italy, and as soon moved to be moody,° and as soon moody to be moved.°

BENVOLIO: And what to?

MERCUTIO: Nay, an° there were two such, we should have none shortly, for
one would kill the other. Thou! Why, thou wilt quarrel with a man that
hath a hair more or a hair less in his beard than thou hast. Thou wilt   15
quarrel with a man for cracking nuts, having no other reason but because
thou hast hazel eyes. What eye but such an eye would spy out such a
quarrel? Thy head is as full of quarrels as an egg is full of meat,° and yet
thy head hath been beaten as addle° as an egg for quarreling. Thou hast

---

30–31. **Conceit . . . ornament:** true understanding, more enriched by the actual reality (of
love) than by mere words, finds more worth in the substance of that reality than in outward
show.   **34. sum up sum:** add up the total.   ACT 3, SCENE 1. **Location:** Verona. A public
place.   **2. Capels:** Capulets.   **7–8. draws . . . drawer:** draws his sword against the tapster or
waiter.   **8. there is no need:** i.e., of his sword.   **10. as hot a Jack:** as hot-tempered a fellow.
11. moody: angry.   **to be moved:** at being provoked.   **13. an:** if.   **18. meat:** i.e., edible matter.   **19. addle:** addled, confused.

quarreled with a man for coughing in the street, because he hath wak- 20
ened thy dog that hath lain asleep in the sun. Didst thou not fall out with
a tailor for wearing his new doublet° before Easter? With another, for
tying his new shoes with old ribbon? And yet thou wilt tutor me from
quarreling!

BENVOLIO: An I were so apt to quarrel as thou art, any man should buy the   25
fee simple° of my life for an hour and a quarter.°

MERCUTIO: The fee simple! O simple!°

Enter Tybalt, Petruchio, and others.

BENVOLIO: By my head, here comes the Capulets.

MERCUTIO: By my heel, I care not.

TYBALT: [*To his companions*]
Follow me close, for I will speak to them. —   30
Gentlemen, good e'en. A word with one of you.

MERCUTIO: And but one word with one of us? Couple it with something:
make it a word and a blow.

TYBALT: You shall find me apt enough to that, sir, an you will give me
occasion.   35

MERCUTIO: Could you not take some occasion without giving?

TYBALT: Mercutio, thou consortest° with Romeo.

MERCUTIO: "Consort"? What, dost thou make us minstrels? An thou make
minstrels of us, look to hear nothing but discords. Here's my fiddlestick;°
here's that° shall make you dance. Zounds,° "consort"!   40

BENVOLIO:
We talk here in the public haunt of men.
Either withdraw unto some private place,
Or reason coldly° of your grievances,
Or else depart;° here all eyes gaze on us.

MERCUTIO:
Men's eyes were made to look, and let them gaze.   45
I will not budge for no man's pleasure, I.

Enter Romeo.

TYBALT:
Well, peace be with you, sir. Here comes my man.

---

22. **doublet:** man's jacket.   26. **fee simple:** outright possession.   **an hour . . . quarter:** i.e.,
my life would last no longer in such circumstances.   27. **simple:** stupid.   37. **consortest:** keep
company with. (But Mercutio quibbles on its musical sense of "accompany" or "play together.")
39. **fiddlestick:** (Mercutio means his sword.)   40. **that:** that which.   **Zounds:** i.e., by God's
(Christ's) wounds.   43. **coldly:** calmly.   44. **depart:** go away separately.

MERCUTIO:

> But I'll be hanged, sir, if he wear your livery.°
> Marry, go before to field,° he'll be your follower;
> Your worship° in that sense may call him "man."   50

TYBALT:

> Romeo, the love I bear thee can afford
> No better term than this: thou art a villain.

ROMEO:

> Tybalt, the reason that I have to love thee
> Doth much excuse the appertaining rage°
> To such a greeting. Villain am I none.   55
> Therefore, farewell. I see thou knowest me not.

TYBALT:

> Boy, this shall not excuse the injuries
> That thou hast done me. Therefore turn and draw.

ROMEO:

> I do protest I never injured thee,
> But love thee better than thou canst devise°   60
> Till thou shalt know the reason of my love.
> And so, good Capulet — which name I tender°
> As dearly as mine own — be satisfied.

MERCUTIO:

> O calm, dishonorable, vile submission!
> *Alla stoccata*° carries it away.   [*He draws.*]   65
> Tybalt, you ratcatcher,° will you walk?

TYBALT: What wouldst thou have with me?

MERCUTIO: Good king of cats, nothing but one of your nine lives, that I
mean to make bold withal,° and, as you shall use me hereafter, dry-beat°
the rest of the eight. Will you pluck your sword out of his pilcher° by the   70
ears? Make haste, lest mine be about your ears ere it be out.

TYBALT: I am for you.   [*He draws.*]

ROMEO:

> Gentle Mercutio, put thy rapier up.

---

48. livery: servant's costume. (Mercutio deliberately mistakes Tybalt's phrase *my man* to mean
"my servant.")   **49. field:** field where a duel might occur.   **50. Your worship:** (A title of honor
used here with mock politeness.)   **54. excuse . . . rage:** mollify the angry reaction appropriate.
60. devise: understand.   **62. tender:** value.   **65. *Alla stoccata:*** at the thrust (Italian); i.e.,
Tybalt, with his fine fencing phrases, *carries it away,* wins the day.   **66. ratcatcher:** (An allusion to Tybalt as king of cats; see 2.4.18.)   **69. make bold withal:** make free with.   **dry-beat:**
beat soundly (without drawing blood).   **70. his pilcher:** its scabbard.

MERCUTIO: Come, sir, your *passado.*°   [*They fight.*]

ROMEO:

Draw, Benvolio, beat down their weapons.   75
Gentlemen, for shame, forbear this outrage!
Tybalt, Mercutio, the Prince expressly hath
Forbid this bandying in Verona streets.
Hold, Tybalt! Good Mercutio!   [*Tybalt under Romeo's arm stabs Mercutio.*]
                                                Away Tybalt° [*with his followers*].

MERCUTIO: I am hurt.
A plague o' both your houses! I am sped.°   80
Is he gone, and hath nothing?

BENVOLIO: What, art thou hurt?

MERCUTIO:

Ay, ay, a scratch, a scratch; marry, 'tis enough.
Where is my page? Go, villain, fetch a surgeon.   [*Exit Page.*]

ROMEO:

Courage, man, the hurt cannot be much.

MERCUTIO: No, 'tis not so deep as a well, nor so wide as a church door, but   85
'tis enough, 'twill serve. Ask for me tomorrow, and you shall find me a
grave° man. I am peppered,° I warrant, for this world. A plague o' both
your houses! Zounds, a dog, a rat, a mouse, a cat, to scratch a man to
death! A braggart, a rogue, a villain, that fights by the book of arithmetic!° Why the devil came you between us? I was hurt under your arm.   90

ROMEO: I thought all for the best.

MERCUTIO:

Help me into some house, Benvolio,
Or I shall faint. A plague o' both your houses!
They have made worm's meat of me. I have it,
And soundly too. Your houses!   *Exit* [*supported by Benvolio*].   95

ROMEO:

This gentleman, the Prince's near ally,°
My very° friend, hath got this mortal hurt
In my behalf; my reputation stained
With Tybalt's slander — Tybalt, that an hour
Hath been my cousin!° O sweet Juliet,   100

---

74. *passado:* forward thrust. (Said derisively.)   79. s.d. *Away Tybalt:* (Some editors assign this
as a speech to Petruchio.)   80. **sped:** done for.   87. **grave:** (Mercutio thus puns with his last
breath.)   **peppered:** finished, done for.   89–90. **by . . . arithmetic:** by the numbers, as in a
textbook on fencing.   96. **ally:** kinsman.   97. **very:** true.   100. **cousin:** kinsman.

Thy beauty hath made me effeminate,°
And in my temper° softened valor's steel!

Enter Benvolio.

BENVOLIO:

O Romeo, Romeo, brave Mercutio is dead!
That gallant spirit hath aspired° the clouds,
Which too untimely here did scorn the earth.   105

ROMEO:

This day's black fate on more days doth depend;°
This but begins the woe others° must end.

[*Enter Tybalt.*]

BENVOLIO:

Here comes the furious Tybalt back again.

ROMEO:

Alive in triumph, and Mercutio slain!
Away to heaven, respective lenity,°   110
And fire-eyed fury be my conduct° now!
Now, Tybalt, take the "villain" back again
That late thou gavest me, for Mercutio's soul
Is but a little way above our heads,
Staying for thine to keep him company.   115
Either thou or I, or both, must go with him.

TYBALT:

Thou, wretched boy, that didst consort him here,
Shalt with him hence.

ROMEO: This shall determine that.   *They fight. Tybalt falls.*

BENVOLIO: Romeo, away, begone!
The citizens are up, and Tybalt slain.   120
Stand not amazed.° The Prince will doom thee death°
If thou art taken. Hence, begone, away!

ROMEO:

O, I am fortune's fool!°

BENVOLIO: Why dost thou stay?   *Exit Romeo.*

---

101. **effeminate:** weak.   102. **temper:** disposition (but with a play on the tempering of a steel
sword).   104. **aspired:** ascended to.   106. **depend:** hang over threateningly.   107. **others:**
other days to come.   110. **respective lenity:** considerate gentleness.   111. **conduct:** guide.
121. **amazed:** dazed.   **doom thee death:** sentence you to death.   123. **fool:** dupe.

Enter Citizens.

FIRST CITIZEN:
Which way ran he that killed Mercutio?
Tybalt, that murderer, which way ran he?   125

BENVOLIO:
There lies that Tybalt.

FIRST CITIZEN: Up, sir, go with me.
I charge thee in the Prince's name, obey.

Enter Prince [attended], old Montague, Capulet, their Wives, and all.

PRINCE:
Where are the vile beginners of this fray?

BENVOLIO:
O noble Prince, I can discover° all
The unlucky manage° of this fatal brawl.   130
There lies the man, slain by young Romeo,
That slew thy kinsman, brave Mercutio.

CAPULET'S WIFE:
Tybalt, my cousin! O my brother's child!
O Prince! O cousin! Husband! O, the blood is spilled
Of my dear kinsman! Prince, as thou art true,   135
For blood of ours shed blood of Montague.
O cousin, cousin!

PRINCE:
Benvolio, who began this bloody fray?

BENVOLIO:
Tybalt, here slain, whom Romeo's hand did slay.
Romeo, that spoke him fair,° bid him bethink°   140
How nice° the quarrel was, and urged withal°
Your high displeasure. All this — utterèd
With gentle breath, calm look, knees humbly bowed —
Could not take truce° with the unruly spleen
Of Tybalt deaf to peace, but that he tilts   145
With piercing steel at bold Mercutio's breast,
Who, all as hot, turns deadly point to point,
And, with a martial scorn, with one hand beats
Cold death aside and with the other sends

---

129. **discover:** reveal.   130. **manage:** conduct.   140. **fair:** civilly.   **bethink:** consider.
141. **nice:** trivial.   **withal:** besides.   144. **take truce:** make peace.

It back to Tybalt, whose dexterity 150
Retorts° it. Romeo he cries aloud,
"Hold, friends! Friends, part!" and swifter than his tongue
His agile arm beats down their fatal points,
And twixt them rushes; underneath whose arm
An envious° thrust from Tybalt hit the life 155
Of stout° Mercutio, and then Tybalt fled;
But by and by comes back to Romeo,
Who had but newly entertained° revenge,
And to 't they go like lightning, for, ere I
Could draw to part them was stout Tybalt slain, 160
And, as he fell, did Romeo turn and fly.
This is the truth, or let Benvolio die.

CAPULET'S WIFE:
He is a kinsman to the Montague.
Affection° makes him false; he speaks not true.
Some twenty of them fought in this black strife, 165
And all those twenty could but kill one life.
I beg for justice, which thou, Prince, must give.
Romeo slew Tybalt; Romeo must not live.

PRINCE:
Romeo slew him, he slew Mercutio.
Who now the price of his dear blood doth owe? 170

MONTAGUE:
Not Romeo, Prince, he was Mercutio's friend;
His fault concludes but° what the law should end,
The life of Tybalt.

PRINCE: And for that offense
Immediately we do exile him hence.
I have an interest in your heart's proceeding; 175
My blood° for your rude brawls doth lie a-bleeding;
But I'll amerce° you with so strong a fine
That you shall all repent the loss of mine.
I will be deaf to pleading and excuses;
Nor tears° nor prayers shall purchase out abuses.° 180
Therefore use none. Let Romeo hence° in haste,

---

151. **Retorts:** returns. 155. **envious:** malicious. 156. **stout:** brave. 158. **entertained:** harbored thoughts of. 164. **Affection:** partiality. 172. **concludes but:** only finishes. 176. **My blood:** i.e., blood of my kinsman. 177. **amerce:** punish by a fine. 180. **Nor tears:** neither tears. **purchase out abuses:** redeem misdeeds. 181. **hence:** depart.

Else,° when he is found, that hour is his last.
Bear hence this body and attend our will.°
Mercy but murders, pardoning those that kill.

Exeunt, [some carrying Tybalt's body].

Act 3, Scene 2°

Enter Juliet alone.

JULIET:
    Gallop apace,° you fiery-footed steeds,°
    Towards Phoebus'° lodging!° Such a wagoner
    As Phaëthon° would whip you to the west
    And bring in cloudy night immediately.
    Spread thy close° curtain, love-performing night,   5
    That runaways'° eyes may wink,° and Romeo
    Leap to these arms, untalked of and unseen.
    Lovers can see to do their amorous rites
    By their own beauties; or, if love be blind,
    It best agrees with night. Come, civil° night,   10
    Thou sober-suited matron all in black,
    And learn° me how to lose a winning match
    Played for a pair of stainless maidenhoods.
    Hood° my unmanned° blood, bating in my cheeks,
    With thy black mantle till strange° love grow bold,   15
    Think° true love acted simple modesty.
    Come, night. Come, Romeo. Come, thou day in night;
    For thou wilt lie upon the wings of night
    Whiter than new snow upon a raven's back.
    Come, gentle night, come, loving, black-browed night,   20

---

182. **Else:** otherwise.   183. **attend our will:** be on hand to hear further judgment.   **Act 3, Scene 2. Location:** Verona. Capulet's house.   1. **apace:** quickly.   **steeds:** i.e., the horses of the sun god's chariot.   2. **Phoebus:** (Often equated with Helios, the sun god.)   **lodging:** i.e., in the west, below the horizon.   2–3. **Such . . . Phaëthon:** i.e., a rash charioteer like Phaëthon, who would quickly bring the day to an end. (Phaëthon was son of the sun god, and was allowed to assume the reins of the sun for a day; not being able to restrain the steeds, he had to be slain by the thunderbolt of Zeus.)   5. **close:** enclosing.   6. **runaways:** (Refers to the horses of the sun chariot that ran away with Phaëthon?)   **wink:** shut, close.   10. **civil:** circumspect, somberly attired.   12. **learn:** teach.   14. **Hood:** cover. (A term in falconry; the hawk's eyes were covered so that it would not *bate* or beat its wings.)   **unmanned:** untamed (in falconry; with a pun on "unmarried").   15. **strange:** diffident.   16. **Think:** i.e., and think.

Give me my Romeo, and when I° shall die
Take him and cut him out in little stars,
And he will make the face of heaven so fine
That all the world will be in love with night
And pay no worship to the garish° sun.   25
O, I have bought the mansion° of a love
But not possessed it, and though I am sold,
Not yet enjoyed. So tedious is this day
As in the night before some festival
To an impatient child that hath new robes   30
And may not wear them. O, here comes my nurse,

Enter Nurse, with cords.°

And she brings news, and every tongue that speaks
But Romeo's name speaks heavenly eloquence.
Now, Nurse, what news? What hast thou there? The cords
That Romeo bid thee fetch?
NURSE: Ay, ay, the cords.   [*She throws them down.*]   35
JULIET:
Ay me, what news? Why dost thou wring thy hands?
NURSE:
Ah, weraday!° He's dead, he's dead, he's dead!
We are undone, lady, we are undone!
Alack the day, he's gone, he's killed, he's dead!
JULIET:
Can heaven be so envious?°
NURSE: Romeo can,   40
Though heaven cannot. O Romeo, Romeo!
Whoever would have thought it? Romeo!
JULIET:
What devil art thou, that dost torment me thus?
This torture should be roared in dismal hell.
Hath Romeo slain himself? Say thou but "Ay,"   45
And that bare vowel "I"° shall poison more
Than the death-darting eye of cockatrice.°

---

21. **I:** (Often emended to *he,* following Quarto 4, but Juliet may mean that when she is dead she will share Romeo's beauty with the world. Dying may also hint at sexual climax.)   25. **garish:** dazzling.   26. **mansion:** dwelling.   31. s.d. **cords:** ropes (for the ladder).   37. **weraday:** i.e., wellaway, alas.   40. **envious:** malicious.   46. **"I":** (Pronounced identically with *ay.*)   47. **cockatrice:** i.e., basilisk, a mythical serpent that could kill by its look.

I am not I, if there be such an "Ay,"
Or those eyes shut,° that makes thee answer "Ay."
If he be slain, say "Ay," or if not, "No."   50
Brief sounds determine of my weal° or woe.

NURSE:
I saw the wound. I saw it with mine eyes —
God save the mark!° — here on his manly breast.
A piteous corpse, a bloody piteous corpse;
Pale, pale as ashes, all bedaubed in blood,   55
All in gore-blood.° I swoonèd at the sight.

JULIET:
O, break, my heart! Poor bankrupt, break at once!
To prison, eyes; ne'er look on liberty!
Vile earth,° to earth resign;° end motion here,
And thou and Romeo press° one heavy bier!°   60

NURSE:
O Tybalt, Tybalt, the best friend I had!
O courteous Tybalt! Honest gentleman!
That ever I should live to see thee dead!

JULIET:
What storm is this that blows so contrary?
Is Romeo slaughtered, and is Tybalt dead?   65
My dearest cousin, and my dearer lord?
Then, dreadful trumpet,° sound the general doom!°
For who is living, if those two are gone?

NURSE:
Tybalt is gone, and Romeo banishèd;
Romeo that killed him, he is banishèd.   70

JULIET:
O God! Did Romeo's hand shed Tybalt's blood?

NURSE:
It did, it did. Alas the day it did!

JULIET:
O serpent heart, hid with° a flowering° face!
Did ever dragon keep° so fair a cave?°

---

49. **those eyes shut:** i.e., if Romeo's eyes are shut (in death).   51. **weal:** welfare, happiness.
53. **God save the mark:** (A familiar oath originally intended to avert ill omen.)   56. **gore-blood:** clotted blood.   59. **Vile earth:** i.e., my body.   **resign:** surrender, return.   60. **press:** weigh down.   **bier:** litter for carrying corpses.   67. **trumpet:** i.e., the last trumpet.   **general doom:** Day of Judgment.   73. **hid with:** hidden by.   **flowering:** i.e., fair, like that of the serpent in the Garden of Eden.   74. **keep:** occupy, guard.   **cave:** i.e., one with treasure in it.

Beautiful tyrant! Fiend angelical!   75
Dove-feathered raven! Wolvish-ravening lamb!
Despisèd substance of divinest show!°
Just° opposite to what thou justly seem'st,
A damnèd saint, an honorable villain!
O nature, what hadst thou to do in hell   80
When thou didst bower° the spirit of a fiend
In mortal paradise of such sweet flesh?
Was ever book containing such vile matter
So fairly bound? O, that deceit should dwell
In such a gorgeous palace!

NURSE: There's no trust,   85
No faith, no honesty in men; all perjured,
All forsworn, all naught,° all dissemblers.
Ah, where's my man? Give me some aqua vitae.°
These griefs, these woes, these sorrows make me old.
Shame come to Romeo!

JULIET: Blistered be thy tongue   90
For such a wish! He was not born to shame.
Upon his brow shame is ashamed to sit;
For 'tis a throne where honor may be crowned
Sole monarch of the universal earth.
O, what a beast was I to chide at him!   95

NURSE:
Will you speak well of him that killed your cousin?

JULIET:
Shall I speak ill of him that is my husband?
Ah, poor my lord,° what tongue shall smooth° thy name
When I, thy three-hours wife, have mangled it?
But wherefore, villain, didst thou kill my cousin?   100
That villain cousin would have killed my husband.
Back, foolish tears, back to your native spring!
Your tributary drops belong to woe,°
Which you, mistaking, offer up to joy.
My husband lives, that° Tybalt would have slain,   105
And Tybalt's dead, that would have slain my husband.

---

77. **show:** appearance.   78. **Just:** precisely (with a play on *justly,* truly).   81. **bower:** give lodging to.   87. **naught:** worthless, evil.   88. **aqua vitae:** alcoholic spirits.   98. **poor my lord:** my poor lord.   **smooth:** speak kindly of.   103. **Your . . . woe:** i.e., you should be shed, offered as a tribute, on some occasion of real woe.   105. **that:** whom.

All this is comfort. Wherefore weep I then?
Some word there was, worser than Tybalt's death,
That murdered me. I would forget it fain,°
But O, it presses to my memory   110
Like damnèd guilty deeds to sinners' minds:
"Tybalt is dead, and Romeo — banishèd."
That "banishèd," that one word "banishèd,"
Hath slain ten thousand Tybalts. Tybalt's death
Was woe enough, if it had ended there;   115
Or, if sour woe delights in fellowship
And needly° will be ranked with° other griefs,
Why followed not, when she said "Tybalt's dead,"
"Thy father," or "thy mother," nay, or both,
Which modern° lamentation might have moved?   120
But with a rearward° following Tybalt's death,
"Romeo is banishèd" — to speak that word
Is father, mother, Tybalt, Romeo, Juliet,
All slain, all dead. "Romeo is banishèd!"
There is no end, no limit, measure, bound,   125
In that word's death; no words can that woe sound.°
Where is my father and my mother, Nurse?

NURSE:
Weeping and wailing over Tybalt's corpse.
Will you go to them? I will bring you thither.

JULIET:
Wash they his wounds with tears? Mine shall be spent,   130
When theirs are dry, for Romeo's banishment.
Take up those cords. Poor ropes, you are beguiled,
Both you and I, for Romeo is exiled.
He made you for a highway to my bed;
But I, a maid, die maiden-widowèd.   135
Come, cords, come, Nurse. I'll to my wedding bed,
And death, not Romeo, take my maidenhead!

NURSE: [*Taking up the cords*]
Hie to your chamber. I'll find Romeo
To comfort you. I wot° well where he is.
Hark ye, your Romeo will be here at night.   140
I'll to him. He is hid at Laurence' cell.

---

109. **fain:** gladly. 117. **needly:** of necessity. **ranked with:** accompanied by. 120. **modern:** ordinary. 121. **rearward:** rearguard. 126. **sound:** (1) fathom (2) express. 139. **wot:** know.

JULIET:

O, find him! Give this ring to my true knight,   [*Giving a ring*]
And bid him come to take his last farewell.   *Exeunt* [*separately*].

ACT 3, SCENE 3°

Enter Friar [*Laurence*].

FRIAR LAURENCE:

Romeo, come forth; come forth, thou fearful° man.
Affliction is enamored of thy parts,°
And thou art wedded to calamity.

[*Enter*] *Romeo.*

ROMEO:

Father, what news? What is the Prince's doom?°
What sorrow craves acquaintance at my hand   5
That I yet know not?
FRIAR LAURENCE: Too familiar
Is my dear son with such sour company.
I bring thee tidings of the Prince's doom.
ROMEO:

What less than doomsday° is the Prince's doom?
FRIAR LAURENCE:

A gentler judgment vanished° from his lips: 10
Not body's death, but body's banishment.
ROMEO:

Ha, banishment? Be merciful, say "death";
For exile hath more terror in his look,
Much more than death. Do not say "banishment."
FRIAR LAURENCE:

Here from Verona art thou banishèd.   15
Be patient, for the world is broad and wide.
ROMEO:

There is no world without° Verona walls
But purgatory, torture, hell itself.
Hence "banishèd" is banished from the world,

ACT 3, SCENE 3. **Location:** Verona. Friar Laurence's cell.   1. **fearful:** full of fear (but also inspiring fear as a tragic figure).   2. **parts:** qualities.   4. **doom:** judgment.   9. **doomsday:** the Day of Judgment, i.e., death.   10. **vanished:** issued (into air).   17. **without:** outside of.

And world's exile° is death. Then "banishèd"   20
Is death mistermed. Calling death "banishèd,"
Thou cutt'st my head off with a golden ax
And smilest upon the stroke that murders me.

FRIAR LAURENCE:
O deadly sin! O rude unthankfulness!
Thy fault our law calls death,° but the kind Prince,   25
Taking thy part, hath rushed° aside the law
And turned that black word "death" to "banishment."
This is dear mercy, and thou seest it not.

ROMEO:
'Tis torture, and not mercy. Heaven is here
Where Juliet lives, and every cat and dog   30
And little mouse, every unworthy thing,
Live here in heaven and may look on her,
But Romeo may not. More validity,°
More honorable state, more courtship° lives
In carrion flies than Romeo. They may seize   35
On the white wonder of dear Juliet's hand
And steal immortal blessing from her lips,
Who even in pure and vestal° modesty
Still blush, as thinking their own kisses° sin;
But Romeo may not, he is banishèd.   40
Flies may do this, but I from this must fly.
They are free men, but I am banishèd.
And sayest thou yet that exile is not death?
Hadst thou no poison mixed, no sharp-ground knife,
No sudden mean of death, though ne'er so mean,°   45
But "banishèd" to kill me? "Banishèd"?
O Friar, the damnèd use that word in hell;
Howling attends it. How hast thou the heart,
Being a divine, a ghostly confessor,
A sin absolver, and my friend professed,   50
To mangle me with that word "banishèd"?

FRIAR LAURENCE:
Thou fond° mad man, hear me a little speak.

---

20. **world's exile:** exile from the world.   25. **Thy fault . . . death:** for your crime the law demands a death sentence.   26. **rushed:** thrust (aside).   33. **validity:** value.   34. **courtship:** (1) courtliness (2) occasion for wooing.   38. **vestal:** maidenly.   39. **their own kisses:** i.e., their touching one another.   45. **mean . . . mean:** means . . . base.   52. **fond:** foolish.

ROMEO:
    O, thou wilt speak again of banishment.
FRIAR LAURENCE:
    I'll give thee armor to keep off that word,
    Adversity's sweet milk, philosophy,
    To comfort thee, though thou art banishèd.   55
ROMEO:
    Yet° "banishèd"? Hang up philosophy!
    Unless philosophy can make a Juliet,
    Displant° a town, reverse a prince's doom,
    It helps not, it prevails not. Talk no more.   60
FRIAR LAURENCE:
    O, then I see that madmen have no ears.
ROMEO:
    How should they, when that wise men have no eyes?
FRIAR LAURENCE:
    Let me dispute° with thee of thy estate.°
ROMEO:
    Thou canst not speak of that° thou dost not feel.
    Wert thou as young as I, Juliet thy love,   65
    An hour but married, Tybalt murderèd,
    Doting like me and like me banishèd,
    Then mightst thou speak, then mightst thou tear thy hair,
    And fall upon the ground, as I do now,
    Taking the measure of an unmade grave.   [*He falls upon the ground.*] 70

    Knock [*within*]

FRIAR LAURENCE:
    Arise. One knocks. Good Romeo, hide thyself.
ROMEO:
    Not I, unless the breath of heartsick groans,
    Mistlike, infold me from the search of eyes.   *Knock.*
FRIAR LAURENCE:
    Hark, how they knock! — Who's there? — Romeo, arise.
    Thou wilt be taken. — Stay awhile! — Stand up.   *Knock.* 75
    Run to my study. — By and by! — God's will,
    What simpleness° is this? — I come, I come!   *Knock.*

---

57. **Yet:** still. 59. **Displant:** uproot. 63. **dispute:** reason. **estate:** situation. 64. **that:** that
which. 77. **simpleness:** foolishness.

Who knocks so hard? Whence come you? What's your will?

[*Going to the door.*]

NURSE: [*Within*]
　　Let me come in, and you shall know my errand.
　　I come from Lady Juliet.
FRIAR LAURENCE:　　　　Welcome, then.　　　　　　[*He opens the door.*]　80

Enter Nurse.

NURSE:
　　O holy Friar, O, tell me, holy Friar,
　　Where's my lady's lord, where's Romeo?
FRIAR LAURENCE:
　　There on the ground, with his own tears made drunk.
NURSE:
　　O, he is even° in my mistress' case,°
　　Just in her case! O woeful sympathy!°　　　　　　　　　　　　85
　　Piteous predicament! Even so lies she,
　　Blubbering and weeping, weeping and blubbering. —
　　Stand up, stand up! Stand, an° you be a man.
　　For Juliet's sake, for her sake, rise and stand!
　　Why should you fall into so deep an O?°　　　　　　　　　　90
ROMEO:　　Nurse!　　　　　　　　　　　　　　　　　[*He rises.*]
NURSE:
　　Ah, sir, ah, sir! Death's the end of all.
ROMEO:
　　Spakest thou of Juliet? How is it with her?
　　Doth not she think me an old° murderer,
　　Now I have stained the childhood of our joy　　　　　　　95
　　With blood removed but little from her own?
　　Where is she? And how doth she? And what says
　　My concealed° lady to our canceled° love?
NURSE:
　　O, she says nothing, sir, but weeps and weeps,
　　And now falls on her bed, and then starts up,　　　　　　　100
　　And "Tybalt" calls, and then on Romeo cries,°
　　And then down falls again.
ROMEO:　　　　　　　　As if that name,

---

84. **even:** exactly.　**case:** situation.　85. **woeful sympathy:** mutuality of grief.　88. **an:** if.
90. **an O:** a fit of groaning.　94. **old:** hardened.　98. **concealed:** secret.　**canceled:** nullified
(by the impending exile).　101. **on Romeo cries:** exclaims against Romeo, calls his name.

Shot from the deadly level° of a gun,
Did murder her, as that name's cursèd hand
Murdered her kinsman. O, tell me, Friar, tell me,   105
In what vile part of this anatomy
Doth my name lodge? Tell me, that I may sack°
The hateful mansion.   [*He draws a weapon, but is restrained.*]
FRIAR LAURENCE: Hold thy desperate hand!
    Art thou a man? Thy form cries out thou art;
    Thy tears are womanish, thy wild acts denote   110
    The unreasonable fury of a beast.
    Unseemly woman in a seeming man,
    And ill-beseeming beast in seeming both!
    Thou hast amazed me. By my holy order,
    I thought thy disposition better tempered.°   115
    Hast thou slain Tybalt? Wilt thou slay thyself,
    And slay thy lady, that in thy life lives,
    By doing damnèd hate upon thyself?
    Why railest thou on thy birth, the heaven, and earth,
    Since birth, and heaven, and earth,° all three do meet   120
    In thee at once, which thou at once wouldst lose?
    Fie, fie, thou shamest thy shape, thy love, thy wit,°
    Which,° like a usurer, abound'st in all,°
    And usest none in that true use° indeed
    Which should bedeck thy shape, thy love, thy wit.   125
    Thy noble shape is but a form of wax,°
    Digressing° from the valor of a man;
    Thy dear love sworn but hollow perjury,
    Killing° that love which thou hast vowed to cherish;
    Thy wit, that ornament to shape and love,   130
    Misshapen in the conduct° of them both,
    Like powder° in a skilless soldier's flask°
    Is set afire by thine own ignorance,
    And thou dismembered with° thine own defense.°
    What, rouse thee, man! Thy Juliet is alive,   135

---

103. **level:** aim.   107. **sack:** destroy.   115. **tempered:** harmonized, balanced.   120. **heaven, and earth:** i.e., soul and body.   122. **wit:** intellect.   123. **Which:** (you) who.   **all:** all capabilities.   124. **true use:** i.e., proper use of your resources, not usury.   126. **form of wax:** waxwork, mere outer form.   127. **Digressing:** if it deviates.   129. **Killing:** if it kills.   131. **conduct:** guidance.   132. **powder:** gunpowder.   **flask:** powder horn.   134. **dismembered with:** blown to pieces by.   **thine own defense:** that which should defend you, i.e., your *wit* or intellect.

For whose dear sake thou wast but lately dead;°
There art thou happy.° Tybalt would kill thee,
But thou slewest Tybalt; there art thou happy.
The law that threatened death becomes thy friend
And turns it to exile; there art thou happy.   140
A pack of blessings light upon thy back,
Happiness courts thee in her best array,
But like a mishavèd° and sullen wench
Thou pouts upon thy fortune and thy love.
Take heed, take heed, for such die miserable.   145
Go, get thee to thy love, as was decreed;
Ascend her chamber; hence and comfort her.
But look thou stay not till the watch be set,°
For then thou canst not pass to Mantua,
Where thou shalt live till we can find a time   150
To blaze° your marriage, reconcile your friends,°
Beg pardon of the Prince, and call thee back
With twenty hundred thousand times more joy
Than thou went'st forth in lamentation.
Go before, Nurse. Commend me to thy lady,   155
And bid her hasten all the house to bed,
Which heavy sorrow makes them apt unto.
Romeo is coming.

NURSE:
O Lord, I could have stayed here all the night
To hear good counsel. O, what learning is! —   160
My lord, I'll tell my lady you will come.

ROMEO:
Do so, and bid my sweet prepare to chide.

NURSE: [*Giving a ring*]
Here, sir, a ring she bid me give you, sir.
Hie you, make haste, for it grows very late.   [*Exit.*]

ROMEO:
How well my comfort° is revived by this!   165

FRIAR LAURENCE:
Go hence. Good night. And here stands all your state:°

---

136. wast . . . dead: i.e., only recently were wishing yourself dead (see l. 70). 137. happy: fortunate. 143. mishavèd: misbehaved. 148. the watch be set: guards be posted (at the city
gates). 151. blaze: publish, divulge. friends: relations. 165. comfort: happiness. 166. here
. . . state: your fortune depends on what follows.

Either be gone before the watch be set,
Or by the break of day disguised from hence.
Sojourn in Mantua. I'll find out your man,
And he shall signify from time to time
Every good hap° to you that chances here.   170
Give me thy hand. 'Tis late. Farewell, good night.
ROMEO:
But that a joy past joy calls out on me,
It were a grief so brief° to part with thee.
Farewell.

                                    Exeunt [separately].   175

Act 3, Scene 4°

Enter old Capulet, his Wife, and Paris.

CAPULET:
Things have fallen out,° sir, so unluckily
That we have had no time to move° our daughter.
Look you, she loved her kinsman Tybalt dearly,
And so did I. Well, we were born to die.
'Tis very late. She'll not come down tonight.
I promise° you, but for your company   5
I would have been abed an hour ago.
PARIS:
These times of woe afford no times to woo.
Madam, good night. Commend me to your daughter.
WIFE:
I will, and know her mind early tomorrow.
Tonight she's mewed up to° her heaviness.°   10
CAPULET:
Sir Paris, I will make a desperate tender°
Of my child's love. I think she will be ruled
In all respects by me; nay, more, I doubt it not.
Wife, go you to her ere you go to bed.
Acquaint her here of my son Paris' love,   15
And bid her, mark you me,° on Wednesday next —
But soft, what day is this?

---

171. **good hap:** fortunate event.   174. **brief:** quickly.   **Act 3, Scene 4. Location:** Verona. Capulet's house.   1. **fallen out:** happened.   2. **move:** persuade.   6. **promise:** assure.   11. **mewed up to:** cooped up with. (A falconry term.)   **heaviness:** sorrow.   12. **desperate tender:** bold offer.   17. **mark you me:** are you paying attention.

PARIS: Monday, my lord.

CAPULET:

Monday! Ha, ha! Well, Wednesday is too soon;
O' Thursday let it be. O' Thursday, tell her,   20
She shall be married to this noble earl.
Will you be ready? Do you like this haste?
We'll keep no great ado — a friend or two;
For hark you, Tybalt being slain so late,°
It may be thought we held him carelessly,°   25
Being our kinsman, if we revel much.
Therefore we'll have some half a dozen friends,
And there an end. But what say you to Thursday?

PARIS:

My lord, I would that Thursday were tomorrow.

CAPULET:

Well, get you gone. O' Thursday be it, then.   30
[*To his Wife.*] Go you to Juliet ere you go to bed;
Prepare her, wife, against° this wedding day. —
Farewell, my lord. — Light to my chamber, ho! —
Afore me,° it is so very late
That we may call it early by and by.   35
Good night.   *Exeunt.*

ACT 3, SCENE 5°

Enter Romeo and Juliet aloft [at the window].

JULIET:

Wilt thou be gone? It is not yet near day.
It was the nightingale, and not the lark,
That pierced the fearful° hollow of thine ear;
Nightly she sings on yond pomegranate tree.
Believe me, love, it was the nightingale.   5

ROMEO:

It was the lark, the herald of the morn,
No nightingale. Look, love, what envious streaks
Do lace the severing° clouds in yonder east.

---

24. **late:** recently.   25. **held him carelessly:** did not regard him highly.   32. **against:** in anticipation of.   34. **Afore me:** i.e., by my life. (A mild oath.)   ACT 3, SCENE 5. **Location:**
Verona. Capulet's orchard with Juliet's chamber window above, and subsequently (l. 68) the
interior of Juliet's chamber.   3. **fearful:** apprehensive, anxious.   8. **severing:** separating.

Night's candles are burnt out, and jocund° day
Stands tiptoe on the misty mountain tops.
I must be gone and live, or stay and die.

JULIET:

Yond light is not daylight, I know it, I.
It is some meteor that the sun exhaled°
To be to thee this night a torchbearer
And light thee on thy way to Mantua.
Therefore stay yet. Thou need'st not to be gone.

ROMEO:

Let me be ta'en; let me be put to death.
I am content, so thou° wilt have it so.
I'll say yon gray is not the morning's eye;
'Tis but the pale reflex° of Cynthia's° brow.
Nor that is not the lark whose notes do beat
The vaulty heaven so high above our heads.
I have more care° to stay than will to go.
Come, death, and welcome! Juliet wills it so.
How is 't, my soul? Let's talk. It is not day.

JULIET:

It is, it is. Hie hence,° begone, away!
It is the lark that sings so out of tune,
Straining harsh discords and unpleasing sharps.°
Some say the lark makes sweet division;°
This doth not so, for she divideth us.
Some say the lark and loathèd toad changed° eyes;
O, now I would they had changed voices too,
Since arm from arm° that voice doth us affray,°
Hunting thee hence with hunt's-up° to the day.
O, now begone! More light and light it grows.

ROMEO:

More light and light, more dark and dark our woes!

Enter Nurse [hastily].

---

9. **jocund:** cheerful.   13. **exhaled:** i.e., has drawn out of the ground. (Meteors were thought to
be vapors of luminous gas drawn up by the sun.)   18. **so thou:** if you.   20. **reflex:** reflection.
Cynthia's: the moon's.   23. **care:** desire, concern.   26. **Hie hence:** hasten away.   28. **sharps:**
notes relatively high in pitch and hence discordant.   29. **division:** variations on a melody, made
by dividing each note into notes of briefer duration.   31. **changed:** exchanged. (A popular saying, to account for the observation that the lark has very ordinary eyes and the toad remarkable
ones.)   33. **arm from arm:** from one another's arms.   **affray:** frighten.   34. **hunt's-up:** a
song or tune to awaken huntsmen and, later, a newly married couple.

NURSE: Madam!

JULIET: Nurse?

NURSE:
Your lady mother is coming to your chamber.
The day is broke; be wary, look about.   [*Exit.*]   40

JULIET:
Then window, let day in, and let life out.

ROMEO:
Farewell, farewell! One kiss, and I'll descend.
                    [*They kiss. He climbs down from the window.*]

JULIET:
Art thou gone so? Love, lord, ay, husband, friend!°
I must hear from thee every day in the hour,
For in a minute there are many days.   45
O, by this count° I shall be much in years°
Ere I again behold my Romeo!

ROMEO: [*From below her window*]   Farewell!
I will omit no opportunity
That may convey my greetings, love, to thee.   50

JULIET:
O, think'st thou we shall ever meet again?

ROMEO:
I doubt it not, and all these woes shall serve
For sweet discourses in our times to come.

JULIET:
O God, I have an ill-divining° soul!
Methinks I see thee, now thou art so low,   55
As one dead in the bottom of a tomb.
Either my eyesight fails or thou lookest pale.

ROMEO:
And trust me, love, in my eye so do you.
Dry sorrow° drinks our blood. Adieu, adieu!   *Exit.*

JULIET:
O Fortune, Fortune! All men call thee fickle.   60
If thou art fickle, what dost thou with him
That is renowned for faith? Be fickle, Fortune.

---

43. **friend:** lover.   46. **count:** method of calculation.   **much in years:** very old.   54. **ill-divining:** prophesying of evil.   59. **Dry sorrow:** (The heat of the body in sorrow and despair was thought to descend into the bowels and dry up the blood.)

For then, I hope, thou wilt not keep him long,
But send him back.

Enter Mother [Capulet's Wife].

WIFE: Ho, daughter, are you up?
JULIET:

Who is 't that calls? It is my lady mother.   65
Is she not down° so late, or up so early?
What unaccustomed cause procures° her hither?

                          [*She goeth down from the window.*]
WIFE:

Why, how now, Juliet?
JULIET: Madam, I am not well.
WIFE:

Evermore weeping for your cousin's death?
What, wilt thou wash him from his grave with tears?   70
An if° thou couldst, thou couldst not make him live;
Therefore, have done. Some grief shows much of love,
But much of grief shows still some want of wit.°
JULIET:

Yet let me weep for such a feeling° loss.
WIFE:

So shall you feel the loss, but not the friend   75
Which you weep for.
JULIET: Feeling so the loss,
I cannot choose but ever weep the friend.
WIFE:

Well, girl, thou weep'st not so much for his death
As that the villain lives which slaughtered him.
JULIET:

What villain, madam?
WIFE: That same villain, Romeo.   80
JULIET: [*Aside*]

Villain and he be many miles asunder. —

---

66. **down:** in bed.   67. **procures:** induces to come. (As indicated by the bracketed stage direction, which is from the first quarto, Juliet, who has appeared until now at her "window" above
the stage, evidently descends quickly to the main stage and joins her mother for the remainder
of the scene. The stage, which before was to have been imagined as Capulet's orchard, is now
Juliet's chamber. Juliet's mother has entered onto the main stage four lines earlier.)   71. **An
if:** if.   73. **wit:** intellect.   74. **feeling:** deeply felt.

God pardon him! I do, with all my heart;
And yet no man like he° doth grieve° my heart.

WIFE:

That is because the traitor murderer lives.

JULIET:

Ay, madam, from the reach of these my hands.   85
Would none but I might venge my cousin's death!

WIFE:

We will have vengeance for it, fear thou not.
Then weep no more. I'll send to one in Mantua,
Where that same banished runagate° doth live,
Shall° give him such an unaccustomed dram°   90
That he shall soon keep Tybalt company.
And then, I hope, thou wilt be satisfied.

JULIET:

Indeed, I never shall be satisfied
With Romeo till I behold him — dead —
Is my poor heart so for a kinsman vexed.   95
Madam, if you could find out but a man
To bear a poison, I would temper° it,
That Romeo should, upon receipt thereof,
Soon sleep in quiet. O, how my heart abhors
To hear him named, and cannot come to him   100
To wreak° the love I bore my cousin
Upon his body that° hath slaughtered him!

WIFE:

Find thou the means, and I'll find such a man.
But now I'll tell thee joyful tidings, girl.

JULIET:

And joy comes well in such a needy time.   105
What are they, beseech your ladyship?

WIFE:

Well, well, thou hast a careful° father, child,
One who, to put thee from thy heaviness,°

---

83. **no man like he:** no man so much as he.   **grieve:** (1) anger (2) grieve with longing. (Juliet speaks to her mother throughout in intentional ambiguities, at ll. 86, 99, 100–02, etc.)   89. **runagate:** renegade, fugitive.   90. **Shall:** who shall.   **dram:** dose. (Literally, one-eighth of a fluid ounce.)   97. **temper:** (1) mix, concoct (2) alloy, dilute.   101. **wreak:** (1) avenge (2) bestow.   102. **his body that:** the body of him who.   107. **careful:** full of care (for you).   108. **heaviness:** sorrow.

Hath sorted° out a sudden day of joy
That thou expects not, nor I looked not for.   110

JULIET:

Madam, in happy time, what day is that?

WIFE:

Marry,° my child, early next Thursday morn,
The gallant, young, and noble gentleman,
The County Paris, at Saint Peter's Church
Shall happily make thee there a joyful bride.   115

JULIET:

Now, by Saint Peter's Church, and Peter too,
He shall not make me there a joyful bride!
I wonder at this haste, that I must wed
Ere he that should be husband comes to woo.
I pray you, tell my lord and father, madam,   120
I will not marry yet, and when I do I swear
It shall be Romeo, whom you know I hate,
Rather than Paris. These are news indeed!

WIFE:

Here comes your father. Tell him so yourself,
And see how he will take it at your hands.   125

Enter Capulet and Nurse.

CAPULET:

When the sun sets, the earth doth drizzle dew,
But for the sunset of my brother's son
It rains downright.
How now, a conduit,° girl? What, still in tears?
Evermore showering? In one little body   130
Thou counterfeits a bark,° a sea, a wind;
For still thy eyes, which I may call the sea,
Do ebb and flow with tears; the bark thy body is,
Sailing in this salt flood; the winds, thy sighs,
Who, raging with thy tears, and they with them,   135
Without a sudden calm,° will overset
Thy tempest-tossèd body. — How now, wife?
Have you delivered to her our decree?

---

109. **sorted:** chosen.   112. **Marry:** i.e., by the Virgin Mary.   129. **conduit:** water pipe, fountain.   131. **bark:** sailing vessel.   136. **Without . . . calm:** unless they quickly calm themselves.

WIFE:
　　Ay, sir, but she will none, she gives you thanks.°
　　I would the fool were married to her grave!　　　　　　140

CAPULET:
　　Soft, take me with you,° take me with you, wife.
　　How? Will she none? Doth she not give us thanks?
　　Is she not proud? Doth she not count her° blest,
　　Unworthy as she is, that we have wrought°
　　So worthy a gentleman to be her bride?°　　　　　　145

JULIET:
　　Not proud you have, but thankful that you have.
　　Proud can I never be of what I hate,
　　But thankful even for hate that is meant love.°

CAPULET:
　　How, how, how, how, chopped logic?° What is this?
　　"Proud," and "I thank you," and "I thank you not,"　　150
　　And yet "not proud"? Mistress minion,° you,
　　Thank me no thankings, nor proud me no prouds,
　　But fettle° your fine joints 'gainst° Thursday next
　　To go with Paris to Saint Peter's Church,
　　Or I will drag thee on a hurdle° thither.　　　　　　155
　　Out, you greensickness° carrion! Out, you baggage!°
　　You tallow-face!°

WIFE: [*To Capulet*]　Fie, fie! What, are you mad?

JULIET: [*Kneeling*]
　　Good father, I beseech you on my knees,
　　Hear me with patience but to speak a word.

CAPULET:
　　Hang thee, young baggage, disobedient wretch!　　160
　　I tell thee what: get thee to church o' Thursday
　　Or never after look me in the face.
　　Speak not, reply not, do not answer me!
　　My fingers itch. Wife, we scarce thought us blest

---

139. will . . . thanks: says "no thank you," she'll have none, no part of it.　141. take . . . you: let me understand you.　143. count her: consider herself.　144. wrought: procured.　145. bride: bridegroom.　148. hate . . . love: i.e., that which is hateful but which was meant lovingly. 149. chopped logic: a shallow and sophistical argument, or arguer.　151. minion: spoiled darling, minx.　153. fettle: make ready.　'gainst: in anticipation of.　155. a hurdle: a conveyance on which criminals were dragged to execution.　156. greensickness: (An anemic ailment of young unmarried women; it suggests Juliet's paleness.)　baggage: good-for-nothing. 157. tallow-face: pale-face.

That God had lent us but this only child;   165
But now I see this one is one too much,
And that we have a curse in having her.
Out on her, hilding!°

NURSE: God in heaven bless her!
You are to blame, my lord, to rate° her so.

CAPULET:
And why, my Lady Wisdom? Hold your tongue,   170
Good Prudence. Smatter° with your gossips, go.

NURSE:
I speak no treason.

CAPULET: O, God-i'-good-e'en!°

NURSE:
May not one speak?

CAPULET: Peace, you mumbling fool!
Utter your gravity° o'er a gossip's bowl,
For here we need it not.   175

WIFE: You are too hot.

CAPULET: God's bread,° it makes me mad!
Day, night, hour, tide,° time, work, play,
Alone, in company, still my care hath been
To have her matched. And having now provided   180
A gentleman of noble parentage,
Of fair demesnes,° youthful, and nobly liened,°
Stuffed, as they say, with honorable parts,°
Proportioned as one's thought would wish a man —
And then to have a wretched puling° fool,   185
A whining mammet,° in her fortune's tender,°
To answer, "I'll not wed, I cannot love,
I am too young; I pray you, pardon me."
But, an you will not wed, I'll pardon you.°
Graze where you will, you shall not house with me.   190
Look to 't, think on 't. I do not use° to jest.
Thursday is near. Lay hand on heart; advise.°

---

168. hilding: worthless person.   **169. rate:** berate, scold.   **171. Smatter:** chatter.   **172. God-i'-good-e'en:** i.e., for God's sake. (Literally, God give you good evening.)   **174. gravity:** wisdom. (Said contemptuously.)   **177. God's bread:** i.e., by God's (Christ's) Sacrament.   **178. tide:** season.   **182. demesnes:** estates.   **liened:** descended.   **183. parts:** qualities.   **185. puling:** whining.   **186. mammet:** doll.   **in . . . tender:** when an offer of good fortune is made to her.   **189. pardon you:** i.e., allow you to depart. (Said caustically.)   **191. do not use:** am not accustomed.   **192. advise:** consider carefully.

An you be mine, I'll give you to my friend;
An you be not, hang, beg, starve, die in the streets,
For, by my soul, I'll ne'er acknowledge thee,   195
Nor what is mine shall never do thee good.
Trust to 't, bethink you. I'll not be forsworn.°   *Exit.*

JULIET:
Is there no pity sitting in the clouds
That sees into the bottom of my grief?
O sweet my Mother, cast me not away!   200
Delay this marriage for a month, a week;
Or if you do not, make the bridal bed
In that dim monument where Tybalt lies.

WIFE:
Talk not to me, for I'll not speak a word.
Do as thou wilt, for I have done with thee.   *Exit.*   205

JULIET:
O God! — O Nurse, how shall this be prevented?
My husband is on earth, my faith in heaven.°
How shall that faith return again to earth,
Unless that husband send it me from heaven
By leaving earth?° Comfort me, counsel me.   210
Alack, alack, that heaven should practice° stratagems
Upon so soft a subject as myself!
What sayst thou? Hast thou not a word of joy?
Some comfort, Nurse.

NURSE: Faith, here it is.
Romeo is banished, and all the world to nothing°   215
That he dares ne'er come back to challenge° you,
Or if he do, it needs must be by stealth.
Then, since the case so stands as now it doth,
I think it best you married with the County.
O, he's a lovely gentleman!   220
Romeo's a dishclout° to him. An eagle, madam,
Hath not so green, so quick,° so fair an eye
As Paris hath. Beshrew° my very heart,

---

197. **be forsworn:** i.e., go back on my word.   207. **my faith in heaven:** (Juliet refers to her marriage vows.)   208–10. **How . . . leaving earth:** i.e., how can I remarry unless Romeo dies.   211. **practice:** scheme, contrive.   215. **all . . . nothing:** the odds are overwhelming.   216. **challenge:** lay claim to.   221. **dishclout:** dishrag.   222. **quick:** keen.   223. **Beshrew:** i.e., cursed be (also at l. 229).

I think you are happy in this second match,
For it excels your first; or if it did not,   225
Your first is dead — or 'twere as good he were
As living here° and you no use of him.
JULIET: Speak'st thou from thy heart?
NURSE:
And from my soul too. Else beshrew them both.
JULIET: Amen!°   230
NURSE: What?
JULIET:
Well, thou hast comforted me marvelous much.
Go in, and tell my lady I am gone,
Having displeased my father, to Laurence' cell
To make confession and to be absolved.   235
NURSE:
Marry, I will; and this is wisely done.   [*Exit.*]
JULIET:
Ancient damnation!° O most wicked fiend!
Is it more sin to wish me thus forsworn,°
Or to dispraise my lord with that same tongue
Which she hath praised him with above compare   240
So many thousand times? Go, counselor,
Thou and my bosom° henceforth shall be twain.°
I'll to the Friar to know his remedy.
If all else fail, myself have power to die.   *Exit.*

ACT 4, SCENE I°

Enter Friar [Laurence] and County Paris.

FRIAR LAURENCE:
On Thursday, sir? The time is very short.
PARIS:
My father Capulet will have it so,
And I am nothing slow to slack his haste.°

---

227. here: i.e., on earth.   **230. Amen:** i.e., yes, indeed, *beshrew* (cursed be) your heart and soul. (But Juliet does not explain this private meaning to the Nurse.)   **237. Ancient damnation:** damnable old woman.   **238. forsworn:** i.e., false to my marriage vows.   **242. bosom:** secret thoughts.   **twain:** separated.   **ACT 4, SCENE I. Location:** Verona. Friar Laurence's cell.   **3. nothing . . . haste:** not at all reluctant in a way that might slacken his haste.

FRIAR LAURENCE:
　You say you do not know the lady's mind?
　Uneven is the course. I like it not.　　　　　　　　　　5
PARIS:
　Immoderately she weeps for Tybalt's death,
　And therefore have I little talked of love,
　For Venus smiles not in a house of tears.°
　Now, sir, her father counts it dangerous
　That she do give her sorrow so much sway,　　　　　　10
　And in his wisdom hastes° our marriage
　To stop the inundation of her tears,
　Which, too much minded° by herself alone,
　May be put from her by society.°
　Now do you know the reason of this haste.　　　　　　15
FRIAR LAURENCE: [*Aside*]
　I would I knew not why it should be slowed. —
　Look, sir, here comes the lady toward my cell.

　Enter Juliet.

PARIS:
　Happily met, my lady and my wife!
JULIET:
　That may be, sir, when I may be a wife.
PARIS:
　That "may be" must be, love, on Thursday next.　　　20
JULIET:
　What must be shall be.
FRIAR LAURENCE:　　　　　That's a certain text.
PARIS:
　Come you to make confession to this father?
JULIET:
　To answer that, I should confess to you.
PARIS:
　Do not deny to him that you love me.
JULIET:
　I will confess to you that I love him.　　　　　　　　25

---

8. **Venus . . . tears:** (1) amorousness isn't appropriate in a house of mourning (2) the planet
Venus does not exert a favorable influence when it is in an inauspicious *house* or portion of the
zodiac. 11. **hastes:** hurries. 13. **minded:** thought about. 14. **society:** companionship.

PARIS:
So will ye, I am sure, that you love me.
JULIET:
If I do so, it will be of more price,°
Being spoke behind your back, than to your face.
PARIS:
Poor soul, thy face is much abused with tears.
JULIET:
The tears have got small victory by that,
For it was bad enough before their spite.° 30
PARIS:
Thou wrong'st it more than tears with that report.
JULIET:
That is no slander, sir, which is a truth;
And what I spake, I spake it to my face.°
PARIS:
Thy face is mine, and thou hast slandered it.
35
JULIET:
It may be so, for it is not mine own. —
Are you at leisure, holy Father, now,
Or shall I come to you at evening Mass?
FRIAR LAURENCE:
My leisure serves me, pensive° daughter, now.
My lord, we must entreat the time alone.°
40
PARIS:
God shield° I should disturb devotion!
Juliet, on Thursday early will I rouse ye.
Till then, adieu, and keep this holy kiss.   *Exit.*
JULIET:
O, shut the door! And when thou hast done so,
Come weep with me — past hope, past cure, past help!
45
FRIAR LAURENCE:
Ah, Juliet, I already know thy grief;
It strains° me past the compass° of my wits.
I hear thou must, and nothing may prorogue° it,
On Thursday next be married to this county.

27. **more price:** greater worth.   31. **spite:** malice.   34. **to my face:** (1) openly (2) about my face.
39. **pensive:** sorrowful.   40. **entreat . . . alone:** i.e., ask you to leave us alone.   41. **shield:** prevent (that).   47. **strains:** forces.   **compass:** bounds.   48. **may prorogue:** can delay.

JULIET:

Tell me not, Friar, that thou hearest of this,   50
Unless thou tell me how I may prevent it.
If in thy wisdom thou canst give no help,
Do thou but call my resolution wise
And with this knife I'll help it presently.°   *[She shows a knife.]*
God joined my heart and Romeo's, thou our hands;   55
And ere this hand, by thee to Romeo's sealed,
Shall be the label° to another deed,
Or my true heart with treacherous revolt
Turn to another, this shall slay them both.°
Therefore, out of thy long-experienced time,°   60
Give me some present counsel, or, behold,
Twixt my extremes° and me this bloody knife
Shall play the umpire, arbitrating that
Which the commission° of thy years and art°
Could to no issue of true honor bring.   65
Be not so long° to speak; I long to die
If what thou speak'st speak not of remedy.

FRIAR LAURENCE:

Hold, daughter. I do spy a kind of hope,
Which craves as desperate an execution
As that is desperate which we would prevent.   70
If, rather than to marry County Paris,
Thou hast the strength of will to slay thyself,
Then is it likely thou wilt undertake
A thing like death to chide away this shame,
That cop'st° with Death himself to scape from it;°   75
And if thou darest, I'll give thee remedy.

JULIET:

O, bid me leap, rather than marry Paris,
From off the battlements of any tower,
Or walk in thievish ways,° or bid me lurk
Where serpents are; chain me with roaring bears,   80
Or hide me nightly in a charnel house,°

---

54. **presently:** at once.   57. **label:** strip attached to a deed to carry the seal; hence, confirmation, seal.   59. **both:** i.e., hand and heart.   60. **time:** age.   62. **extremes:** extreme difficulties.   64. **commission:** authority.   **art:** skill.   66. **so long:** so slow.   75. **That cop'st:** you who
would encounter or negotiate with; or, a thing that would cope.   **it:** i.e., shame.   79. **thievish
ways:** roads frequented by thieves.   81. **charnel house:** vault for human bones.

O'ercovered quite with dead men's rattling bones,
With reeky° shanks and yellow chopless° skulls;
Or bid me go into a new-made grave
And hide me with a dead man in his tomb — 85
Things that, to hear them told, have made me tremble —
And I will do it without fear or doubt,
To live an unstained wife to my sweet love.

FRIAR LAURENCE:

Hold, then. Go home, be merry, give consent
To marry Paris. Wednesday is tomorrow. 90
Tomorrow night look that thou lie alone;
Let not the Nurse lie with thee in thy chamber.
Take thou this vial, being then in bed,
[*Showing her a vial*]
And this distilling° liquor drink thou off,
When presently through all thy veins shall run 95
A cold and drowsy humor;° for no pulse
Shall keep his native° progress, but surcease;°
No warmth, no breath shall testify thou livest;
The roses in thy lips and cheeks shall fade
To wanny° ashes, thy eyes' windows fall 100
Like death when he shuts up the day of life;
Each part, deprived of supple government,°
Shall, stiff and stark and cold, appear like death.
And in this borrowed likeness of shrunk death
Thou shalt continue two-and-forty hours, 105
And then awake as from a pleasant sleep.
Now, when the bridegroom in the morning comes
To rouse thee from thy bed, there art thou dead.
Then, as the manner of our country is,
In thy best robes uncovered on the bier 110
Thou shalt be borne to that same ancient vault
Where all the kindred of the Capulets lie.
In the meantime, against° thou shalt awake,
Shall Romeo by my letters know our drift,°
And hither shall he come; and he and I 115

---

83. **reeky:** reeking, malodorous. **chopless:** without the lower jaw. 94. **distilling:** infusing.
96. **humor:** fluid, moisture. 97. **his native:** its natural. **surcease:** cease. 100. **wanny:** wan, pale. 102. **supple government:** control of motion. 113. **against:** anticipating when.
114. **drift:** plan.

Will watch thy waking, and that very night
Shall Romeo bear thee hence to Mantua.
And this shall free thee from this present shame,
If no inconstant toy° nor womanish fear
Abate thy valor in the acting it.   120
JULIET: [*Taking the vial*]
Give me, give me! O, tell not me of fear!
FRIAR LAURENCE:
Hold, get you gone. Be strong and prosperous°
In this resolve. I'll send a friar with speed
To Mantua, with my letters to thy lord.
JULIET:
Love give me strength, and strength shall help afford.°   125
Farewell, dear Father!   *Exeunt* [*separately*].

ACT 4, SCENE 2°

Enter Father Capulet, Mother [*Capulet's Wife*], *Nurse, and Servingmen, two or three.*

CAPULET:
So many guests invite as here are writ.   [*Exit one or two Servingmen.*]
Sirrah, go hire me twenty cunning° cooks.
SERVINGMAN: You shall have none ill,° sir, for I'll try° if they can lick their
fingers.
CAPULET: How canst thou try them so?   5
SERVINGMAN: Marry, sir, 'tis an ill cook that cannot lick his own fingers;
therefore he that cannot lick his fingers goes not with me.
CAPULET: Go, begone.   [*Exit Servingman.*]
We shall be much unfurnished° for this time.
What, is my daughter gone to Friar Laurence?   10
NURSE: Ay, forsooth.
CAPULET:
Well, he may chance to do some good on her.
A peevish self-willed harlotry it is.°

Enter Juliet.

---

119. **toy:** idle fancy.   122. **prosperous:** successful.   125. **help afford:** provide help.   ACT 4,
SCENE 2. **Location:** Verona. Capulet's house.   2. **cunning:** skilled.   3. **none ill:** no bad
ones.   **try:** test.   9. **unfurnished:** unprovided.   13. **A peevish . . . is:** i.e., she's a silly good-
for-nothing.

NURSE:
See where she comes from shrift with merry look.

CAPULET:
How now, my headstrong, where have you been gadding?°   15

JULIET:
Where I have learned me to repent the sin
Of disobedient opposition
To you and your behests,° and am enjoined
By holy Laurence to fall prostrate here,   [*Kneeling*]
To beg your pardon. Pardon, I beseech you!   20
Henceforward I am ever ruled by you.

CAPULET:
Send for the County! Go tell him of this.
I'll have this knot knit up tomorrow morning.

JULIET:
I met the youthful lord at Laurence' cell
And gave him what becomèd° love I might,   25
Not stepping o'er the bounds of modesty.

CAPULET:
Why, I am glad on 't. This is well. Stand up.   [*Juliet rises.*]
This is as 't should be. Let me see the County;
Ay, marry, go, I say, and fetch him hither.
Now, afore God, this reverend holy friar,   30
All our whole city is much bound° to him.

JULIET:
Nurse, will you go with me into my closet°
To help me sort° such needful ornaments
As you think fit to furnish me tomorrow?

WIFE:
No, not till Thursday. There is time enough.   35

CAPULET:
Go, Nurse, go with her. We'll to church tomorrow.
                                    Exeunt [*Juliet and Nurse*].

WIFE:
We shall be short in our provision.
'Tis now near night.

CAPULET: Tush, I will stir about,
And all things shall be well, I warrant thee, wife.

---

15. **gadding:** wandering. 18. **behests:** commands. 25. **becomèd:** befitting. 31. **bound:** indebted. 32. **closet:** chamber. 33. **sort:** choose.

Go thou to Juliet, help to deck up° her.   40
I'll not to bed tonight. Let me alone.
I'll play the huswife° for this once. — What ho! —
They are all forth. Well, I will walk myself
To County Paris, to prepare up him
Against tomorrow. My heart is wondrous light,   45
Since this same wayward girl is so reclaimed.   *Exeunt.*

ACT 4, SCENE 3°

Enter Juliet and Nurse.

JULIET:

Ay, those attires are best. But, gentle Nurse,
I pray thee, leave me to myself tonight;
For I have need of many orisons°
To move the heavens to smile upon my state,
Which, well thou knowest, is cross° and full of sin.   5

Enter Mother [Capulet's Wife].

WIFE:

What, are you busy, ho? Need you my help?

JULIET:

No, madam, we have culled° such necessaries
As are behooveful° for our state° tomorrow.
So please you, let me now be left alone,
And let the Nurse this night sit up with you,   10
For I am sure you have your hands full all
In this so sudden business.

WIFE: Good night.
Get thee to bed and rest, for thou hast need.

Exeunt [Capulet's Wife and Nurse].

JULIET:

Farewell! God knows when we shall meet again.
I have a faint° cold fear thrills° through my veins   15
That almost freezes up the heat of life.
I'll call them back again to comfort me.

---

40. **deck up:** dress, adorn.   42. **huswife:** housewife.   ACT 4, SCENE 3. Location: Verona.
Capulet's house; Juliet's bed, enclosed by bedcurtains, is thrust out or is otherwise visible.
3. **orisons:** prayers.   5. **cross:** contrary, perverse.   7. **culled:** picked out.   8. **behooveful:**
needful.   **state:** ceremony.   15. **faint:** producing faintness.   **thrills:** pierces, shivers.

Nurse! — What should she do here?
My dismal scene I needs must act alone.
Come, vial.   *[She takes out the vial.]*   20
What if this mixture do not work at all?
Shall I be married then tomorrow morning?
No, no, this shall forbid it. Lie thou there.   *[She lays down a dagger.]*
What if it be a poison which the Friar
Subtly hath ministered to have me dead,   25
Lest in this marriage he should be dishonored
Because he married me before to Romeo?
I fear it is; and yet methinks it should not,
For he hath still° been tried° a holy man.
How if, when I am laid into the tomb,   30
I wake before the time that Romeo
Come to redeem me? There's a fearful point!
Shall I not then be stifled in the vault,
To whose foul mouth no healthsome air breathes in,
And there die strangled ere my Romeo comes?   35
Or, if I live, is it not very like,°
The horrible conceit° of death and night,
Together with the terror of the place —
As° in a vault, an ancient receptacle,
Where for this many hundred years the bones   40
Of all my buried ancestors are packed;
Where bloody Tybalt, yet but green° in earth,
Lies festering in his shroud; where, as they say,
At some hours in the night spirits resort —
Alack, alack, is it not like that I,   45
So early waking, what with loathsome smells,
And shrieks like mandrakes° torn out of the earth,
That° living mortals, hearing them, run mad —
O, if I wake, shall I not be distraught,
Environèd with all these hideous fears,°   50
And madly play with my forefathers' joints,
And pluck the mangled Tybalt from his shroud,
And in this rage,° with some great° kinsman's bone

29. **still:** always. **tried:** proved. 36. **like:** likely (also at l. 45). 37. **conceit:** idea. 39. **As:** namely. 42. **green:** new, freshly. 47. **mandrakes:** (The root of the mandragora or mandrake resembled the human form; the plant was fabled to utter a shriek when torn from the ground.) 48. **That:** so that. 50. **fears:** objects of fear. 53. **rage:** madness. **great:** i.e., of an earlier generation, as in *great*-grandfather.

As with a club dash out my desperate brains?
O, look! Methinks I see my cousin's ghost   55
Seeking out Romeo, that did spit° his body
Upon a rapier's point. Stay,° Tybalt, stay!
Romeo, Romeo, Romeo! Here's drink — I drink to thee.

[*She drinks and falls upon her bed, within the curtains.*]

Act 4, Scene 4°

Enter Lady of the House [Capulet's Wife] and Nurse.

WIFE:
Hold, take these keys, and fetch more spices, Nurse.
NURSE:
They call for dates and quinces in the pastry.°

Enter old Capulet.

CAPULET:
Come, stir, stir, stir! The second cock hath crowed.
The curfew bell hath rung; 'tis three o'clock.
Look to the baked meats,° good Angelica.   5
Spare not for cost.
NURSE: Go, you cotquean,° go,
Get you to bed. Faith, you'll be sick tomorrow
For this night's watching.°
CAPULET:
No, not a whit. What, I have watched ere now
All night for lesser cause, and ne'er been sick.   10
WIFE:
Ay, you have been a mouse-hunt° in your time,
But I will watch you from such watching° now.   *Exeunt Lady and Nurse.*
CAPULET:
A jealous hood,° a jealous hood!

Enter three or four [Servingmen] with spits and logs, and baskets.

Now, fellow, what is there?

---

56. **spit:** impale. 57. **Stay:** stop. **Act 4, Scene 4. Location:** Scene continues. Juliet's bed remains visible. 2. **pastry:** room in which pastry was made. 5. **baked meats:** pies, pastry. 6. **cotquean:** i.e., a man who acts the housewife. (Literally, a cottage housewife.) 8. **watching:** being awake. 11. **mouse-hunt:** i.e., hunter of women. 12. **watch ... watching:** i.e., keep an eye on you to prevent such nighttime activity. 13. **A jealous hood:** i.e., you wear the cap of jealousy.

FIRST SERVINGMAN:

Things for the cook, sir, but I know not what.   15

CAPULET:

Make haste, make haste. [*Exit First Servingman.*] Sirrah, fetch drier logs.

Call Peter. He will show thee where they are.

SECOND SERVINGMAN:

I have a head, sir, that will find out logs

And never trouble Peter for the matter.

CAPULET:

Mass,° and well said. A merry whoreson,° ha!   20

Thou shalt be loggerhead.° [*Exit Servingman.*] Good faith, 'tis day.

The County will be here with music straight,°

For so he said he would. I hear him near.   *Play music* [*within*].

Nurse! Wife! What ho! What, Nurse, I say!

Enter Nurse.

Go waken Juliet, go and trim° her up.   25

I'll go and chat with Paris. Hie, make haste,

Make haste. The bridegroom he is come already.

Make haste, I say.   [*Exit Capulet.*]

ACT 4, SCENE 5°

[*The Nurse goes to the bed.*]

NURSE:

Mistress! What, mistress! Juliet! Fast,° I warrant her, she.

Why, lamb, why, lady! Fie, you slugabed!

Why, love, I say! Madam! Sweetheart! Why, bride!

What, not a word? You take your pennyworths° now.

Sleep for a week; for the next night, I warrant,   5

The County Paris hath set up his rest°

That you shall rest but little. God forgive me,

Marry, and amen! How sound is she asleep!

I needs must wake her. Madam, madam, madam!

20. **Mass:** by the Mass.   **whoreson:** i.e., fellow. (An abusive term used familiarly.)   21. **log-gerhead:** (1) put in charge of getting logs (2) a blockhead.   22. **straight:** straightway, immediately.   25. **trim:** dress.   ACT 4, SCENE 5. Location: Scene continues. Juliet's bed remains visible.   1. **Fast:** fast asleep.   4. **pennyworths:** small portions (of sleep).   6. **set up his rest:** firmly resolved. (From primero, a card game, where it means "staked his reserve." The Nurse speaks bawdily.)

Ay, let the County take you in your bed;   10
He'll fright you up, i' faith. Will it not be?   [*She opens the bedcurtains.*]
What, dressed, and in your clothes, and down again?
I must needs wake you. Lady, lady, lady!
Alas, alas! Help, help! My lady's dead!
O, weraday,° that ever I was born!   15
Some aqua vitae,° ho! My lord! My lady!

[*Enter Capulet's Wife.*]

WIFE:
What noise is here?
NURSE: O lamentable day!
WIFE:
What is the matter?
NURSE: Look. look! O heavy° day!
WIFE:
O me, O me! My child, my only life!
Revive, look up, or I will die with thee!   20
Help, help! Call help.

Enter Father [Capulet].

CAPULET:
For shame, bring Juliet forth. Her lord is come.
NURSE:
She's dead, deceased. She's dead, alack the day!
WIFE:
Alack the day, she's dead, she's dead, she's dead!
CAPULET:
Ha! Let me see her. Out, alas! She's cold.   25
Her blood is settled,° and her joints are stiff;
Life and these lips have long been separated.
Death lies on her like an untimely frost
Upon the sweetest flower of all the field.
NURSE:
O lamentable day!
WIFE: O woeful time!   30

---

15. **weraday:** wellaway, alas.   16. **aqua vitae:** strong alcoholic spirits.   18. **heavy:** sorrowful.
26. **settled:** congealed.

CAPULET:
Death, that hath ta'en her hence to make me wail,
Ties up my tongue and will not let me speak.

Enter Friar [Laurence] and the County [Paris, with Musicians].

FRIAR LAURENCE:
Come, is the bride ready to go to church?
CAPULET:
Ready to go, but never to return.
O son, the night before thy wedding day   35
Hath Death lain with thy wife. There she lies,
Flower as she was, deflowered by him.
Death is my son-in-law, Death is my heir;
My daughter he hath wedded. I will die
And leave him all; life, living,° all is Death's.   40
PARIS:
Have I thought long° to see this morning's face,
And doth it give me such a sight as this?
WIFE:
Accurst, unhappy,° wretched, hateful day!
Most miserable hour that e'er time saw
In lasting° labor of his pilgrimage!   45
But one, poor one, one poor and loving child,
But one thing to rejoice and solace in,
And cruel Death hath catched° it from my sight!
NURSE:
O woe! O woeful, woeful, woeful day!
Most lamentable day, most woeful day   50
That ever, ever I did yet behold!
O day, O day, O day! O hateful day!
Never was seen so black a day as this.
O woeful day, O woeful day!
PARIS:
Beguiled,° divorcèd, wrongèd, spited, slain!   55
Most detestable Death, by thee beguiled,
By cruel, cruel thee quite overthrown!
O love! O life! Not life, but love in death!

---

40. **living:** means of living, property.   41. **thought long:** looked forward to.   43. **unhappy:**
fatal.   45. **lasting:** unceasing.   48. **catched:** snatched.   55. **Beguiled:** cheated.

CAPULET:

Despised, distressèd, hated, martyred, killed!
Uncomfortable° time, why cam'st thou now   60
To murder, murder our solemnity?°
O child! O child! My soul, and not my child!
Dead art thou! Alack, my child is dead,
And with my child my joys are burièd.

FRIAR LAURENCE:

Peace, ho, for shame! Confusion's° cure lives not   65
In these confusions. Heaven and yourself
Had part in this fair maid; now heaven hath all,
And all the better is it for the maid.
Your part° in her you could not keep from death,
But heaven keeps his part in eternal life.   70
The most you sought was her promotion,°
For 'twas your heaven° she should be advanced;
And weep ye now, seeing she is advanced
Above the clouds, as high as heaven itself?
O, in this love you love your child so ill   75
That you run mad, seeing that she is well.
She's not well married that lives married long,
But she's best married that dies married young.
Dry up your tears, and stick your rosemary°
On this fair corpse, and, as the custom is,   80
And in her best array, bear her to church;
For though fond nature° bids us all lament,
Yet nature's tears are reason's merriment.°

CAPULET:

All things that we ordainèd festival°
Turn from their office° to black funeral: 85
Our instruments to melancholy bells,
Our wedding cheer to a sad burial feast,
Our solemn hymns to sullen° dirges change,

---

60. **Uncomfortable:** comfortless. 61. **solemnity:** ceremony, festivity. 65. **Confusion's:** calamity's. 69. **Your part:** i.e., the mortal part. 71. **promotion:** social advancement. 72. **your heaven:** i.e., your idea of the greatest good. 79. **rosemary:** symbol of immortality and enduring love; therefore used at both funerals and weddings. 82. **fond nature:** foolish human nature. 83. **nature's . . . merriment:** that which causes human nature to weep is an occasion of joy to reason. 84. **ordainèd festival:** intended to be festive. 85. **office:** function. 88. **sullen:** mournful.

Our bridal flowers serve for a buried corpse,
And all things change them° to the contrary.   90

FRIAR LAURENCE:

Sir, go you in, and, madam, go with him,
And go, Sir Paris. Everyone prepare
To follow this fair corpse unto her grave.
The heavens do lour° upon you for some ill;°
Move° them no more by crossing their high will.   95

Exeunt. Manet° [*Nurse with Musicians*].

FIRST MUSICIAN:

Faith, we may put up our pipes and be gone.

NURSE:

Honest good fellows, ah, put up, put up!
For well you know this is a pitiful case.   [*Exit.*]

FIRST MUSICIAN:

Ay, by my troth, the case may be amended.°

Enter Peter.°

PETER: Musicians, O, musicians, "Heart's ease."° "Heart's ease." O, an you   100
will have me live, play "Heart's ease."

FIRST MUSICIAN: Why, "Heart's ease"?

PETER: O, musicians, because my heart itself plays "My heart is full."° O,
play me some merry dump° to comfort me.

FIRST MUSICIAN: Not a dump we! 'Tis no time to play now.   105

PETER: You will not, then?

FIRST MUSICIAN: No.

PETER: I will then give it you soundly.

FIRST MUSICIAN: What will you give us?

PETER: No money, on my faith, but the gleek;° I will give you the minstrel.°   110

FIRST MUSICIAN: Then will I give you the serving-creature.

PETER: Then will I lay the serving-creature's dagger on your pate. I will
carry no crotchets.° I'll re° you, I'll fa° you. Do you note° me?

---

90. **them:** themselves.   94. **lour:** threaten.   **for some ill:** on account of some sin.   95. **Move:**
i.e., anger.   s.d. *Manet:* she remains onstage.   99. **case . . . amended:** (1) things generally
could be much better (2) the instrument case could be repaired.   s.d. *Enter Peter:* (The second quarto has *Enter Will Kemp*, well-known comic actor and member of Shakespeare's company, for whom Shakespeare evidently intended this role and so named him in the manuscript.)
100, 103. **"Heart's ease," "My heart is full":** (Popular ballads.)   104. **dump:** mournful tune or
dance.   110. **gleek:** jest, gibe.   **give you the minstrel:** insultingly term you a minstrel, i.e.,
vagabond.   113. **carry no crotchets:** (1) endure no whims (2) sing no quarter notes.   **re, fa:**
musical notes.   **note:** (1) heed (2) set to music.

FIRST MUSICIAN: An you re us and fa us, you note us.

SECOND MUSICIAN: Pray you, put up your dagger and put out° your wit.   115

PETER: Then have at you with my wit! I will dry-beat° you with an iron
wit, and put up my iron dagger. Answer me like men:
> "When griping griefs the heart doth wound,
>   And doleful dumps the mind oppress,
>   Then music with her silver sound"° —   120

Why "silver sound"? Why "music with her silver sound"? What say you,
Simon Catling?°

FIRST MUSICIAN: Marry, sir, because silver hath a sweet sound.

PETER: Pretty! What say you, Hugh Rebeck?°

SECOND MUSICIAN: I say "silver sound" because musicians sound° for   125
silver.

PETER: Pretty too! What say you, James Soundpost?°

THIRD MUSICIAN: Faith, I know not what to say.

PETER: O, I cry you mercy° you are the singer. I will say for you. It is "music with her silver sound" because musicians have no gold for sounding:°   130
> "Then music with her silver sound
>   With speedy help doth lend redress."   *Exit.*

FIRST MUSICIAN: What a pestilent knave is this same!

SECOND MUSICIAN: Hang him, Jack! Come, we'll in here, tarry for the
mourners, and stay° dinner.   *Exeunt.*   135

Act 5, Scene 1°

Enter Romeo.

ROMEO:
> If I may trust the flattering° truth of sleep,
> My dreams presage some joyful news at hand.
> My bosom's lord° sits lightly in his throne,
> And all this day an unaccustomed spirit
> Lifts me above the ground with cheerful thoughts.   5

---

115. **put out:** display.   116. **dry-beat:** thrash (without drawing blood).   118–20. "When . . .
sound": (From Richard Edwards's song "In Commendation of Music," published in *The Paradise of Dainty Devices,* 1576.)   122. **Catling:** (A catling was a small lutestring made of cat-
gut.)   124. **Rebeck:** (A rebeck was a fiddle with three strings.)   125. **sound:** make music.
127. **Soundpost:** (A soundpost is the pillar or peg that supports the sounding board of a
stringed instrument.)   129. **cry you mercy:** beg your pardon.   130. **have . . . sounding:** i.e.,
are paid only silver for playing.   135. **stay:** await.   Act 5, Scene 1. **Location:** Mantua.
A street.   1. **flattering:** favorable (but potentially illusory).   3. **bosom's lord:** i.e., heart.

I dreamt my lady came and found me dead —
Strange dream that gives a dead man leave to think! —
And breathed such life with kisses in my lips
That I revived and was an emperor.
Ah me, how sweet is love itself possessed°
When but love's shadows° are so rich in joy!

Enter Romeo's man [Balthasar, booted°].

News from Verona! How now, Balthasar,
Dost thou not bring me letters from the Friar?
How doth my lady? Is my father well?
How fares my Juliet? That I ask again,
For nothing can be ill if she be well.

BALTHASAR:
Then she is well, and nothing can be ill.
Her body sleeps in Capels' monument,
And her immortal part with angels lives.
I saw her laid low in her kindred's vault
And presently took post° to tell it to you.
O, pardon me for bringing these ill news,
Since you did leave it for my office,° sir.

ROMEO:
Is it e'en so? Then I defy you, stars!
Thou knowest my lodging. Get me ink and paper,
And hire post-horses. I will hence tonight.

BALTHASAR:
I do beseech you, sir, have patience.
Your looks are pale and wild, and do import°
Some misadventure.

ROMEO: Tush, thou art deceived.
Leave me, and do the thing I bid thee do.
Hast thou no letters to me from the Friar?

BALTHASAR:
No, my good lord.

ROMEO: No matter. Get thee gone,
And hire those horses. I'll be with thee straight.   *Exit [Balthasar].*

---

10. itself possessed: actually enjoyed.   **11. shadows:** dreams.   **s.d.** *booted:* wearing riding
boots — a conventional stage sign of traveling.   **21. presently took post:** at once started off in
haste; or, with post-horses.   **23. office:** duty.   **28. import:** signify.

Well, Juliet, I will lie with thee tonight.
Let's see for means.° O mischief, thou art swift   35
To enter in the thoughts of desperate men!
I do remember an apothecary° —
And hereabouts 'a dwells — which late I noted°
In tattered weeds,° with overwhelming brows,°
Culling of simples.° Meager° were his looks;   40
Sharp misery had worn him to the bones;
And in his needy shop a tortoise hung,
An alligator stuffed, and other skins
Of ill-shaped fishes; and about his shelves
A beggarly account° of empty boxes,   45
Green earthen pots, bladders, and musty seeds,
Remnants of packthread, and old cakes of roses°
Were thinly scattered to make up a show.
Noting this penury, to myself I said,
"An if° a man did need a poison now,   50
Whose sale is present° death in Mantua,
Here lives a caitiff° wretch would° sell it him."
O, this same thought did but forerun my need,
And this same needy man must sell it me.
As I remember, this should be the house.   55
Being holiday, the beggar's shop is shut.
What, ho! Apothecary!

[*Enter Apothecary.*]

APOTHECARY: Who calls so loud?
ROMEO:
Come hither, man. I see that thou art poor.
Hold, there is forty ducats.° [*He shows gold.*] Let me have
A dram of poison, such soon-speeding gear°   60
As will disperse itself through all the veins
That the life-weary taker may fall dead,

---

35. **for means:** by what means.   37. **apothecary:** druggist.   38. **which . . . noted:** whom lately I noticed.   39. **weeds:** garments.   **overwhelming brows:** eyebrows jutting out over his eyes.   40. **simples:** medicinal herbs.   **Meager:** impoverished.   45. **beggarly account:** poor array.   47. **cakes of roses:** petals pressed into cakes to be used as perfume.   50. **An if:** if.   51. **present:** immediate.   52. **caitiff:** miserable.   **would:** who would.   59. **ducats:** gold coins.   60. **soon-speeding gear:** quickly effective stuff.

And that the trunk° may be discharged of breath
As violently as hasty powder fired
Doth hurry from the fatal cannon's womb.   65

APOTHECARY:

Such mortal° drugs I have, but Mantua's law
Is death to any he° that utters° them.

ROMEO:

Art thou so bare and full of wretchedness,
And fearest to die? Famine is in thy cheeks,
Need and oppression starveth° in thy eyes,
Contempt and beggary hangs upon thy back.   70
The world is not thy friend, nor the world's law;
The world affords no law to make thee rich.
Then be not poor, but break it, and take this.

APOTHECARY:

My poverty but not my will consents.   75

ROMEO:

I pay thy poverty and not thy will.

APOTHECARY:

Put this in any liquid thing you will
And drink it off, and if you had the strength
Of twenty men it would dispatch you straight.

                    [*He gives poison, and takes the gold.*]

ROMEO:

There is thy gold — worse poison to men's souls,   80
Doing more murder in this loathsome world
Than these poor compounds that thou mayst not sell.
I sell thee poison; thou hast sold me none.
Farewell. Buy food, and get thyself in flesh. —
Come, cordial° and not poison, go with me   85
To Juliet's grave, for there must I use thee.   *Exeunt [separately].*

---

63. **trunk:** body.   66. **mortal:** deadly.   67. **any he:** anyone.   **utters:** issues, gives out.   70.
starveth: are revealed by the starving look.   85. **cordial:** restorative for the heart.

ACT 5, SCENE 2°

Enter Friar John to Friar Laurence.

FRIAR JOHN:

Holy Franciscan friar! Brother, ho!

Enter [Friar] Laurence.

FRIAR LAURENCE:

This same should be the voice of Friar John.
Welcome from Mantua! What says Romeo?
Or if his mind° be writ, give me his letter.

FRIAR JOHN:

Going to find a barefoot brother out — 5
One of our order — to associate° me
Here in this city visiting the sick,
And finding him, the searchers of the town,°
Suspecting that we both were in a house
Where the infectious pestilence did reign, 10
Sealed up the doors and would not let us forth,
So that my speed° to Mantua there was stayed.°

FRIAR LAURENCE:

Who bare my letter, then, to Romeo?

FRIAR JOHN:

I could not send it — here it is again —
Nor get a messenger to bring it thee, 15
So fearful were they of infection.   [*He gives a letter.*]

FRIAR LAURENCE:

Unhappy fortune! By my brotherhood,
The letter was not nice° but full of charge,°
Of dear° import, and the neglecting it
May do much danger. Friar John, go hence. 20
Get me an iron crow° and bring it straight
Unto my cell.

FRIAR JOHN: Brother, I'll go and bring it thee.   *Exit.*

FRIAR LAURENCE:

Now must I to the monument alone.

ACT 5, SCENE 2. Location: Verona. Friar Laurence's cell.   4. mind: thoughts.   6. associate: accompany.   8. searchers of the town: town officials charged with public health (and especially concerned about the *pestilence* or plague).   12. speed: successful journey, progress.   stayed: prevented.   18. nice: trivial.   charge: importance.   19. dear: precious, urgent.   21. crow: crowbar.

Within this three hours will fair Juliet wake.   25
She will beshrew° me much that Romeo
Hath had no notice of these accidents;°
But I will write again to Mantua,
And keep her at my cell till Romeo come —
Poor living corpse, closed in a dead man's tomb!   *Exit.*

Act 5, Scene 3°

Enter Paris, and his Page [bearing flowers, perfumed water, and a torch].

PARIS:
  Give me thy torch, boy. Hence, and stand aloof.°
  Yet put it out, for I would not be seen.
  Under yond yew trees lay thee all along,°
  Holding thy ear close to the hollow ground.
  So shall no foot upon the churchyard tread,   5
  Being° loose, unfirm, with digging up of graves,
  But thou shalt hear it. Whistle then to me
  As signal that thou hearest something approach.
  Give me those flowers. Do as I bid thee. Go.
PAGE: [*Aside*]
  I am almost afraid to stand alone   10
  Here in the churchyard, yet I will adventure.   [*He retires.*]
PARIS: [*Strewing flowers and perfumed water*]
  Sweet flower, with flowers thy bridal bed I strew —
    O woe! Thy canopy° is dust and stones —
  Which with sweet water nightly I will dew,°
    Or wanting° that, with tears distilled by moans.   15
  The obsequies° that I for thee will keep
  Nightly shall be to strew thy grave and weep.   *Whistle Boy.*
  The boy gives warning something doth approach.
  What cursèd foot wanders this way tonight,
  To cross° my obsequies and true love's rite?   20
  What, with a torch? Muffle° me, night, awhile.   [*He retires.*]

Enter Romeo and [Balthasar, with a torch, a mattock,° and a crowbar].

---

26. **beshrew:** i.e., reprove.   27. **accidents:** events.   ACT 5, SCENE 3. **Location:** Verona. A churchyard and the vault or tomb belonging to the Capulets.   1. **aloof:** to one side, at a distance.   3. **all along:** at full length.   6. **Being:** i.e., the soil being.   13. **canopy:** covering.   14. **dew:** moisten.   15. **wanting:** lacking.   16. **obsequies:** ceremonies in memory of the dead.   20. **cross:** interrupt.   21. **Muffle:** conceal.   s.d. *mattock:* pickax.

ROMEO:

    Give me that mattock and the wrenching iron.°   [*He takes the tools.*]

    Hold, take this letter. Early in the morning

    See thou deliver it to my lord and father. [*He gives a letter and takes a torch.*]

    Give me the light. Upon thy life I charge thee,   25

    Whate'er thou hearest or seest, stand all aloof

    And do not interrupt me in my course.°

    Why I descend into this bed of death

    Is partly to behold my lady's face,

    But chiefly to take thence from her dead finger   30

    A precious ring — a ring that I must use

    In dear employment.° Therefore hence, begone.

    But if thou, jealous,° dost return to pry

    In what I farther shall intend to do,

    By heaven, I will tear thee joint by joint   35

    And strew this hungry churchyard with thy limbs.

    The time and my intents are savage-wild,

    More fierce and more inexorable far

    Than empty° tigers or the roaring sea.

BALTHASAR:

    I will be gone, sir, and not trouble ye.   40

ROMEO:

    So shalt thou show me friendship. Take thou that.   [*He gives him money.*]

    Live, and be prosperous; and farewell, good fellow.

BALTHASAR: [*Aside*]

    For all this same,° I'll hide me hereabout.

    His looks I fear, and his intents I doubt.°   [*He retires.*]

ROMEO:

    Thou detestable maw, thou womb° of death,   45

    Gorged with the dearest morsel of the earth,

    Thus I enforce thy rotten jaws to open,

    And in despite° I'll cram thee with more food. [*He begins to open the tomb.*]

PARIS:

    This is that banished haughty Montague

    That murdered my love's cousin, with which grief   50

    It is supposèd the fair creature died,

---

22. **wrenching iron:** crowbar.   27. **course:** intended action.   32. **dear employment:** important business.   33. **jealous:** suspicious.   39. **empty:** hungry.   43. **For all this same:** all the same.   44. **doubt:** suspect.   45. **womb:** belly.   48. **in despite:** defiantly.

And here is come to do some villainous shame
To the dead bodies. I will apprehend him.   [*He comes forward.*]
Stop thy unhallowed toil, vile Montague!
Can vengeance be pursued further than death?   55
Condemnèd villain, I do apprehend thee.
Obey and go with me, for thou must die.

ROMEO:

I must indeed, and therefore came I hither.
Good gentle youth, tempt not a desperate man.
Fly hence and leave me. Think upon these gone;°   60
Let them affright thee. I beseech thee, youth,
Put not another sin upon my head
By urging me to fury. O, begone!
By heaven, I love thee better than myself,
For I come hither armed against myself.   65
Stay not, begone. Live, and hereafter say
A madman's mercy bid thee run away.

PARIS:

I do defy thy conjuration,
And apprehend thee for a felon here.

ROMEO:

Wilt thou provoke me? Then have at thee, boy!   [*They fight.*]   70

PAGE:

O Lord, they fight! I will go call the watch.   [*Exit.*]

PARIS:

O, I am slain! [*He falls.*] If thou be merciful,
Open the tomb, lay me with Juliet.   [*He dies.*]

ROMEO:

In faith, I will. Let me peruse this face.
Mercutio's kinsman, noble County Paris!   75
What said my man when my betossèd soul
Did not attend him as we rode? I think
He told me Paris should have married Juliet.
Said he not so? Or did I dream it so?
Or am I mad, hearing him talk of Juliet,   80
To think it was so? O, give me thy hand,
One writ with me in sour misfortune's book.

60. gone: dead.

I'll bury thee in a triumphant grave.   [*He opens the tomb.*]
A grave? O, no! A lantern,° slaughtered youth,
For here lies Juliet, and her beauty makes   85
This vault a feasting presence° full of light.
Death, lie thou there, by a dead man interred.   [*He lays Paris in the tomb.*]
How oft when men are at the point of death
Have they been merry, which their keepers° call
A lightening° before death! O, how may I   90
Call this a lightening? O my love, my wife!
Death, that hath sucked the honey of thy breath,
Hath had no power yet upon thy beauty.
Thou art not conquered; beauty's ensign° yet
Is crimson in thy lips and in thy cheeks,   95
And death's pale flag is not advancèd° there.
Tybalt, liest thou there in thy bloody sheet?°
O, what more favor can I do to thee
Than with that hand that cut thy youth in twain
To sunder his° that was thine enemy?   100
Forgive me, cousin! Ah, dear Juliet,
Why art thou yet so fair? Shall I believe
That unsubstantial° Death is amorous,
And that the lean abhorrèd monster keeps
Thee here in dark to be his paramour?   105
For fear of that I still° will stay with thee
And never from this palace of dim night
Depart again. Here, here will I remain
With worms that are thy chambermaids. O, here
Will I set up my everlasting rest°   110
And shake the yoke of inauspicious stars
From this world-wearied flesh. Eyes, look your last!
Arms, take your last embrace! And, lips, O you
The doors of breath, seal with a righteous kiss
A dateless bargain° to engrossing° death!   [*He kisses Juliet.*]   115

---

84. **lantern:** turret room full of windows.   86. **feasting presence:** reception chamber for feasting.   89. **keepers:** attendants.   90. **lightening:** exhilaration (supposed to occur just before death).   94. **ensign:** banner.   96. **advancèd:** raised.   97. **sheet:** shroud.   100. **his:** i.e., my (Romeo's) own.   103. **unsubstantial:** lacking material existence.   106. **still:** always.   110. **set . . . rest:** (See 4.5.6. The meaning is, "make my final determination," with allusion to the idea of repose.)   115. **dateless bargain:** everlasting contract.   **engrossing:** monopolizing, taking all; also, drawing up the contract.

Come, bitter conduct,° come, unsavory guide,
Thou desperate° pilot, now at once run on
The dashing rocks thy seasick weary bark!
Here's to my love. [*He drinks.*] O true apothecary!
Thy drugs are quick. Thus with a kiss I die.　　　　　　　[*He dies.*]　120

Enter [at the other end of the churchyard] Friar [Laurence] with lantern, crow, and
spade.

FRIAR LAURENCE:
Saint Francis be my speed!° How oft tonight
Have my old feet stumbled at graves! Who's there?
BALTHASAR:
Here's one, a friend, and one that knows you well.
FRIAR LAURENCE:
Bliss be upon you. Tell me, good my friend,
What torch is yond that vainly° lends his light　　　　　　　125
To grubs° and eyeless skulls? As I discern,
It burneth in the Capels' monument.
BALTHASAR:
It doth so, holy sir, and there's my master,
One that you love.
FRIAR LAURENCE:　　Who is it?
BALTHASAR:　　　　　　　　Romeo.
FRIAR LAURENCE:
How long hath he been there?
BALTHASAR:　　　　　　　　Full half an hour.　　　　　　　130
FRIAR LAURENCE:
Go with me to the vault.
BALTHASAR:　　　　　　　　I dare not, sir.
My master knows not but I am gone hence,
And fearfully did menace me with death
If I did stay to look on his intents.
FRIAR LAURENCE:
Stay, then, I'll go alone. Fear comes upon me.　　　　　　　135
O, much I fear some ill unthrifty° thing.

---

116. **conduct:** guide (i.e., the poison). 117. **desperate:** reckless, despairing. 121. **be my speed:** prosper me. 125. **vainly:** uselessly. 126. **grubs:** insect larvae. 136. **unthrifty:** unfortunate.

BALTHASAR:

As I did sleep under this yew tree here
I dreamt my master and another fought,
And that my master slew him.

FRIAR LAURENCE: [*Advancing to the tomb*]   Romeo!

Alack, alack, what blood is this which stains   140
The stony entrance of this sepulcher?
What mean these masterless and gory swords
To lie discolored by this place of peace?   [*He enters the tomb.*]
Romeo! O, pale! Who else? What, Paris too?
And steeped in blood? Ah, what an unkind° hour   145
Is guilty of this lamentable chance!
The lady stirs.   [*Juliet wakes.*]

JULIET:

O comfortable° Friar, where is my lord?
I do remember well where I should be,
And there I am. Where is my Romeo?   [*A noise within.*] 150

FRIAR LAURENCE:

I hear some noise. Lady, come from that nest
Of death, contagion, and unnatural sleep.
A greater power than we can contradict
Hath thwarted our intents. Come, come away.
Thy husband in thy bosom there lies dead,   155
And Paris, too. Come, I'll dispose of thee
Among a sisterhood of holy nuns.
Stay not to question, for the watch is coming.
Come, go, good Juliet. [*A noise again.*] I dare no longer stay.

                                        Exit [*Friar Laurence*].

JULIET:

Go, get thee hence, for I will not away.   160
What's here? A cup, closed in my true love's hand?
Poison, I see, hath been his timeless° end.
O churl,° drunk all, and left no friendly drop
To help me after? I will kiss thy lips;
Haply° some poison yet doth hang on them,   165
To make me die with a restorative.   [*She kisses him.*]
Thy lips are warm.

---

145. **unkind:** unnatural.   148. **comfortable:** comforting.   162. **timeless:** (1) untimely (2) everlasting.   163. **churl:** miser.   165. **Haply:** perhaps.

Enter [Paris's] Boy and Watch [at the other end of the churchyard].

FIRST WATCH: Lead, boy. Which way?
JULIET:
    Yea, noise? Then I'll be brief. O happy° dagger!   [*She takes Romeo's dagger.*]
    This is thy sheath. There rust, and let me die.   [*She stabs herself and falls.*]   170
PAGE:
    This is the place, there where the torch doth burn.
FIRST WATCH:
    The ground is bloody. Search about the churchyard.
    Go, some of you, whoe'er you find attach.°   [*Exeunt some.*]
    Pitiful sight! Here lies the County slain,
    And Juliet bleeding, warm, and newly dead,   175
    Who here hath lain this two days burièd.
    Go tell the Prince. Run to the Capulets.
    Raise up the Montagues. Some others search.   [*Exeunt others.*]
    We see the ground whereon these woes do lie,
    But the true ground° of all these piteous woes   180
    We cannot without circumstance° descry.

Enter [some of the Watch, with] Romeo's man [Balthasar].

SECOND WATCH:
    Here's Romeo's man. We found him in the churchyard.
FIRST WATCH:
    Hold him in safety° till the Prince come hither.

Enter Friar [Laurence], and another Watchman [with tools].

THIRD WATCH:
    Here is a friar, that trembles, sighs, and weeps.
    We took this mattock and this spade from him   185
    As he was coming from this churchyard's side.
FIRST WATCH:
    A great suspicion. Stay° the Friar too.

Enter the Prince [and attendants].

---

169. **happy:** opportune.   173. **attach:** arrest, detain.   180. **ground:** basis (playing on the literal meaning in l. 179).   181. **circumstance:** details.   183. **in safety:** under guard.   187. **Stay:** detain.

PRINCE:
What misadventure is so early up
That calls our person from our morning rest?

Enter Capels [Capulet and his Wife].

CAPULET:
What should it be that is so shrieked abroad? 190
CAPULET'S WIFE:
O, the people in the street cry "Romeo,"
Some "Juliet," and some "Paris," and all run
With open outcry toward our monument.
PRINCE:
What fear is this which startles° in our ears?
FIRST WATCH:
Sovereign, here lies the County Paris slain, 195
And Romeo dead, and Juliet, dead before,
Warm and new killed.
PRINCE:
Search, seek, and know° how this foul murder comes.
FIRST WATCH:
Here is a friar, and slaughtered Romeo's man,
With instruments° upon them fit to open 200
These dead men's tombs.
CAPULET:
O heavens! O wife, look how our daughter bleeds!
This dagger hath mista'en, for lo, his house°
Is empty on the back of Montague,
And it mis-sheathèd in my daughter's bosom! 205
CAPULET'S WIFE:
O me! This sight of death is as a bell
That warns my old age to a sepulcher.

Enter Montague.

PRINCE:
Come, Montague, for thou art early up
To see thy son and heir now early down.

---

194. **startles:** cries alarmingly.   198. **know:** learn.   200. **instruments:** tools.   203. **his house:** its scabbard.

MONTAGUE:

  Alas, my liege, my wife is dead tonight;   210

  Grief of my son's exile hath stopped her breath.

  What further woe conspires against mine age?

PRINCE: Look, and thou shalt see.

MONTAGUE: [*Seeing Romeo's body*]

  O thou untaught!° What manners is in this,

  To press° before thy father to a grave?   215

PRINCE:

  Seal up the mouth of outrage° for a while,

  Till we can clear these ambiguities

  And know their spring, their head,° their true descent;

  And then will I be general of your woes°

  And lead you even to death.° Meantime forbear,   220

  And let mischance be slave to patience.°

  Bring forth the parties of° suspicion.

FRIAR LAURENCE:

  I am the greatest, able to do least,

  Yet most suspected, as the time and place

  Doth make° against me, of this direful murder;   225

  And here I stand, both to impeach and purge

  Myself condemnèd and myself excused.°

PRINCE:

  Then say at once what thou dost know in this.

FRIAR LAURENCE:

  I will be brief, for my short date of breath°

  Is not so long as is a tedious tale.   230

  Romeo, there dead, was husband to that Juliet,

  And she, there dead, that Romeo's faithful wife.

  I married them, and their stol'n marriage day

  Was Tybalt's doomsday, whose untimely death

  Banished the new-made bridegroom from this city,   235

  For whom, and not for Tybalt, Juliet pined.

  You, to remove that siege of grief from her,

---

214. untaught: ill-mannered youth. (Said with affectionate irony.) **215. press:** hasten, go.
216. outrage: outcry. **218. spring . . . head:** source. **219. be . . . woes:** be leader in lamentation. **220. to death:** i.e., (1) as far as the dead bodies (2) so far in lamentation that we shall
seem dead. **221. let . . . patience:** i.e., submit patiently to our misfortune. **222. of:** under.
225. make: conspire, tell. **226–27. to . . . excused:** to accuse myself of what is to be condemned in me, and to exonerate myself where I ought to be excused. **229. date of breath:**
time left to live.

Betrothed and would have married her perforce°
To County Paris. Then comes she to me,
And with wild looks bid me devise some means   240
To rid her from this second marriage,
Or in my cell there would she kill herself.
Then gave I her — so tutored by my art —
A sleeping potion, which so took effect
As I intended, for it wrought° on her   245
The form° of death. Meantime I writ to Romeo
That he should hither come as this° dire night
To help to take her from her borrowed grave,
Being the time the potion's force should cease.
But he which bore my letter, Friar John,   250
Was stayed° by accident, and yesternight
Returned my letter back. Then all alone
At the prefixèd hour of her waking
Came I to take her from her kindred's vault,
Meaning to keep her closely° at my cell   255
Till I conveniently could send to Romeo.
But when I came, some minute ere the time
Of her awakening, here untimely lay
The noble Paris and true Romeo dead.
She wakes, and I entreated her come forth   260
And bear this work of heaven with patience.
But then a noise did scare me from the tomb,
And she, too desperate, would not go with me,
But, as it seems, did violence on herself.
All this I know, and to the marriage   265
Her nurse is privy;° and if aught in this
Miscarried by my fault, let my old life
Be sacrificed some hour before his° time
Unto the rigor of severest law.

PRINCE:
We still° have known thee for a holy man.   270
Where's Romeo's man? What can he say to this?

---

238. **perforce:** by compulsion.   245. **wrought:** fashioned.   246. **form:** appearance.   247. **as this:** this very.   251. **stayed:** stopped.   255. **closely:** secretly.   266. **privy:** in on the secret.   268. **his:** its.   270. **still:** always.

BALTHASAR:
   I brought my master news of Juliet's death,
   And then in post° he came from Mantua
   To this same place, to this same monument.
   This letter he early° bid me give his father,   [*Showing a letter*]   275
   And threatened me with death, going in the vault,
   If I departed not and left him there.
PRINCE: [*Taking the letter*]
   Give me the letter. I will look on it.
   Where is the County's page, that raised the watch?
   Sirrah, what made° your master in this place?   280
PAGE:
   He came with flowers to strew his lady's grave,
   And bid me stand aloof, and so I did.
   Anon comes one with light to ope the tomb,
   And by and by my master drew on him,
   And then I ran away to call the watch.   285
PRINCE:
   This letter doth make good the Friar's words,
   Their course of love, the tidings of her death;
   And here he writes that he did buy a poison
   Of a poor 'pothecary, and therewithal°
   Came to this vault to die, and lie with Juliet.
   Where be these enemies? Capulet, Montague,   290
   See what a scourge is laid upon your hate,
   That heaven finds means to kill your joys° with° love.
   And I, for winking at° your discords, too
   Have lost a brace of° kinsmen. All are punished.   295
CAPULET:
   O brother Montague, give me thy hand.
   This is my daughter's jointure,° for no more
   Can I demand.
MONTAGUE: But I can give thee more,
   For I will raise° her statue in pure gold,

---

273. **post:** haste.   275. **early:** early in the morning.   280. **made:** did.   289. **therewithal:** i.e., with the poison.   293. **kill your joys:** (1) destroy your happiness (2) kill your children. **with:** by means of.   294. **winking at:** shutting my eyes to.   295. **a brace of:** two.   297. **jointure:** marriage portion.   299. **raise:** (The Quarto 2 reading, *raie*, is defended by some editors in the sense of "array," make ready.)

That whiles Verona by that name is known   300
There shall no figure at such rate° be set
As that of true and faithful Juliet.

CAPULET:
As rich shall Romeo's by his lady's lie;
Poor sacrifices of our enmity!

PRINCE:
A glooming peace this morning with it brings;   305
 The sun, for sorrow, will not show his head.
Go hence to have more talk of these sad things.
 Some shall be pardoned, and some punishèd;
For never was a story of more woe
Than this of Juliet and her Romeo.   [*Exeunt.*]   310

FINIS

301. **rate:** value

Textual Notes for Romeo and Juliet

These textual notes are not a historical collation, either of the early quartos and the early folios or of more recent editions; they are simply a record of departures in this edition from the copy text. The reading adopted in this edition appears in boldface, followed by the rejected reading from the copy text, i.e., the second quarto of 1599. Only major alterations in punctuation are noted. Changes in lineation are not indicated, nor are some minor and obvious typographical errors.

Abbreviations used:
Q1 the first quarto of 1597
Q2 the second quarto of 1599
s.d. stage direction
s.p. speech prefix

Copy text: the second quarto of 1599, except for 1.2.53–1.3.34, for which Q1 is the prior authority.

Act 1, Scene 1. 22. **it in:** [Q1] it. 60. s.p. **Citizens:** Offi. 63. s.p. **Capulet's Wife:** Wife. 79. **Verona's:** Neronas. 107. **drave:** drive. 134. **his:** is. 140. **sun:** same. 164. **create:** [Q1] created. 166. **well-seeming:** [Q1] welseeing. 176. **grief to:** [Q1] grief, too. 179. **lovers':** [Q1] loving. 189. **Bid a:** [Q1] A. **make:** [Q1] makes. 193. **markman:** mark man. 198. **unharmed:** [Q1] vncharmd. 205. **makes:** make.
Act 1, Scene 2. 14. **The earth:** Earth. 32. **on:** one. 38. **written here:** written. Here. 45. **One:** [Q1] on. 69. **and Livia:** [Q1] Liuia [Q2]. 78. **thee:** [Q1] you [Q2]. **fires:** fier. [Q1]
Act 1, Scene 3. 12. **an:** [Q2] a [Q1]. 18. **shall:** [Q1] stal [Q2]. 33. **wi' th':** [Q1: with] with the [Q2]. 50. s.p. [and elsewhere]. **Wife:** Old La. 66. **disposition:** [F] dispositions. 67, 68. **honor:** [Q1] houre. 100. **it fly:** [Q1] flie. 104. s.p. [and elsewhere] **Wife:** Mo.
Act 1, Scene 4. 7–8: [Q1; not in Q2]. 23. s.p. **Mercutio:** Horatio. 39. **done:** [Q1] dum. 42. **Of:** Or. 45. **like lamps:** [Q1] lights lights. 47. **five:** fine. 57. **atomi:** [Q1] ottamie. 59–61: [these lines follow line 69 in Q2]. 66. **film:** Philome. 69. **maid:** [Q1] man. 72. **O'er:** [Q1] On. 74. **on:** one. 76. **breaths:** [Q1] breath. 80. **parson's:** Persons. 81. **dreams he:** [Q1] he dreams. 90. **elflocks:** Elklocks. 111. **fofreit:** [Q1] forfeit.
Act 1, Scene 5. s.d. [Q2 adds: "Enter Romeo"]. 1. s.p. **First Servingman:** Ser [also at lines 6 and 12]. 3. s.p. **Second Servingman:** 1. 9. s.p. **Third Servingman:** 2. 12. s.p. **Fourth Servingman:** 3. 14. s.p. **Capulet:** Capu [also at lines 33 and 37]. 15. **a bout:** about. 92. **ready:** [Q1] did readie.
Act 2. **Chorus.** 1. s.p. **Chorus:** [not in Q2]. 4. **matched:** match.
Act 2, Scene 1. 7. **Nay . . . too:** [assigned in Q2 to Benvolio]. 10. **one:** [Q1] on. 11. **Pronounce:** [Q1] prouaunt. **dove:** [Q1] day. 13. **heir:** [Q1] her. 14. **trim:** [Q1] true. 32. **open-arse, and:** open, or.
Act 2, Scene 2. 16. **do:** [Q1] to. 20. **eyes:** [Q1] eye. 41–42. **nor any . . . name:** ô be some other name / Belonging to a man. 45. **were:** [Q1] wene. 58. **not yet:** yet not. 82. **pilot:** Pylat. 83. **washed:** [Q1] washeth. 92–93. **false . . . They:** false at louers periuries. / They. 101. **more coying:** [Q1] coying. 110. **circled:** [Q1] circle. 149, 151. s.p. **Nurse:** [not in Q2]. 150, 151. s.p. **Juliet:** [not in Q2]. 163. **than mine:** then. 170. **years:** [Q1] yeare. 180. **gyves:** giues. 187. **Sleep . . . breast:** [Q1: assigned in Q2 to Juliet]. 189–90. [preceded in Q2 by an earlier version of lines 1–4 of the next scene, in which "fleck-led darkness" reads "darknesse fleckted" and "and Titan's fiery wheels" reads "made by *Tytans* wheeles"].
Act 2, Scene 3. 2. **Check 'ring:** [Q1] Checking. 4. **fiery:** [Q1] burning. 51. **wounded. Both our:** wounded both, our. 85. **not. She whom:** [Q1] me not, her.
Act 2, Scene 4. 17. s.p. **Benvolio:** [Q1] Ro. 25–26. **phantasimes:** phantacies. 29. **pardonme's:** pardons mees. 34. **but a:** a. 94. **for himself:** [Q1] himself. 170. **dog's:** dog. 176. s.d. **Exeunt:** Exit.
Act 2, Scene 5. 5. **glide:** glides. 11. **three:** there. 15. **And:** M. And. 26. **I had:** [Q1] I.

ACT 2, SCENE 6. 18. gossamer: gossamours. 27. music's: musicke.
ACT 3, SCENE 1. 2. Capels are: Capels. 59. injured: iniuried. 65. *stoccata:* stucatho. 80. your houses: houses. 95. soundly too. Your: soundly, to your. 109. Alive: He gan. 111. fire-eyed: [Q1] fier end. 124, 126. s.p. First Citizen: Citti. 153. agile: [Q1] aged. 171. s.p. Montague: Capu. 179. I: [Q1] It. 184. s.d. Exeunt: Exit.
ACT 3, SCENE 2. 1. s.p. Juliet: [not in Q2]. 9. By: And by. 47. darting: arting. 49. shut: shot. 51. of my: my. 60. one: on. 72. It . . . did: [assigned in Q2 to Juliet]. 73. O . . . face: [assigned in Q2 to Nurse]. 76. Dove-feathered: Rauenous douefeatherd. 79. damnèd: dimme. 143. s.d. Exeunt: Exit.
ACT 3, SCENE 3. s.d.: [Q2 has "Enter Friar and Romeo"]. 39. [Q2 follows with a line: "This may flyes do, when I from this must flie"]. 43. [printed in Q2 before line 40]. 52. Thou: [Q1] Then. 61. madmen: [Q1] mad man. 70. s.d. Knock: Enter Nurse, and knocke. 73. s.d. Knock: They knocke. 75. s.d. Knock: Slud knock. 80. s.d. Enter Nurse: [at line 78 in Q2]. 110. denote: [Q1] deuote. 117. lives: [Q1] lies. 144. pouts upon: puts vp. 168. disguised: disguise.
ACT 3, SCENE 4. 10. s.d. [and elsewhere] Wife: La. 13. be: me.
ACT 3, SCENE 5. 13. exhaled: exhale. 19. the: the the. 31. changed: change. 36. s.d. Enter Nurse: Enter Madame and Nurse. 54. s.p. Juliet: Ro. 67. s.d. [bracketed s.d. from Q1]. 82. pardon him: padon. 130–31. body . . . a bark: body? / Thou counterfeits. A bark. 139. gives: giue. 142. How? Will: How will. 151–52. proud . . . Thank: proud mistresse minion you? / Thanke. 160. s.p. [and elsewhere] Capulet: Fa. 172. s.p. and text Capulet O, God-i'-good-e'en: Father, ô Godigeden. 173. s.p. Nurse: [not in Q2]. 182. liened: liand.
ACT 4, SCENE 1. 7. talked: [Q1] talke. 45. cure: [Q1] care. 46. Ah: [Q1] O. 72. slay: [Q1] stay. 78. off: [Q1] of. 83. chopless: [Q1] chapels. 85. his tomb: his. 98. breath: [Q1] breast. 100. wanny: many. 110. In: Is [Q2 follows with a line: "Be borne to buriall in thy kindreds graue"]. 111. shalt: shall. 115. and he: an he. 116. waking: walking. 126. s.d. Exeunt: Exit.
ACT 4, SCENE 2. 3, 6. s.p. Servingman: Ser. 13. willed: wield. 37. s.p. [and elsewhere] Wife: Mo. 46. s.d. Exeunt: Exit.
ACT 4, SCENE 3. 49. wake: walke.
ACT 4, SCENE 4. 1. s.p. [and elsewhere] Wife: La. 12. s.d. Exeunt: Exit. 15. s.p. First Servingman: Fel. 18. s.p. Second Servingman: Fel. 21. Thou: Twou. faith: father. 23. s.d.: [at line 21 in Q2].
ACT 4, SCENE 5. 41. long: [Q1] loue. 51. behold: bedold. 65. cure: care. 65–66. not . . . Heaven: not, / In these confusions heauen. 82. fond: some. 96. s.p. First Musician: Musi. 99, 102. s.p. First Musician: Fid. 99. by: [Q1] my. [Q2 has s.d. here: "Exit omnes"]. s.d. Enter Peter: Enter Will Kemp. 105. s.p. First Musician: Minstrels [and subsequently in this scene indicated by *Minst* or *Minstrel*]. 116. Then . . . wit: [assigned in Q2 to 2 M]. 119. And . . . oppress: [Q1; not in Q2]. 124, 127. Pretty: [Q1] Prates. 135. s.d. Exeunt: Exit.
ACT 5, SCENE 1. 15. fares my: [Q1] doth my Lady. 17, 27, 32. s.p. Balthasar: Man. 24. e'en: in. defy: [Q1] denie. 33. s.d.: [at line 32 in Q2]. 76. pay: [Q1] pray.
ACT 5, SCENE 3. 3. yew: [Q1] young. 21. s.d. [Balthasar]: [Q1] Peter. 40, 43. s.p. Balthasar: Pet. 68. conjuration: commiration. 71. s.p. Page: Boy [Q1; s.p. missing in Q2 and line treated as a s.d.] 102. fair: faire? I will beleeue. 107. palace: pallat. 108. [Q2 has four undeleted lines here: "Depart againe, come lye thou in my arme, / Heer's to thy health, where ere thou tumblest in. / O true Appothecarie! / Thy drugs are quicke. Thus with a kisse I die."]. 123. s.p. [and elsewhere] Balthasar: Man. 137. yew: yong. 168. s.p. First Watch: Watch [also at lines 172, 195, 199]. 171. s.p. Page: Watch boy. 182. s.p. Second Watch: Watch. 183, 187. s.p. First Watch: Chief. watch. 187. too: too too. 190. shrieked: shrike. 194. our: your. 199. slaughtered: Slaughter. 201. [Q2 has a s.d. here: "Enter Capulet and his wife"]. 209. early: [Q1] earling. 232. that: thats. 274–75. place . . . This: place. To this same monument / This. 281. s.p. Page: Boy. 299. raise: raie.

PART TWO

—— ✕ ——

Cultural Contexts

Italy

>‹

The Idea of Italy for Shakespeare's English Audience

In fair Verona, where we lay our scene

(Romeo and Juliet, Prologue, line 2)

The Renaissance, the rebirth of classical art and culture after the hiatus of the middle ages, began in Italy some two hundred years before it came to England in the age of Shakespeare. In Shakespeare's plays, Italy serves both as a foreign place, a reference point for a sophisticated yet alien culture, and as the literary source for many of the plots. Although Italian drama is arguably "the most significant case of appropriation of an alien culture," such appropriation was not a neutral fact (Marrapodi 2). That Shakespeare was irredeemably indebted to a country which maintained faith in the religion England officially rejected, namely Catholicism, was a circumstance that may have created conflicting attitudes toward characters who inhabit the discursive space (that is, the imaginary textual space) marked by *Romeo and Juliet*'s Italian setting. For some Elizabethans, such as Roger Ascham whose book *The Schoolmaster* is excerpted below, Italian literature was a dangerously foreign and corrupting influence, especially in translation. The Italian source and setting of this play, far from determining a single interpretation, open up multiple avenues to some of the play's central themes.

A NEWLY DISCOVERED LOVE STORY

Luigi da Porto (1485–1529), *Novella Novamente Ritrovata d'uno Innamoramento* (Venice, 1535; first published in 1530, also in Venice under the title, *Historia novellamente ritrovata di due nobili amanti* or "The recovered story of two noble lovers").

This charming frontispiece to da Porto's Italian novella shows an act of exchange between the lovers. Juliet gives Romeo a letter, while Cupid, the mischievous god of love, aims his arrow at Juliet's heart. This woodcut illustration is in the style of an emblem, a highly symbolic image that emphasizes iconographic meaning, or as Randle Cotgrave defined it in his *Dictionary of the French and English Tongues* (1611), "a picture . . . expressing some particular conceit." These were extremely popular in the Renaissance.

Da Porto, the author of this novella, was a soldier in the Venetian army and a friend of the Italian poet and literary theorist Pietro Bembo (1470–1547). The full title, *Novella novamente ritrovata d'uno innamoramento: Il quale*

FIGURE 3 *Frontispiece*

successo in Verona nel tempo del Signor Bartholomeo de la Scala: Historia jocondissima, "A newly discovered story of an enamourment, which takes place in Verona in the time of Signor Bartholomeo de la Scala: A Most Jocund Story," implies that the author takes the story to be a real historical event and the "jocund," or jovial, ending refers not to the lovers' suicide but to the families' reconciliation. In this version, published in Venice in 1535 (first published there in 1530 under the title *Historia novellamente ritrovata di due nobili amanti*), the characters' names are almost the same as Shakespeare's: Giulietta Capelletti and Romeo Montecchi, Marcuccio (the Mercutio figure), and Friar Lorenzo (the Franciscan). Although many earlier stories involve certain plot elements reminiscent of Shakespeare's *Romeo and Juliet,* da Porto's is the first version that constitutes an unambiguous antecedent to the play and the first to set the action in Verona. His most immediate predecessor, for example, Tommaso Guardati (c. 1410–1475), known as Masuccio Salernitano, who wrote a version of the tale in a collection of fifty short stories or *Cinquante Novelle,* sets the story in Siena and the banished lover is exiled to Alexandria (see Bullough 1: 269–76; *Norton* 865; Prunster; Caso). Although Salernitano's protagonists are named Mariotto and Giannozza, his story does include a Friar, a sleeping potion, an angry father, and a fatal quarrel. The most startling difference from Shakespeare's story is that Salernitano's Mariotto (the Romeo figure) is captured and beheaded on his return to Siena.

Da Porto, as we have noted, presents the story as having its origins in historical fact and specifies the time period by indicating that the lovers lived in the days of Bartholomeo del la Scala. There were families called Capelletti and Montecchi, who belonged to different political factions, in thirteenth-century Italy; however, the Montecchi were from Verona and the Capelletti hailed from Cremona. Historically, the only connection between them is that they are mentioned by the famous Italian poet, Dante, in his *Purgatorio* as examples of civil strife. Nonetheless, although it is unlikely that there is any historical truth to the legend of the lovers, a balcony purporting to be Giulietta's and a tomb are still popular tourist sites in Verona today (see Gibbons 34).

There is no evidence that Shakespeare had direct access to da Porto's text, or indeed to any of the subsequent French and Italian treatments of the lovers' story. However, *previous* English versions of the story relied heavily on continental sources. These were William Painter's (1540?–1594) "Rhomeo and Julietta," in volume 2 of his well-known collection of prose translations, *Palace of Pleasure* (1567) (a book attacked in 1582 by moralist Stephen Gosson), and Arthur Brooke's (d. 1563) long poem, *The Tragical History of Romeus and Juliet* (1562). These English renditions made use of the French version by Pierre Boaistuau (c. 1517–1566) published in François Belleforest's *Histoires Tragiques* (Tragic Stories) (1599). Boaistuau used two earlier versions of the story: da Porto's and Matteo Bandello's (1485–1561) *Romeo e Giulietta* (1554). Note that iterability, that is, the extent to which the story is recyclable, rather than originality is the prized quality in a Renaissance story line.

PLOT AND PLACE

The story of *Romeo and Juliet* as Shakespeare inherited it came from many Italian sources, including Mascussio Salernitano, Luigi da Porto, and Matteo Bandello (Lombardo 148). However, the most direct influence on the play is Arthur Brooke's English versified version of the Italian story set in Verona, *The Tragical History of Romeus and Juliet* (1562):

> There is beyond the Alps, a town of ancient fame
> Whose bright renown yet shineth clear, Verona men it name,
> Built in a happy time, built on a fertile soil,
> Maintained by the heavenly fates, and by the townish toil.
> The fruitful hill above, the pleasant vales below,
> The silver stream with channel deep, and that through the town
>   doth flow,
> The store of springs that serve for use, and eke[1] for ease
> And other more commodities which profit may and please,
> To fill the hungry eyes of those that curiously behold
> Do make this town to be preferred above the rest
> Of Lombard towns, or at least compared with the best.   (1–11)

The world of "fair Verona" to which Shakespeare alludes noticeably lacks documentary specificity in the play, such as a description of the city and its topography. Shakespeare never mentions the Roman amphitheater in Verona observed by the Elizabethan traveler Fynes Moryson, or the splendid palaces in Mantua mentioned by another English traveler Thomas Coryate. Similarly, the fact that Mantua (the town in which Romeo visits the apothecary shop) was renowned as the birthplace of the ancient poet Virgil has no place in Shakespeare's play (Locatelli 79). Nor does the fact that the city was the home of Baldassare Castiglione, author of *The Courtier*, one of the most famous political and cultural handbooks of the Renaissance, merit so much as a passing remark. Indeed, we can tell as much about Shakespeare's idea of Italy from what he leaves out as from what he includes. Angela Locatelli itemizes these omissions as follows: "Shakespeare never mentions the Palazzo Ducale, the Palazzo del Capitano, the Domus Magna, the Castle of San Georgio and the Basiliche of Santa Barbara and Sant' Andrea. He ignores the important waterways linking the town to the Adriatic" (Locatelli 79). The point is not, of course, as Locatelli explains, to imply that *Romeo and Juliet* is impaired by these omissions, but rather that "the credibility of a dramatist does not depend on factual evidence" (Locatelli 80).

---

[1] **eke**: also.

How important then is geographical locale to the play given that Shakespeare evinces little or no particular investment in its details? We might begin to think about this in relation to several of Shakespeare's other plays that are set in Italian cities: Obviously, Venice is the location for *The Merchant of Venice* and the protagonists of *Two Gentlemen of Verona* hail from the city of Romeo and Juliet's tragic demise; *Julius Caesar* and parts of *Antony and Cleopatra* are set in Rome; *The Taming of the Shrew* is set in the university town of Padua. As Jean Howard points out: "Verona, Milan, Mantua, and Padua are places of which characters speak, but the names often are used interchangeably and seem collectively to be Shakespeare's shorthand for 'Italy' rather than distinct places" (Howard in *Norton* 77). The Verona of *Romeo and Juliet*, indeed, seems to stand more for urban life in Italy than for a precisely specified Veronese culture and landscape.

For all that, in all these instances Italy functions as much more than merely backdrop. As Michele Marrapodi puts it, the Italianate setting was "semantically overdetermined for the Elizabethans" (Marrapodi vii). That is to say, the idea of Italy had very specific and, crucially, somewhat negative connotations for Shakespeare's audience. Although associated with both ancient and new learning, Italy as home of the papal seat was virtually synonymous with Catholicism, or, as English Protestants derisively called it "papistry." Attending this construction of Italy as the religious "other" was the idea, mistakenly derived from *The Prince*, Niccolo Machiavelli's political handbook, that the Italians engaged in quasi-demonic political manipulations as their preferred method of government (Praz 162). When comparing the two countries, the English rather predictably often found England to be superior to Italy. The anonymous author of a tract on London who may have been English or foreign, pointed out that the city was governed "not by cruel viceroys, as is Naples or Milan, neither by proud Podesta [the chief magistrate of a medieval Italian republic], as be most cities in Italy . . . but by a man of trade or a mere merchant, who not withstanding, during the time of his magistracy, carries himself with . . . honorable magnificence in his port, and ensigns of estate" (Archer 50).

It is tempting to explain English suspicions by the fact that it was an island, isolated relative to Italy, which was part of the continent of Europe and therefore more open to foreign influences especially through trade. However, by the late sixteenth century this was no longer true. London in particular was very connected with the wider world, and so to some extent, at least for lack of a solid empirical explanation, English xenophobia remains unfathomable. Italians were often regarded by English travelers and cultural commentators as fundamentally different in matters of social and religious practice and more than faintly associated with sexual impropriety.

At the same time, Italy often served as a sort of fictional London, an exotic mirror of the metropolis, a place where writers could experiment with issues deemed too sensitive or too threatening to be set in the familiar surroundings of contemporary London. All these connotations are important because, as Agostino Lombardo points out:

> Shakespeare's Italy is a country in which "real" features — social, historical, geographical, political, cultural — are inextricably intertwined with the imaginary. His Italy is the product of the written and oral traditions, and of the imagination, and is itself a mask behind which are hidden the features and problems of London and England. Italy is an Elizabethan myth fed by a thousand sources, not least by the travelers who "narrate" it. Italy is the Papal State, the courts of the Renaissance, Machiavelli; it is desire, nostalgia, utopia; it is the stage on which anything can happen — loves, murders, political intrigue, tragedies, comedies. (Lombardo 144–45; see also Locatelli 69–84)

For Elizabethans, then, Italy is both a real and a symbolic geographical location, both a place and an image whose contours are more often defined in the imagination than they are by direct experience of the country. This is especially true for Shakespeare because, despite speculation that he might have visited the Italian duchy of Mantua with the earl of Southampton in 1593, there is no conclusive evidence that Shakespeare ever left England (Locatelli 79).

SEX AND THE CITY

What can we learn about the city of Verona from the play's references to it? In particular, what can we glean about the operations of gender and the place of sexuality both in Verona and in its cultural analog, the city of London: "Three civil brawls . . . / Have thrice disturbed the quiet of our streets / And made Verona's ancient citizens / Cast by their grave-beseeming ornaments / To wield old partisans" (1.1.76–81); "sirrah, trudge about / Through fair Verona" (1.2.34–35); "all the admirèd beauties of Verona" (1.2.84); "Younger than you / Here in Verona, ladies of esteem / Are made already mothers" (1.3.70–72)? Even from that juxtaposition of lines in which the city's name is mentioned, we get a sense of the predominant and sometimes antithetical or conflicting energies of Verona: youth and age, sexuality, especially reproductive female sexuality ("beauties" and young mothers), and violence. While we do see Capulet's servant "trudge about" to find those who are to be invited to his feast, by and large encounters in the street have a certain volatility, the spark of confrontation rather than the civil exchanges that bespeak a sense of social cohesiveness.

Verona is a place where, as Ann Jenalie Cook has pointed out, "all passion is at the boil — choler, grief, hatred — sexual passion. . . . Emotional intensity so pervades the society that it constantly erupts into public broils, private highjinks, secret sorrows, magical fantasies, dark premonitions" (Cook 30). When Romeo is exiled from Verona for killing Tybalt he expresses his despair about separation from Juliet in terms of the loss of the city in a way that summons up the primordial exile figured in the biblical loss of Eden:

> There is no world without Verona walls
> But purgatory, torture, hell itself.
> Hence "banishèd" is banished from the world,
> And world's exile is death.   (3.3.17–20)

These walls may be an amplified version of those Romeo has breached in his nocturnal encounter with Juliet: "The orchard walls are high and hard to climb, / And the place death, considering who thou art" (2.2.63–64). The walls of what was known in the period as the *hortus conclusis* or the enclosed garden, figure female virginity as male property, whose incursion, rather like Adam eating the forbidden fruit, promises death.

In London, the river Thames bordered the city to the south; it was walled on the other sides. At night, the city gates were shut and the bellman set out to patrol the streets as Bow Bell rang with the cry:

> Remember the clocks,
> Look well to your locks,
> Fire and your light,
> And God give you good night
> For now the bell ringeth.   (Salgado 1)

Built in Roman and medieval times to keep invaders out, in the Renaissance walls come to define the space and identity of city life, which contrasted very sharply in terms of governance, resources, and population not only with rural, but also with small-town life (Orlin 345). The city, like the orchard, was a walled enclosure susceptible to the threat of violation. For London, that threat was more figurative than literal. *Literally,* the exploding population led to disputes about property boundaries, about walls, fences, rights of access, trespass, and related problems that arose from living at close quarters in an urban environment (Orlin 345). *Figuratively,* however, walls represented professedly impregnable boundaries, even though the actual metropolis had

long expanded far beyond the city walls. City spaces were intensely gen-
dered and London itself was conceived of as feminine. The streets were
ostensibly open to both sexes and travelers remarked on the relative freedom
of English women (compared to those on the continent) to leave their
houses as they pleased. For all that, as Laura Gowing maintains: "Women's
use of the streets, fields and civic spaces of early modern London was neither simple nor free. The rhetoric of enclosure and the identification of
female mobility with sexual and economic disorder shaped female identities
and women's use of space. In this context, women's part in street life could
be self-conscious and anxious" (Gowing, "Freedom" 145). Perhaps that is
why, with the exception of the Nurse, we see men rather than women
"abroad" in Verona, out on the open street. When the Nurse does venture
forth to deliver Juliet's message she is subject to sexual ribbing and ridicule,
a susceptibility to which she is generically predisposed as the comic, garru-
lous obverse of the contained body and demeanor of the chaste housewife:

> An old hare hoar,
> And an old hare hoar,
> Is very good meat in Lent.
> But a hare that is hoar
> Is too much for a score,
> When it hoars ere it be spent.   (2.4.108–13)

Mercutio taunts the Nurse with this obscene song with its pun on hoar and
"whore." Essentially, he is calling the Nurse a "retread," a woman whose sexual desirability is long past, only fit for a period of sexual scarcity ("Lent").
Since misogyny, even though we may not approve of it, is often funny,
should we read this encounter as harmless bawdy? Or is this jibing something more sinister, on the verge of sexual violence?

> NURSE: Scurvy knave! I am none of his flirt-gills. I am none of his
> skains-mates. [To Peter.] And thou must stand by, too, and suffer every
> knave to use me at his pleasure!
> PETER: I saw no man use you at his pleasure. If I had, my weapon
> should quickly have been out; I warrant you, I dare draw as soon as
> another man . . .   (2.4.123–27)

Whatever our interpretation, we should bear in mind that it is an encounter
in the open street in which the Nurse's riposte to Mercutio's charge that she
is an old whore — "flirt-gills" (whores) and "skains-mates" (dagger bearing
companions) — derives from the lexicon of urban London. The Nurse
pleads for protection from her fellow servant and the wordplay on "use"
(coitus), "pleasure" (coitus/orgasm), "weapon" (penis), "draw" (to take one's

FIGURE 4 *The City of Verona, from John Speed,* A Prospect of the Most Famous Parts of the World *(1676). John Speed (1552–1629) was a historian and cartographer who produced numerous and important maps of England, Wales, and Ireland, and was noted for his "very rare and ingenious capacity in drawing and setting forth of maps and genealogies, and other very excellent inventions."[2] Panoramic views of European cities were very popular during the period. There were many such images of London often printed from metal engravings (which Speed's Verona is not), for example, the view of the city in 1625 done by the Dutch engraver Claes Jansz Visscher (Schoenbaum,* The Globe *58–59).*

penis out of one's britches) may intimate sexual violence, even gang rape. Sex in this city is always, it seems, potentially if not actually deadly.

As I have indicated, there are several issues to be raised about what the city of Verona might have meant to Shakespeare's audience, but the central question seems to be did the audience identify as Londoners with the problems of Verona, or were those problems viewed as signs of a degenerate and alien culture? In the absence of a definitive answer, our best approach is to look at the writings of the period. The excerpts below include admiration for the beauty of Italy, horror at the differences between Italian and English culture, and attempts at objective description. Also included, by way of

---

[2] *Dictionary of National Biography.* The *DNB* is a very useful tool for finding out about people who lived in Shakespeare's England. The project was founded in 1882 by George Smith and the volumes were edited in 1917 for Oxford University Press by Leslie Stephen and Sidney Lee. A new *DNB* is now underway and will be soon available.

showing the other side of the coin, so to speak, is a brief account of the experience of Italians in London.

→ FYNES MORYSON

From His Ten Years Travel   *1611*

In part because of burgeoning foreign trade, travel writing was an immensely popular genre during this period. Such narratives contained advice to travelers, reasons for travel, and translations of geographies (such as Richard Eden's *The Decades of the New World, or West India,* 1555), as well as descriptions of the process of travel and of places visited in Europe and beyond. The latter category included Richard Hakluyt's *Principal Navigations, Voyages, and Discoveries of the English Nation* (1589), and Samuel Purchas's *Purchas His Pilgrimage* (1613). Thomas Coryate, who traveled in Europe, the Middle East, and Asia and died far from England in Surat, was the author of *Coryat's Crudities* (1611). His description of himself as the "Odcombian leg-stretcher" (he came from Odcome in Somerset and was a prodigious walker) gives some indication of the sheer physical demands that nearly all travel entailed.

Although Shakespeare does not address travel directly, except for very local journeys from Verona to Mantua in *Romeo and Juliet,* he does tap into the popularity of travel literature in his Italian comedy *Two Gentlemen of Verona,* written not long before the love tragedy:

> He wondered that your Lordship
> Would suffer him to spend his youth at home,
> While other men, of slender reputation
> Put forth their sons . . .
> Some to discover islands far away   (1.3.4–9)[1]

The play opens with a commentary on the urge to travel, its dangers as well as its importance as an aspect of education, which is in a sense surprising since there is no evidence that Shakespeare himself ever traveled abroad: "Home keeping youth, have ever homely wits" (1.1.3); "I . . . would entreat thy company, / To see the wonders of the world abroad, / Than (living dully slug-gardized[2] at home) / Wear out thy youth with shapeless idleness" (1.1.5–8); "[S]ave your ship from wreck, / Which cannot perish having thee aboard"

---

[1] All references to Shakespeare not from *Romeo and Juliet* are to *The Norton Shakespeare.*
[2] **sluggardized:** becoming idle.

Fynes Moryson, *His Ten Years Travel through the Twelve Dominions of Germany, Bohmerland* [Bohemia], *Switzerland, Netherland, Denmark, Poland, Italy, Turkey, France, England, Scotland, and Ireland* (London, 1611), 173, 176.

(1.1.136–37). It is interesting to compare this sentiment to the complete insularity of Romeo, who never demonstrates any desire (quite the contrary, in fact) to venture beyond Verona's walls. Robert Burton, author of *The Anatomy of Melancholy* (1621) counseled travel as a remedy for disconsolate young men like Romeo:

> There is no better Physic for a melancholy man than change of air and variety of places, to travel abroad and see fashions. For peregrination[3] charms our senses with such unspeakable and sweet variety, that some account him unhappy that never traveled, a kind of prisoner, and pity his case that from his cradle to his old age beholds the same still; still, still, the same, the same. (Burton, 1632 edition, 126)

There were, in fact, mixed views of travel in the period and the debate surely indicates an increase in travel to Europe especially among the gentry. Writers like Purchas were well aware of its benefits but despaired of its effects on some Englishmen; he comments in particular on the deleterious effects of visiting Italy, or at least Naples:

> As for gentlemen, travel is accounted an excellent ornament to them: and therefore many of them coming to their lands sooner than to their wits, adventure themselves to see the fashions of other countries, whence they bring home a few smattering terms, flattering garbs[4] . . . foolish guises and disguises, the vanities of neighbor nations (I name not Naples) without furthering of their knowledge of God, the world or themselves. (Purchas, preface)

Others, such as Joseph Hall writing in 1617 before he became Bishop of Norwich, protested in his *Quo Vadis? A Just Censure of Travel as it is Commonly Undertaken by the Gentlemen of Our Nation* that the English were better to read books about travel and "learn to keep their sons at home" (quoted in Rye xxvii). Indeed, we might wonder whether Moryson's narrative (much like Shakespeare's representation of Verona in the play itself) fueled readers with the desire to see Italy for themselves or whether it confirmed a conviction that Italy was a dangerous place that the English might do well to avoid.

The following excerpt is from one of England's earliest travel writers, Fynes Moryson (c. 1566–1630?), who was educated at Peterhouse in Cambridge before embarking on his travels in 1591 at the age of about twenty-five. He professed that he had an "innated desire" from his childhood to see foreign countries. He visited almost all of Europe before returning to "blessed England" in 1595. Despite the misfortune of having had his cloak and his money stolen while in France, this was the first of many journeys he made through Europe. Moryson's travelogue of these journeys, known as *An Itinerary,* ultimately amounted to over nine hundred pages (see Hadfield, *Literature* 4; and *Amazons* 81–82).

---

[3] **peregrination:** moving about.   [4] **flattering garbs:** stylish dress.

From *His Ten Years Travel*

It is unlawful to wear a sword without license of the Magistrate, either at *Milan, Cremona, Mantua,* or almost any city of *Italy;* only at *Venice* and *Padua,* and the cities of that state, strangers may wear swords, and only the wearing of pistols or shortguns is forbidden. . . .

From *Vincenza* I rode thirty miles to *Verona* in a most pleasant plain (tilled after the manner of *Lombardy*) lying on my left hand towards *Italy,* farther than I could see and having fruitful hills on my right hand towards the Alps, abounding with vines, growing low upon short stakes, and yielding rich wines. I entered *Verona* on the East side, by the Bishop's gate called *Porta del vescon.* They write that the city was of old called *Berona,* by the name of the founder thereof; but the Friar *Leander* of *Bologna* writes that the city was built by *Tuscans,* and had the name of the family *Vera,* and was after rebuilt. . . . This most fair city is built in the form of a lute, the neck whereof lies towards the West, on which side the River *Athesis* (running towards the East) doth not only compass the city, but runs almost through the center of the body of this lute, so as the less part of the body lies on the North side of the River. The banks of *Athesis* (vulgarly[5] called L'Adice) are joined together with three bridges of stone, and one of marble, and are adorned on both sides with many ruins of an old theater, and old triumphal arches. The city is compassed with a wall of brick, and is seated towards the South upon the end of a large stony plain, and towards the other sides upon pleasant hills, rising towards the distant mountains. It is not built with the houses cast out towards the streets, and supported with arches to avoid rain, as other cities are in those parts: but the building of the houses is stately, and the Cathedral Church is remarkable for the antiquity, as likewise the Church of Saint *Anastasius*[6] for the great beauty thereof; and towards the walls the ground lies void of houses, as the manner is in strong towns. It hath a pure air, and is ennobled by the civility and ancient nobility of the citizens, who are endowed with a cheerful countenance, magnificent minds, and much inclined to all good literature. . . .

On the North-side of the city without the walls, is the mountain *Baldo,* hanging over the city, and famous for the great plenty of medicinal herbs, and upon the side of this mountain, within the walls, are no buildings, but only a strong fort.

On the south side lies the way to Mantua (23 miles distant).

---

[5] **vulgarly:** commonly.   [6] **Saint Anastasius:** Pope who was canonized 399–401 A.D.

→ ROGER ASCHAM

From The Schoolmaster

1570

Roger Ascham (1515–1568) was educated at Cambridge and served as tutor from 1548 to 1550 to the young Princess Elizabeth. He was later secretary to Sir Richard Moryson, who was the English Ambassador to Charles V (Holy Roman Emperor from 1519 to 1558), and from 1553 served as Latin secretary to both Edward VI and Queen Mary, Elizabeth's older sister who was Catholic. In 1558, Elizabeth, now queen, reinstated Ascham to his post as private tutor before giving him a prebend (a portion of land held from a cathedral chapter — essentially, he was paid by the cathedral) in Yorkshire. Although it is unfinished, Ascham's treatise on pedagogy, *The Schoolmaster*, is his most famous work.

This text relates to the play not only because of what it says about Italy, but because it is a book about how, from a pedagogical point of view, one might shape the youth of the nation. Clearly, for Ascham, Italy is a place to be viewed with a certain critical and skeptical distance and a place that holds particular dangers for young men.

THE FIRST BOOK TEACHING THE BRINGING UP OF YOUTH.

. . . Sir Richard Sackville,[1] that worthy gentleman of worthy memory, as I said in the beginning, in the Queen's privy chamber at Windsor, after he had talked with me, for the right choice of a good wit in a child for learning, and of the true difference betwixt quick and hard wits, of alluring young children by gentleness to love learning, and of the special care that was to be had, to keep young men from licentious living, he was most earnest with me, to have me say my mind also, what I thought, concerning the fancy that many young gentlemen of England have to travel abroad, and namely to lead a long life in Italy. His request, both for his authority, and good will toward me, was a sufficient commandment unto me, to satisfy his pleasure, with uttering plainly my opinion in that matter. Sir quoth I, I take going thither, and living there, for a young gentleman that both not go under the keep and guard of such a man, as both, by wisdom can, and authority dare rule him, to be marvelous dangerous. And why I said so then, I will declare at large now: which I said then privately, and write now openly, not because I do condemn, either the knowledge of strange and diverse tongues, and

---

[1] **Sir Richard Sackville:** (d. 1566), first cousin of Anne Boleyn, member of Parliament and privy councilor, knighted in 1549.

Roger Ascham, *The Schoolmaster, or Plain and Perfect Way of Teaching Children the Latin Tongue* (London, 1570), 23–28.

namely the Italian tongue, which next the Greek and Latin tongue, I like and love above all other, or else because I do despise the learning that is gotten, or the experience that is gathered in strange countries: or for any private malice that I bear to Italy: which country, and in it, namely Rome, I have always specially honored: because, time was, when Italy and Rome, have been to the great good of us that now live, the best breeders and bringers up of the worthiest men, not only for wise speaking, but also for well being, in all civil affairs, that ever was in the world. But now that time is gone, and though the place remain, yet the old and present manners, do differ as far, as black and white, as virtue and vice. Virtue once made that country mistress over all the world. Vice now maketh that country slave to them, that before, were glad to serve it. All men saith it: They themselves confess it, namely such as be best and wisest amongst them. For sin, by lust and vanity, hath & doth breed by every where, common contempt of God's word, private contention in many families, open factions in every city: and so making themselves bond, to vanity and vice at home, they are content to bear the yoke of serving strangers abroad: Italy now, is not that Italy, that it was wont to be: and therefore now, not so fit a place, as some do count it, for young men to fetch either wisdom or honesty from thence. For surely, they will make other but bad scholars, that be so ill masters to themselves. Yet, if a gentleman will needs travel into Italy, he shall do well, to look of the life, of the wisest traveler that ever traveled thither, set out by the wisest writer that ever spake with tongue, God's doctrine only excepted: and that is Ulysses[2] in Homer.[3] Ulysses and his travel, I wish our travelers to look upon, not so much to fear them, with the great dangers that he many times suffered, as to instruct them, with his excellent wisdom, which he always and every where used. . . .

Therefore if wise men will needs send their sons to Italy, let them do it wisely, under the keep and garb of him, who, by his wisdom and honesty, by his example and authority, may be able to keep them safe and sound, in the fear of God, in Christ's true religion, in good order and honesty of living: except they will have them run headlong into over many jeopardies, as Ulysses hath done many times. . . .

I know diverse noble personages, and many worthy gentlemen of England, whom all the Siren[4] songs of Italy, could never untwine from the matter of God's word: nor no enchantment of vanity, overturn them, from the fear of God, and love of honesty.

---

[2] **Ulysses:** Ulysses (Odysseus) joined the Greeks in the Siege of Troy; his adventures on his way home to Penelope, his wife, are the subject of Homer's *Odyssey*. [3] **Homer:** the blind Greek poet of the eighth century B.C.E., reputedly the author of the *Odyssey* and *Iliad*. [4] **Siren:** female figures in Greek mythology who lured unwary seafarers to their rocky isle with enchanting music.

But I know as many, or more, and some, sometime my dear friends, for whose sake I hate going into that country the more, who, parting out of England fervent in the love of Christ's doctrine, and well-furnished with the fear of God, returned out of Italy worse transformed, then ever was any in Circe's[5] court. I know diverse, that went out of England, men of innocent life, men of excellent learning, who returned out of Italy, not only with worse manners but also with less learning: neither so willing to live orderly, nor yet so able to speak learnedly, as they were at home, before they went abroad. And why: Plato, that wise writer, a worthy traveler himself, telleth thy cause why. He went into Sicily, a country, no nearer Italy, by sight of place, than Italy that is now, is like Sicily that was then, in all corrupt manners and licentiousness of life. Plato found in Sicily, every city full of vanity, full of factions, even as Italy is now. And as Homer, like a learned poet, doth feign that Circe, by pleasant enchantments, did turn men into beasts, some into swine, some into asses, some into foxes, some into wolves, etc. Even so Plato, like a wise philosopher, both plainly declare, that pleasure, by licentious vanity, that sweet and perilous poison of all youth, both engender in all those, that yield up themselves to her, four notorious properties. . . .

The first, forgetfulness of all good things learned before: the second, dullness to receive either learning or honesty ever after: the third, a mind embracing lightly the worse opinion, and barren discretion to make true difference betwixt good and ill, betwixt truth, and vanity: the fourth a proud disdainfulness of other good men, in all honest matters.

. . . But I am afraid, that over many of our travelers into Italy, do not eschew the way to Circe's court: but go, and ride, and run, and fly thither, they make great haste to come to her: they make great suit to serve her: yea, I could point out some with my finger, that never had gone out of England, but only to serve Circe in Italy. Vanity and vice, and any license to ill living in England was counted stale and rude unto them. And so, being mules and horses before they went, return very swine and asses home again: yet every where very foxes with subtle and busy heads: and where they may, very wolves, with cruel malicious hearts. A marvelous monster, which, for filthiness of living, for dullness to learning himself, for wittiness in dealing with others, for malice in hurting without cause, should carry at once in one body, the belly of a swine, the head of an ass, the brain of a fox, the womb of a wolf. If you think, we judge amiss, and write too sore against you, hear, what the Italian saith of the English man, what the master reporteth of the scholar: who uttereth plainly, what is taught by him, and what is learned by you, saying: . . . that is to say, you remain men in shape and fashion, but

[5] **Circe's:** Circe, a seductive enchantress who transformed Ulysses' men into swine.

become devils in life and condition. This is not, the opinion of one, for some private spite, but the judgment of all, in a common proverb, which riseth, of that learning, and those manners, which you gather in Italy: a good schoolhouse of wholesome doctrine: and worthy masters of commendable scholars, where the master had rather defame himself for his teaching, than not shame his scholar for his learning. A good nature of the master, and fair conditions of the scholars. And now choose you, you Italian English men, whether you will be angry with us, for calling you monsters, or with the Italians, for calling you devils, or else with your own selves, that take so much pains, and go so far, to make yourselves both. If some yet do not well understand, what is an English man Italianated, I will plainly tell him. He, that by living, & traveling in Italy, bringeth home into England out of Italy, the religion, the learning, . . . policy, the experience, the manners of Italy. That is to say, for religion, papistry, or worse: for learning, less commonly than they carried out with them: for policy, a factious heart, a discoursing head, a mind to meddle in all men's matters: for experience, plenty of new mischiefs never known in England before: for manners, variety of vanities, and change of filthy living. These be the enchantments of Circe, brought out of Italy, to mar men's manners in England, which, by example of ill life, but more by precepts of some books, of late translated out of Italian into English, sold in every shop in London, commended by honest titles, the sooner to corrupt honest manners, dedicated over boldly to virtuous and honorable personages, the easier to beguile simple & innocent wits. It is pity, that those, which have authority and charge to allow and disallow books to be printed, be no more circumspect herein, than they are. Ten sermons of Paul's Cross[6] do not so much good for moving men to true bearing, as one of those books do harm, with enticing one to ill living. Yea, I say farther, those books tend not so much to corrupt honest living, as they do to subvert true religion. More papists be made, by your merry books of Italy, than by your earnest books of Louvain.[7] And because our great physicians do wink at the matter, and make no count of this sore, I though not admitted one of their fellowship, yet having been many years an apprentice of God's true religion, and trust to continue a poor journeyman therein all days of my life, for the duty I owe, and love I bear, both to true doctrine, and honest living, though I have no authority to amend the sore my self, yet I will declare my good will, to discover sore to others.

---

[6] **Paul's Cross:** famous London pulpit.   [7] **Louvain:** French site of Catholic seminary and printing press; thus, Catholic books published as part of the Reformation polemic do less damage to good, English Protestants than Italian secular materials.

... Therefore, when the busy and open papists abroad, could not, by their contentious books, turn men in England fast enough, from truth and right judgment in doctrine, then the subtle and secret papists at home, procured bawdy books to be translated out of the Italian tongue, whereby over many young wills and wits allured to wantonness, do now boldly condemn all severe books that [tend] to honesty and godliness. In our forefathers' time, when papistry, as a standing pool, covered and overflowed all England, few books were read in our tongue, saving certain books of chivalry, as they said for pastime and pleasure, which, as some say, were made in monasteries, by idle monks, or wanton chansons.[8] ... They open, not fond and common ways to vice, but such subtle, cunning, new, and diverse shifts, to carry young wills to vanity, and young wits to mischief, to teach old bawds, new school points, as the simple head of an English man is not able to invent, nor never was heard of in England before, yea when papistry overflowed all. Suffer these books to be read, and they shall soon displace all books of godly learning. For they, carrying the will to vanity, and marring good manners, shall easily corrupt the mind with ill opinions, and false judgment in doctrine: first, to think ill of all true religion, and at last to think nothing of God himself, one special point that is to be learned in Italy, and Italian books. And that which is most to be lamented, and therefore more needful to be looked to, there be more of these ungracious books set out in print within these few months, than have been seen in England many score years before. And because our English men made Italians, can not hurt, but certain persons, and in certain places, therefore these Italian books are made English, to bring mischief enough openly and boldly, to all states great and mean, young and old, every where.

And thus you see, how will enticed to wantonness, doth easily allure the mind to false opinions: and how corrupt manners in living, breed false judgment in doctrine: how sin and fleshliness, bring forth sects and heresies: And therefore suffer not vain books to breed vanity in men's wills, if you would have God's truth take root in men's minds.

That Italian that first invented the Italian proverb against our English men Italianated, meant no more their vanity in living, than their lewd opinion in religion: for in calling them devils, he carrieth them clean from God: and yet he carrieth them no farther than they willingly go themselves, that is, where they may freely say their minds to the open contempt of God, & all godliness, both in living and doctrine.

---

[8] **chansons:** singers.

→ THOMAS NASHE

From The Unfortunate Traveler, or the Life of Jack Wilton   *1594*

Thomas Nashe (1567–c.1601) graduated from St. John's College, Cambridge in 1582. He was a prolific satirist capable of the most biting invective, and for his part in writing the lost comedy *The Isle of Dogs* (1597), he was jailed in the Fleet prison for several months. There has been some debate among historians and critics about whether Nashe himself ever traveled to Italy. Although the old *Dictionary of National Biography* (*DNB*) asserts unequivocally that Nashe went to Italy just after Cambridge, Ronald McKerrow observes:

> The question is, do the references to Italy and Italian affairs in *The Unfortunate Traveler* show more acquaintance with the country than could be derived from maps, books, and the conversation of those who had been there? Is there anything in the work that suggests personal observation? . . . I think there is not. In fact I believe that a careful perusal of the book would bring any reader to the almost certain conclusion that the writer had as little actual knowledge of the places in which he lays his scenes as Shakespeare had of Venice, of Verona, or of Bohemia.   (13)

Whether or not he ever went to Italy, Nashe certainly claimed to emulate an Italian in his work, none other than the infamous Pietro Aretino (1492–1556), whose writing contained, alongside flattery and libel, a strongly pornographic emphasis. The latter is not much evident in Nashe's prose works, though it is certainly apparent in his *Choice of Valentines,* a poem about a dildo.

The Unfortunate Traveler figures in literary history because, as a popular prose story of the reckless adventures of the page Jack Wilton, it is a precursor of the novel. Like Shakespeare's *Venus and Adonis* (1593) and *The Rape of Lucrece* (1594), the book is dedicated to the earl of Southampton, who seems to have had a particular interest in Italianate culture.

At my first coming to Rome, I, being a youth of the English cut, wore my hair long, went appareled in light colors, and imitated four or five sundry nations in my attire at once; which no sooner was noted, but I had all the boys of the city in a swarm wondering about me.

I had not gone a little farther, but certain officers crossed the way of me, and demanded to see my rapier: which when they found (as also my dagger) with his point unblunted, they would have hauled me headlong to the

Thomas Nashe, *The Unfortunate Traveler, or the Life of Jack Wilton* (1594), ed. Ronald B. McKerrow, *The Works of Thomas Nashe,* vol. 2 (London, 1904–10), 281–301.

Strappado,[1] but that with money I appeased them: and my fault was more pardonable in that I was a stranger, altogether ignorant of their customs.

Note, by the way, that it is the use in *Rome* for all men whatsoever to wear their hair short: which they do not so much for conscience sake, or any religion they place in it, but because the extremity of the heat is such there that, if they should not do so, they should not have a hair left on their heads to stand upright when they were scared with sprites. And he is counted no gentleman amongst them that goes not in black: they dress their jesters and fools only in fresh colors, and say variable garments do argue unsteadiness and inconstancy of affections.

The reason of their straight ordinance for carrying weapons without points is this: The Bandittos, which are certain outlaws that lie betwixt *Rome* and *Naples,* and besiege the passage, so that none can travel that way without robbing. Now and then, hired for some few crowns, they will steal to *Rome* and do a murder, and betake them to their heels again. Disguised as they go, they are not known from strangers; sometimes they will shroud themselves under the habit of grave citizens. In this consideration, neither citizen or stranger, gentleman, knight, marquis, or any may wear any weapon endamageable upon pain of the Strappado. I bought it out; let others buy experience of me better cheap.[2]

To tell you of the rare pleasures of their gardens, their baths, their vineyards, their galleries, were to write a second part of *The Gorgeous Gallery of Gallant Devices.* Why, you should not come into any man's house of account, but he had fish-ponds and little orchards on the top of his leads.[3] If by rain or any other means these ponds were so full they need to be sluiced or let out, even of their superfluities they made melodious use, for they had great wind instruments instead of leaden spouts, that went duly on consort,[4] only with this water's rumbling descent. I saw a summer banqueting house belonging to a merchant, that was the marvel of the world, & could not be matched except God should make another paradise. It was built round of green marble like a theater with-out: within there was a heaven and earth comprehended both under one roof: The heaven was a clear overhanging vault of crystal, wherein the sun and moon and each visible star had his true similitude, shine, situation, and motion; and, by what enwrapped art I cannot conceive, these spheres in their proper orbs observed their circular wheelings and turnings, making a certain kind of soft angelical murmuring music in their often windings & going about; which music the philosophers

---

[1] **Strappado:** torture technique; here, the place of punishment. [2] **I bought it out; . . . of me better cheap:** let others learn at my expense. [3] **on the top of his leads:** a roof garden. [4] **duly on consort:** poured out together.

say in the true heaven, by reason of the grossness of our senses, we are not capable of. For the earth, it was counterfeited in that likeness that Adam lorded over it before his fall. . . .[5]

O *Rome*, if thou hast in thee such soul-exalting objects, what a thing is heaven in comparison of thee, of which *Mercator's* globe[6] is a perfecter model than thou art? Yet this I must say to the shame of us Protestants; if good works may merit heaven, they do them, we talk of them. Whether superstition or no makes them unprofitable servants, that let pulpits decide: But there you shall have the bravest ladies, in gowns of beaten gold, washing pilgrims' & poor soldiers' feet, and doing nothing, they and their waiting maids, all the year long, but making shirts and bands[7] for them against they come by in distress. Their hospitals are more like noblemen's houses than otherwise; so richly furnished, clean kept, and hot perfumed, that a soldier would think it a sufficient recompense for all his travel and his wounds, to have such a heavenly retiring place. For the pope and his pontificalibus[8] I will not deal with; only I will dilate unto you what happened whilst I was in *Rome*.

So it fell out that it being a vehement hot summer when I was a sojourner there, there entered such a hot-spurred[9] plague as hath not been heard of: Why, it was but a word and a blow, Lord have mercy upon us, and he was gone. Within three quarters of a year in that one city there died of it a hundred thousand; look in Lanquet's *Chronicle*[10] and you shall find it. To smell of a nosegay[11] that was poisoned, and turn your nose to a house that had the plague, it was all one. The clouds, like a number of cormorants that keep their corn till it stink and is musty, kept in their stinking exhalations, till they had almost stifled all *Rome's* inhabitants. Physicians' greediness of gold made them greedy of their destiny. They would come to visit those with whose infirmity their art had no affinity; and even as a man with a fee should be hired to hang himself, so would they quietly go home and die presently after they had been with their patients.[12] All day and all night long car-men did nothing but go up and down the streets with their carts and cry, Have you any dead bodies to bury? and had many times out of one house their whole load: one grave was the sepulchre of seven score, one bed was the altar whereon whole families were offered. . . .

---

[5] **Adam . . . fall:** paradise ruled by Adam; i.e., Eden.   [6] *Mercator's* **globe:** map of the globe drawn by sixteenth-century Dutch cartographer Gerard Mercator.   [7] **bands:** bandages. [8] **pontificalibus:** pontificate; that is, a group of high-level clerics.   [9] **hot-spurred:** virulent. [10] **Lanquet's *Chronicle*:** Thomas Lanquet's *Chronicle of the World* (1521–45).   [11] **nosegay:** small, fragrant bouquet.   [12] **Physicians' . . . patients:** out of greed, doctors visited plague-stricken patients whom they had no means to cure, causing the doctors to contract the disease themselves.

If thou dost but lend half a look to a *Roman's* or *Italian's* wife, thy porridge shall be prepared for thee, and cost thee nothing but thy life. Chance some of them break a bitter jest on thee, and thou retort it severely, or seem discontented: go to thy chamber, and provide a great banquet, for thou shall be sure to be visited with guests in a mask the next night, when in kindness and courtship thy throat shall be cut, and the doers return undiscovered. Nothing so long of memories as a dog; these *Italians* are old dogs, & will carry an injury a whole age in memory. I have heard of a box on the ear that hath been revenged thirty years after. The *Neapolitan*[13] carrieth the bloodiest mind, and is the most secret fleering[14] murderer: whereupon it is grown to a common proverb, *I'll give him the Neapolitan shrug,* when one intends to play the villain and make no boast of it.

The only precept that a traveler hath most use of, and shall find most ease in, is that of Epicharmus,[15] *Vigila, & memor sis ne quid credas:* Believe nothing, trust no man; yet seem thou as thou swallowed all, suspected none, but were easy to be gulled[16] by every one. *Multi fallere docuerunt* (as *Seneca* saith) *dum timent falli:* Many by showing their jealous suspect of deceit have made men seek more subtle means to deceive them.

Alas, our Englishmen are the plainest dealing souls that ever God put life in: they are greedy of news, and love to be fed in their humors and hear themselves flattered the best that may be. Even as *Philemon,* a comic poet, died with extreme laughter at the conceit of seeing an ass eat figs; so have the *Italians* no such sport as to see poor English asses how soberly they swallow Spanish figs, devour any hook baited for them. . . .

Italy, the paradise of the earth and the epicure's heaven, how doth it form our young master? It makes him to kiss his hand like an ape, cringe his neck like a starveling,[17] and play at hey pass, repass, or come aloft,[18] when he salutes a man. From thence he brings the art of atheism, the art of epicurizing,[19] the art of whoring, the art of poisoning, the art of sodomitry.[20] The only probable good thing they have to keep us from utterly condemning it is that it maketh a man an excellent courtier, a curious carpet knight: which is, by interpretation, a fine close lecher, a glorious hypocrite. It is now a privy note amongst the better sort of men, when they would set a singular mark or brand on a notorious villain, to say, he hath been in *Italy.*

---

[13] *Neapolitan:* one from Naples.   [14] **fleering:** fleeing or deceitful.   [15] **Epicharmus:** (c. 550–460 B.C.E.), a writer who gave artistic form to comedy; he was born in Greece but lived and worked in Syracuse, Sicily.   [16] **gulled:** conned.   [17] **starveling:** someone starving.   [18] **hey pass, repass, or come aloft:** Italian gestures.   [19] **the art of epicurizing:** fine dining.   [20] **the art of sodomitry:** sex between men.

→ WILLIAM THOMAS

From The History of Italy   *1549*

William Thomas was executed in 1554 by the Catholic queen, Mary I, on the charge that he played a role in the attempted coup against her known as the Wyatt Conspiracy of 1553–54. He vainly sought to thwart his prosecutors by attempting suicide. This failure meant that Thomas instead endured the protracted agony of the rack. An appalling instrument of torture, the rack was a frame with a roller at either end, to which the wrists and ankles were tied, so that the victim's joints were stretched in excruciating pain when the rollers turned.

Despite its tragic and hideous conclusion, Thomas's life had held much promise. He was born in Wales and probably educated at Oxford. Thomas became a much respected Italian scholar, spending part of his life in Italy. In 1550, he became clerk of the privy council to King Edward VI and served as Edward's political instructor. When he translated *Voyages* by the fifteenth-century Italian writer Barbaro, he dedicated the volume to the king. Thomas's political success during this reign was in part attributable to the fact that he remained a firm adherent of the new Protestant religion despite his time in Catholic Italy. Thomas's future seemed secure, especially when he was rewarded with a prebend (a portion of land held from a cathedral chapter; see p. 167) at St. Paul's in London along with numerous other preferments. Alas, when Mary came to the throne in 1553, the tide turned rapidly, and Thomas lost everything, including his life. This, the first English book on Italy, was written in the midst of a craze for Italian culture.

THE DESCRIPTION OF ITALY

Italy containeth in length from Augusta Pretoria unto Otranto, 1,020 miles: and in breadth from the river Varo in Provance, to the river Arsia in Friuli (which is the broadest place), 410 miles and in the narrow places, as from the mouth of Pescara to the mouth of Tiber, 126 miles. So that to compass it by sea from Varo to Arsia, are 3,038 miles, which with the 410 miles by land, maketh the whole circuit to be 3,448 miles. Thus it appeareth, that it is almost an island, closed on the east side with the sea Adriaticum, and on the south and west with the sea Tirrhenum, which is a part of the great sea Mediterraneum. And from the north it hath the mightiest mountains of all Europe called Alps, which divideth it from all other regions.

William Thomas, *The History of Italy. A Book Exceedingly Profitable to Be Read Because It Entreateth of the State of Many and Divers Commonweals* (London, 1549), 1–6v, 200v–01.

The fashion (as Pliny[1] describeth it) is like unto an oak leaf with the stalk: but it endeth in manner of the Amazon's target.[2]

It hath a very temperate and wholesome air, fertile fields, pleasant hills, barful[3] pastures, shadowing woods, plenty of all kind of trees and groves, abundance of corn, vines, and olives: good wools, fair cattle, and so many springs, fountains, lakes, rivers, and havens, that it is an open lap to receive the trade of all countries: and as it were to offer all men help it seemeth willingly to put itself into the sea.

It lieth between the sixth hour and the first of the winter in manner half way between the equinox and the pole: between (I say) the heat of the sun and the cold of the north. For the city of Bononia[4] (where the great resort of scholars from all nations is wont to be) standeth almost in the heart of Italy, and hath in his elevation 44 degrees: for that dividing the quarter from the equinox to the Septentrion into 90 according to the rule of cosmography, and taking the one half thereof, which is 45, the difference is little, to prove that Italy is in the middest between the extremities of heat and cold. And saying then, that temperature is it that most of all other comforteth, nourisheth and maintaineth nature: it must needs follow, that this being one of the most indifferent regions, must be very pleasant, delicate and abundant.

This little discourse I have made to the intent the wise may the better understand the cause of those things, that to my purpose I must hereafter treat upon.

The Commodities of Italy

If I should go about to describe unto you particularly how commodious the country is, as well to the traffic of them that live by merchandise, as the good life of them that love their rest, it should be enough alone to occupy an whole volume, but because I would seem no more tedious in this, than I covet to do in all the rest, I say:

First for merchandise, Italy as an heart or knot of these parts on our half of the world, is the principal place of recourse of all nations that occupy any thing of importance far from home. For like as with us in England the most merchants of the realm resort to London, to utter[5] their own wares, and to

---

[1] **Pliny:** Roman author (23–79 C.E.) who wrote *The Natural History.*   [2] **is like unto an oak leaf . . . Amazon's target:** Amazons were a mythical race of women warriors famed for their skill with bow and arrow. The entire sentence refers to the shape of Italy ("target" here means a small form of shield).   [3] **barful:** fenced.   [4] **Bononia:** Bologna.   [5] **utter:** sell; Shakespeare uses this same word to describe the sale of the poison to Romeo (5.1.67).

buy such other as make for their purposes: even so they of France, of Spain, of Germany, and of all other westerly places, that covet the merchandise of Syria, Egypt, Cyprus, Candia,[6] Constantinople, and those other easterly parts, as jewels, drugs, spices, perfumes, silks, cotton, sugar, malmseys[7] and other like: resort much commonly into Italy with their wools, clothes, linen, leather, metals and such other, to Genoa, Milan, Venice, Ancona, Messina, Naples, or to some of those places, whereas traffic is used: and there meeting with Jews, Turks, Greeks, Moors and other easterly merchants, selling the one they buy the other.

Then for pleasure, he that hath means to pay for that he taketh, shall have in Italy what he can reasonably desire: fine bread, singular good wines both strong and small, flesh of all sorts both wild and tame, fowl of all kinds both water and land, fish as well of the sea as of the fresh water, but specially such plenty of delicate fruits, as would make a man leave flesh, fowl and fish to eat them: namely in the summer. I mean the melons, pepons,[8] pomegranates, oranges, lemons, citrons,[9] and sweet grapes: besides these figs, apples, pears, peaches, plums and olives, with a thousand other of that sort. And it is not to be marveled at, though (as the same goeth) the Italian be a small eater of flesh. For though here before I have commended the temperature of Italy to be compatible with any other country: yet must you understand, that in summer the sun is somewhat fervent, and in time of that heat, the lightness of those sweet fresh fruits is better digested than the heaviness of flesh or fish, which would not there be so lightly digested. As I myself have proved, that before time could in manner brook no fruit, and yet after I had been a while in Italy I fell so in love withal, that as long as I was there, I desire no more meat: because me thought nothing more wholesome, specially in summer. And all be it, the heat be (as I have said) somewhat fervent, yet it exceedeth not so much at the hottest, as the winter cold is temperate at the coldest. For at the most the cold there endureth not three months of the twelve and some years in manner you shall feel no winter at all.

These rehearsed commodities, with infinite other, too long here to treat of, together with the loving company of the Italians (who in manner make more of strangers than of their own) do cause the infinite resort of all nations that continually is seen there. And I think verily, that in one region of all the world again, are not half so many strangers as in Italy: specially of gentlemen, whose resort thither is principally under pretense of study. For there are diverse famous cities, that be privileged with great libraries for all

---

[6] **Candia:** Crete.   [7] **malmseys:** strong, sweet wines.   [8] **pepons:** pumpkins.   [9] **citrons:** citrus fruit.

scholars that come: as Padua, Bononia, Pavia, Ferrara, Pisa, and others: in every one of the which, are excellent learned men, waged for the reading of philosophy, of the civil laws, and of all the liberal sciences. Besides excellent masters of music to sing and play on all manner of instruments, and the best masters of fence at all weapons that can be found. So that all kinds of virtue may there be learned: and therefore are those places accordingly furnished: not of such students alone, as most commonly are brought up in our universities (mean men's children set to school in hope to live upon hired learning) but for the more part of noblemen's sons, and of the best gentlemen: that study more for knowledge and pleasure, than for curiosity or lucre.[10] For lightly there passeth no shrovetide[11] without running at the tilt,[12] tourneying,[13] fighting at the barriers, and other like feats of arms, handled and furnished after the best sort: the greatest doers whereof are scholars.

This last winter lying in Padua, with diligent search I learned that the number of scholars there was little less than fifteen hundred: whereof I dare say, a thousand at the least were gentlemen.

OF THE ITALIAN CUSTOMS

The inheritance of lands in Italy goeth by gavelkind,[14] that is to where, one brother as good part as another. So that if a count, (which is as much to say as an earl) have twenty sons, every one of them is called count, and the youngest hath as good part in his father's lands and goods, as the eldest: unless it be in the estates of princes, as of Mantua, Ferrara, Urbino, and such others, which the best ever more enjoyeth. And by this mean it is come to pass, that in process of time, with change from wealth to poverty, there be diverse earls and marquesses without land or goods, retaining nevertheless the glory of that name to them and theirs for ever.

But to speak of the gentlemen, that have whereof worshipfully to live (which for the most part do commonly profess arms) me seemeth, that none other nation is like them in majesty.

. . . I grant, that in the expense or love of his [the Italian's] money for a stranger he is wary, and will be at no more cost than he is sure either to save by, or to have thank for: wherein I rather can commend him than otherwise. But this is out of doubt, a stranger can not be better entertained, nor more honorably entreated than amongst the Italians.

---

[10] **lucre:** wealth. [11] **shrovetide:** shrove Tuesday, the day before Ash Wednesday, the beginning of Lent, the forty-day period leading up to Easter. [12] **at the tilt:** mounted armed contest with javelins. [13] **tourneying:** the tournament at arms. [14] **gavelkind:** system of inheritance in which land was divided among offspring rather than bequeathed to the eldest son, as in primogeniture.

They are very modest in their apparel, fine in trimming of their houses, and exceeding neat at their table. But above all other they are sober of speech, enemies of ill report, and so tender over their own good name (which they call their honor) that whosoever speaketh ill of one of them, shall die for it, if the party slandered may know it, and find time and place to do it. Whereof there is a use grown amongst them, that few gentleman go abroad unarmed. And though some in this case do discommend them, yet mine opinion doeth rather allow than blame them. For the scare of further dangers maketh men so wary of their tongues, that a man may go twenty years through Italy without finding reproach or villainy, unless he provoke it himself.[15]

And if one gentleman happen to defame another, many times the defamed maketh his defiance by a writ called Cartello, and openly challengeth the defamer to fight in camp: so that there are seen sometime worthy trials between them.

And it is true, that many years ago, such contention hath grown amongst them that almost the whole nation hath been divided into part-takings, as Guelfi and Ghibellini:[16] imperial and French, with other like: which hath been occasion of much manslaughter, and consequently of their aforesaid continual use in wearing of armor. But at this day those open contentions are wonderfully abated, whether it proceed of wariness or of wisdom I can not tell.

Finally in one thing I can singularly commend them, that they will not lightly meddle with other men's matters, and that when they hear ill report, they do their best to cover the slander, saying that no man liveth without fault: or with some other such reason. But like as I could reckon in the Italians' commendation many things more than are here rehearsed, even so on the other side if I were disposed to speak of vice, I might happen to find a number as ill as in any other men: which are better untouched than spoken of. For whereas temperance, modesty, and other civil virtues excel in the number of the Italian nobility, more than in the nobility of any other nation that I know: so undoubtedly the fleshly appetite with unnatural heat and other things in them that be vicious, do pass all the terms of reason or honesty.

And yet it is not to be forgotten, that these gentlemen generally profess three things: the first is arms, to maintain withal his honor: the second is love, to show himself gentle and not cruel of nature: and the third is learning, to be able to know, to understand, and to utter his opinion in matters of weight. . . .

[15] This contradicts the opinion of Moryson and Nash (p. 166 and 173) that wearing weapons was barred in Italy.
[16] **Guelfi and Ghibellini:** the Guelphs and the Ghibellines were rival parties in medieval Germany and Italy, which supported the papal party and the Holy Roman emperors respectively.

As for the women,
Some be wonders gay,
And some go as they may,
Some at liberty do swim afloat,
And some would feign but they can not.
Some be merry, I wote[17] well why,
And some beguile the husband, with finger in the eye.
Some be married against their will,
And therefore some abide MAIDENS still.
In effect they are women all,
Ever have been and ever shall.

But in good earnest the gentlewomen generally, for gorgeous attire, apparel and jewels, exceed (I think) all other women of our known world. I mean as well the courtesans as the married women. For in some places of Italy, specially where churchmen do reign: you shall find of that sort of women in rich apparel, in furniture of household, in service, in horse and hackney,[18] and in all things that appertain to a delicate lady, so well furnished, that to see one of them unknowingly, she should seem rather of the quality of a princess, than of a common woman. But because I have to speak hereafter in particular, I will forbear to treat any further of them in this place. . . .

Of the Estate of Mantua

The city of itself is very fair and strong, and standeth richly, by reason the countries about are plain, and no less plentiful than the other parts of Lombardy be. It is strong, because the river of Meltio (or Mentio as some call it) falling out of the lake of Garda through the town of Peshciera, passeth to the Po by Mantua, and maketh about it such a pool, that three parts of the city are defended with the breadth of a quarter of a mile of water every way: which in some places is deep, and in some shallow, that it can not be passed with boats. And then in the necessary places such bulwarks are made to defend, that it seemeth impossible to be won by assault on that side.

And for the fourth part, which is toward the west, it is very well fortified with strong walls and bulwarks, and a large ditch well-watered: besides that the ground on that side is in manner all marsh, or at the least so rank, that in the driest of summer there can none artillery pass: so that the city is undoubtedly one of the strongest that I have seen.

---

[17] **wote:** know.   [18] **hackney:** carriage.

The dominion that the Duke hath is not great, neither of circuit nor of revenue. For at the best (as I have been informed) the rents never passed a 100,000 ducats a year, and many times it hath been much less, by reason it is not standing, but riseth of customs and casualties.

It is true, that the state is much increased by reason of Monferrato, that the last Duke had by the marriage of his wife, so that now the Duke of Mantua's rents by estimation are reckoned at 130,000 ducats or there abouts.

And as for notable buildings in Mantua, other than such as be universal in the goodly cities of Italy, I find none, saving certain proper lodgings that the Duke Federico deceased, hath made on the fourth part of his palace: which undoubtedly are gallant and rich. Wherefore proceeding now to the original of the citizens and city, with the success thereof hitherwards.

THE ORIGINAL OF MANTUA

By agreement of most authors I find that the people of Mantua are descended of those ancient Tuscans that before the siege of Troy departed out of Lydia in Asia, and under the leading of their prince Tirieno, came and inhabited the region of Italy. Part of which Tuscans, choosing afterwards the place of Mantua for their habitation, built the city, before the coming of Aeneas[19] into Italy, and before the edification of Rome, more than 300 years. The captain of which people at that time was named Ogno, a very expert man in astronomy, or in the science of divination. For his virtue in which science, following the Greek word Mantia, he named the city Mantua. . . .

[19] **Aeneas:** Trojan hero who founded a new kingdom in Italy after the fall of Troy.

G. B. A. F.

→ *From* A Discovery of the Great Subtlety and Wonderful Wisdom of the Italians   *1591*

This book, whose author is unknown, was translated from French and undoubtedly thought suitable for the English market because of its anti-Italian and anti-Catholic stance. The views expressed here were certainly not uncommon or unusual in England at this time. In juxtaposing this work with *Romeo and Juliet,* we glimpse something of the cultural contradiction entailed in the heavy reliance on Italian literary materials, on the one hand, and the loathing Italians

G.B.A.F., *A Discovery of the Great Subtlety and Wonderful Wisdom of the Italians* (London, 1591), 1–3.

themselves often inspired in the English, on the other. Certainly, "fascination" with Italy did not necessarily entail unqualified admiration, but rather the articulation of cultural difference in terms often weighted more toward repulsion than attraction. One wonders if those in Shakespeare's audience who shared G. B. A. F.'s views of the Roman religion and of Italians would have suspended their disapprobation for the course of *Romeo and Juliet*. Or would they have withheld their sympathy entirely from the lovers' plight?

Chapter 1, A Description of Italy, and the Causes of the Subtlety[1] of That Nation.

The Italians inhabit the right arm of the continent of Europe, which hath Spain in place of the head, France for the stomach, for the belly Germany, and Denmark for the left arm. . . . That which produceth such effects in Italy is the moderate temperature of the climate, situated in a subtle air near unto the sea everywhere, without any excess heat or cold: and beside, another cause is the trading and great dealing that the Italians have with the people of Asia, of Africa, and Europe, as also with the Flanders or a great part of them with whom they haunt and live. By reason whereof, besides that they are of themselves very witty and subtle headed, all cunning flights, crafty conveyances, and deceitful cozenages,[2] are so proper and common to them, whereby they can fetch under other people, and are so cunning to finger from them their money, and can, moreover, so closely cover their actions that of a thousand hardly one could ever come within them to perceive their juggling. For as any deceit or cozenage finely handled, is not perceived but of those which know it, and look very near unto it, deceiving those which have their eye but on the natural and external show: so there are none but those which curiously seek out the beginning, the progress and advancements of the Roman and Italian government, and the means whereby they have drawn money from other nations of the earth, since the time of Romulus[3] to this present day, who can find out their fetches and shifts,[4] or discover the masks wherewith they are disguised, to advance and enrich themselves by the overthrow and pillage of others. Albeit, it is not enough when we have gone so far, if besides we throw not away the mufflers which deprive us of sound and true judgment in things of this world, as are custom, hate, love, obstinacy, and envy, which are even so many plagues & corruptions, overthrowing quite the judgment and clear understanding of man in all things: for if custom carry us away, the Italian may prevail, not only of an hundred, but of more than a thousand & five hundred years, which was the very time

---

[1] **Subtlety:** sly, underhanded. [2] **cozenages:** con tricks. [3] **Romulus:** founder of Rome.
[4] **fetches and shifts:** chicanery.

that Julius Caesar, an Italian, pillaged and ruined not only France, but also all other parts of Europe. Therefore we should deserve to be commanded and gnawed to the bare bone, for ever hereafter, as well as in time past, that could look to these matters no sooner. The cause of all have been but our blind affections which pervert us in true judgment, the which now we must needs cut off, to have only reason for our guide, which is the true & essential difference, that separateth man from other animals, & maketh him judge truly of all things: otherwise we rob ourselves of the most excellent and precious jewel we have, to become as bestial as the brute beasts. From hence springeth then also the cause of so great diversity of opinions on our continent, the principal and chiefest part of the world, for that some suffer themselves to be governed by the clear light of reason & understanding, and other some let themselves be carried away headlong with their own affections and customs, and this is the cause why the inhabitants of the oriental Asia under the dominion of the great Khan of Tartary,[5] whose empire is two thousand leagues in longitude, do hold him for the son of God in earth, . . . and why Christendom is so troubled by reason of the Romish constitutions, which some believe to be holy and necessary to salvation, and others altogether condemn: being none other means of reconciliation amongst us, but to cast away these blind mufflers of customs, hatred, and consideration of loss or gain, & to suffer our selves to be directed by the clear light of the heavenly word, by the unsearchable works of God, and by lively reason clarified with authentic histories of time. Putting but this in practice once, we shall soon discover, and clearly see with our eyes the wonderful deep subtleties of Italians, and hereafter beware how we be overwrought by their policies.

[5] **the great Khan of Tartary:** Genghis Khan (1202–1227), the ruler of central Asia extending Eastward from the Caspian sea and his lineage.

➜ ANDREAS FRANCISCUS

From A Description of the Author's Journey from Trento to London
1497

The following is an excerpt from a text written in Latin by an Italian traveler, Andreas Franciscus. We know nothing about his reasons for journeying to England other than those expressed in the slim account he has left us. Since he

Andreas Franciscus, *Itinerarium Britanniae, A Description of the Author's Journey from Trento to London by the Route of Germany and Flanders* (1497) from *Two Italian Accounts of Tudor England,* trans. C. V. Malfatti (Barcelona, 1953), 36–38.

refers to his journey as a "legation," he may have been an envoy from one of the Italian states. Though this excerpt is dated earlier (1497) than most of the documents included here, Franciscus's account nonetheless conveys the experience of a foreigner in England, and the degree of xenophobia that existed many years before the English Reformation added religious fuel to its flames.

Now I shall say something about the inhabitants, their culture and methods of government, thinking that readers will find no less entertainment in these. Londoners have such fierce tempers and wicked dispositions that they not only despise the way in which Italians live, but actually pursue them with uncontrollable hatred, and whereas Bruges[1] foreigners are hospitably received and complimented and treated with consideration by everybody, here the Englishmen use them with the utmost contempt and arrogance, and make them the object of insults. At Bruges we could do as we liked by day as well as by night. But here they look askance at us by day, and at night they sometimes drive us off with kicks and blows of the truncheon. Some of the men are exceptionally tall. All exercise themselves in a marvelous way with great bows made of yew wood, with which they practice continually outside the walls. They also fight with them on foot in such a way as to show that they have been enthusiastically trained in this from their earliest youth.

. . . [B]ut they delight in banquets and variety of meat and food, and they excel everyone in preparing them with an excessive abundance. They eat very frequently, at times more than is suitable, and are particularly fond of young swans, rabbits, deer and sea birds. They often eat mutton and beef, which is generally considered to be better here than anywhere else in the world. This is due to the excellence of their pastures. They have all kinds of fish in plenty and great quantities of oysters which come from the sea-shore. The majority, not to say everyone, drink that beverage[2] I have spoken of before, and prepare it in various ways. For wine is very expensive, as the vine does not grow in the island; nor does the olive, and the products of both are imported from France and Spain. In certain places, mainly inland, silver and iron are found. But although there is abundance of these, gold is very scarce and copper scarcer still: they import it from Germany.

The first governor of this town is an Englishman and is called Mayor, and has great power and authority; this dignity cannot be bestowed on a man unless he has served the apprenticeship in the trade guilds, a rule said to be established by law among them. . . .

---

[1] **Bruges:** a city in northwest Belgium.   [2] **that beverage:** beer.

CHAPTER 2

Between Men

———————————— >< ————————————

Relationships between Men

> Young Romeo is it? . . .
> 'A bears him like a portly gentleman,
> And, to say truth, Verona brags of him
> To be a virtuous and well governed youth.   (1.5.61–65)

When a character's virtues are described by an enemy, as Romeo's are here by Capulet at the feast, the audience can be in no doubt that they are virtues indeed. Capulet describes Romeo as "a portly gentleman," that is, as someone who carries himself like a well-mannered gentleman. Though the feud between the Capulet and Montague families makes it impossible, the audience also glimpses in these words the potential for a father-in-law and son-in-law relationship.

Capulet's reflection on Romeo as an ideal of Veronese masculinity offers a sharp contrast to the belligerent Tybalt, who is merely "a saucy boy" (1.5.80). From his father's perspective, however, Romeo is far closer to adolescence than manhood:

> BENVOLIO: My noble uncle, do you know the cause [of Romeo's despondency]?
> MONTAGUE: I neither know it nor can learn of him.

BENVOLIO: Have you importuned him by any means?
MONTAGUE: Both by myself and many other friends.
    But he, his own affections' counselor,
    Is to himself — I will not say how true,
    But to himself so secret and so close,
    So far from sounding and discovery,
    As is the bud bit with an envious worm
    Ere he can spread his sweet leaves to the air
    Or dedicate his beauty to the sun.
    Could we but learn from whence his sorrows grow,
    We would as willingly give cure as know.   (1.1.131–42)

What does Shakespeare's audience glean from this exchange about the Montague household and especially about the relation between sons and their fathers in Verona? The language of this passage, especially the image of Romeo being literally too wrapped up in himself ("to himself so secret and so close") to flower into manhood, echoes the eloquent meditation on youthful masculinity in the sonnets: "Thou that art now the world's fresh ornament, / And only herald to the gaudy [joyful] spring, / Within thine own bud buriest thy content [happiness]" (1.9–11). Similarly, the concern with Romeo's melancholy foreshadows the brooding intensity of Hamlet, whose protracted adolescence proves a powerful contribution to the play's tragedy. The bud that never opened was a common Renaissance image of youth that never reached maturity: "The canker galls the infants of the spring / Too often before their buttons be disclosed" [i.e., disease kills before buds have chance to open] (*Hamlet* 1.3.39–40). There is always a danger that the promise of youth will go unfulfilled, especially given the unfavorable odds of simply surviving into adulthood in early modern England. In the treatment of emergent masculinity in Shakespeare's poem *Venus and Adonis,* there is the sense that to blossom into manhood is to render oneself subject to old age and mortality. But not to flower at all is equally parlous, so that Adonis's care for his virginity, his refusal to become a fully sexual adult, leads only to death: "Bud, and be blasted" (142).

The dangers inherent in maturation, then, are both intensified and given very concrete form in the Montague-Capulet feud. The audience is left to ponder the ultimate source of the tragedy. Does it reside in the "ancient enmity" between the Montagues and Capulets, or does it lie even more deeply embedded in the psychologically morose and socially turbulent nature of young men?

Young men in the play are something of a mystery, locked up in their bedrooms "so secret and so close," engaged in the business of growth and maturation. Friar Laurence's concerns parallel those of Romeo's father, and it is telling that just as Romeo arrives at his cell, he offers an analogy between plant and human potential: "Within the infant rind of this weak flower / Poison hath residence and medicine power" (2.3.23–24). Potency resides precisely in the early stages of plant development, but it is here not simply the capacity to mature or die, but, "In man as well as herbs" (2.3.28), the dual potential for good and evil. Even beyond the violence of the feud, then, the shadow of death hangs over the youth of Verona, and however sympathetically Romeo is presented on stage, like the "infant rind," he contains both the power of God-given "grace" and simultaneously "rude will" (2.3.28), or the baser (sensual and avaricious) aspects of human desire.

For all that, young people remain the ornaments of the city: "Verona brags of him" (1.5.64). Romeo is, as the Nurse describes him, "like an honest gentleman, / And a courteous, and a kind, and a handsome, / And, I warrant, a virtuous" (2.5.53–55). Even though she is an unreliable character witness, this corroborates Capulet's more sober and discriminating observations. We see Romeo's "portly bearing" in action when he intervenes in the fatal quarrel that kills Mercutio and Tybalt, a scene that is recapitulated by Benvolio in his report to the Prince. Romeo "spoke him fair" (3.1.140), "With gentle breath, calm look, knees humbly bowed" (3.1.143). Eloquent and diplomatic, he is also capable of valor: "swifter than his tongue / His agile arm beats down their fatal points, / And twixt them rushes" (3.1.152–54).

All relationships between men, including family, marriage, and class relationships in Verona, are underscored and ultimately riven by the violence in whose context they take shape. Such is the problem of what Coppélia Kahn has so aptly called "Coming of Age in Verona," in which sexual bonds with women are pitted against allegiances between men (Kahn 82–103). In his failure to rescue Mercutio, Romeo experiences a conflict of allegiance between his friends and his bride: "Thy beauty hath made me effeminate, / And in my temper softened valor's steel!" (3.1.101–02). Notably, Romeo identifies Juliet as the source of his weakness after Mercutio receives the fatal wound. He feels he has in some way betrayed his friendship with Mercutio by trying to negotiate with Tybalt: "My very [true] friend, hath got this mortal hurt / In my behalf" (3.1.97–98). Indeed, Mercutio is a figure of enormous interest in part because he represents an allegiance not based on family identity; he is not a kinsman of Romeo, he is his "very friend."

We do, however, learn something of Mercutio's own kin network from Romeo's statement that Mercutio is "the Prince's near ally" (3.1.96). Mercutio is presumably one of "a brace of kinsmen" (5.3.295) Escalus says he has lost in the feud. This remark suggests the extent of the damage to the social and familial infrastructure of Verona caused by the feud. That is, it extends beyond immediate members of the Capulet and Montague household to the likes of ostensibly non-aligned persons such as Mercutio and the Prince. For Mercutio is the only kinsman to the Prince we know by name, and he seems to have no blood ties to the feuding factions. This is evidenced not only by his dying curse: "A plague o' both your houses!" (3.1.80, 87–88, 93), but also by the fact that he is both Romeo's friend *and* invited to the Capulet ball: "Mercutio and his brother Valentine" (1.2.67). Of course, we never see Mercutio's brother in the play, nor is he ever mentioned again. Joseph Porter has pointed out the potential significance of this omission because in Shakespeare's *Two Gentlemen of Verona* (written c. 1593–95), Valentine "the constant lover is tested by his fickle friend Proteus's temporary rivalry in love" (Joseph Porter 5). In fact, Proteus tries to rape Valentine's beloved, Silvia, but when Valentine discovers Proteus in the attempt, Proteus's remorse moves Valentine not only to forgive his friend, but to offer Silvia to him as a sign of their renewed friendship. This is an enormously disturbing rendition of male amity for most modern audiences, in part because, as Jean Howard points out, it "participates both in the celebration of male friendship and to some extent in the comic deflation of male-female love" (*Norton* 79). The name Valentine, seen in this light, reflects something of Mercutio's character. Certainly, Romeo feels his love for Juliet as a betrayal of Mercutio. There is no such crisis in the relationship between Romeo and his cousin Benvolio, who appears to be languishing for a woman at the opening of the play when he tells Montague he measured "his [Romeo's] affections by my own" (1.1.113). However, Benvolio disappears unaccountably from the play after act 3, not even reappearing to mourn the lovers' deaths (Joseph Porter 2).

Mercutio is also given to speculating on Romeo's sexual activity in a way that makes Romeo the object of his libidinal energies:

> If love be blind, love cannot hit the mark.
> Now will he sit under a medlar tree
> And wish his mistress were that kind of fruit
> As maids call medlars when they laugh alone.
> O, Romeo, that she were, O, that she were
> An open-arse, and thou a poppering pear!
> Romeo, good night. I'll to my truckle bed   (2.1.34–40)

Mercutio associates Romeo's mistress with the medlar or "open-arse" fruit, so called because it resembles the clefts and folds of human flesh. Here, the vulgar implication is that women are penetrable via the anus as well as the vagina, but the sodomitically explicit image of the "open-arse" seems to imply also Romeo's own "o," that is his own anus, and not just that of his mistress. Blind love here is the figure of Cupid, unable to "hit the mark." A further implication is that the phallus that is limp at the prospect of vaginal penetration would revive at the prospect of intercourse with "[A]n open-arse," that is, with a rectum, or perhaps with a man, instead.

Romeo's "R's," both the letter of his name and a pun on "arse," make him the potential object of Mercutio's bawdy pun on "the whole depth of my tale" (2.4.79), that is, the penetrative reach or the length of his penis (see Goldberg, "Open R's" 218–35). In an important interpretation of this passage, Bruce Smith has argued that "it is not Juliet's pudenda that Mercutio jokes about but Romeo's." This is so, he claims, "because the image of anal sex climaxes a whole series of earlier jokes to which Romeo's member supplies the point." When Mercutio is killed, asks Smith, is he "an exemplar of male violence and misogyny? A martyr to male friendship? A victim of sexual desire that he cannot, will not, or must not acknowledge directly? Mercutio is all three." (Smith, *Shakespeare* 63–64).

Like Mercutio, the play itself is obsessed with phallic objects from the opening references to "standing" (erection) and naked weapons (taking out the penis) to Mercutio's insistent use of phallic imagery. "The bawdy hand of the dial is now upon the prick of noon" (2.4.91–92) suggests, for example, the fondling of an erect penis. Elsewhere he counsels: "If love be rough with you, be rough with love; / Prick love for pricking, and you beat love down" (1.4.27–28). Love, or Cupid, pricks his victims with his arrow, so Mercutio advises a quasi-violent sexual response, the use of Romeo's own "prick" in the sexual act, "pricking" the boy god Cupid as a form of retribution (see also Radel 92). This is also a pun that appears in Shakespeare's Sonnet 20 and one that has provoked questions about Shakespeare's own sexual identity (see Chedgzoy 167–70).

Critics have long noted the sexual connotations of the homosocial bonds between young men on the streets of Verona, and especially those of Mercutio's insistently sexual banter with Romeo, which in performance can even be played as laddish vulgarity, "saucy" and "full of ropery" as the Nurse describes it (2.4.117–18). There is also a twinge of sexual jealousy, or at least sexual exclusion in Mercutio's "You gave us the counterfeit fairly last night" (2.4.38) and "I'll to my truckle bed" (2.1.40). Elizabethan rooms had a standing bed and the truckle bed for the attending page or lady's maid. This was usually on casters and was pushed under the standing bed during the daytime. The truckle bed may connote Mercutio's potential exclusion from the marital bed.

How would an Elizabethan audience have interpreted the relationship between Romeo and Mercutio? Would they have assumed that the homoerotic was a necessary and perhaps even unremarkable aspect of the homosocial? One of the difficulties in answering this question is that, as

THE ENGLISH GENTLEMAN

FIGURE 5

Two Men Embracing, from Richard Brathwaite, *The English Gentleman* (London, 1633).

Jeffrey Masten has argued that, like many Latin mottos, this one is something of a brain-teaser, possibly meaning "The love of virtue is sure" or even, "A secure love is a virtue" (see Masten 28), or even "Steadfast is the love based on inclination" (*Norton* 78). However, *Certus Amor Morum Est* is a quotation from Ovid's treatise on cosmetics, *Medicamina Faciei Femineae,* and in context it means "The love which is based on moral qualities is a sure one." The passage goes on to say that time will destroy a beautiful face with wrinkles, implying that time *does not* destroy moral qualities such as, say, compassion. Brathwaite's text itself emphasizes qualities we might more readily associate with romantic partnerships than with platonic friendship, such as constancy: "[H]ow consequent a thing it is to show ourselves *constant* in the *choice* of our *acquaintance*" (Brathwaite 272):

> Certainly, every faithful *friend* should be as a brother . . . So, I say, should friends and acquaintance be to one another; not in preying or feeding one upon another, as if all were fish that came to net, for this were to make no difference or distinction betwixt friend or foe, but for some intendment of private benefit to dissolve the strict bond of *friendship*. Whereas a *friend,* being indeed a man's *second self,* or rather an individuate companion to himself, (for there is one soul which ruleth two hearts, and one heart which dwelleth in two bodies) should be valued above the rate of any outward good. . . . How highly then are we to value the possession of a good *friend,* who partakes with us in our comforts and discomforts, in the frowns and fawns of fortune, showing himself the same both in our weal and woe? (297–98)

The embrace depicted far exceeds modern notions of the appropriate greeting for mere acquaintances, which to us denotes a far lesser species of amity than friendship as such. *Acquaintance* is itself a word used in a very ambiguous context by Shakespeare in Sonnet 20, when he asserts that the young man has "a woman's gentle heart but not acquainted" with "false women's fashion," that is, duplicitous female behavior. The "quaint" in "acquainted" is an obscene early modern pun on "cunt," meaning either that the young man has no sexual dealings with women, or that he is sexually like them.

Alan Bray points out, "Elizabethan society was one of those which lacked the idea of a distinct homosexual minority" (Bray, "Homosexuality" 40). Similarly, "friend," rather than meaning simply someone for whom one had special fondness "pointed to that network of subtle bonds amongst influential patrons and their clients, suitors, and friends at court" ("Homosexuality" 42; see also Shannon). As Mario DiGangi points out, "The 'homosocial' and the homoerotic . . . overlapped to a greater extent, and with less attendant anxiety in the early modern period than would later be possible under a modern regime of sexuality" (DiGangi 2). James I, for example, wrote to his favorite, George Villiers, duke of Buckingham, in terms that now we would use only to a lover: "God so love me as I desire only to live in the world for your sake, and that I had rather live banished in any part of the earth with you than live a sorrowful widow's life without you" (reproduced in Bergeron 174). Indeed, if Shakespeare had included a letter from Juliet to Romeo in exile, we would not be surprised to find the expression of such romantic sentiments. Because, as Nicholas Radel points out, "The early modern period simply would not have made the distinction between behaviors that, for us, demarcate homosexual and heterosexual identity" (92), it is impossible to prove whether James's language is indeed that of a lover or simply the discourse of passionate friendship (see Bergeron 28–29).

We can get a sense of the difference between early modern sexuality and our own notions of it when we consider, for example, that it is *not* intimacy with Mercutio that makes Romeo effeminate, but his erotic desire for Juliet: "thy beauty hath made me effeminate" (3.1.101). It is tempting to see this as a complete reversal on contemporary notions of sexual identity in which masculinity is secured by heterosexual alliance. However, even today, in some bastions of aggressively heterosexual masculinity, truly intimate relations with women, as opposed to the use of women for sexual gratification, may well be considered a weakness, a tempering of "valor's steel."

The situation of male sexual identity in the Renaissance remains complex. On the one hand, there is no ontological difference between same-sex desire and heterosexual desire and yet "sodomy" was very much a proscribed and stigmatized though completely incoherent category of behavior (DiGangi 4–5; Bray, "Homosexuality" 14–16). It is important to emphasize that *sodomy* is in early modern England far more than a synonym for our word *homosexuality*, or even the early modern term *buggery* (Stewart xxi; Goldberg, "Open R's" 19). Sexual relations between men and with animals was proscribed by a law of 1553: "[T]he detestable and abominable vice of buggery committed with mankind or beast." No one, however, seems to have received a punishment for this behavior, at least not for homosexual activity alone (*Norton* 26). In contrast to *buggery* per se, *sodomy* was understood as disorderly sexual conduct that exceeded the mere fact of sex between men. Sodomy was in some ill-defined way potentially subversive, a threat to "the status quo of male homosocial relations" (Radel 93). In other words, sex between men *combined with* any number of possible social circumstances or ingredients — class transgression or political intrigue, for example, could potentially constitute sodomy. When Tybalt says, "Mercutio, thou consortest with Romeo" (3.1.37), is he trying to make a veiled, politically convenient accusation of sodomy (Radel 93)? Certainly, Tybalt returns to the same line of insult when he threatens Romeo after Mercutio's death: "Thou, wretched boy, that didst consort him here, / Shalt with him hence" (3.1.117–18). Mercutio's witty retort in act 3 implies he is aware of the full range of meanings that "consort" may carry, including the sense of sexual liaison: "'Consort'? What, dost thou make us minstrels?" (3.1.38).

While there remain considerable interpretive difficulties around male sexual practices and identities in this period, what is clear is that *Romeo and Juliet* contains a range of sexual discourses and practices that have been, until the very recent advent of queer theory and criticism, largely subsumed in favor of an interpretation of the play as an irredeemably "straight" tragedy. This erasure of the play's homoerotic dimension was impossible on the early modern stage, not least because Juliet was played by a male actor (see Callaghan, Helms, and Singh 61; Callaghan, *Shakespeare* 7). The first encounter between the lovers, after all, as Paul Hammond points out, requires the actors to join hands, then lips: "It is for spectators to decide what it is that they see, even though playwrights may from time to time wish to remind them of the boy actor behind the female role" (Hammond 45; see also Sinfield 1–20).

FIGHTING

At the opening of the play, the Capulet servants Samson and Gregory define themselves within completely masculine terms of identification as servants of the house of Capulet, as parties to a violent "quarrel" "between our masters and us their men" (Radel 93). Part of this violence is then directed against the women of the house of Montague whom they joke about raping:

> SAMSON: . . . I will push Montague's men from the wall and thrust his maids to the wall.
> GREGORY: The quarrel is between our masters and us their men.

> SAMSON: 'Tis all one. I will show myself a tyrant: when I have fought
>   with the men, I will be civil with the maids — I will cut off their heads.
> GREGORY: The heads of the maids?
> SAMSON: Ay, the heads of the maids, or their maidenheads. Take it in
>   what sense thou wilt. (1.1.14–21)

This is both an exchange about sexuality *between men* and simultaneously, a misogynous and potentially violent discourse *against women*. The passage is an example of a phenomenon described by Eve Sedgwick: "In any male-dominated society, there is a special relationship between male homosocial (*including* homosexual) bonds and the institution for maintaining and transmitting patriarchal power over women" (Sedgwick 127). In other words, violence is not so much the opposite of sex (either heterosexual or homosexual), its antithesis, but rather its instrument. Indeed, Samson and Gregory go on to make explicit the synonymy of "flesh" (penis) "tool" and "weapon," as the specifically sexual implements of the feud in the antagonism that ensues when the Montagues arrive: "Do you bite your thumb at us, sir?" (1.1.35). Since this is the case, when we consider violence in the play, we should not assume that it inhabits a completely different social space from the issues of male-male eroticism and male friendship, described above. Rather, we might consider violence as another type of relationship between men, and one that might be as potentially fraught with eroticism as the bonds of amity.

Violence was also in many ways integral rather than antithetical to the dynamics of kinship: the family that slayed together stayed together, as Lawrence Stone once wonderfully remarked. As we shall see in later sections of this chapter, feuding clans were a real threat to centralized sovereign power in this era. Elizabeth I had to contend, for example, with the rebellion of the northern earls in 1569, and even as late as the 1620s, there were pitched battles between armed retainers in the Strand (see Stone, *Crisis* 250–57).

FENCING MANUALS

> Thou hast quarreled with a man for coughing in the street, because he
> hath wakened thy dog that hath lain asleep in the sun. (3.1.29–21).

Swordfighting, or fencing, in Elizabethan London was a predominantly male sport. Taught and practiced in the fencing schools, it was enormously popular and used both in competition and military and civil combat. Enthusiasts followed the intricacies of swordplay with intense relish. Violence had always been something of a sport in England, but with the increased avail-ability in early Elizabethan England of the murderously efficient rapier, a two-edged sword that allowed a man to pierce his opponent through with a nimble thrust, it became a passion (Stone, *Crisis* 243). Gone were the cum-bersome and heavy broadswords and longswords, which required the trouble and tedium of heaving weapons out of the armory; rapiers were light enough to be worn as the fashionable accoutrement of a gentleman. When ire flared, it was possible to draw on an opponent almost anywhere with the long, light rapier and to do so with a reach far greater than that afforded by any conventional weapon.

The readiness of these new arms prompted increased endeavors on the part of the Crown to curb public violence. These new weapons made per-sonal assault much more dangerous. As Lawrence Stone points out:

> In spite of the substantial numbers involved and the fact that all combat-ants were armed, there was relatively little actual killing in the sixteenth century. . . . [T]he main reason was that the standard weapons used were the heavy sword with a single cutting edge and the buckler or shield. These weapons allowed the maximum muscular effort and the most spec-tacular show of violence with the minimum threat to life and limb. Fight-ing with them was not much more dangerous than all-in wrestling. (Stone, *Crisis* 243)

The rapier was a much more deadly weapon, needle sharp and able to pene-trate the body with vastly less exertion than the obsolete broad sword that Montague calls for in act 1. Playwright Ben Jonson was arraigned at the Old Bailey in October 1598 for the manslaughter of fellow actor Gabriel Spencer. The indictment charged that he

> with a certain sword of iron and steel called a Rapier, of the price of three shillings, which he then and there had in his right hand and held drawn, feloniously and willfully struck and beat the same Gabriel, then and there with the aforesaid sword giving to the same Gabriel Spencer, in and upon the same Gabriel's right side, a mortal wound, of the depth of six inches and of the breadth of one inch, of which mortal wound the same Gabriel Spencer then and there died instantly. (Quoted in Edelman 175)

In contrast, however, the kind of unintentional fatality that results in Mer-cutio's death was certainly very familiar in early modern London. While still in his teens in 1567, Edward, the seventeenth Earl of Oxford acciden-tally killed his servant with a rapier, and in 1598 the fifth earl of Sussex, like Romeo, seriously wounded one of his own men while trying to break up a quarrel (Stone, *Crisis* 243). However, because the code of the duel involved only the principals in the quarrel rather than large numbers of armed retainers, this in itself curbed the power of the nobility who were now more often compelled to rely on their own fencing skills (Stone, *Crisis* 245).

Efforts to curb violence were only partly successful as the duel became the most fashionable way to settle a quarrel. While the duel had the advantage (on the whole) of confining the broil to two combatants, it occurred so frequently that James I felt rapier fighting undermined the stability of the realm. Although the *vendetta,* as the name implies, was a distinctly Italian phenomenon, Lawrence Stone has shown that feuds were waged even in the center of London until at least the 1630s. This demonstrates how dangerous the shared identity of kinship groups might be and how they had the potential to turn against the crown. Indeed "the protocols of fighting" that inform the play not only facilitate the mechanics of plot but also add political implications, "producing a narrative driven by social disorder through violence" (Stone, *Family* 83). On the stage this violence is figured both in terms of plot and of the stage properties it requires: swords and bucklers, the old-fashioned long sword belonging to Juliet's father, the rapiers of the young men of Verona, daggers, knives, and clubs. With the dagger that penetrates Juliet's bosom, the violence of Verona eventually penetrates the private world of the lovers, and even, sacrilegiously, the resting place of the dead.

The swordplay in *Romeo and Juliet* was probably precisely choreographed, for spectators were likely to have had sophisticated knowledge of, and even firsthand experience in the art of fencing. There were a number of fairly distinct national styles: Spanish (employed by Tybalt in his counted paces), English (generally regarded at the time as rather retrograde), and Italian. Had there been a World Cup in sword fighting, the Italians would undoubtedly have won it. *Romeo and Juliet* includes a plethora of Italian fencing terms, including *passado* (2.4.23; 3.1.74) (a pass or step forward or a side step), *punto reverso* (2.4.23) (a thrust delivered at the attacker's left side, usually over the opponent's weapon with the hand in supination, i.e., knuckles down, nails up), *hay* (2.4.23) (meaning "have at you now"), and *alla stoccata* (3.1.65) (meaning "at the thrust," reaching the enemy *under* the sword, hand, or dagger). None of these terms appears in Arthur Brooke's *Romeus and Juliet,* Shakespeare's source (Homer 164; 167). Clearly, fencing was a specifically dramatic element and one which had singular appeal for Shakespeare's audiences. As a very refined form of violence, swordplay distinguished itself from the mere thuggery of the lower orders. When menials like Samson and Gregory are equipped with weapons, are their "washing blow[s]" the powerful but relatively straightforward strokes of those more used to handling blunt instruments than rapiers? When Samson urges

"Gregory, remember thy washing blow" (1.1.50) at the start of the affray in act 1 scene 1, would the audience have recognized two aspiring fencers or two servants who were inept swordsmen? Certainly, Tybalt, "The very butcher of a silk button" (2.4.21), Mercutio, Romeo, and Benvolio demonstrate unequivocally accomplished swordsmanship, a dexterity and agility that lend heightened dramatic tension to their armed encounters.

Although there is no dueling as such in the play — no one sets a pre-arranged time for combat — Tybalt does send Romeo a challenge:

> BENVOLIO: Tybalt, the kinsman to old Capulet,
>   Hath sent a letter to his father's house.
> MERCUTIO: A challenge, on my life. (2.4.6–8)

In his compelling account of martial arts in the Renaissance, Sydney Anglo writes:

> [T]he habit of carrying arms and of being trained in the arts of killing did not merely induce men to duel. Such training also informed their behavior outside the formal structures of challenge and reply, and of rules seeking to impose equality on the combatants. There were many upper-class fools prepared to observe the niceties, but there must have been a far greater number of belligerents sufficiently intelligent to ensure that violence was, as far as possible, weighted in their favor — whether this meant knifing an enemy in the back, blinding him with a handful of grit, or throwing a tankard of ale in his face before kicking him in the testicles. (37)

The decade in which *Romeo and Juliet* was written saw not only the publication of major works on the topic of fencing by Saviolo and Silver (excerpted below), but also Giacomo di Grassi's *His True Art of Defense* (1594) and Sir William Segar's *The Book of Honor and Arms* (1590). (Part of the latter was an abridgement of the second book of Saviolo's *Practice*.) In addition, we know (from references in the plays of Shakespeare's contemporaries) that the work of the Spanish master Jeronimo Sanchez de Carranza, *De la Filosofia de las Armas* (1569), was also available in England. Carranza taught the technique of "complement," that is, complementing the steps of an opponent, almost dancing with him, and doing so with mathematical precision. This is the "book of arithmetic" (3.1.89–90) to which Mercutio derisively refers and involved diagrams on the floor and walls of the fencing studio to aid the combatant (Homer 188; Soens 124). This is what makes Tybalt "captain of compliments" (2.4.18–19), That his pacing "keeps time, distance, and proportion" (2.4.19–20); and that "he swung about his head and cut the winds" (1.1.98) also identify him with the Spanish school of fencing.

Swordsmanship and the skill attendant upon it served as an elegant rationalization for violence. While local administration was perfectly competent to deal with most lower-class disorders in Elizabethan England, they were usually unable to address quarrels among the nobility, be they duels fought out in a moment of ire, or longstanding feuds. More important, there was no really effective mechanism to punish the guilty among the landed classes. If they were at all held to account, nobles would arrive at the quarter sessions (local court sessions of limited jurisdiction that sat quarterly) or assizes (the periodic court sessions held throughout England and Wales) with a following of armed retainers and threaten the court (Stone, *Crisis* 230–31). The feuding Russell and Berkeley houses, for example, brought 500 armed men with them to court at Worcester, and the retinues of Lord Morley and his antagonist, Lord Strange, began a bloody affray at the Lancaster assizes of 1581. In 1558 in Fleet Street, in the heart of the city of London, Sir John Perrot and William Phelippes, supported by their men, set to fighting, and in that street alone there were further skirmishes between aristocrats and their retainers in 1573, 1578, and 1596 (Stone, *Crisis* 231–32). The Strand was another popular and central location for armed conflict between noblemen in London. Violence that took place at Smithfield, a less populated urban location, was more in the way of what we might call private conflict, where assignations for duels might be made rather than the more public feuding that saw pitched battles in the streets of London itself. One contemporary, Edmund Howes, in his continuation of Stowe's *Annals* describes it as follows:

> This field commonly called West Smithfield, was for many years called Ruffians hall, by reason it was the usual place of affrays and common fighting, during the time that sword and buckler were in use. . . . This manner of fight was frequent with all men, until the fight of the rapier and dagger took place and then suddenly the general quarrel of fighting abated which began about the 20th year of Queen Elizabeth [1579], for until then it was usual to have 'frays, fights, and quarrels, upon the Sundays and holidays . . . (quoted in Levenson 92)

It is to a location of this type that Benvolio urges Mercutio and Tybalt to withdraw: "We talk here in the public haunt of men. / Either withdraw unto some private place, / Or reason coldly of your grievances, / Or else depart; here all eyes gaze on us" (3.1.41–44). The Prince has, of course, forbidden such combat specifically in the streets of Verona, but it is not clear whether such conduct would be tolerated if it occurred in "some private place." Interestingly, no one considers moving out of the public space for rational discussion; the only alternative considered is that of adjourning to have the confrontation without state censure. Benvolio's reluctance to stage the conflict openly suggests that Escalus's prohibition has had some impact on him, even if it is not shared by his more quarrelsome contemporaries.

The focus for much of the fighting action in London was St. Paul's Cathedral, the very heart of the Elizabethan city. (The cathedral was not Sir Christopher Wren's great edifice, which now stands in the same location, but an earlier building.) In the center of the churchyard at St. Paul's Cross, important proclamations were made, such as the news of the defeat of the Spanish Armada in 1588. But there were strong contemporary criticisms of the use to which St. Paul's, and St. Paul's walk (the middle aisle of the cathedral) was made by men from the fencing schools who sought to try their swordsmanship in a real fight. One bishop in 1561 complained about the uses of the cathedral: "The south alley for popery and usury, the north for simony, and the horse fair in the midst for all kinds of bargains, meetings, brawlings, murders, conspiracies" (Salgado 9).

Despite the urgency of ire and popularity of bloodshed, there were considerable moral contradictions involved not only in the practice of dueling but in the matter of sword fighting in general, which concerned the ethics of vengeance. As Sir William Segar observed in the preface to *The Book of Honor and Arms* (1590):

> The cause of all quarrel is injury and reproach, but the matter of content is justice and honor. . . . True it is, that the Christian law willeth men to be of so perfect patience, as not only to endure injurious words, but also quietly to suffer every force and violence. Not withstanding for so much as none (or very few men) have attained such perfection, the laws of all nations, for avoiding further inconveniences, and the manifestation of truth, have (among many other trials) permitted, that such questions as could not be civilly proved by concession, witness, or other circumstances, should receive judgment by fight and combat, supposing that God (who only knoweth the secret thoughts of all men) would give victory to him that justly adventured his life, for truth, honor and justice. (A2–3)

Segar sidesteps the indisputable fact that Christian ethics forbade revenge and tries to reconcile his principles with a plea to God's providence, in which God supposedly supports the victor in any fair fight. Christian pacifism, in Segar's view, would make a man a doormat, and so training in combat becomes a pragmatic necessity. This ethical uncertainty surfaces less directly in other tracts of the period, and by and large the gory reality of "purple fountains" (1.1.72) and "bloody hands" (1.1.73) enacted in the play is obscured by the emphasis of the fencing manuals on skill and precision. Violence is here refined into an art far removed from the grim realities of death. In this there is something of the surprise and even annoyance expressed by Mercutio when he discovers that the sport of swords can end his life: "A plague o' both your houses . . . to scratch a man to death" (3.1.87–89).

→ RICHARD BARNFIELD

From The Affectionate Shepherd   *1594*

Containing the Complaint of Daphnis for the Love of Ganymede.
Amor plus mellis, quam fellis est.[1]

Barnfield (1574–c. 1626) was born in Shropshire and attended Brasenose College, Oxford. He is thought to have later studied law at Gray's Inn, although no record to this effect survives. Whether or not he was officially enrolled at one of the Inns of Court (essentially, the colleges at which young men studied for a legal career), Barnfield was certainly part of the social milieu of ambitious young men anxious to demonstrate their talents in the world, clamoring for recognition and social advancement. More than anything, the Inns of Court was a cultured metropolitan environment where young men exchanged poetry to please and impress other young men with their eloquence. The *Dictionary of National Biography* (1917) makes the following telling (and homophobic) observation about the insistently homoerotic tenor of Barnfield's verses:

> All his best early pieces, and especially his sonnets, are dedicated to a sentiment of friendship so exaggerated as to remove them beyond wholesome sympathy. Even in the Elizabethan age, when great warmth and candor were permitted, the tone of these sonnets was felt to be unguarded. It is only of late that something like justice has been done to the great poetical qualities of Barnfield, to his melody, picturesqueness, and limpid sweetness.

Barnfield seems to have spent his early life in the company of literary notables of the time such as Thomas Watson and Frances Meres, and (very

---

[1] *Amor plus mellis, quam fellis est:* love is a matter more of sweetness than of bitterness; probably derives from Plautus, *Cistellaria*, 1.1.170, "amor et melle et felle fecunissimus," "love is most fertile both in sweetness and bitterness"; see note 30.

Richard Barnfield, *The Affectionate Shepherd. Containing the Complaint of Daphnis for the Love of Ganymede* (London, 1594), 79–86.

probably) Shakespeare. He stopped writing at the age of twenty-four, and was long believed to have retired to a quiet life in the country, proof of which was allegedly found in a will recording that Barnfield had a son, Robert, and a granddaughter, Jane (Klawitter 19). This fact was taken to support the belief that homosexual practices in early modern England were not at all at odds with patrilineal inheritance, marriage, and heterosexuality as dominant and normative social structures.

However, this view has been recently overturned by Andrew Worrall, who unearthed evidence that the records of Barnfield's so-called return to heterosexuality in the countryside refer not to the poet but to the poet's father. Worrall claims also that there were legal attempts to disinherit Barnfield in favor of his younger brother, Robert. According to Worrall, Barnfield died in 1620 or 1626, apparently unmarried and estranged from his family (Worrall 25–38). Worrall's discovery lends support to Claude J. Summers's concern that: "In promulgating the idea that there were no homosexuals (by whatever name) in Renaissance England, only individuals who committed sodomitical acts without ever recognizing themselves as sodomites, . . . gay theorists have trapped Renaissance 'sodomites' within a hegemonic ideology that denies them either self-awareness or agency" (Summers 9). Once again, however, rather than resolving the issue of how we read male sexuality in early modern England and in *Romeo and Juliet,* what we know about Barnfield merely adds to its complexity.

The following excerpts are from Barnfield's gracefully written variation on the second eclogue[2] of the Latin poet, Virgil. The "Ganymede" of the title is a mythical reference to Jove's cup-bearer and boy-lover, who was for the Elizabethans synonymous with a young male whore (see Stewart xvii). The book is dedicated to the woman who had spurned Sir Philip Sidney, Lady Penelope Rich. She was the Stella of Sidney's *Astrophil and Stella* and mistress of Charles Blount, Lord Mountjoy, whom she later married after divorcing her first husband, Lord Rich.

The poet identifies himself as the forlorn shepherd, Daphnis, and there is considerable critical speculation about the ostensibly "real" identities of the poem's other characters. While there was undoubtedly political innuendo as poems were circulated among courtiers and young men from the Inns of Court, it is probably a mistake to read these verses as puzzles rather than as poems, as if they could be deciphered with an allegorical key. Rather, Barnfield's poetry is, as Bruce Smith has observed, "a precisely imagined sexual fantasy . . . Barnfield's quite distinctive 'interpersonal script' for homosexual lovemaking" (Smith, *Homosexual* 100). In this, Barnfield's sexual imagination may parallel that of Mercutio's, and his verses offer a context for the play's unrelenting use of phallic puns as well.

---

[2] **eclogue:** a pastoral verse dialogue, that is, a dialogue set in an artificial, idealized and literary version of the countryside.

From *The Affectionate Shepherd*

Scarce had the morning star hid from the light
Heaven's crimson canopy with stars bespangled,
But I began to rue th'unhappy sight
Of that fair boy that had my heart entangled;
    Cursing the time, the place, the sense, the sin;   5
    I came, I saw, I viewed, I slipped in.

If it be sin to love a sweet-fac'd boy,
(Whose amber locks trussed up in golden tramels[3]
Dangle adown his lovely cheeks with joy,
When pearl and flowers his fair hair enamels)   10
    If it be sin to love a lovely lad;
    Oh then sin I, for whom my soul is sad.

His ivory-white and alabaster skin
Is stained throughout with rare vermillion red,
Whose twinkling starry lights do never blin[k]   15
To shine on lovely *Venus* (Beauty's bed:)
    But as the lily and the blushing rose,
    So white and red on him in order grows.

. . . .

Oh would she[4] would forsake my *Ganymede*,   25
Whose surged love is full of sweet delight,
Upon whose forehead you may plainly read
Loves pleasure, grav'd in ivory tables bright:
    In whose fair eyeballs you may clearly see
    Base love still stained with foul indignity.   30

Oh would to God he would but pity me,
That love him more than any mortal wight![5]
Then he and I with love would soon agree,
That now cannot abide his suitor's sight.
    O would to God (so I might have my fee)[6]   35
    My lips were honey, and thy mouth a bee.

Then shouldst thou suck my sweet and my fair flower
That now is ripe, and full of honey-berries:
Then would I lead thee to my pleasant bower

---

[3] **tramels**: nets, ties.   [4] **she**: Guendolena, queen of beauty in the poem, see line 97.   [5] **wight**:
person.   [6] **so I might have my fee**: get sexual satisfaction; have my love returned.

Filled full of grapes, of mulberries, and cherries;   40
   Then shouldst thou be my wasp or else my bee,
   I would thy hive, and thou my honey bee.

I would put amber bracelets on thy wrists,
Coronets of pearl about thy naked arms:
And when thou sits at swilling *Bacchus'*[7] feasts   45
My lips with charms should save thee from all harms:
   And when in sleep thou tookest thy chiefest pleasure,
   Mine eyes should gaze upon thine eyelids' treasure.

And every morn by dawning of the day,
When *Phoebus*[8] riseth with a blushing face,   50
Silvanus[9] chapel-clerks shall chant a lay,
And play thee hunts-up in thy resting place:
   My cote[10] thy chamber, my bosom thy bed;
   Shall be appointed for thy sleepy head.

And when it pleaseth thee to walk abroad,   55
(Abroad into the fields to take fresh air:)
The meads with *Flora's*[11] treasure should be strode,
(The mantled meadows, and the fields so fair.)
   And by a silver well (with golden sands)
   I'll sit me down, and wash thine ivory hands.   60

And in the sweltering heat of summer time,
I would make cabinets for thee (my love:)
Sweet-smelling arbors made of eglantine[12]
Should be thy shrine, and I would be thy dove.
   Cool cabinets of fresh green laurel boughs   65
   Should shadow us, ore-set[13] with thick-set yews.

Or if thou list[14] to bathe thy naked limbs,
Within the crystal of a pearl-bright brook,
Paved with dainty pebbles to the brims;
Or clear, wherein thyself thy self mayst look;   70
   We'll go to *Ladon*,[15] whose still trickling noise,
   Will lull thee fast asleep amidst thy joys.

---

[7] *Bacchus':* god of intoxication, both of the spiritual and alcoholic kinds.   [8] *Phoebus:* Apollo, the sun god.   [9] *Silvanus:* forest deity.   [10] **cote:** cottage.   [11] *Flora's:* goddess of the flowers.   [12] **eglantine:** the sweetbrier flower.   [13] **ore-set:** overset; overlaid.   [14] **thou list:** you want.   [15] *Ladon:* a river in Arcadia (paradisal pastoral landscape).

Or if thou't go unto the riverside,
To angle for the sweet freshwater fish;
Arm'd with thy implements that will abide   75
(Thy rod, hook, line) to take a dainty dish;
    Thy rods shall be of cane, thy lines of silk,
    Thy hooks of silver, and thy baits of milk.

Or if thou lov'st to hear sweet melody,
Or pipe a round upon an oaten reed,[16]   80
Or make thy self glad with some mirthful glee,
Or play them music whilst thy flock doth feed;
    To *Pan's* own pipe I'll help my lovely lad,
    (*Pan's* golden pipe) which he of *Syrinx*[17] had.

Or if thou darest to climb the highest trees   85
For apples, cherries, medlars,[18] pears, or plums,
Nuts, walnuts, filberts, chestnuts, cervices,[19]
The hoary peach, when snowy winter comes;
    I have fine orchards full of mellowed fruit;
    Which I will give thee to obtain my suit.   90

Not proud *Alcinous*[20] himself can vaunt,[21]
Of goodlier orchards or of braver trees
Than I have planted; yet thou will not grant
My simple suit; but like the honey bees
    Thou suckest the flower till all the sweet be gone;   95
    And lov'st me for my coin till I have none.

Leave *Guendolen* (sweet heart) though she be fair
Yet she be light; not light in virtue shining:
But light in her behavior, to impair
Her honor in her chastity's declining;   100
    Trust not her tears, for they can wantonize,
    When tears in pearl are trickling from her eyes.

If thou wilt come and dwell with me at home;
My sheepcote[22] shall be strowed with new green rushes:
We'll haunt the trembling prickets[23] as they roam   105
About the fields, along the hawthorn bushes;

---

[16] **oaten reed:** pipe; a musical instrument. [17] *Syrinx:* nymph transformed into a reed. [18] **medlars:** a fruit. See p. 207. [19] **cervices:** a fruit. [20] *Alcinous:* king of the island of Phaeacia; he had a huge palace garden. [21] **vaunt:** boast. [22] **sheepcote:** sheep pen. [23] **prickets:** young bucks.

I have a pie-bald cur to hunt the hare,
So we will live with dainty forest fare.

Nay, more than this, I have a garden plot,
Wherein there wants nor herbs, nor roots, nor flowers;   110
(Flowers to smell, roots to eat, herbs for the pot,)
And dainty shelters when the welkin[24] lowers:
  Sweet-smelling beds of lilies, and of roses,
  Which rosemary banks and lavender encloses.

There grows the gillyflower, the mint, the daisy   115
(Both red and white), the blue-veined violet:
The purple hyacinth, the spike to please thee,
The scarlet died carnation bleeding yet;
  The sage, the savory, and sweet marjoram,
  Hyssop, thyme, and eye-bright, good for the blind and dumb.   120

The pink, the primrose, cowslip, and daffodil,
The harebell blue, the crimson columbine,
Sage, lettuce, parsley, and the milk-white lily,
The rose, and speckled flower called sops in wine.
  Fine pretty kingcups, and the yellow boots,   125
  That grows by rivers, and by shallow brooks.

And many thousand more (I cannot name)
Of herbs and flowers that in gardens grow,
I have for thee: and conies[25] that be tame,
Young rabbits, white as swan, and black as crow,   130
  Some speckled here and there with dainty spots:
  And more I have two milk and milk-white goats.

All these, and more, I'll give thee for thy love;
If these, and more, may 'tice[26] thy love away:
I have a pigeon-house, in it a dove,
Which I love more than mortal tongue can say: 135
  And last of all, I'll give thee a little lamb
  To play withal, new-weaned from her dam.

But if thou wilt not pity my complaint,
My tears, nor vows, nor oaths, made to thy beauty;   140
What shall I do? But languish, die, or faint,
Since thou dost scorn my tears, and my soul's duty:

---

[24] **welkin:** firmament; the expanse of the heavens.   [25] **conies:** rabbits.   [26] **'tice:** entice.

And tears contemned, vows and oaths must fail;
And where tears cannot, nothing can prevail.

Compare the love of fair Queen *Guendolen*   145
With mine, and thou shalt see how she doth love thee:
I love thee for thy qualities divine,
But she doth love another swain above thee:
   I love thee for thy gifts, she for her pleasure;
   I for thy virtue, she for beauty's treasure.   150

And always (I am sure) it cannot last,
But sometime Nature will deny those dimples:
Instead of beauty (when thy blossom's past)
Thy face will be deformed, full of wrinkles:
   Then she that lov'd thee for thy beauty's sake,   155
   When age draws on, thy love will soon forsake.

But I that lov'd thee for thy gifts divine,
In the December of thy beauty's waning,
Will still admire (with joy) those lovely eine,[27]
That now behold me with their beauty's baning.[28]   160
   Though January will never come again,
   Yet April years will come in showers of rain.

When will my May come, that I may embrace thee?
When will the hour be of my soul's joying?
Why dost thou seek in mirth still to disgrace me?   165
Whose mirth's my health, whose grief's my heart's annoying.
   Thy bane my bale, thy bliss my blessedness,
   Thy ill my hell, thy weal my welfare is.

Thus do I honor thee that love thee so,
And love thee so, that so do honor thee,   170
Much more than any mortal man doth know,
Or can discern by love or jealousy:
   But if that thou disdainst my loving ever;
   Oh happy I, if I had loved never! *Finis.*

Plus fellis quam mellis amor.[29]   175

---

[27] **eine:** eyes.   [28] **baning:** life-destroying, woe-inducing.   [29] *Plus fellis quam mellis amor:* Love is a matter more of bitterness than of sweetness.

FIGURE 6 *Medlars, or Open Arses, from* The Great Herbal *(1529). As the full title of this book explains,* The Great Herbal *aims to "giveth perfect knowledge and understanding of all manner of herbs [and] their gracious virtues which God hath ordained for our prosperous welfare and health." Early modern remedies were derived from plants, and it is precisely this science in which Friar Laurence has considerable expertise. As we see, plant extracts could also be used for poisons.*

The emphasis of the Herbal *is on the medicinal properties of plants, fruits, and flowers. Its relevance to the documents in this section, however, is that the medlar (whose Latin horticultural name is* mespilus germanica*) depicted here, was thought to resemble the cleft of the posterior or the pudenda. In other words, the fruit constitutes a visual pun, and this is particularly significant in relation to* Romeo and Juliet, *a play that puns relentlessly not just to interject humor onto the somber tragic scene, but, as Stephen Greenblatt points out, "to cram into brief utterances more meanings than language would ordinarily hold" (* Norton *867; see also Bly 64). The* medlar *is mentioned by Mercutio (2.1.35) and in Barnfield's profoundly homoerotic poem,* The Affectionate Shepherd *(line 86). It illustrates (because of its resemblance to the human backside) the early modern preoccupation with the confusion or reversal of all that is back to front, "preposterous." (See Parker 186–213.) That is, what was literally "posterior," the backside, could subvert the proper order of front before back, "arsie versie" ("ass backwards") (Parker 186).*

→ VINCENTIO SAVIOLO

From His Practice

Vincentio Saviolo was a popular Italian fencing master in Elizabethan London who came to England from Padua in 1590. He taught at the fencing college that had been established in 1576 by the Italian master Rocco Bonnetti and his famous assistant, Jeronimo. Saviolo advocated the theory that the point of the weapon is quicker than the edge and professed to be able to teach his pupils how to thrust two feet farther than any possible rival. Despite rivalry between English and Italian fencing masters, the Englishman George Silver declared him to be "one of the valiantest fencers that ever came from beyond the seas" (Morton, n.p.).

Practice was dedicated to Robert Devereux, the second earl of Essex (1566–1601), who distinguished himself as a soldier and favorite of Elizabeth I. As one of the court's most dashing noblemen, he was the very model of English masculinity — at least until his ignominious fall from grace. Just as it is in Shakespeare's Verona, Elizabethan manhood was vulnerable on many fronts, and Essex was executed in 1601 for attempted rebellion.

Saviolo is particularly important in relation to *Romeo and Juliet* because Shakespeare has Mercutio ridicule his fashionable theories in the play. Saviolo's manual, published in 1595, is contemporaneous with *Romeo and Juliet,* and there is no doubt that at that time his ideas about fencing were popular, indeed sensational, in Elizabethan London. Furthermore, John Florio, who knew Saviolo, described him in *Florio's Second Fruits* (1591) as "that Italian [who] looks like Mars himself, and he is most patient, neither doth he go about to revenge any injury that is offered him, unless it touch his credit and honor very far" (Homer 188–89).

Saviolo's text takes the form of a dialogue between Vincentio and his student, Luke. While a considerable portion of the text is devoted to the description of various "wards," that is fencing postures and strategies, Saviolo also discusses the causes of quarrels and what justifies "going into the field" in order to engage in combat. Saviolo had in mind prearranged duels, in which one man issued a challenge to another and demanded that he meet him at a set time to settle the dispute by means of armed combat. Saviolo conceded, however, that there were also times when a man would try to provoke an enemy upon a chance meeting in order to secure an advantage over him. All such fighting was undertaken to maintain one's honor and redress any insult, perceived or actual. Saviolo's student in this dialogue, Luke, expresses concern about fighting and killing friends. Defending one's person, his master assures him, requires that the

Vincentio Saviolo, *Vincentio Saviolo His Practice in Two Books. The First Entreating the Use of the Rapier and the Dagger. The Second, of Honor and Honorable Quarrels* (London, 1595), 209–45, 266–69, 336–39.

combatant nurture hatred rather than ambivalence about killing a friend. A combatant may find himself, then, as Romeo does in the play, compelled to murder a man he does not really hate. The ideal combatant was, of course, the morally as well as physically disciplined warrior who did not rush into the fray at the merest slight. But reality was somewhat different, and some men found any excuse to pick an ostensibly honorable quarrel. Once the duel had begun, all notions of peace were actively dangerous, and Saviolo clearly anticipates the situation in which Romeo finds himself, that is, where intervening in the fight brings not the peaceful cessation of conflict but only fatal results.

Book I

VINCENTIO: For your rapier, hold it as you shall think most fit and commodious for you, but if I might advise you, you should not hold it after this fashion, and especially with the second finger in the hilt, for holding it in that sort, you cannot reach so far either to strike direct or cross blows, or to give a feign or thrust, because your arm is not free and at liberty.

LUKE: How then would you have me hold it?

VINCENTIO: I would have you put your thumb on the hilt and the next finger toward the edge of the rapier, for so you shall reach further and strike more readily.

LUKE: You have fully satisfied me concerning this matter, but I pray you proceed and show me how I must stand upon my guard, or assail mine enemy.

VINCENTIO: So I will, and as before I have told you of diversity of teachers and variety of wards, so in this point also must I tell you that men's fashions are diverse, for some set upon their enemies in running, and there are other which assail them with rage and fury after the fashion of rams, and both these sorts of men for the most part are slain and come to misfortune, as may be seen in many places of such like fights. Which I speak not as though those two fights were not good for him which knows how to use them, because that sometimes they are very necessary, according as a man finds his enemy prepared with his weapon but then they must be done with time and measure, when you have got your enemy at an advantage, with great dexterity and readiness. But as for me I will show you the wards which I myself use, the which if you well mark and observe, you cannot but understand the art, and withal keep your body safe from hurt and danger.

LUKE: At this present I take wonderful delight in your company, and nothing pleaseth me so much as this discourse of yours, to hear you give me the reasons of those things which so much concern the life and honor of a man: wherefore perform that which you have promised, wherein you shall not only pleasure me, but many other gentlemen and noble men will think themselves to have received a favor at your hands, therefore begin I pray you.

VINCENTIO: That which I have promised you I will now perform, therefore I say, that when a teacher will begin to make a scholar, (as for me I will begin with the single rapier, and at this weapon will first enter you,[1] to the end you may frame your hand, your foot, and your body, all which parts must go together, and unless you can stir and move all these together, you shall never be able to perform any great matter, but with great danger) I come therefore to the point and say, that when the teacher will enter his scholar,[2] he shall cause him to stand upon this ward, which is very good to be taught for framing the foot, the hand, and the body: so the teacher shall deliver the rapier into his hand, and shall cause him to stand with his right foot foremost, with his knee somewhat bowing, but that his body rest more upon the left leg, not steadfast and firm as some stand, which seem to be nailed to the place, but with a readiness and nimbleness, as though he were to perform some feat of activity, and in this sort let them stand both to strike and to defend themselves. Now when the master hath placed his scholar in this sort, and that the scholar hath received his rapier into his hand, let him make his hand free and at liberty, not by force of the arm, but by the nimble and ready moving of the joint of the wrist of the hand, so that his hand be free and at liberty from his body, and that the ward of his hand be directly against his right knee and let the teacher also put himself in the same ward, and hold his rapier against the middle of his scholar's rapier, so that the point be directly against the face of his scholar, and likewise his scholar's against his, and let their feet be right one against another, then shall the master begin to teach him, moving his right foot somewhat on the right side in circle wise, putting the point of his rapier under his scholar's rapier, and so giving him a thrust in the belly.

LUKE: And what then must the scholar do?

VINCENTIO: At the selfsame time the scholar must remove with like measure or counter-time with his right foot a little aside, and let the left foot follow the right, turning a little his body on the right side, thrusting the point of his rapier at the belly of his teacher, turning readily his hand that the fingers be inward toward the body, and the joint of the wrist be outward. In this sort the said scholar shall learn to strike and not be stricken,

---

[1] **will first enter upon:** will be your first introduction. [2] **enter his scholar:** begin to instruct his students.

FIGURE 7 *Two Men Fencing, from Vincentio Saviolo*, His Practice, *1595. This picture demonstrates how to position the body in combat. The markings on the floor, like the "mathematical" fighting Mercutio derides ("a villain, that fights by the book of arithmetic!" [3.1.89–90]), shows the number of paces between the combatants as well as the width of the stance required in order to execute the maneuver. Note here the formal dress of the swordsmen, especially the tall, feathered hats, part of the fashionable accoutrement of a gentleman.*

as I always advise the noblemen and gentlemen with whom I have to deal, that if they cannot hit or hurt their enemy, that they learn to defend themselves that they be not hurt. Then to make the scholar more ready, the teacher shall cause his scholar first to part, wherefore he shall remove with his right foot on the right side a little in circle-wise as the master did before to the scholar.

LUKE: What then must the master or teacher do?

VINCENTIO: At the same time that the scholar removeth his foot, the teacher shall play a little with stirring of his body, and with his left hand shall beat away his scholar's rapier from his left side, and shall remove his right foot behind his left striking a cross blow at the head.

LUKE: And the scholar, what shall he do?

VINCENTIO: When I remove with my foot and lift up my hand, let the scholar pass with his left foot where his right was, and withal let him turn his hand, and not lose the opportunity of this blow, which must be a feign in manner of a thrust under his rapier, and let him lift up his hand with his ward that he be guarded and lie not open, meeting with his left hand the rapier of his teacher, and let him not beat aside the blow with his rapier for he endangereth the point and brings his life in hazard, because he loseth the point: But I will go forward. At the selfsame time that the scholar goes back, the master shall play a little, and shifting his body shall break the same imbroccata[3] or feign outward from the left side, removing with his left foot, which must be carried behind the right, and withal shall give a mandritta[4] at the head of his scholar, at which time the scholar must remove with his right foot, following with his left, and let him turn his rapier hand as I have said, and that the scholar observe the same time in going back as the teacher shall, to the end that his point may be toward the belly of his master, and let him lift up his other hand with his ward on high, that he be not stricken on the face with the mandritta, or in the belly with the thrust or stoccata. Wherefore at the selfsame time that the scholar shall deliver the aforesaid stoccata to the teacher, the teacher shall yield and shrink with his body, and beat the stoccata outward on the left side, and shall bring his right foot a little aside with the same measure, and shall beat aside the imbroccata of his master with his left hand outward from the left side, and withal shall deliver the like imbroccata of countertime to the teacher, but only to the face, and then the master shall go back with his right foot toward the left side of his scholar, in breaking with his left hand the said imbroccata outward from the left side, and shall strike a downright blow to his head, because that by beating aside his feign with his hand, he shall find him naked and without guard.

LUKE: And what then, cannot the scholar defend himself?

VINCENTIO: Yes, very easily with a ready dexterity or nimbleness, for at the same time that the master shall give the said mandritta, the scholar shall do nothing else but turn the point of his foot toward the body of his master, and let the middest of his left foot directly respect the heel of the right, and let him turn his body upon the right side, but let it rest and stay upon the left, and in the same time let him turn the rapier hand outward in the stoccata or thrust, as I have given you to understand before, that the point be toward the belly of his master, and let him lift up his hand

---

[3] **imbroccata:** a thrust with the hand pronated (knuckles forward, palm outward) passing over the opponent's hand and downward.   [4] **mandritta:** any cut made from right to left.

and take good heed that he come not forward in delivering the said stoccata, which is half an incartata,[5] for how soever little he should come forward, he would put himself in danger of his life: and believe me, every
man which shall not understand these measures and principles, incurs
the danger of his life: and who so despiseth these grounds which are necessary as well for the school as the combat, it may be to his confusion and
dishonor, and loss of his life: wherefore every one which makes profession of this art, should seek to learn and understand them. . . .

LUKE: But I pray you of friendship tell me, if a man were to go into the
field with some friend of his whom he would be loathe to kill, should not
these mandrittas be good to wound him, and not put him in danger of
his life, I pray you therefore tell me your opinion, and how a man in
respect of his honor were to use and order himself, put the case he would
not kill his friend, but would willingly save and keep him from harm?

VINCENTIO: I will speak mine opinion of these things which concern a
man's life and honor, and first I would with every one which is challenged
into the field, to consider that he which challengeth him, doth not
require to fight with him as a friend, but as an enemy, and that he is not
to think any otherwise of his mind but as full of rancor and malice
towards him: wherefore when you see one with weapons in his hand that
will needs fight with you, although he were your friend or kinsman, take
him for an enemy, and trust him not, how great a friend or how nigh of
kin soever he be, for the inconvenience that may grow thereby, is seen in
many histories both ancient and modern. But when you see the naked
blade or weapon, consider that it means redress of wrong, justice, and
revenge: and therefore if he be your friend that will needs fight with you,
you may tell him that you have given him no cause, nor offered any
wrong, and if any other have made any false report, & that he is to prove
and justify it, that for your self, if by chance without your knowledge you
have offended him, that you are ready with reason to satisfy him and
make amends. But if they be matters that touch your honor and that you
be compelled to accept of the combat, do the best you can when you have
your weapon in your hand, and consider that fights are dangerous, and
you know not the mind and purpose of your enemy, whom if you should
chance to spare, afterwards peradventure he may kill you or put you in
danger of your life, especially when you use the mandritta or right blows:
for if he be either a man skillful at his weapon, or fierce or furious, he may
peradventure do that to you, which you would not do, (when you might)

---

[5] **incartata:** a circular step forward and to the right made by passing the left foot behind the
right.

to him. Wherefore if he be your friend go not with him into the field, but if you go, do your best, because it seemeth childish to say, I will go and fight, but I will spare and favor him. For if you were the valiantest man in the world, and had no mind to do him any harm, yet when you see the fury and malice of your enemy, you shall be forced, as it were, to do that you thought not to do, for which you may peradventure be sorry, and disquieted in mind as long as you live, as well in respect of friendship, if you kill your friend, as for the punishment which the laws will inflict and lay upon you, whether it be loss of goods, imprisonment, or death. And on the other side, if you be slain or wounded, it is no excuse for you to say afterward, that you favored him & did not so much as you might, for in such a case every man will think as he [likes] so that if your enemy were the most coward and base man that might be, yet he shall be counted the more valiant and brave man. Therefore if it happen that some friend of yours hath a quarrel against you, tell him that you will not have anything to do with him: and fight with your enemy, not with your friend: neither account him your friend that will fight with you: well you may be his friend, but you shall find him to be your enemy. Therefore whensoever you see any man draw upon you, stay not until he do his pleasure, and trust him not, for he hath not his weapon drawn to no purpose: and if in that sort he will talk of the matter with you, cause him to stand aloof off, and so let him speak: for of the inconvenience that hath grown thereby we have many examples, as I will show you more at large by and by. I would wish that everyone should beware to offend any man either in words or deeds, and if you have offered offense, seek to make amends, as a civil and honest man should, and suffer not the matter to grow to such extremity and inconvenience, as we see examples everyday, whereby God is highly displeased. And amongst others I will tell you of an accident which hath happened in *Padua*, where I myself was born, of a master of fence called M. *Angelo* of *Alezza*, who many years brought up, maintained, and taught a nephew of his, in such sort, that he became a very sufficient and skillful man in this art. Which his nephew, whereas by reason should have been loving and faithful to him, as to his own father, having so long eaten of his bread, and received from him so many good turns, especially having been brought up by him from his childhood and infancy, he did the quite contrary, for his Uncle *Angelo* yet living and teaching scholars, he openly did teach and play with many, and by that means came acquainted with many gentlemen, so that he set up a school of fence, and began to teach, enticing away many which were scholars of his Uncle *Angelo*. A part truly very vile, and of an unkind, unthankful man. Whereupon the said *Angelo* complained of this injury and wrong offered by his nephew, to a gentleman who was his scholar and loved him entirely, showing how his nephew had not only impaired his credit, but defrauded him of the aid and help which he looked for at his hands, having brought him up, as I have said, and especially being now grown old. Which nephew (as he said) in respect of kindred, bringing up, and teaching of his art and skill, was bound to have showed him all friendship and courtesy. Hereupon the gentleman, *Angelo* his scholar, promised to seek redress, although he was a friend also unto the nephew of *Angelo*. And so, by bad happenstance, finding the said nephew of *Angelo,* told him that for the wrong offered to his master and uncle, he would fight with him, and therewithal put hand to his weapon: the other refused to fight with him because he was his friend: but the gentleman told him that if he would not defend himself he would run him through: as he did indeed, for whilst he stood upon terms, and would not do his best to defend himself, he ran him quite through the body. Therefore when a man sees anyone with a drawn weapon, let him take care to defend himself, because it is not a matter of friendship. But I think verily in this man, that the justice of God and his own conscience took away all courage and wit of defending himself. And this was the end of his unthankfulness, which God would not leave unpunished. And if all unthankful and treacherous men were so served after the same sort, I think there would not be found so many: and truly of all vices, I take this unthankfulness to be one of the greatest that is incident to man. Therefore to conclude this matter, I would counsel and advise everyone, to give as small occasion of offense any way unto any as may be, and especially unto his friend, to whom he is in any sort beholding: but when that he is forced to lay hand on his weapon, to do the best he can, as well in respect of his credit, as for to save his own life.

LUKE: Verily this example which you have here brought in, is very good and necessary, as well to instruct and teach a man not to trust his enemy when he seeth him coming with his weapon in his hand, as also to warn these unthankful men to be more true and faithful. . . .

VINCENTIO: M. Luke, if all men were lovers of virtue as your self is, these things would be held in greater account, but through the love of vices, wherewith men are carried away, they are little regarded, wherefore I will do my best endeavor to instruct you and all others that are lovers of virtue, imparting unto them that knowledge which God hath given me. Therefore for your better understanding, I will first show you how this ward is good, either to offend or defend, and chiefly with the single sword and the glove, which is most in use among gentlemen, and therefore I advise you and all other to learn to break the thrusts with the left hand, both stoccataes and imbroccataes, as I purpose to show you.

LUKE: But I pray you tell me, is it not better to break with the sword, than with the hand: for (me thinketh) it should be dangerous for hurting the hand.

VINCENTIO: I will tell you, this weapon must be used with a glove, and if a man should be without a glove, it were better to hazard a little hurt of the hand, thereby to become master of his enemy's sword, than to break with the sword, and so give his enemy the advantage of him.

Moreover, having the use of your left hand, and wearing a gauntlet or glove of mail, your enemy shall no sooner make a thrust, but you shall be ready to catch his sword fast, and so command him at your pleasure: wherefore I wish you not to defend any thrust with the sword, because in so doing you lose the point. . . .

LUKE: But I pray you why do you use so many stoccataes and imbroccataes?

VINCENTIO: Because they may learn the just time and measure, and make the foot, hand and body readily agree together, and understand the way to give the stoccata and imbroccata right: so that these principles are very necessary, and will serve for the rapier and dagger, therefore whosoever will make a perfect scholar, let him show the principles of his ward.

LUKE: I perceive very well, that these things which you have spoken of, are to be done with great agility and quickness, but especially by the master, if he intend to make a perfect scholar, because the master often putteth himself in danger, and the scholar regardeth him not, neither is his hand firm: and therefore the master must be respective two ways: in saving himself, and not hurting his scholar. . . .

LUKE: But I pray you instruct me a little further concerning time.

VINCENTIO: As soon as your rapier is drawn, put your self presently in guard, seeking the advantage, and go not leaping, but while you change from one ward to another, be sure to be out of distance, by retiring a little, because if your enemy be skillful, he may offend you in the same instant. And note this well, that to seek to offend, being out of measure, and not in due time, is very dangerous: wherefore as I told you before, having put yourself in guard, and charging your adversary, take heed how you go about, and that your right foot be foremost, stealing the advantage by little & little, carrying your left leg behind, with your point within the point of your enemy's sword, and so finding the advantage in time and measure, make a stoccata to the belly or face of your enemy, as you shall find him unguarded. . . .

. . . And remember, that whilst your enemy striketh his mandritta, you deliver a thrust or stoccata to his face, for the avoiding of which, he must needs shrink back, otherwise he is slain: and how little so ever your enemy is wounded in the face, he is half undone and vanquished,

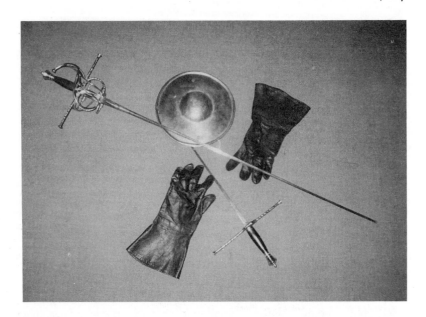

FIGURE 8 *Renaissance Weaponry. Photograph by Milan Petricevic of rapier, gauntlets, buckler, and dagger, from the collection of The Sword Academy, Calgary, Alberta, Canada.*

Every man in this play is armed, and arms figure as augmentations and ornaments of manhood. Weapons also feature prominently as consumer items in the city of London. Sold at haberdashers' shops, they are as much ornament as caps and glasses and other less dangerous items of urban accoutrement. Thomas Smith observes in A Discourse of the Commonweal of this Realm of England *(1549):*

> I have seen within these sixty years, when there were not of these haberdashers that sell French or Milan caps, glasses, daggers, swords, girdles [belts] and such things, not a dozen in all London. And now from the Tower to Westminster along, every street is full of them; and their shops glisters and shine of ... gay daggers, knives, swords, and girdles, that is able to make any temperate man to gaze on them and to buy somewhat.   (Quoted in Archer, "Material" 189)

The weapons pictured above are:

buckler: small wooden or metal (Renaissance) shield, usually round.

dagger: knife with no edge, often worn as a fashion accessory; used for thrusting only.

gauntlet: a protective glove, usually of mail or leather.

rapier: slender civilian and urban weapon that became fashionable in the Renaissance.

whether by chance it fall out that the blood cover and hinder his fight, or that the wound be mortal, as most in that part are: and it is an easy matter to one which knows this play, to hit the face, although everyone understands not this advantage. And many there are which have practiced and do practice fence, and which have to deal with those which understand these kind of thrusts or stoccatas, and yet cannot learn to use them, unless these secrets be shown them. Because these matters are for fight and combat, not for play or practice. . . .

. . . There are many which oftentimes by chance and hap, do many things in fight, of which if a man should ask them a reason, they themselves know not how they have done them. And sometimes men very sufficient and skillful at their weapon, are hurt, either by their evil fortune, that they suffer themselves to be carried away and overmastered too much with choler and rage, or else for that they make no account of their enemy. Wherefore as well in this ward as in the other, take heed that you suffer not yourself to be blinded and carried away with rage and fury.

LUKE: I perceive very well that the secrets of this noble art are very great, & that with great travail and pains a man must come to the knowledge and skill both to rightly understand and practice it, for otherwise I see, that by very small error a man comes in danger of his life.

BOOK II

. . . It were an endless thing for me to rehearse all the examples that I have heard, concerning this vice of insolency, which are infinite, and happen daily in all countries, by reason of the little regard that is had in the bringing up of young men: and so I will only exhort every man to take heed lest himself fall into like folly.

I will not omit to speak of a certain vice, and part not to be used by a gentleman, seeing it proceedeth of rare cowardice: which is, when a man having fallen out with one or other, and wanting courage to deal with him in single fight, procureth base and cowardly means by the help of some of his friends, with whom he plotteth how they may circumvent his enemy. And so watching him at some time or other, will draw upon him, as if he had met him by chance, who thinking upon no villainy, without any suspicion at all, likewise draweth to defend himself, as a man ought to do, which when the other plotters espy standing afar off, draw near as strangers to them both, and unwilling any hurt should be done on either side, whereas they most traitorously will either themselves impart a thrust by the way, or so strike his weapon, that his enemy may take occasion to hurt him: which villainy (for I

think no term bad enough to express it by) you may escape, if you take heed when anyone draweth upon you, that none else come near you, willing them to retire, with protestation, that you will take them as your enemies, if they do not: for by reason that you know them not, they cannot but like of your protestation, if they mean you no evil, seeing that you not knowing them cannot assure yourself of their good affection towards you, and care of your safeguard. Therefore in any case, at such time as you shall happen to be enforced to defend yourself on the sudden, let no man come near you, for it is very dangerous: and I speak this because I have seen the like done very often, and found it confirmed by great experience. And to say something of parting, I will by the way declare thus much. That he that will part two that are fighting, must go betwixt them both, having great regard that he neither hindreth one more than the other, nor suffereth the one more to endanger his enemy than the other: and if more come to part than one, they must divide themselves, and some come on one side, and some on the other, taking great heed that neither of them be any way either prejudiced, or favored: wherefore I do not mislike with the great Duke of Florence his opinion, who upon pain of great forfeiture, forbade all men to part those that should fight, for he would have them suffered to fight 'til they parted themselves, and if anyone chanced to be hurt, they should blame themselves, seeing they were the only cause thereof.

If the like were used in all places, I think we should not have so much quarreling by half as we daily see among gentlemen: for surely many will be very ready upon no occasion to draw upon a man, only because he knoweth that he shall not be suffered to fight.

Some others there be, who to wreak themselves upon their enemies will do it by a third means, by gifts or promises, persuading some needy fellow to pick a quarrel, with their enemy, whom either the poor fellow hurteth or killeth, and so incureth danger of death: or at the least is hurt or maimed himself. Therefore I could with every man to meddle with his own quarrels only, neither revenging his own wrong, by another, nor wreaking other men's injuries by himself, unless he have a good reason to the contrary, as in diverse cases a man may honestly and honorably both entreat others to revenge his wrongs, and be also entreated of others.

There be also some gentlemen so careless, that being in company with honest gentlemen, think that whatsoever folly they commit, the company will be ready to defend them, and so will either scoff or jibe with them that pass by, or use some knavish trick toward someone that is not of their company, or fall a-quarrelling with one or other whom they think good, and so having set many together by the ears, they are the first that will run away, or hide themselves in some corner 'til all be done. By my counsel therefore shall no man be so fond as to back any, or take part with any that are so void of discretion or government. . . .

All which I have here said, because I have myself had experience thereof. And these be the things whereof quarrels proceed; which beginning but between two or three, sometimes are so far increased, that whole families are wrapped in quarrels and broils, which oftentimes are not ended without great hurt and bloodshed. Every man ought therefore to know how to behave himself in these cases, and not to presume upon his own skill or knowledge, but to learn how he ought to proceed in matters of combats or quarrels: For a man may daily learn more than he knoweth, & especially they that want experience: seeing it is a matter seldom seen, that he shall be able to know what is good, that hath not had some trial of that which is evil. According to a verse of Petrarch, "Every one must learn to his cost": which saying pertaineth especially to young men, who for the most part can never learn to govern themselves aright, until such time as they have had experience of some mishap or other, concerning either their goods, life, or credit. But as nothing is so dangerous but may be prevented, so in this point, that men take good heed and arm themselves with the sure shield of sound counsel and advice, that they may easily avoid such errors as I have in these my advertisements discovered and made known for their profit and commodity.

➔ GEORGE SILVER

From Paradoxes of Defense   *1599*

> O sweet Juliet,
> Thy beauty hath made me effeminate,
> And in my temper softened valor's steel!   (3.1.100–02)

George Silver wrote a counterblast to Saviolo, whom he viewed as a foreigner misleading Englishmen and bringing them to their premature deaths. He argued for the use of the indigenous English short sword over the imported rapier. The rapier served as a sort of extension of phallicity, as Bruce Smith observes: "As devices for violating the persons of other people, rapiers function as the ulti-

---

George Silver, *Paradoxes of Defense. Wherein Is Proved the True Grounds of Fight to Be in the Short Ancient Weapons, and That the Short Sword Hath Advantage Over the Long Sword or Rapier* (London, 1599), 1–6, 55–56.

mate extension of the male body into social space" (Smith, *Shakespeare* 32). In a sense, this is not dissimilar to Silver's objections to the rapier, which he said were limited in combat to thrusting maneuvers only and so offered effective defensive strategies. There is an intense and unambivalent xenophobic jealousy of Saviolo in the *Paradoxes*, but we should probably not therefore dismiss Silver's arguments as mere chauvinism. Writing at the end of the nineteenth century when swords still had some, albeit diminished, practical use for infantry army officers, Cyril G. R. Matthey, a captain in the London Rifle Brigade, produced an edition of Silver's works for training purposes. Matthey particularly commended Silver's emphasis on defense and claimed that "the manner in which he treats his own method of defence and attack . . . as opposed to that of the Italian school of his day, clearly proves that he had thoroughly thought out the system which he advocated, and that he had reduced it to a science practically of his own creation, which is remarkable at any rate for much common sense, and in some respects, perhaps, for teaching of a unique kind" (Matthey xvii).

Essentially the techniques described in the treatise made no distinction between the swordsmanship of the duelist, with all its attendant etiquette, and that of the soldier — in other words between training a fencer and training a warrior for battle. The Company of the Masters of Defense of London, (to which it is usually assumed Silver belonged) was the officially recognized guild of the teachers of fencing in and around the city. Perhaps on account of this, a certain degree of moral probity is emphasized in the text. For example, Silver argued that a man should rather "endure an injury than seek revenge" (Aylward 69).

Paradoxes of Defense, **wherein is proved the true grounds of fight to be in the short ancient weapons, and that the short sword hath advantage of the long sword or long rapier. And the weakness and imperfection of the rapier-fights displayed. Together with an admonition to the noble, ancient, victorious, valiant, and most brave nation of Englishmen, to beware of false teachers of defense, and how they forsake their own natural fights: with a brief commendation of the noble science or exercising of arms.**

To the right honorable, my singular good lord, Robert Earl of Essex and Ewe, Earl Marshal of England, Viscount Hereford, Lord Ferrers of Chartley, Bourchier and Lovaine, Master of the Queen Majesty's Horse, and of the Ordinance, Chancellor of the University of Cambridge, Knight of the most noble Order of the Garter, and one of her Highness's most honorable Privy Council.

Fencing (Right Honorable) in this new-fangled age, is like our fashions, every day a change, resembling the chameleon, who altereth himself into all colors save white: so fencing changeth into all wards save the right. That it is so, experience teacheth us: why it is so, I doubt not but your wisdom doth conceive. There is nothing permanent that is not true, what can be true that is uncertain? How can that be certain, that stands upon uncertain grounds? . . . [T]he mind desirous of truth, hunts after it, and hating false-hood, flies from it, and therefore having missed it once, it assays the second time: if then he thrives not, he tries another way: . . . and if all these fail him, yet he never faileth to change his weapon, his fight, his ward . . . for because men desire to find out a true defense for themselves in their fight, therefore they seek it diligently, nature having taught us to defend ourselves, and art teaching how. . . . But though we often chop and change, turn and return, from ward to ward, from fight to fight, in this unconstant search, yet we never rest in any, and that because we never find the truth: and therefore we never find it, because we never seek it in that weapon where it may be found. For, to seek for a true defense in an untrue weapon, is to angle on the earth for fish, and to hunt in the sea for hares: truth is ancient though it seem an upstart: our forefathers were wise, though our age account them foolish, valiant though we repute them cowards: they found out the true defense for their bodies in short weapons by their wisdom, they defended themselves and subdued their enemies, with those weapons and their valor. And (Right Honorable) if we will have this true defense, we must seek it where it is, in short swords, short staves,[1] the half pike,[2] partisans,[3] gloves,[4] or such like weapons of perfect lengths, not in long swords, long rapiers, nor frog pricking poinards.[5] . . . To prove this, I have set forth these my *Paradoxes,* different I confess from the main current of our outlandish teachers, but agreeing I am well assured to the truth, and tending as I hope to the honor of our English nation. The reason which moved me to adventure so great a task, is the desire I have to bring the truth to light, which hath long time lain hidden in the cave of contempt, while we like degenerate sons, have forsaken our forefathers virtues with their weapons, and have lusted like men sick of a strange ague, after the strange vices and devices of Italian, French and Spanish fencers, little remembering, that these apish toys could not free Rome from Brennus' sack,[6] nor France from King Henry the fifth his conquest. To this desire to find out truth the daughter of time . . . I was also moved, that by it I might remove the great loss of our English gallants, which we daily suffer by these imperfect fights. . . . If that man were now alive, which beat the master for the scholar's fault, because he had no better instructed him, these Italian fencers

---

[1] **staves:** poles, staffs.   [2] **half pike:** half-spear.   [3] **partisans:** long-handled spears.   [4] **gloves:** mail-covered gauntlets.   [5] **poinards:** stabbing knives, a sort of English stiletto.   [6] **Brennus' sack:** sack of Rome by the Gauls led by Brennus in 387 B.C.

could not escape his censure, who teach us offense, not defense, and to fight, as Diogenes's scholars were taught to dance,[7] to bring their lives to an end by art. . . . Is it valor for a man to go naked against his enemy? . . . But that which is most shameful, they teach men to butcher one another here at home in peace, wherewith they cannot hurt their enemies abroad in war. For, your Honor well knows, that when the battles are joined, and come to the charge, there is no room for them to draw their bird-spits,[8] and when they have them, what can they do with them? Can they pierce his corslet[9] with the point? Can they unlace his helmet, unbuckle his armor, hew asunder their pikes with a stoccata, a reversa, or a dritta, a stramason,[10] or other such like tempestuous terms? No, these toys are fit for children, not for men, for straggling boys of the camp to murder poultry, not for men of honor to try the battle with their foes. Thus I have (Right Honorable) for the trial of the truth, between the short sword and the long rapier, for the saving of the lives of our English gallants, who are sent to certain death by their uncertain fights, & for abandoning of that mischievous and imperfect weapon, which serves to kill our friends in peace, but cannot much hurt our foes in war, have I at this time given forth these *Paradoxes* to the view of the world. . . . And so I humbly commend this book to your Lordship's wisdom to peruse, and your honor to the highest to protect in all health and happiness now and ever.

Your Honors in all duty,
George Silver.

An admonition to the noble, ancient, victorious, valiant, and most brave nation of Englishmen. George Silver having the perfect knowledge of all manner of weapons, and being experienced in all manner of fights, thereby perceiving the great abuses by the Italian teachers of offense done unto them, the great errors, inconveniences, & false resolutions they have brought them into, have enforced me, even of pity of their most lamentable wounds and slaughters, & as I verily think it my bounden duty, with all love and humility to admonish them to take heed, how they submit themselves into the hands of Italian teachers of defense, or strangers whatsoever; and to beware how they forsake or suspect their own natural fight, that they may by casting off of these Italianated, weak, fanatical, and most devilish and imperfect fights, and by exercising of their own ancient weapons, be

---

[7] **as Diogenes's scholars were taught to dance:** Diogenes was a philosopher who used a stick to deter would-be scholars, thus making them dance about to avoid a beating.   [8] **bird-spits:** Silver's mocking term for rapiers.   [9] **corslet:** garment, often made of mail, covering the torso.
[10] **a stoccata, a reversa, or a dritta, a stramason:** a thrust, a reverse, a cut from the right, a vertical cut to the head.

restored, or achieve unto their natural, and most manly and victorious fight again, the dint and force whereof many brave nations have both felt and feared. Our ploughmen have mightily prevailed against them, as also against masters of defense both in schools and countries, that have taken upon them to stand upon schooltricks and juggling gambolds:[11] whereby it grew to a common speech among the country-men, "Bring me to a fencer, I will bring him out of his fence tricks with good downright blows, I will make him forget his fence tricks I will warrant him." I speak not against Masters of Defense indeed, they are to be honored, nor against the science, it is noble, and in mine opinion to be preferred next to divinity; for as divinity preserveth the soul from hell and the devil, so doth this noble science defend the body from wounds & slaughter. And moreover, the exercising of weapons putteth away aches, griefs, and diseases, it increaseth strength, and sharpeneth the wits, it giveth a perfect judgment, it expelleth melancholy, choleric and evil conceits, it keepeth a man in breath, perfect health, and long life. It is unto him that hath the perfection thereof, a most friendly and comfortable companion when he is alone, having but only his weapon about him, it putteth him out of all fear, & in the wars and places of most danger it maketh him bold, hardy, and valiant.

And for as much as this noble and most mighty nation of Englishmen, of their good natures, are always most loving, very credulous, & ready to cherish & protect strangers: yet that through their good natures they never more by strangers or false teachers may be deceived, once again I am most humbly to admonish them, or such as shall find in themselves a disposition or desire to learn their weapons of them, that from henceforth as strangers shall take upon them to come hither to teach this noble & most valiant, & victorious nation to fight, that first, before they learn of them, they cause a sufficient trial of them to be made, whether the excellency of their skill be such as they profess or no, the trial to be very requisite & reasonable, even such as I myself would be content withal, if I should take upon me to go in their country to teach their nation to fight. And this is the trial: they shall play with such weapons as they profess to teach withal,[12] three bouts apiece with three of the best English Masters of Defense, & three bouts apiece with three unskillful valiant men, and three bouts apiece with three resolute men half drunk. Then if they can defend themselves against these Masters of Defense, and hurt, and go free from the rest, then are they to be honored,

---

[11] **juggling gambolds:** frolics. Silver means showmanship, which he deplores.   [12] Here Silver inserts a textual note: "A great favor to give them choice of their weapons, because professors of arms ought to be skillful with all manner of weapons."

cherished, and allowed for perfect good teachers, what countrymen soever they be: but if of any of these they take foil,[13] then are they imperfect in their profession, their fight is false, & and they are false teachers, deceivers and murderers, and to be punished accordingly, yet to worse punishment unto them I wish, than such as in their trial they shall find.

There are four especial marks to know the Italian fight is imperfect, & that the Italian teachers and setters forth of books of defense, never had the perfection of the true fight.

The first mark is, they seldom fight in their own country unarmed, commonly in this sort, a pair of gauntlets[14] upon their hands, and a good shirt of mail upon their bodies.[15] The second mark is, that neither the Italians, nor any of their best scholars do never fight, but they are most commonly sore hurt, or one or both of them slain.

The third mark is, they never teach their scholars, nor set down in their books any perfect lengths of their weapons, without the which no man can by nature or art against the perfect length fight safe, for being too short, their times are too long, and spaces too wide for their defense, and being too long, they will be upon every cross that shall happen to be made, whether it be done by skill or chance, in great danger of death; because the rapier being too long, the cross cannot be undone in due time, but may be done by going back with the feet; but that time is always too long to answer the time of the hand, therefore every man ought to have a weapon according to his own stature: the tall man must have his weapon longer than the man of mean[16] stature, or else he hath wrong in his defense, & the man of mean stature must have his weapon longer than the man of small stature, or else he hath wrong in his defense; & the man of small stature must beware that he feed not himself with this vain conceit, that he will have his weapon long, to reach as far as the tall man, for therein he shall have great disadvantage, both in making of a strong cross, and also in uncrossing again, and in keeping his point from crossing, and when a cross is made upon him, to defend himself, or endanger his enemy, or to redeem his lost times. . . .

The fourth mark is, the crosses of their rapiers for true defense of their hands are imperfect, for the true carriage of the guardant[17] fight, without the which all fights are imperfect.

---

[13] **foil:** light weapon used in fencing. [14] **gauntlets:** protective combat gloves. [15] Here Silver inserts a textual note: "Yet they persuade us that the cross of the rapier without hilt or gauntlet is sufficient." [16] **mean:** average. [17] **guardant:** defensive.

If the sword be longer, you can hardly vncrosse without going backe with your feet. If shorter, thē you can hardly make a true crosse without putting in of your feet, the which times are too long to answer the time of the hand.

The like reasons for the short staffe, half Pike, Forrest bill, Partisan, or Gleue, or such like weapons of perfect length.

Of six chief causes, that many valiant men thinking of themselves by their practices to be skillful in their weapons, are yet many times in their fight sore hurt, and many times slain by men of small skill, or none at all.

... The fifth cause is, their weapons are most commonly too long to uncross without going back with the feet.

The sixth cause is, their weapons are most commonly too heavy both to defend and offend in due time, & by these two last causes many valiant men have lost their lives.

≺ FIGURE 9 *Posed Swordsman, from George Silver,* Paradoxes of Defense *(1599). As an instruction and training manual for men at arms, this book included several illustrations all designed to allow the reader to imitate the postures described in the text. In contrast to the images that accompany the fencing manuals, Silver's combatant is outside (as we see from the sprigs of grass around his feet) rather than in a fencing hall, and wearing a breastplate — ready for a pre-scheduled encounter at arms. The instructions describe how to position the feet when executing a crossing maneuver with a sword and dagger.*

The issues to which Silver addressed himself are apparent in the writings of the great English travel writer Fynes Moryson, who writes that

> Englishmen, especially being young and inexperienced, are apt to take all things in snuff. Of old they were fenced with bucklers as with a rapier, nothing was more common with them than to fight about taking the right or the left hand or the wall, or upon any unpleasing countenance. But at this day they scorned such men, and esteem them of an idle brain who for ridiculous or trifling causes run the trial of single fight. And the cause why single fights are more rare in England at these times is the dangerous fight at the single rapier. (Moryson quoted in Aylward 62)

Moryson also comments explicitly on attempts to curb violence in Italy. "It is unlawfull to wear a sword without licence of the Magistrate, wither at Milan, Cremona, Mantua, or almost any City of Italy; only at Venice and Padua, and the Cities of that State, strangers may wear Swords, and only the wearing of Pistols or shortguns is forbidden" (Moryson 173).

Of the false resolutions and vain opinions of rapier-men, and of the danger of death thereby ensuing.

It is a great question, & especially amongst the rapier-men, who hath the advantage of the thruster, or of the warder. Some hold strongly, that the warder hath the vantage: others say, it is most certain that the thruster hath the vantage. Now when two do happen to fight, being both of one mind, that the thruster hath the vantage, they make all shift they can, who shall give the first thrust: as for example, two Captains at Southampton . . . fell at strife, drew their rapiers, and presently, being desperate, hardy or resolute, as they call it, with all force and over great speed, ran with their rapiers one at the other, & were both slain. Now when two of the contrary opinion shall meet and fight, you shall see very peaceable wars between them: for they verily think that he that first thrusteth is in great danger of his life, therefore

with all speed do put themselves in ward, or stoccata, the surest guard of all
other, as Vincentio[18] saith, and thereupon they stand sure, saying the one to
the other, thrust and thou dare. . . . These two cunning gentlemen standing
long time together, upon this worthy ward, they both depart in peace,
according to the old proverb: It is good sleeping in a whole skin. Again if
two shall fight, the one of opinion, that he that thrusteth hath the vantage,
and the other of opinion, that the warder hath the vantage, then most commonly the thruster being valiant, with all speed thrusteth home, and by reason of the time and swift motion of his hand, they are most commonly with
the points of their rapiers, or daggers, or both, one or both of them hurt or
slain; because their spaces of defense in that kind of fight, are too wide in
due time to defend, and the place being won, the eye of the patient by the
swift motion of the agent's hand, is deceived. Another resolution they stand
sure upon for their lives, to kill their enemies, in the which they are most
commonly slain themselves: that is this: When they find the point of their
enemy's rapier out of the right line, they say, they may boldly make home a
thrust with a passata,[19] the which they observe, and do accordingly: but the
other having a shorter time with his hand, as nature many times teacheth
him, suddenly turning his wrist, whereby he meeteth the other in his passage just with the point of his rapier in the face or body. And this false resolution hath cost many a life.

*That the cause that many are so often slain, and many sore hurt in fight
with long rapiers is not by reason of their dangerous thrusts, nor cunningness
of that Italianated fight, but in the length and unwieldiness thereof.*

It is most certain, that men may with short swords both strike, thrust, false
and double, by reason of their distance and nimbleness thereof, more dangerously than they can with long rapiers: and yet when two fight with short
swords, having true fight, there is no hurt done: neither is it possible in any
reason, that any hurt should be done betwixt them of either side, and this is
well known to all such as have the perfection of true fight. By this it plainly
appeareth, that the cause of the great slaughter, and sundry hurts done by
long rapiers, consisteth not in long reach, dangerous thrusts, nor cunningness of the Italian fight, but of the inconvenient length, and unwieldiness of
their long rapiers: whereby it commonly falleth out, that in all their actions
appertaining to their defense, they are unable, in due time to perform, and

---

[18] **Vincentio:** Vincentio Saviolo, an Italian fencing master and instructor. (See pp. 208–20.)
[19] **passata:** pass.

continually in danger of every cross, that shall happen to be made with their rapier blades. . . .

[T]he hilt . . . serveth to defend the head as the hand, and is a more sure and strong ward, than is the blade of the rapier. And further, understand this for truth, that in guardant and open fight, the hand without an hilt lieth open to most blows that shall be stroken by the agent. . . .

Rapiers having no hilts to defend the head, the rapier-man is driven of necessity to lie at the variable fight or low ward, and being there he can neither defend in due time, head, face, nor body from the blows or thrusts of him, that shall fight out of the guardant or open fight, but is continually in great danger of the agent, for these causes following. First, because his space is too wide to defend his head from blow or thrust. Secondly his pace standing upon that fight, will be of necessity too great or too narrow: if too narrow, too weak: if too large, his weight and number of his feet, are too great to endanger him, that is upon his guardant or open fight. . . .

. . .

Now, O you Italian teachers of defense, where are your stoccatas, imbroccatas, mandrittas, puntas, & punta reversas, stramisons, passatas, carricados, amazzas, & incartatas,[20] & playing with your bodies, removing with your feet a little aside, circle-wise winding of your bodies, making of three times with your feet together, marking with one eye the motion of the adversary, & with the other eye the advantage of thrusting? What is become of all these juggling gambolds, apish devices, with all the rest of your squint-eyed tricks, when as through your deep studies, long practices, & apt bodies, both strong and agile, you have attained to the height of all these things? What then availeth it you, when you shall come to fight for your lives with a man of skill? You shall have neither time, nor place, in due time to perform any one of them, nor guardant nor open fight safely to keep out a man of skill, a man of no skill, or scholar of your own teaching, from the true place, the place of safety, the place of uncertainty or mischief, the place of wounds or death, but are there enforced to stand in that mischievous, uncertain, dangerous, and most deadly place, as two men having lost in part their chiefest fences, most furiously with their rapiers or poinards, wounding or slaying each other.

Thus endeth the imperfect fights of the rapier with all manner of weapons or instruments thereto appertaining, with their imperfections, through the true grounds and rules of the art of arms, truly displayed & brought to light.

[20] **stoccatas . . . & incartatas:** fancy Italian maneuvers.

Keeping the Peace

> [T]he Prince expressly hath
> Forbid this bandying in Verona streets   (3.1.77–78)

The following proclamations address the issue of urban violence. Proclamations were ordinances issued by monarchs with the advice of the privy council. These declarations had legal force, and were actually proclaimed (read aloud) in towns across the country. To this purpose, the proclamation was also accompanied by a royal writ addressed to officers, such as sheriffs and mayors, giving directions about when and where the proclamation was to be publicly delivered (Larkin and Hughes ix–xi). Proclamations were usually issued to enforce already existing statute law or to articulate that law in response to specific circumstances or local needs.

In *Romeo and Juliet,* we see Escalus deliver his own rather ineffective "proclamation" in act 1: "If ever you disturb our streets again / Your lives shall pay the forfeit of the peace" (1.1.83–84). Events conspire to endow this statement with the force of a prediction because, of course, lives are paid for the disturbance of the peace, but not by virtue of the Prince's edict. We might consider how the proclamations contextualize the play's representation of sovereign power and the attempt to enforce law. In Verona, the power of young men is not just an inconvenience but a direct threat to the state and to the rule of law. Similarly, in Elizabethan England, a society without a police force, a standing army, and all the other elements of state power that we take for granted, there was an obsessive concern about how to enforce law and quell social disorder. In the play the watch, for example, who arrive at the monument (5.3.168) after the lovers' deaths, are the rudimentary and ineffective local arm of the law. Shakespeare makes a mockery of their disorganization and stupidity in *Much Ado About Nothing,* but here they constitute a pitifully belated attempt to execute the Prince's authority. Indeed, local officers such as justices of the peace, sheriffs, and the watch were often hard pressed to deal with the heavy amount of work they were required to undertake for little or no pay. One justice, Sir George Manners of Haddon, prayed "for better times and fortunes than always to live a poor base Justice, recreating myself in sending rogues to the gallows" (Stone, *Crisis* 391).

Ultimate responsibility for upholding the law in Shakespeare's Verona lies with Escalus, who indeed acknowledges his culpability in the tragedy, "for winking at your discords" (5.3.294). Does the play urge greater control of the forces that threaten to subvert the social order? Could the tragedy have been avoided if, in the chain of male power in Verona, fathers exercised more control over sons and princes over subjects? Or are the energies of love and hate primordial forces in the face of which sovereign power and legal authority are utterly impotent?

→ QUEEN ELIZABETH I

Proclamation Enforcing Statutes of Apparel   *May 6, 1562*

This proclamation charges that rapiers are now being worn not for the purpose of defense, which is clearly regarded as legitimate, but for "murder and evident death." These new, longer, sharper blades are designed for the swift and efficient execution of an opponent.

. . . And whereas an usage is crept in, contrary to former orders, of wearing of long swords and rapiers, sharpened in such sort as may appear the usage of them can not tend to defense, which ought to be the very meaning of wearing of weapons in times of peace, but to murder and evident death, when the same shall be occupied: her majesty's pleasure is that no man shall, after ten days next following this proclamation, wear any sword, rapier, or any weapon in their stead, passing the length of one yard and half a quarter of blade at the uttermost, neither any dagger above the length of twelve inches in blade, neither any buckler with a sharp point or with any point above two inches of length, upon pain of forfeiting the sword or dagger passing the said length, and the buckler made otherwise than is prescribed, to whomsoever will seize upon it, and the imprisonment of his body that shall be found to wear any of them, and to make fine at her majesty's will and pleasure. And if any cutler or other artificer shall, after the day of the publication hereof, sell, or have within his shop or house to be sold, or shall make or cause to be made, any rapier, sword, dagger, or buckler contrary to this order, to forfeit the same, his body to be imprisoned, and to make fine at the Queen's Highness' pleasure, and to remain in prison till the said fine be fully satisfied; and being taken with the fault the second time never to be permitted after to use that occupation; which in the court is to be executed by the officers aforesaid, in the city and liberties by the mayor and court of aldermen, and such as by them shall be appointed in that sort, as well ser-geants as others beforesaid; in Westminster, the suburbs, and other privileged

---

places, by the officers of the same, in towns corporate by the mayor and other head officers, and in all other places by the justices of peace.

And finally her majesty straightly chargeth as well the said Lord Steward, Treasurer, and Comptroller of the household, as the Lord Chamberlain, vice-chamberlain and such as under them shall be appointed and assigned, the Mayor of London and all other mayors, sheriffs, bailiffs, constables and all justices of peace, all principals and ancients of the Inns-of-Court and Chancery, the chancellor and vice-chancellor of both the universities, and the heads of halls and colleges of the same, and all other her highness' officers and ministers, each of them in their jurisdictions, to see these orders being set forth and confirmed by her majesty's proclamation, to be duly and speedily executed in form aforesaid, as they will answer for the contrary at their perils, and will avoid Her Highness' displeasure and indignation.

➜ QUEEN ELIZABETH I

Proclamation Prohibiting Unlawful Assembly under Martial Law
June 20, 1591 [1594]

This document speaks to one of the obsessions of Elizabethan society, namely, how to prevent rioting. The concern here is not the upper classes who might organize rebellion against the crown like the Northern Earls in 1569 or the Earl of Essex in 1601, but the lower orders, the menials of the society who had little to gain from obedience. Enforcing the law was a matter of giving "better direction . . . to officers of justice," and the addition of a "provost martial" [officer-in-chief] to the ranks of the ordinary officers. Martial law was declared and ordinary law suspended during times of war or civil emergency, and Tudor monarchs showed little hesitancy in invoking its powers whenever they felt the necessity to maintain order, especially concerning religion. The provost martial, under the declared conditions of martial law, could summarily execute suspects without giving them the benefit of trial by jury. This was rough justice indeed and it constitutes a stark contrast to the ineffective edicts of Escalus in Shakespeare's Verona.

Proclamation 735, "Prohibiting Unlawful Assembly under Martial Law" (June 20, 1591), in *Tudor Royal Proclamations, Vol. 3: 1588–1603*, ed. James F. Larkin and Paul L. Hughes (New Haven: Yale UP, 1969), 82–83. (The proclamation should be dated 1594.)

The Queen's majesty, being informed of sundry great disorders committed in and about her city of London by unlawful great assemblies of multitudes of a popular sort of base condition, whereof some are apprentices and servants to artificers and to such like as are not able or not disposed to rule their servants as they ought to do, and some attempting to rescue out of the hands of public officers such as have been lawfully arrested; whereby her majesty's peace hath been of late notably violated and broken to the dishonor of her majesty's government, and chiefly for lack of due correction in time of such manifest offenders by the officers of her city and others in the places around and about her city:

For reformation whereof her majesty hath had conference with her council of the most ready means both for punishment of such offenses already committed and for stay of the like, and to that purpose doth most straightly charge all her officers both in the city and in places near to the city in the counties of Middlesex, Kent, Surrey, and Essex, that have authority to preserve the peace and to punish the offenders of the peace, that they do more diligently to the best of their power see to the suppression of all offenders against the peace, and specially of all unlawful assemblies; upon pain to be not only removed from their offices but to be also punished as persons maintaining and rather comforting such offenders.

And because these late unlawful assemblies and routs are compounded of sundry sorts of base people, some known apprentices such as are of base manual occupation, and some others wandering idle persons of condition of beggars and vagabonds, and some coloring their wandering by the name of soldiers returned from the war:

Therefore her majesty hath, for better direction to her officers of justice, and for the inquisition and knowledge of all such kind of persons so either unlawfully gathering themselves in companies or wandering about like vagabonds without any known manner of honest living, notified her pleasure to her council to prescribe certain orders to be published in and about the said city which she will have straightly observed; and for that purpose meaneth to have a provost martial with sufficient authority to apprehend all such as shall not be readily reformed and corrected by the ordinary officers of justice; and them without delay to execute upon the gallows by order of martial law. And this her majesty's commandment she willeth to be duly observed, upon pain of her indignation.

→ QUEEN ELIZABETH I

Proclamation Enforcing Earlier
Proclamation against Handguns

December 2, 1594

While there are no firearms in *Romeo and Juliet,* there is a very powerful image of a gun in act 3, scene 3. Romeo asks the Nurse about Juliet's reaction to his murder of her cousin Tybalt:

> NURSE: O, she says nothing, sir, but weeps and weeps,
>   And now falls on her bed, and then starts up,
>   And "Tybalt" calls, and then on Romeo cries,
>   And then down falls again.
> ROMEO: As if that name,
>   *Shot from the deadly level of a gun,*
>   Did murder her, as that name's cursèd hand
>   Murdered her kinsman.   (3.3.99–105, my italics)

The sense here is that of all the weapons in the play, the lovers are themselves the most sure instruments of one another's deaths. To love, at least in this society, is, in effect, to kill. Gunpowder images in the play intimate the explosive and incendiary nature of desire: "These violent desires have violent ends / And in their triumph die, like fire and powder, / Which as they kiss consume" (2.6.9–11); "that the trunk may be discharged of breath / As violently as hasty powder fired / Doth hurry from the fatal cannon's womb" (5.1.63–65).

Despite such references, the following proclamation probably strikes most readers as distinctly un-Shakespearean, that is, as something which, though it is a burning issue in twenty-first-century United States culture, does not comport with our notion of the quaint and less violent world that we (erroneously) associate with Elizabethan England. Violence was, in fact, endemic to Elizabethan society, and Shakespeare's representation of it is more than merely decorative (see Sharpe 86–87). Interestingly, too, this proclamation repeated an earlier one, perhaps because the first was ineffective.

The Queen's Majesty, hearing by credible report that there are great disorders lately grown in sundry parts of her realm, and specially in and about her city of London and in the usual highways towards the said city and to Her Majesty's court, by common carrying of dags otherwise called pistols, to the terror of all people professing to travel and live peaceably, and (which is

---

Proclamation 766, "Enforcing Earlier Proclamation against Handguns" (December 2, 1594), in *Tudor Royal Proclamations, Vol. 3: 1588–1603,* ed. James F. Larkin and Paul L. Hughes (New Haven: Yale UP, 1969), 141–42.

most to Her Majesty's grief) by the usage whereof certain persons have been of late in sundry places slain with such pieces: hereupon, hath called to her remembrance that she hath by former proclamations published straightly forbidden the carrying not only of such dags but also of other longer pieces as calivers[1] and such like in places and times not allowable for service.[2] By which proclamations, as first by one in very few words, in May the first of her reign Her Majesty, reciting the statute of her noble father, King Henry VIII, in the 33rd year of his reign, against the riding with handguns and dags under the length of three-quarters of a yard, commanded the same to be observed, and charged all her justices of peace at their next sessions to make inquisition of the observation thereof and to see the same statute duly executed. And for that by process of time the due execution thereof hath ceased and the disorders grown much greater, not only in open carrying such dags but also in a device to have secretly small dags commonly called pocket dags,[3] and in wearing also secretly coats of armor commonly called privy coats, whereby many robberies and frays have been increased and become unpunished; Her Majesty did in the 21st year of her reign by another open proclamation, expressing the disorders and dangers hereby ensuing, command that both her former proclamation concerning the prohibition of dags should be speedily put in execution; and added thereto her further commandments and prohibitions against a disorder in carrying and shooting with handguns and calivers within two miles of the place of Her Majesty's residence, and near to towns and men's houses, where there was no cause of musters to show the same, nor any places ordained for exercise; and against the wearing of privy coats and doublets of defense by such as thereby moved quarrels and frays upon other quiet subjects unarmed; and in conclusion of the same latter proclamation Her Majesty did also command all her officers in any city or town to make search for all manner of such small dags called pocket dags, and specially in shops and houses of artificers that do use to make the same, and those to take and keep in their possession, giving the owners testimonial of the receipt thereof to the end if there should be seen good cause they might have a reasonable recompense.

All which former commandments and prohibitions appearing in this time to be as necessary, or rather more to be duly executed, than before time, Her Majesty doth newly now command to be presently executed; wherewith Her Majesty chargeth all her justices of peace, and specially, now at the first sessions that shall be kept after Christmas in all counties, diligently to be given in charge, and by juries the defaults to be presented and punished.

---

[1] **calivers:** an early form of portable gun or harquebus, which could be fired without being placed on a stand. [2] **not allowable for service:** not permitted. [3] **dags:** handguns.

And for more certainty to have the same so executed, Her Majesty commandeth the *custos rotulorum*[4] every county and the recorders in all cities being justices of peace to make certificate in writing to Her Majesty's council in the Star Chamber[5] within the space of eight days from the beginning of every Hilary term[6] how this Her Majesty's present proclamation hath been in the said first sessions executed; and so yearly to certify the like in every Hilary term until the same be otherwise directed by admonition from her majesty's said council to cease from the same.

And although hereby the carriage of dags is generally prohibited, yet the carriage thereof shall not be prohibited to persons appointed to come to musters as horsemen with dags to serve therewith, or to be used by any of Her Majesty's ministers or their servants for their more surety to carry Her Majesty's treasure, or to bring her revenue to places appointed; so as always the carriage of such dags be in open sort to be manifestly seen to all persons. . . .

[4] *custos rotulorum:* keeper of the rolls, generally the most senior justice of the peace in the county. [5] **Star Chamber:** one of the most important courts in the late sixteenth and early seventeenth centuries. For the Crown it had the advantage that the judges were the members of the privy council and no jury was present. This made it one of the favorite courts of the monarchs and one of the most unpopular among the populace. It was abolished in 1641. [6] **Hilary term:** a term or session of the High Court beginning January 13.

→ KING JAMES I

Proclamation Prohibiting the Publishing of Any Reports or Writing of Duels

October 15, 1613

A challenge, on my life. (2.4.8)

This proclamation is aimed not just at dueling itself, but at quelling its immense popularity among those eager to devour tales of armed combat. King James I considered that written reports of duels amounted to "proclamations" or edicts on the part of private persons and therefore represented a direct subversion of his sovereign authority. Like Escalus, James declared that offenders would be banished from the royal court (presence) for the term of seven years, a threat that seems to have had the intended effect.

In September 1613 there were five duels that occasioned public comment, and

King James i, "A Proclamation prohibiting the publishing of any reports or writings of Duels" (October 15, 1613), in *Stuart Royal Proclamations, Vol. 1: Royal Proclamations of King James I 1603–1625*, ed. James F. Larkin and Paul L. Hughes (Oxford: Clarendon P, 1973), 295–96.

the earl of Essex's challenge to Henry Howard supplied the immediate provocation for this royal proclamation. Essex and Howard went to Flanders to fight, but authorities there intervened and prevented the encounter (Larkin and Hughes 295). James needed to control his bellicose nobles, whose quarrels constituted both a real and symbolic threat to his sovereignty. When he issued this proclamation nearly twenty years after *Romeo and Juliet* was written, James I made a fervent endeavor to suppress dueling, making all the acts associated with the practice, including incitement, delivery of a challenge or response to a challenge, acting as a second, and so on, liable to a trial in the Star Chamber.[1] James was far more effective in this respect than the rather Escalus-like Elizabeth, and insisted "on the immediate and final authority of the Crown in all issues of honour" (Larkin and Hughes vii).

Because among other bitter fruits that these unlawful and bewitching duels have produced; there is none more dangerous for the sequel, more contemptuous against Our authority, and more godless against the Divine Majesty, than is the publication, as it were before the sun and moon, of men's arrogant conceits of their own valor: We have thought it high time to prevent the same, finding it now to be a common custom, which doth daily come to Our ears; that men no sooner find themselves barred or crossed by any intervening occasion of their blood thirsty and revenging appetite, for destruction either of themselves, or their party in the field; but presently must come forth a writing to be published to the world; which is nothing else, than a proclamation or edict as far as in him lieth; thereby either shifting or excusing their former slowness, or accusing their party for not duly meeting them in their preposterous haste to their own ruins: Wherein We observe three great and main offenses; One against both God and Us, that they dare presume to set forth to the world without shame, their own vindictive and bloody humor upon so unjust a ground; For no quarrel of any subjects can be lawful, except in defense of their prince or their country, the revenging of all private wrongs only belongs to Us (under God,) into whose hand he hath put the sword for that purpose; The next is their offense against Us, in daring to presume so far upon Our special prerogative,[2] as to take upon them to make any publication of their pleasure, the power whereof is only in Us; The third and last is, that thereby is a new seed sown

---

[1] **Star Chamber:** court so named for the star pattern on the ceiling; one of the most important courts of the period. For the Crown it had the advantage that judges were members of the privy council and no jury was present. This made it one of the favorite courts of the monarchs and one of the most unpopular among the people. [2] **Our special prerogative:** rights pertaining only to the sovereign.

of quarrels, whereupon quarrels do not only become immortal, but multiply: For when as We shall have taken the pains to cause Our marshals to agree a quarrel, whereupon We and all honest men have reason to account it as utterly extinct upon such publication; both the parties and the seconds (if any be) are anew brought upon the stage again, and not only by that means may it happen, that the parties shall again fall out who before were agreed; but even their friends, and peradventure other friends who had nothing to do with the matter, must upon that back reckoning fall by the ears together: Nay, if it should chance one or both of the parties to be killed in the first quarrel, if such sort of publication should be made by any of the seconds: It is enough to renew a quarrel either between those seconds, or some of the nearest of their kin who were killed before: And so shall quarrels become immortal, and their memory renew, whereas the best remedy against all sins and offenses is forgetfulness.

For remedy whereof, We do hereby declare, that whosoever shall after the publication of this Our pleasure,[3] presume to put in writing, or publish any discourse of the manner, either of their meetings appointed with their parties, or their fighting, or of any part of that quarrelous business: We will have them to be brought *ore tenus*,[4] or otherwise, as the case shall require in the Star Chamber, and there to be punished at the discretion and censure of that court for their high contempt against Us; to be hereafter banished the court, of Us, Our dearest bedfellow, and the prince Our son for the space of seven years; And (which is heaviest of all) We do protest for Our own part, We will never account of them but as of cowards: For We do ever hold it the part of a man to show his courage, when he is put to it in action: but he that seeks his reputation from many voices amongst the people, We will ever account it to proceed from the knowledge and jealousy of his own weakness, as if a man could not win honor, but *per emendicata suffragia*[5] among the ordinaries.[6] And if any man should find himself grieved with any whisperings, or rumors spread abroad, misreporting the carriage of any such matter, he may resort to our Commissioners' Marshall, who shall right him in his reputation, if they find he be wronged.

---

[3] **Our pleasure:** sovereign will.   [4] *ore tenus:* that now holds.   [5] *per emendicata suffragia:* to beg favor.   [6] **ordinaries:** the common people.

➜ WILLIAM FLEETWOOD

Report to Lord Burghley   *June 18, 1584*

My naked weapon is out. Quarrel. I will back thee.   *(1.1.27)*

When we consider violence in *Romeo and Juliet,* what comes most readily to mind is probably Mercutio's fight with Tybalt and Romeo's fatal intervention. However, it is important to remember that Shakespeare emphasized the antagonisms of the lower orders too, particularly the way in which the servants took up their masters' quarrel, and indeed, it is with such an episode that the play begins.

In Shakespeare's London servants took up their masters' fights, but they also engaged in sometimes fierce altercations with young men of higher rank on their own behalf. However, despite fairly regular instances of riot and disorder in the city, Ian Archer argues that London in the later sixteenth century was free of the kind of serious unrest that might undermine the fabric of government and the structures of authority that sustained it. This remained true even though the city's rulers faced problems attendant upon population explosion, soaring inflation, plague, harvest failure, poverty, and crime, conditions that were exacerbated in the 1590s. As in Verona, in London social stability depended on the solidarity of the elite and its relationship with the crown in sustaining that solidarity (see Archer, *Pursuit* 17).

Similarly, disturbances in London were often far from arbitrary, occurring not because rioters identified with feuding clans, but because of occupational solidarity among guilds and the formation of communities in the livery companies that were determined by factors other than location. This meant that people did not have to be physically proximate in order to decide to come together to revolt against authorities. Livery, that is, a uniform worn by members of a given trade, offered a ready-made identity that particularly threatened the social order because it did not rely on geographical proximity, but on the idea of a shared identity stemming from labor in the same trade. That solidarity could be mobilized in acts of class antagonism such as the Feltmakers' riot in Southwark in 1592, which "united inhabitants of the borough with residents of the Blackfriars liberty on the other side of the river" (Archer, *Pursuit* 82–83).

At the end of June 1595, a thousand apprentices marched on Tower Hill apparently with the intention of ransacking gunmakers' shops and hanging the Lord Mayor of the city. For the rest of the summer, the capital was subject to martial law, and five apprentices were accused of levying war against the Crown and were hanged, drawn, and quartered for it. London had been plagued by

Fleetwood to Lord Burghley, June 18, 1584, from *Queen Elizabeth and Her Times,* ed. Thomas Wright (London, 1883), 226–31.

such violent disorders since the 1580s (Archer, *Pursuit* 1–2). Rioters were over-whelmingly young men, prone to attack particular targets, especially brothels and theaters. But was the city of London so vulnerable to violent unrest merely as the result of uncontainable youthful male energy? Or were riots, uprisings, and other instances of social disorder the predictable, and motivated result of protest by a menacing underclass? In June 1581, for example, in the wake of a vio-lent altercation between apprentices and the servants of Sir Thomas Stanhope in Smithfield, Thomas Butcher, a brewer, was accused of inciting a thousand apprentices "to make a rebellion against the gentlemen & servingmen." The youth named Butcher was being whipped for the offense when he was rescued by a mob of apprentices (Archer, *Pursuit* 3–4). This was in no way an isolated incident, and some of these affrays, such as the first William Fleetwood dis-cusses in his report, bear the characteristics of class antagonism.

The document refers to a series of riots outside the Curtain theater in 1584. This began in a "broil" (a fight) between an apprentice and a gentleman, which led to an attack on the Inns of Court. Lincoln's Inn was an especially prominent target through the 1590s. There, well-educated young men (like the young John Donne) were trained in the law. The gentleman in this disturbance fumed that "the apprentice was but a rascal, and some were little better than rogues that took upon them the name of gentlemen, and said the 'prentices were but the scum of the world" (quoted in Archer, *Pursuit* 4). Fleetwood reported the inci-dent, along with a log of events from the same week, to Lord Burghley. Fleet-wood was the Recorder of London, the Corporation's principal secretary, and was described by his contemporary, John Stow, as "a grave and learned lawyer, skillful in the customs of the City" (Graves 209). Here, and in general, the theater figures as a magnet for violence and social disturbance. While Fleet-wood reports other more minor incidences, such as fighting over a prostitute, the greatest perceived threat seems to be that posed by the lower orders. When Sir Henry Lee's nephew is arrested, Fleetwood insists that he be detained in a "sweet, clean" house rather than the prison. Lee (1530–1610) was a wealthy landowner, man at arms, and master of the ordnance (weapons and ammuni-tion) who made a vow of chivalry at a tournament in 1559 that each year he would uphold Elizabeth's honor against all comers. So Fleetwood did not treat his nephew like a common murderer, even though he had mortally wounded two men. He told Burghley, in a comment reminiscent of "the fiery Tybalt" (1.1.96), that "the gentleman . . . is wild."

Report to Lord Burghley

Right honorable, and my very good Lord, upon Whit Sunday[1] there was a very good sermon preached at the new churchyard near Bethlehem, whereat my Lord Mayor was with his brethren. And by reason[2] no plays were the same day, all the city was quiet.

Upon Monday I was at the court, and went to Kingston to bed, and upon Tuesday I kept the law day[3] for the whole liberty of Kingston, and found all quiet and in good order. There lieth in Kingston Sir John Savage, of Cheshire, with his lady, at Mr. Henry Grises his house, the which is at the vicarage.

That night returned to London, and found all the wards full of watches.[4] The cause thereof was for that near the Theater or Curtain, at the time of the plays, there lay an apprentice sleeping upon the grass; and one Challes alias Grostock did turn upon the toe upon the belly of the same prentice; whereupon this apprentice start up, and after words they fell to plain blows. The company increased of both sides to the number of 500 at the least. This Challes exclaimed and said, that he was a gentleman, and that the apprentice was but a rascal, and some there were little better than rogues, that took upon them the name of gentlemen, and said the apprentices were but the scum of the world. Upon these troubles, the apprentices began the next day, being Tuesday, to make mutinies and assemblies, and did conspire to have broken the prisons, and to have taken forth the apprentices that were imprisoned. But my Lord and I having intelligence thereof, apprehended four or five of the chief conspirators, who are in Newgate,[5] and stand indicted of their lewd demeanors.

Upon Wednesday, one Brown, a serving man in a blue coat, a shifting fellow,[6] having a perilous wit of his own, intending a spoil if he could have brought it to pass, did at the Theater door quarrel with certain poor boys, handicraft apprentices, and struck some of them; and lastly, he, with his sword, wounded and maimed one of the boys upon the left hand. Whereupon there assembled near a thousand people. This Brown did very cunningly convey himself away, but by chance he was taken after and brought to Mr. Humphrey Smith, and because no man was able to charge him, he dismissed him. And after this, Brown was brought before Mr. Young, where he used himself so cunningly and subtly, no man being there to charge him,

---

[1] **Whit Sunday:** the feast of the descent of the Holy Spirit upon the Apostles after Christ's resurrection.   [2] **by reason:** because.   [3] **law day:** attendance at the quarter sessions.   [4] **wards full of watches:** the districts of London were heavily guarded.   [5] **Newgate:** a prison.   [6] **shifting fellow:** a suspicious character.

that there also he was dismissed. And after I sent a warrant for him, and the constables with the deputy, at the Bell in Holborne,[7] found him in a parlor, fast locked in, and he would not obey the warrant, but by the means of the host he was conveyed away; and then I sent for the host and, caused him to appear at Newgate, at the sessions of oyer and terminer,[8] where he was committed until he brought forth his guest. The next day after he brought forth himself, and so we indicted him for his misdemeanors. This Brown is a common cozener,[9] a thief, and a horse-stealer, and coloreth all his doings here about this town with a suit that he hath in the law against a brother of his in Staffordshire. He resteth now in Newgate.

Upon the same Wednesday at night, two companions, one being a tailor and the other a clerk of the Common Pleas,[10] both of the Duchy, and both very lewd fellows, fell out about a harlot, and the tailor raised the prentices and other light persons, and thinking the clerk was run into the Lyon's Inn, ran to the house with 300 at the least, broke down the windows of the house, and struck at the gentlemen. During which broil,[11] one Raynolds, a baker's son, came into Fleet Street, and there made solemn proclamation for cloaks.[12] The street rose and took and brought him unto me. And the next day we indicted him also, for this misdemeanor, with many other more.

Upon Wednesday, Thursday, Friday, and Saturday, we did nothing else but sit in commission, and examine these misdemeanors. We had good help of my Lord Anderson, and Mr. Sackforth.

Upon Sunday, my Lord sent two aldermen[13] to the court, for the suppressing and pulling down of the Theater and Curtain, for all the Lords agreed thereunto, saving my Lord Chamberlain and Mr. Vice-Chamberlain; but we obtained a letter to suppress them all. Upon the same night I sent for the Queen's players, and my Lord of Arundel his players, and they all well nigh obeyed the Lords' letters. The chiefest of Her Highness's players advised me to send for the owner of the Theater, who was a stubborn fellow, and to bind him. I did so. He sent me word that he was my Lord of Hunsdon's man, and that he would not come to me; but he would in the morning ride to my Lord. Then I sent the under-sheriff for him, and he brought him to me; and at his coming he shouted me out very justice.[14] And in the end I showed

---

[7] **the Bell in Holborne:** a tavern in an area of London known as Holborn. [8] **sessions of oyer and terminer:** legal sessions of hearing in order to determine whether there is a case to answer. [9] **cozener:** con man. [10] **Common Pleas:** one of the main law courts. [11] **broil:** affray; fight. [12] **cloaks:** Raynolds seems to have declared he would attack persons attired in cloaks. [13] **aldermen:** civic authorities. [14] **he shouted me out very justice:** he demanded to know by what authority I arrested him.

him my Lord his master's hand, and then he was more quiet. But . . . for it he would not be bound. And then I minding to send him to prison, he made suit that he might be bound to appear at the oyer and terminer, the which is tomorrow, where he said that he was sure the court would not bind him, being a councilor's man. And so I have granted his request, where he is sure to be bound, or else is likely to do worse.

Upon Sunday, at afternoon, one brewer's man killed another at Islington. The like part[15] was done at the White Chapel, at the same time.

The same Sunday, at night, my Lord Fitzgerald, with a number of gentlemen with him, at Moorgate, met a tall young fellow, being an apprentice, and struck him upon the face with his hat. Whereupon my Lord and his company were glad to take a house, and did scarcely escape without great danger. The sheriff came and fetched him to his house, where he lodged; and imprisoned one Cotton, that procured my Lord to misuse the apprentice. The same night at Aldersgate Street, an apprentice was put in the cage, and the cage was broken by a number of lewd fellows, and I hearing thereof did send my men for him, and sent him to the Counter,[16] where tomorrow he shall answer for his misdemeanor with others. . . .

The eldest son of Mr. Henry I hear upon Monday, being yesterday, fought in Cheapside[17] with one Boat, that is, or lately was, Mr. Vice-Chamberlain's man; and all was which of them was the better gentleman, and for taking of the wall.[18]

This day Mr. Cheney, of the Boyes, brought me his youngest son, being nephew to Sir Henry Lee, and would needs have me to send him to Bridewell,[19] where he had provided a chamber for him. But I would not agree thereunto, but sent him to be kept with my Lord of Winton's bailiffs house, the which is a place both sweet and clean. The young gent hath hurt two, whereof I learn they are like to die. The gentleman, as I can perceive, is wild, *et lucidus inter valla*.[20] And even now cometh in my Lord of Winton's bailiff, and telleth me that he is glad to hire three men to keep him both day and night in this extreme frenzy.

This Wednesday morning, the oyer and terminer sat at Newgate, for the quieting of the daily and nightly brawls. There appeared my Lord Fitzgerald, and one Cotton of eighteen years of age, (more bold than wise) a marvelous audacious youth, standing altogether upon his gentry. It so fell out,

---

[15] **like part:** same thing. [16] **Counter:** a prison. [17] **Cheapside:** a lower-class suburb of London. [18] **for taking of the wall:** starting a street fight ostensibly about which side of the pavement one man will allow the other to walk on. [19] **Bridewell:** a prison. [20] *et lucidus inter valla:* with lucid intervals.

that, by due examination, my Lord of Kildare's son dealt very wisely, well, and circumspectly, without any manner of evil behavior in any manner of wise. Mr. Wynter, son and heir of Mr. George Wynter, deceased, was there, and advised my Lord so to do for time's experience. Mr. Doctor Lewes, and the Admiral commission, have made him a man of good understanding. . . .

CHAPTER 3

Loving and Marrying

><

Thy good heart's oppression   (1.1.171)

Freedom in love is arguably literature's most persistent and pervasive theme, but when Shakespeare wrote *Romeo and Juliet* it was also one of the most controversial social topics of the time. As we noted in our discussion of enforced marriage in the introduction (see pp. 23–29), the kernel of the problem was whether or not individuals had the right to choose for themselves their future husbands or wives, or whether they ought to submit to the choice made for them by their parents or social superiors.

The choice of a marriage partner became increasingly controversial throughout the course of the sixteenth century primarily as a consequence of the Reformation. Protestant reform in relation to marriage was in part a reaction to the hypocrisy of the medieval Catholic Church, which, while it formally asserted that a monastic life devoted to God was the highest form of existence, in practice permitted morally dissolute behavior by ostensibly celibate clergy. Thus marriage became a newly respected condition in the Protestant religion, and married chastity, not sexual abstinence, was now espoused as the highest virtue and model of a godly life. The success of these new ideals, however, required that marriage partners take their vows of their own free will and not because of parental pressure or social coercion.

Crucially, unless they were fellows at one of the colleges of the universities where old traditions died hard, Protestant clergy themselves were permitted and even encouraged to marry. Protestant clerics therefore had a vested interest in matters pertaining to marriage as their Catholic forbears did not. Indeed, one of the most visible signs of difference between the English Catholic Church and the Protestant one that superceded it after the mid-Tudor Edwardian reformation was the fact that clergy were as likely to have wives and families as members of their congregations.

While the Protestant Reformation aimed at cleansing the Church of corrupt practices that had bedeviled it in the later medieval period, there were some (the Puritans) who sought more radical measures, and who hoped to "purify" the Church, not just reform it. Thus, the spectrum of belief and practice in the reformed English (Anglican) Church ranged from those who wished for a return to Catholicism, to those who felt reform had gone far enough, to radical Protestant churchmen who felt that change had hardly begun. All this fueled debates about obedience and hierarchy in the church and in the commonwealth, as well as debates about marriage. But while doctrinal positions on matters such as hierarchy panned out fairly neatly in accordance with religious affiliation, those on marriage very often did not.

In general, however, the reformed status of marriage had the corollary effect of suggesting the equality of marriage partners, men and women. This was a dangerous idea in such a profoundly patriarchal society and one around which many writers had to do a great deal of fast footwork. For all the *potential* of Protestant ideals of marriage to endow women with the same rights as men, it is certainly not true, as scholars once believed, that the Puritan doctrine of marriage revolutionized the status of women and invariably advocated freedom of choice in marriage (Davies 563–80). No Puritan was likely to uphold the right of his child to marry a Catholic, for example. Further, orthodox Elizabethan political and religious ideology held that the family was a microcosm of the state. This meant that if it was permissible to disobey fathers in the domestic realm over the matter of choosing a spouse, then, by analogy, the way was open for sweeping changes in the structure of political authority. In effect, legitimizing a child's right to choose a spouse over the duty to obey a parent was, when taken to its fullest extreme, akin to endorsing treason (see Callaghan, *Woman and Gender* 14–22; Dolan, *Dangerous* 59–88). To maintain the status quo, it was imperative, then, to limit the divisiveness caused by sharply different religious interests and beliefs by enforcing orthodox Anglican doctrine and removing nonconformists (those who did not toe the line) from their posts. All of these burning issues of the day about social and political order and the nature of power, about the rights of individuals in general and women in particular (though the term *rights* did not begin to be used in this context until a hundred years later), about whether disobedience to authority could ever be justifiable — in other words, all the issues about personal and political freedom — constellated around the issue of choosing a mate. So while we tend to think of selecting a life partner as pertaining only to the limited sphere of personal relations, this was far from the case.

Marriage in early modern England was also a mark of social maturity, and to enter into it was to change one's estate in a definitive and public way. (The clandestine marriage of Romeo and Juliet, and especially the fact that they never actually live together, singularly fails as such a public marker.) Apart from the completely dispossessed, everyone in Shakespeare's England had personal experience relating to the regulations governing courtship and marriage. Shakespeare's own daughter, Judith, in Lent 1616 married Thomas Quiney (a man who had already fathered one illegitimate child and who was to father another during the course of their marriage). The couple were subsequently disciplined by the consistory court (the bishop's court for ecclesiastical offences) for failing to get a license to marry during the Lenten period (see Schoenbaum, *Documentary;* Cook 9).

While people in secular life occasionally voiced their opinions about enforced marriage, clergymen and "divines" (experts in theological matters who had been trained at Oxford and Cambridge, the only universities in England at the time), proffered their opinions far more often. As a result, several of the documents that follow were written by clergymen. Selections include stern warnings against disobeying parental authority, insistent threats about how choosing the wrong partner leads not just to adultery but to spiritual and social ruin, as well as practical advice about how to choose a spouse. The excerpts printed here also represent both benign and belligerent parenting styles.

The discourse on choice of a spouse is both pervasive and fraught with contradiction. Many early moderns sense that choice is central to personal happiness, while others argue that it is more prudent to follow parental choice in marriage. In our selections there is a range of opinion — sometimes within the work of a single writer. Further, some texts emphasize either obedience or choice as aspects of godly behavior, while others are concerned more with pragmatics than with piety. Whatever their opinion on choice in marriage, Protestant churchmen shared the widespread disapproval of clandestine marriage, which was associated with Catholic nuptial rites. That the lovers of Verona are, in many ways, distinctly Catholic, may, as we noted in the introduction, have made them decidedly less sympathetic to an Elizabethan audience than they seem to contemporary theatergoers.

A further problem is that when we examine the discourses on enforced marriage, the doctrinal affiliation of the writer is not always clear. Although Catholicism was officially outlawed and Puritanism severely censured, it is sometimes quite difficult to attribute specific religious opinions to particular individuals. This is partly because the threat of censure and punishment mitigated against frank expression of belief, but also because religious identity was so much in flux that it rarely exhibited itself in stable and neatly segregated categories.

In the play's emphasis on marriage as the appropriate conclusion of heady romance, Shakespeare departs from literary precedent and participates in a historical shift in the ideal of romantic love. Juliet is not the cold, chaste Petrarchan lady, who, like Rosaline, refuses Romeo's love; instead, she reciprocates on the specific condition (one which, significantly, she and not Romeo introduces) of marriage — an aim that Petrarchanism never takes as its objective. The second part of this chapter deals with the literary discourses of this period, which seem to counter all social prescription with their emphasis on the centrality of subjective emotional life and sexual longing over all other notions of familial or social duty. Under this rubric, we will consider several famous poems of the period, including sonnets by Petrarch, Shakespeare, and Sidney. While canonical literary texts are usually considered simply as part of the *aesthetic,* rather than the *social* context for another literary work, it is important to understand the vital role played by literature in framing views and opinions about love and marriage.

→ CHARLES GIBBON

From A Work Worth the Reading   *1591*

Charles Gibbon (fl. 1589–1604)[1] attended Cambridge university, though there is no record of his graduation. He probably took holy orders (that is, became a clergyman). He wrote six books on a variety of topics, including what the *Dictionary of National Biography* suggests is his greatest contribution, a treatise in favor of progressive taxation. Writers on marriage were not, then, the "experts" we see interviewed on breakfast television today but people with wide-ranging interests in social issues. This is evident within the text of *A Work Worth the*

---

[1] When the exact dates of a person's birth and death are unknown, it is customary to refer to the period in which they were active, or in which they "flourished," of which "fl." is the abbreviated form.

Charles Gibbon, *A Work Worth the Reading* (London: Thomas Orwin, 1591), 1–16.

Reading itself: the first portion of the book is devoted to enforced marriage, but later sections address matters such as the disinheriting of first-born sons and whether hierarchy exists in heaven. The text at hand takes the form of a dialogue where two speakers address different sides of the argument for and against enforced marriage. In the dialogue, Philogus represents the rights of children over those of their parents in the choice of a marriage partner, while Tychius represents parental prerogative. This mode of addressing an issue was used widely in the Elizabethan educational system, where students were encouraged to argue in *utramque partem*, that is, on both sides of the question (Altman 3). Gibbon requires his reader to weigh the various arguments in order to decide about the justice of marriage arrangements that do not have the full consent of the couple who are to be married. Notably, the preface to the "indifferent," that is, the non-specialist reader (not reprinted here) emphasizes the difference, or rather the superiority, of the treatise versus all forms of fictional writing as the difference between "a pleasant story and a grave discourse." Although imbued with a clear sense of purpose, the dialogic form of the argument that follows allows the author not to position himself clearly on one side of the argument, compelling us to ask if he is indeed neutral, or if he obliquely demonstrates the superiority of one argument over another.

As in many Renaissance texts, there is considerable emphasis on biblical precedent, that is, on using examples from the Bible to prove and substantiate one's point. The Bible is a tremendously flexible text, and both of Gibbon's fictional debaters claim it for their side of the argument. References to the Old Testament, in particular, often led to discussion of social and sexual practices such as polygamy, remarriage after divorce, or the sale of children, which were related to Elizabethan practice only as very exaggerated or extreme manifestations of, for example, adultery, marriage after annulment, or marrying children off for money. As Ann Jenalie Cook points out, polygamy and the sale of children were neither sanctioned in Shakespeare's England, nor, despite the theater's tendency to favor the outrageous as an appropriate focus for drama, represented, at least in these exacerbated forms, on the stage (Cook 11). Marriage with infidels, atheists, idolaters, however, was another matter. As a result of religious rifts left by the Reformation, Protestants often regarded their Catholic neighbors as image worshippers who were little better than infidels, and children married spouses their parents considered impious. Moreover, on stage there were many accounts of intermarriage between all manner of foreigners, from marauding Turks to Moorish kings. In *The Tempest*, for example, Claribel has been married by her father to the King of Tunis. There were also stories of marriages across differences of belief and religion. Chaucer recounts the marriage of Celia, a Roman virgin, who is married against her will to Valerian, and who persuades him on their wedding night to embrace baptism and celibacy.

Gibbon's dialogue begins not with a discussion of marriage but with a discussion of class, in particular whether class differences are natural and God-given or man-made, whether genteel and noble behavior, which ostensibly defined the gentry, was innate or socially produced. This argument relates to the question of enforced marriage in that if gentility is not inevitably related to wealth and class status, it is inappropriate for fathers to try to marry their daughters to rich men: men of gentle manners and good character are to be found just as much among those who are not wealthy. For modern readers the issue of enforcement seems to be about whether young people should have autonomy from their parents in terms of their sexual desires, but for people in early modern England, the debate is far more concerned with whether public, communal, and familial considerations about wealth, power, and property take priority over matters of personal affection. In a sense, the debate is about whether marriage is primarily a public or a private agreement.

Gibbon's book also indicates that coercion itself was not necessarily the central problem in the debate about enforced marriage. The first examples concern compelling one's young daughter to marry an old man, that is, someone who is clearly unsuitable. There is not, however, a great deal of concern about compelling a child to marry someone like Paris, who would be deemed "suitable" by any reasonable measure. The idea of "misliking" and rejecting someone suitable just because one prefers someone else is not at issue here. However, the example of the aged suitor is important in this argument too because the exposition of the argument around this matter poses questions about women's desire. Would a young woman really feel sexual attraction for an old husband? Philogus claims that an old man is repellent to a young woman because he is "nothing answerable to his daughter's desire" and that she "will rather be martyred than married to him." He argues, contra Juliet's initial promise to bend her affections to her father's will, that a maid cannot "matcheth her self after another's liking." In these instances, female desire has the power to disrupt received notions of social and spiritual hierarchy. Not only may a poor man be as upstanding as any gentleman, but potentially "the Prince hath no privilege above the poor." Although Tychicus strenuously denies it, there is a suggestion here of the fundamental equality of all human beings, a notion that would be taken up fifty years later by radical sects during the English Revolution. For Philogus, the right to choose one's own marriage partner is a fundamental human freedom, "[E]ither let us link to our own liking or else better unborn, than living." Though these arguments are compelling to modern readers, Elizabethans might have been more swayed by Tychicus's perspective that "children are the goods of the parents," who must submit to their parents in all things, and so the father may give them to whomever he wishes. However, even Tychicus finally concedes that parents have no power to compel children to marry if they wish to remain celibate instead, "neither may they enforce them to any match, if their children mislike." But in cases where a daughter wishes neither to remain single nor to marry the man her father has chosen for her, Tychicus claims she must do her father's bidding.

Tychicus argues that these days, no one cares about the piety of a potential groom, but only about his wealth: "be he atheist, be he papist, be he newter [nothing at all], we respect not the man but his money." Just as Jews married Gentiles, it is not necessarily wrong for parents to marry children outside their racial or religious group. Tychicus's argument at this point, far from being a fairly conservative defense of parents' rights, becomes one which implicitly questions the assumption that marrying someone "proper and well disposed" necessarily entails marrying someone reasonably like oneself, within one's clan or community, or within the confines of one's own religious allegiance. Philogus's response raises a further problem, namely the potential contradiction between the authority of God and the authority of a parent, which is certainly one of the flash points of conflict within patriarchal structure. By professing allegiance to a higher authority, that of God, children might circumvent parental authority altogether.

The argument concludes with some agreement that, at least in the case of marrying an old man, a maid should not be coerced into marriage. That such an obvious point needs to be argued so carefully is instructive in itself, and along the way both characters in the dialogue offer stringent critiques of contemporary marriage arrangements.

From *A Work Worth the Reading*

Whether the Election of the Parents Is to Be Preferred before the Affection of Their Children in Marriage.

The speakers are Philogus and Tychicus: two lovers of learning.

PHILOGUS: There is an old verse which retains his old virtue being as credible for antiquities as truth; It is this:

> When Adam digg'd and Eve span
> who was then a gentleman?
> Then came a rich churl[2] and gathered good,
> and so came in the gentle blood.

Wherein appears that the ground of gentility began with goods: for (as the wiseman saith) *have not all men one entrance into life and a like going out* . . . Are we not equal by creation, heirs by adoption, brothers by profession, and yet it is a strange thing to see what preciseness of pedigrees, and difference of bloods there is amongst us. The days have been, that kings would bestow their daughters upon plain men, and yet thought it

---

[2] **churl:** person of low birth.

no disparagement of blood, as Saul, who bestowed his daughter Michal (1 Samuel 18:27) upon David being but a simple shepherd; that lords would have matched their sons with mean men's daughters, and yet account it no blemish to their birth, as Shechem the son of Hamor, who joined with Dinah, the daughter of Jacob, he was a lord's son that ruled a whole country (Genesis 34:1–2), she a plain man's daughter that dwelt in tents (Genesis 25:27). The time was when rich men would have taken poor women to their wives, and yet never made any respect of their portions, as Boaz did Ruth; he was a man of great authority and riches (Ruth 2:1), as some think Judge of Israel (Judges 12:8), she, a poor woman, that gleaned upon his land for her living. But now it is no match amongst us, where the parties be not answerable in birth, and agreeable in abilities, where indeed the best gentility consist in piety, and the most wealth in contentment.

I thought good to use this preamble for this purpose. There is old Cleanthes an ancient gentleman, who is adorned as well with the affluency of fortune, for great possessions, as with the excellency of nature, for good properties; he hath amongst many children but one daughter (yet a sister to every son); this maid is very desirous to marry, and hath made her choice of such a one, as is both of a goodly composition of body, and of godly disposition of mind. Yet as he is proper and well disposed, so he is very poor, insomuch as her father by reason of the baseness of his lineage, and barrenness of his living, will not allow of her liking, but hath appointed her another, which both by parentage and portion may countervail her calling and his contentment, yet nothing answerable to his daughter's desire, because for his years he may rather be her father than her husband, which as he cannot be the first, so he is so far from the latter that she will rather be martyred than married to him; now in this case whether is the affection of the children to be preferred before the election of the father.

TYCHICUS: You produce your preamble (as it seemeth) to impugn and reprove such as (upon circumstances of parentage and possessions) will permit or prohibit marriage, and therefore before I answer your proposition, I will say somewhat to your protestation. You bring an old verse to prove that gentility began with goods. Indeed goods in these days add a grace to many, yet gentry hath not his beginning all of one ground. Some have been base born, yet came to great estimation, not by their possessions, but by their valiant exploits, as Jephthah, being son of a harlot (Judges 11:1) became Judge of Israel (Judges 12:7). Others have been poor and yet came to great promotion, not for their wealth, but their wisdom; as Joseph who being an abject of his brethren (Genesis 37:4) became fellow to king Pharoah, and was made governor over all Egypt (Genesis 41:40) and in these days amongst us, many come to preferment, not for their living, but learning, not by progeny, but prowess, not by deserving, but descent: notwithstanding I affirm your sayings that as touching the bare birth, a king hath no better beginning than a beggar, or in respect of the ordinary end, the prince hath no privilege above the poor, for as both proceed from a woman, so both shall feed the worms; yet that followeth not although all be made of one metal, none should be more excellent in majesty, or albeit none be noble by nature, any should not be renowned by calling: for as many differ in degrees of dignity, so according to their title and authority they are to be preferred, and what renown the predecessor doth purchase by his life, it descendeth by succession to his posterity after him. You proceed further and say, that kings would bestow their children upon plain men, and for proof you bring in Saul's daughter and David? This example nothing availeth: for David had her, not by intercession, but upon condition, if he had not slain Goliath he had gone without her (1 Samuel 17:25). Yet are you advised of David's answer after he should have her, *What am I* (saith he) *and what is my life, or the family of my father in Israel, that I should be son-in-law to the king* (1 Samuel 18:18). Herein he doth show his unworthiness to match with such a man's daughter (I mean for pedigree, not for piety) & this argueth that in those days they had a special respect of parentage? And lords (say you) would match with mean men's children, & for this you infer Shechem and Dinah; you must note, although he were a lord's son he played a lead part to deflower her, & therefore no doubt it was the filthiness of the fact that forced him to marry her. Yea & rich men (say you) would take poor women to their wives, as Boaz did Ruth, still you strive against the stream, for Boaz was her kinsman, & therefore was to take her by the title of affinity according to God's law as it was commanded. *If brethren dwell together, & one of them die & have no son,* (as she had not) *the wife of the dead shall not marry to a stranger, but his kinsman shall go in to her and take her to wife, and do the kinsman's office to her* (Deuteronomy 25:5–7). So that your preamble is impertinent: for where parties be matched equally according to their birth and abilities there is ever best agreement. Now to your question: *whether the election of the father is to be preferred before the affection of the child.* This is as easy to answer as to ask: The ten commandments teach children to honor and submit themselves to their parents, therefore if the contract & couple contrary to their contentation, they rather rebel than obey them.

PHILOGUS: It is true indeed but you know the common by-word, it is the eye of the master, that fatteth the horse, and the love of the maid that maketh the liking, she that matcheth herself after another's mind, is like him that fitteth his foot by another's last:[3] one is often wrong with his shoes in the wearing, the other often vexed with her husband after wedding, either let us link to our own liking or else better unborn, than living.

TYCHICUS: Your talk tendeth only to sensual circumstances altogether preposterous from the proposition: for the word of God hath given parents great prerogative over their children, even in this matter concerning marriage; insomuch as no contract (much less any conjunction) can be lawful unless the parents allow it, according as it is written: *If a woman vow a vow unto the Lord and bind herself by a bond being in her father's house in the time of her youth, and her father hear her vow & bond wherewith she hath bound herself, and her father hold his peace concerning her, then all her vows shall stand, and every bond wherewith she hath bound herself shall stand. But if her father disallow her the same day that he heareth all her vows and bonds wherewith she hath bound herself, they shall not be of value, and the Lord will forgive her: because her father disallowed her* (Numbers 30:4–6). Hereof it is that where the maid was taken away and abused, albeit she was afterward married to the man that did it, yet he was to pay a piece of money to her father, because he had not his preconsent, as it is written, *If a man entice a maid that is not betrothed and lie with her, he shall endow her and take her to his wife. If her father refuse to give her to him, he shall pay money according to the Dowry of Virgins* (Exodus 22:16–17). It is more fully confirmed in Deuteronomy 22:28–29. *If a man find a maid that is not betrothed, and take her and lie with her and they be found, then the man that lay with her, shall give unto the maid's father fifty shekels of silver, and she shall be his wife, because he hath humbled her, he cannot put her away all his life,* yea Saint Paul himself doth approve the superiority of parents in this respect, for (saith he) *If any man think that it is uncomely for his virgin, if she pass the flower of her age, and need so require let him do what he will, he sinneth not: let them be married* (1 Corinthians 7:36). And hereto agreeth the same saying of the wise man, *Marry thy daughter, and so thou shalt perform a weighty work* (Ecclesiastes 30). I could amplify the matter very much, but these are sufficient to resolve you, that children cannot match without their parents' consent.

PHILOGUS: Alas, you do not consider the innumerable inconveniences that be incident to those parties which be brought together more for lucre[4] than love, more for goods than good will, more by constraint than consent, nay more than that, you do little weigh the inequalities of years, the contrariety of natures between age and youth. Is there no difference

---

[3] **last:** a block or form used in the making of shoes.   [4] **lucre:** wealth.

between the withered beech and the flourishing bay tree, no opposition between frost and flowers, or is it possible that oxen unequally yoked should draw well together? If you would confer all these circumstances together with the accidents you shall find that such a husband is a hell to a tender virgin, and that such a marriage is the beginning of all misery, and no doubt he that bestows his daughter no better, shall abridge her grief, by following her to the grave. So that I conclude, seeing marriage is of great moment, not for a month but a whole lifetime, there is no reason, but he or she that entereth into that bond, should make their own bargain: because it is they that must abide by it.

TYCHICUS: You still continue your carnal positions, to confirm your crazed opinion, as though the prescript rule of God's book were to be impugned by the natural reason of man's brain. If a man may give his goods to whom he will, he may as well bestow his children where he thinketh best, for children are the goods of the parents. So it seemeth by that which God himself said to Satan, when he earnestly desired to deal with Job, *All that he hath* (saith the Lord) *be in thy hands* (Job 1:12). If you look into the old law, you shall find that parents might sell their children to supply their necessity, as appears in Exodus 21:7: *If a man sell his daughter to be a servant & etc.* . . . Laban did little better than make a benefit of his daughters before he bestowed them: For by Jacob's servitude it appeareth he made a sale of them, and so they could say themselves afterward (Genesis 31:15). Therefore if parents had this great privilege then (which is almost importable) why should they be barred of this benefit now, not in selling but in bestowing them (which is so reasonable); you allege it is good reason they should make their own bargain, because they must abide it, as though parents would seek the prejudice of their own children, but what liberty of liking had Leah to Jacob, who instead of her sister Rachel was brought to his bed (Genesis 29:23). This argueth that parents would dispose their children at their pleasure.

PHILOGUS: I perceive by your speech you so much prefer the parents, that you altogether enjoin their children to an inconvenience; that is, not to match to their own liking but as their parents list,[5] as though they ought not to show as well a fatherly affection, as they look for filial obedience.

TYCHICUS: You mistake both the matter and my meaning, for albeit parents ought to yield their consent to their children's choice, yet they have not power to provoke them to marry, if necessity urgeth not, hereof sayeth Paul: *He that standeth firm in his heart that he hath no need, but hath power over his own will, and hath so decreed in his heart that he will keep his*

---

[5] **list:** desire.

virgin he doth well (1 Corinthians 7:37). Neither may they deprive them of that remedy if they cannot live continent, *for it is better to marry than burn* (1 Corinthians 7:9), nay more than that, the parents must presently provide for them as a duty enjoined to them, which the same apostle proveth in these words, *Let them be married* (1 Corinthians 7:36), neither may they inforce them to any match, if their children mislike, we have example thereof in Rebecca, for when the servant (who should have her) whom Abraham sent was requested that she might remain ten days before their departure, his expedition was such that he had rather go away without her than tarry to take her: whereupon her parents called her, to ask her consent, and to know whether she would go with that man or no, her answer was, she would (Genesis 24:27 & etc.). This argueth that parents must not use any coaction, where their children have no disposition to the party.

PHILOGUS: Yet all this is to no purpose to the question I propose, for the maid neither meaneth to live single as a virgin, yet she cannot be suffered to match to her mind, as she would do: now in this case whether may the perversity of the parents hinder the choice of the child?

TYCHICUS: It is needless to add a double answer to a single question, or to demand a reason where there is no doubt, your word perversity, is so termed of the willful, but it is taken for prudency amongst the wise, for they know that it is the property of parents, not to deal frowardly[6] but fatherly with their children, and to bestow them not as they desire, without discretion; but as is most expedient, with circumspection: but admit, that parents be sometimes perverse, shall children be pernicious, or (as we commonly say) drive out one nail with another? God forbid, they must win them by petition, not provocation, by obedience, not obstinacy. The parents' joy depends upon their children, and therefore their evil placing, turn to their displeasure, did not Esau by taking wives, contrary to his father's will, procure his sorrow, insomuch as his mother said, *It should not avail her to live if his brother Jacob did bestow himself so* (Genesis 27:46), let then the example of Esau dehort[7] the disobedient which care more to please their fancies than their fathers, and let Jacob be an imitation to the dutiful, which prefer their fathers' precept before their own pleasure: and to resolve you more fully will I show some apparent examples that shall approve the submission of children to their parents in this respect: Sechem, the son of a lord having deflowered Dinah, although (by reason of the filthiness of the fact) it was more time for him

[6] **frowardly:** obstinately.   [7] **dehort:** chastise; from *de haut en bas,* in a condescending or superior manner.

to marry the maid than to motion[8] the matter, yet before he would marry he craved his father's good will, as appeareth in the text for it is there said, *He said to his father Hamer, get me this maid to wife* (Genesis 34:1 & etc.). If the consent of parents was observed as a principle amongst the very infidels, how much more ought we to be careful of it that be Christians; Samson was Judge of Israel, and a strong and valiant man, yet falling in love with Delilah he did not satisfy his lust without his father's liking: for he said to his father, *Give me her to wife* (Judges 14:2). Ruth was content to be ruled by Naomi her mother-in-law, yea even in this matter concerning her marriage (Ruth 3:5), then how much more ought we to submit our consents to our natural parents? Many such examples I could infer, but these may satisfy a sensible man in a reasonable matter.

PHILOGUS: I have permitted your speech hitherto, not because I could not prevent your apology, but that I was desirous to learn what you could allege and now I plainly see, that a fierce stream hath no stay, if it be not stopped in time, nor your arguments an end, if they be not intercepted; to the matter, I confess that children are commanded to obey their parents, yet I affirm they must not in many things approve their proceedings, for their limits are prescribed, *They must obey them in the Lord: for this is right,* (saith Paul), (Ephesians 6:1) if parents will provoke their children to marry with Infidels they may not: for they have no warrant by the word of God (2 Corinthians 6:14).

TYCHICUS: Yet the same apostle saith, *The unbelieving husband is sanctified by the believing wife, and the unbelieving wife is sanctified by the husband* (1 Corinthians 7:14). What say you to this?

PHILOGUS: . . . [T]he end he chiefly aimeth at, was to premonish the unmarried not to match in that manner as appeareth in the 2 Corinthians 6:14–15. *Be not* (saith he) *unequally yoked with infidels:* then he showeth a reason, *for what fellowship hath righteousness with unrighteousness, & what communion hath light with darkness, and what concord hath Christ with Belial, or what part hath the believer with the infidel?* So having answered your objection, I will iterate where you interrupted me: As children may not intercommon with infidels, so their parents may not urge them to match with idolaters, or such like because it is prohibited.

TYCHICUS: And yet it is nothing respected in these days, for in marriages amongst us, we make no regard of godliness, but goods, of righteousness, but riches, how well, but how wealthy, they be made: be he atheist, be he papist, be he newter,[9] we respect not the man, but his money, not his life, but his living, not his profession, but his promotion; and therefore I see

---

[8] **motion:** begin marriage negotiations.   [9] **newter:** of no religion.

no reason, but that they may deal with idolaters. The Israelites a chosen people of God did intercovenant with the Gentiles which were great idolaters (Judges 3:6). Solomon that prudent king took the daughter of king Pharaoh (1 Kings 3:1) & David that holy man, matched with the daughter of king Saul, yet Pharaoh and Saul were gross idolaters.

PHILOGUS: I see you strive to wring water out of the pumice,[10] or else you would never waste the time with such words, doth it follow because most in marriage have regard of goods, that I by their example should impair God's glory, why we are taught, not to follow a multitude in evil. Did the Israelites intercovenant with the Gentiles? Why they did contrary to the commandment of God (Deuteronomy 7:3). Yet the Lord did not let them pass unpunished (Judges 3:8). Did Solomon marry an idolatrous wife? Why he was drawn to idolatry by them, & what followed: he incurred the wrath of God for his wickedness (1 Kings 11:14). As for that act of David it cannot animate us, neither is it expedient for any to presume of God's power, without his will. Now having answered your digression, I will proceed where I left, I say still, that the glory of God not the motions of men, his praise not their practices are to be preferred in every thing, as in this matter concerning marriage; we ought indeed to obey our earthly parents, yet we must not dishonor our eternal father, for we are taught by the apostle Peter *to obey God more than man* (Acts 5:29). We ought to love our worldly parents, yet we must not offend our heavenly father: for, *He that loveth father & mother more than me is not worthy of me*, (saith Christ) (Matthew 10:37). We ought to fear our natural parents, that have governance of our bodies, yet we must be more afraid of our celestial father, which preserves both body and soul, and is able to cast them into hell fire (Matthew 10:28). Whereupon I ground my argument, that if parents will profit and impose upon their children such a match as tendeth more to profit than piety, more to content their greedy desire for lucre than their children's godly choice for love, as this man hath done to his daughter, neither they nor this maid ought to depend on their parents in this point: what greater occasion of incontinency can be given, than to match a young and lusty maid against her own mind, with an infirm and decrepit person to satisfy another's pleasure? What a cross contract this would be and shall not the maid (who hath made a fit choice to her own mind) marry, unless she take such an old man, against her mind? What say you, shall the severity of her father abridge her liberty, or deprive her of the lawful remedy? Nay more than that, shall the maid increase in sin for want of her desire, because her father will not

---

[10] **wring water out of the pumice**: get water out of a stone.

yield his consent, unless it be to her disliking? I say no: the apostle telleth us, *It is better to marry than burn*, and yet she shall keep her within the bounds of obedience, because she doth it not of purpose in contempt of her parents, but in regard of God's glory to avoid the occasion of evil.

TYCHICUS: Indeed I must needs confess that to match a young maid with an old man, it is miserable: nay then that which is more admirable, some man that hath lived single above sixty years, will (upon a little fleshly fancy) needs to the world; yet he will sooner angle for a frog than a fish; I mean, he will sooner catch a light minion than couple with a grave matron, and as the world doth wonder at him for his wantonness, in making such a match, so his kindred which did hope to have good of him, are deceived by this means: for he will so much respect the trifling tricks of his coffer, that he will not care to cast off the tried love of his kindred, whom of a long time he hath put in hope of some great promotion by his death (which no doubt by their duty & diligence they have deserved) and at last doth recompense them with this delusion, by his life to give all to his young wife, fie[11] upon flesh that rageth so furiously, & of men that have no more modesty, & of age that yields no better gravity (for the grace of man consists not in proportion, but properties; nor the glory of age in gray hairs, but in gravity). The days have been that men would not have their possessions go out of the name (Ruth 4:5), but these account more of their filthy pleasure than their posterity. Moses made a law in Israel, that he hath had no issue,[12] should give his inheritance to such as were of his consanguinity, for sale of such to some of his affinity (Numbers 27:8 & etc.), but these do more regard their greedy lust than a godly law. We shall read in the Old Testament that they might not sell any parcel of their possessions from their kindred (Ruth 4). Then with what conscience may these give all away from them? Good God what a strange thing is this, that those which go holding down their heads as though they would drop into their graves, should be casting up their eyes a-doting after girls, when it were more meeter[13] for them to make a covenant with death than a contract with a damsel: but it seemeth such have lived longer for their years than their virtues, that neither the decrepidity of their age, nor the imbecility of their bodies, can bridle their concupiscence,[14] but they must further their infirmities by their own follies; the young flesh of Abishah (say they) did foster David in his age, this giveth a great light to their levity, as though David would make his deathbed, a place of beastliness, when the text saith *He knew her not* (1 Kings 1:4), and

---

[11] **fie:** exclamation of outraged propriety.   [12] **he hath had no issue:** he had not had children.
[13] **more meeter:** more fitting.   [14] **concupiscence:** lust.

to cover their dotage, they will carry this cloak for an excuse, *It is better to marry than burn* (as though rotten wood could take fire so fast). It is lawful for them to marry I confess, yet not expedient . . . the original of such a marriage is grounded upon no goodness, for he taketh her upon a burning unbridled lust, she him upon a lewd desire of living, the sight of such nuptials are ridiculous, for who sees them that in derision will not say, the old horse has got him a young filly, the success of such a contract is sorrowful: for there is no greater rage than the jealousy of man (saith Solomon) (Proverbs 6:34), it is as cruel as death (Canticles 3:6), and who can be more jealous than an old man over his young wife: the end of such a uniting is but evil, for imbecility and debility is a mean to cause his wife's inconstancy. Then what reason should move the old man to make such a match, or what maid well-disposed will match with such a man, my reason is: It is not sufficient for us to do well, but therewith to avoid the occasion of evil, although she be of an honest conversation, yet the taking of such an old huddle,[15] will give occasion to the world to judge the worst.

[15] **huddle:** a bent old fellow.

→ JOHN STOCKWOOD

From A Bartholomew Fairing for Parents   *1589*

John Stockwood (d. 1610), was a schoolmaster and divine. He studied at Oxford, Cambridge, and Heidelberg, and was vicar of Tunbridge in Kent as well as headmaster of the grammar school there. In contrast to this text, most of his writings were translations of works by continental reformers. His is a decidedly tub-thumping Protestantism concerned with the evils and what he calls the "enormities" (the moral outrages) of his time. In concert with his brand of religious thinking, Stockwood believes human beings are inherently depraved, and saved from their baseness only by the sober moral strictures of reformed religion.

The title *Bartholomew Fairing* refers to the annual fair on the feast day of St. Bartholomew and suggests his book is like one of the novelties to be purchased there, or alternatively, a form of chastisement.

John Stockwood, *A Bartholomew Fairing for Parents, to Bestow upon Their Sons and Daughters, and for One Friend to Give unto Another; Showing That Children Are Not to Marry, without the Consent of Their Parents, in Whose Power and Choice It Lieth to Provide Wives and Husbands for Their Sons and Daughters* (1589), 11–17, 21–24, 26–27, 33, 38, 41–50, 56, 67, 74–88, 90–91.

That Marriages Are Not to Be Made
without the Consent of Parents.

Among many other vices, wherewith the world at this day is full fraughted, insomuch that the very elements themselves, together with the rest of the creatures . . . do groan under the burden of them, looking for a change, from the vanity whereunto they are made subject through the sin of man, that they may be restored unto the glorious liberty of the sons of God, this one is neither the least nor the last, whereby youth for the most part is grown into such a pass, that forgetting all childlike affection and dutiful obedience unto father and mother in the highest point of subjection, the which they owe unto them in this life, and wherupon dependeth their making or marring (as they say) together with the continual joy or sorrow of their parents they wholly follow their own will and let out the reins unto their own unbridled & unsettled lusts, making matches according to their own fickle fantasies, and choosing unto themselves yokefellows after the outward deceivable direction of the eye, nothing regarding the sound advice of a mind guided with the knowledge & fear of God, the which counseleth to respect the inward graces and ornaments of the soul, & not to be enamored with the outward garnishing, beauty, bravery and decking of the body. And hereof it comes to pass, that men in their marriages following the manners of the sons of the first forlorn world, seeing the daughters of men to be beautiful & pleasing unto the eye, take unto themselves of all that they like, not waiting or staying for the choice of their parents, by whose authority, if they ought to be directed in the matters of smaller weight and less importance, as now is so shameless and void of grace, that he dare to deny, how much more are they then to be ruled by their grave advice in this which chiefly concerneth God's glory, their own welfare, the cheering and rejoicing of them that have begotten them.

. . . For marriage being the means the which God himself hath ordained and sanctified for the propagation and increase of mankind, that being taken in hand in his fear, a godly seed being multiplied & grown up here on earth the same may be blessed to the constitution & making of a church, the which may serve him in holiness and righteousness: when the same is taken in hand with the breach of his commandment, so far off is it, that any blessing is to be hoped for, that contrariwise is hot indignation and heavy curse hangeth over that house & family, where the parties which are the principal pillars and upholders of the same, are linked and tied together in such a band of wedlock, whose links & enclosings are not fastened and coupled together with the necessary and lawful assent and liking of the parents, whose authority & consent ought to bear the chiefest sway, and strike like-wise the greatest stroke in this most holy and heavenly action. And like as marriage is begun & enterprised in the fear of God according to his word, there God is well pleased, there the parties so matched live together in a joyful agreement and liking the one of the other, there God is honored and served in sincerity and truth, there the children, when God giveth them, with the rest of the family are instructed and brought up in the knowledge of religion, and grounds of faith: so on the other side, the regard of that which God especially commandeth, being shut out of our marriages, there must needs ensue his dislike, and displeasure, there is ire and discord, there God's honor is neglected, there household discipline and Christian instruction of such as belong unto our charge, goeth utterly to wreck, and is nothing at all regarded. And no marvel: for, if where God blesseth, all things go well and do prosper, then consequently where he curseth, there nothing thriveth, hath good success, or goeth happily forward. . . .

. . . [I]t shall plainly appear, that not only the consent of father & mother is chiefly requisite in the case of marriage, but also in the former ages and more ancient times of this world, always declining from better to worse, that the choice it self of wives for the sons, and husbands for the daughters, rested wholly in the power & authority of the parents, insomuch that not only the better sort of the children of the godly referred the whole care of their bestowing this way unto the provident election of their fathers and mothers, but the very heathen themselves that were not altogether past grace, and had clean shaken of the yoke of dutiful obedience, would not so much as once vouchsafe to hear of the motion of any match for themselves in the state of wedlock, except the choice of their fathers & mothers had gone before.

. . . [W]e ought not to do unto others that thing, the like whereof we would be grieved and offended, they should do unto us: I appeal to the conscience of all graceless sons and daughters, as now a days (the more is the pity) in too great multitudes betroth themselves in marriage . . . against the will of their fathers and mother, whether that they would take it in good part at the hands of their children, if they should in like manner provide themselves of wives and husbands, their good will and consent being not first obtained before, if there be none having any conscience at all, but that the same duly examined every night when he goeth unto his bed, telleth him that he would not thus himself be served: let this rule then be sufficient to teach him, that he also ought not to marry without the well-liking and agreement of his father and mother. . . .

. . . [C]hildren are worthily to be reckoned among the goods and substance of their fathers, . . . as those which are more nearly linked and joined unto them, and which cost them more dearly, being flesh of their flesh, and bone of their bone, and without whom, they had never been: so that they owe themselves wholly unto them in all manner of obedience and dutiful affection, and shall in seeking to betroth themselves at their own pleasures, not regarding to have the good will and leave of their parents, deal as preposterously, and overthwartly,[1] as if the goods should go about to dispose the owner and possessor of the same, and not be disposed and ordered by those unto whom the possession and property of the same doeth by right and equity belong and appertain. . . .

And it seemeth not to be much impertinent from this place, the which we read in the book of Numbers concerning vows, . . . that the vows which were made by the children without the privity[2] and consent of the fathers, and of the wives without the liking and allowance of their husbands were altogether unlawful and of no force. And the reason according, to true meaning of the place, is given by the best interpreters, because neither children, nor wives are . . . at their own liberty and appointment, but under the rule and government of others, namely of their parents and husbands. As therefore to make a vow unto the Lord, being in itself and of its own nature an holy and acceptable action unto God, and wherewith he is well pleased, is notwithstanding in children unlawful, because it is such an action as they only may perform which are free and at their own disposition, the which they are not: so in like manner to consent in matrimony, although in itself it be both honest & lawful, yet is it not an action of force in children, without the consent and allowance of their parents, because that children are not free & at their own liberty, but by the laws both of God and man tied and bound unto the subjection of their fathers. . . .

Besides all this what clearer evidence can we have on our side, than the fifth commandment, in which children are commanded to honor their fathers and mothers, with a blessing promised to those which perform the same: whereby we gather by the nature of contraries, that there is a curse also belonging unto all those children that shall dishonor them. And in that God willeth that the parents by their children should be honored, he meaneth, that they should in all humility and modesty reverence them, with all dutiful submission, be obedient unto them, and with all willingness show themselves thankful for their procreation, education, sustentation,[3] and all other benefits, that under God they have received from them. . . . Obedience herein showeth forth itself, in that willingly without murmuring or grudging we be willing to be ordered, directed, guided, and ruled by them, being ready to do all lawful things the which they command us, & to refrain from those things the which they shall forbid us. . . .

---

[1] **overthwartly:** presumptuously.   [2] **privity:** knowledge.   [3] **sustentation:** sustenance.

... [W]e are taught, that not only in the commandments of our parents, but also of all other our superiors be they kings, rulers or magistrates of any other condition whatsoever, all which are comprehended under the name of parents, that if they enjoin us to do any thing against that obedience which we owe unto God, we are not indeed violently to resist, but we must with patience abide such punishment as they shall lay upon us, rather than in obeying them we should disobey God, unto whom of good right we are bound above and before all others be they of never so high and excellent places. For there is a double obedience, that is, a certain first, chief, & most sovereign obedience the which is proper and belongeth unto God, and a secondary or inferior obedience the which is due and appertaining unto men. So that in all our actions whatsoever belongeth unto this life this is a most general rule the which admitteth or receiveth none exception: *God must be obeyed before, or rather than men.* To return therefore unto the matter in hand, the obedience of children to their parents must (I grant) be limited and bounded within the rails and lists of our obedience peculiar unto God, that is to say, children are no further to obey the commandments of their parents, than so far forth as the same be answerable and agreeable unto the commandments of God. ...

It will here peradventure be said, that God by making this law [that parents must *not* make marriages between their sons & daughters & those of non-Christian nations], setteth not down an order the which he would have generally to be observed of the parents in all matches of their children, yea even with their own people and nation, but only directeth them what they should do concerning marriage of their sons and daughters among those seven accursed nations,[4] & this also to prevent a mischief, least that by making and joining any such affinity, they might be pulled and drawn away from the true worship and service of God unto idolatry and superstition. I answer, that God, when he gave unto them this commandment, had indeed an especial regard to meet with beforehand this danger of having his people carried by such matches to run a whoring after strange gods. ...

... Yet do I not think the contrary, but that in those ages, like as in our time there were many both sons and daughters, which are like unruly colts and untamed heifers could not be brought unto this pass, nor yet be yoked within this bow, but the sturdy frowardness of some certain, is not disproof of the dutiful obedience of the better sort, neither was there any more required of the fathers, than that according unto God his commandment, so far as in them lay, they should do their parts to keep their children within

---

[4] **accursed nations**: refers to the biblical prohibition against marrying people of nations that practice idolatry, for example in Deuteronomy 7.

this compass: that is to say, they were to provide matches for them within their own people, to charge them in regard of that honor, the which by God his commandment they did owe unto them, that they yielded unto their fathers' choice, and having gone thus far, they have sufficiently done that which unto them belonged, and for the rest, they were to leave their ruleless children unto the judgments of God, and correction of the magistrate, who in cases of disobedience, where the authority of parents could bear no sway, was by God himself appointed to minister correction according unto the quality of the transgression.

. . . I will shut up this place with an authority taken out of the prophet Jeremiah, & with the judgment of M[onsieur] Calvin[5] (a most worthy instrument of Christ in his church in our time) upon the same, the which shall strike this matter stone dead (as they say) and so go on to other proofs, and these shall serve as a strong nail to fasten all the rest together. . . .

. . . Calvin writeth after this manner, Whereas (saith he) the prophet willeth them to *take wives for their sons, and to give their daughters to be married*, this is according to the lawful order and course of nature, because that this were too preposterous, or overthwart[6] and topsy-turvy dealing, that young men and maidens, should get them either husbands or wives at their own lust and pleasure. God therefore in this place speaketh according unto the common rule, when as he commandeth young men to be linked in matrimony no otherwise, but by the commandment of their parents and maidens also not to marry any husbands, but such as to whom they shall be given. Here you may see in a few words confirmed that, which in so many I have at large set down before: where first it is to be noted, that children's marrying according to the choice of their parents, is a thing commanded by God. Secondly, that it is agreeable unto the law of nature. Thirdly, that it was a general rule and common practice. Fourthly, that the contrary dealing is preposterous and overthwart, and as far out of square and order, as if the cart should be placed and set before the horse. And mark further, that in all these places . . . God saith not, that parents if they will, may provide wives for their sons, and husbands for their daughters: That it were meet[7] and requisite that it should be so, but useth everywhere the imperative mood, that is commandeth that it be so, and leaveth it not at random to our discretion to choose whether we will have it to be so, or otherwise, to that end that we should know, that if we that are parents shall neglect our daughters in this behalf, we shall not pass away with the matter slightly and lightly, as if it

---

[5] **Calvin:** John Calvin, author of *The Institutes of the Christian Religion* and radical Protestant who headed the church in Geneva.   [6] **overthwart:** crossed or confused.   [7] **it were meet:** it is appropriate; only proper.

were a jest & a trifle, but that we shall answer for it, as for a transgression and breach of his commandment.

Having therefore given this brief caveat and warning blow unto fathers and mothers to think hereafter more advisedly upon their duties in bestowing their children, I take my leave and farewell of this reason, giving all young men and maidens in like manner to understand, that if they shall henceforth refuse to be ordered and directed by their parents, they shall be found rebels against God, transgressors against the law of nature, breakers of the common rule and custom of all well-governed children, and such, so far as in them, would bring in all confusion and disorder, in altering and changing God's own course, to set up and establish their own unbridled lust and lawless affection.

. . . The purpose . . . in this place is to give counsel unto parents, what course they were best to take for their children concerning their bestowing of them in marriage, or letting them remain single, according unto the assured and certain knowledge that they have of their ability to live chaste, or their need, otherwise to use that lawful remedy, the which God hath ordained against fornication, which is to marry, so that those which have the gift of chastity, he would not have constrained to join themselves in wedlock, nor those which are not able to, be forced to live single. This is briefly the sum of the place. Concerning those children that cannot live single, he willeth their parents to look unto them betimes, least that their too long differing and delaying the matter breed some inconvenience. . . . [P]arents when their children come once to such years, that they are ready to marry, should in due time have consideration hereof, not giving occasion, by causing them stay too long, either to be derided, or laughed to scorn as stale bachelors, or otherwise to be suspected of bad husbandry, or housewifery, or of pride and disdaining all others, being so nice & coy, that they think none fine enough to match withal, or that there is in them some secret & hidden vice or infirmity the which maketh them unfit for marriage, or otherwise of covetousness, because they are loath to depart with money towards their maintenance, protracting & delaying the time longer than the nature and disposition of their sons & daughters will bear, so that by their means being thus deferred and put off, when as they are not able any longer to forbear, their parents neglecting to provide that remedy for them the which God hath ordained, they burn in lust and commit folly. Their fathers and mothers therefore perceiving that so it ought to be, that is, their children without fear of some inconvenience cannot tarry any longer unmarried, ought worthily to have this wife care for them, in time to provide them of fit and honest matches. . . . Thus we see how pregnant and plentiful a text this is to teach that it lieth in the parents to make due choice for their children in the

case of matrimony: And because that small regard is had hereof in many
now-a-days, hence it cometh that some children give themselves over unto
the lusts of the flesh, in committing shameful & filthy fornication; others,
contrary unto the laws both of God and nature, break to the duties of their
fathers, and unnaturally, and not child-like, without the privity & consent of
their parents make their own matches & the same for the most part so unto-
ward, that they bring the gray hairs of their parents unto their grief and sorrow to the grave, and themselves besides wastefully spending all that they
have, live all their life long in continual and daily home brawls and household strifes and discords.

You therefore that be fathers and mothers I most earnestly and heartily
exhort and beseech you for the love of God and in the tender bowels and
mercy of Jesus Christ our most gracious redeemer, that you will at length
awake, and rouse up your selves out of this deadly sleep of carelessness,
wherewith you have been long oppressed, making little or none accounts at
all of this weighty and necessary duty of providing virtuous wives and husbands for your sons and daughters, delay the time henceforth no longer, . . .
lay off all rigorous austereness and bitterness, and in the spirit of levity and
mildness, question and confer, talk and reason with your sons and daughters, when they be come unto ripe years, that you may learn how they are
inclined concerning marriage, or sole life: and if it be so that you think, that
through bashfulness and shamefulness they will not dare to deal plainly with
you, nor freely to unfold their minds unto you as they would do unto some
of their familiars, let it not grieve you to use this wise policy to fish out their
purpose by some of their friends, unto whom being great[8] with them, they
will not be afraid to utter the very bottom of their hearts and inmost secrets.
And when you shall have found, that it is safest for your honor, and meetest
for their present estate, that you provide for them to marry, go about the
same in the fear of God accordingly, with faithful and earnest prayer unto
God. . . .

. . . [Let it be proven further that] if . . . God the father made the choice
of us his church to be a wife for Jesus Christ his son . . . [h]ow much more
then ought earthly fathers seek out meet wives & husbands for their sons
and daughters. . . .

Here is to be noted, that God not only created the woman, but also
brought her unto Adam to espouse and betroth her unto him, and delivered
her & joined her unto him for his wife. . . . But God would not that either
Adam, or the woman, should do any of these things, upon their own heads.
Wherefore he himself joined them together, & brought the woman unto

---

[8] **great:** close.

Adam, delivered and betrothed her being formed, & made for lawful company sake. . . .

. . . [W]e will conclude and shut up this point with the testimony of M. Luther,[9] the thunderbolt of Germany, whom we have reserved unto this last place, not for that he is the least among my witnesses, who worthily ought to be accounted of even with the very foremost for his most profitable service done unto the church of God, but because he doth very evidently and clearly with great courage and boldness of heart set down his judgment in this cause writing upon the 14th chapter of the book of Genesis: Therefore (saith he) do I handle this place, albeit odious or hateful: Because Isaac doth not marry a wife, where he pleaseth, but is forbidden of his father to marry one of the land of Canaan, and his father himself doth carefully provide his son of a wife, and his son with all willingness doth obey his father. For daily experience doth teach, that those privy and stolen contracts are the cause of great mischiefs, daily brawls, strifes, perjuries, and murders, and also the most shameful plague and garboil[10] of the church and commonwealth. So the popish Canonists[11] do nothing else but seek to tear asunder the church and trouble the world because of their doltish & unlearned canons.[12] And shall we suffer them to bring in so many mischiefs into our churches? Let the devil wink at this, and no other man: nay rather I myself will excommunicate all those doctors,[13] than that we will tolerate and bear in our churches their wicked and ungodly sentences & judgment.

And some pretty space after, he hath these words: The doctrine therefore of this place is, that parents ought to provide their sons and daughters of honest marriage: Although . . . parents do sometimes abuse their power and authority, and will compel their children to marry with those whom they love not, the which cometh often to pass in the great families of noble men. They are to be found fault withal, because they carry no spark of a fatherly mind & affection, but are blocks & stocks, they have not that same natural love towards their children. In such a case let the pastor of the church, or the civil magistrate set in their authority; because that this is not a fatherly power, but a tyranny. We therefore do so diligently urge the authority of parents, first because of the commandment & ordinance of God, the examples of the scriptures, and the civil laws. Secondly because of that notable wickedness being unto all godly and honest parents very grievous, the which hath ranged in the world in all ages: namely that when as they have brought

---

[9] **Luther:** Martin Luther, German Reformer and former Augustine friar who essentially began the Reformation by nailing his ninety-five theses on the door of the church at Wittenberg. [10] **garboil:** tumult. [11] **popish Canonists:** Catholic theologians or experts in canon (church) law. [12] **canons:** clergy; theologians. [13] **doctors:** doctors of the church, theologians.

up their children godly and honestly, that they might be heirs of their fathers' goods, afterwards there have been some found, they not knowing of it and against their wills, the which by deceit and subtlety have over-reached and compassed[14] the maidens and honest young men, that they should by stealth marry with those, the which were both of small honesty and also unfit for them, and unto their parents most unwelcome.

The pope hath set open a window and a broad gate unto these horrible offenses, and hath made a way for bawds, that they might steal away men's sons and daughters for me, for thee, for every one of us. Shall we think these things to be suffered, or defended? But they say that men must look diligently unto the keeping of their children, & have an especial care of them. But how can this be in so great wickedness and untowardness of men? How easily are the plain and simple meaning minds corrupted, and beguiled?

. . . Let not a young man, whose age is fit for marriage, be afraid to open his mind unto his parents: that he is in love with an honest maiden, and desire, that they will give her him to wife. For albeit this seem to be a token of lust scarce comely, yet let them know that God his mercy doth cover the same in marriage, & hath given a remedy for this disease. Let them therefore humble themselves before their parents, and plainly and freely say unto them: my dear father, my good mother, give me such a young man, or such a maiden, whom I love. And if she be worthy to be matched with thee, or worthy of thine affinity, or thy parents', thine honest parents will not deny thee, albeit the dowry or wealth be not answerable. Such marriages cannot choose but be happy and prosperous, and God of his infinite goodness doth bless, pardon, and cover the heat of lust as it were with the cover of marriage. Yea, moreover the holy scripture doth allow, and allege for example the love and speech of the bridegroom and bride. Thus God pardoneth the filthiness, and miserable lust, wherein we are born, and that which more is, doth beautify and honest the same with lawful marriage. . . . [I]f henceforeward the parents shall either of negligence or sluggishness leave of their duty in providing of honest matches for their children, or their sons and daughters contemptuously and stubbornly refuse to stand unto their godly and Christian choice, ignorance will no longer serve to excuse the fault on either side, but that it must needs follow, that the servant that knoweth his master's will, and doth it not, the same shall be beaten with many stripes. Let fathers therefore on whom the charge by God his commandment lieth to take wives for their sons, and to provide husbands for their daughters, take diligent heed hereunto, that they abuse not this their power and

---

[14] **over-reached and compassed:** unscrupulous, ambitious suitors have sought to capture and ensnare the affections of honest young folk.

authority over their children . . . let them abstain from all rigor and rough-
ness, and beware that they turn not their fatherly jurisdiction and government into a tyrannical sourness and waywardness, letting their will go for a
law and their pleasure for a reason, according unto that old, but both Tiger
and Tyrant like saying: Look what I command, that will I have, my will
standeth for a reason. For the rule of the parents over their children ought to
resemble the government of good princes towards their subjects, that is to
say, it must be mild, gentle, and easy to be borne. . . . [T]hey must carry such
an even and upright hand in their government, that they may by love seek to
win the hearts of those over whom they are set, to be firm and sure towards
them, and not to keep them under awe and subjection by fear. For, whom
men fear, they hate, and him whom they hate, his death they wish. I speak of
servile or slavish fear, not of that child-like and reverent fear, the which both
the subjects owe unto their princes, and the children unto their parents, and
the which both the one and the other easily obtain at the hands of such as
are under their government, by their equal, upright and moderate behavior
towards them.

It doth therefore stand parents greatly in hand, that in making choice for
their children they be free from all sinister and corrupt affection, and that
for lucre[15] & covetousness they seek not to thrust such matches upon their
children, as they cannot brook, nor like well of. . . . Fathers therefore as they
are by good right to choose, so ought they not in truth to constrain & compel. For of all other matters, the consent of the children in marriage ought to
be most free . . .

The children can say for themselves, we are old enough, and therefore
able enough to make our own choice: we see it to be daily practiced by others, yea and peradventure we do know (as having heard our parents sometimes in their merriments to brag of the same) our fathers have matched
without the consent of their parents, and have all this notwithstanding done
well enough, and lived very well: why therefore should not we also do the
like? The question here is not, what children in regard either of age or wit
are able for to do but what God hath thought meet & expedient, nay,
straightly charged and commanded that they should do. For there are many
children found sometimes far to exceed their fathers in wit and in wisdom,
yea and in all other gifts both of mind & body, yet is this no good reason
that they should take upon them their fathers' authority. The wife may not
therefore be a master, because she hath more knowledge sometimes than her
husband, but she must obey, & the husband is to rule, because that God
hath willed that it should be so. . . . And whereas it is said, that our parents

---

[15] **lucre:** money.

have matched without the choice & consent of their parents, therefore we also will choose for ourselves according unto our own liking, besides that the breach of duty in the father doth not excuse the like disobedience in his son: what art thou that thinkest it not enough that thou go unto the devil thyself unless thou have thy father to go with thee also for company? For as thy sin of disobedience, if God grant thee not repentance of the same, shall in his justice press thee down even unto hell. . . .

. . . As for . . . not granting unto the father's choice in the cause of contrary religion, it is confirmed flatly by the counsel of the Apostle, where he willeth that we should not draw the yoke with infidels, which if it hold in other cases of the affairs of this life, much more ought it to be of force in marriage matters, marriage (I mean) hereafter to be made and not such as are already made, for where the knot is once already knit, there disparity, or unequalness in religion is no just cause of separation. . . .

And whilst I give this counsel unto the parents, I would not have the children think that I discharge them of this duty. . . . [Sons] are not at all once so much as to make the least motion of marriage unto the daughter, unless before they have obtained the good will and liking of the father. For in these cases let the daughters . . . say unto their suitors: My father and my mother have to determine and dispose of my marriage, this is a matter not belonging nor appertaining unto me. . . .

. . . [I]t maketh me astonished and amazed, to hear that a great many, and the same otherwise very civil and honest, are to be found almost in all places, the which not only do not dislike of this shameful disorder [that of taking marriage partners without parental consent], but hold it as it were but a sport and a play, . . . and defend this notorious kind of shameless thievery (for so I will not fear to call it) the which also doth far better deserve to be punished with death, than a great many crimes that are punished with the same. . . . Wilt thou condemn him that stealeth away thy beast, and justify him that robbeth thee of thy daughter? The law of God appointeth death unto such as steal men's children & sell them into slavery of the body, & what then thinkest thou is their offence which steal men's daughters against the consent of their parents, to live all their life time in whoredom & adultery, which is a spiritual slavery and bondage of the soul. . . .

But it may be answered hereunto, not by the sheep-stealers, but by the maid-stealers, that they have the consent and goodwill of the maiden, and that peradventure so far forth, that she hath in most earnest manner, yea even with tears, and for all the love sake that ever was between them, made request and suit unto them to carry and convey her away, and by some secret means to be married unto them &c. This is indeed a very plausible color, and such as carries a great show of reason among many, but is in truth the very worst plea that they could possibly have made for themselves of all others. For do they not see, how by this means they do not alone quite cast and clean overthrow themselves, but also accuse and condemn the party, whom they have after this sort seduced and enticed? . . . And because that such manner of contracts are altogether by God his word unlawful, therefore in carnally knowing the one the other (the which for the most part is the best end of these bad compacts) they have committed fornication, heaping as it were drunkenness unto thirst, that is to say, committing one sin in the neck of another, the which may not here by be excused. . . .

→ THOMAS HILDER

From Conjugal Counsel: or, Seasonable Advice, Both to Unmarried, and Married Persons   *1653*

Juliet's father conforms to the dramatic type of the *senex iratus*, the old man who opposes love matches in comedies until all his opposition is undone and the play ends in triumphant nuptials. Capulet threatens Juliet, but the real-life father Thomas Hilder exhibits instead touching concern that his children select marriage partners who will bring them happiness. Hilder urges his children to be submissive to God, not as slaves, but precisely *as children*. This is a benign rendition of early modern patriarchy, and even though it is published mid-century, the tender parenting it represents merit its inclusion here.

Hilder directs much of his counsel to his son. In Shakespeare's play we see parental concern about Romeo only in act 1; for the most part, Romeo confides in and takes advice from Friar Laurence rather than his own father. Hilder situates his authorial identity as an aging father who, from what he tells us, reproduced rather late in life: Samuel, Mehetabel, and Anne. Hilder does not play the distant patriarch laying down the law, but the affectionate parent who has an intimate relationship with his offspring: "the yearning bowels, and rowling affections of your tender-hearted father." When Hilder directs his fatherly advice toward his son, however, we learn that the child's mother, Margaret, died in childbirth. It follows then, that Hilder had not one but two wives in the autumn of his years, and he strikes the reader as a loving and affectionate husband.

Crucially, Hilder tells young men who are to be married that they must consider the responsibilities attendant upon marriage. These entail not merely a

Thomas Hilder, *Conjugal Counsel: or, Seasonable Advice, Both to Unmarried, and Married Persons* (London, 1653), sig. 65–A2, 1–63.

relationship with a wife, but authority over her as well as over any children and servants the couple may have. After Hilder has described all the spiritual gifts marriage requires, he offers counsel on more practical matters such as achieving "a ripening age before marriage," and the issue of livelihood, or "calling." Prayer is recommended as the first and surest means of finding a "meet helper," that is, a suitable partner. In the course of this discussion, Hilder mentions that a man who marries a woman without consent cannot expect to get her "portion" or dowry. Quoting 2 Corinthians 6:14, Hilder, like many commentators of the period, cautions against marrying with infidels, which he interprets as marrying a person who is without grace. In sharp contrast to the overwhelmingly secular nature of literary writings of the period, Hilder insists on grace as a quality above beauty and above wealth as a qualification of a potential wife. Beauty is not a quality to be dismissed, since its absence can breed repulsion and loathing, and it is not in itself a negative quality, but physical attractiveness should not become the object of the relationship.

Hilder has hard words for those parents who compel their children to marry despite their aversion to their marriage partner. He holds such parents responsible for the worst marital abuses: brawling, and even poisoning and plotting to do away with an unwanted spouse. While Hilder is stern with parents, he is equally adamant that children should not marry against their parents' wishes. While such equanimity may indeed be admirable, it does not solve the knotty problems surrounding unions where children cannot secure their parents' consent, no matter how they try. Hilder insists on "honorable means" in the choice of a wife, which implies that he would have little sympathy for elopement or clandestine marriage.

DEDICATORY EPISTLE

The Author's Paternal Advice to His Children

Now my dear Children, because I am convinced that it is the duty of a father to seek the complete happiness of his children, both internal and external, and though chiefly the good of their souls, in relation to a better life, yet in a second place, the good also of their bodies, and their outward comfortable enjoyments in this terrestrial world, I cannot therefore omit, in order to your well-being here, to communicate unto you some advice, in reference to the change of your conditions by marriage, if the Lord be pleased to bring you to such a time for seasonableness, and to give you opportunities to embrace the same. Let me tell you, that for you to enjoy meet[1] helpers in that estate, you may reckon to be one of the greatest outward favors that God doth bestow on his children to sweeten their condition otherwise

---

[1] **meet:** suitable.

mixed with diverse afflictions in this life. . . . I shall here take the liberty to add in general this one thing: . . . that it is a rule, case, and maxim in divinity, that whatsoever action any one is call'd to perform, which is of high concernment, (especially to God's glory,) and relates to the good of man, and but once (in probability) to be done his whole life, and which being done is unalterable . . . (Daniel 5:8–12), there is required more than ordinary caution and circumspection in the undertaking and managing of the same. Now the entering into the marriage estate is an action of the same nature before expressed; nay, to speak properly, it is that action, and none but it that fully answers the description beforesaid; and if so, then judge you what singular care should fill your hearts and heads when you mind marriage, and use the means conducible for that end.

Dear hearts, I cannot but think it necessary to acquaint you concerning this poor piece ensuing, which is denominated *Conjugal Counsel,* that the original copy of it was compiled six and twenty years since . . . (it being then in my intentions to make it public,) . . . but that those times did obstruct it, since which time it hath lain even as dead and buried; but (my choicely beloved ones,) now God having (in the riches of His grace) bestowed you on me, (who are as dear to me as my own soul) what could I do less than seek your complete happiness? And I apprehending this poor work might contribute a small piece thereto (by the blessing of God) I could not be so unjust to detain it from you. Truly, (next the seeking the glory of God) I have chiefly for your sakes made it obvious to public view. . . . And now my poor hearts, on whom can I so properly bestow it as on you, who are bone of my bone, and flesh of my flesh? I have two especial reasons, amongst many, to write this Epistle Dedicatory to you: First, to manifest my cordial love to your souls. Secondly, that hereby I may oblige you to endear it the more, and to make it your rule to walk by. . . .

Much endeared Children, you cannot but remember that I have acquainted you, that I cannot but conceive my abode here with you is short, and I may truly say, my desire is to depart this life and to be with Christ, which for me is best of all, yet to remain in the flesh is more profitable for you (Philippians 1:23–24). But however the Lord be pleased to deal with me, I hope your mother will discharge her duties toward you both for soul and body, and will endeavor to walk before you in good examples, and that may prove to you all matter of joy and singular comfort.

But you my dear son, I must here take the liberty to tell you (and I cannot do less) that you are descended from the loins of a most choice and precious mother (who by divine providence lost her natural life in being a means to bring you forth to live in this world). Truly, I might here dip a golden pen in odoriferous oil, and therewith write an encomium[2] of her, both of her life, and of her death. She was indeed a *Margaret* by name and much more by sweetness of nature;[3] but above all, by the super-abundant grace of God toward her, and in her, she was of a most transcendent, exemplary, and holy life. She did (through the grace of God) walk sweetly with her Savior in all pious ways; she did highly prize the means of grace; she did really hold forth the power of godliness in an unblameable conversation; she was frequent in secret prayer; and let me tell you (to your comfort) she hath lodged in the bosom of God (by the assistance of the Holy Spirit, and in the meditation of her dear Savior) many an ardent and most affectionate prayer for your poor soul while she was here in the flesh; which I doubt not but the Lord will return answer of (through his free grace) upon your head and heart, upon your body and upon your soul. She was full of the overflowings of love to her most unworthy (yet much endeared) comfort. She was of a very peaceable and amiable life toward all persons. She did live much in a little time; and as she was of an exact life (in comparison of most,) so through the infinite grace of God she ended her days in the peace of a good conscience, and did enjoy peace with God which passeth understanding (Philippians 4:7, Psalms 37:37). God gave her the white stone, and therein the new name written, which none knew but herself who received it[4] (Revelations 2:17). She was full of heavenly raptures, and divine manifestations of the love of God to her soul on her deathbed. She went not out by death like the snuff of a stinking candle, leaving an ill favor behind, but like Juniper, or the choicest of sweet perfumes. . . . She lived like a saint, and died like a daughter of the most high God: To her to live was Christ, and her death was gain (Philippians 1:21). . . .

My very dear and choicely beloved Children, I have been somewhat longer in this Epistle Dedicatory than I intended at the first, but the strength of my affections to your souls hath carried me forth in this way. Truly, the good of those precious souls of yours I desire to seek as the good of my own. . . . Thus my dear, sweet, and precious Children I take my leave of you in this kind, and subscribe myself what I am, and desire to remain (by the grace of God) to the end of my life, . . . Your dear, tender-hearted and most affectionate father to love and serve you, Thomas Hilder.

---

[2] **encomium:** praise.   [3] *Margaret* **by name . . . nature:** "Margaret" is from the Greek for pearl; in other words, she was a jewel by virtue of her temperament.   [4] **God gave her . . . who received it:** quotation from the Book of Revelations about the messages to be given to those who attend to the voice of the Holy Spirit, which speaks directly to the soul of the believer.

CONJUGAL COUNSEL

When the omnipotent, immense, all-powerful, and all-glorious Jehovah, had made and perfected that impermanent structure of the celestial and terrestrial world, and all creatures in general contained in them, man only excepted, the Lord did then consult with himself (as we may say) about making man in his own image and likeness (Genesis 1:26), which he accordingly did. . . . [T]o consummate and complete man's outward full and sweet enjoyments, the Lord God resolves to make man a meet help, because he saw it not good for man to be alone . . . which accordingly he did, for he made woman of a rib taken out of a man . . . which *Adam* owns peculiarly. . . . Therefore the Lord joins them together in marriage, and so makes them one flesh. . . . And then institutes marriage to be an ordinance in his church to the end of the world; and saith, a man shall forsake father and mother and cleave unto his wife, for they twain shall be one flesh. . . . And the apostle [Mark] saith, *Marriage is honorable among all men, and the bed undefiled* (Hebrews 13:4). From all which places there is a full confirmation, that God (and that in man's innocence) did ordain matrimony, and that matrimony is an holy ordinance of God.

. . . [F]rom men and women's unlawful entering into this (otherwise blessed) state of life, and their unholy use of it, doth spring, first dishonor to God, who did institute marriage; secondly, accessory to the sin of those that condemned the ordinance, and are afraid to enjoy it, rather choosing an unclean and beastly life. And lastly, an occasion of others rash and inconsiderate running into this estate, to the ruin of themselves and posterity, and the increase of many poor families: to the great prejudice of church and commonwealth, and diverse other evils are hence produced. . . .

If it be again demanded, how may a man know when he is fit to enter into the marriage condition?

I answer, there is a threefold fitness which every man must have in some competent measure, before he use means to change his single life for the marriage estate: first, spiritual gifts; secondly, fitness of age; thirdly, fitness of estate or outward ability for such a condition. . . .

When a man enters into that estate, he becomes the husband of a wife, and in process of time the father of children, and the master of servants, and these souls are committed to his charge, and God hath made him a watchman over them. Now if souls be not well-governed by such as have the charge of them, they will go astray, (if not lost forever). . . .

. . . Beloved, every Christian is as well a prophet in his own house to teach, as a king to rule, or as a priest to offer the sacrifice of prayer to God. . . . [A] family is a society, and (if godly) a church. Now in all societies or churches there must be discipline exercised, and good government maintained. . . .

. . . A man must have wisdom to walk before his wife and family in giving good examples unto them, that they (seeing his wife and Christian carriage in everything) may be provoked to follow him. . . .

. . . Therefore for domestic government too; impatience is a gangrene, which eats out the heart and vitals of love, a man (much more a Christian) must not give sharp words, much less fall to blows for every trivial offense, for that will discourage (especially) young people, and dull their spirits; it will sometimes be a man's discretion to look but with half an eye upon a fault, yet he may give a loving admonition, which will be sufficient where good natures are especially to be found. . . .

The second qualification to be considered of before-hand, is fitness of age. . . . [T]here must be maturity and ripeness both in body and mind for that estate, or else the entrance into it is unlawful. . . .

The third and last qualification, or consideration before marriage, is, to see a fitness in estate for such a condition of life. The marriage estate brings with it great charge and expense, therefore, before this fall upon a man, he had need to see some probable ways and means to carry him through all. . . . But these things premised occasions a question to be propounded, and that is, whether a man may not marry until he have lands, or stocks in money, or in goods and chattels?[5] I answer, that in case a man have neither of them, yet if God have given him an honest calling, and a heart to depend upon divine providence in the use of lawful means, and in special find himself (through free grace) to have an interest in the promises of God for all good things; he may conclude his call to marriage is as clear as the call of any person in the world. . . . God hath promised, *the hand of the diligent shall make rich,* (Proverbs 10:4). . . .

A second, and clear ground, demonstrating a man's call to enter into the marriage life, is, when the Lord is pleased to deny him the gift of chastity and continency . . . for when it is wanting, a man is disabled to keep his soul and body for to be the temple of the Holy Ghost. . . . [I]t is time I say, for thee then to look about thee, and to use that remedy which God hath sanctified and appointed for thy spiritual and corporal benefit; *To avoid fornication let* (saith the Apostle) *every man have his own wife,* etc. (1 Corinthians 7:2); it is better to marry than to burn by carnal lusts, and fleshly concupiscence.[6] . . .

. . . Truly, they speak most profanely, and are every way unworthy of the comfort that marriage doth afford, that say, a woman is a necessary evil, we

---

[5] **chattels:** movable possessions.   [6] **concupiscence:** sexual appetite.

may rather say she is a singular and necessary good; yet understand she is only so, when she answers the end God made her for, that is, a meet helper, (and it is such a one that in the sequel of this small treatise I shall endeavor to put thee on, and stir thee up to seek) such a one will fit (as we say) for every occasion, both in prosperity and adversity, in sickness and in health. Next the glory of God, she will spend and be spent for the good of thee and thine; she will help bear thy burdens of every kind, she will sympathize and condole with thee in all thy sufferings: In her bosom there is a passage to receive in any secrets thou shalt think fit to impart, but no vent to let them out at to thy danger or disgrace; she will apply herself, and imply her parts of grace to help thee with spiritual cordials in times of spiritual desertion; she will labor to further thee in the religious and civil government of thy family, both of children and servants. She will be ready to draw with thee (as a true yoke-fellow) in the plow of thy calling, to the utmost of her knowledge and strength with all dexterity: She will with much frugality manage thy family-expense; she will labor to help thee against thy infirmities, to prevent them if possible, however to conceal them; she will labor to comfort thee in times of sorrow and losses; . . . lastly she will put forth her self to her uttermost power with much pains of body, and with much and enlarged, dear, and tender affections of heart to help thee in times of loss of health, and when thou liest conflicting with grievous pains, and burdensome (and perhaps loathsome) diseases. . . .

. . . And by the way let me add, that happy are those wives that are obtained by the faithful prayers of their husbands: For they shall be best beloved, and most prized, because they are received by their husbands as a love-token sent them from heaven. . . . The same course must thou take for to obtain this mercy for thy self; and thou mayest receive encouragement to walk first in this way of seeking God by prayer, before any other means used. . . . As he that takes a wife without consent of parents can look for no portion with her; so be sure that he that takes a wife without the Lord's consent (as he doth in a sense that begs her not of him by prayer) can look for no comfort, and comfort is the portion which God gives with his daughters; nay, on the contrary, such a man may expect discomfort instead of comfort, and a curse instead of a blessing. God knows how to meet with thee, and to cause all thy gourds of comfort to wither; make thy self certain of this. . . .

If it be demanded, what those inward qualifications be that make a woman a meet helper? I answer, the first is Grace, or the manifestation of the true fear of God in the heart, by the fruits of holiness in the life. . . .

In the second place, the chief qualification of a good wife (next saving grace) is sweet disposition of nature, that she be of a quiet and peaceable spirit . . . A cross and tart nature in a wife un-wifes her. . . .

In the third place, to make an addition to thy comforts in the marriage estate, be very careful in thy choice to satisfy thine eye, both in the person and favor of such a one as thou wouldst enjoy for thy comfort, both in bed, and at board. . . . [S]trength of affections between married persons is a sovereign antidote against all uncleanness. And how can strength of affections be expected where there is not satisfaction in each others' persons? . . . It is true, that . . . beauty is vanity . . . But that hath been only in relation to the making it the object of thy love, for so it is vain and sinful; yet it hath its use, and some eyes must have many grains of it too to make a well-accomplished wife for them. Here by the way, how much then are those parents to blame, that strain their power over their children beyond due limits, in laying engagements and commands on them as like of such persons for husbands, and wives, for them, as they shall think most meet, which if they will not (because many times they cannot, by reason they are not able to close in their hearts and affections with their persons and favors) then they must be frown'd upon, called disobedient children, and disinherited, cast off as if they were but a bastard generation: But if this (in a special manner) be not a provoking children to wrath and a discouraging of them, I know not what it is; which sin of parents the Apostle forbids (Colossians 3:21). Now in the fear of God let parents be admonished to beware of this sin, of enforcing their children to accept of such husbands, and wives, as themselves only chose without, nay, against the free consent of their children. But if parents will not be exhorted to the contrary, let them know, that they are in a high degree accessory to all the brawlings and contentions that fall out after such marriages between their children, and they must answer before the bar of God's tribunal for all breach of covenant, all marriage-bed defilement, for all poisonings, or other bloody plots to take away the natural lives of either person; and they are guilty of all disorders, of all non-performance of family duties, of all dishonor brought to God by their children in the marriage estate, and (so by undeniable consequence) of their children's damnation for such sins, though the children are accountable before God for their own sins too. . . .

In the fourth place, if thou would have a meet helper thou must look at fitness of age in that woman whom thou desirest to be thy wife; or else how canst thou expect meet help from her in all conditions; if a man of fit age for marriage choose a girl for his wife, or if a young man marry with an old woman, and expect furtherance from such in that estate of life, they befool themselves; for the girl stands in need of a dame to instruct her in all points of womanhood to fit her for to be a good wife, and the old woman stands in need of a nurse to wait on her in her decrepit age. . . . Now though it be not convenient that a woman of eight or ten years older than the man should be joined in marriage with him, yet no man of understanding dare deny, but that it may be lawful, provided that the woman be not past child-bearing, and withal, be of an able and healthful constitution. But if other wise, two special ends of marriage are frustrated, and then it is a sin against God, and nature too, to be so joined in marriage. But when a man about twenty-six years old shall be married to a maid of about twenty, or a man about thirty years old shall marry with a maid about twenty-four, such conjunctions are of good report; and such persons, as they are youthful together, so they grow aged together, and are never estranged in their affections one towards another, if other qualifications also correspond. And besides, the fruit of such marriages ordinarily (by the blessing of God) is to have children betimes in youthful days, when their parents can best care for them, and take pains with them, which children, if the Lord give them grace, prove as a staff or support to their parents, (under God) in their old age, which is a blessing abundantly desirable. . . .

The fifth qualification necessary to make a woman a meet helper, is, to be descended from the loins of godly parents . . . [T]hou mayest warrantably take a wife from *India* (whose parents were heathens,) from *Rome,* from *Spain,* or out of any profane and irreligious family, provided, that herself be a sincere convert, a godly, pious, and religious woman; for it is not her parents and thee, but she and thou that make but one flesh; this premised, I say, it is necessary to marry a wife out of a godly family . . . for hereby the covenant of grace runs to them in the fuller stream. . . .

The sixth qualification which is necessary to be looked after in the choice of a wife, is, a competent outward estate; . . . it is unlawful for a man to mind a portion with his wife, because it is the duty of parents to lay up portions for, & to give portions to their children (2 Corinthians 12:14). . . . [A] man may look at portion with a wife, because he cannot live at so low a rate when he is married as he could when he was a single man, and his wife doth increase (or help to increase) this his charge, therefore there is all the reason in the world she should bring some additional maintenance; *For money answereth all things,* saith Solomon (Ecclesiastes 10:19). We have a proverb, that money will keep love warm. . . .

The seventh qualification (or necessary ingredient) to make a woman a meet helper, is frugality or good housewifery. . . . [W]hat advantage will it be to a man to have a great portion with his wife, if she be expensive, wasteful, profuse, & prodigal in her carriage. . . . [W]hat she brings in with a rake she will disperse with a fork. . . . Such a woman will soon bring herself, her husband, and children to a morsel of bread. . . . Oh these are worse than highway thieves. . . .

The eighth and last qualification to be eyed by thee in a woman whom thou would enjoy as thy wife, is so much education and breeding as is necessary in a woman in relation to thy rank and condition . . . For as an absurd, clownish, and sordid behavior ill becomes a man, so all unworthy, fliggish,[7] hoydenly carriage[8] as ill becomes a woman. And herein I appeal to all rational and intelligible persons of both sexes. The complete and comely behavior of woman, both at home and abroad, is an ornament both to herself and husband, and if thou be a wise man thou wilt be ashamed to see the contrary in thy wife . . .

Thirdly, if thou dost desire to have a good wife, and a meet helper, thou must labor by honest and just means to obtain the consent of parents on both sides, which if thou be wanting in, thy marriage will be rather cursed of God than blessed, and thou shalt have cause rather to mourn, than to rejoice in that condition; for thou must be convinced in this, that the very essence of marriage is the agreement of the parties, and the consent of parents. Great is the interest that parents have in their children, and the power that God hath invested them with over them. First, for their interest in them, as the Apostle saith in another case, *You are not your own, but are bought with a price* (1 Corinthians 6:19–20). So may I say to children, You are not your own, but you are bought with a price; your parents have bought you, (for though to speak most properly God be the giver of children, as no man nor angel can deny, for children are the inheritance of the Lord, and the fruit of the womb is his reward (Psalm 127:31) . . .). [Y]et in some sense parents may be said to have bought their children, for their mothers buy them dear, they conceive them, bear them, and bring them into the world with great pain and grief, sometimes children cost their mothers their lives in childbirth, or child-bed. . . . The tree doth sometimes wither and die that the fruit may live: And when children are born they cost both fathers and mothers much pain, cost, grief, and fear in bringing them up. . . . Besides, what heart-breaking pains doth parents take to leave some maintenance for their children? . . . [W]e may conclude this much, That it is an offense and a sin of an high nature for children to bestow themselves in marriage without, much more if against, the free consent of their parents . . . [Y]et mistake me not, I dare not think, much less say, that parents have a power to force their children against their own wills to marry or be married as they please; I only intend, that though children must have their own free consents to marry with such or such a person, that yet they may not, nor lawfully cannot without the consent of their parents . . . [I]n God's book . . . for them to bestow

---

[7] **fliggish:** flighty.   [8] **hoydenly carriage:** ill-mannered behavior.

themselves in marriage thus without . . . the consent of their parents, is a capital breach of the fifth, seventh, and eighth commandments of the Decalogue: First, they transgress against the fifth commandment, for therein God commands them *to honor their father and mother.* . . . Secondly, these undutiful children do violate the seventh commandment, where in God saith, *Thou shalt not commit adultery.* Now this is a most undeniable truth, that those who presume to step into the marriage condition, in a way point blank to that which God hath ordained, never lawfully enter into such a condition; . . . if two be not lawfully married, they be not man and wife, then what they are you may easily determine: You may say they are a couple of unclean persons, or a whoremonger and a whore, and so they will be till they labor to be humbled for their unclean societies, and for their disobedience against God and their parents. . . . Lastly, they transgress against the eighth commandment, for therein God saith, *Thou shalt not steal.* Now such as marry against the consent of parents are the greatest thieves in the world. You may remember that I told you that children are dearer to their parents than all that besides they enjoy, and that they have bought them very dear: Now if thieves break the eighth commandment, then surely these that thus marry against their parents' consent, being thieves, do break that commandment. . . .

Yet, before we proceed thereto, here falls in a case of conscience, . . . whether a man may under no consideration bestow himself in marriage against the consent of parents? This is necessary to be spoken to in this place for some poor soul may object, and say,

> I apprehend in my self a clear call to change my single condition, and to enjoy the marriage estate, for I find my self in some poor measure fit for it; God having graciously bestowed on me those gifts before spoken of in some degrees; and this I am sure of, I am unfit for the single life, having not the gift of chastity, but upon all occasions burn with fleshly concupiscence, to God's dishonor, and to the wasting of all my spiritual comforts. I have used those means you mention to obtain a good wife, and by God's gracious providence I have found out a maid largely qualified to make a good wife; and now the obstacle is, my parents like it not that I should enjoy her as my wife, and that because she hath too much of the fear of God in her, as they think, and not outward portion[9] so much as they would have me enjoy with a wife; and truly, I have long waited for their consents, and used the best means I can to enjoy the same, but do even despair of ever gaining of

---

[9] **outward portion:** dowry.

it; now Sir, I beseech you, give me a word or two of counsel and direction what I shall do in this case.

I answer, dear heart, I condole thy condition, and cannot but sympathize with thee; I see thou art in a conflicting estate with the devil, with thy corruptions, and with thy unnatural and degenerate parents; yet there is some balm in *Gilead*[10] for thee. . . . Then (I say) in the fear of the Lord set apart a day, two, or three, to seek God by fasting, humiliation and prayer, there bewail thy own sins in general, that they may have had an influence on the hearts of thy parents to bind them up and harden them against thee; . . . and rent the caul[11] of thy heart before the Lord by unfeigned humiliation, and implore His mercy for pardon and reconciliation. Then in a second place seek to God to humble thee likewise for thy parents' sin. Thirdly, seek God to humble thy parents for their iniquities, and to pardon their sin. Lastly, seek God to be gracious to thee in wheeling their hearts toward thee. Now when thou hast this done, and yet hast not prevailed, beg the prayers of such as have an interest in God, both for thy self, and for thy parents; which done, if no cloud yet appear for thy comfort so big as a man's hand, then desire some godly ministers and other worthy Christians to grapple with thy parents by persuasive arguments tending to the melting their frozen hearts, and for the turning them toward thee. Now if none of these means can prevail, then wait a convenient time, expecting some comfort for thee, but if none come, and that thy necessities remain still for the enjoyment of the marriage estate, then now thou art bound to obey God rather than man: God commands thee to marry, though thy parents forbid thee. In such a case, I am confident, that thou shalt not sin by marriage against the unreasonable desires of thy parents. Mind that of the Apostle (Ephesians 6:1), *Children obey your parents in the Lord, for that is right*. Parents must not be obeyed but in the Lord. God is the father of souls and spirits, now the spirit is the better part of a man, we must obey our spiritual father rather than our earthly. When the Apostle had spoke of subjection to our early fathers (Hebrews 13:9), he adds, *Shall we not much rather be in subjection to the father of spirits, and live*. To draw a conclusion, Obey thy heavenly father's call in this particular, and with all humility and thankfulness enter into the marriage condition; yet one thing let me add, thou must labor to carry thy self with much care in the humble observance of thy parents in all lawful things, and to counsel thy wife to do the same, and then thou knowst not but that the Lord may give thee in their hearts, to thine, and thy yoke-fellows great comfort even after marriage. . . .

[10] **balm in** *Gilead:* biblical reference (Jeremiah 8:22) to a gold-colored aromatic resin with soothing and antiseptic properties. [11] **caul:** membrane.

→ HENRY SWINBURNE

From A Treatise of Spousals   *1686*

Henry Swinburne (c. 1560–1623) was a judge in the Prerogative Court (that is, the court that dealt with the probate of wills) at York. Written in 1600, but printed in 1686, this treatise describes legal and social practices current in Shakespeare's time. It is the first work written in England on the subject of marriage contracts, or "spousals," and it differs from the advice books and clerical writings on marriage in that it is a specifically legal work. Prior to its publication, as the printer's preface maintains, the manuscript circulated among lawyers who used the book but were reluctant to publish it for fear of doing themselves out of business. The issues covered here concern the age at which a couple can be said to be physically and psychologically mature enough to enter into the state of matrimony and the question of public versus private and secret contracts. The term "private contracts" covered a range of practices, from a couple's merely declaring themselves married with or without witnesses, to being married by a minister without the presence of the couple's family. These distinctions were important because marriages could be legally contested unless conjugality was definitively established.

Canon law, that is, ecclesiastical law made by bishops, in 1604 forbade a priest "to marry anyone under the age of twenty-one without the assurance of parental consent, upon pain of suspension from his office" (Cook 18). Were it not for the fact that the canons of 1604 were never ratified by Parliament, this would have made the marriage of a couple like Romeo and Juliet illegal.

The issue of age is of particular relevance to *Romeo and Juliet* because Shakespeare makes Juliet considerably younger than she is in Arthur Brooke's poem, his source for the story, where she is sixteen. Capulet alludes to her youth when he tells Paris, "My child is yet a stranger in the world" (1.2.8). Note too that in expressing his concern about Juliet's age, his vocabulary echoes Swinburne's discussion of "the ripe age at marriage": "Let two more summers wither in their pride / Ere we may think her ripe to be a bride" (1.2.10–11).

SECTION II. THE DEFINITION OF SPOUSALS.

1. . . . Spousals are a mutual promise of future marriage, being duly made between those persons, to whom it is lawful. In which definition I observe three things especially: *One,* that this promise must be mutual; *Another,* That it must be done *rightfully,* duly; *The last,* by them to whom it is lawful.

Henry Swinburne, *A Treatise of Spousals, or Matrimonial Contracts: Wherein All the Questions Relating to That Subject Are Ingeniously Debated and Resolved. By the Late Famous and Learned Mr. Henry Swinburne, Author of the Treatise of Wills and Testaments* (London, 1686), 5–7, 24–50, 193–202.

2. First, whereas this promise is described to be *mutual,* it proveth that it is not sufficient if either of the parties alone do promise: And therefore if the man (for example) say to the woman, *I do promise that I will marry thee:* But the woman doth not make the like promise to the man; or contrariwise, the woman doth promise, but not the man, this is a lame contract (having as it were but one leg) and so not being able to walk upright, is not of any force of law. Neither is the silent party in this case presumed to consent, unless the consent appear, either by words, or at least by sufficient conjectures. As when the father or mother do contract spousals, or promise marriage for their child; for the child's silence in this case (being present and hearing the same) is taken for a consent and approbation thereof; though it be otherwise, if any other person than the parents take upon him to speak, or answer for the party; for there the party's silence doth not prove any consent at all.

3. Secondly, whereas this promise is to be done *right,* duly, we are to consider that this word *right* being strictly understood hath relation only to the formalities of the act or contract; but being understood in a more ample signification, it comprehendeth whatsoever is included within the compass of the word *recte* [right], namely whatsoever doth respect the justice and equity of the matter. In this definition it seemeth to comprehend both the one and the other, and so this promise of marriage must not only be *formal,* but *just and right* also.

4. Concerning the form, so precise were the ancient Romans in the observation thereof, that they did not for a long time admit any other manner of contracting spousals, but by *stipulation;* that is to say, by a certain conception of words consisting of question and answer: for example, the one party asking, *Wilt thou marry me?* The other answering, *I will.* Nevertheless, forasmuch as it is the consent alone of the parties whereby this knot is tied, and whereby this *dispensation* or *affiance* is sufficiently wrought, being the very substance (and as it were the life and soul) of this contract; therefore the necessity of observing that former prescript form of stipulation was not without just cause abolished, and liberty granted to contract spousals by whatsoever form of words, or by any other means, as *writing, signs, tokens, etc.* whereby this mutual consent might appear; and so at this present, there is no one *form* of *dispensation* more lawful than another, but it is sufficient if the consent of the parties do appear by any form.

5. Concerning the *justice and equity* of spousals (if we shall extend this word *right* so far) we may learn, that seeing the same must be just and right as well as formal, all unjust and wrongful means and causes thereof, as *violence, threats, fraud,* with such sinister practices and errors likewise are excluded.

6. Thirdly, by these words of the definition . . . made between those parties to whom it is lawful, we may easily collect, that it is not lawful for every person to contract spousals, namely, not for *infants* before they be *seven* years old; not for any person prohibited to contract matrimony, as they which be of *kin* within the Levitical Degrees,[1] and such as be already married, with many persons more ranged in a more ample field than is here allowed to conduct them.

Section VII. Of Spousals Contracted by Children betwixt Infancy and Ripe Age.

1. The second age to be regarded in persons contracting spousals is *childhood*, which age how far it reacheth is needful to be known: Children therefore, in respect of their age, are so termed of some, until they be twice seven years old; of some till they be thrice seven years old, that is one and twenty, sometimes children are so called until they be of the age of two and twenty years, sometimes until they be of the age of eighteen, sometimes until they be twenty, and sometimes till they be five and twenty, according to the variety of the *subjected matter* and meaning of the author. . . .

2. By children in this place, I understand them which have exceeded their *infancy*, but have not as yet attained to that age wherein nature (by the providence of God) bestoweth corporal ability of performing the act of generation; these children the laws civil and ecclesiastical, do call *impuberes*,[2] as it were young plants, without buds or blossoms, being the outward signs of inward vigor, and they are also called *pueri*, as some conjecture *quasi puri*, that is, pure, or as virgins clean from carnal pollution: . . . but let the names go, and come we to the thing it self, *pueritia*,[3] childhood is the age betwixt *infancy* and *ripe age* fit for marriage.

3. During this age, children cannot contract matrimony or spousals *de presenti*,[4] but only *de futuro*,[5] which excellent conclusion is not only adorned with sundry limitations or importance, but enriched with many profitable questions.

4. The first limitation is . . . for the good or benefit of peace, and therefore if two princes, after long or cruel wars, concluding a friendly peace, do for more assured confirmation thereof match their children in marriage, this *marriage* the laws do tolerate as lawful, being made upon such urgent cause, though otherwise for diverse wants the same were unlawful.

---

[1] **Levitical Degrees:** degrees of consanguinity or nearness of blood relation recorded in the book of Leviticus.   [2] *impuberes:* underage; prepubescent.   [3] *pueritia:* childhood.   [4] *de presenti:* at the present.   [5] *de futuro:* in the future.

5. The second limitation is . . . when *natural ability* to pay the marriage debt[6] doth supply the want of age, . . . albeit the laws do not presume any man or woman to be able to perform the act of generation, until a certain number of years (hereafter described) be accomplished: Nevertheless if it do appear, that in the meantime, and before the expiration of those years, they are able to perform the act aforesaid, then it is lawful for them to contract spousals *de presenti*, or to marry.

6. Thirdly, albeit children cannot contract spousals *de presenti* so effectually, that the same shall enjoy the very force and virtue proper thereunto, yet observing the form of spousals *de presenti* in their contract, as [*I do take thee to my husband, I do take thee to my wife, etc.*] this contract is not utterly void, but by the interpretation of the law, obtaineth the force of spousals *de futuro:* Divers[7] (I deny not) of the ancient lawyers were of a contrary opinion for a long time, holding, that if by these words the parties did intend to contract matrimony, then the contract was utterly void, not having any force either of *matrimony* or of *spousals:* Not of matrimony, because if they would, they could not make any such contract: Not of spousals, because albeit they might, yet they did not intend to make any such contract: And so either because they could not, or would not, the contract did not prevail at all, either as matrimony, or as spousals; howbeit in the end this opinion was dashed by later laws made for that purpose, whereby it was and is established, that if two children do contract spousals by words of present time, intending also thereby to contract matrimony, yet this contract shall prevail as spousals *de futuro;* and so it is if one of the parties be of ripe age, the other not.

7. Fourthly, by what means spousals contracted during *infancy,* and therefore void at the beginning, are notwithstanding afterwards made strong and confirmed, namely by mutual cohabitation, by kissings, by embracings, by giving and receiving of gifts and tokens, etc., or by words, expressing the continuance and perseverance of the mutual consent; as by calling each other husband and wife: By the same means practiced, after the parties be of *ripe age,* fit for marriage, are those spousals by them contracted in their *minority* by words of present time (being then spousals *de futuro* by interpretation of law only) resolved or turned into matrimony, from that time enjoying the same properties and effects belonging to spousals *de presenti,* contracted betwixt persons of full and perfect age, unless the parties, after they be come to perfect age, do first *dissent,* and so dissolve the contract before they consent: As for their dissent before they come to perfect age, it hindreth not the exchange or passage of the contract from spousals (so

---

[6] **pay the marriage debt:** have sex, especially sex leading to reproduction.   [7] **divers:** several.

termed by interpretation of law) to matrimony, by any the means aforesaid. Howbeit this is to be diligently noted in this place, that spousals *de futuro* properly so called, those I mean which are contracted by words of future time, . . . before the *parochial pastor* or *minister*, and other honest witnesses. The time of manifesting this dissent, is so soon as he or she shall attain to ripe age, or years of consent; for to dissent before that time, is to no purpose; and to prolong the same afterwards is dangerous. Now if any desire to know when the parties are said to be of ripe age, or of years of consent, let him read the next paragraph.

SECTION IX. OF RIPE OR LAWFUL AGE FOR MARRIAGE.

1. The third age now to be considered is *ripe age*, that is to say, that age wherein it is lawful not only to contract spousals, but also to solemnize true, perfect, and indissoluble matrimony, and thereby effectually to become husband and wife, both before God and his church; which age, when it doth begin, is now to be discussed. . . . [M]y meaning in this place is to unfold, at what age by the laws ecclesiastical of this realm, now in force, it is lawful to contract, not spousals only, but true and perfect matrimony.

2. Understand therefore, That a man so soon as he hath accomplished the age of *fourteen* years, and a woman so soon as she hath accomplished the age of *twelve* years, may contract true and lawful and individual matrimony, in case there be no other impediment to hinder the same: The reason is, that because at these years the man and the woman are not only presumed to be of discretion, and able to discern betwixt good and evil, and what is for their profit and disprofit; but also to have natural and corporal ability to perform the duty of marriage, and in that respect are termed *puberes*, as it were plants, now sending forth buds and flowers, apparent testimonies of inward sap, and immediate messengers of approaching fruit. And albeit this age may seem over-tender and over-timely to prevent those inconveniences so long ago foreseen by *Lycurgus*,[8] *Plato*, and the rest, yet considering the Lord and maker of all creatures, . . . hath by divine providence, for the propagation of his church, proclaimed an universal liberty. . . . [T]his liberty is to be denied to none, whom otherwise the Almighty hath naturally disposed and enabled to increase and multiply; considering also, that like as the little sparks are to be extinguished at the very first, least afterwards they mount to

---

[8] **Lycurgus:** ninth-century ruler and law giver of Sparta. He too had considered questions of marriage and the age at which people were suited to marry. He did not believe that children were the property of their parents.

an unquenchable flame: So whosoever have any such sparks of natural provocation, whereby their hearts may be kindled, or set on fire by ungodly lusts. To these persons, albeit very young, the remedy against lust is not to be denied, especially seeing it is *better to marry than to burn.* . . .

3. But what may be the reason wherefore women are sooner ripe than men? . . . Because the female bodies are more *tender* and *moister* than the *male:* And so men's bodies being harder and drier, they are more slow in ripening; and women's bodies, because they are softer and moister, are more quickly ripe; like as it is to be seen in plants and fruits, whereof that which is more soft and moist is sooner ripe, than that which is hard and dry. And this I take to be the *best* reason, and is agreeable to that which followeth, namely, that even that fruit which is sooner ripe, doth sooner decay: So women as they are sooner able, so they sooner become unable to bring forth than men to beget.

4. The former rule standing upon these reasons and foundations agreeable to the law of God and nature, is thus extended: First, albeit he or she have not fully accomplished their several[9] ages of *fourteen* and *twelve* years at the time of the marriage, the same peradventure[10] being solemnized within *one, two,* or *three* days next before the expiration of those several years, yet is the marriage of no less force than if the last hours of those years had also been expired.

5. The second ampliation[11] is, that albeit he that hath accomplished the age of fourteen years at the time of the marriage, be not then *able to pay* the debt which he oweth to his wife, yet by the received opinion (though some dissent) the matrimony is not therefore by and by to be adjudged void, but she is to expect until he have over-reached the *eighteenth* year of his age, . . . and if then also he be unable to pay his due, at the instance of the woman the marriage may be dissolved, unless the judge, upon the consideration of the qualities of the persons, shall grant a longer time.

6. The third ampliation is, That after the expiration of fourteen and twelve years, men and women, how old soever they be, may lawfully marry, notwithstanding any prohibition of former laws. And albeit not women only in process of time become barren and fruitless, but men also (if we may believe the learned) are at length (*viz.* after eighty years) deprived and spoiled of the ability of getting children, in whom, if any heat or warmth be then left, whereby by nature or by art they are provoked, this act is not of force for procreation, which was the cause wherefore sometimes they might

---

[9] **several:** respective.   [10] **peradventure:** perhaps.   [11] **ampliation:** elaboration.

not marry; yet nevertheless so beneficial are the laws *civil* and *ecclesiastical* in these days, to them that be disposed to marry, that none are barred by lapse of any years. . . .

SECTION XIV. OF PUBLIC AND PRIVATE SPOUSALS.

1. Fourthly, spousals be either public or private; public spousals are they which are contracted before sufficient witnesses, and wherein are observed all other solemnities requisite by the ecclesiastical law: For so careful were the ancient law-makers to avoid those mischiefs, which commonly attend upon *secret* and *clandestine* contracts, that they would have the same solemnities observed in contracting spousals, which be requisite in contracting matrimony; Which solemnities what they are shall afterwards be declared: Private spousals are they, at the contracting whereof, are omitted some of those solemnities aforesaid, but especially when as there be no *witnesses present* at the contract: In which case these questions following are usually propounded.

2. First, whether such secret contracts be good in law, yea, or no? And it seemeth they are not good . . . But the law doth forbid all persons to make *secret* contracts of spousals, or matrimony; and that justly, considering the manifold discommodities depending thereupon, namely, for that hereby it cometh to pass oftentimes, that the parties secretly contracting, are otherwise formally affianced, or so near in blood that they cannot be married; or being free from those impediments, yet do they alter their purposes, denying and breaking their promises, whence perjuries, adulteries, and bastardies, with many more intolerable mischiefs do succeed; and therefore such secret pacts, covenants, and contracts are worthily reputed, as if they had not been made at all . . . Wherefore seeing secret contracts cannot be proved, it is all one in effect, as if they were not.

3. Others are of another opinion, holding the contract for firm and indissoluble; for the confirmation whereof, they allege a very round text, extant in the body of the law, the words are these . . . Secret marriages are done indeed against the law, but being contracted, cannot be dissolved; Yielding this reason, that because these solemnities are not of the substance of spousals, or of matrimony but consent only; for (as another text saith) . . . Naked consent is sufficient to make spousals; And therefore if bare consent is sufficient, these solemnities are not so necessary as without the which spousals cannot consist, being no more than accidents, the which (as the logicians teach us) may be either present or absent, without the destruction of the principal subject; so that it may be justly inferred, that the only want of solemnity doth not hurt the contract.

4. To the reasons whereupon the contrary conclusion is collected, it is thus answered: First, that no pact, no covenant, no contract, shall be thought to be made betwixt them, whom the law doth prohibit to contract, etc. That's true, when the act is simply forbidden, but when the act is not simply forbidden, but only in respect of some quality, which is not of the substance thereof; Then the act done without that *quality*, is not to be accounted for undone; now to contract spousals is not simply forbidden, but in some respects only; And therefore being done without the observation of those unsubstantial circumstances, is not to be reputed for undone.

5. As for the other reason, that not to appear, and not to be, are both one in law, that's true . . . Before man, not before God; for the church indeed doth not judge of secret and hidden things, whereof there is no appearance. But most true it is, that almighty God . . . before him bare conscience alone is as a thousand witnesses; Wherefore I do admonish thee, that have in truth contracted secret matrimony, that thou do not marry any other person; for doubtless this thy pretended marriage, how lawful soever it may seem in the eye of man, who judgeth only according to the outward appearance, is nothing, but mere adultery in the infallible sight of God's just judgment, whose justice rewards every man according to his works, and before whose tribunal thou must at last appear to give an account of this thy foul misdeed.

6. But now admit thou art willing to marry, and the other party is not only unwilling, but utterly denieth the intent or consent to any marriage; Whether in this case mayest thou with safe conscience marry elsewhere? It seemeth at the first view, That thou canst not marry so long as the other party liveth, to whom thou didst so assuredly give thy faithful promise of matrimony, as appeareth by thine own concession, making a full and strong proof against thy self: Nevertheless, the case being rightly scanned, I am of their opinion which hold that thou may with safety, not of law only, but of conscience also, proceed to marry any other person.

7. First, seeing the other party constantly denieth the intent and consent of marriage, for his or her part, without which consent, as well on the behalf of that other party, as on thine own behalf, it is a clear case, that no matrimony can consist, neither in law nor in conscience, for the consent must be mutual and reciprocal, as I have often confirmed. Is it possible for a man to be a husband without a wife? Or a woman to be a wife without a husband? Seeing (I say) the other party so constantly denieth this necessary consent, thou mayest safely from thy conscience act according to this constant denial, and persuading thy self that the same is true, then art thou at liberty to marry elsewhere, without any let in law, or scruple in conscience.

8. This case thus absolved, let us vary the case a little. A man and a woman are first secretly, yet truly and before God, contracted in matrimony

mutually giving their full and perfect consent to the other therein; afterwards the man is publicly contracted to another woman in matrimony, the former woman practices all good means, as well by suit as otherwise, to recover him for her husband, but prevaileth not, for want of sufficient proof; Whether may she with safe conscience marry another husband? Albeit this question may seem to appertain to the determination of divines, yet will I adventure to signify mine own opinion, having first resolved another question preparatory thereunto; which question is this.

9. A man doth secretly (I mean without the presence of witnesses) contract spousals or matrimony with one woman, and afterwards publicly and before a sufficient number of witnesses, doth make the like contract with another woman; after which second contract the former woman chargeth him, and he likewise *confesseth* that he was formerly contracted unto her, whether in this case, shall the former secret contract, or the second public contract prevail?

10. It seemeth, because the same being (in truth) first made, this truth now appearing by the confession of both parties, is to be preferred before the second public contract . . . [by] the tribunal of the infallible judge, to whom all things (how soever secret) be all naked and open; but also in courts . . . of mortal men, whose judgment is directed according to that which appeareth, and is proved. And as no man can die with two testaments at once, so no man can live with two wives at once: Howbeit testaments and contracts be in this point, of a contrary condition; for of testaments the latter is the better, and maketh void the former; but of contracts, the former is the better and maketh void the latter; Wherefore, the man having first given his faith to one woman, cannot afterwards give the same to another woman. And so the former contract, albeit at the first secret, yet afterwards published and made known, is to be preferred before the second public contract.

11. Others nevertheless (whose opinion is generally received) are of this judgment, That howsoever, before God, the secret pre-contract, though it were never published, is to be preferred before the like subsequent contract, how soever public; yet before his church it is otherwise; neither is the sole confession of both the parties, pretending themselves to be pre-contracted, in secret sort, betwixt themselves alone, to be credited in prejudice of a sufficiently rectified contract, and proved by witnesses; because otherwise it were a very easy matter for such, as were truly contracted, under pretense of a pre-contract, at their pleasures whensoever they were displeased either with other, to undo the undoubted contract, by suborning one, of whom they had better liking, to affirm a former secret contract: A mischievous inconvenience in no wise to be tolerated.

12. As concerning the reason of the contrary opinion, *viz.* That the truth is to be preferred when it appeareth. That's true, if it appear by lawful and sufficient proof; but the sole confession of the parties, is not a lawful or sufficient proof, in prejudice of another contract lawfully and sufficiently proved, by the testimony of witnesses. Indeed if it were not in prejudice of another contract, the bare confession of the parties would suffice: Or if this confession of both the parties were made before the second contract was made, then also peradventure it might suffice against the second contract, because at that time the confession cannot be suspected of any collusion; But the confession being made after the time of the second contract, which contract is proved by two sufficient witnesses, in this case, not only the confession of the parties is not sufficient to prove a pre-contract, but also if besides the confession of the parties, there were *one witness* who did likewise depose of the same pre-contract; yet were not the testimony of this one witness joined with the parties' confession, able to overthrow the second contract, proved by two able witnesses. Likewise the testimony of one witness, together with a common *voice and fame* of a pre-contract, is not able to overthrow the second contract proved by two sufficient witnesses; for this conclusion is commonly received, that when the proof of the second contract is more clear than of the former contract, there the second contract is to be preferred, saving in these cases following, *viz.* When the second contract is made depending the suit, about the former contract; for the contract made depending the suit loseth that privilege, which otherwise it should enjoy; Or when the second contract is made under this condition, if there be no pre-contract before going, or if the pre-contract be frustrate and void, or when the former contract comprehendeth spousals *de presenti,* the other spousals *de futuro;* or when as over and besides this one witness and fame, there be other adjutants or helpers, such as may suffice to induce the judge to give sentence for the former contract: In these cases the former contract proved by one witness with the fame, etc. is preferred before the second contract proved by two entire witnesses.

13. Another question incident to secret contracts, is this, a man and a woman are first secretly, yet truly and before God contracted, either of them mutually giving their full and perfect consent thereunto; Afterwards the man is publicly contracted to another woman; The former woman practiceth all good means as well by suit as otherwise, to recover him for her husband, but prevaileth not for want of sufficient proof; In this case whether may she with safe conscience marry another husband? It seemeth that she may, for having endeavored to the utmost of her power, not able to continue any longer; It were not only against law, but against reason and equity, that

294 | LOVING AND MARRYING

she should be bound to an *impossibility;* And therefore of two evils (whereof the one is inevitable) the less is to be chosen, that is to say, it is better for her to marry than to burn in the fire of lust and concupiscence.[12]

14. Contrariwise it seemeth that she may not; for he and she being once very husband and wife before God, the woman is in subjection to the man, and is bound unto him while he liveth, nor is delivered, until the man be dead; So that if while the man liveth, she take another husband, before God it is adultery; only then, when her husband is dead, she is at liberty to marry with whom she will in the Lord, and not before; unless this be true that by reason of the husband's adultery, she may marry another, (of which question we shall have better opportunity to discourse more at large in another place;) or unless in contracting spousals, the consent of parents be necessary, the which being awanting in the former contract, the spousals therefore may be broken without peril; (of which question also I mean to deliver my opinion hereafter); or unless the former contract contained spousals *de futuro,* and the second *de presenti;* for then also the former spousals are dissolved, and the party at liberty to marry elsewhere, both in law and conscience; and by the opinion not of lawyers only, but of divinities also. . . .

[12] concupiscence: sexual appetite.

→ JOHN DONNE

Letter to Sir George More   *1602*

In what was to become one of the most famous marriages in literary history, John Donne (1573–1631) eloped with Ann More in December 1601, after a secret courtship of the type frowned on by virtually everyone who ever put pen to paper on the matter in early modern England. The poet was dismissed from his post as secretary to Sir Thomas Egerton, Lord Keeper (chancellor), who was the bride's uncle, and Donne was imprisoned until the marriage was finally ratified by the archbishop of Canterbury in April 1602. The bride was still a minor at the time of her wedding, and her father was in the process of finding her a suitable match. The couple did not break the news to her father immediately, in part because he was given, rather like Capulet, to violent fits of rage.

Donne's career did not recover from the match until at last he took holy orders in 1615; he became dean of St. Paul's Cathedral in 1621. What Donne suffered from marrying Ann without the consent of her kin offers compelling evi-

---

John Donne, Letter to Sir George More (2 February 1602), in *John Donne,* ed. John Carey (Oxford: Oxford UP, 1990), 86–87.

dence of the social ostracism and financial ruin that might result from an impru-
dent match. We know that Donne was an avid playgoer, but we do not know
whether his conceptions of romance were influenced by the plays he would have
seen in London, which would have no doubt included *Romeo and Juliet*
(although the dramatic voice of his poetry certainly bears the imprint of that
influence). However, we do know that marriage without parental consent, in
this case at least, resulted in tragedy of a singularly material kind. Donne is
reputed to have written to his wife the following, which may well sum up the
unfortunate outcome of their marriage:

John Donne,   Ann Donne,   Un-done.

In his *Life of Donne* (1640) Izaak Walton wrote of Donne's marriage:

> [L]ove is a flattering mischief . . . a passion! That carries us to commit
> *errors* with as much ease as whirlwinds remove feathers, and begets in us
> an unwearied industry to the attainment of what we desire. And such an
> industry did . . . bring them secretly together . . . and at last to a marriage
> too, without the allowance of those friends [parents and kinfolk] whose
> approbation always was, and ever will be necessary to make even a virtu-
> ous love become lawful.   (Quoted in Bald, 131)

Donne clearly had not expected such dire consequences to ensue from his
rash marriage.

The damage to Donne's career represents, however, only his side of the story.
Sir George, as John Carey points out, "suspected that his daughter's seducer was
a crypto-Catholic" (Carey, *Life* 58), and indeed, Donne had been brought up in a
Catholic family. Furthermore, Ann's father was troubled by Donne's reputation
as a libertine. Donne writes: "That fault was laid to me of having received some
gentlewomen before" (Carey, *Life* 58). Donne was in fact widely known to be, as
contemporary Sir Richard Baker put it, "a great visitor of ladies" (Carey, *Life* 58).
Nor was it merely that Donne was poorer and of a lower social status than Ann.
Rather Sir George seems to have been not unreasonably concerned about
Donne's debts and the rakish lifestyle that had led to their accumulation in the
first place. Ann's father had nine children, but only one of his four sons survived
to marriageable age; all of Ann's four sisters married country gentlemen with
wealth and position. Upon learning of Ann's marriage, More initiated proceedings before the High Commission, presumably in an attempt to get the marriage annulled, and as a result, though the marriage was declared "good and
sufficient," two of Donne's friends who had served as witnesses to the wedding
were imprisoned in the Marshalsea prison while the groom himself was committed to the Fleet (Bald 135). In a sense, Ann More was fortunate: in 1600,
Anne Barnes was imprisoned for a year for secretly marrying Walter Aston, the
ward of Sir Edward Coke (pronounced Cook), Queen Elizabeth's attorney general (Bald 132).

Ann More was sixteen or seventeen years old at the time while Donne was twenty-nine, and rather than living happily ever after, the pair lived for a long time in severely straitened circumstances (Carey, *Life* 59). The lives of Ann More and John Donne may represent what might have happened had Romeo and Juliet survived their tragedy and lived through the opposition of their kindred. Ann was pregnant virtually every year of her marriage, while Donne craved intellectual society and more sophisticated company than that afforded by his domestic circumstances. Two years after their marriage was declared legal, Donne embarked on a year's travel — and this was not to be his only lengthy departure from home. Although Donne may have remained faithful to his wife, only a few years later he was telling the stunning Lucy, countess of Bedford, that she was "God's masterpiece" (Carey, *Life* 64). In a way that parallels Romeo and Juliet's language of idolatry, in one of the Holy Sonnets written later in his life when Donne finally found respectability in a career in the church, he admits to God what he used to say in his "idolatry" to "all my profane mistresses." Donne was not, of course, unique in this rhetoric. Rather, it is part of the convention of love poetry, which served not only aesthetic uses in the construction of lyrics, but which was also embedded in the social practice of courtship and practical arts of seduction.

The letter below claims that both Donne and Ann had "adventured equally" — that is, that she had not been seduced or abducted by him.

Letter to Sir George More

S_{ir},

If a very respective fear of your displeasure, and a doubt that my Lord[1] (whom I know out of your worthiness to love you much) would be so compassionate with you as to add his anger to yours, did not so much increase my sickness as that I cannot stir, I had taken the boldness to have done the office of this letter by waiting upon you myself, to have given you truth and clearness of this matter between your daughter and me, and to show to you plainly the limits of our fault, by which I know your wisdom will proportion the punishment. So long since as her being at York House, this had foundation, and so much then of promise and contract built upon it, as without violence to conscience might not be shaken. At her lying in town this last Parliament, I found means to see her twice or thrice. We both knew the obligations that lay upon us, and we adventured equally; and about three weeks before Christmas we married. And as at the doing there were not used above five persons, of which I protest to you by my salvation there was

---

[1] **Lord:** Egerton; Donne's employer.

not one that had any dependence or relation to you, so in all the passage of it did I forbear to use any such person, who by furthering of it might violate any trust or duty towards you. The reasons why I did not fore-acquaint you with it (to deal with the same plainness that I have used) were these. I knew my present estate less than fit for her. I knew (yet I knew not why) that I stood not right in your opinion. I knew that to have given any intimation of it had been to impossibilitate the whole matter. And then having these honest purposes in our hearts, and those fetters in our consciences, methinks we should be pardoned if our fault be but this, that we did not, by fore-revealing of it, consent to our hindrance and torment. Sir, I acknowledge my fault to be so great as I dare scarce offer any other prayer to you in mine own behalf than this, to believe this truth, that I neither had dishonest ends nor means. But for her whom I tender much more than my fortunes or life (else I would I might neither joy in this life, nor enjoy the next), I humbly beg of you that she may not to her danger feel the terror of your sudden anger. I know this letter shall find you full of passion; but I know no passion can alter your reason and wisdom, to which I venture to commend these particulars: that it is irremediably done; that if you incense my Lord, you destroy her and me; that it is easy to give us happiness, and that my endeavours and industry, if it please you to prosper them, may so make me somewhat worthier of her. If any take the advantage of your displeasure against me, and fill you with ill thoughts of me, my comfort is, that you know that faith and thanks are due to them only that speak when their information might do good; which now it cannot work towards any party. For my excuse I can say nothing, except I knew what were said to you. Sir, I have truly told you this matter, and I humbly beseech you so to deal in it as the persuasions of nature, reason, wisdom and Christianity shall inform you; and to accept the vows of one whom you may now raise or scatter, which are that as my love is directed unchangeably upon her, so all my labours shall concur to her contentment, and to show my humble obedience to yourself.

> Yours in all duty and humbleness,
> J. Donne

From my lodgings by the Savoy,
2 February, 1602
To the Right Worshipful Sir George More, Kt.[2]

---

[2] Kt.: Knight.

From The Canzoniere

begun c. 1327

When Mercutio says, "Now is he for the numbers that Petrarch flowed in" (2.4.33), he acknowledges that Romeo has become a poet-lover participating in a discourse that constitutes the most significant celebration of Renaissance femininity. "Numbers" are the metrical count of a love poem. However, this elevated, poetic ideal of woman may have had little influence on or even no connection with the treatment and lives of real women. Only a small proportion of people, more men than women, were literate in Renaissance England. Petrarchanism was a very courtly, elite, stylized literary paradigm, and since it described the changing moods and nuances of male desire, there was little opportunity for even aristocratic women to enter the privileged confines of this poetic discourse. (See pp. 3–4 on Petrarchanism in general and Dubrow 263–67 on its importance in *Romeo and Juliet*.) Although Petrarchanism treated women primarily as objects, some English women did, despite the odds, enter the discourse. These included Isabella Whitney, a gentlewoman from Cheshire, and the ultra-aristocratic Mary Wroth, daughter of Robert Sidney and niece of Sir Philip Sidney, the author of the famous prose romance *Arcadia* (Jones 36–52; 118–22).

Whatever the gender politics and permutations that followed in the wake of Petrarch's poetry, however, it is important to recognize the lyrical achievement of the *Canzoniere*.

3

It was the day the sun's ray had turned pale
with pity for the suffering of his Maker
when I was caught (and I put up no fight),
my lady, for your lovely eyes had bound me.

It seemed no time to be on guard against   5
Love's blows; therefore, I went my way
secure and fearless — so, all my misfortunes
began in midst of universal woe.

Love found me all disarmed and saw the way
was clear to reach my heart down through the eyes,   10
which have become the halls and doors of tears.

Francesco Petrarch, *The Canzoniere or Rerum Vulgarium Fragmenta* (begun c. 1327), trans. Mark Musa (Bloomington: Indiana UP, 1996) 4–18.

It seems to me it did him little honor
to wound me with his arrow in my state
and to you, armed, not to show his bow at all.

11

In sun or shade I've never seen you, lady,
remove that veil of yours
since you discovered my so great desire
that every other wish fades in my heart.

While I carried my loving thoughts in secret,   5
the ones that kill my heart with their desire,
I saw your face adorned with pity then;
but when Love made you conscious of my feelings,
your blond hair took the veil immediately,
your loving gaze withdrew into itself.   10
What I most longed for in you I have lost;
it is the veil that rules me,
which to my death, in warmth or cooler weather,
covers the sweet light of your lovely eyes.

12

If my life can resist the bitter anguish
and all its struggles long enough for me
to see the brilliance of your lovely eyes,
lady, dimmed by the force of your last years,

and your fine golden hair changing to silver,   5
and see you give up garlands and green clothes,
and your face pale that in all my misfortunes
now makes me slow and timid to lament,

then love at least will make me bold enough
so that I may disclose to you my suffering,   10
the years, the days, the hours, what they were like;

and should time work against my sweet desires,
at least it will not stop my grief receiving
some comfort brought by late arriving sighs.

13

When Love within her lovely face appears
now and again among the other ladies,
as much as each is less lovely than she,
the more the wish I love within me grows.

I bless the place, the time and hour of the day 5
that my eyes aimed their sights at such a height
and say: "My soul, you must be very grateful
that you were found worthy of such great honor.

"From her to you comes loving thought that leads,
as long as you pursue, to highest good, 10
esteeming little what all men desire:

"there comes from her all joyous honesty
that leads you by the straight path up to Heaven —
already I fly high upon my hope."

17

A bitter rain of tears pours down my face
blowing with a wind of anguished sighs
should my eyes turn to look at you alone
for whom I am divided from mankind.

There is no doubt your sweet and soothing smile 5
does calm the ardor of all my desires
and rescues me from burning martyrdom
as long as I keep my gaze fixed in you;

but then my spirits suddenly turn cold
when I see, as you leave, those fated stars 10
turning their gentle motion from my sight.

Let loose, at last, by those two amorous keys,
the soul deserts the heart to follow you,
and deep in thought it tears itself away.

Grotesque Parody of Female Beauty, from Charles Sorel, *The Extravagant Shepherd: or, the History of the Shepherd Lysis An Anti-Romance Written Originally in French and Now Made English*, translated by John Davies (London, 1654).

Thomas Roche, commenting on the literary language of love, which makes bizarre parallels between the beloved's beauty and a series of precious objects, writes: "Only with the artist's literalization of the sonneteers' metaphors does the monstrous force of those words hit us. The question for us as literary critics is whether the parody begins with the artistic representation that shows so clearly the monstrous fatuity of the metaphors or whether the parody is inherent in the poet's choice of metaphor" (383). When eyes are literally stars or diamonds, teeth literally pearls, and hair literally gold wire, beauty is transformed into a grotesque parody of itself. The ideal of beauty is rendered as a nightmare vision of ugliness — hideously funny, but hideous all the same. Such imagery is intrinsic to Petrarchan rhetoric. Laura's mouth is described by Petrarch, for example, as *"di perle / piena et di rose"* or "full of pearls and roses" (Dubrow 43). Nancy Vickers writes: "Laura is always presented as a part or parts of a woman. When more than one part figures in a single poem, a sequential, inclusive ordering is never stressed. Her textures are those of metal and stones; her image

FIGURE 10

is that of a collection of exquisitely beautiful disassociated objects. Singled out among them are hair, hand, foot, and eyes: golden hair trapped and bound the speaker; an ivory hand took his heart away; a marble foot imprinted the grass and flowers; starry eyes directed him in his wandering" (Vickers 267).

169

Full of a loving thought, that makes me stray
from all the rest and go the world alone,
I steal myself away from me at times
and search for her alone whom I should flee;

I see her walking by so sweet and hard   5
that my soul shakes, about to take to flight,
for such an army of armed sighs she leads,
this lovely one, Love's enemy and mine.

It's true, if I'm not wrong, I see a ray
of pity on her cloudy and proud brow   10
that clears in part the sorrow in my heart;

then I collect her soul, and once decided
to show my hurt to her, I find there is
so much to tell her, I dare not begin.

→ SIR PHILIP SIDNEY

Sonnet 9   *1591*

In the following poem, the tormented Astrophil pursues the divine Stella. This
relationship never achieves consummation. In fact, the closest Astrophil comes
to gaining Stella's love is when he steals a kiss from her while she is asleep. This
poem is part of a much longer and ostensibly autobiographical sequence in
which Astrophil represents the poet Sir Philip Sidney (1554–1586), author of the
prose romance the *Arcadia*, while Stella figures Lady Penelope Rich. Sidney's
infatuation certainly comports with the Petrarchan model, in that despite having known her before her marriage to Lord Rich, he seems to have developed a
passionate interest in Penelope Devereux (as she then was) only *after* her marriage. In real life, far from being the model of virtue the poet describes, "Stella,"
then the mother of six children, left her husband for Charles Blount, Lord
Mountjoy.

The Englishing of Petrarch, even while it demonstrated a definite continuity
with the much earlier Italian prototype, was far more secular. For Petrarch,
Laura was the poet's means of contact with God, whereas in England, the lady
was the means by which the poet-lover came to know himself. Stella's beauty

---

Sir Philip Sidney, Sonnet 9 in *Astrophil and Stella. Wherein the Excellence of Sweet Poesie Is Concluded* (London, 1591).

reflects the Platonic notion that beauty is a mirror of virtue, and she possessed all the standard Petrarchan features: skin white as alabaster, lips like coral (porphyry was a stone that resembled red coral), pearly teeth, and eyes ("windows" through which her celestial being views the world) made of black glossy touchstones. When rubbed these stones were thought to attract light objects such as straws, and the poem even suggests that the straw becomes combustible. These eyes have power over the poet, they touch him, even though he and Stella do not literally touch.

Queen Virtue's Court, which some call Stella's face,
Prepared by Nature's chiefest furniture,
Hath his front built of alabaster pure;
Gold is the covering of that stately place;[1]
The door, by which sometimes comes forth her grace,   5
Red porphyr[2] is, which lock of pearl makes sure,
Whose porches rich (which name of cheeks endure)
Marble mixed with red and white do interlace;
The windows[3] now through which this heav'nly guest[4]
Looks o'er the world, and can find nothing such   10
Which dare claim from those lights the name of best,
Of touch[5] they are, that without touch doth touch,
Which Cupid's self from beauty's mine did draw:
Of touch they are, and poor I am their straw.[6]

[1] Gold . . . place: her hair is like gold.   [2] porphyr: a very hard red stone.   [3] windows: eyes.
[4] heav'nly guest: Stella, or Stella's spirit, who as a star is literally heavenly (i.e., of the heavens).
[5] touch: a black, shiny stone.   [6] their straw: friction created by the touch causes the straw to ignite.

→ WILLIAM SHAKESPEARE

Sonnet 130   1609

Shakespeare appropriates and modifies Petrarchan conventions in the love scenes between Romeo and Juliet, and we know he was much occupied with Petrarchan motifs at the time of the play's composition because this is also the period during which he composed the sonnets. Sonnet 130 is most famous for its inversion of economastic tropes (the rhetoric of praise) in an anti-blazon tradition, written deliberately against the conventional blazon, or feature-by-feature

William Shakespeare, *Shakespeare's Sonnets* (London, 1609).

description of the lady. The poet's love object here, traditionally known as "the dark lady," does not resemble conventional beauty in any of its aspects: in fact she represents its antithesis with dark ("dun") skin, black rather than golden hair, smelly (or at least, nondescript rather than sweet) breath, an ordinary sort of voice and gait. And yet, for all that, the poet loves her, though there is a possible joke at the end that he loves her as much as any maligned ("belied") woman. In *Romeo and Juliet,* Shakespeare toys with the exhausting hyperbole of the panegyric (a formal eulogistic composition praising the lady), and in this poem, he reverses the tedious repetition of conventional encomium, which consisted of elaborate conceits in praise of a typecast mistress (see Kerrigan 19).

My mistress' eyes are nothing like the sun;
Coral is far more red than her lips' red.
If snow be white, why then, her breasts are dun;
If hairs be wires, black wires grow on her head.
I have seen roses damasked, red and white,   5
But no such roses see I in her cheeks;
And in some perfumes is there more delight
Than in the breath that from my mistress reeks.
I love to hear her speak, yet well I know
That music hath a far more pleasing sound.   10
I grant I never saw a goddess go:
My mistress when she walks treads on the ground.
    And yet, by heaven, I think my love as rare
    As any she belied with false compare.

✦ Solemnization of Matrimony   1559

Whereas in our own culture the wedding is the high point of soap operas and movies, we do not actually see the wedding of Romeo and Juliet. At the end of act 2, when the Friar announces that "Holy Church [will] incorporate two in one" (2.6.37), we are led to believe that the wedding takes place between the acts,

Solemnization of Matrimony in *The Book of Common Prayer,* from *Liturgical Services, Liturgies and Occasional Forms of Prayer Set forth in the Reign of Queen Elizabeth,* ed. William Keating Clay (Cambridge, 1847), 217–24; it was revised extensively thereafter. The *First Prayer Book of Edward VI* was published in 1548 and its use was enforced by the Act of Uniformity 1549. It was revised in 1552, repealed during the reign of Mary Tudor, and then revived as the *Elizabethan Book of Common Prayer* in 1559.

between the hasty betrothal and the tragic brawl of act 3. Religious rituals were in any case prohibited from the Renaissance stage. The wedding ceremony itself, especially the giving of rings, had become controversial because it was regarded as popish by the more strictly Protestant members of the population.

First the banns[1] must be asked three several Sundays or holydays, in the time of service, the people being present after the accustomed manner.

And if the persons that would be married dwell in divers parishes, the banns must be asked in both parishes, and the Curate[2] of the one parish shall not solemnize Matrimony betwixt them, without a certificate of the banns being thrice asked from the Curate of the other parish. At the day appointed for solemnization of Matrimony, the persons to be married shall come into the body of the church with their friends and neighbours. And there the Priest shall thus say.

Dearly beloved friends, we are gathered together here in the sight of God, and in the face of his congregation, to join together this man and this woman in holy matrimony, which is an honourable estate, instituted of God in paradise, in the time of man's innocency: signifying unto us the mystical union, that is betwixt Christ and his church: which holy estate Christ adorned and beautified with his presence and first miracle that he wrought in Cana[3] of Galilee, and is commended of Saint Paul to be honourable among all men, and therefore is not to be enterprised, nor taken in hand unadvisedly, lightly or wantonly, to satisfy men's carnal lusts and appetites, like brute beasts that have no understanding; but reverently, discreetly, advisedly, soberly, and in the fear of God: duly considering the causes for the which matrimony was ordained. One was, the procreation of children, to be brought up in the fear and nurture of the Lord, and praise of God. Secondly, it was ordained for a remedy against sin, and to avoid fornication, that such persons as have not the gift of continency, might marry, and keep themselves undefiled members of Christ's body. Thirdly, for the mutual society, help and comfort, that the one ought to have of the other, both in prosperity and adversity: into the which holy estate these two persons present come now to be joined. Therefore if any man can shew any just cause, why they may not lawfully be joined together, let him now speak: or else hereafter for ever hold his peace.

[1] banns: church announcement of a forthcoming marriage. [2] Curate: assistant priest.
[3] Cana: wedding feast at Cana where Jesus transformed water into wine.

And also speaking to the persons that shall be married, he shall say.

I require and charge you (as you will answer at the dreadful day of judgment, when the secrets of all hearts shall be disclosed) that if either of you do know any impediment why ye may not be lawfully joined together in Matrimony, that ye confess it. For be ye well assured, that so many as be coupled together otherwise than God's word doth allow, are not joined together by God, neither is their Matrimony lawful.

At which day of marriage, if any man do allege and declare any impediment why they may not be coupled together in Matrimony by God's law or the laws of this Realm: and will be bound, and sufficient sureties with him, to the parties, or else put in a caution to the full value of such charges as the persons to be married doth sustain to prove his allegation: then the solemnization must be deferred unto such time as the truth be tried. If no impediment be alleged, then shall the Curate say unto the man,

N.[4] wilt thou have this woman to thy wedded wife, to live together after God's ordinance in the holy estate of Matrimony? Wilt thou love her, comfort her, honour and keep her, in sickness, and in health? And forsaking all other, keep thee only to her, so long as you both shall live?

The man shall answer, "I will." Then shall the Priest say to the woman,

N. wilt thou have this man to thy wedded husband, to live together after God's ordinance in the holy estate of Matrimony? Wilt thou obey him and serve him, love, honour, and keep him, in sickness and in health, and forsaking all other, keep thee only unto him, so long as you both shall live?

The woman shall answer, "I will." Then shall the Minister say,

Who giveth this woman to be married unto this man?

---

[4] *N.:* the name of the bride or groom.

And the Minister receiving the woman at her father or friend's hands, shall cause the man to take the woman by the right hand, and so either to give their troth to the other. The man first saying.

I *N.* take thee *N.* to my wedded wife, to have and to hold from this day forward, for better, for worse, for richer, for poorer, in sickness, and in health, to love and to cherish, till death us depart, according to God's holy ordinance: and thereto I plight thee my troth.

Then shall they loose their hands, and the woman taking again the man by the right hand shall say.

I *N.* take thee *N.* to my wedded husband, to have and to hold from this day forward, for better, for worse, for richer, for poorer, in sickness, and in health, to love, cherish, and to obey, till death us depart, according to God's holy ordinance: and thereto I give thee my troth.

Then shall they again loose their hands, and the man shall give unto the woman a ring, laying the same upon the book with the accustomed duty to the Priest and Clerk. And the Priest taking the ring, shall deliver it unto the man, to put it upon the fourth finger of the woman's left hand. And the man taught by the Priest shall say.

With this ring I thee wed: with my body I thee worship: and with all my worldly goods I thee endow. In the name of the Father, and of the Son, and of the Holy Ghost. Amen.

Then the man leaving the ring upon the fourth finger of the woman's left hand, the Minister shall say.

O eternal God, creator and preserver of all mankind, giver of all spiritual grace, the author of everlasting life: Send thy blessing upon these thy servants, this man and this woman, whom we bless in thy name; that as Isaac and Rebecca lived faithfully together, so these persons may surely perform and keep the vow and covenant betwixt them made, whereof this ring given and received is a token and pledge, and may ever remain in perfect love and peace together, and live according unto thy laws: through Jesus Christ our Lord. Amen.

Then shall the Priest join their right hands together, and say.

Those whom God hath joined together, let no man put asunder.

Then shall the Minister speak unto the people.

Forasmuch as *N.* and *N.* have consented together in holy wedlock, and have witnessed the same before God and this company, and thereto have given and pledged their troth, either to other, and have declared the same by giving and receiving of a Ring, and by joining of hands: I pronounce that they be man and wife together. In the name of the Father, and of the Son, and of the Holy Ghost. Amen.

And the Minister shall add this blessing.

God the Father, God the Son, God the Holy Ghost, bless, preserve, and keep you: the Lord mercifully with his favour look upon you, and so fill you with all spiritual benediction and grace, that you may so live together in this life, that in the world to come you may have life everlasting. Amen.

Then the Ministers or Clerks going to the Lord's table, shall say or sing, this Psalm following.

Blessed are all they that fear the Lord, and walk in his ways.
For thou shalt eat the labour of thy hands: O well is thee, and happy shalt thou be.
Thy wife shall be as the fruitful vine: upon the walls of thy house.
Thy children like the olive branches: round about thy table.
Lo, thus shall the man be blessed: that feareth the Lord.
The Lord from out of Sion[5] shall bless thee: that thou shalt see Jerusalem in prosperity, all thy life long;
Yea, that thou shalt see thy children's children: and peace upon Israel.
Glory be to the Father. &c.
As it was in the. &c.

---

[5] **Sion:** Zion, i.e., home of the Hebrew people.

Or else this Psalm following.

God be merciful unto us and bless us: and show us the light of his counte-
nance, and be merciful unto us.
That thy way may be known upon the earth: thy saving health among all
nations.
Let the people praise thee (O God): yea let all the people praise thee.
O let the nations rejoice and be glad: for thou shalt judge the flock right-
eously, and govern the nations upon the earth.
Let the people praise thee (O God): let all the people praise thee.
Then shall the earth bring forth her increase: and God, even our God, shall
give us his blessing.
God shall bless us, and all the ends of the world shall fear him.
Glory be to the Father. &c.
As it was in the. &c.

The Psalm ended, and the man and the woman kneeling afore the Lord's
table: the Priest standing at the table, and turning his face toward them,
shall say,

Lord have mercy upon us.

ANSWER.   Christ have mercy upon us.
MINISTER.   Lord have mercy upon us.

Our Father which art in heaven. &c.
And lead us not into temptation.

ANSWER.   But deliver us from evil. Amen.
MINISTER.   O Lord save thy servant, and thy handmaid.
ANSWER.   Which put their trust in thee.
MINISTER.   O Lord send them help from thy holy place.
ANSWER.   And evermore defend them.
MINISTER.   Be unto them a tower of strength.
ANSWER.   From the face of their enemy.
MINISTER.   O Lord, hear our prayer.
ANSWER.   And let our cry come unto thee.

The Minister.

O God of Abraham, God of Isaac, God of Jacob, bless these thy servants, and sow the seed of eternal life in their minds, that whatsoever in thy holy word they shall profitably learn, they may in deed fulfil the same. Look, O Lord, mercifully upon them from heaven, and bless them. And as thou didst send thy blessing upon Abraham and Sara to their great comfort: so vouchsafe[6] to send thy blessing upon these thy servants, that they obeying thy will, and always being in safety under thy protection, may abide in thy love unto their lives end: through Jesus Christ our Lord. Amen.

This prayer next following shall be omitted, where the woman is past child birth.

O merciful Lord and heavenly Father, by whose gracious gift mankind is increased: we beseech thee assist with thy blessing these two persons, that they may both be fruitful in procreation of children, and also live together so long in godly love and honesty, that they may see their children's children, unto the third and fourth generation, unto thy praise and honor: through Jesus Christ our Lord. Amen.

O God, which by thy mighty power hast made all things of nought; which also, after other things set in order, didst appoint that out of man (created after thine own image and similitude) woman should take her beginning: and knitting them together, didst teach that it should never be lawful to put asunder those, whom thou by matrimony hadst made one; O God which hast consecrated the state of matrimony to such an excellent mystery, that in it is signified and represented the spiritual marriage and unity betwixt Christ and his church: Look mercifully upon these thy servants, that both this man may love his wife, according to thy word (as Christ did love his spouse the Church, who gave himself for it, loving and cherishing it even as his own flesh:) And also that this woman may be loving and amiable to her husband as Rachel, wise as Rebecca, faithful and obedient as Sara, and in all quietness, sobriety, and peace be a follower of holy and godly matrons: O Lord, bless them both, and grant them to inherit thy everlasting kingdom: through Jesus Christ our Lord. Amen.

---

[6] **vouchsafe:** condescend to grant or bestow.

Then shall the Priest say,

Almighty God, which at the beginning did create our first parents Adam and Eve, and did sanctify and join them together in marriage: pour upon you the riches of his grace, sanctify and bless you, that ye may please him both in body and soul, and live together in holy love, unto your lives' end. Amen.

Then shall begin the Communion, and after the Gospel shall be said a sermon, wherein ordinarily (so oft as there is any marriage) the office of a man and wife shall be declared, according to holy scripture: or if there be no sermon, the Minister shall read this that followeth.

All ye which be married, or which intend to take the holy estate of matrimony upon you: hear what holy scripture doth say, as touching the duty of husbands toward their wives, and wives toward their husbands. Saint Paul (in his Epistle to the Ephesians, the fifth chapter) doth give this commandment to all married men.

Ye husbands love your wives, even as Christ loved the church, and hath given himself for it, to sanctify it purging it in the fountain of water, through thy word, that he might make it unto himself a glorious congregation, not having spot or wrinkle, or any such thing, but that it should be holy and blameless. So men are bound to love their own wives as their own bodies. He that loveth his own wife, loveth himself: for never did any man hate his own flesh, but nourisheth and cherisheth it, even as the Lord doth the congregation: for we are members of his body, of his flesh and of his bones.

For this cause shall a man leave father and mother, and shall be joined unto his wife, and they two shall be one flesh. This mystery is great: but I speak of Christ and of the congregation. Nevertheless, let every one of you so love his own wife, even as himself.

Likewise the same Saint Paul (writing to the Colossians) speaketh thus to all men that be married. Ye men, love your wives, and be not bitter unto them.

Hear also what Saint Peter the apostle of Christ, which was himself a married man, saith unto all men that are married. Ye husbands, dwell with your wives according to knowledge: Giving honour unto the wife as unto the weaker vessel, and as heirs together of the grace of life, so that your prayers be not hindered.

Hitherto ye have heard the duty of the husband toward the wife.
Now likewise, ye wives, hear and learn your duty toward your husbands,
even as it is plainly set forth in holy scripture.

Saint Paul (in the forenamed Epistle to the Ephesians, fifth chapter) teacheth you thus: Ye women, submit yourselves unto your own husbands as unto the Lord: for the husband is the wife's head, even as Christ is the head of the Church. And he is also the Saviour of the whole body. Therefore as the church or congregation is subject unto Christ, so likewise let the wives also be in subjection unto their own husbands in all things. And again he saith: Let the wife reverence her husband. And (in his Epistle to the Colossians) Saint Paul giveth you this short lesson. Ye wives, submit yourselves unto your own husbands, as it is convenient in the Lord.

Saint Peter also doth instruct you very godly, thus saying: Let wives be subject to their own husbands, so that if any obey not the word, they may be won without the worst by the conversation of the wives, while they behold your chaste conversation coupled with fear: whose apparel let it not be outward, with braided hair and trimming about with gold, either in putting on of gorgeous apparel: but let the hid man which is in the heart, be without all corruption, so that the spirit be mild and quiet, which is a precious thing in the sight of God. For after this manner (in the old time) did the holy women which trusted in God apparel themselves, being subject to their own husbands: as Sara obeyed Abraham, calling him lord; whose daughters ye are made, doing well, and being not dismayed with any fear.

The new married persons (the same day of their marriage)
must receive the Holy Communion.

CHAPTER 4

Family Life

———————————— >‹— ————————————

My child is yet a stranger in the world   (1.2.8)

The household, rather than the family, was the fundamental unit of Elizabethan society; it consisted of parents, children, and often a substantial
number of servants. The government of the household was thought to be a
microcosm of the government of the commonwealth, and fathers were
understood to function as sovereigns in the domestic realm. In early modern
England there was not the emphasis that there is now on the nuclear
family — parents and their biological offspring in isolation from the rest of
society. Nor was this an era in which men went out to work and women
stayed home. Because capitalism had just emerged as an economic system,
people did not, on the whole, sell their labor to others who owned the means
of production (that is, the workplace and all its tools, animals, and equip-
ment). As a result, men and women tended to work in the same environ-
ments even though they were engaged in gender differentiated tasks.
Protestant writing on marriage stressed the sense of shared enterprise and
companionship as a source of both joy and solace. Henry Smith in *A Preparative to Marriage* (1591) wrote: "[I]n all Nations the day of marriage was
reputed the joyfullest day in all their life. And is reputed still of all, as
though the sun of happiness began that day to shine upon us, when a good

wife is brought unto us. Therefore one sayeth, that marriage doth signify *merriage*, because a playfellow is come to make our age merry" (11–12).

Marriage as the central relationship within the household, however, existed within a dense context of other social alliances, and with other classes of society. Thus, when young people married, they relied not only on parents (who themselves depended on an array of social connections in order to negotiate a match), but on a wide-ranging network of kin and "friends." Laura Gowing reminds us:

> Prominent in the social world of courtship were friends. In the context of marriage, "friends" were a very special group, a particular kind of kin who advised or intervened in marriage plans. Kinship in early modern England operated flexibly, dependent on social contexts in the case of marriage . . . [I]t extended to non-biological ties through a framework that was about trust and responsibility rather than blood relationships.
> (*Domestic* 148)

This was vitally important, since in London alone, forty-seven percent of daughters had lost their fathers by age twenty, and girls were understood to need quasi-parental supervision in making a match in a way that boys were not (Gowing, *Domestic* 148, 151). Crucially, families of any wealth or property sought to make alliances with one another to improve their social standing, or as one letter of the period put it when discussing a land negotiation: "Good cousin the good consent I have of you and in that my father's house and yours is linked together in so sure a bond of amity." Such language connotes not merely warm feelings, but also expressions of shared material and political interest.

The contextual documents in this chapter show the Elizabethan household in operation — celebrating, working, caring for infants, making marriage negotiations, organizing connections with other families, and quarreling among themselves. Above all else, we get a sense of the tremendous labor that goes into the family's attempt to survive and reproduce, not merely on the biological level, but, even more importantly, at the level of property and social status.

Early modern texts on the family also reveal a boundary between private and public, personal and communal, that is strikingly different from today's. The documents that follow are windows into the homes and hearts of people living in early modern England, and what we see there is often not what we might expect. Emotional issues and family matters, for example, are nearly always tied in some way to issues of property and its transmission across the generations. In other words, the letters of a family, the regrets of a mother who did not breastfeed, and the diary of an upper-class woman, are *private* but they are not *personal* revelations in the manner of modern autobiography. As we read the materials that follow, then, we should bear in mind that our scholarly and historical objective here is to *contextualize* the issues of family in *Romeo and Juliet,* and not to *contemporize* them.

➔ RICHARD DAY

A Prayer of Children for Their Parents   *1581 and 1590*

The prayer below asks God to bless the child's parents and stresses the obedience of the child to both the parents and to God. The child also asks not to cause his parents "any trouble," which might of course mean that she or he would have to submit to a marriage of his or her parents' choosing, especially since making them happy was seen as akin to making God happy.

Lord God, whose will it is that next thy self we should yield most honor to our fathers and mothers: for as much as among the duties of natural love, it is not the least to sue unto thy goodness for the welfare of our parents: I beseech thee preserve my father and mother, with all their household, first in the love of thy religion, and next in safety from all encumbrance and grief both of body and mind.

And unto me, grant that they may not have any trouble by my means: And finally, that I may enjoy the favor of them, & they the favor of thee, which art the sovereign Father of all. Amen.

Correspondence of the Bagot Family

In contrast to the normative and prescriptive tone of the conduct books on marriage and family life, the following unpublished letters from members of the Bagot family of Blithfield in Staffordshire give something of the flavor of the trials of love and marriage as vital aspects of early modern family dynamics in the lives of the English gentry. We glimpse the writers of these letters in the throes of their lives: arranging marriages, parenting, growing

---

Richard Day, *A Book of Christian Prayers* (London, 1581 and 1590, bound together), 49–50.

up, accepting and rejecting marriage proposals, eloping, marrying well, and living (at least as far as we can tell) happily ever after, and occasionally, coming to a bad end.

The letters included here cover the period between circa 1587 and 1622. When viewed all at once, this correspondence seems to compress time and events so that they take on an almost soap-opera character. They are arranged in family units, rather than chronologically, so that the reader can best make sense of the progress of family affairs across the generations. These letters demonstrate above all the wide network of kin involved in any single marriage alliance. All kinds of people, including friends (a term that in early modern parlance might include close and very distant relatives of the couple as well as people who were not related), had some form of social obligation to the parties involved, which gave them a vested interest in the match. In these letters, we read of third parties intervening on behalf of couples who have married without waiting for full parental authority, negotiating as delicately as possible on behalf of others, softening the blow of rejection, or complaining about the financial settlement. This correspondence indicates the fully material dimensions of marriage; mutual affection is one consideration for a match, certainly, but it is often far down the list of concerns about finances and property. From a twenty-first-century point of view, which places so much emphasis on the emotional aspects of long-term relationships, it is surprising that perhaps only one of these letters approximates a love letter. In fact, we see very little of the marriage principals (i.e., the couple or proposed couple): They rarely act for themselves or on their own behalf. Rather, their elders and social superiors are the ones who are actively engaged in the delicate, diplomatic art of match-making. Marriage is clearly a means of upward mobility, but the advances of many of these marriages probably constitute only what Freud later described as "the narcissism of small differences."

Another notable fact about this correspondence is that a startling number of these liaisons are between people who are neighbors and/or distant relatives. The network of kinship, then, was a key component of the fabric of this society, but it was also one that did not, despite laws governing consanguinity (that is, how near a blood relation one was permitted to marry), preclude erotic attachment. All of the letters below speak far more to the desire to maintain social and familial ties rather than to sever them, and this remains so despite all threats and Capulet-like thunderings to the contrary.

The letters that follow, unlike nearly everything else in this volume, are *not* modernized. Instead, they are transcribed exactly as they appear on the manuscript page, although contractions (the early modern habit of leaving some letters out) are expanded, as are suspensions (not putting in the last few letters of a word). The early modern "v" has been converted to "u" and "i" to "j." Otherwise, the letters retain their original spelling and the linguistic richness of the period. Readers who encounter difficulty with words should try sounding them out phonetically in order to catch the meaning. Readers should also notice that the proficiency of the writing often depends upon the gender, class, or profession of the writer, all of which factors determined the degree of the writer's literacy.

In 1587, Richard Bagot discovered that his daughter Margaret had secretly married William Trew, a member of the household of Queen Elizabeth's favorite, Robert, earl of Essex. Like Capulet, he can barely contain his rage in the following letter to another son-in-law, and in his fury, Bagot clearly wants to contest the legality of the marriage on the grounds of its being clandestine. Margaret and her father, however, were not ultimately estranged, and eventually, with the intervention of various other members of the family, peace was restored (Wrottesley 83–84).

→ RICHARD BAGOT

Letter to Richard Broughton   *June 3, 1587*

To the right Worshipfull my lovinge Sonne in Lawe, Richard Broughton esquire give these.

Sir my daughters lewde dealings in this her matche, hath not a litle trobled me and her mother, which if it be a mariage, (as I rest doubtfull) I way [weigh] it not so much as the maner of yt [it], the practizes wherof are so dishonest to her self, as hardly wilbe recovered, besydes discredit to others. Upon knowledge of yt [it] I turned her away to him to Chartley, wher they remayne, as I thinke by direccion from my Lord, who hath written two sundry letters to me in his behalf to pardon the offence, and not to cast her off, wherin I shall desyre you to satisfye his Lordship, that at his request I am contended to forgive the fault, but as yet I can not digest such a villainy in him, as at his departing hence, in Lent last, upon communicacion of the matter, protested by others, ther was not any promise or contract betwixte them, nether it was ever his intention to requyre it at her hands, wher now it apperes [appears] they were maried, wherin if she have don well I shalbe right glad, otherwise she hath made to much hast, and seinge she wold not

---

be ruled by me, I will rule my purse, which shall make me better hable [able] to helpe the rest and so god give them joye and some sorrowe, as they have given us cause of grief.

––––––––

The following letter was written in November 1589 by Lord Lumley to his friend Richard Bagot. The connection between these two men is their shared interest in Richard Rugeley (c. 1564–1623), who is Lord Lumley's nephew and Bagot's godson. Young Richard has rather hastily married Mary Rugeley. Though Mary bore the same surname as her husband prior to the marriage, she was not so closely related to him that concerns about consanguinity (nearness of blood relation) proved an impediment to the match. Bagot seems to have been involved in marriage negotiations between the two young people, but they have alienated their parents by rushing ahead with a clandestine marriage without their parents' consent.

It is not clear why the couple rushed into marriage. If the bride was pregnant, it would probably have been in the interests of the parents to move ahead with the nuptials. Some marriage negotiations were extraordinarily protracted: Richard Bagot, who was ambitious about the marriage prospects of his own son, Walter, took ten years to make him a match after he entertained the first "motion of marriage" (that is the initiation of negotiations toward a match). Wealthy parents might enter into negotiations with several potential spouses for their child, who would not be married until financial and property arrangements satisfied all parties concerned. Given the possibility that negotiations could be either protracted or aborted, it may have been that the lovers were simply impatient. We will never know.

What is clear, however, is that while Richard and Mary flout their parents' wishes, like Romeo and Juliet, they do so within the appropriate bounds of class. Unlike Shakespeare's play, however, every effort is made by the elders to integrate these young people into the existing social order and to secure their livelihood with the mate of their choice.

→ LORD JOHN LUMLEY[1]

Letter to Richard Bagot Esquire and Deputy Lieutenant within the County of Staffordshire

November 25, 1589

After my harty comendacions whereas I doo understand by my nephewe Richard Rugeley your godsone, that at the request of his father it pleased you to take somuche paines as to travell unto Mr. Rugeley of Hawkeshurst at which tyme you with other frends that were there assembled togeather had some talke as concerning assuraunce of lands on both parts, and also a joincture in respect of a marriage to be had betwene my said nephewe and Mr. Rugeleys daughter of Hawkshurst. Sythence [since] which tyme the younge couple, have with more speede then was meete coupled themselves togeather in marriage without the consent and pryvitie of their parents, to the utter subversion and undooing of the younge couple, if yt [it] be not providently forseene and wrought by some speciall frend of theirs. Wherefore forasmuche as I doo understand that you may doo asmuche with their parents as any man in Staffordsheire, it hath caused me to wryte these fewe lynes unto you, (as our desiring their good) which is, that you will take somuche paynes for me, as to conferre with their fathers to the end that those speaches and promysses that have been delivered and made by them both may be performed accordingly, both in the assuraunce of their lands and otherwayes for joyncture, for their maintenance, according to a survey taken in Callenswood. And in this dooing you shall not onely occasion me (though unacquainted with you) to doo you any pleasure that is in me, but I hope shall geve cause both to the parents and children to thinck themselves very greatly beholding unto you, for so frendly and needefull a labor as this is, for the good of them all, where with moste hartely [heartily] I comytt [commit] to you gods good favor. From my house Nonesuche. This xxvth [25th] of November 1589.

Your very lovyng frend
Lumley

---

[1] **Lord John Lumley:** Lumley (1547–1609) was a Catholic who, apart from a brief spell in the Tower of London (arrested in September 1569 and released in April 1573), was spared the worst consequences of his religious choice. His imprisonment was the result of his involvement with the earl of Arundel in intrigues and plots for the restoration of the Catholic religion and the marriage of Mary Queen of Scots to the duke of Norfolk. He was arrested but never convicted as a recusant. Lumley's fortunes recovered sufficiently to allow him to act as commissioner in several state trials including, surprisingly, that of Mary Queen of Scots, October 1586. See Cokayne, 276–9.

Folger ms. L.a.628

Despite the intervention of a peer of the realm, we know that Lord Lumley's letter did not resolve everything instantly because Mary's father wrote to Richard Bagot (L.a.772) over a year later, in December 1590, complaining that the legal documents drawn up in accordance with Lord Lumley's request were inadequate. However, the tone of the letter was one of persistence, as negotiations continued quite a long time after the marriage with Rugeley, who was especially concerned about his own profit from the match. Indeed, that marriage negotiations often rumbled on long after the actual nuptials indicates that a wedding, in and of itself, did not resolve the problems between neighbors and kin in the way that the drama often leads us to believe they do. Though he was not the parent of the groom, Lumley at least suggested he was interested in the economic welfare of the couple, whereas Rugeley made no pretension toward such concern. Neither correspondent even mentions the emotional ties at stake, which would likely be paramount today.

THOMAS RUGELEY

Letter to Richard Bagot   *December 12, 1590*

To the righte worshipfull Mr. Bagotte, Lyeutenant of Staffordshire geve these with speede.

Righte worshipfull, with my hartie commendacions and thankes for my greate cheare [cheer] and your paynes taken betwixte my brother[1] Rygdley [Rugeley][2] and me. Sir I have sente you herein inclosed a copye of the articles that you sente me. Sir this copye is suche as dothe not convey anye commoditie to my sonne in Lawe and daughter other than a moitye [a designated part] of Calingewood, and when they shall receive the commoditye thereof I knowe not. Wherfore my requeste is you woulde call into your handes the articles of covenante in frendshippe by you and Mr. Savage at the requeste of my Lorde Lumley by me and my brother Ridgley appoynted

---

[1] **my brother:** the bride's father-in-law, whom the writer refers to as his "brother" in the same sort of generic way in which people of the period used the ubiquitous "cousin" to refer to all manner of people to whom they had some form of social or familial affinity.   [2] **Rygdley:** because there was no standardized orthography (spelling) in the period, like Shakespeare himself, who also signed his name "Shakespere" (see pp. 33–34), people frequently gave different versions of their names, and here Rugeley spells the name "Rydgley."

and there sette downe for I am persuaded that those and these do farre dis-
agree for as touchinge the articles concerninge my brother Ridgley there is
nothing either in possession or joynture to my daughter if it fortune
Richarde Ridgley, my sonne in lawe, to dye or for xxi [21] yeares or three
Lives[3] after the decesse of my brother Ridgely or his wife comprised in these
articles. Sir as touchinge the articles by you sette downe betwixte us I truste
you do not thinke me so simple to reserve no estate to my self for myne
owne life nor yet for xxi yeares or three Lyves but absolutely to passe away
all and to receive nothinge agayne as by these articles it would seme I
shoulde have done but by goddes grace I meane to have a further consideracion herein unlesse I perceive a further commoditie to be comynge suche as
I was promysed and expected. Thus ceasing any further to trouble you, I
commytte you to the tuicion of the almightie. Hawkesyarde, the xiith day of
December 1590.

> Youres to commaunde in that he may,
> Thomas Rydgley [sic]

[3] **three Lives:** standard legal term meaning three generations.

In the following letter, the man in the highway is the now much older
Richard Rugeley, whose eldest son, Simon, was at Cambridge at this time
and was involved in a secret matrimonial scheme with the daughter of Sir
Henry Skipwith; Sir Henry favored the union. Walter Bagot was engaged
by Sir Henry (his brother-in-law) to further the match, and so a chance
meeting with Rugeley became the perfect opportunity to tell Simon's father
of the mutual affection between his son and Jane Skipwith. Rugeley was
shocked and declared he knew nothing of this unauthorized courtship.[1]
Further, he told Bagot that he had already begun negotiations with another
gentleman, and that matters with him awaited only Simon's completing his
education. Bagot relayed all this information to Sir Henry. At this point, a
match between Simon and Jane did not look promising. This letter emphasizes that the children are almost incidental to the negotiations between the
parents, and that in this instance at least, Richard Rugeley does not know
his son's heart. Jane, in contrast, may have conveyed her feelings to her
father, Sir Henry, and so they possibly had a closer relationship. On the

[1] Richard Rugeley is the subject of Lord Lumley's letter to Richard Bagot (p. 318). As a young
man, Rugeley had married Mary Rugeley (a distant relative) without the parents' consent. Now
his son, Simon, seems to be involved in a similar affair.

other hand, Jane may have simply been prodded into the courtship by her father for reasons of social and financial advantage.

We do not know how Simon and Jane met, but it could have been when Simon was on his way to university, because traveling gentlemen commonly stopped at the houses of relations and connections. The connection between the Rugeleys and the Skipwiths was not close, but there was nonetheless a connection: Rugley's great-grandmother was Jane, daughter to Walter Bagot's great-grandfather, Lewis Bagot. In early modern society, relationships so distant were neither forgotten nor ignored.

→ WALTER BAGOT

Letter to Henry Skipwith   *1620/21*

Presently upon your departure from my howse I went after my huntsmen, but before I could meete with them it was my happ in the high waye to incounter the gentleman you required mee to conferre withall concerninge the mutuall lykinge betwixt his sone and your daughter. And thinkinge good to take the opportunetie of so convenient a time and place cawsed him to staye and told him that I was required by you to make their affeccions knowen unto him and withall that yf [if] the match might bee to his contentment you wold streane your self and abilitie to geve a portion answereable to your estate and yf [if] some reasonable time maye bee geven for payement I thought it wold bee answereable to his expectacion. Hee made some staye to speake, and I told him it was a matter of importance and therefore I required him to consider upon it and at better leasure (yet so soone as hee wold bee pleased) to geve me an answere. Hee told mee the matter was straunge unto him for hee had never suspected any such affeccion in his soone and further sayed hee was acquainted with you and thought him selfe much beholden unto you for your pleane and gentlemanlyke dealinge with him but his soone was yet younge and hee desired rather to have him folow his booke [further his education] then to affecte mariadge, and that I shold very spedely heare more from him when hee had better considered the matter. So at that time parted from mee and went to his sister Mrs. Aspinall whose daughter your neighbour Mr. Coats hath maried. In the eveninge hee returned and came to my howse where hee found mee and my wefe walkinge and then told us hee could not rest untill hee had geven a more resolute answere which was as before that hee desired his soone shold still folow his booke and further that there had bin a motion of mariadge betwixt his soone and the daughter of a gentleman of good worth in this contrie but that the further proceedinge was only stayed for his studies sake that hee might bee of more ripe years to make his choyce and that hee had promised in the meane time to forbeare conference with any other, which hee was resolved (god willinge) to performe requiringe I wold make the same knowen unto you for his resolute answere and that hee held himselfe much beholden to you for your worthie and gentlemanlyke proceedinge in the whole course of this busines.

Given the circumstances of her own marriage in 1589 described on pages 318–319, one might expect that when Mary Rugeley had children of her own, she would have permitted them freedom of choice in marriage. That was far from the case, and it is Mary who, in the next letter, is said to have had the strongest objections to the marriage of her son Simon to Henry Skipwith's daughter, Jane, and was prepared to disinherit her son of the lands that were part of her own jointure, that is those over which she retained control after her own marriage. Despite these threats and protestations, Simon did marry Jane and was not disinherited, and we know this because in Richard Rugeley's funeral certificate, dated 5 July 1623 (quoted in Salt V, 257), Simon was called the son and heir, and was said to have married Jane Skipwith and by her had issue, a son who died young. Walter Bagot was Rugeley's cousin and Sir Henry Skipwith, Bagot's brother-in-law. Hence Richard Rugeley addresses his letter to his *cousin* Bagot, but the consanguinity was not a close one.

→ RICHARD RUGELEY

Letter to Walter Bagot

March 1621

To the right worshipful my verry lovinge cozen Walter Bagott, esquire, at Blithfield deliver this.

Right worshipful I must thinke myself forever most bounden unto you for your love booth nowe and at all tymes. Sir after it pleased you to acquainte mee with this matter from Mr. Skipwith I coulde not rest untill I had sent my wiffe to my soone in Cambridge to know how all thinges stoode. And he hath answered his mother that he is free from the gentillwoman,

---

Folger ms. L.a.771

and that he hath clearely left hir and will never come neere hir againe. He confesseth that they [Jane and her family. Note, this is a group enterprise] weare desirous to have married with him, but his answeare was that he would doe nothinge without his parents consent, the which I hope will prove true and therefore I make noe doubt but that allthinges are nowe dissolved. For upon Mr. Skipwiths writinge unto me I answered him that I had allready provided a Match for my soone in our owne sheere and that if my soone would not be ruled by me I would make another my heire. And for my wiffe (how it is reported I know not) but I know shee is as vehement against it as my selfe, and hath vowed that if it should have been a Match he should never have enjoyed any part of hir landes.

And soe with my humble commendacions unto you, and to my good cozen your loving bedfellow giving hir thankes for hir kind remembrance I take leave and rest.

Yours forever to commaund,
Richarde Ruggeley

———

That interest in an upcoming marriage might be primarily economic is nowhere more evident than in the category of "wards," where feudal marriage held unyielding sway. Wards were children who inherited their parents' estate during their minority. During the reigns of Elizabeth and James, the court of wards dealt with these cases, not, it must be emphasized, to ensure the emotional welfare of the children, but to ensure that property and power relations were properly maintained. A wardship, that is, to be named guardian to a ward, was extremely valuable because the recipient could not only subsequently marry his own child to a wealthy heir, but also, during the child's minority, he was entitled to the income from the ward's lands. This issue was a crucial one, as Joel Hurstfield points out, because "[Elizabethans] were beginning to ask themselves whether they were free to live and work and marry as they pleased or were still governed by harsh — and unyielding — feudal customs of the past" (Hurstfield xiv). As a result, monarchs doled out wardships as favors for services rendered.

In one such case, Walter Bagot, himself the father of nine children, got the lucrative wardship of Humphrey Okeover (1609–1639), whose father had died in 1610 when he was an infant. Walter planned to have Humphrey marry one of his daughters, Lettice, a plan foiled when the young man secretly married a woman called Martha Cheney (the name is also spelled Cheyney in this period). While it is tempting to regard this incident as one of the triumph of love over Bagot's selfish financial motives, this would be a hasty and indeed erroneous reading. Humphrey was not an orphan — only his father died in 1610. His mother went on to marry Sir Oliver Cheney, who had a daughter, none other than Martha, by a previous marriage. Thus, instead of being coerced into marriage by his guardian, it looks instead as if Humphrey was simply persuaded into marriage by his mother and her husband, who thereby kept Humphrey's estate in the family. Humphrey was very young indeed at the time of the marriage to Martha, barely fourteen, and yet Bagot claimed that he had him married in infancy to his daughter Lettice.

The following is an account of events immediately before and after the marriage of Humphrey Okeover to Martha Cheney. The wardship of Humphrey had been given to Walter Bagot's wife, Elizabeth, by the earl of Salisbury, Robert Cecil, who was the master of the court of wards. All did not go as planned when Humphrey married Martha Cheney, allegedly *without* the knowledge of Martha's father, Sir Oliver Cheney, who claimed he knew nothing about their marriage.

→ **WALTER BAGOT**

Letter to an Unidentified Man   *n. date*

Right honorable yf [if] matter of importance had not enforced me to have written I wold not have presumed to troble you with idle letters to withdrawe or hinder you in your honorable imployment. But having lately susteaned great wronge and beeinge muche abused by my old adversarie Sir Oliver Cheney and his wicked lady the mother of younge Okeover, whose wardship was geven unto my wiefe by the late Erle of Salisburie her cosen germain,[1] and afterward passed under the great seale of England, and the saied ward (at the earnest desier of his then lyvinge father and the said lady his then wiefe) was maried unto my daughter (boath inphants) by the mutuall consent of us their parents. The ward hath at Candlemas [February 2 — feast of purification of the Virgin Mary] now one yeare sithence accomplished his age of consent, viz., fourteen years and within twoo dayes after maried to Sir Oliver his daughter. In what maner I have bin abused in the cariadge of this busines were over tediose to troble your Honor withe report. But now there chifest defence in the Court of Wards (where I expect my remedie) is to alledge that I was only putt in trust to procure the wardship

---

[1] **cosen germain:** first cousin.

for her use and that the Erle of Salisburie neaver made any such graunt ether to my wiefe or mee.

———

Marriages of infants were lawful and not uncommon. But such a marriage, though so called, was not quite a marriage unless the parties confirmed it as such after reaching the ages of consent — fourteen for a boy, twelve for a girl. The marriage of Humphrey and Lettice was never confirmed.

Bagot, it appears, had carelessly allowed his ward to visit his mother when he was close to fourteen. Once his mother got her hands on him she married him to her stepdaughter, Martha Cheney. Bagot took the matter to the court of wards because he had been defrauded of the value of the ward's marriage. The outcome of the case is not known, but Bagot was prosecuting it right up to the time of his death. Bagot seems to have offered to sell the marriage to Sir Oliver, and £2,000 may have been the price.

The following letter was written when Humphrey was back in Bagot's grasp. The lawyer Edmund Waring (the son-in-law of Bagot's sister Ann Broughton) advises that Humphrey be compelled to acknowledge before the congregation his marriage since infancy to Lettice. Then he should consummate the marriage. If he refuses he could be held by force as Bagot's ward. Refusal of marriage rendered a ward liable to payment, out of his estate, of the full value of the marriage, which was usually far more than the guardian had paid for the wardship (a fate such as befell the earl of Southampton; see p. 23).

→ EDMUND WARING

Letter to Walter Bagot
February 21, 1619/20

In asmuche as a marriage hathe alredy beene I know not well how it stands with the rules of the ecclesiastic Lawe to marry the same persons agayne. But now havinge his person eyther he is really your sonn in law or ward. Yf [If] your sonn in law then lett him before your mynister in the face of the congregacion acknowledge the same by suche words or acts as that lawe dyrecteth but yf it were myne owne case I would surely request Mr. Chauncellor's [presumably the Chancellor of the Diocese of Lichfield and Coventry] opynion and perservere at such act as he shall dyrect in this kynd. Yf voluntary acceptance be then lett them bed together (with modest instruc-

---

cions) and Gods blessing. Yf otherways, deteyne him perforce: he is yours *quoad* [to this extent] property, but not any of his fellowes. Howbeit yf fayre words may prevayle it is the best course of staying him. He may returne to his mother at next byrth day. Your articles as I remember leave you to your remedy agaynst him at law yf he refuse. Yet yf he do so you may tender him the other daughter yf she be xii [twelve] [Mary, the "other daughter" referred to was only ii at the time of this letter]. However now com to your parley upon even termes with possession of your ward, in any case a strong gard over him, not in armes but in judgment and discreete parts such as for no sleyte may be deceyved in his escape. Yf he denye to take Let [an abbreviation of "Lettice"] to wyfe let that denyall be as well wytnessed as you desyre the acceptance to have beene.

Now sir you have abruptly what I can advise and as reddyly should you have myne attendance for that or any other servyce to you yf I were able but I had such a bruse that day I was with you as not able now to ryde or goe a myle for my lyf. I pray god helpe me I feare I have hurt me muche.

So hastely I leave longer circumstance render my love to you and my good Aunt, with all yours.

Ever remayning yours unfaynedly,
Ed. War

———

The following letter is from Sir John Ferrers. He had planned to begin marriage negotiations with Sir Simon Weston of Lichfield (who was to serve as an intermediary) about a union between his own daughter and a son of Bagot's. But his daughter insisted she wanted to lead a single life for some years, and Ferrers, though much displeased, could not compel her to marry against her inclination. We don't know the identity of Sir John's daughter, or which Bagot son (Lewis or Harvey) she is supposed to marry, or why she decided to remain single. That the names of these children are not so much as mentioned speaks volumes. Also notable is the emphasis on the love between the two parties — not the love between the couple on whose behalf these marriage negotiations have been undertaken, but that between Sir John Ferrers and Walter Bagot.

What is fascinating about this letter is the way Sir John described his attempts to persuade his daughter to marry, and the fact that he did not begin to do so until fairly well into preliminary negotiations with Bagot. First, he attempted to discover how well disposed she was to marriage — and here the emphasis was on the state of matrimony rather than on her feelings about this particular potential husband. In a pattern similar to that of *Romeo and Juliet,* when his own attempts at negotiation failed, his wife stepped in to attempt to persuade her further. But this young woman, whose age we do not know, was firm in her decision not to marry for some time. The young woman's relationship with her father appears to have been distant since it was only when he tried to proceed with marriage negotiations that she told him she had resisted her aunt's earlier attempts to find her a husband in London. We do not know whether this aunt had acted independently or in concert with the wishes of the girl's father. Whatever the case, despite the obvious desire of her family to have her married, her father nonetheless conceded to her wishes, declaring that "God hath his secret decree in all things," and that in a matter of this nature, coercion would be inappropriate. In other words, he arrived at a decision diametrically opposed to that of Capulet.

At least on the face of it, the letter presents us with a daughter who resisted marriage and a father who conceded to her wishes. But of course, it is possible that Sir John was extricating himself from an alliance about which he had become reluctant. If the son referred to was the wastrel Lewis Bagot, Sir John might, as we will see from subsequent letters, have had powerful incentive to retreat from the match.

→ SIR JOHN FERRERS

Letter to Walter Bagot   *April 20, 1610*

Good Sir where as there hath bene a motion betwene us for a marriage betwext your sonne and my daughter, which hath bene intertayned to my understandinge with greate love on ether syde, and wee having referred our selves to Sir Simon Weston, and appoynted a day to meet att Lichfielde concerninge some further speche of this busines, where I dowted not wee shold have concluded to the good lykinge of all parties, and therefore I thought fitt to acquaint my daughter what I intended to doe, and require for her, and to try how shee stode affected to a married lyfe, which I had not done before, presuminge she wolde willingely have referred her affections that way wholly to the discression of my selfe and her mother, whose answere I will truly deliver to you shee humbly desiered me to pardonne her afferminge with ernest protestations, that shee had no cause to dislyke your sonne, but acknowledge his worth and deserts respectively and aledged her owne sicknes, desieringe to live a single lyfe for some few yeares. Shee also acquainted me with the lyke motions made unto her, beinge att London, by my sister Newtons meanes and confessed that shee had intreated her Aunte to forbeare to move any such matter unto her, although shee knew I much desiered to bestow her, and sent her thither most chefly for that purpose, which answere much discontentinge I acquainted my wyfe with itt, who delte with her to the same purpose, as I had done before, and receved the lyke answere from her, I know god hath his secret decree in all things, and although this unexpected accident much greeveth both me and my wyfe, yett wee are unwillinge in a busines of this nature, to urge her any further att this tyme. And therefore we doe both earnestly desier that as this begonne in love so howsoever itt shall take successe itt may breed no unkynd conceit butt wee remayne as I will ever be

Your true and constant Frend
Jo: fferrers
Tamworth, this xxth [20th] of Aprill

———

There were two girls in one generation of this family, first cousins in fact, bearing the name Jane. One of them, as we have seen, eloped with Simon Bagot, and as far as we know, attained the much desired goal of marital felicity, even if she did so by less than conventional means. We have no letters from this Jane, only letters pertaining to her elopement and clandestine marriage. The other Jane, born in 1589, eventually marries Sir George Throckmorton, but only after a very messy and misguided romance with her first cousin Lewis Bagot, the ne'er-do-well eldest son of Walter Bagot.

Jane is especially interesting because we have letters from her written in her own hand. She writes lovingly to Lewis, her beloved, and penitently to Lewis's father, Walter. Once Jane was removed from the danger of an ill-chosen love match, however, we never hear from her again, and it is perhaps telling that in this collection of letters as a whole, women tend to put pen to paper when they are in the throes of crisis rather than when they are in the midst of domestic happiness. For instance, though not reproduced here, the unhappily married Lettice, who was earlier married as an infant to Humphrey Okeover (he who married Martha Cheyney as an adolescent, see above, pp. 324–27), writes to her relatives for help. So the glimpse we get of womens' lives inclines more toward the tragic than may be accurate. Interestingly, too, in this correspondence, we find Jane's stepmother (also called — inconveniently — Jane Skipwith) weighing in about the romance with Lewis.

Neither Jane Bagot nor Jane Throckmorton followed the prescripts of the conduct literature — in fact, both engaged in singular acts of disobedience — and neither of them seems to have had their lives ruined by doing so. While disgruntled fathers and other relatives might have thundered threats of ruin and disinheritance, eventually, all parties involved seem to have accommodated themselves to their situations without taking drastic action. That is, there seems to have been considerable effort made to maintain rather than sever familial and social ties, and certainly in the case of Jane Throckmorton, women's reputations do not seem to be quite as vulnerable as we might imagine. Remarkable also is the way in which this family was quasi-incestuously intertwined in matters of love, marriage, and property. While taking great care not to breech laws of consanguinity (blood relation) during this period, people did marry neighbors to whom they also had some, albeit fairly distant, ties of kinship. Thus, when Juliet professes her love for Tybalt, we should not dismiss this as being a demonstration of a clearly platonic connection between them, a point emphasized by the punning eroticism of her own declaration of outrage at his death. The object of Juliet's rage and sexual longing is deliberately doubled rather than being merely ambiguous. Whatever the implications of Juliet's words, there is an unquestionably amatory echo in Jane Skipwith's address to her cousin Lewis as "My best beloved cousin."

It may be tempting to read Jane as the plucky heroine who falls in love but is thwarted by a testy uncle until we know the full facts of the case. Lewis Bagot, Jane's beloved, led a dissolute life in London that ended in his early death in 1611. How that death came about is unclear, though from the evidence of an investigation ordered by his father after his death, it seems possible that he died as a result of injuries inflicted in a duel after he was pressured to marry the woman with whom he had been cohabiting: "He told them he could not marry her nor would marry her, but give other satisfaction as he might, and if that would not content them, if they would have further satisfaction he would meet either of them in the field and give them satisfaction with his sword, and bade them take what course they could in it, for he would not marry her" (Folger ms. L.a.355). This report also stated that Lewis's mistress had also pretended to be his wife: "[t]hey were told that she had married one Mr. Baggot, son to a great gent in Staffordshire and a mere kinsman to the Lord Treasurer, and that she said Mr. Bagot and her friends also did keep all things secret for fear of his father's displeasure, but one day she was like to come to great preferment, and this excuse was made to the churchwardens" (Folger ms. L.a.355).

In the following letter, Lady Markham informs her brother-in-law Walter Bagot that Jane, her stepdaughter, has assured her that she will break off the betrothal between herself and Bagot's son Lewis since it is displeasing to Bagot.

JANE SKIPWITH (ROBERTS), LADY MARKHAM

Letter to Walter Bagot   *September 20, 1610*

C̲otes Leics.[1]

    Sir I hope the gentellmen which cam from you to me aboute the buissnis [business] betwixte your sonne and my daughter in lawe [i.e. stepdaughter] hath fully satisfyed you that there is noe suche thinge as you did muche suspecte there were, and I am fully perswaded of my daughter that she will never speake with your sonne agayne of that matter. And for your better satisfaccion she hath wrytten to you to let you understande the truethe, under her owne hand, good brother I beseeche you pardon that which is paste, [past] and impute it to theyr younge yeares, and want of experience it may bee theye thoughte because they have hard [heard] and knowne the lyke matches have bene made betwixt them which hath beene as neare of kinred as they be made them presume to thinke it might be lawfull for them to doe the lyke, but boothe your sonne and my daughter as they have tolde me were never minded to make a matche without your good will, and wheras you are perswaded that your sonne hathe beene many tymes at Coates, often he hath not benne, but when he cam he was very wellcome to me, and I proteste I did not knowe there was any suche matter in hand till of late, and when I did knowe, I did advise them as well as I could, not to be overforwarde but take good counsell of theyr frendes, and so I hope they will when eyther of them shall marry, I hope my cossen your sonne will by all meanes endeavor to purchase your favour, and become an obedient chyld to you and his mother, which comffortes God send you and all that have children and so with my kynde commendaciones to you and my sister your wyfe I reste ever

Your lovinge Sister,
Jane Skipwith

I am sory for the discomfort that is fallen to Sir Edmund Bushey and his lady, I heare that god hath taken my cossen ther daughter Hawfford. She

---

[1] **Cotes Leics.**: Coates, Leicestershire.

Folger ms. L.a.850

dyd of a consumption I fear the gref will be great both to your father and mother god send them comforte

→ JANE SKIPWITH

Letter to Lewes Bagot   *April 14, 1610*

To my good frend Mr Lewes Bagott give this
My best beloved cosin,

I am very glad to here from you that you ar well, and I would have you thinke that it tis one of the greates comfordes [comforts] I have in this world to here of your wellfarer [sic]. I am very sory to here that your father is still in that humer [humor] of offering you more wifes [wives] but as for this shee hathe a great porshone [portion], wich I thinke if I hade, hee would not so much mislike of mee as hee dothe; and besides shee is honorabell wich dothe goe fare with most men nowe dayes; but I protest I writ not this out of any mistrust I have of your love; for I have ever found it more then I have desserved; yett I know not what [I] shall deserve, and thus with my best wishes for your good fortune; and happynes in all your bussines I rest ever

> Your truly loving frende while I breath
> Jane Skipwith

My sisters love may not bee forgotten to you; lett mee here you as soone as you can.

Folger ms. L.a.854 (see this letter on p. 333.)

FIGURE 11 *Letter of Jane Skipwith to Lewes Bagot. It is interesting to compare this* ➤ *correspondence to the letters in* Romeo and Juliet. *In the play, letters, whose precise contents we never see, function almost entirely as practical communications between the lovers themselves and between Friar Laurence and Romeo; they constitute strategies of a thoroughly pragmatic nature, such as the arrangement of meeting times and places. When these missives fail, it is not because of some rhetorical error on the part of the writer but because, in accordance with traditional dramatic device, delivery was thwarted. The most important instance of this is when the Friar's letter fails to reach Mantua because of an outbreak of plague. While it is important to remember that then (even more than now) letters might be subject to misdirection as a result of unreliable carriers and that the physical act of transporting them was often long and arduous, Jane's letter suggests that the real obstacle to communication is the difficulty of disclosing one's heart and of interpreting the silence of one's lover.*

My best beloued cosin.

I am very glad to here from you that you
ar well, and I would haue you thinke
that it is one of the greates comfortes I
haue in this world to here of youe well
fares. I am very sory to here that your
father is still in that humor of offering you
more wifes; but as for this shee hathe a great
porshone, with I thinke if I haue, hee would
not so much mislike of mee as hee dothe, and
besides shee is honorabell with clothe gee faee
with most men now adayes; but I protest I
writ not this out of any mistrust I haue
of your loue; for I haue euer found it more then
I haue desserued, yett I know not what shall
desserue, and thus with my best wishes for yr
good fortune, and happyes in all your busines
I rest euer

the xiiii of
Aprill

                              your truly louing
                              frende while I breath

                              Jane Skipwith

my sisters loue
may not bee for
gotten to you, lett mee here
you as sowne as you can

→ JANE SKIPWITH

Letter to Walter Bagot

1611

My good Unckel; I am very sorye that this matter hathe beene soe troubbellsome unto you; and I beeseche you have so charetabell a concete of mee; as to Impuit it to want of witte and yeres: I have harde [heard] of such maches[1] which made me the more to give here [ear] to this but never to bee soe forward in it as to mache with out your concente; and since I heare that it dothe discontent you I am very sory that it was ever mosshoned [motioned]: and am fully resoulefed [resolved] never to here more of that matter; and good unckel I hope you have not soe harde a concette of mee; as thinke I cane forgett my good father['s] carefull advice to mee by his letter; which was I should bee thankfull to all from whom I receved any good; and if I should be found gilty of ingrattitued [ingratitude] to you whom I have receved soe much love and kindnes from that as lounge as I leve [long as I live] I must thinke my selfe much bound unto for: I should thinke my selfe unworthy of your love; and all though this for atime hath beene a meanes to with drawe your love from mee and your sonne; yett I hope wee shall in joye it againe. I protest I should thinke my selfe very happy if I might bee assuered of your frendsheepe againe; which I feare I have hassarded with this rashe busines and thus humblly craving your love and my Aunts' I rest

> Your neece to command in what you please;
> Jane Skipwith

[1] **such ma[t]ches:** marriages between first cousins.

Folger ms. L.a.135

→ WALTER BAGOT

Letter to Henry Skipwith[1]

1611

Sir I did wryte unto my much esteemed Lady your mother in lawe in September last desiringe to bee satisfied from her whether there were ether mariadge or contracte past betwixt my disobedient soone and my neece your sister or not which I greatly suspected. I receaved her kynd answere which

[1] **Henry Skipwith:** Jane's brother.

Folger ms. L.a.135

(in respecte of that reverend opinion I hold of her virtues) I well not sus-
pecte but at that time was the pleane truthe (a denyall of boath) first in her
owne opinion and secondly by my neece in her letters with a protestacion
shee would neaver hereafter geve care into any such motion. Callinge to
rememberance her fathers letters whoe advised her ever to bee thankfull to
her friends. Not withstandinge her protesacions my gracelesse sonne now
affirmeith there is such promise past bewtixt them as can not bee revoked.
Hee hath withdrawen his obedience from mee and hath continuewed in
a base infamouse place in Godwins howse in London since Christmas till
Saturdaye last. Charged to bee the father of a bastard child begotten on a
base strumpet servant to a gentlewoman of this contrie and taken in bed
with her cooke a maried man. For this his wicked lyfe his obstinate disobe-
diense and infinite others lewde condicions I have rejected him purposinge
(god willinge to disinherit him). And whilest I live meane to withdrawe all
my maynteanance from him. Yf [If] these shewe the fruits of true affeccon
unto my neece I praye god send them as much joye together as I receave
comfort by them. This much I thought good out of my love to make you
acquainted with whome it shall please you to imparte yt [it] to I leave to
your good consideracion. And so rest your lovinge unckle.

––––––––

The following is endorsed "Lewes [*sic*] his last letters," and indicates that
Walter Bagot's bad seed was on his deathbed, possibly as the result of an
injury received in a violent altercation in London. Too late, he was penitent
and resolved to reform himself and give up his dissolute life. Of all the stories we overhear in this correspondence, this is the one with a definitively
tragic ending. It is not the suicide of lovers but the willful self-destruction of
youth and promise. Whereas Shakespeare's play emphasizes the tragedy of
the lovers, Lewis Bagot bears a closer parallel to Tybalt or Mercutio. The
play here separates sex and violence from one another in the sense that unlike Benvolio or Romeo we never see these characters in the throes of a relationship. In contrast, the real-life Lewis appears to have succumbed to both
sex and violence as instruments of his ruin.

→ LEWES BAGOT

Letter to Walter Bagot

1610

To the worshipfull his good and lovinge father Mr. Wallter Bagot att Blithe-feild give these:

Sir

If hetherto I have spent the beginninge of my tyme in that uncivill kinde of behaviour that I have beene a disparagement to my house and a disgrace to my selfe yet I hope you will out of your fatherly love bee as willinge to forgive and forgett as I unfaynedly will be most dutifull to you and by gods grace to amend my misspent tyme and lead the rest of my life in such a civill manner that shall bee bothe pleasinge to God and noe thinge att all distast-full to you, or any of my frends: tyme paste [past] can hardly be recalled and it is never too late to doe well. I knowe Sir it is my duty to honor and obeye you my parents, and I pray God I may no longer live than to expresse my duty to you and my mother: not onely in woord, but allsoe in deed. Though your just displeashure att mee, may bee a motive against my submission; yet I beseech you to pardon this my bouldnes and the follies of my ill spent tyme, and the too little acknowledgement, and performance of my duty, (I humbly beseeche you for Gods sake) to forgive and take once again your loste sonne to mercy and thincke uppon mee with the eye of pitty and com-passion and not accordinge to my deserts. With humble and harty desier of yours and my mothers blessinge I humbly take leave and rest.

Your ever dutyfull and obedient sonne
Lewes Bagot

The following letter from Robert Broughton refers to Lewis Bagot's recent death and urges his father to discharge a debt of £100, for which he was surety.

→ **ROBERT BROUGHTON**

Letter to Walter Bagot

1611

To the Worshipfull my approved good unckle Mr. Wallter Bagott esquire at his howse at Blithfeild this be delivered.

Sir:

I am sory that my ill fortune and occasion should be such that now I can write you no good newes & must be troublesome to crave your favoure to helpe my misfortune. The unexpected death of my cosen I assure my selfe yow have heard of and the mannor of his death I know will be made knowne unto you. His penitency at his departure and desire of your forgiveness I hope will obtaine your pardon for his former mispent tyme, and I doubt not but but [sic] his father allmightie will forgive him. For my selfe I must earnestly intreate your favoure that whereas out of my naturall, and intire love to him I was bound in Michaelmas Terme [university term starting in October and ending in November] last togaither with him selfe (uppon his extreame necessity and earnest meanes and intreaty) to save two harmlesse that were bound for 100£ for him and his owne use (as his man knoweth): you will be pleased out of your love and kindnesse to us both as to see yt [it] discharged with what conveniencie yow may. If hee had lived I had before this bin discharged, and now yf [if] you be not good to mee my fortunes are overthrowne. What my troubles and my estate is yow know and would my estate afford it I would not be this troublesome to you but Ducum telum necessitas [needs must]. In your love to mee I hope yow will releive mee and graunt this suite in the performance whereof yow shall ever bind mee to continue your unfayned lovinge cosen to command.

Robert Broughton

Folger ms. L.a.282

———

Although mothers rarely took part in the more formal and financial aspects of marriage negotiation, Elinor Cave[1] (wife to Sir Thomas, Walter Bagot's brother-in-law) writes because her husband's resources have been so far

---

[1] **Elinor Cave:** Cave's own jointure was confirmed by an Act of Parliament in 1606 (House of Lord's Record Office, 3 James I OA 41).

depleted by the marriage of her eldest daughter to the Welshman, Sir John Wynn, that there was not enough left to come up with the £3,000 Sir John Egerton was asking for the marriage of one of Elinor's younger daughters with his son. Clearly, Elinor likes Egerton's son and he is clearly taken with her daughter. Sir John's financial goals are here the only apparent impediment to the match, and they turned out to be insurmountable: Elinor's daughter and Egerton's son were never married.

→ LADY ELINOR CAVE

Letter to Walter Bagot   *September 22, 1606*

Good brother. Heare hath byn with mee younge Mr. Egerton ever since his departure from Blyfeeld, and to whome I am verie much beholdinge for the good affection hee beareth to my daughter. Hee hath brought mee a noat of his fathers land, which contayned thus much; that his father is contented to deliver £300: a yeare for a joynter [jointure][2] for his wife; and to make upp that three hundred pownds, two thowsands a yeare to desende uppon the heires of them boath; yett I thought sumwhat strange of the noate in respect itt had not Sir John Egertons name subscribed to itt, if hee weare privy to itt, the which the younge gentleman assureth mee hee is; And farther the younge gentleman letteth mee understand that his father looketh for no less than three thowsand pound with my daughter; and doth thinck itt ympossible to drawe itt to a less sum; If you remember att my cominge out of wales I had sum talke with you about this motion; and I wished that if Sir Johan Egerton would stand uppon soe great a sum hee might bee certyfyed that my husbands habillitie was not able to answere itt, for beinge of late soe drawne downe by my daughter Wynns marriage. Hee is not able to begynn to paye an other portion with out good tyme bee given. It is this opinion I have of the younge gentleman, that if I weare able to answere Sir John's Expectacon [expectation], I doe not know anye gentleman in the world that I would soner entertaynne. The younge gentleman doth much ymportune mee that you should writt unto his father in his

---

[2] **jointure:** the portion of a woman's dowry that reverts to her possession after her husband's death, or that always remains hers throughout the marriage.

behalfe and therfore I pray you satisfie hym hearein. And thus not doubtinge of your love att all tymes to bee ready to doe mee any kyndness that lyeth in your power, and with my best remembraunce to my sister assuringe you I desire to live no longer than I maye be found

Your true lovinge sister
Elianor Cave

I pray you remember mee most kyndly to my Aunt, my nephew Lewes; my coosen Ann; and the rest of my younge coosens.

Sir Thomas Cokayne, of Ashbourne, Derbyshire (1519–1592), grew up in the household of George, earl of Shrewsbury, and came into a large inheritance in 1538. He claimed that Jane Okeover "procured" his son to elope with her and thus defended young Cokayne against the charge of abduction. We do not know if the matter went to court because the records for Staffordshire quarter sessions are not extant. Whatever happened, Tom and Jane were married, and Jane was widowed in 1584. The charges Sir Thomas makes about Jane could just as easily be made about Shakespeare's Juliet, and it suggests that although the story of the lovers was not new, given the more positive outcome of real-life elopements, Shakespeare's audience might well have been far more surprised than we are by the tragic outcome of events.

→ **SIR THOMAS COKAYNE**

Letter to Richard Bagot ⠀⠀⠀⠀⠀⠀⠀⠀*May 28, 1579*

Right worshipful and my olde good friend. I have nowe just occasion to prove your frendshepe, I am geven to understande that Mr. Okeover and his man Parker, ether the one or bothe, contrarie to their othes, goe about to procure a privy sessions agaynst my sonne who playinge a yonge [young] mans parte as yt [it] should seeme went about to take away his daughter and yet faylled therof and was procured by the gentillwoman soe to doe. I trust to have your especiall frendshepe herein, prayinge you to advertize mee of the day and place of your sittinge. Thus with my hartie commend[ations] to

---

Folger ms. L.a.392

you and good Mrs. Bagott with all your childeren, I commytt you to gods almightie protecsion, Ashbourne, this xxviii [28th] of May 1579.

Yours as his owne,
Thomas Cokayne

To the right worshipfull and my assured frend Richarde Bagott, Esquyre, at Blythfild, geve thess. hast hast.

————

In the following letter, we learn that Walter Bagot's sister refused to marry Christopher Brooke; what is interesting here is she did not make the decision on her own, though Walter Bagot insists that *he* had nothing to do with it and wishes she had accepted. Is Bagot put out by the fact that Brooke did not tell him he intended to propose to his sister? The negative outcome might indicate that things had not developed between the couple and so there was no need to tell anyone, but the very next sentence admits that Walter has heard from others how much Brooke liked his sister. Brooke does not seem to have negotiated very well. He would clearly have done better to work directly through Walter. It is interesting, too, that Bagot's sister apparently tried to defer to her brother in making her decision about this proposal and that Bagot felt it imperative to respond to Brooke himself. The woman's agency, here at least, seems to have been overshadowed by negotiations between men. If Brooke had been counting on his beloved making an independent decision, he was sadly mistaken.

→ WALTER BAGOT

Letter to Christopher Brooke   *December 4, 1598?*

Good Mr Brooke I have received your letters wherin you wryte you do acknoledge your self much bounden unto mee and indebtted for many kyndnesses, but wherupon such bond or debt ariseth I knowe not unlesse you account a littel ordinary intertaynment such curtesie the which yf [if] far better and greater might no waye have requited your present paynes or former desertes. I am not so apte to conceave displeasure, espetially with my good frends as upon small occasion to condemne them and therfore doe not blame your secresie but commend your wisdome in beeing secrete unlesse there had bin greater occasion than by the sequele appeareth ther was why you shold have made any others than allredy were acquainted with it. I did indeed before that here of that good lykinge you had of my sister. I delivered unto her your letters beeinge sent together with my owne from my sister Trew and will deale with you as with one I account amongst the number of my best frends which is in the playnest maner I can. She made me acquainted with the contents of your letters and required my assistance in drawinge an answere which I urged her unto. I refused for divers causes, (1) because I had bin unacquainted with the matter before (2) because I knew your desier was to have it proceed from her selfe, and lastly in regard others were present whome I was assured she wold rather acquaint with her secrets than my selfe with whose privitie and assistance she hath sent you answere as hath best seemed unto her and them. Yf it had bin better to your content-ment it shold better have contented mee. I have seene it truly Sir I thinke you in every waye deserving to bee matched with my sister. I account you very well worthie of her yf the affeccions of the other were answerable unto my owne. And what event soever matters shall have hereafter, I can not but think my selfe many wayes beholden unto you which I hartily desier I maye as well performe in deedes as promise in words, etc. December 4.

People had been complaining about the marriage of Katherine Lowe to Richard Bagot's son, Anthony. It is not clear why the marriage was regarded as unsuitable. At any rate, Martin Heton, dean of Westminster and later bishop of Ely, asked Bagot to make it appear to the world that Katherine had made an appropriate match. Heton said he was chiefly instrumental in the marriage and that he supported the young woman's choice. In this instance, the churchman, rather as did Friar Laurence, defended mutual affection against other interests represented by those who found the union objectionable.

→ MARTIN HETON

Letter to Richard Bagot   *June 18, 1594*

To the right worshipfull my very loving frend Mr. Richard Bagott, Esquire, att his house att Blithfeild.

Good Sir ytt [it] hath pleased god to dispose the affections of your sonne Mr. Anthonie Bagott and my cozen Katherine Lowe one towards the other whereatt because offence ys [is] taken and wrong ys done unto my brother [brother-in-law] Symon Weston, and some of her frends shewe them selves displeased att ytt I hope you will strayne your selfe a little that ytt may appeare to the world that shee shall bee aswell bestowed uppon your sonne as uppon some others whereunto I am the more bould earnestly to intreat you because otherwise her frends would bee ready to lay great blame uppon mee, who must needes bee found to have bynne the cheefest worker in ytt. I write not this as doubtinge but you will performe as muche or more than your two sonnes have promised for you but because the gentlewoman hath affiance in mee and next unto her owne likeinge, by mee was leadd to the choise of your sonne I cannot but bee carefull of her. I hope bothe you and Mrs. Bagott your wyfe shall have joy and comforte in ytt.

And so with remembrance of my hartie comendations and my wives [wife's], to you and Mrs. Bagott your good wyfe I committ you bothe to the grace and protection of allmightie god. From Winchester the 18 of June 1594.

Your very assured loving frend,
Martin Heton

Folger ms. L.a.539

Mothering

Two of the documents that follow address the issue of nursing, while Anne Clifford's diary entry records the life of an aristocratic mother whose maternity is neither her sole nor her primary preoccupation. The main role of the well-to-do woman in the early modern household, as stage directions to this edition indicate, was as "Wife" and "Lady of the House" (4.4). Typically, wealthier women, unlike their lower-class counterparts, were alienated from the labors of child-rearing principally because they hired wet-nurses to suckle their offspring. Significantly, however, one of the objections voiced by

Elizabeth (Knyvett) Clinton in her argument that well-to-do women should breastfeed their own children is that one should not expose them to the dubious manners and morals of many wet-nurses. Thus, Shakespeare's rendition of the Nurse draws both on prevailing cultural stereotypes as much as on social practice.

In dramatic terms, the Nurse is a character type celebrated in popular culture, a comic-grotesque figure whose outrageously indecorous behavior represents fecundity and amoral exuberance. Thematically, this characterization is appropriate because the Nurse is culturally associated with the wholly somatic aspects of maternity, and is quite cut off from the cultural ideal of motherhood, which in comparison with the excess and exaggeration of the comic-grotesque, seems limited and inflexible, inadequate in face of the breadth of life. In terms of popular, "carnivalesque" culture, such gross physiologism with its emphasis on the physical body is entirely positive. The grotesque or carnivalesque emphasis here (see Paster; Bakhtin) counters the cultural tendency to divorce spirit from flesh and ideals from material reality. The Nurse comically deflates Lady Capulet's high-flown conceit about Paris as an ornate volume, "this precious book of love" (1.3.88), "gold clasps locks in the golden story" (1.3.93), with jokes about sex and pregnancy—in other words, the reality of adult sexual life. However, in grounding and earthing the abstract and the ideal, the comic grotesque also admits mortality, not as tragedy, but as an exacerbated form of human fallibility. Notably, both the Nurse's husband and daughter are dead, and she observes presciently, in act 2, that "rosemary" — the herb of remembrance strewn on corpses — "and Romeo begin both with a letter" (2.4.167–68).

→ ELIZABETH (KNYVETT) CLINTON, COUNTESS OF LINCOLN

From The Countess of Lincoln's Nursery   *1622*

And she was weaned — I never shall forget it —
Of all the days of the year, upon that day;
For I had then laid wormwood to my dug . . .
When it did taste the wormwood on the nipple
Of my dug and felt it bitter, pretty fool,
To see it tetchy and fall out wi' th' dug!   (1.3.25–27, 31–33)

Elizabeth (Knyvett) Clinton, *The Countess of Lincoln's Nursery* (Oxford, 1622), 1–21.

Aristocratic women commonly hired wet-nurses to feed their infants, a process that went on rather longer than in our own day. By the Nurse's calculations, for example, Juliet was almost three years old when she was weaned. However, the practice of putting children out to nurse came under some scrutiny in the early seventeenth century. The account below is by Elizabeth Clinton, the mother of eighteen children, who regrets not breastfeeding her own babies and who exhorts other mothers to nourish their own children. She was not the only commentator on the topic; in 1622 churchman William Gouge's influential treatise *Domestical Duties* included a lengthy section on the virtues of women breastfeeding their own offspring.

Clinton's tract is addressed to her daughter-in-law, Bridget, so it is an interesting example of communication between women across the generations and also assumes an audience of literate women who are actively involved in the business of childrearing. This contrasts with the lack of mothering in *Romeo and Juliet*, conveyed by the fact that, as the Nurse notes, Juliet's mother was in Mantua when her daughter was weaned.

... Because it hath pleased God to bless me with many children, and so caused me to observe many things falling out to mothers, and to their children; I thought good to open my mind concerning a special matter belonging to all child-bearing women, seriously to consider of: and to manifest my mind the better, even to write of this matter, so far as God shall please to direct me; in sum, the matter I mean, *is the duty of nursing due by mothers to their own children.*

In setting down whereof, I will first show, that every woman ought to nurse her own child; and secondly, I will endeavor to answer such objections, as are used to be cast out against this duty to disgrace the same.

The first point is easily performed. For it is the express *ordinance* of God that mothers should nurse their own children, & being his ordinance they are bound to it in conscience. This should stop the mouths of all repliers, for *God is most wise,* and therefore must needs know what is fittest and best for us to do: & to prevent all foolish fears, or shifts,[1] we are given to understand that he is also *all sufficient,* & therefore infinitely able to bless his own ordinance, and to afford us means in ourselves (as continual experience confirmeth) toward the observance thereof.

If this (as it ought) be granted, then how venturous are those women that dare venture to do otherwise, and so to refuse, and by refusing to despise that order, which the most wise and almighty God hath appointed, and in stead thereof to choose their own pleasures? Oh what peace can there be to

---

[1] **shifts:** changes, especially of mood.

these women's consciences, unless through the darkness of their under-standing they judge it no disobedience?

And then they will drive me to prove that this nursing, and nourishing of their own children in their own bosoms is God's ordinance; They are very willful, or very ignorant, if they make a question of it. For it is proved suffi-ciently to be their duty, both by God's word, and also by his works.

By his word it is proved, first by *examples,* namely the example of *Eve.* For who suckled her sons Cain, Abel, Seth, etc., but herself? Which she did not only of mere necessity, because yet no other woman was created; but especially because she was their mother, and so saw it was her duty: and because she had a true natural affection, which moved her to do it gladly. Next the example of *Sarah* the wife of *Abraham;* For she both gave her son *Isaac* suck, as doing the duty commanded of God: And also took great com-fort, and delight therein, as in a duty well pleasing to herself; whence she spoke of it, as of an action worthy to be named in her holy rejoicing. Now if *Sarah,* so great a *princess,* did nurse her own child, why should any of us neglect to do the like, except (which God forbid) we think scorn to follow her, whose daughters it is our glory to be, and which we be only upon this condition, that we imitate her well-doing. Let us look therefore to our wor-thy pattern, noting withal, that she put herself to this work when she was very old, and so might the better have excused herself, than we younger women can: being also more able to hire, and keep a nurse, than any of us. But why is she not followed by most in the practice of this duty? Even because they want her virtue, and piety. This want is the common hindrance to this point of the woman's obedience; for this want makes them want love to God's precepts, want love to his doctrine, and like step-mothers, want due love to their own children.

But now to another worthy example, namely that excellent woman *Han-nah,* who having after much affliction of mind obtained a son of God, whom she vowed unto God, she did not put him to another to nurse, but nursed him her own self until she had weaned him, & carried him to be consecrate unto the Lord: As well knowing that this duty of giving her child suck, was so acceptable to God, as for the cause thereof she did not sin in staying with it at home from the yearly sacrifice: but now women, especially of any place, and of little grace, do not hold this duty acceptable to God, because it is unacceptable to themselves: as if they would have the Lord to like, and dislike, according to their vain lusts.

To proceed, take notice of one example more, that is, of the *Blessed Vir-gin:* as her womb bare our *Blessed Savior,* so her paps[2] gave him suck. Now

---

[2] **paps:** breasts.

who shall deny the own mothers' suckling of their own children to be their duty, since every godly matron hath walked in these steps before them: *Eve* the mother of all the living; *Sarah* the mother of all the faithful; *Hannah* so graciously heard of God; *Mary* blessed among women, and called blessed of all ages. And who can say but that the rest of holy women mentioned in the holy scriptures did the like; since no doubt that speech of that noble dame, saying, who would have said to *Abraham* that *Sarah* should have given children suck? was taken from the ordinary custom of mothers in those less corrupted times.

And so much for proof of this office, and duty to be God's ordinance, by his own *Word* according to the argument of *examples:* I hope I shall likewise prove it by the same word from plain *precepts.* First from that *precept,* which willeth the younger women to marry, and to *bear* children, that is, not only to *bear* them in the womb, and to bring them forth, but also to *bear* them on their knee, in their arms, and at their breasts: for this *bearing* a little before is called nourishing, and bringing up: and to enforce it the better upon women's consciences, it is numbered as the first of the good works, for which godly women should be well reported of. And well it may be the first, because if holy ministers, or other Christians do hear of a good woman to be brought to bed, and her child to be living; their first question usually is, whether she herself give it suck, yea, or no? if the answer be she doth, then they commend her: if the answer be she doth not, then they are sorry for her.

And thus I come to a second *precept* I pray you, who that judges aright; doth not hold the suckling of her own child the part of a true mother, of an honest mother, of a just mother, of a sincere mother, of a mother worthy of love, of a mother deserving good report, of a virtuous mother, of a mother winning praise for it? All this is assented to by any of good understanding. Therefore this is also a *precept,* as for other duties, so for *this* of mothers to their children; which saith, whatsoever things are true, whatsoever things are honest, whatsoever things are just, whatsoever things are pure, whatsoever things be worthy of love, whatsoever things be of good report, if there be any virtue, if there be any praise, think on these things, these things do and the God of peace shall be with you.

So far for my promise, to prove by the word of God, that it is his ordinance that women should nurse their own children: now I will endeavor to prove it by his *works:* First by his *works of judgment;* if it were not his ordinance for mothers to give their children suck, it were no *judgment* to bereave them of their milk, but it is specified to be a great *judgment* to bereave them hereof, & to give them dry breasts, therefore it is to be gathered, even from hence, that it is his ordinance, since to deprive them of means to do it, is a punishment of them.

I add to this *the work that God worketh in the very nature of mothers,* which proveth also that he hath ordained that they should nurse their own children: for by his secret operation, the mother's affection is so knit by nature's law to her tender babe, as she finds no power to deny to suckle it, no not when she is in hazard to lose her own life, by attending on it, for in such a case it is not said, let the mother fly, and leave her infant to the peril, as if she were dispensed with: but only it is said *woe to her,* as if she were to be pitied, that for nature to her child, she must be unnatural to herself: now if any then being even at liberty, and in peace, with all plenty, shall deny to give suck to their own children, they go against nature: and show that God hath not done so much for them as to work any good, no not in their nature, but left them more savage than the dragons, and as cruel to their little ones as the ostriches.[3]

Now another *work* of God, proving this point is the *work of his provision,* for every kind to be apt, and able to nourish their own fruit: there is no beast that feeds their young with milk, but the Lord, even from the first ground of the order of nature; *grow, and multiply;* hath provided it of milk to suckle their own young, which every beast takes so naturally unto, as if another beast come toward their young to offer the office of a dame unto it, they show according to their fashion, a plain dislike of it: as if nature did speak in them, and say it is contrary to God's order in nature, commanding each kind to increase, and multiply in their own bodies, and by their own breasts, not to bring forth by one dame, and to bring up by another: but it is his ordinance that every kind should both bring forth, and also nurse its own fruit.

Much more should this work of God prevail to persuade women, made as man in the image of God, and therefore should be ashamed to be put to school to learn good nature of the unreasonable creature.[4] In us also, as we know by experience, God provideth milk in our breasts against the time of our childrens' birth, and this he hath done ever since it was said to us also, *increase, and multiply,* so that this work of his provision showeth that he tieth us likewise to nourish the children of our own womb, with our own breasts, even by the order of nature: yea it showeth that he so careth for, and regardeth little children even from the womb, that he would have them nursed by those that in all reason will look to them with the kindest affection, namely their mothers; & in giving them milk for it, he doth plainly tell them that he requires it.

Oh consider, how comes our milk? Is it not by the direct providence of God? Why provides he it, but for the child? The mothers then that refuse to

---

[3] **ostriches:** believed to be uncaring towards their young.   [4] **the unreasonable creature:** animals not possessed of rationality.

nurse their own children, do they not despise God's providence? Do they not deny God's will? Do they not as it were say, *I see, O God, by the means thou hast put into me, that thou wouldst have me nurse the child thou has given me, but I will not do so much for thee*. Oh impious, and impudent unthankfulness; yea monstrous unnaturalness, both to their own natural fruit born so near their breasts, and fed in their own wombs, and yet may not be suffered to suck their own milk.

And this unthankfulness, and unnaturalness is oftener the sin of the *higher*, and the *richer sort*, than of the meaner, and poorer, except some nice and proud idle dames, who will imitate their betters, till they make their poor husbands beggars. And this is one hurt which the better rank do by their ill example; egg, and embolden the lower ones to follow them to their loss. Were it not better for *us greater persons* to keep God's ordinance, & show the meaner their duty in our good example? I am sure we have more helps to perform it, and have fewer probable reasons to allege against it, than women that live by hard labor, & painful toil. If such mothers as refuse this office of love, & of nature to their children, should hereafter be refused, despised, and neglected of those their children, were they not justly requited according to their own unkind dealing? I might say more in handling this first point of my promise; but I leave the larger, and [more learned] discourse hereof unto men of art, and learning: only I speak of so much as I read, and know in my own experience, which if any of my sex, and condition do receive good by, I am glad: if they scorn it, they shall have the reward of scorners. I write in modesty, and can reap no disgrace by their immodest folly.

And so I come to the last part of my promise; which is to answer objections made by divers[5] against this duty of mothers to their children.

First it is objected that *Rebeckah*[6] had a nurse, and that therefore her mother did not give her suck of her own breasts, and so good women, in the first ages, did not hold them to this office of nursing their own children. To this I answer; that if her mother had milk, and health, and yet did put this duty from her to another, it was her fault, & so proveth nothing against me. But it is manifest that she that *Rebeckah* calleth her nurse, was called so, either for that she most tended her while her mother suckled her: or for that she weaned her: or for that during her nonage,[7] and childhood, she did minister to her continually such good things as delighted, and nourished her up. For to any one of these the name of a nurse is fitly given: whence a good wife is called her husband's nurse: and that *Rebeckah's* nurse was only such a one,

[5] **divers**: several people.   [6] **Rebeckah**: Rebecca, wife of Isaac, Genesis 24:67.   [7] **nonage**: infancy.

appeareth, because afterward she is not named a *nurse,* but a *maid,* saying: Then *Rebeckah* rose, and her maids; now maids give not suck out of their breasts, never any virgin, or honest maid gave suck, but that *blessed one*[8] from an extraordinary, & blessed power.

Secondly it is objected, that it is troublesome; that it is noisome to one's clothes;[9] that it makes one look old, etc. All such reasons are uncomely, and unchristian to be objected: and therefore unworthy to be answered, they argue *unmotherly affection, idleness, desire to have liberty to gad from home, pride, foolish fineness, lust, wantonness,* & the like evils. Ask *Sarah, Hannah,* the *Blessed Virgin,* and any modest loving mother, what trouble they accounted it to give their little ones suck? Behold most nursing mothers, and they be as clean and sweet in their clothes, and carry their age, and hold their beauty, as well as those that suckle not: and most likely are they so to do; because keeping God's *ordinance,* they are sure of God's *blessing:* and it hath been observed in some women that they grew more beautiful, and better favored, by very nursing their own children.

But there are some women that object fear: saying that they are so weak, & so tender, that they are afraid to venture to give their children suck, least they endanger their health thereby. Of these, I demand, why then they did venture to marry, and so to bear children; and if they say they could not choose, and that they thought not that marriage would impair their health: I answer, that for the same reasons they should set themselves to nurse their own children, because they should not choose but do what God would have them to do: and they should believe that this work will be for their health also, seeing it is ordinary with the Lord to give *good stomach, health,* and *strength* to almost all mothers that take this pains with their children.

One answer more to all the objections that use to be made against giving children suck, is this, that now the hardness, to effect this matter, is much removed by a late example of a *tender young lady,* and you may all be encouraged to follow after, in that wherein she hath gone before you, & so made the way more easy, and more hopeful by that which she findeth possible and comfortable by God's blessing, and no offence to her *Lord* nor herself: she might have had as many doubts, and lets,[10] as any of you, but she was willing to try how God would enable her, & he hath given her good success, as I hope he will do to others that are willing to trust in God for his help.

Now if any reading these few lines return against me, that it may be I my self have given my own children suck: & therefore am bolder, and more busy to meddle in urging this point, to the end to insult over, & to make them to be blamed that have not done it. I answer, that whether I have, or have not

---

[8] *blessed one:* the Virgin Mary.   [9] **noisome to one's clothes:** messy.   [10] **lets:** objections.

performed this my bounden duty, I will not deny to tell my own practice. I know & acknowledge that I should have done it, and having not done it, it was not for want of will in my self, but *partly I was overruled by another's authority,* and *partly deceived by some's ill counsel, & partly I had not so well considered of my duty in this motherly office,* as since I did, when it was too late for me to put it in execution. Wherefore being pricked in heart for my undutifulness, this way I study to redeem my peace, first by *repentance* towards God, humbly and often craving his pardon for this my offence: secondly by *studying how to show double love to my children,* to make them amends for neglect of this part of love to them, when they should have hung on my breasts, & have been nourished in mine own bosom: thirdly *by doing my endeavor to prevent many Christian mothers* from sinning in the same kind, against our most loving and gracious God.

And for this cause I add unto my performed promise, this short exhortation: namely I beseech all godly women to remember, how we *elder* ones are commanded to instruct the *younger,* to love their children, now therefore love them so as to do this office to them when they are born, more gladly for *love* sake, than a *stranger,* who bore them not, shall do for *lucre's* sake. Also I pray you to set no more so light by God's blessing in your own breasts, which the holy Spirit ranketh with other excellent blessings, if it be unlawful to trample under feet a cluster of grapes, in which a little wine is found, then how unlawful is it to destroy and dry up those breasts, in which your own child (and perhaps one of God's very elect, to whom to be a nursing father, is a king's honor; and to whom to be a nursing mother is a queen's honor) might find food of sincere milk, even from God's immediate providence, until it were fitter for stronger meat? I do know that the Lord may deny some women, either to have any milk in their breasts at all, or to have any passage for their milk, or to have any health, or to have a right mind: and so they may be letted[11] from this duty, by *want,* by *sickness,* by *lunacy,* etc. But I speak not to these: I speak to you, whose *consciences* witness against you, that you cannot justly allege any of those impediments.

Do you submit yourselves, to the pain and trouble of this ordinance of God? Trust not other women, whom *wages hires* to do it, better than your selves, whom *God, and nature ties* to do it. I have found by grievous experience, such dissembling in nurses, pretending sufficiency of milk, when indeed they had too much scarcity; pretending willingness, towardness, wakefulness, when indeed they have been most willful, most froward, and most slothful, as I fear the death of one or two of my little babes came by the default of their nurses. Of all those which I had for eighteen children, I had

[11] **be letted:** be excused.

but two which were thoroughly willing, and careful: divers have had their children miscarry in the nurse's hands, and are such mothers (if it were by the nurse's carelessness) guiltless? I know not how they should, since they will shut them out of the *arms of nature,* and leave them to the will of a *stranger;* yea to one that will seem to *estrange* herself from her *own child,* to give suck to the *nurse-child:* This she may feign to do upon a *covetous composition,* but she frets at it in her mind, if she have any natural affection.

Therefore be no longer at the trouble, and at the care to hire others to do your *own work:* be not so *unnatural* to thrust away your own children: be not so *hardy* as to venture a *tender babe* to a *less tender heart:* be not *accessory* to that disorder of causing a *poorer woman to banish her own infant,* for the entertaining of a *richer woman's child,* as it were, bidding her *unlove her own to love yours.* We have followed *Eve* in transgression, let us follow her in obedience. When God laid the sorrows of conception, of breeding of bringing forth, and of bringing up her children upon her, & so upon us in her loins, did she reply any word against? Not a word; so I pray you all mine own *daughters,* and others that are still child-bearing reply not against the duty of suckling them, when God hath sent you them.

Indeed I see some, if the weather be wet, or cold; if the way be foul; if the church be far off, I see they are so coy, so nice, so lukewarm, they will not take pains for their *own souls,* alas, no marvel if these will not be at trouble, and pain to nourish their *children's bodies,* but fear God, be diligent to serve him; approve all his ordinances, seek to please him; account it no trouble, or pain to do any thing that hath the promise of his blessing: and then you will, no doubt, do this *good, laudable, natural, loving duty* to your children. If yet you be not satisfied, inquire not of such as refuse to do this: consult not with your own conceit: advise not with flatterers: but ask counsel of sincere, and faithful preachers. If you be satisfied, then take this with you, to make you do it cheerfully. Think always, that having the child at your breast, and having it in your arms, you have *God's blessing* there. For children are God's blessings. Think again how your babe crying for your breast, sucking heartily the milk out of it, and growing by it, is the *Lord's own instruction,* every hour, and every day, that you are suckling it, instructing you to show that you are his *new born babes,* by your earnest desire after his word, & the sincere doctrine thereof, and by your daily growing in grace and goodness thereby, so shall you reap pleasure, and profit. Again, you may consider, that when your child is at your breast, it is a fit occasion to move your heart to pray for a blessing upon that work; and to give thanks for your child, and for ability & freedom unto that, which many a mother would have done and could not; who have tried & ventured their health, & taken much pains, and yet have not obtained their desire. But they that are fitted every way for this *commendable act,* have certainly great cause to be thankful: and I much desire that God may have glory and praise for every good work, and you much comfort, that do seek to honor God in all things. *Amen.*

→ HENRY SMITH

From A Preparative to Marriage   *1591*

Henry Smith (c. 1550–1591) was a Puritan divine and a famous Elizabethan preacher. Despite his popularity, he was suspended from his ministry in 1588 as a result of his Puritanism. None other than the great and powerful Lord Burghley, Elizabeth's chief minister, intervened to have him restored to his clerical duties.

At a time when most aristocratic children were sent out to a wet-nurse, Smith espoused the more homely practice of breastfeeding as the more "natural" one. The poor, he observed, do not have the luxury to suffer from the inability to succor children. Smith also took up the nursing analogy in relation to fathers. The father of the family was understood to give his wisdom to the family as a sort of metaphorical milk. This analogy was not unique to Smith and was widely used in political and religious writing of the period (see Shuger, ch. 6).

Another significant factor here is the context in which Smith's treatment of breastfeeding occurs, just prior to a discussion of how to instruct children in catechism. Physical and moral well-being are thus placed on a par with one another, without any sense that matters of health and religion occupy distinct or discrete discursive sites.

After their duties one to another,[1] they must learn their duties to their family. One compareth the master of the house to the *seraphin*,[2] which came and kindled the prophets' zeal: so he should go from wife to servants, and from servants to children, and kindle them in the zeal of God, longing to teach his knowledge as a nurse to empty their breasts. Another sayeth, that a master in his family hath all the offices of Christ: for he must rule, and teach, and pray; rule like a king, teach like a prophet, pray like a priest. To show how a godly man should behave himself in his household, when the Holy Ghost speaketh of the conversion of any housekeeper, lightly he sayeth, that the man believed with all his household. As *Peter* being con-

---

[1] **one to another:** husband and wife.   [2] *seraphin:* the highest of the nine orders of angels.

Henry Smith, *A Preparative to Marriage. The Sum Whereof Was Spoken at a Contract [wedding], and Enlarged After* (London, 1591), 88–105.

verted, must convert his brethren; so the master being converted, must convert his servants. . . . This is reported also of *Joseph* and *Mary* for an example, that they went up every year with all their family to worship at *Jerusalem*, that their children and their servants might learn to know God as well as they. These examples be written for householders, as other are for magistrates, and ministers, and soldiers, that no calling might seek further than the Scripture for instruction. Wherefore as you are masters now, and they your servants, so instruct them and train them, as if you would show what masters they should be hereafter.

After the care of their souls, they must care for their bodies, for if the laborer is worthy of his hire which laboreth but a day, what is the servant worth which laboreth every day? . . . Therefore because cruel & greedy masters should not use them too hardly, God remembered them in his creation, and made every week one day of rest, wherein they should be as free as their masters: so God pityeth the poor laborer from heaven, and every Sabbath looks down upon him from heaven, as if he should say, one day thy labors shall have an end, and thou shalt rest for ever as thou resteth this day.

By this we see, as *David* did limit *Joab*[3] that he should not kill *Absalom*, so God hath bound masters that they should not oppress their servants. Shall God respect thine more than thou? Art thou made fresher to thy labor by a little rest, and is not thy servant made stronger by rest to labor for thee? . . . He which counteth his servant his slave, is in an error, for there is difference between believing servants, and infidel servants: the infidels were made slaves to the *Jews*, because God hated them, and would humble them, but their brethren did serve them like helpers, which should be trained by them.

It is not a base nor a vile thing to be called a servant, for our Lord is called a servant, which teacheth Christians to use their servants well for Christ's sake, seeing they are servants too, and have one master Christ. As *David* speaketh of man, saying *Thou hast made him a little lower than the angels:* so I may say of servants, that God hath made them a little lower than children, not children, but the next to children, as one would say inferior to our children, or sons in law: and therefore the householder is called *paterfamilias*, which signifieth a father of his family, because he should have a fatherly care over his servants, as if they were his children, and not use them only for their labor like beasts. Beside, the name of a servant doth not signify suffering, but doing: therefore masters must not exercise their hands upon them, but set their hands to work: and yet as God layeth no more upon his servants than he makes them able to bear; so men should lay no more upon their servants than they are able to bear. . . .

---

[3] **Joab:** one of the sons of King David's sister.

Next unto servants instruction and labors, must be considered their corrections. As *Paul* sayeth, *Fathers provoke not your children to wrath:* So may I say, Masters provoke not your servants to wrath, that is, use such reproves, & such corrections, that you do not provoke them, but move them, that you do not exasperate them, but win them; for reviling words and unreasonable fierceness, doth more hurt than good. . . . For while a child, or scholar, or servant doth think that he is reproved for love. Or beaten with reason, it makes him think of his fault and be ashamed: but when he seeth that he is rebuked with curses and beaten with staves,[4] as though he were hated like a dog, his heart is hardened against the man which correcteth him, and the fault for which he is corrected, & after he becometh desperate, like a horse which turneth upon the striker: and therefore think that God even then chides you whensoever you chide in such rage. For though there be a fault, yet some things must be winked at, & some things forgiven, and some things punished with a look; for he which takes the forfeit of every offense shall never rest, but vex himself more than his servant. . . .

Lastly, we put the duty toward children, because they come last to their hands. In Latin children are called *pignora,* that is pledges, as if I should say, a pledge of the husband's love to the wife, and a pledge of the wife's love toward the husband: for there is nothing which doth so knit love between the man and the wife, as the fruit of the womb. . . . If a woman have many defects . . . yet this is the amends which she makes her husband to bring him children, which is the right wedding ring that sealeth and maketh up as it were the marriage. When their father and mother fall out, they perk up between them like little mediators, and with many pretty sports make truce when other dare not speak to them. Therefore now let us consider what these little ones may challenge of their parents, which stayed them instead of lawyers.

The first duty is the mother's, that is, to nurse her child at her own breasts, as *Sarah* did *Isaac:* & therefore *Isaiah* joineth the nurse's name and the mother's name both in one, and calleth them *nursing mothers:* showing that mothers should be the nurses. So when God chose a nurse for *Moses,* he led the handmaid of *Pharaoh's* daughter to his mother, as though God would have none to nurse him but his mother. After, when the son of God was born, his father thought none fit to be his nurse but the virgin his mother. The fountains of the earth are made to give water, & the breasts of women are made to give suck. Every beast, and every fowl, is bred of the same that did bear it, only women love to be mothers, but not nurses. Therefore if their children prove unnatural, they may say thou followest thy mother, for she

---

[4] **staves:** wooden staffs.

The Nurse.
Give suck
no more,
for I am at
the door.

The Infant.
Lo, this
little heart:
I strike with
my dart.

FIGURES 12 AND 13 *The Nurse and the Infant, from Richard Day,* A Book of Christian Prayers *(London, 1590). These images are part of the tradition known as the* danse macabre *and represent the threat of death even at moments when the life force seems strongest. See pages 400, 442 for a greater discussion.*

was unnatural first in locking up her breasts from thee, and committing thee forth like a cuckoo to be hatched in the sparrow's nest. Hereof it comes that we say, he sucked evil from the dug, that is, as the nurse is affected in her body or in her mind, commonly the children draweth the like infirmity from her, as the eggs of a hen are altered under a hawk: yet they which have no milk can give no milk; but whose breasts have this perpetual drought? Forsooth it is like the gout,[5] no beggars may have it, but citizens or gentlewomen. In the 9 of *Hosea,*[6] dry breasts are named for a curse; what lamentable hap have gentlewomen to light upon this curse more than other? Sure if their breasts be dry as they say, they should fast & pray together that this curse might be removed from them.

[5] **gout:** a disease that inflames the smaller joints, especially the big toe, which was thought to be caused by consumption of rich food and wine.   [6] **9 of *Hosea*:** Hosea 9:14, "Give them a miscarrying womb and dry breasts."

The next duty is, *Catechize child in his youth, and he will remember it when he is old.* This is the right blessing which fathers and mothers give to their children, when they cause God to bless them too. The wrong mother cared not though the child were divided,[7] but the right mother would not have it divided: so wicked parents care not though their children be destroyed, but godly parents would not have them destroyed but saved, that when they have dwelt together in earth, they may dwell together in heaven. As the midwife frameth the body when it is young and tender, so the parents must frame the mind while it is green and flexible, for youth is the seed time of virtue. They which are called fathers, are called by the name of God, to warn them that they are in stead of God to their children, which teacheth all sons. What example have children but their parents? And sure the providence of God doth ease their charge more than they are aware; for a child will learn better of his father, than of any other. And therefore we read of no schoolmasters in the Scripture but the parents: for when Christ sayeth to the *Jews, If ye be the sons of Abraham, ye will do the works of your father Abraham.* He showeth that sons use to walk in their father's steps whether they be good or bad. It is a marvelous delight to father & mother when people say that their children are like them: but if they be like them in goodness, it is as great a delight to other as to the parents: or else we say that they are so like, that they are worse for it. Well doth *David* call children arrows, for if they be well bred they shoot at their parents' enemies, & if they be evil bred they shoot at their parents. Therefore many fathers want a staff to stay them in their age, because they prepared none before. . . . Are not children called the fruit of their parents? Therefore as a good tree is known by bringing forth good fruit, so parents should show their goodness in the good education of their children which are their fruit. For this cause the *Jews* were wont to[8] name their children so when they were born, that ever after if they did but think upon their names, they would put them in mind of that religion which they should profess, for they did signify something that they should learn. An admonition to such as call their children at all adventures, sometimes by the names of dogs even as they prove after. In the I *Kings* 2:2 we have *David* instructing his sons: In *Genesis* 3:9, *Jacob* correcting his sons: and in *Job* I, *Job* praying for his sons: These three put together, instructing, correcting, and praying, make good children and happy parents.

Once Christ took a child and set him in the midst of his disciples, and said, *He which will receive the kingdom of heaven, must receive it as a little child.*

---

[7] **The wrong mother . . . divided:** Solomon resolved a dispute between two women telling them he would cut in two the child they fought over on the assumption that the real mother would object to such a drastic settlement (I Kings 3:26).   [8] **were wont to:** had a tendency to.

Showing that our children should be so innocent, so humble, and void of evil, that they may be taken for examples of the children of God. Therefore in 1 *Psalms* 27:4 children are called the heritage of the Lord, to show that they should be trained as though they were not mens' children but God's, that they may have God's heritage after. Thus if you do, your servants shall be God's servants, and your children shall be God's children, and your house shall be God's house, like a little church when others' are like a den of thieves. . . .

→ **LADY ANNE CLIFFORD**

From The Diary of the Lady Anne Clifford   *1616–1619*

Anne Clifford (1590–1676) was countess of Dorset, Pembroke, and Montgomery. Her diary tells of her first marriage to Richard Sackville, earl of Dorset. Her second wedding, six years after Dorset's death in 1624, was to the earl of Pembroke, even though she had suffered a disfiguring attack of smallpox shortly after Dorset's death "which disease did so martyr my face, that it confirmed more and more my mind never to marry again, though ye providence of God caused me after to alter that resolution."

The daughter of the wealthy and powerful third earl of Cumberland, Anne was an heiress, although to take possession of all she had inherited, she had to spend thirty-eight years of her life (with the staunch support of her mother during the latter's lifetime) in protracted litigation over her lands in Westmoreland. This property had belonged to her father, and it became hers only after all the male heirs had died (David Clifford x). Her profligate husband, Dorset, continually pressured her to renounce the claim in favor of ready cash, but she prevailed, secured her lands, and went on to exert considerable power and influence quite independent of male control before she died at age eighty-six. Unlike Juliet and "Capulet's wife," she had been very close to her own mother and their correspondence survives (Williamson 150; see also David Clifford i–xv).

Anne bore Dorset five children, of whom the three boys died and the two girls survived (Spence 78). "The child" referred to in the excerpts below is her eldest daughter, Margaret, who was plagued with childhood sickness even though she survived to adulthood. Other children in the diary were not so lucky — there are accounts of dead babies littered throughout the narrative. The diary here elaborates the alarmingly high rate of infant mortality in early modern England. These tragic facts constitute the social reality that frames the

Anne Clifford, *The Diary of the Lady Anne Clifford*, with an introductory note by Vita Sackville-West (London: William Heinemann, 1923), 21–31, 48–58, 66–69, 74–75, 82–83, 86–89, 104–12.

Lady Anne Clifford only Daug
and hair to George Earl of
Cumberland She First Married
to Richard Earl of Dorset after
to Philip Herbert Earl of
Pembroke

ÆTATE SVE 30
1620

FIGURE 14 *Lady Anne Clifford at Age Thirty. Born at Skipton Castle on January 30, 1590, Anne Clifford (1590–1676) fought resolutely for thirty-eight years to obtain her rightful inheritance to her family's impressive estates. She is also admired for commissioning the restoration of her castles, which were damaged in the Civil War. This painting by an unknown artist depicts Anne at age thirty, before smallpox ravaged her complexion.*

death of Susan, the Nurse's own child in *Romeo and Juliet*. She tragically shadows the infancy of Juliet, while the sexual maturity of the aptly named Susan *Grindstone* (1.5.7; the name puns on coital friction) onomastically ghosts and reiterates the Nurse's earlier reference to her daughter.

Clearly Anne both enjoyed and worried about her daughter's development. We see little Margaret as a toddler learning to walk with leading strings (a sort of early modern baby harness), just at the stage that the Nurse describes Juliet: "For then she could stand high-lone; nay, by the rood, / She could have run and waddled all about" (1.3.37–38). The kind of intimate information about Juliet's infancy afforded us by the Nurse is here provided by Margaret's own mother. In Anne's home, as in the Capulet household, and indeed in most early modern dwellings of people of social rank, there was considerable interaction with social inferiors, and so we find Anne donating to servants, clothes Margaret has outgrown.

From *The Diary of the Lady Anne Clifford*

MARCH 1616

Upon the 20th in the morning my Lord William Howard with his son, my cousin [her husband's first cousin]. William Howard and Mr. John Dudley came hither to take the answer of my Mother and myself which was a direct denial to stand to the judges' award.[1]

APRIL 1616

Upon the 1st came my cousin Charles Howard and Mr. John Dudley with letters to show that it was my Lord's[2] pleasure that the men and horses should come away without me and so after much falling out betwixt my Lady[3] and them all the folks[4] went away there being a paper drawn to show that they went away by my Lord's direction and contrary to my will.

At night I sent 2 messengers to my folks to entreat them to stay. For some 2 nights my mother and I lay together and had much talk about this business.

Upon the 2nd I went after my folks in my Lady's coach she bringing me a quarter of a mile in the way where she and I had a grievous and heavy parting. . . .

Upon the 11th I came from London to Knole where I had but a cold

---

[1] **the judges' award:** the outcome of the lawsuit over Anne's inheritance.   [2] **my Lord's:** a reference to Anne's husband, Sir Richard Sackville, third earl of Dorset.   [3] **my Lady:** a reference to Anne's mother, Lady Margaret Russell, countess of Cumberland.   [4] **folks:** servants.

welcome from my Lord. My Lady Margaret met me in the outermost gate and my Lord came to me in the drawing chamber.

Upon the 12th I told my Lord how I had left those writings which the judges and my Lord would have me sign and seal behind with my mother. . . .

Upon the 17th came Tom Woodgatt from London but brought me no news of my going up which I daily look for.[5]

Upon the 18th Baskett [Gentleman of the Horse] came hither and brought me a letter from my Lord to let me know this was the last time of asking me whether I would set my hand to this award of the judges.

Upon the 19th I returned my Lord for answer that I would not stand to the award of the judges what misery soever it cost me. This morning the bishop of St. David's and my little child [Anne's daughter, Lady Margaret] were brought to speak to me.

About this time I used to rise early in the morning and go to the standing in the garden, and taking my prayer book with me beseech God to be merciful to me in this and to help me as he always hath done.

May 1616

Upon the 1st Rivers came from London in the afternoon and brought me word that I should neither live at Knole or Bolebrooke.

Upon the 2nd came Mr. Legg [the steward] and told divers[6] of the servants that my Lord would come down and see me once more which would be the last time that I should see him again.

Upon the 3rd came Baskett down from London and brought me a letter from my Lord by which I might see it was his pleasure that the child should go the next day to London, which at the first was somewhat grievous to me, but when I considered that it would both make my Lord more angry with me and be worse for the child, I resolved to let her go, after I had sent for Mr. Legg and talked with him about that and other matters and wept bitterly.

Upon the 4th being Saturday between 10 and 11 the child went into the litter to go to London, Mrs. Bathurst and her two maids with Mr. Legge and a good company of the servants going with her. In the afternoon came a man called Hilton, born in Craven, from my Lady Willoughby to see me which I took as a great argument of her love being in the midst of all my misery.

---

[5] [**Anne Clifford's marginal note**]: "Upon the 17th my mother sickened as she came from prayers, being taken with a cold chillness in the manner of an ague [chills and fever] which afterwards turned to great heats and pains in her side, so as when she was opened, it was plainly seen she had an imposthume (i.e., an abscess)." [6] **divers:** several.

Upon the 8th I dispatched a letter to my mother.

Upon the 9th I received a letter from Mr. Bellasis how extreme ill my mother had been and in the afternoon came Humphrey Godding's son with letters that my mother was exceeding ill and as they thought in sore danger of death — so as I sent Rivers presently to London with letters to be sent to her and certain cordials and conserves.[7]

At night was brought to me a letter from my Lord to let me know his determination was, the child should go live at Horseley, and not come hither any more so as this was a very grievous and sorrowful day to me.

Upon the 10th Rivers came from London and brought me word from Lord William that she was not in such danger as I fear'd, the same day came the steward from London, whom I expected would have given warning to many of the servants to go away because the audits was newly come up.[8]

Upon the 11th being Sunday before Mr. Legge went away I talked with him an hour or two about all the business and matters between me and my Lord, so as I gave him better satisfaction and made him conceive a better opinion of me than ever he did.

A little before dinner came Matthew [my Lord's favorite] down from London, my Lord sending me by him the wedding ring that my Lord Treasurer and my old Lady were married withall and a message that my Lord would be here the next week, and that the child would not as yet go down to Horsley and I sent my Lord the wedding ring that my Lord and I was married with; the same day came Mr. Marsh [attendant to Anne's mother] from London and persuaded me much to consent to this argument.

The 12th at night Grosvenor [gentleman usher] came hither and told me how my Lord had won £200 at the cocking match and that my Lord of Essex and Lord Willoughby who was on my Lord's side won a great deal and how there was some unkind words between my Lord and his side and Sir William Herbert and his side. This day my Lady Grantham sent me a letter about these businesses between my Uncle Cumberland and me and returned me an answer.

All this time my Lord was in London where he had all and infinite great resort coming to him. He went much abroad to cocking, to bowling alleys, to plays and horse races, and commended by all the world. I stayed in

---

[7] cordials and conserves: alcohol and vegetable based preparations used for medicinal purposes.
[8] [Anne Clifford's marginal note]: "Upon the 10th early in the morning I wrote a very earnest letter to beseech him that I might not go to the little house that was appointed for me, but that I might go to Horsely and sojourn with my child, and to the same effect I wrote to my sister Beauchamp. [Anne, daughter of Robert Earl of Dorset, married to Lord Beauchamp, great grandson of the Protector Duke of Somerset]."

the country having many times a sorrowful and heavy heart, and being condemned by most folks because I would not consent to the agreements, so as I may truly say, I am like an owl in the desert.

Upon the 13th being Monday, my Lady's footman Thomas Petty brought me letters out of Westmoreland, by which I perceived how very sick and full of grievous pains my dear mother was, so as she was not able to write herself to me and most of her people about her feared she would hardly recover this sickness, at night I went out and pray'd to God my only helper that she might not die in this pitiful case. The 14th Richard Jones came from London to me and brought a letter with him from Matthew the effect whereof was to persuade me to yield to my Lord's desire in this business at this time, or else I was undone for ever.

Upon the 15th my Lord came down from London and my cousin Cecily Neville, my Lord lying in Leslie Chamber and I in my own. Upon the 17th my Lord and I after supper had some talk about these businesses, Matthew being in the room where we all fell out[9] and so parted for that night. Upon the 18th being Saturday in the morning my Lord and I having much talk about these businessees, we agreed that Mr. Marsh should go presently down to my mother and that by him I should write a letter to persuade her to give over her jointure[10] presently to my Lord and that he would give her yearly as much as it was worth.

This day my Lord went from Knole to London.[11]

Upon the 20th being Monday I dispatch'd Mr. Marsh with letters to my mother about the business aforesaid. I sent them unsealed because my Lord might see them.

My brother Compton [brother-in-law] and his wife kept the house at West Horsley and my brother Beauchamp and my sister his wife sojourned with them so as the child was with both her aunts. Upon the 22nd Mr. Davy's came down from London and brought me word that my mother was very well recovered of her dangerous sickness. By him I writ a letter to my Lord that Mr. Amherst [sargeant at law and steward] and Mr. Davy might confer together about my jointure to free it from the payment of debts and all other incumbrances. . . .

---

[9] **fell out:** quarreled.   [10] **her jointure:** the portion of a woman's dowry that reverts to her possession after her husband's death, or that always remains hers throughout the marriage.
[11] **[Anne Clifford's marginal note]:** "Upon the 20th went my child to W. Horsley. . . . Upon the 24th being Friday between the hours of 6 and 9 at night died my dear mother at Broome in the same chamber where my father was born, 13 years and 2 months after the death of Queen Elizabeth and 10 years and 7 months after the death of my father, I being 26 years old and 5 months and the child 2 years old wanting a month. . . ."

JANUARY 1617

. . . Upon the 18th being Saturday I went presently after dinner to the Queen to the drawing chamber where my Lady Derby told the Queen how my business stood and that I was to go to the King[12] so she promised me she would do all the good in it she could. When I had stay'd but a little while there I was sent for out, my Lord and I going through my Lord Buckingham's chamber who brought us into the King, being in the drawing chamber. He put out all that were there and my Lord and I kneeled by his chair sides when he persuaded us both to peace and to put the whole matter wholly into his hands, which my Lord consented to, but I beseech'd His Majesty to pardon me for that I would never part from Westmoreland[13] while I lived upon any condition whatsoever. Sometimes he used fair means and persuasions and sometimes foul means but I was resolved before so as nothing would move me. . . . At this time I was much bound to my Lord for he was far kinder to me in all these businesses than I expected and was very unwilling that the King should do me any public disgrace.[14] . . .

Upon the 20th, I and my Lord went presently after dinner to the Court, he went up to the King's side about his business, I went to my Aunt Bedford in her lodging where I stay'd in Lady Ruthven's chamber till towards 8 o'clock about which time I was sent for up to the King into his drawing chamber when the door was lock'd and nobody suffered to stay here but my Lord and I, my Uncle Cumberland, my cousin Clifford, my Lords Arundel, Pembroke, Montgomery, Sir John Digby. For lawyers there were my Lord Chief Justice Montague and Hobart, Yelverton the King's solicitor, Sir Randal Crewe that was to speak for my Lord and I. The King asked us all if we would submit to his judgment in this case. My Uncle Cumberland, my cousin. Clifford, and my Lord answered they would, but I would never agree to it without Westmoreland at which the King grew in a great chaff. My Lord of Pembroke and the King's solicitor speaking much against me, at last when they saw there was no remedy, my Lord fearing the King would do me some public disgrace, desired Sir John Digby would open the door, who went out with me and persuaded me much to yield to the King. My Lord Hay came to me to whom I told in brief how this business stood. Presently after my Lord came from the King when it was resolved that if I would not come to an agreement there should be an agreement made without me. We

---

[12] the King: King James I.   [13] Westmoreland: Anne Clifford's ancestral family estate.
[14] [Anne Clifford's marginal note]: "The Queen [i.e., James' wife, Anne of Denmark] gave me a warning not to trust my matters absolutely to the King lest he should deceive me."

went down, Sir Robert Douglas and Sir George Chaworth bringing us to the coach, by the way my Lord and I went in at Worcester House to see my Lord and Lady and so came home this day. I may say I was led miraculously by God's providence, and next to that I trust all my good to the worth and nobleness of my Lord's disposition for neither I nor anybody else thought I should have passed over this day so well as I have done.

Upon the 22nd the child had her 6th fit of the ague[15] in the morning. Mr. Smith went up in the coach to London to my Lord to whom I wrote a letter to let him know in what case the child was and to give him humble thanks for his noble usage towards me at London. The same day my Lord came down to Knole to see the child.

Upon the 23rd my Lord went up betimes to London again. The same day the child put on her red baize[16] coats.

Upon the 25th I spent most of my time in working and in going up and down to see the child. About 5 or 6 o'clock the fit took her, which lasted 6 or 7 hours.

Upon the 28th at this time I wore a plain green flannel gown that William Punn made me, and my yellow taffety waistcoat. Rivers used to read to me in Montaigne[17] and Moll Neville in the *Fairy Queen*.

Upon the 30th Mr. Amherst the preacher came hither to see me with whom I had much talk. He told me that now they began to think at London that I had done well in not referring this business to the King and that everybody said God had a hand in it.

FEBRUARY 1617

Upon the 4th should have been the child's fit but she miss'd it. Achin came presently after dinner with a letter to Tom the groom, to meet my Lord at Hampton Court with his hunting horses. At night Thomas Woodgate came from London and brought a squirrel to the child, and my Lord wrote me a letter by which I perceived my Lord was clean out[18] with me and how much my enemies have wrought against me.

Upon the 6th the child had a grudging of her ague again at night. . . .

Upon the 7th presently after dinner Mr. Oberton and I had a great deal of talk, he telling me how much I was condemned in the world and what strange censures most folks made of my courses, so I as I kneeled down to

---

[15] **ague:** fever and chills.   [16] **baize:** a coarse, woolen material with a long nap.   [17] **Montaigne:** Michel de Montaigne, skeptical philosopher and essayist (1533–92).   [18] **clean out:** fed up.

my prayers and desired God to send a good end to these troublesome businesses, my trust being wholly in Him that always helped me.

Upon the 12th the child had a bitter fit of her ague again, insomuch I was fearful of her that I could hardly sleep all night, so I beseeched God Almighty to be merciful to me and spare her life. Rivers came down presently from London and told me that the judges had been with the King divers times about my business, but as yet the award is not published, but it is thought that it will be much according to the award that was formerly set down by the judges. He told me that he had been with Lord William who, as he thought, did not like the agreement considering how he had heretofore shewn himself in the business.

After supper the child's nose bled which I think was the chief cause she was rid of her ague.

Upon the 13th the King made a speech in the Star Chamber[19] about duels and combats, my Lord standing by his chair where he talked with him all the while, being in extraordinary grace and favour with the King.

Upon the 19th I sent Mr. Edward's man to London with a letter to my Lord to desire him to come down hither. All this day I spent with Marsh who did write the chronicles of 1607, who went in afterwards to my prayers, desiring God to send me some end of my troubles that my enemies might not still have the upper hand of me.

Upon the 16th my Lord came hither from London before dinner and told me how the whole state of my business went and how things stood at the court.

Upon the 17th about 8 o'clock in the morning my Lord returned to London.

At night Mr. Asken came and brought me a letter from Lady Grantham and told me a great deal of news from London, and I signed a bill to give him £7 at his return from Jerusalem.

This day I gave the child's old clothes to Legge for his wife.

Upon the 21st the child had an extreme fit of the ague and the doctor set by her all the afternoon and gave her a salt powder to put in her beer. Upon the 22nd Basket went up with the great horses to my Lord because my Lord intended to ride a day's journey with the prince. Legge came down and brought me word that the King would make a composition and take a

---

[19] **Star Chamber:** court so named for the star pattern on the ceiling; one of the most important courts of the period. For the Crown, it had the advantage that judges were members of the privy council and no jury was present. Thus, it was one of the favorite courts of the monarchs and one of the most unpopular among the people.

course to put me from my right to the lands, so as if I did not consider of it speedily it would be too late and how bitter the King stood against me.

My sister Compton sent to borrow £77 so I sent her 10 twenty shilling pieces.

Upon the 27th I spent my time in working and hearing Mr. Rose read the Bible and walking abroad.

My Lord writ me word that the King had referred the drawing and perfecting the business to the solicitor.

My soul was much troubled and afflicted to see how things go, but my trust is still in God, and compare things past with things present and read over the Chronicles.

MARCH 1617[20]

Upon the 1st after supper my mother Dorset [stepmother-in-law] came hither to see me and the child.

Upon the 3rd Petley [under farrier] and Tom went to Buckhurst with my Lord's horses and hounds to meet my Lord there, by whom I wrote a letter to my Lord to beseech him that he would take Knole on his way as he goes to London.

Upon the 5th Couch puppied in the morning. The 8th I made an end of reading Exodus with Mr. Ran. After supper I play'd at Glecko[21] with the steward and as I often do after dinner and supper.

Upon the 9th Mr. Ran said service in the chapel but made no sermon. In the afternoon I went abroad in the garden and said my prayers in the standing. I was not well at night so I ate a posset[22] and went to bed.

The 11th we perceived the child had two great teeth come out so that in all she had now 18. I went in the afternoon and said my prayers in the standing in the garden and spent my time in reading and working[23] as I used to do. The time grew tedious so as I used to go to bed about 8 o'clock and did lie a-bed till 8 the next morning.

Upon the 12th I wrote to my Lord, to Sir Walter Raleigh, Marsh, &c.

The 13th made an end of Leviticus with Mr. Ran. I sent by Willoughby a little jewel of opal to Lady Frenchard's girl.

The 14th I made an end of my Irish stitch cushion. This afternoon Basket came from London and told me that my Lord and my uncle were agreed and the writings sealed.

---

[20] [Anne Clifford's marginal note]: "About this time the curtain in the child's room was let up to let in the light which had been close shut up for 3 weeks or a month before."　[21] **Glecko:** a card game.　[22] **posset:** a hot, milk-based drink curdled with ale.　[23] **working:** needlework.

The King set forward this day on his journey to Scotland, the Queen and Prince going with him to Theobalds.[24] . . .

APRIL 1617

. . . The 26th I spent the evening in working and going down to my Lord's closet where I sat and read much in the Turkish History and Chaucer.

The 28th was the first time the child put on a pair of whalebone bodice.

My Lord went a hunting the fox and the hare. . . . About this time my Lord made the steward alter most of the rooms in the house, and dress them up as fine as he could, and determined to make all his old clothes in purple stuff for the gallery and drawing chamber.

MAY 1617

Upon the 1st I cut the child's strings off from her coats and made her use togs alone,[25] so as she had two or three falls at first but had no hurt with them.

The 2nd the child put on her first coat that was laced with lace, being of red baize.

The 3rd my Lord went from Buckhurst to London, and rid it in four hours, he riding very hard, a hunting all the while he was at Buckhurst and had his health exceeding well.

The 7th my Lord Keeper rode from Dorset House to Westminster in great pomp and state, most of the lords going with him, amongst which my Lord was one.

The 8th I spent this day in working, the time being very tedious unto me as having neither comfort nor company, only the child.

The 12th I began to dress my head with a roll without a wire.

I wrote not to my Lord because he wrote not to me since he went away. After supper I went with the child who rode the piebald nag that came out of Westmoreland to Mrs. ———. The 14th the child came to lie with me, which was the first time that ever she lay all night in a bed with me since she was born.

The 15th the child put on her white coats and left off many things from her head, the weather growing extremely hot. . . .

---

[24] [Anne Clifford's marginal note]: "The 14th being Friday my uncle Cumberland and my cousin Clifford came to Dorset House where my Lord and they signed and sealed the writings and made a final conclusion of my business [my inheritance] and did what they could to cut me off from my right, but I referred my cause to God. . . . [25] made her use togs alone: Lady Margaret is learning to walk without the use of "strings," a sort of early modern baby harness.

FIGURE 15 *Sir Richard Sackville. This painting by William Larkin (1580–1619) depicts Anne Clifford's profligate husband, Richard Sackville (1589–1624), third earl of Dorset, in all his finery. Lady Anne married him in 1609.*

The 17th the steward came from London and told me my Lord was much discontented with me, for not doing this business, because he must be fain[26] to buy land for the payment of the money which will much encumber his estate.

Upon the 18th Mr. Wolrich came hither to serve me, he bringing me news that all Westmoreland was surrender'd to my Uncle Cumberland. . . .

This time my Lord's mother did first of all sue out of her thirds[27] which was an increase of trouble and discontent to my Lord.

The 25th my Lord St. John's tailor came to me hither to take measure of me and to make me a new gown. In the afternoon my cousin Russell wrote me a letter to let me know how my Lord had cancelled my jointure he made upon me last June when I went into the North, and by these proceedings I may see how much my Lord is offended with me and that my enemies have the upper hand of me. I am resolved to take all patiently, casting all my care upon God. His footman told me that my cousin Russell and my Lady Bedford were agreed, and my Lord Herbert and his Lady, and that the next week they were to seal the writings and the agreement, which I little expected.

The 27th I wrote a letter to my Lord to let him know how ill I took his cancelling my jointure, but yet told him I was content to bear it with patience, whatsoever he thought fit.

The 29th I wrote a letter to my sister Beauchamp and sent her a lock of the child's hair. I wrote a letter to my sister Compton and my Aunt Glenham, I being desirous to win the love of my Lord's kindred by all the fair means I could. . . .

JULY 1617

. . . The 16th Lady Wootton came here on horseback, she and my Lord having lain that night at Sir Percival Hart's, and so hunted a deer as far as Otford; she stay'd not above an hour in regard she saw I was so resolutely bent not to part with Westmoreland. . . .

The same night [the 20th] Dr. Donne came hither.

The 27th I went to church (being Sunday) forenoon and afternoon, Dr. Donne preaching and he and the other strangers dining with me in the great chamber.

The 31st I sat still, thinking the time to be very tedious.

---

[26] **fain:** contented.   [27] **sue out of her thirds:** portions appointed women as part of the dowry agreement, especially in the event that they became widows.

AUGUST 1617

. . . The 2nd my brother Compton came hither before supper, my Lord came from London, this time of his being here he lying in my chamber.

The 3rd in the afternoon we had much falling out about the house which my Lord would have me undertake, which I refused in regard things went so ill with me. This night the child lay all night with my Lord and me, this being the first night she did so.

The 4th in the morning my Lord went to Penshurst but would not suffer me to go with him although my Lord and Lady Lisle sent a man on purpose to desire me to come. He hunted and lay there all night, there being my Lord of Montgomery, my Lord Hay, my Lady Lucy, and a great deal of other company, yet my Lord and I parted reasonable good friends, he leaving with me his grandmother's ring. . . .

DECEMBER 1617[28]

The 8th I was not very well, and Mr. Thomas Cornwallis the groom porter came hither.

The 9th I spent in talking with him of Queen Elizabeth and such old matters at the court.

The 10th my Lord went to Buckhurst where all country gentlemen met him with their greyhounds. All the officers of the house went to Buckhurst where my Lord kept feasting till the 13th at which time all the gentlemen went away. . . .

The 15th came Sir H. Nevill's lady, I carried her up to my closet and shewed her all my things and gave her a pair of Spanish leather gloves.

The 22nd my Lord and all the household removed to London, the child going before in a litter.

The 25th Christmas Day Mr. —— [blank in MS.] preached in the chapel and my Lord and I dined below, there being great housekeeping all this Xmas at Dorset House.

The 28th I went to church in my rich night gown and petticoat, both my women waiting upon me in their liveries,[29] but my Lord stayed at home. There came to dine Mrs. Levisey and a great company of the neighbors to eat venison.

---

[28] [Anne Clifford's marginal note]: "The 2nd the child grew ill with a cough and a pain in her head so as we feared the small-pox, but it proved nothing for within 8 days she recovered. About this time Lady Rich was brought to bed of a son, her sixth child. I should have christened it, but it died in 3 or 4 days." [29] **liveries:** servants' uniforms.

Now I had a great desire to have all my father's sea voyages written, so I did set Jones to inquire about these matters.

JANUARY 1619

. . . The 29th in the morning died my sister Beauchamp's daughter Mrs. Anne Seymour in the same house her father died in 2 months before; the child was opened, it having a corrupt body, so it was put in lead[30] and the day following Legge brought it to Knole, which day was my birthday, I being now 29 years old.

The 31st my cousin Russell's wife was brought to bed of a son (it being the 7th child) at Chiswick, which was christened in the Church privately and was named Francis.

FEBRUARY 1619[31]

The 1st carried Lord Beauchamp's child from Knole, where it had stood in his chamber, to Withyham, where it was carried in the vault, so now there was an end of the issue of that marriage which was concluded soon after mine.

The 2nd . . . I made pancakes with my women in the great chamber.

The 10th Walter Coniston began to read St. Austin [*sic:* St. Augustine] of the City of God to me, and I received a letter from Mr. Davis with another enclosed in it of Ralph Coniston, whereby I perceived things went in Westmoreland as I would have them. . . .

In Sir Thomas Lake's place Sir George Calvert was sworn secretary. My Lord should have gone to London the 24th of this month but I entreated him to stay here the 25th, because on that day 10 years I was married, which I kept as a day of jubilee to me, so my Lord went not till the 27th, at which time he rid on horseback by reason of the great snow and was so ill after his journey that whereas he intended to return two or three days he stay'd nine or ten.

The 28th Sunday the judges came to Sevenoaks. I did often receive letters from Mr. Davis and Marsh by which I perceived my motion to Sir John Suckling on his behalf took good effect, and that businesses went well to my

---

[30] **it having a corrupt body, so it was put in lead:** was buried in a lead casket to prevent further contagion.   [31] **[Anne Clifford's marginal note]:** "About this time Lord William caused my cousin Clifford to come before the Lords of the Council about northern business, so as the spleen increased between them more and more and bred faction in Westmoreland, which I held to be a very good matter for me."

liking in Westmoreland, by reason of difference between Lord William and my cousin Clifford.[32]

MARCH 1619

The 2nd the Queen died at Hampton Court between two and three in the morning, the King was then at Newmarket. Legge brought me the news of her death about two in the afternoon, I being in the bed chamber at Knole where I had the first news of my mother's death about the same hour. (Legge told me my Lord was about to take some physic of Mr. Smith and as he could not come from London these four or five days yet.) She died in the same room that Queen Jane, Harry 8th's [Henry VIII] wife died in. . . .

JUNE 1619

. . . The 6th Sunday I heard neither sermon or prayers because I had no coach to go to church. All this week I spent at my work and sometimes riding abroad. My cousin Maria read Ovid's *Metamorphoses* to me. . . .

The 23rd my Lord went up to London to take up certain bonds which he did discharge with part of my portion.

The 24th my Lord received the last payment of my portion which was £6,000, so as he hath received in all £17,000. . . .

JULY 1619

The 2nd my Lord and Sir Henry Vane played at bowls. This night my Lady Margaret was 5 years old so as my Lord caused her health to be drank throughout the house. . . .

22nd my Lady Margaret began to sit to Mr. Van Somer for her picture.

The 27th about this time my Lady Bedford had the smallpox and had them in that extremity that she lost one of her eyes. About this time my cousin Clifford's wife was brought to bed at Lanesboro of a son, which lived not seven hours and was christened Francis and was buried there. The same day Lord Rutland and Lady Katherine Manners came and dined here from the Wells and in the evening went to London.

---

[32] [Anne Clifford's marginal note]: "About the 20th the King fell into an extreme fit of the stone [kidney stones] at Newmarket, so as many doubted of his recovery, and the prince rid down post to see him, most of the great ladies about the town put themselves in mourning and did watch the queen's corpse at Denmark House which lay there with much state.

"The queen dowager of Denmark was alive when her daughter queen Anne of England died."

FIGURE 16 *Lady Margaret Sackville at Age Four. Paul Van Somer (c. 1556–1621) painted this image of four-year-old Margaret Sackville (1614–1676), Lady Anne Clifford's first daughter and "the child" so frequently mentioned in the diaries, in 1618. The artist was born in Antwerp and died in London, where he worked later in his life. He also executed a portrait of James I.*

August 1619

The 14th my cousin Mary and I had a bitter falling out. The 15th being Sunday I went not to Church at all. I fell out with Kate Burton and swore I would not keep her and caused her to send to her father.

The 18th Sir Edward Burton came hither and I told him I was determined I would not keep his daughter. . . .

The 30th my Lord sat much to have his picture drawn by Van Somer, and one picture was drawn for me.

FEASTING

"Preparing a Feast," by Jan Sadeler, from L. F. Salzman, *England in Tudor Times: An Account of Its Social Life and Industries* (London, 1926).

The greatest feasts were celebrated at Christmas, though there were also feasts tied to the church calendar, as well as feasts to celebrate royal and civic occasions such as triumphs and pageants, or the annual observance of the monarch's accession day and birthday. The wealthy, of course, entertained on a lavish scale producing sumptuous feasts for royal visitors and dignitaries, but ordinary people might also participate in such festivities, for instance, as members of a guild or parish (Cressy, *Bonfires* xi).

In Arthur Brooke's *Romeus and Juliet*, which, as we have noted, was Shakespeare's primary source, the lovers meet at a Christmas feast, and by Easter they are dead. The feast celebrated at the Capulet house in *Romeo and Juliet*, however, may be related to the summer festival of Lammastide, celebrating the first fruits of the harvest at the beginning of August to which the play specifically alludes. Lammas Eve is July 31, Juliet's birthday, and Lammas is directly opposed in the calendar to Shrovetide, the beginning of Lent (Berry, *Feminine* 42; see also Laroque 48). Juliet is herself connected both with Lammas feasting and with its macabre antithesis because she is referred to as "a feasting presence" (5.3.86) in the tomb and "the dearest morsel of the earth" (5.3.46) upon which death's "detestable maw" [devouring mouth] (5.3.45) has

FIGURE 17

"gorged" itself (5.3.46). Having been a feast for Romeo when they met at the Capulet ball, she is now a feast for death in this sad termination of fruitfulness.

The cultural logic whereby death constitutes an integral aspect of festivity is an ancient one. Traditionally, feasts marked the recurrence of natural events in the cosmic cycle, whose circumference is infinite, reaching beyond all human notions of time into the realms of timelessness where life and death are mutually constitutive, and in terms of which there can, of course, be no distinction between comedy and tragedy. In this earlier understanding of festival, death was not the antithesis of festival but a vital component of the cycle of change and renewal. Because historically such festivity was linked to moments of social crisis, breaking points that were not amenable to control from the top of the social hierarchy, there was, according to Russian theorist Mikhail Bakhtin (1895–1975), an endeavor to replace them with "official" festivities, such as those sanctioned by the church. The "official" feast tended toward an emphasis on the perennial and unchanging, the status quo, a man-made order of things, which attempted to excise the rupture and spontaneity inherent in the rhythms of nature.

Lammas, August 1, a celebration of ancient and obscure origin, harks back to this earlier form of festivity, untrammeled by political and moral dictates and prohibitions. Although not recognized by the ecclesiastical calendar, Lammas was always noted in almanacs of the period, and both Lammas and its seasonal opposite, Candlemas, February 2 (the feast forty days after the birth of Jesus, of the purification of the Blessed Virgin and the presentation of Christ in the temple), were days when traditionally rents were paid (Cressy, *Bonfires* 29). Lammas was also a day when fairs were held, a day of what Bahktin calls the "carnivalesque," the temporary inversion of all social hierarchy. On this day, there was a traditional treat of bread and beer (Cressy, *Bonfires* 24). The early English church observed the feast as a harvest festival, at which loaves of bread were consecrated, made from the first ripe corn. It was also popularly known as the "Gule of August," so that when the Nurse calls Juliet "Jule," the audience would undoubtedly have recognized the pun.

Pagan and Catholic festivals, then, both excised by Protestantism, survived in the popular commemoration of Lammas (Duffy 47). Catholic saints days in the period of late July and early August included the feasts of St. Thomas Becket (7 July), St. Mary Magdalene (22 July), St. James the Apostle and St. Christopher (July 25), St. Anne (July 26), and St. Lawrence (August 10). Although officially abolished, these feast days did not always go unmarked even in state celebrations, such as the coronation of James I and Anne of Denmark, which occurred on July 25, the feast of St. James and the eve of St. Anne's Day (Berry, *Feminine* 35; see also Berlin 47–60).

SEPTEMBER 1619

The 21st. All this week I spent with my sister Compton; and my sister Sackville, being sad about an unkind letter from my Lord.

OCTOBER 1619

. . . The 2nd Kate Burton went away from serving me to her Father's house in Sussex.[33]

This 10th Mary was brought to bed of a boy. The same night I began to be ill. . . .

Upon the 18th at night the Fire Dog play'd with fire,[34] so as I took cold with standing in the window. . . .

The 29th . . .

This night the drawing chamber chimney was on fire so that I supped in the new drawing chamber with my Lord. After this I never stirred out of my own bedchamber till the 23rd of March.

NOVEMBER 1619

. . . Upon the 8th shortly after supper when I came into my chamber I was so ill that I fell into a swoon which was the first time I ever swooned. . . .

About this time I received letters . . . by which I perceived how ill things were likely to go in Westmoreland.[35] . . .

The 29th all the ladies hereabout being very kind to me all the time of my not being well. This day I received a letter and a box of sweetmeats[36] from my cousin Hall which was brought to me by one of his tenants, to whom I gave a good reward, returned her a letter of many thanks.

DECEMBER 1619

. . . After supper my Lord and I had a great falling out, he saying that, if ever my land came to me I should assure it as he would have me.

The 18th my Lord came and supped with me in my chamber, which he had not done before since his coming from London, for I determined to keep my chamber, and did not so much as go over the threshold of the door. . . .

---

[33] [**Anne Clifford's marginal note**]: "Upon the 2nd I began to think I was quick with child so as I told it to my Lord, my sister Sackville, and my sister Compton."   [34] **Fire Dog play'd with fire:** celestial display similar to the aurora borealis.   [35] [**Anne Clifford's marginal note**]: "All this winter my Lady Margaret's speech was very ill so as strangers cannot understand her, besides she was so apt to take cold and so out of temper that it grieved me to think of it. I verily believe all these inconveniences proceed from some distemper in her head."   [36] **sweetmeats:** delicacies.

→ SIR HUGH PLATT

From Delights for Ladies to Adorn Their Persons, Tables, Closets, and Distillatories
1609

Most contemporary productions of *Romeo and Juliet* leave out the first lines of act 1, scene 5, in which a servant asks his fellow servant to save him a piece of marzipan: "Good thou, save me a piece of marchpane" (1.5.6). This is because modern productions tend to focus on the nuclear family more than on the household and its wider network of relations. Moreover, modern productions tend to give a sense merely of joyous bustle, whereas in Shakespeare's text, the preparations for the Capulet ball and for Juliet's marriage to Paris in act 4, scene 4 clearly involve the labor of a host of servants presided over by the "Lady of the House," as the scene direction to 4.4. informs us. The text is also very specific about the ingredients of a feast: "marchpane," (1.5.6), "spices" (4.4.1), and "dates and quinces" (4.4.2), among others.

Marzipan or "marchpane" (the early modern version of almond paste) became popular in England with the advent of sugar from the New World. Sugar was sold in large conical sugar loaves, and it had to be refined after purchase. Refining was a complicated task which involved boiling and then adding lime juice, oil, and egg whites until the mixture became a thick syrup. After this, it was left in molds over night so that the molasses would drain out of the white sugar. Then the sugar was left to dry and harden before being stored in paper (Sim 150). Alison Sim explains that for Elizabethans, making marzipan was a labor intensive luxury food:

> [M]aking it must have been an exercise in patience as the almonds had first to be blanched to remove their skins, then finely ground in a mortar. The sugar had to be "the finest refined" to start with, and then it had to be sieved through fine linen, which would have given it the texture of modern powdered sugar. The paste would usually be shaped or molded into some elaborate form. Finally, it would be intricately decorated, with icing made of sugar and rosewater, with colored comfits [seeds, spices, or fruit covered with sugar], or it might even be gilded, and then baked in an oven. (Sim 153)

The author of the following treatise on confection, Sir Hugh Platt (1552–1608), though interested in literature in his youth, was primarily an inventor and writer on agriculture and gardening. In 1592 he exhibited a series of mechanical inventions to privy councilors and eminent citizens of London, and in 1594 published *The Jewel House of Art and Nature, Containing divers rare and profitable*

Sir Hugh Platt, *Delights for Ladies, to Adorn Their Persons, Tables, Closets, and Distillatories with Beauties, Banquets, Perfumes & Waters. Read, Practice and Censure*, with an introduction by G. E. Fussell and Kathleen Rosemary Fussell (London; 1609, rpt. 1948), 24–25.

Inventions, together with sundry new Experiments in the Art of Husbandry, Distillation and Moulding. Delights is a publication that continues in this vein, consisting of a collection of recipes for cooking, for preserving fruits, distilling, cosmetics, and housewifery in general. Platt was knighted in 1605 for his ingenious inventions, which included "coal balls" (a mixture of coal, clay, and other substances to serve as a means of fuel economy) and English wine made from grapes grown at Bethnal Green.

From *Delights for Ladies to Adorn Their Persons, Tables, Closets, and Distillatories*

To Make an Excellent Marchpane Paste to Print Off in Molds for Banqueting Dishes.

Take to every Jordan almond blanched, three spoonfuls of the whitest refined sugar you can get, sieve your sugar, and now and then as you see cause put in two or three drops of damask rosewater, beat the same in a smooth stone mortar, with great labor, until you have brought it into a dry stiff paste, one quartern[1] of sugar is sufficient to work at once.

Make your paste into little balls, every ball containing so much by estimation as will cover your mold or print, then roll the same with a rolling pin, upon a sheet of clean paper, without strewing any powdered sugar either upon your paste or paper. There is a country gentlewoman whom I could name, which venteth[2] great store of sugar cakes made of this composition. But the only fault which I find in this paste is, that it tasteth too much of the sugar, and too little of the almonds, and therefore you may prove the making thereof with such almonds, which have had some part of their oil taken from them by expression, before you incorporate them with the sugar, and so happily you may mix a greater quantity of them with the sugar, because they are not so oily as the other. You may mix cinnamon or ginger in your paste, & that will both grace the taste, and alter the color; but the spice must pass through a fair sieve: you may steep your almonds in cold water all night, & so blanch them cold, and being blanched, dry them in a sieve over the fire. Here the garble[3] of almonds will make a cheap paste.

---

[1] **one quartern:** a quarter of various weights and measures.   [2] **which venteth:** who sells.
[3] **garble:** refuse of spices or nuts, in this case almonds — i.e., what is left over after they have been blanched.

FIGURE 18 *Costumes of Venetian Men and Women* (Habiti d'huomeni et donne Venetia), *by Giacomo Franco, 1609. Feasts and celebrations punctuated the Elizabethan
calendar with cycles of dearth and plenty, luxury foods and abstinence. At feasting
times, the houses of the wealthy were appropriately prepared for guests. The main room
was the hall, which served as a dining-room, drawing room, and place for festivities.
When meals were served, tables consisting of leaves hinged together and laid on trestles
were carried in or taken down from their place against the walls. Capulet may refer to
such tables being removed preparatory to clearing the hall for a dance, when he cries,*

> *A hall, a hall! Give room! And foot it, girls.*
> *[To Servingmen.] More light, you knaves, and turn the tables up,*   (1.5.24–25)

*The feast depicted in this image is a masked ball, popular all over Europe but especially in
Italy, which adds the* frisson *of uncertain identity — on which the love of Romeo and
Juliet initially depends — to the general holiday mood. We are told specifically that Romeo,
Mercutio, and Benvolio attend the Capulet ball as masquers, and at 1.4.29, Mercutio dons
a visor. What is not so clear, however, is whether or at what point Romeo is masked.*

CHAPTER 5

Friars

———————————————————— ✦ ————————————————————

Holy St. Francis   (2.3.65)

St. Francis be my speed   (5.3.121)

Friars were one of the most powerful symbols of the Protestant critique of pre-Reformation Christianity, and the character of Friar Laurence focused some of the post-Reformation dilemmas that confronted Shakespeare's audience as they watched *Romeo and Juliet*. Modern critical response to the Friar has been divergent: for some he is the voice of good sense and moderation who valiantly attempts to reconcile the warring families, while for others, he is weak and meddlesome, responsible for the bulk of the catastrophe. E. A. J. Honigmann goes so far as to suggest that Shakespeare's portrait of the Friar is sympathetic and indicative of Shakespeare's own Catholic sympathies (Honigmann 122). In contrast, theater productions of the play tend to emphasize his weakness, and he is usually regarded as an essentially comic character, even though the events he is consulted about lead inexorably toward death (Rozett 156). Whatever his shortcomings, Friar Laurence is a far less egregious character than the friars in the farce about necromancy written by Robert Greene (1560–1592), *Friar Bacon and Friar Bungay,* or the friar who is a devil in disguise in Christopher Marlowe's *Dr. Faustus.*

Friar Laurence is introduced as "ghostly [meaning spiritual] father," "a divine, a ghostly confessor, / A sin absolver" (3.3.49–50); Juliet's father calls him "reverend holy friar" (4.2.30) and the Prince recognizes him as "a holy man" (5.3.270). While Brooke's Juliet (that is, the Juliet of Shakespeare's source) worries that if the potion does not work, she will become a laughing-stock, Shakespeare's Juliet is concerned that the Friar is trying to kill her in order to save himself from disgrace:

> What if it be a poison which the Friar
> Subtly hath ministered to have me dead,
> Lest in this marriage he should be dishonored,
> Because he married me before to Romeo? (4.3.24–27).

Given the degree of trust that circumstances require her to place in Friar Laurence, Juliet's doubts are perhaps understandable, and she finally determines that "he hath still been tried a holy man" (4.3.29).

As the ejaculation "Holy St. Francis" attests, Laurence is a Franciscan, as he is in earlier versions of the story. Shakespeare's source, Arthur Brooke's poem *Romeus and Juliet,* specifically mentions that Laurence was "Out of saint Francis church" (line 2693), and in Luigi da Porto's 1530 Italian version of the story, Friar Lorenzo was also identified as a Franciscan. Shakespeare's play offers a glimpse of the Franciscan brotherhood of Verona and Mantua in the interaction between Friar Laurence and Friar John: "Holy Franciscan friar! Brother, ho!" (5.2.1). Act 5, scene 2, the brief scene between the two brothers of the order, serves at this point in the play largely to cover the heavy machinery of the plot that is working its way toward the tragic catastrophe. It does, however, provide some indication of the work and lifestyle of the Franciscans. In Friar John's report, we glimpse their poverty (they go barefoot) and their ministrations to the sick, even those afflicted with the plague:

> Going to find a barefoot brother out —
> One of our order — to associate me
> Here in this city visiting the sick,
> And finding him, the searchers of the town,
> Suspecting that we both were in a house
> Where the infectious pestilence did reign,
> Sealed up the doors and would not let us forth (5.2.5–11)

Plague ravaged the population of London in several outbreaks during Shakespeare's lifetime. Theaters, courts, and other institutions were closed and the houses of infected people marked so they could be avoided while wealthier people often fled the city to avoid the risk of contagion. Thus, an Elizabethan audience would have been familiar with the problem of travel during outbreaks of plague, and sensitive to the plight of those who were left to die in isolation from the rest of the community.

This scene (5.2) is also the one in which Friar Laurence asks for a crowbar, "an iron crow" (line 21), in order to get into the monument. It provides a sense that he is capable of active intervention in worldly events beyond the confines of secluded monasticism, namely works of charity and care of the sick. There is also a reference here to one of the rules of the order, namely that friars were not to travel alone, which is why John needs someone to "associate me." The point was somewhat belabored in Brooke's *Romeus and Juliet:* "And for because in Italy it is a wonted guise [habit], / That friars in the town should seldom walk alone, / But of their covenant ay [ever] should be accompanied with one / Of his profession" (Brooke, lines 2488–91). Nonetheless, Shakespeare did not choose to omit this information, and so the scene contains the potential for audiences to see the friars as charitable, godly men, *or* as ineffectual go-betweens whose bizarre papist rules of living fail, with ultimately tragic consequences, to save Romeo and Juliet.

What then was the spectrum of opinion on friars in Shakespeare's time? What were the ideological and religious positions available in relation to monasticism and especially toward the Franciscans? In engaging these questions, we need to recognize the sharp difference between medieval piety and the Tridentine concepts of religion (those developed at the beginning of the Counter-Reformation at the Council of Trent, 1545–63, which sought to respond both to Protestantism and to abuses that had developed within the Roman Catholic church). It is possible that Shakespeare deliberately associated the Friar with medieval piety, even though in post-Reformation England the friar had become the symbol (as he is in Marlowe's *Faustus*) of absolute corruption.

In 1500 there were approximately 900 monastic communities in England (Youings 143). In the early sixteenth century, these numbers declined, in part because of a shift in theological emphasis from communal to personal piety, to the point that many houses were no longer viable. Henry VIII's chief advisor in the 1520s, Cardinal Thomas Wolsey, closed twenty-nine smaller houses between 1524 and 1529; Thomas Cromwell (1485–1540), appointed by Henry VIII as the deputy governor of the Church of England, set about dissolving all religious communities with an unprecedented messianic zeal. Cromwell dispatched a team of assessors to travel around the country in order to interview members of religious orders and catalog the income and possessions of their houses. This was recorded in a document known as *Valor Ecclesiasticus* (1535). The following year Parliament passed the Act of

Suppression, which outlawed religious communities: It required the "surrender" of all monastic property to the Crown as well as the dissolution of the larger religious communities. The act offered ample moral justification, complaining against "vicious, carnal and abominable living, daily used and committed among the little and small abbeys, priories, and other religious houses of monks, canons and nuns" (quoted in Stewart 46). While there was undoubtedly a certain amount of truth in these allegations, and while there were problems of maintaining the rules of monastic order, it is important to remember that most of the information about specific sexual abuses was garnered from disgruntled members of religious orders, and the "moral" justification for the dissolution was outweighed by the financial motivations of the Crown. Religious communities were actually dissolved not for religious and moral reasons but for economic and political ones (Baskerville 14; Youings 144–45). By confiscating monastic property the Crown increased its estate by nearly £200,000 per annum (Youings 145). By 1547, however, at the end of Henry VIII's reign, well over half these properties had been sold. Elizabeth, short of money to finance wars and patronage, disposed of virtually all that was left from Henry's monastic land grab.

Despite the Henrican and Cromwellian portrayal of friars as corrupt, some were extraordinarily zealous reformers. Indeed, Martin Luther, who instigated the Reformation in Germany, had been an Austin friar, while the English zealot John Bale, who was one of the period's most ardent polemicists against the evils of monastic life, had himself been a Carmelite friar. Bale's autobiography, *The Vocation of John Bale* (1553), denounced the religious life as one of utter moral depredation and claimed that prayer itself, at least as practiced by the friars, was merely idolatry. From this error, according to Bale, there followed no end of moral abominations: "[T]he impertinent idolater must therewith be also a filthy adulterer or most detestable sodomite. It is his just plague (Romans 1). We cannot stop it" (quoted in Stewart 56). A former Dominican friar, Prior Richard Ingworth, Suffragan Bishop (that is, an assistant or subsidiary bishop) of Dover, led the "visitation" to the monasteries ordered by Cromwell. "My friar's heart was gone two years before my habit," Ingworth declared (Baskerville 234), and indeed he was ruthless in the execution of his commission. Some former friars, like the Franciscan Gilbert Berkeley, fared well under the new regime. He became bishop of Bath and Wells in 1559 (Baskerville 236). If some friars adopted the new religion, others clung to the old and suffered the consequences, like one Friar Stone, who was "parboiled" at Canterbury in 1538, or Friar Forrest, burned at Smithfield the same year (Baskerville 235).

Communities of friars, containing an estimated 550 persons, were all dissolved in England in the course of a single year, 1538. There were four orders of friars: Franciscan, Carmelite, Austin, and Dominican. Because of their commitment to an ideal of Christian poverty, the Crown had much less to gain from the confiscation of their houses. The friars themselves were in a much more parlous position than the more wealthy dispossessed religious monastic houses such as the Benedictines, Cistercians, Augustinians, and Carthusians. There were only about twenty-five Franciscans in London at the time of the surrender, even though they retained a very popular role in praying for the dead and comforting the afflicted (Baskerville 227). The medical knowledge possessed by the friars was extremely valuable, and one of the most eminent medical men of the period, Dr. Simon Ludford, was a former Franciscan. In Luigi da Porto, *Novella Novamente Ritrouvata d'uno Innamoramento* (Venice, 1535), the friar is "a great philosopher and experimenter in things natural and magical" (Bullough 1:270). In the middle ages, Franciscans were known for their skills in the natural philosophy, chemistry, and in all the arts of healing (Bowden 267). Though in the play there are no associations of Friar Laurence with the interest in spiritualism attributed to friars, Romeo clearly has had much recourse to his wisdom (see Baskerville 232). Upon receiving the news of his banishment, however, Romeo finds the Friar's consolations inadequate: "Hang up philosophy! / Unless philosophy can make a Juliet" (3.3.57–58). Is the Friar suggesting substantive spiritual consolation, or is he simply out of touch with the young men of Verona?

The popularity of the Franciscan order in particular is due in part to its founder, St. Francis of Assisi. St. Francis, a rich young man who renounced his wealth to devote his life to the service of the poor, was one of the most venerated saints in medieval Europe. Whereas some Protestants saw prayers to the saints as idolatrous, Catholics saw the saints as people who had overcome their faults and frailties to achieve a life lived in the imitation of Christ, a life illuminated by compassion and unconditional love. For Catholics, statues of Francis, Christ, the Virgin Mary, or the saints were not idolatrous images — substitutes for the living presence of God — but rather objects for contemplation that served as windows into the divine presence. Looking through that window, so to speak, in the discipline of prayer and meditation, Catholics believed they might achieve an intimation of the power and presence of the deity. This was certainly the Counter-Reformation thinking among educated Catholics, but medieval Catholicism had fostered the notion of saints and clergy as "conjures" — as endowed with magical powers with which they could manipulate the world around them. Protestantism helped reform this notion, insisting on purity of heart and life as the signs of

Christ rather than on the flashy so-called miracles attributed to so many saints. Many medieval accounts of martyrs, for instance, strike the modern reader as a sort of comic-horror genre in their ludicrous exaggerations of saintly endurance and miraculous powers: saints with all limbs gone and their heads hacked off still speaking out and refusing to die. While Protestantism eschewed hagiography (the worshipful biographies of saints popular in medieval Catholicism), at least in its official forms up until the mid-seventeenth century, it also spurned mysticism. The inner life was important, but it was important so that "conscience," a sort of vigilant superego, could ensure proper godly behavior. Contemplation was no longer a significant aspect of spiritual life, but was instead replaced by an emphasis on outward conformity to social dictates and inwardly, by the repression of all temptation.

Mendicant friars — friars who, in obedience to their vow of poverty, were forbidden to hold property and therefore relied on alms (charitable donations) — such as St. Francis and his followers — were committed to a life of poverty. This meant that they followed Christ's injunction, "Consider the lilies of the field, how they grow; they toil not, neither do they spin; And yet I say unto you, That even Solomon in all his glory was not arrayed like one of these" (Matthew 7:28–29). The idea here is that "the Lord will provide," that in completely surrendering to God, all concerns about worldly well-being should be secondary to the principle purpose in life — finding the Kingdom of God: "[S]eek ye first the kingdom of God . . . and all these things shall be added unto you" (Matthew 7:32). Prior to its corruption, this notion implied God should be the focus of life, even through the process of providing the necessities of daily living. The poor, whose poverty Franciscans were committed to share, were not just objects of charity for the Franciscans but rather individuals who shared the divine identity of Christ. This notion accorded with the Gospel injunction: "Inasmuch as ye have done it unto one of the least of these my brethren, ye have done it unto me" (Matthew 25:41). As such, to share the lot of the poor and to minister to their needs was understood to be an immense privilege against which no worldly comfort or wealth could possibly measure.

These ideas, conceived in spiritual purity by Francis, were vulnerable to abuse. A life of poverty, originally understood as sharing the life of the poor and seeing in them nothing less than the image of Christ, became an excuse and even a license for a life of idleness; relying on the power of God in all things became the idea that members of religious orders had a right to expect the secular community to support and maintain them in considerable luxury. This hypocrisy enraged Protestant martyrologist John Foxe because it distorted Christ's teachings and used them to rationalize and cloak greed and corruption — the very antitheses of Christian values. For instance, some monasteries not only relied on the financial support of the laity (parishioners), but actively engaged in extorting money from it. Foxe refers to the corruption of the friars as "ingling" which, though it is used by Foxe to mean devious behavior, in the early modern period has distinctly sexual connotations. *Ingle* was a derisive term for a homosexual, and anti-Catholic diatribes of the period repeatedly insinuated that monastic living in single-sex communities was not a sign of renunciation of the flesh, but merely an opportunity for sodomy.

Through the medieval period, monastic orders became increasingly corrupt. Far from adhering to the vows of poverty, chastity, and obedience, many monks were downright avaricious and lecherous. In Shakespeare's source (Brooke), the Friar is much more the stereotype of corruption than he is in Shakespeare. When Romeus kills Tybalt in Brooke's version, he goes to the Friar's cell:

> He sought some where unseen, to lurk a little space,
> And trusty Lawrence secret cell, he thought the surest place.
> In doubtful hap aye best, a trusty friend is tried,
> The friendly friar in this distress, doth grant his friend to hide.
> A secret place he hath, well sealed round about,
> The mouth of which, so close is shut, that none may find it out
> But room there is to walk, and place to sit and rest,
> Beside, a bed to sleep upon, full soft and trimly dressed.
> The floor is planked so with mats, it is so warm,
> That neither wind, nor smoky damps have power him ought to harm
> Where he was wont in youth his fair friends to bestow.
> (Bullough, lines 1263–73)

"Fair friends" suggests that there are illicit sexual encounters in the Friar's past, and Brooke's preface to the reader leaves little doubt about his opinion of the Friar: "superstitious friars (the naturally fit instruments of unchastity)." He also accuses the lovers of "using auricular confession (the key of whoredom, and treason) for furtherance of their purpose" (Bullough, line 284).

In Shakespeare's version, Romeo suggests that Juliet use the excuse of going to confession as a pretext for their nuptials: "Bid her devise / Some means to come to shrift this afternoon, / And there she shall at Friar Laurence' cell / Be shrived and married" (2.4.143–46). But shrift is not only an excuse; the implication is that the couple should receive absolution prior to marriage, which, according to Catholic doctrine, is a sacrament. In England, however, the sacrament of confession was a practice proscribed as a heresy after 1530:

Confession auricular, absolution, and penance, are neither necessary, nor profitable in the church of God; it is sufficient that the sinner do say I know myself a sinner; it is sufficient for a man or woman to make their confession to God alone; confession is but a whispering in a priest's ear, and is as well to be made a multitude being present, as secretly; it is as lawful at all times to confess to a layman as to a priest; the ghostly father cannot give or enjoin any penance at all; auricular confession is only invested and ordained to have the secret knowledge of men's hearts, and to pull money out of their purses. (Quoted in Hughes 127)

As Alan Stewart points out, there was a sort of "sexualization of the confessional" (Stewart 59) in this period: "In the context of the Reformation, the confession had taken on a dangerously political character, as conservative priests were accused of exploiting the sanctity of the confessional to attack innovatory ideas. More generally, it was seen as an indecently close situation for a man and a woman to be in . . ." (Stewart 58).

When we consider Friar Laurence, it is important to remember that there were Catholics in England despite the Reformation, and there were people, then as now, whose spiritual lives did not conform to any of the official religious designations whatever the form of their external religious practice. This was a period in which people were trying to decide what external form spiritual life should take. Paradoxically, both Catholics and Protestants sought to define the relation between the spiritual and the material. For Catholic monks, the spirit was to be found in avoiding the quest for wealth and material things — although they found little or no contradiction in ornamenting the space and instruments of religious ritual. For Protestants, the spirit was to be found in a communion with God that eschewed all sacred objects, ornaments, images, and religious paraphernalia, although they found little or no contradiction in the possession of worldly wealth. At least in their purest forms, both faiths sought, despite all their bloody struggles and theological squabbles, the means of making a connection with a God who could not be seen.

→ ST. BONAVENTURE

From The Life of the Most Holy Father St. Francis

1595, 1635

This tiny and beautiful book is an edition of the life of St. Francis first published in English translation in 1595 in Douai, France, home to many Catholic exiles from Protestant England. Douai was the site of an English Catholic seminary founded by Cardinal William Allen in 1568, as well as Franciscan and Benedictine monasteries, and Scots and Irish colleges. The author of this biography was St. Bonaventure (1221–1274), a Franciscan philosopher and theologian who was cardinal and bishop of Albano. The book was written in the midst of bitter controversy about the status of the mendicant orders (those friars living entirely on alms) in the medieval church. Bonaventure entered the Franciscan Order of the Friars Minor in about 1243, was sent from Italy to the University of Paris, and received his "licentiate" in 1248. This gave him the right to teach publicly, which he did with great success, until he was forced to desist in the face of violent criticism of friars by secular professors at the university. What is interesting about this is that it is clear that friars were under attack even in pre-Reformation Europe and particularly in France. However, the problem was not simply a matter of secular criticism from outside the order: When Bonaventure was elected Minister General of the Friars Minor in 1257, the order was rife with internal dissent between those who argued for the literal observance of the original rules of the order, especially the adherence to the vow of poverty, and those who argued for change.

Bonaventure intervened in the dispute, instituting a program for reform and had extremists in the order tried for heresy (two were perpetually imprisoned). His *Life of St. Francis* was officially approved as the standard biography — Bonaventure ordered the destruction of all others, a move that, predictably, provoked sharp criticism of his methods. His death in Lyons in 1274 is thought to be the result of poisoning.

Though Bonaventure's administration was subject to much criticism, he was known as an intensely spiritual and holy man, not only in his role as the author of profoundly influential philosophical and theological writings, but also in his personal piety and humility. After his death, numerous miracles were attributed to him. Dante placed him among the saints in his *Paradiso*, and the Vatican itself recognized him as a saint in 1482. Bonaventure was especially venerated in the city of his death, and his remains, apparently undecayed, were moved to a new church in 1434. So while Lyons was the site of the incident of Franciscan chicanery in Foxe, as we shall see later in this chapter, it was also the site of intense Franciscan devotion.

St. Bonaventure, *The Life of the Most Holy Father St. Francis . . . Now Lately Translated into Our English Tongue* (Douai, 1635), 173–77, 249–55.

In Bonaventure's account, St. Francis is a very different type of monk from the corrupt, well-fed friars who had abandoned their ascetic vows for a life of carnal pleasures. The episodes of his life included below described his preternatural affinity with animals as well as the profound mystical experience in which he received the stigmata, the wounds of Christ.

. . . [A]lso on a time, a young leveret[1] was given alive unto the servant of God: which being set free on the ground, when as it might have gone which way it would, yet being by the good father called unto him, it came forthwith running and leaping into his bosom which cherishing with great affection, he seemed to have compassion thereof as a mother hath towards her child: and warning it with sweet words not to let it self so to be taken again gave it free leave to depart. But being put oftentimes upon the ground and returning always into the father's bosom again (as if it had some secret feeling, of the inward piety of his loving heart) at length by the father's commandment he was carried by the brethren, unto some safer parts to depart. . . .

Another time also walking with one of the brethren, nigh unto the marsh lands of Venice, he found a great multitude of birds, sitting and singing in the thicket. Upon a sight whereof, he said to his companion, *Our sisters the birds, do praise the creator: let us therefore go into the midst among them, and there let us sing our praises and canonical hours,[2] to our Lord.* And being entered into the midst of them the birds never stirred out of their places: and because for their chirping noise, the holy man and his brother could not hear one another in saying their hours; he therefore turning himself to the birds; spoke this unto them: *Ye birds, my sisters, leave of your singing until we have performed the due praises we owe to God.* The birds presently ceased all manner of noise: and continued all that while in silence, until the said hours & praises being leisurely performed, they were licensed by the saint of God to sing again. But so soon as the man of God had given this license unto them, they presently betook themselves to their former singing. . . .

This angelical man St. Francis, was never accustomed to be idle: but like the heavenly spirits, in *Jacob's* ladder,[3] he did either ascend unto God, or descend unto his neighbor. For the time which was granted unto him for his merit, he had learned so prudently to divide, that some part, he did with great labor bestow upon his neighbor, and the rest, he did dedicate, to the

---

[1] leveret: hare.   [2] *canonical hours:* prayers known as the "divine office," which are to be recited at specific hours of the day.   [3] *Jacob's* ladder: "And he [Jacob] dreamed, and behold a ladder set up on the earth, and the top of it reached to heaven: and behold the angels of God ascending and descending on it" (Genesis 28:12).

SERAPHICVS PATER S. FRANCISCVS
Vidi alterum Angelum, ascendentem ab ortu
solis, habentem signum Dei VIII. Apoc.7

FIGURE 19

St. Francis Enraptured, from St. Bonaventure, *The Life of the Most Holy Father St. Francis (1635)*.

Born of wealthy parents in Assisi, Italy, Francis (c. 1182–1226) had been groomed to follow in the footsteps of his father, a successful cloth merchant. However, self-doubt, illnesses, and dreams prodded him toward religious contemplation. He eventually rejected his family's wealth, stripping publicly before his father, the bishop of Assisi, and other onlookers in a defiant, if flamboyant, show of his emerging asceticism. He took a vow of poverty, wore a simple robe, and walked barefoot, preaching and begging for alms.

A charismatic speaker, he soon attracted followers; after three years, they were recognized by Pope Honorius III in 1223 as the Order of Friars Minor, more commonly called the Franciscans. The friars filled their days preaching, caring for the needy, including lepers, and performing manual labor. Unlike Cistercians, Franciscans sought town life and refused to be cloistered, preferring that their ministries bring them in direct contact with layfolk. Eventually, Franciscan fraternal groups could be found throughout Italy, France, Spain, Germany, the Holy Land, and England.

In 1219, during the Fifth Crusade, Francis traveled to the Holy Land to preach to the Muslims and was granted an audience with the Sultan Melek al-Kamil. Although Francis's efforts to convert the Muslim leader failed, and his proposed armistice between the Christians and the Muslims was rejected by Christian leaders, the Franciscan order was granted custody of the Christian shrines then under Muslim control.

Returning to Assisi, Francis resigned as minister general of the order in 1220, turning to a life of prayer and fasting at a mountain retreat north of Assisi called La Verna. It was here, in 1224, in a state of ecstasy, that he received the stigmata, the reproduction of the wounds of Christ on his own body. His hands and feet bore nail holes that bled, his brow let blood as if encircled by a thorny crown, and his side gaped open as if from the thrust of a spear. St. Francis of Assisi was the first of a number of stigmatics to bear the marks of the Passion of Christ, the presence of which confirmed for the devout the godliness of the afflicted individual and the divinity of Jesus Christ.

quiet of contemplation. And therefore when according to the necessity of place and time he had been conversant, in procuring the salvation of others, withdrawing himself from the disquietness of the multitudes, he always betook himself, to some secret part of the wilderness, and place of rest: that attending there more freely unto the service of God: if any dust had cleaved unto him, by means of humane conversation, he might so shake it off again. Two years therefore before he rendered up his soul to heaven: he was by divine providence, after many labors, brought into a high place apart, which is called the mount of *Alverna*. And whilst he did, in that place, according to his wonted manner, begin to fast the Lent . . . enjoying the sweetness of divine contemplation, more abundantly than formerly he accustomed, and being set on fire, with a more burning flame of heavenly desires, he began yet in a more abundant measure, to feel the good gifts of God sent down from heaven upon him. He was carried up aloft, not as a curious searcher of the majesty of God, so to be oppressed by his glory, but as *a faithful and prudent servant*, seeking the will of God, whereunto he most earnestly in all things did conform himself. And therefore it was, by God's oracle inspired unto him that in opening of the book of the Gospel, *Christ* would reveal unto him, what should be most acceptable unto God, in him, and concerning him. Having therefore betaken himself to prayer with much devotion, he caused the Gospel book taken from the Altar in the name of the Holy Trinity, to be opened by his companion, a man of great devotion and holiness. Now in three times opening of the book always the Passion of our Lord[4] occurred: he therefore full of God's spirit, did well understand, that as he had imitated *Christ* in the actions of his life, so ought he before his departure from this world, be conformable unto him in the afflictions and dolors[5] of his Passion. And albeit that through continual austerity of his life past, and of his continually bearing the cross of our Lord he was now but weak of body, yet was he nothing terrified: but was more forcibly animated to the sustaining of martyrdom. For the burning love of good *Jesus*, had increased in him, to lamps of fire & flames: so that many waters, were not able to quench his so prevalent charity. Being therefore with seraphical[6] fervor borne up aloft into God, & by the sweetness of compassion, transformed into him, who by his surpassing charity would vouchsafe to be crucified. One morning about the feast of the exaltation of the holy cross, while he did pray on the side of the hill: he saw a *seraphin*,[7] with six wings all fiery and full of glorious light, descending down from the heavens. And as he came with a swift flight, to that place of the air which was near to the

---

[4] **Passion of our Lord:** the suffering and death of Christ. [5] **dolors:** sorrows. [6] **seraphical:** angelic. [7] *seraphin:* highest of the nine orders of angels.

man of God: there appeared between his wings, the form of a man crucified, having his hands and feet stretched out, in manner of a cross, and fastened unto a cross. Two of his wings were lifted up above his head, two were stretched forth to fly, & two did cover his whole body. At the beholding whereof he was exceedingly amazed: and there entered his heart, a joy mingled with sorrow. For he rejoiced, in that gracious aspect, whereby he perceived himself to be beholden of *Christ,* under the form of a *Seraphin:* but the fastening to the Cross, did transpierce his soul, with a sword, of compassionate grief. He much wondered in the beholding of so strange a vision: knowing well, that the infirmity of Passion, could by no means agree with the immortality of a Seraphicall spirit. But in the end he herehence perceived, (our Lord revealing the same unto him,) that therefore this vision, was by the providence of God, in such manner presented unto his sight, that he the friend of *Christ* might foreknow, that he was wholly to be transformed into the likeness of *Christ* crucified: not by the martyrdom of his flesh: but by the burning inflammation of his mind.

The vision therefore, disappearing, did leave a wonderful heat in his heart, and a no less wonderful impression of signs, in his flesh. For presently there began to appear in his hands and feet, the signs of nails: even as a little before he had seen them, in the figure of the crucified man. For his hands and feet seemed to be, in the middest, pierced through with nails: the heads of the nails appearing in the inner part of his hands, and the outward parts of his feet: but the points of them on the contrary sides. . . . His right side also, as being pierced through with a spear, was covered over with a red scar: which oftentimes casting out holy blood, did stain his tunic and drawers.

→ JOHN FOXE

From Acts and Monuments 1583

John Foxe (1516–1587), martyrologist (he compiled the most extensive list of Protestant martyrs ever written), studied at Magdalene College, Oxford. During the reign of Catholic Mary Tudor (1553–58), Elizabeth's elder half-sister, Foxe was forced to flee England and live in Frankfurt and Basle. Foxe worked as a reader in a printing house in Basle and, from that time on, was closely associated with the printing trade and with the London printer John Day. He was virulently anti-Catholic and spent his life in service of the Protestant cause.

John Foxe, *Acts and Monuments of matters most special and memorable, happening in the Church* (London, 1583), 1291–92.

Foxe's fiercely anti-Catholic polemic was commonly known as "The Book of Martyrs," detailing as it did the trials of "true Christians" in the face of "papistry." There were numerous editions of the book, and one was chained along with the Bible in every church in post-Reformation England. In the text below, Foxe denounces the corrupt practices of the Franciscan monks, who though they have taken a vow of poverty, try to cozen all they can out of their parishioners, in this episode by staging the appearance of a spirit in order to denounce a dead woman whose husband has refused to give them money. Stories of this sort abounded in the period.

That the priests in the episode below are referred to as "conjurers" is another standard element of anti-Catholic propaganda, though in this case they are quite literally conjuring. The "conjuring tricks" Protestants objected to were the quasi-magical powers they felt priests claimed when they offered the Mass and "transformed" the bread and wine into the body and blood of Christ. This was a theological dispute that led to a tremendous controversy about the nature of the Eucharist. Catholics believed that the bread literally transformed into the body of Christ (the doctrine of transubstantiation), while Luther held to the principle of consubstantiation, that is, that the bread remained bread even if infused with Christ's presence. A third proposition, maintained by the Calvinists, was that the bread and wine were entirely symbolic. There were numerous variations on these positions, but essentially what was at stake was whether any material thing could represent or contain (host) the living presence of God. We see traces of this dispute in the derisive reference Foxe makes to the pyx, which was the elaborate container used for keeping the Eucharist or host, and which occasionally was displayed by Catholics for veneration. The Renaissance pyx was often a very ornate, bejewelled object, which fueled Protestant charges of idolatry. They claimed that Catholics were worshipping the golden calf, which in the Old Testament, the children of Israel (the Jews) are specifically commanded to abjure.

While there was undoubtedly corruption in many religious houses, Foxe is far from being an unbiased reporter of the events he relates, and he never presents himself as such. Whereas for modern writers, asserting one's neutrality is how one asserts that what one has written is "true," for Foxe the unabashed assertion of his zealous Protestantism, defined by virulent anti-Catholicism, would assure his acceptance among English Protestants.

From *Acts and Monuments*

THE INGLING OF THE FRIARS ESPIED

The mayor's wife of the city of Orleans provided in her will to be buried without any pomp or solemnity. For when any departeth there, in some places the bellmen are hired to go about the city, and in places most frequented to assemble the people with the sound of the bell, & there to declare the names and the titles of those parties deceased, also where and when they were buried, exhorting the people to pray for them. And when the corpse is carried forth, the most part of the begging friars go withal to the church, with many torches and tapers carried before them, and the more pomp and solemnity is used, the more is the concourse of people. But this woman (as I said) would have none of all this gear done for her. Wherefore her husband which loved her well, followed her mind herein, and gave unto these greedy cormorants the friars, which waiting for their prey (in whose church she was buried besides her father and her grandfather) five crowns for a reward: whereas they gaped for a great deal more. And afterward when he cut down a wood and sold it, the friars craving to have part thereof freely and without money, he denied them, this took them wonderful grievously, and where as they loved him not before, they devised now a way to be revenged, saying that his wife was damned everlastingly.

The workers of the tragedy were Colyman, and Steven of Arras, both doctors of divinity: and the first in deed was a conjurer, and had all his trinkets and furniture concerning such matters, in a readiness, and they used the matter thus. They set a young man which was a novice above over the vault of the church, and when they came to mumble up their matins[1] at midnight after their accustomed manner, he made a wonderful noise and shrieking aloft. Then went this Colyman to crossing and conjuring, but the other above would not speak. Being charged to make a sign to declare if he were a dumb spirit, he rustled and made a noise again, and that was the sign and token.

When they had laid this foundation, they went to certain of the chiefest in all the city, and such as favored the most, and told them what a heavy case was chanced, yet did they not utter what it was, but entreated them to take the pains to come to their service at night. When they were come, and the service was begun, he that was aloft, made a great noise. Being demanded what he would, and what he was, he signified that he might not speak, then was he commanded to answer to their interrogatories by signs and tokens. Now, was there a hole made for the purpose, where by laying to his ear, he might hear and understand what the conjurer said unto them. There was also a table at hand, and when any question was asked, he struck and beat upon the table, so that he might be heard beneath. Then first the conjurer demanded to know whether he were any of them that had been buried there. After that, reckoning up many of their names in order, whose bodies had been buried there, at the last he named the mayor's wife. Here he made a sign that he was the spirit of that woman. Then he asked whether he were

---

[1] **matins**: morning prayers.

damned, and for what defect or offense? Whether it were for covetousness, pride, or lechery, or not doing the works or charities, or else for this new sprung up heresy and Lutheranism? Moreover, what was the cause that he made such a noise, and was so unquiet? Whether it was ere the body being buried within holy ground should be dug up again and carried to some other place? To all these things he answered by signs in like case as he was commanded: whereby he affirmed, or denied everything, striking twice or thrice upon the table.

When he hath thus signified that Luther's heresy was the cause of her damnation, and that her body must be taken up, the friars decried the citizens that were present, to bear witness of such things as they had seen and heard, and set their hands to it in writing. But they taking advisement least they should both offend the mayor and bring themselves in trouble, refused to subscribe. Notwithstanding, the friars took the pyx[2] with the host and the Lord's body[3] (as they call it) and all their saints' relics, and carried them to another place, and there said they masses: which they are wont[4] to do by the pope's law, when a church is suspended, and must be hallowed again, and when the bishop's official heard of this, he came together to understand the matter better, and associating to him certain honest men, he commanded the friars to conjure in his presence, and would have appointed certain to go up to the vault, to see if any spirit did there appear. But Steven of Arras was sore against it, and exhorted them earnestly that they should not so do, saying that the spirit ought not to be molested. And albeit the official did earnestly urge them to conjure before him, yet could they not bring them to it. In the mean time, the mayor making his friends privy[5] to what he would do, went to the king, and informed him of the whole matter. And because the friars trusting to their immunities and privileges, refused to come in judgment, the king chose certain out of the court of *Parlement* at Paris, to examine the matter, and gave them full authority to do. Whereupon they were carried to Paris, and constrained to make answer, but they would confess nothing. Then they were sent again to prison, and kept apart one from another, and the novice was kept in Fumeus house as a senator, and being oftentimes examined, he would confess nothing, fearing lest he should be after murdered of them for slandering their order. But when the judges promised him that he should have no harm: and should come no more to the friars hands, he declared to them the whole matter in order, and being brought before the others, he avouched the same. But they, albeit they were

---

[2] **pyx:** vessel in which the consecrated host is kept and occasionally displayed for veneration on the altar. [3] **the Lord's body:** alludes to the Catholic belief in transubstantiation, the literal presence of Jesus in the Eucharistic bread. [4] **wont:** enjoined. [5] **privy:** party.

convicted, and in manner taken with the deed, yet refused they their judges, and bragged of their privileges: but it was altogether in vain, for they were condemned in open judgement, that they should be carried again to Orleans, and committed to prison, and afterwards brought openly to the Cathedral Church, and so to the place of punishment where malefactors are executed, and there should make open confession of their wickedness.

But even at the same time chanced a persecution against the Lutherans, which was the cause that this sentence, albeit it was too gentle for so great offense, was not put in execution. For, because the name of the Lutherans was most odious, they feared lest the punishment of these men should not have been so much thought to be due for their offense, as done in reproach of the order: and many thought that whatsoever should be done to them, it would be to the Lutherans a pleasant spectacle, and cause them much to rejoice.

This order of the Franciscans was esteemed of the common people very holy: so that what time they were carried out of Paris, certain women moved with pity, followed them unto the gate of the university with many tears and sighs.

After they came to Orleans, and were bestowed in several prisons, they began to boast again of their liberties and privileges, and at length, after long imprisonment, they were discharged and set at liberty without any further punishments. Had not these persecutions before mentioned settled the matter, the King[6] had determined, as it was certainly reported, to pluck down their house, and make it even with the ground.

[6] the King: French King Francis I, ruled 1515–1547.

→ EDMUND SPENSER

From The Faerie Queene   1590

The rosary referred to in the excerpt that follows is the Catholic prayer comprised of one Pater Noster (the Our Father) and ten Hail Marys (the Ave), repeated five times with beads to aid as a counter. In Spenser's allegorical schema, any character who recites these prayers is an idolatrous papist and a villain. The evil arch-villain Archimago, whose name means someone who manipulates images, stands in Spenser's poem for the evils of idolatry and ritual that he ascribes to Catholicism. Like the pyx in Foxe, the rosary is presented as papist

Edmund Spenser, The Faerie Queene, Book 1, Canto 1 (London, 1596), 29–37.

paraphenalia that, far from enabling people to apprehend the divine, serves as a gaudy, fetishistic substitute for God.

The social ramifications of the shift in belief from Catholicism to Protestantism were many, but among them was the fact that on Paternoster Row in London, the narrow street immediately north of St. Paul's churchyard where rosaries were made and sold, trade stopped virtually overnight. Protestants tended to regard images as misleading illusions and distractions from God, whose presence was always, for them, unmediated by objects and persons. Because they sought a direct, personal connection with God, Protestants regarded all forms of mediation with the deity not just as erroneous, but as actively idolatrous, and often satanic. In the excerpt below, Archimago disguises himself as a holy friar hermit, but as soon as he has lured the Red Cross Knight into his snare, he uses magical spells to conjure up the devil from hell. In this instance, Spenser equates Catholicism, especially in its ascetic and monastic manifestations, with the occult and the terrible forces of darkness. In contrast to Archimago, Red Cross is the emblem of the good Protestant Christian whose purpose is to do battle with worldly temptation and protect the pure, one, true (i.e., Protestant) church, symbolized by the lady Una.

From *Book I*

Canto I

At length they chaunced to meet upon the way
    An aged Sire, in long blacke weedes yclad,[1]
    His feete all bare, his beard all hoarie[2] gray,
    And by his belt his booke he hanging had;
    Sober he seemde, and very sagely sad,   5
    And to the ground his eyes were lowly bent,
    Simple in shew, and voyde of malice bad,
    And all the way he prayed, as he went,
And often knockt his brest,[3] as one that did repent.

He faire the knight saluted, louting[4] low,   10
    Who faire him quited,[5] as that courteous was:
    And after asked him, if he did know
    Of straunge adventures, which abroad did pas.
    Ah my deare Son (quoth he) how should, alas,

---

[1] **blacke weedes yclad:** dressed in black.   [2] **hoarie:** grey or white with age.   [3] **knockt his brest:** put his right fist to his heart in gesture of penitence, or the *mea culpa*.   [4] **louting:** bowing.
[5] **faire him quited:** responded similarly.

Silly[6] old man, that lives in hidden cell, 15
Bidding his beades[7] all day for his trespas,[8]
Tidyngs of warre and worldly trouble tell?
With holy father sits not with such things to mell.[9]

But if of daunger which hereby doth dwell,
And homebred evil ye desire to heare, 20
Of a straunge man I can you tidings tell,
That wasteth all this countrey farre and neare.
Of such (said he) I chiefly do inquere,
And shall you well reward to shew the place,
In which that wicked wight[10] his dayes doth weare: 25
For to all knighthood it is foule disgrace,
That such a cursed creature lives so long a space.

Far hence (quoth he) in wastfull wildernesse
His dwelling is, by which no living wight
May ever passe, but thorough great distresse. 30
Now (sayd the Lady) draweth toward night,
And well I wote,[11] that of your later fight
Ye all forwearied be: for what so strong,
But wanting rest will also want of might?
The Sunne that measures heaven all day long, 35
At night doth baite[12] his steedes the *Ocean* waves emong.

Then with the Sunne take Sir, your timely rest,
And with new day new worke at once begin:
Untroubled night they say gives counsell best.
Right well Sir knight ye have advised bin, 40
(Quoth then that aged man;) the way to win
Is wisely to advise: now day is spent;
Therefore with me ye may take up your In
For this same night. The knight was well content:
So with that godly father to his home they went. 45

A little lowly Hermitage it was,
Downe in a dale, hard by a forests side,
Far from resort of people, that did pas
In travell to and froe: a little wyde
There was an holy Chappell edifyde, 50

---

[6] **Silly:** simple.   [7] **Bidding his beades:** saying his rosary.   [8] **trespas:** sins.   [9] **mell:** meddle.
[10] **wight:** person.   [11] **wote:** know.   [12] **baite:** abate, rest.

Wherein the Hermite dewly wont to say
His holy things each morne and eventyde:
Thereby a Cristall streame did gently play,
Which from a sacred fountaine welled forth alway.

Arrived there, the little house they fill,
   Ne looke for entertainement, where none was:
   Rest is their feast, and all things at their will;
   The noblest mind the best contentment has.
   With faire discourse the evening so they pas:
   For that old man of pleasing wordes had store,
   And well could file his tongue as smooth as glas;
   He told of Saintes and Popes, and evermore
He strowd[12] an *Ave-Mary* after and before.

The drouping Night thus creepeth on them fast,
   And the sad humour loading their eye liddes,
   As messenger of *Morpheus*[13] on them cast
   Sweet slombring deaw, the which to sleepe them biddes.
   Unto their lodgings then his guestes he riddes:
   Where when all drownd in deadly sleepe he findes,
   He to his study goes, and there amiddes
   His Magick bookes and artes of sundry kindes,
He seekes out mighty charmes, to trouble sleepy mindes.

Then choosing out few wordes most horrible,
   (Let none them read) thereof did verses frame,
   With which and other spelles like terrible,
   He bad awake black *Plutoes* griesly Dame,[14]
   And cursed heaven, and spake reprochfull shame
   Of the highest God, the Lord of life and light;
   A bold bad man, that dar'd to call by name
   Great *Gorgon*,[15] Prince of darknesse and dead night,
At which *Cocytus* quakes, and *Styx*[16] is put to flight.

55

60

65

70

75

80

---

[12] strowd: strewed, said. [13] *Morpheus:* deity of sleep. [14] *Plutoes* griesly **Dame:** Pluto's wife, Proserpina, queen of hell. [15] *Gorgon:* Demogorgon, the progenitor of all the gods. [16] *Cocy-tus . . . Styx:* rivers of hell.

CHAPTER 6

Death and the Stars

———————————————————————→✦←———————————————————————

Menace me with death   (5.3.133)

One of the remarkable facts about *Romeo and Juliet* is that it was written at approximately the same time as one of Shakespeare's greatest comedies, *A Midsummer Night's Dream*. This is extraordinary because comedy and tragedy seem to be diametrically opposite forces. But critics have pointed out that *Romeo and Juliet* not only contains comic characters like the Nurse and servants, but also bears a structural propensity toward comedy. The basic framework of the play, namely the young couple whose parents oppose their union, is the staple formula for a happy ending in which such obstacles are overcome. In part, what makes the play's tragic ending so poignant is that things could so easily have been otherwise; the structural debt to comedy heightens the sense of the futility in the death of the young lovers. On the other hand, the grim shadows of death loom like a veil over this play from the outset. Romeo's dark melancholy, his fatalistic sense that things will not turn out well, reiterates and gives depth to the chorus's fourteen-line summary of the tragic events to come. Yet, no matter how cosmically predestined or socially predetermined the deaths of these lovers might be, they both consciously choose suicide; in other words, they actively decide to be the mortal instruments of their own destiny.

In many ways, the complexities of Shakespeare's treatment of untimely death in this play reflect the period's own multi-layered response to mortality. While the grave was in one sense the final resting place, it was also a place of macabre animation, where matter was devoured and regurgitated in the endless natural cycles, which represented simultaneously the triumph of life and the annihilation of individual identity. The figure used to represent this paradox in the Renaissance was that of the *danse macabre* or *Totentanz* (the French and German terms, respectively for the dance of death) in which the skeletal figure of death gyrates to demonstrate its peculiar vitality, the irrepressible vigor of its wormed rottenness. The *danse* is an interesting parallel to the conventional Christian notions of death and resurrection, in which the soul transcends the mortal body in its progress to heaven, waiting until the end of the world and the Last Judgment for the resurrection of all bodies. Death, in other words, was not in the Renaissance a phenomenon of clean finality, of pure cessation. Rather it was a point of crossing over — from one side to the other, but also back and forth — between this world and the next. Death confounded rather than clarified natural boundaries.

Renaissance thinking about death, even in its most Christian formulation — the mystery of Christ's crucifixion and resurrection — was also very much imbued with pagan and especially classical ideas about death. Here death was allegorized as Thanatos or Mors, the twin brother of sleep. These religious and philosophical notions of death also combine with death as the crucial, crowning element of tragedy as a literary genre. *Romeo and Juliet* is of course one of Shakespeare's two great love tragedies (the other is *Antony and Cleopatra*), in which, instead of taking as its focus the fall of a single tragic protagonist, the play emphasizes the tragedy of lovers. In plays of this type, tragedy is not just about the demise of an individual but about the definitive conclusion and ultimate consummation of a sexual relationship (see Callaghan, *Woman and Gender* 9–33). While death conceived as an absolute negation of identity cannot be imaged or represented, its detritus — bones, decay, earth — serve as metonymic substitutions (signs that stand in for death). Similarly, since death cannot be directly described, it can only be approached in terms of similitude; that is, as what it is like — sleep, or orgasm. Indeed, the connection between death and its cultural shadows is made insistently throughout the period. For example, sexual intercourse was sometimes referred to as "the shaking of the sheets," a phrase that also meant the dance of death in the shaking of the winding sheet, or shroud, in which a corpse was wrapped before burial. The play too makes this connection between sex and death, spending a great deal of time with death in some of its most grotesque and macabre aspects, particularly in relation to Juliet's "double dying" (her ersatz death followed by her suicide) (see Berry,

The bones of the
ded ſhall appeer
aboue ÿ ſepulkers

FIGURE 20 *The bones of the dead shall appear above the sepulchers. This wood-cut borderpiece in the macabre style from Richard Day's* A Book of Christian Prayers *(1590) gruesomely illustrates the horrific mortality rates of early modern Europe.*

Feminine 21–43). We see Juliet awake alone to the horror of the Capulet monument where so many bodies, ancient and fresh, are interred, in what becomes the consummation of her fatal marriage, not to Romeo, but to death itself (Wymer 116–18), something she unwittingly predicted on first seeing Romeo: "If he be marrièd, / My grave is like to be my wedding bed" (1.5.131–32). The imagery of the last act of the play reinforces this point: "Alack, alack, what blood is this which stains / The stony entrance of this sepulcher" (5.3.140–41). As Coppélia Kahn observes, in act 5, "The blood-spattered entrance to the tomb that has been figured as a womb recalls both a defloration or initiation to sexuality and a birth. Juliet's wedding bed is her grave, as premonitions had warned her, and three young men, two of them her bridegrooms, all killed as a result of the feud, share it with her" (Kahn 101).

Michael Neill has argued that in the early modern period, death was increasingly secularized. Early moderns were, he argues, more concerned with what the deceased had achieved and represented in this world than with what might happen in the next. Neill writes "that the extraordinary burgeoning of tragic drama in late Elizabethan and Jacobean England was a crucial part of this secularizing process: tragedy . . . was among the principle instruments by which the culture of early modern England reinvented death" (Neill 3). This secularization of death may constitute a species of denial about mortality, domesticating the terrors of death by confining the concerns of the culture to the solidly material horizons of daily living. On the other hand, secularization may be a way of looking squarely at what remains at the end of life rather than gazing off into the hereafter.

Whatever the conceptual understanding of death, early moderns certainly had far more direct experience of it than we do. No trained personnel from hospitals and funeral parlors conveniently dispatched cadavers, and dead family members and plague victims made mortality an integral part of daily living. When Juliet's body is strewn with rosemary (4.5.79–80), early moderns would have registered simultaneously the herb's association with remembrance and the knowledge that its sharp odor offset the stench of putrefaction (see Cressy, *Birth* 454). Dying was a physical fact with real, material consequences, not simply a literary trope that might provide the convenient conclusion to a play.

The documents below contextualize early modern understanding of death, or rather the ways in which death and its approach and after-effects were dealt with by the living. The Church of England funeral rite, alongside the controversy over funeral monuments and ideas about poison, suicide, fate, and astrological predestination, serve to expand and elaborate what we usually understand to be, or perhaps *want* to be, the dramatic closure, or denouement, the narrowing of the text's issues as the play reaches its final moments, its own demise at the end of performance. In terms of these contexts, there is nothing resembling "finality" about the play. Rather, these cultural documents compel us to reconsider some of our critical certainties about dramatic tragedy.

Love and Death

→ JACQUES FERRAND

From Erotomania
1640

This is the English translation of a book printed in France in 1623 and written by a noted "doctor of physic," whose medical credentials lend authority to his pronouncements about love. Ferrand addresses love melancholy as a genuine psychological problem complete with observable symptoms. He was not unique in this approach. In England, Robert Burton's *Anatomy of Melancholy* (1620), a

---

Jacques Ferrand, *Erotomania or A Treatise Discoursing of the Essence, Causes, Symptoms, Prognostics, and Cure of Love or Erotic Melancholy* (Oxford, 1640), 82–93, 101–04, 106, 107, 110–20.

treatise devoted to the entire spectrum of mental maladies, quotes the final couplet of *Romeo and Juliet* as evidence that lovers:

> lose themselves, their wits, and make shipwreck of their fortunes all together: madness, to make away themselves and others, violent death . . . if this passion continue, it makes the blood hot, thick, and black, and if the inflammation get into the brain with continual meditation and waiting, it so dries it up that madness follows, or else they make away themselves.   (Burton 763–64; Dickey 269–83)

There was a pervasive sense in the culture that "immoderate" love was a disease. In the extract from Ferrand below, he emphasizes, just as literary discourse on the subject does, that lovers were "wounded" through the eyes upon the sight of the object who thereby becomes beloved. Also, Ferrand ends the chapter with the case of young men in the throes of passion. One youth is prevented from self-destruction only by the intervention of his parents, who, rather like Romeo's parents, express care and concern about his welfare. Another is nearly suicidal because he cannot marry the woman he loves — a maidservant. Ferrand does not say why, though it seems that the fact that the woman was of a lower class ("she was no fit match for him") was the hindrance to their union.

Chapter X. Whether Love-Melancholy Be an Hereditary Disease, or No.

Aristotle[1] is of opinion, that he that is not like his parents, is in some sort a monster. . . . For in such cases, nature seems to have come short of her end, and hath begun to degenerate; and that sometimes of necessity, as in the bringing forth of women, for the propagation of the species; and sometimes also through some defect of the matter; and lastly by reason of some external causes amongst which, the genethliacal[2] astrologers place the influence of the stars and . . . the change of the seasons, and nature of the climate. But the Arabian physicians attribute the greatest power in these matters to the imagination, and endeavor to prove their assertion by many forcible arguments, and also by particular instances, borrowed out of diverse other authentic authors.

   This similitude and resemblance that is required in children, consists in three things, that is, either in the *species*, sex, or accidents. The first of these depends on the specifical difference, & the formative faculty; the second on the complexion & temperature of the seed, the menstrual blood, and the

---

[1] *Aristotle:* there were two major prevailing theories of medicine in this period, one derived from the Greek philosopher Aristotle, and the other from Galen (see note 3 below).
[2] **genethliacal:** natal astrology, i.e., astrology based on the date and time of birth.

matrix (womb), according to *Galen:*[3] and the last bears a proportion to the difference of formative faculty, not specifical, as the first, but individual; which residing in the seed, and being restrained by the matter which hath the impression fixed on it, receives from it the Virtue to produce individuals, semblable properties,[4] qualities, and other accidents to the individual from which they spring. Now these corporal qualities which are derived from the parents to the children, are such only as are in the parts informed in such sort, as that they have already contracted a habitude. So that those properties and qualities that depend of the superior faculties, and which are more noble than the formative; as the sensitive, imaginative, and rational; cannot possibly be hereditary? Otherwise a learned physician should necessarily beget a son as learned in his faculty as himself, without any study at all. Neither yet are those diseases hereditary, which are not habitual, as fever, pleurisy, catarrhs,[5] and those intemperatures which are not confirmed: but those only are hereditary, that are habitual in the parents, and by continuance of time confirmed; whether they be in the whole body, or only in the principal parts of the same. And for this cause we may observe, that choleric men beget choleric children; and weak infirm men, beget the like children. Men of courage, and of strong bodies, beget stout and valiant children; & so those that have their generative parts of a hot and dry temperature, beget children of the same constitution, and consequently, as *Galen* says, inclined to lust. . . . Notwithstanding *Fernelius,*[6] in his first book . . . affirms, that children do not inherit those diseases only that are . . . in habit, but some other also: for that we often find children to be subject to agues,[7] pleurisy, catarrhs, and the like, because their mothers had the same diseases, when they travailed with[8] them.

So that hence we may conclude, that those children that are begotten of such parents as have been so besotted with love, as that they have at length become melancholy withal, are in danger of inheriting the same disease; unless peradventure the seed of one of the parents corrected this fault in the other: or else it be prevented by good education, and discipline. And it is also probable that those that are inclined to love, through the intemperature either of the whole body, or else of the principal parts; and not by the depravation of the imaginative faculties as the greatest part of lovers are, will beget children subject to the same disease.

---

[3] *Galen:* physician and philosopher (129–210 C.E.) who practiced in Rome after being a *therapeutes* or "attendant" of the healing god Asclepius in his home town of Pergamun. He synthesized the work of Hippocrates and the Greek medical tradition.   [4] **semblable properties:** resemblances.   [5] **catarrhs:** infections of the mucous membrane.   [6] *Fernelius:* Joannes Fernelius (1497–1558), physician.   [7] **agues:** chills and fever.   [8] **travailed with:** were pregnant with.

Chapter XI. The Different Kinds
of Love-Melancholy.

I shall not here reckon up all the several *loves, Cupids,* or *veneres,*[9] mentioned by authors. . . . But my purpose in this place is, to show you the different kinds of passionate love, or erotic melancholy, wherein sometimes the imagination only is depraved, and sometimes both the judgment and discourse, together with the imagination.

Galen, speaking of this disease, in diverse places of his works, sayeth, that the dotage[10] of melancholy persons differeth, according as the imagination is diversely affected . . . There are some so blinded with their unruly desires, that they can love *Hecuba* as well as *Helen, Thersites* as *Achilles.*[11] Others are so besotted with this passion, that they place their love on inanimate and senseless things: as those of whom *Ælian,* and *Philostratus*[12] make mention, who were so desperately enamored of a marble statue, that they died with the very grief they conceived, for that the Senate of *Athens* refused to sell them those idols, they so much adored. *Xerxes* is reported to have been enamored of a tree: *Alkidias* the Rhodian of a statue of *Cupid* of *Praxiteles'* workmanship: *Charicles* of the statue of *Venus: Narcissus* and *Eutelides* of their own pictures. Notwithstanding *Aristotle* in his Morals says, that that love which is born to inanimate things, cannot properly be called love, because a man cannot reciprocally be beloved by them again: and because one cannot define in them that good, wherein consists the essence of love.

And here omitting to speak of the filthy brutish loves of *Myrrha, Valeria, Tustulanaria, Canace, Aristonymus, Fulvius, Tellus, Pasiphae, Phaedra, Phyllis,*[13] and others, of whom as it is reported by *Plutarch, Ovid, Ælian,* and others, both poets and historians, some have basely lusted after their fathers; others, their mothers, and brothers; and some have doted even upon beasts: I shall only discover to you the several symptoms that distinguish Love-Melancholy into diverse kinds of *species.* For we may observe, that love is sometimes attended on by jealousy, and sometimes it is free from it: some love is furious, and sometimes again it is mild and temperate. In like manner doth the diversity of regions and climes much conduce to the distinguishing of the

---

[9] *veneres:* sexual love.   [10] the dotage: mental deterioration.   [11] they can love *Hecuba* as well as *Helen, Thersites* as *Achilles:* figures from the Trojan war, i.e., sometimes the libidinal impulse is such that it cares not what object gratifies it — the ancient Hecuba or the young and beautiful Helen.   [12] *Ælian,* and *Philostratus:* writers on natural history.   [13] *Myrrha . . . Phyllis:* reference to various forms of what the author regards as sexual depravity or excess. Myrrha, for example, the mother of Adonis, bore him as the result of an incestuous union with her father. Phyllis fell in love with one of the sons of Theseus and, despairing of his return to her, committed suicide, only to be turned into an almond tree. These myths were most famously recorded in *Metamorphoses* by the Roman poet Ovid, who died in about 18 C.E.

several kinds of love. And therefore it is observed, that the eastern people pursue their desires, without either moderation, or discretion; yet in a kind of base servile way. Those that inhabit the more southern parts, love with impatience, rage, and fury: those that inhabit the western countries are very industrious in their love: and the northern are very slowly moved or touched with love.

The wily Italian in courting his mistress, cunningly dissembles his love, and insinuates himself into her favor by pleasant discourses, sonnets, and verses, composed in her praise: and if he be so happy as to enjoy her, he is presently jealous of her, and like a prisoner, keeps her up under lock and key: but if he fail in his suit, he then begins to hate her, as much, as before he loved her; and will not stick to do her any mischief that lies in his power.

The eager and impatient Spaniard, being once enflamed with these desires, running headlong on in his love, & without intermission follows his suit; and with most pitiful lamentations complaining of the fire that consumes him, invocates and adores his mistress. But when at length by any the most unlawful means he hath compassed his desires; he either grows jealous of her, and so perhaps cuts her throat; or else basely prostitutes her for money: But if he cannot effect his purpose, he is then ready to run mad, or kill himself.

The effeminate Frenchman endeavors to win his mistress's affection by fair honest means, entertaining her with songs, and pleasant discourses. If he chance to be jealous of her, he tortures himself extremely, and weeps and laments his own unhappiness: But if she chance to put a trick upon him, and deceive him at last; he then begins to brave it, and casts his opprobrious and injurious terms upon her, and sometimes too falls to down-right violence. And if he have once compassed his desires, and enjoyed her, he presently neglects her and begins to look after a new one.

The German is of a disposition quite contrary to that of the Spaniard: for he comes on in his love by degrees, & takes fire by little and little: And when he is once inflamed, he proceeds with art and judgment, and endeavors to win his mistress' favor by gifts. If he be once jealous of her, he withdrew his liberality: if she deceiveth him, he makes little stir about it; and if he speeds in his faith his love grows as soon as cold again. . . .

In brief, the most certain differences of love, are taken from the variety of the complexion of those that are affected with this malady. If a sanguine man love one of the same complexion this love proves happy and full of delight. But if two choleric persons meet together, this is rather a slavery, than true love, it is so subject to outrages and anger, notwithstanding the nearness of their complexions. There is less danger in the love that happens betwixt a choleric person and a sanguine: for these will be sometimes in, and sometimes out. The love that falls out betwixt a melancholy and a sanguine person, may be happy enough, for here the sweetness of the sanguine disposition will easily correct the untowardliness of the melancholy. But if this latter chance to join with the choleric, it oft proves rather a plague, than love; and the end of it for the most part is despair. . . .

CHAPTER XIII. WHETHER OR NO A PHYSICIAN MAY BY HIS ART FIND OUT LOVE, WITHOUT CONFESSION OF THE PATIENT.

Galen, in that book of his, . . . boasts how that himself had found out the love of a fellow that was servant to a knight in Rome, that had purposely made his knees to swell, by rubbing them with the juice of *Thapsia,* that so he might not be able to wait on his master into the field, but might stay at home, and by this means have the fitter opportunity to enjoy his mistress. And in his book *de Pracog* he relates the manner, how he discovered the love of *Justus* his wife, who was enamored of one *Pylades:* and that, merely by feeling her pulse very hard, and observing withal her countenance, as he named him to her. . . .

Anacreon the poet makes great boasts of his own skill in this particular, in his last ode after this manner.

> By marks, our horses bear,
> We straight know whose they are.
> By his tiare,[14] a man
> May know the Parthian.[15]
> And so, at first sight, I
> An amorist descry.
> For in his breast's a sign,
> By which I can divine.

For as soon as ever *Cupid* hath kindled this fire within their hearts, they are constrained presently to lay open their breasts, and cry out for help. The heat of these flames oftentimes discovers itself in the cheeks, where it presents the beholder's eye with as many various colors, as the rainbow wears. . . .

> Who's he, that can hide fire? whose brighter rays,
> The more restrain'd, the more themselves betray.
> Nor can love be by any art suppressed,
> Where each blush tells the secrets of the breast.

---

[14] **tiare:** tiara, i.e., head-dress.   [15] **Parthian:** Parthia was an empire (247 B.C.E.–228 C.E.) west of the Euphrates (modern-day Iran); Parthians were horse warriors who presented a major challenge to the Roman Empire.

And for this cause *Diotimus* in *Plato's Conviv.*[16] says, that love inherits this from his mother *Penia,* to be always . . . naked, and without a covering. And for this cause the poets also always feign him to be naked, because, as *Erasmus*[17] in his *Adages* observes, love cannot be converted. For, not the eyes alone, but even the tongue also, and the cheeks themselves by their blushes will necessarily discover it. Yet notwithstanding all these manifest signs of love, together with their frequent sighings, continual complaints, importunate praises of their mistresses, and the like: the lover still believes his desires are so closely carried, as that the quickest apprehension cannot discover them: whereas indeed they lie open, and exposed to every eye. . . .

Chapter XIV. Signs Diagnostic of Love-Melancholy.

As this disease finds its first passage into the inward parts of the body through the eyes: so do they give the first assured and undoubted tokens of the same: For as soon as ever this malady hath seized on the patient, it causeth a certain kind of modest cast of the eye. . . .

But if the party be over far gone with this disease, the eyes begin then to grow hollow, and dry, (unless perhaps some unkindness, or denial from their mistress, or else her absence moisten them with a tear or two:) and you shall observe them to stand, as if they were either in some deep contemplation, or else were earnestly fixed in beholding something or other that much delighted them.

And if the lover's eyes be thus discomposed, and out of order; how much more think you is his heart? For you shall see him now very jocund and laughing; and presently within a moment he falls a weeping, and is extreme sad: then by and by again he entertains himself with some pleasant merry concepts, or other; and within a short space again is altogether as sad, pensive, and dejected as before. . . .

To this we may add their excessive talking, which proceeds from the fullness of their heart. For love, says *Plutarch,*[18] is naturally a great babbler, especially when it chanceth to light upon the commendation of those things that are its objects. For that lovers have a strong desire to induce all others to the belief of that whereof themselves are already persuaded: which is, that they love nothing but what is absolutely perfect, both for goodness, beauty and profit: and they would willingly have these opinions of theirs confirmed also

---

[16] *Plato's Conviv.:* Plato's *Symposium.*   [17] *Erasmus:* (c. 1469–1536) Dutch humanist, friend of Sir Thomas More.   [18] *Plutarch:* Mestrius Plutarchus, known as Plutarch (45–125 C.E.) from Chaeronea in Greece. He wrote *Plutarch's Lives,* biographies of famous Greeks and Romans.

by all other men's judgments. This is that which moved *Candaules*[19] to bring *Gyges* into his bed-chamber, and there to let him have a perfect view of the naked beauties of his wife. Unless you will rather say, that the reason that those that are in love, talk so much, is, to exercise their persuasive faculty, that so by this means they may render themselves the more worthy of their mistress's love. . . .

> Twas not *Ulysses*[20] form, but sweet discourse,
> That did, to seek his love, the sea-nymphs force. . . .

By the signs we have already set down, and by his languishing countenance did *Fonadab* discover that *Amnon,*[21] King *David's* son, was enamored of some princess, or great personage. For those that are in love . . . have always a kind of languishing countenance, and that too without any apparent cause. . . .

There is besides, no order or equality at all in these gestures, motions, or actions: and they are perpetually sighing, and complaining without cause. . . . In like manner did *Erasistratus* discover the love of *Antiochus,* to his step-mother: for so soon as ever she but entered into the chamber, his color changed, his speech was stopped, his looks were smiling, and pleasant, or else . . . steadfastly bent upon their object: his face burned, and he was all in a sweat, his pulse beat very disorderly, and lastly his heart failed him: he grew pale, amazed, astonished often: with other such like symptoms, which . . . are wont[22] to appear in melancholy lovers. . . .

Galen, Erasistratus, and all our modern physicians, add to these, the unequal and confused beating of the pulse: And *Galen* boasts, that by these signs joined together, he discovered the miserable doting of *Justus* his wife upon *Pylades.* I had found . . . that she had neither fever, nor any other corporal disease; so that I presently conjectured that she was in love. And when, because that at the naming of *Pylades,* her color changed, her pulse beat unequally and with diverse motions, . . . I concluded that she was in love with *Pylades.* . . . [T]here is a . . . question raised by our modern physicians, whether or no there is a certain distinct kind of pulse by which love is discovered . . . and the more learned sort of physicians, maintains the negative: and that, because that rational love is an affection of the brain, as likewise

---

[19] *Candaules:* from Herodutus' *Histories* (c. 440 B.C.E.). King Candaules made his servant, Gyges, watch his wife undress in order to prove that she was the most beautiful woman in the world. However, his wife saw Gyges, surmises what Candaules was doing, and the next day conspired with Gyges to murder her husband and take over the kingdom. [20] *Ulysses:* Ulysses (Odyseus) joined the Greeks in the siege of Troy. His return to Penelope, his wife, is the subject of Homer's *Odyssey* (c. 800 B.C.E.). [21] *Amnon:* reference to the life of King David (1085–1015 B.C.E.) recorded in 1 *Chronicles.* [22] **are wont:** tend.

irrational and dishonest love is of the liver; but neither of them of the heart, (as we have already demonstrated) which suffers no whit at all in love, but only by sympathy.

Yet I deny not, but that by the pulse it is possible to know a passionate lover, by reason of the stirring of the spirits: for which cause, *Avicen*[23] says, that if one would know the name of such a one's mistress, he must feel his pulse, and at the same instant name the party whom he suspects to be the cause of his malady, to take some occasion or other to commend her beauty, sweetness of behavior, parentage, attire, or qualities of mind: for at the same time . . . you shall perceive, sayeth he, a strange alteration in the motion of the pulse, and it will be very unequal, and oftentimes interrupted. . . .

Christophorus à Vega adds to these signs here set down, another, which in my opinion seems to be of little or no moment: and that is, that those that are in love, will not eat grapes; because that this kind of fruit filleth the stomach and belly with wind, and this institution oppressing the midriff, and hindering the motion of the heart, disturbeth respiration, and suffers them not to sigh at their pleasure.

By the greater part of these signs, when I first began to practice in this faculty at *Agen*, the place of my birth, in the year 1604. I discovered the foolish dotings of a young scholar of that city, who was desperately gone in love, and made his complaint unto me, that notwithstanding all the medicines that had been prescribed him by the physicians of that place . . . he could neither enjoy his sleep, nor take delight in any thing in the world; but was so full of discontent, that he was feign to retire from *Toulouse* to *Agen*, hoping by this change of air to find some mitigation of his grief: whereas, contrary to his expectation, he found himself in a far worse state than before. When I considered his relation, and withal saw him to be a young man, and affected with the griefs and discontents without any cause, whom but a little before I had known jovial and merry: and perceived withal his countenance to be grown pale, yellowish, and of a sad decayed color; his eyes hollow; and all the rest of body in reasonable good plight: I began to suspect it was some passion of the mind that thus tormented him: & then considering his age, and his complexion, which was sanguine, and his profession; I certainly concluded that his disease was love. And as I was urgent upon him to let me know the external cause of his malady, there comes by chance a handsome servant-maid of the house about some business or other into the room where we were, and was the means of discovering the true ground of his disease. For she coming in at the instant as I was feeling his pulse, I perceived it suddenly vary its motion, and beat very unequally; he presently grew pale,

[23] *Avicen:* Persian philosopher (908–1037 C.E.).

and blushed again in a moment, and could hardly speak. At the last seeing himself as it were taken tardy,[24] he plainly confessed the true cause of this his distemper; but withal refused to admit of any other cure but from her that had given him the wound: and therefore entreated me to desire the mother of the damsel to give her consent that he might marry her; presuming that his father, notwithstanding she was no fit match for him, would not deny him that contentment, on which his life and safety depended. . . . But this marriage could not be effected: the young man in the mean time grows worse and worse in a desperate manner, till at length a fever seizes on him, together with a violent spitting of blood. This amazes him; and seeing no other means of safety, he is at length persuaded to follow my directions: and so by such physic as I prescribe him, he was at length perfectly cured of his malady.

A like story to this may you read of a cure wrought upon a merchant of *Arles*, who had continued for the space of six months distracted with love: and had he not been prevented by the care of his parents, he had killed himself.

But what need we trouble our selves to seek so far for examples of this kind, seeing that there is hardly a disease more frequent in our eyes than this of love, if we are able but to distinguish betwixt it, and the other kinds of melancholy; a madness, and the suffocation of the matrix: with which diseases, this of love hath great affinity.

[24] **taken tardy**: discovered.

→ *From* An Act Concerning Physicians   *1540*
and

→ ROYAL COLLEGE OF PHYSICIANS OF LONDON

From Pharmacopoeia Londinensis   *1618*

> Such mortal drugs I have, but Mantua's law
> Is death to any he that utters them   (5.1.66–67)

Pharmacopoeia Londinensis (or the *London Pharmacopoeia*[1]) was first printed in Latin in May 1618 but then immediately superceded by a new edition in December. It was the first English attempt at the official regulation of medicines and their content. Apothecaries were to follow the *Pharmacopoeia* in compounding their *materia medica* (medicines). While continental pharmacopoeias were locally enforced, this London edition produced by the Royal College of Physicians (founded under Henry VIII in 1518 by the physician and clergyman Thomas Linacre) was to be the standard for the whole realm.

The College of Physicians was itself modeled after guild-like associations of physicians and apothecaries in Italy. Acts of Parliament in 1540 (see pp. 416–18) and 1553 authorized the Royal College of Physicians to examine the stocks of apothecaries, whose ranks included druggists, distillers, sellers of water and oils, and preparers of chemical medicines. These categories of persons were officially recognized practitioners of pharmaceutical practice. As George Urdang has pointed out, a belief that Providence had supplied each country with "the natural remedies necessary for combating diseases peculiar to that region" combined with a growing nationalistic ideology, led to the desire for state standards in the second half of the sixteenth century (Urdang 9).

The *Pharmacopoeia* was written not by an individual but compiled by the College of Physicians, or more accurately by a committee of "examiners" who were assigned the task of reforming the manufacture and dispensation of drugs,

---

[1] A pharmacopoeia is a book, written in Latin, containing a selected list of drugs, chemicals, and medicinal preparations with descriptions of them, tests for their identity, purity, and strength, and formulas for making the preparations, especially one issued by an official authority and recognized as a standard (*Webster's 3rd New International Dictionary*).

An Act Concerning Physicians (London, 1540) in *Statutes of the Realm*, vol. 3, 1509–1541 (London: House of Commons, 1819), 793.

Royal College of Physicians of London, *Pharmacopoeia Londinensis, A Brief of His Majesty's Royal Proclamation Commanding All Apothecaries of This Realm to Follow This Pharmacopoeia Lately Compiled by the College of Physicians of London* (London, 1618), reproduced in facsimile, with a historical introduction by George Urdang (Madison: State Historical Society of Wisconsin, 1944), 4–6.

FIGURE 21 *An Apothecary, from Ambroise Paré,* Works *(1634). The illustration here to the writings of the famous French physician Ambroise Paré shows an apothecary or doctor making a medicinal compound. It serves as a visual analog to Romeo's detailed description of the apothecary's shop with its "tortoise hung, / An alligator stuffed, and other skins . . . / Green earthen pots, bladder, and musty seeds" (5.1.42–46 ff.).*

or as they called it *"examen dispensatorii nostri,"* or "the examination of our dispensary" in 1589 (Urdang 12). The committee, working sporadically until 1618, included the immensely learned Thomas Moffett (1553–1604), who had studied in Basel and was also author of a treatise on silkworms, and Launcelot Browne, father-in-law of William Harvey who "discovered" the circulation of the blood. Another member of the committee called Thomas Frier or Fryer (d. 1623) had studied in Italy at Padua. Probably the most colorful (and certainly one of the most prominent) members of this committee was Sir William Paddy (1554–1634), physician to James I. Paddy is an interesting figure, not only because of his interest in new scientific and medical discourses, but also because he had an affair with the wife of one of the king's Scottish courtiers, who, when he discovered the affair, threatened to cut off Paddy's testicles:

> You have heard I am sure of a great danger Sir William Paddy lately escaped at Barn Elms, where the house was assaulted by Sir John Kennedy by night with a band of furious Scots, who besides their warlike weapons came furnished . . . with certain snippers and searing irons, purposing to have used him worse than a Jew, with much more ceremony than circumcision. Sir William having the alarm given him, fled like a valiant knight out at a back door, leaving his breeches behind him, and the lady by his sweet side went tripping over the plains in her smock with her petticoat in her hand till they recovered the next castle, and now he walks London streets with three or four men in defense of his dimissaries [testicles]. (Lee 113)

It is worth remembering that this committee was made up of flesh-and-blood individuals, many of whom were colorful and interesting characters.

On the more serious business of regulating the administration of drugs and poisons, the 1553 act sought "the better Reformation of divers enormities happening to the Commonwealth by the evil using and undue administration of Physic" (*Statutes of the Realm* 4:207). In 1617 the Society of Apothecaries of London was granted a royal charter, in yet another attempt to regulate the trade. In Italy, by the fifteenth century, poisoning had become an art commonly referred to as *Venemosa Italiana* (*venenum* is the Latin for poison) (see Grier). In *Romeo and Juliet* the apothecary of act 5, scene 1, is not the only one who deals in dangerous drugs; Friar Laurence does also. He is presented as a proficient herbalist whose knowledge, while potentially life-saving, is also associated with poison and necromancy.

The most famous case of poisoning in England of this period occurred some years after Shakespeare's play was written. Sir Thomas Overbury was the victim and the murderer was Lady Frances Howard who wanted to get rid of him in order to pave the way for her divorce from the earl of Essex and remarriage to James I's favorite, Robert Carr. Overbury's objections to such irregular proceedings appear to have led to the killing. At Howard's trial in 1615, it was alleged that astrologer-physician Simon Forman had supplied her with poison through an intermediary, Anne Turner, who was later hanged. Intimate letters from Howard to Forman were produced as evidence. These letters addressed him as "sweet Father," suggesting, perhaps, a relationship of pastoral care such as that Juliet has with the Friar (Salgado 102–03).

From *An Act Concerning Physicians*

In most humble wise shown unto your Majesty your true and faithful subjects and liege men[1] the president of the corporation of the commonality and fellowship of the science and faculty of physic in your city of London and the Commons and fellows of the same. That whereas diverse of them, many times having in cure as well some of the lords of your most honorable council and diverse times many of the nobility of this realm as many other of your faithful and liege people, cannot give their attendance to them and other their patients with such diligence as their duty were and is to do, by reason they be many times compelled as well within the city of London and suburbs of the same as in other towns and villages to keep watch and ward, and be chosen to the office of constable and other offices[2] unquieting and to the pill[3] of their patients by reason they cannot be conveniently attended. It may therefore please your most excellent Majesty with the assent of your Lords Spiritual and Temporal and the Commons in this present Parliament assembled and by the authority of the same, to enact, ordain, and establish that the president of the said commonality and fellowship for the time being, and the Commons and fellows of the same, and every fellow thereof that now be or at any time hereafter shall be, their successors and the successors of every of them, at all time and times after the making of this present act shall be discharged to keep any watch or ward in your said city of London or the suburbs of the same or any part thereof. And that they nor any of them shall be chosen constable or any other officer in the said city or suburbs: And that if at any time hereafter the said president for the time being or any of the said Commons or fellows for the time being by any ways or means be appointed or elected to any watch or ward, office of constable or any other office within the said city or suburbs . . . the same appointment or election to be utterly void and of none effect; any order custom or law to the contrary before this time used in the said city notwithstanding.

And that it may please your most Royal Majesty by the authority aforesaid that it may be further enacted, ordained, and established for the commonwealth and surety of your loving subjects of this your realm in and for the administration of medicines to such of your said subjects as shall have need of the same, that from henceforth the said president for the time being commons and fellows and their successors may yearly, at such time as they

---

[1] **liege men:** sworn vassals or faithful followers. [2] **by reason . . . other offices:** physicians can't always attend their patients because of pressing civic duties. [3] **the pill:** something unpleasant but unavoidable.

shall think most meet and convenient for the same, elect and choose four persons of the said commons and fellows of the best learned, wisest, and most discrete such as they shall think convenient and have experience in the said faculty of physic. And that the said four persons so elected and chosen, after a corporal oath to them ministered by the said president or his deputy, shall and may by virtue of this present act have full authority and power, as often as they shall think meet[4] and convenient, to enter into the house or houses of all and every apothecary now or any time hereafter using the mystery or craft of an apothecary within the said city only to search, view, and see such apothecary wares, drugs, and stuffs as the said apothecaries or any of them have or at any time hereafter shall have in their house or houses; And all such wares, drugs, and stuffs as the said four persons shall then find defective, corrupted, and not meet nor convenient to be ministered in any medicines for the health of men's body the same four persons, calling to them the warden of the said mystery of apothecaries within the said city for that time being or one of them, shall cause to be burnt or otherwise destroy the same as they shall think meet by their discretion: And if the said apothecaries or any of them at any time hereafter do obstinately or willingly refuse or deny the said four persons, yearly elected and chosen as is beforesaid, to enter into their said house or houses for the causes, intent, and purpose before rehearsed, that then they and every of them so offending contrary to this act for every time that he or they do so offend to forfeit an 100 shillings, the one half to your Majesty and the other half to him that will sue for the same by action of debt, bill, plaint or information in any of the king's courts wherein no wager of law, essoin,[5] or protection shall be allowed: And if the said four persons or any of them so elected and chosen as before is said, do refuse to be sworn, or after his said oath to him or them administered do obstinately refuse to make the said search and view ones in the year at such time as they shall think most convenient by their discretions, having no lawful impediment by sickness or otherwise to the contrary, that then for every such willful and obstinate default of every of the said four persons making default to forfeit 40 shillings.

And forasmuch as the science of the physic doth comprehend, include, and contain the knowledge of surgery as a special member and part of the same, therefore be it enacted that any of the said company or fellowship of physicians, being able, chosen, and admitted by the said president and fellowship of physicians, may from time to time as well within the city of London as elsewhere within this realm practice and exercise the said science of

---

[4] meet: appropriate. [5] essoin: excuse for non-appearance in court.

physic in all and every his members and parts, any act, statute, or provision made to the contrary notwithstanding.

From *Pharmacopoeia Londinensis*

Whereas by our special commandment there hath been of late compiled in the Latin tongue by the College of Physicians of London a book entitled *Pharmacopoeia Londinensis* etc. And whereas through the great care and industry of the said College, the foresaid *Pharmacopoeia Londinensis* now perfected, and is a work greatly tending to the public good of our subjects, and we minding that all falsehood, differences, varieties, and uncertainties in making or composing of medicines, and distilling of oils, or waters, hereafter be utterly taken away and abolished: And that in the time to come the manner and form prescribed by the said book should be generally and solely practiced by apothecaries in their compositions of medicines, and distillation of waters for all such things as are therein named and prescribed: We therefore desirous in all things, to provide for the common good of our subjects, and intending to settle and establish the general use of the said book in this realm of England do hereby signify and declare our royal will and pleasure to be, and hereby straightly require, charge, and command all and singular apothecaries, within this our realm of England or the dominions thereof, that they and every of them, immediately after the said *Pharmacopoeia Londin:* shall be printed and published; do not compound, or make any medicine, or medicinal receipt, or prescription; or distill any oil, or waters, or other extractions that are or shall be in the said *Pharmacop Londin:* mentioned and named after the ways and means prescribed or directed, by any other books or dispensatories whatsoever, but after the only manner and form that hereby is, or shall be directed, prescribed, and set down by the said book, and according to the weights and measures that are or shall be therein limited, and not otherwise etc. upon pain of our high displeasure, and to incur such penalties and punishment as may be inflicted upon offenders herein for their contempt or neglect of thou our royal commandment. Willing and commanding also hereby all mayors, sheriffs, justices of peace, constables etc. Given at our Palace of Whitehall 26th of April in the 16th year of our reign of England, France, and Ireland, and of Scotland the 51st. 1618.

The king's most Excellent Majesty hath not only commanded the publishing of this book, but hath farther been graciously pleased to grant full and sole privilege unto John Marriot of London, Stationer (and printer of this work), his executors, administrators, deputies, and assigns, for 21 years next ensuing, to imprint, or cause to be imprinted, and to sell, assign, and dispose of, to his and their best benefit and avail, this book, and books, as well in the Latin as English tongue, as also in any other language or tongue whatsoever: straightly prohibiting any other during the said time, to imprint or cause to be imprinted, to import, or utter, or sell, or cause to be imported from any parts beyond the seas, uttered, or sold, the said book or books, or any part thereof within any of His Majesty's realms and dominions (without the special license, and consent of the said John Marriot his executors, administrators, deputies, and assigns first had and obtained in that behalf) upon pain of His Majesty's high displeasure, and to forfeit five pounds of lawful English money for every such book or books, or any part, or parts thereof imprinted, imported, uttered, or sold contrary to the true meaning of this privilege, beside the forfeiture of every such book or books, etc. as more at large appeareth by His Majesty's letters patents dated the twentieth of March in the fifteenth year of His Majesty's reign of England, France, and Ireland and of Scotland the fiftieth. 1618.

→ NICHOLAS CULPEPER

From Pharmacopoeia Londinensis ####### *1654*

The following excerpt is from the sixth edition of the *Pharmacopoeia*, translated by Nicholas Culpeper (1616–1654). Like Simon Forman, he was a writer and practitioner of astrology and medicine. Culpeper warns against the self-destructive tendency to overdose with opiates, but recognizes that there is little he can do to prevent such behavior.

WATCHING

I desire the ignorant to be very cautious in taking Opiates; I confess it was the urgent importunity of friends moved me to set down the Doses; they may do wise men very much good, and therefore I consented: if people will be mad and do themselves mischief, I can but warn them of it, I can do no more.

Take juice of Henbane, Lettice, Plantane, Poppy, Mandrake leaves, Ivy and Mulberry leaves, Hemlock, Opium, Ivy berries in powder, of each a like

Nicholas Culpeper, trans., *Pharmacopoeia Londinensis: or the London Dispensatory Further adorned by the Studies and Collections of the Fellows, Now Living in the Said College* (1654), 63.

quantity, mix them well together, and then put a sponge into them, and let them drink them all up, dry the sponge in the Sun, and when you would have any body sleep lay the sponge at his nose, and he will quickly sleep, and when you would have him wake, dip another sponge in Vinegar and hold to his nose, and he will wake as soon.

→ RICHARD DAY

A Prayer to be Said at Our Going into Bed   *1581*

and

A Prayer When We Be Ready to Sleep   *1590*

In the play, we see Juliet in the everyday activity of going to bed, but on this occasion her sleep will literally mimic death. The connection between sleep and death was something of which the Elizabethans were acutely conscious, and before surrendering themselves to the arms of Morpheus, the classical deity of sleep, Elizabethans carefully squared themselves with God. Day (1552–c. 1607), who compiled and printed this work, was also a translator and clergyman.

A Prayer to Be Said at Our Going into Bed

When the day is ended, we give ourselves to rest in the night: so when this life is ended, we rest in death. Nothing resembleth our life more than the day, nor death more than sleep, nor the grave, more than the bed. Vouchsafe, therefore, O Lord our governor, & defender, both to shield us now living, unable to help our selves from the craftiness and assaults of our cruel enemy:[1] and also to call us then to thee, when we shall be yet more unable at the finishing of the race of this life,[2] not for our own deserts, but for thy own mercy sake: that we may live and walk with thee forever. And now let us so fall asleep in thee, as thou only, and those exceeding great, & incredible good things may in such wise be present always before us by the insight of our minds, as we may not be absent from thee, no not even in sleep: that such dreams may both keep our beds, and bodies, pure & undefiled, and also cheer our hearts with that blessed joy of thine. In truth whereof I will fall asleep and take my rest, through our Lord and Savior Jesus Christ, Amen.

[1] **our cruel enemy:** Satan.   [2] **the race of this life:** an allusion to St. Paul: "I have fought the good fight, I have run the race to the finish."

Richard Day, *A Book of Christian Prayers* (London, 1581, 1590), 9–10.

A Prayer When We Be Ready to Sleep

Take me into thy protection, O Lord Jesus Christ our defender: & grant that while my body sleepeth my soul may wake in thee, and cheerfully, and joyfully behold the happy and gladsome heavenly life, wherein thou art sovereign with thy father and the holy ghost: and the angels, and holy souls of men are most blessed fellow citizens for ever and ever, Amen.

Astrology

One area in which the complex interrelation between the lyrical and the social emphasized in this edition can be seen most vividly is in the play's references to the stars. Juliet is likened to the sun, a standard Petrarchan allusion, and one emphasized by her name (July is the month when the sun is at its zenith). These are all very conventional poetic tropes. Petrarch's Laura is "starry-eyed" as can be, and Sir Philip Sidney's sonnet sequence, *Astrophil and Stella*, is named for "Astrophil" ("star-lover") and "Stella" ("star"). The play's references to the stars also suggest the passage of time in the movement of the heavenly spheres from day to night and through the course of the seasons, about all of which there was new, scientific information available in this period. Ideas about astrologically predestined events were beginning to be contested by scientific empiricism. Shakespeare gives us a sense of the emotion between the lovers and the movement toward tragic catastrophe (the lovers are simultaneously starry-eyed and star-crossed), and at the same time he invokes skepticism about astrology and about notions of temporality that were residual, if not obsolete, by the late sixteenth century.

Among images of light in the heavens that suffuse the play, the most prominent allusions to the stars are perhaps when Romeo declares Juliet's eyes are "two of the fairest stars in all the heavens" and Juliet pleads that Night take Romeo when he dies and "cut him out in little stars." In contrast to these intensely lyrical moments, celestial light is invoked even in the apparently mundane and insignificant image of "carrying coals" at the play's opening (1.1.1), a fiery image associated with the heat of July (Berry, *Feminine* 41). The stars operate in one sense to foreshadow and even preordain the play's tragic conclusion: the "star-crossed lovers," "a consequence yet hanging in the stars," "the yoke of inauspicious stars." But they also work to place the events depicted at a specific moment in the calendar, and to foster the play's sense of causality and precise temporality. Philippa Berry has argued that the play's insistent specificity about time can be seen in that the "fateful date" of the lovers' first meeting is probably the eve of the day of July 16 (Berry, *Feminine* 33). July is the season of intense heat, popularly referred to as the "dog days," and is reflected in the play's fiery passions and explosive violence: "The day is hot, the Capels are abroad, / And if we meet we shall not scape a brawl, / For now, these hot days, is the mad blood stirring" (3.1.2–4) (see Fitter 154–83). Such associations were more than casual or traditional connections between weather and temperament, for the month of July was indeed a period of riots and social disturbance in England throughout the reigns of Elizabeth and James. We know that Shakespeare shared more than a passing interest in this phenomenon because he wrote *A Midsummer Night's Dream*, whose pivotal character is Bottom the weaver, onomastically (that is, by his name) located in the lowest reaches of the social order and associated with social turbulence. Heavenly fire, then, can work either as a twinkling aesthetic ornament of romantic ardor, or, like the "coals" that signal the heat of the fatal quarrel in the first scene, can signal the flaring of social unrest.

Because the sun travels through the sky in the course of a year, the stars have periods of visibility known as heliacal rising. In Britain, when Sirius,

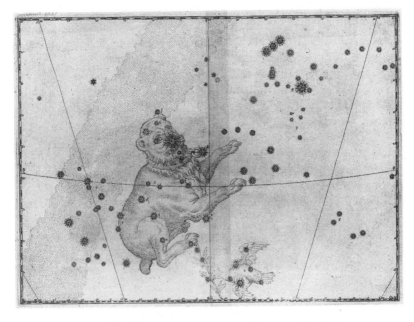

FIGURE 22 *Canis Major, from John Bayer,* Uranometria *(1603).*

the chief star of the constellation Canis Major, depicted as a dog, rises at dawn, the sun is in Leo:

> In this stellar calendar, the latter part of July and most of August was described as the "canicular" or dog days, since this was the time of the heliacal rising [the risings and settings of a star most nearly coincident with those of the sun while yet visible] near the sun of the brightest star in the sky, Sirius, chief star of the constellation Canis Major. (Berry 39)

Elizabethan almanacs, annual calendars of months and days, provided, among other things, the dates of the dog days of high summer, a time when it was widely believed dangerous to take any medicine (Capp 65). Thus, people in Shakespeare's audience would have likely recognized that it was not an auspicious time for Juliet to accept a sleeping potion and that it was probably not a period of good business for apothecaries, such as the impoverished one Romeo consults in Mantua. Further, the Dog Star's hot, noxious breath or vapors was insistently associated with pestilence, and thus with the plague that impedes Romeo's receipt of the Friar's letters (Eade 18).

Although there was enormous controversy about the efficacy and accuracy of astrological speculations and predictions, almost everyone of means had a nativity horoscope drawn up for them when they were born. Ellis Bomelius cast the nativity horoscope for Elizabeth I, even though some of his later predictions about trouble for the realm led authorities to imprison him, ostensibly for practicing physic without a license (Wright 361). Furthermore, since the divisions between scientific thinking and quasi-magical speculation (most obviously in the relation between astrology and astronomy) were not at all clear, astrological influences were a well-established element of medicine, and astro-physicians like Simon Forman enjoyed enormous success and popularity (though this might also be, in part, attributed to the fact that he bedded most of his female clientele) (see Traister). Yet, both astrology and medicine represent systematic attempts to explain natural phenomena according to rigorous scientific principles. Astrology involved a close alignment with mathematics. The famous Dutch humanist Desiderius Erasmus derisively linked mathematicians with astrologers in *The Praise of Folly* (1511) on the grounds that both were "figure casters":

> To this philosophical brotherhood belong all those who give out that they can foretell future events by observing the position of the stars. And they predict occurrences of the most prodigious proportions. Talk of marvels of magic! Why, they dwindle to insignificance when compared with the astounding wonders which astrologers declare to us are about to be. Yet — fortunate men — they find gullible people enough in the world to swallow their wildest announcements! (Quoted in Salgado 91)

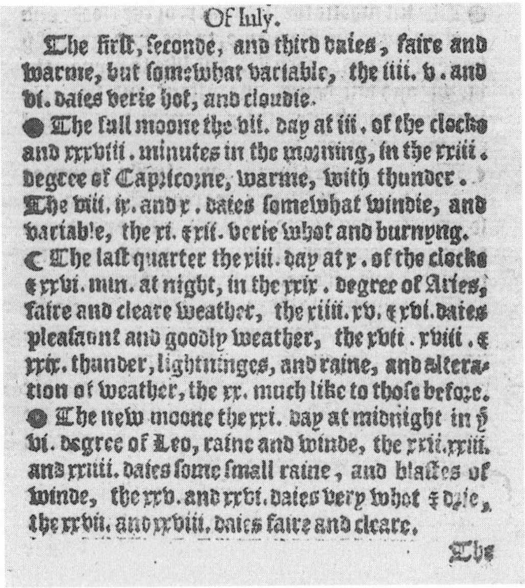

Of Iuly.

The first, seconde, and third daies, faire and warme, but somewhat variable, the iiii. v. and vi. daies verie hot, and cloudie.

● The full moone the vii. day at iii. of the clocke and xxviii. minutes in the morning, in the xiiii. degree of Capricorne, warme, with thunder. The viii. ix. and x. daies somewhat windie, and variable, the xi. xii. verie whot and burnyng.

☾ The last quarter the xiii. day at x. of the clocke & xxvi. min. at night, in the xix. degree of Aries, faire and cleare weather, the xiiii. xv. xvi. daies pleasaunt and goodly weather, the xvii. xviii. & xix. thunder, lightninges, and raine, and alteration of weather, the xx. much like to those before.

● The new moone the xxi. day at midnight in ⸿ vi. degree of Leo, raine and winde, the xxii. xxiii. and xxiiii. daies some small raine, and blastes of winde, the xxv. and xxvi. daies very whot & drie, the xxvii. and xxviii. daies faire and cleare.

The

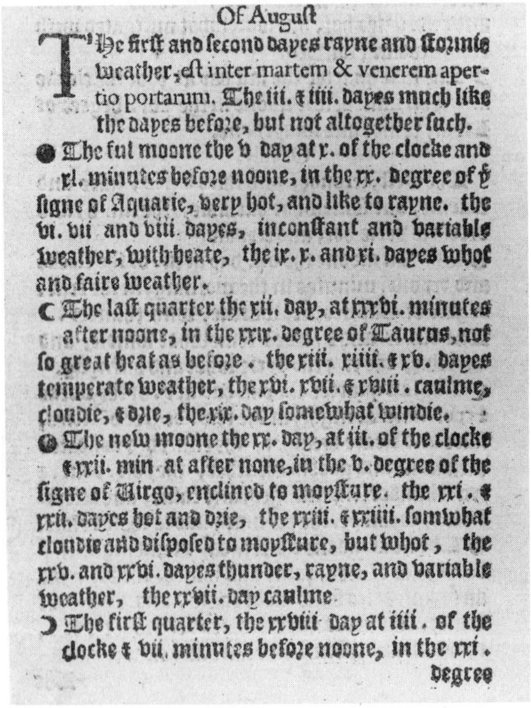

Of August

The first and second dayes rayne and stormie weather, est inter martem & venerem apertio portarum. The iii. & iiii. dayes much like the dayes before, but not altogether such.

● The full moone the v. day at x. of the clocke and xl. minutes before noone, in the xx. degree of ⸿ signe of Aquarie, very hot, and like to rayne. the vi. vii. and viii. dayes, inconstant and variable weather, with heate, the ix. x. and xi. dayes whot and faire weather.

☾ The last quarter the xii. day, at xxxvi. minutes after noone, in the xix. degree of Taurus, not so great heat as before. the xiii. xiiii. & xv. dayes temperate weather, the xvi. xvii. & xviii. caulme, cloudie, & drie, the xx. day somewhat windie.

● The new moone the xx. day, at iii. of the clocke & xxii. min. at after none, in the v. degree of the signe of Virgo, enclined to moysture. the xxi. & xxii. dayes hot and drie, the xxiii. & xxiiii. somwhat cloudie and disposed to moysture, but whot, the xxv. and xxvi. dayes thunder, rayne, and variable weather, the xxvii. day caulme.

☽ The first quarter, the xxviii. day at iiii. of the clocke & vii. minutes before noone, in the xxi. degree

FIGURE 23 *Prognostications, from Thomas Buckminster, A New Almanac (1571).*

¶ Iuly hath XXXI. dayes.

Ghe Sunne ryseth at three of the clocke liij. minutes.
Setteth at viij. of the clocke, and vij. minutes.

The length of the day is xvi.houres.xiiij.minutes.
The nyght is vij. houres. xlvj. minutes.

i		Octa Ioh. Bap	Scorp. 1.	7
ij	a	Visita. of Mary	Scor. 14	56
iij	b	Gregory confess.	pio. 29.	11
iiij	c	Cerincendeth	Sagi. 13	36
v	d	Ioe virgin.	tarius.28	29
vi	e	Octa. of Peter.	Cap. 13.	24
vij	f	Deposi.of Grim	corne.28.	26
viij	g	Dog days begin	Aqua.13.	23
ix	a	Cyrpl bishop	rius. 28.	10
x	b	Vit.brethr.mar.	Pisce.12	40
xi	c	Nabor & Felir.	Pisce.26	51
xij	d	Transl.of Bene.	Aries.10	39
xiij	e	Sunne in Leo.	Aries.24.	4
xiiij	f	Transl.of Swy.	Tau. 7.	6
xv	g	Transl. of Osm.	rus. 19.	42
xvi	a	Eustase virgin.	Gem. 2.	13
xvij	b	Kenelme kyng.	Gem. 14.	20
xviij	c	Arnulph byshop	Gem.26.	17
xix	d	Ruffine & Iustin	Can. 8.	10
xx	e	Margaret virg.	cer. 19.	36
xxi	f	Praxed virgin.	Leo 1.	12
xxij	g	Mary Magda.	Leo 13.	4
xxiij	a	Appolin virgin.	Leo 24.	49
xxiiij	b	Fast.	Virg. 6.	53
xxv	c	Iames apostle.	Virg. 18	57
xxvi	d	An Mr. moth.	Libra. 1.	4
xxvij	e	Seuen slepers.	Libra. 13	40
xxviij	f	Sampson bysh.	Libr. 26.	43
xxix	g	Martha virgin.	Scor.10.	4
xxx	a	Abdon & Senn.	pio. 23.	53
xxxi	b	German byshop	Sagit.8.	0

● The full mone the vij. day at three of the clock xxviij. minutes in the mornynge warme, with thunder.

☽ The laste quarter the xiij.day atk. of the clocke & xxvi. minutes at nyght, fayre & cleare weather.

● The new mone the xxi. day at mydnyght rayne.

☽ The first quarter the xxix.dai at viij.of ś clocke xrb. minutes at nyght some small mislynges.

B i

FIGURE 24 *Table for July, from Thomas Buckminster,* A New Almanac *(1571).*

¶ August hath XXXI. daye ﹅.

The Sunne ryſeth at iiij. of the clocke xxxvij. minutes,
Setteth at vij. of tye clocke, and xxiij. minutes,

The day is xiiii. houres, and xlvi. minutes.
The nyght is ix. houres, and xiiii. minutes.

i	c	Lammas day,	Sagit 22	27	
ij	d	Stephan byſſ,	Capzi 7	10	
iii	e	Inuent, of Ste,	cozne 22	5	
iiii	f	Iuſtine pzieſt,	Equa 7	12	● The full mone
b	ᵹ		rius 22	4	the b.day at x.
bi	a	Cräſſi. of chziſt.	Piſces 6	40	of the clocke and
vij	b	Feaſt of Ieſus,	Piſce 21	3	xl. minutes befoze
biii	c	Cyzneck & ſoch,	Aries 4	51	noone very hotte,
ix	d	Romane martir,	Aries 18	56	lyke to rayne.
x.	e	Laurence martir	Tau 2	17	
xi	f	Ciburt martir,	rus 15	24	☾ The laſt quar-
xii	ᵹ	Clarebirgin,	Taur 28	7	ter the xii. day
xiii	a	Hyppolite birgin	Gem 10	37	xxrbi . minutes
xiiii	b	Sun in Uirgo,	Gem 22	48	after noone , not
xb	c		Can 4	59	ſo great heate as
xbi	d	Roche martir,	ccr 16	56	befoze.
xbii	e	Octa, of Lauren	Canc. 28	30	
xbiii	f	Dog dayes ende,	Leo 10	21	● The new mone
xix	ᵹ	Magnus martir	Leo 22	16	the xx . daye at
xx.	a	Ledoute biſhop,	Uirgo 4	4	three of the clock
xxi	b	Barnard confeſ	Uirg. 16	10	and xxii.minutes
xxii	c	Athanaſ, martir	Uirg. 28	24	clined to moiſture
xxiii	d	Feſt	Libza 10	47	
xxiiii	e	Bartholo, apoſt.	Libza 23	27	
xxb	f	Lewes kyng,	Scoz 6	35	☽ The firſt quar-
xxbi	ᵹ	Seuerin biſhop,	pio 19	55	ter the xxbiii.
xxbii	a	auguſtin confeſſ	Sagit 3	40	day at foure of the
xxbiii	b	John beheaded,	tarius 17	45	clocke and ſeuen
xxix	c	Rufine martir,	Capzi 2	15	minutes in the
xxx	d	Felix & Audect,	cozne 16	50	moznyng lyke to
xxxi	e	Paultne biſhop.	Aqua 1	32	rayne.

FIGURE 25 *Table for August, from Thomas Buckminster,* A New
Almanac *(1571).*

Erasmus's skepticism about astrology, however, was by no means a position shared by all the intellectual elite.[1] Among the influential scholars of the Italian Renaissance, for example, Marsilio Ficino (1433–1499), one of the most important translators of Plato (from the Greek into Latin), was ambivalent about astrology in general but persisted in an interest in astrological medicine. His student Giovanni Pico della Mirandola (1463–1494), however, wrote a twelve-volume treatise refuting astrology, *Disputationes Adversus Astrologiam Divinatricem* (*Treatise against Astrological Divination*), at a moment when astrologers were immensely popular in the courts of Italian noblemen (Tester 207). In Shakespeare's England, humanist opinion about astrology was similarly divided. Francis Bacon (1561–1626),[2] who is recognized by posterity as one of the greatest names in the history of science, did not dismiss astrology. He writes in Book 3 of *The Advancement of Learning:* "As for Astrology, it is so full of superstition, that scarce anything can be discovered in it. Not withstanding, I would rather have it purified than altogether rejected. . . . [T]here is no fatal necessity in the stars but that they rather incline than compel" (quoted in Tester 220–21). The last assertion is especially relevant to *Romeo and Juliet* and to whether we see the tragic couple as victims of fate compelled by forces beyond their own making, or, if not entirely responsible for their tragic choices, as caught somewhere in between free will and astrological predetermination.

Because it pointed to the operations of the supernatural in human life, astrology was often linked with so-called papist superstition. However, all three forms of belief — Catholic piety with its saints and sacraments, Protestant asceticism, and astrological belief founded on observations about the constellation of the stars dating back to before recorded history — were current in England during Shakespeare's lifetime. When practiced by a magus and polymath like John Dee (1527–1609), who was an early supporter of the then highly suspect Copernican theory that the earth revolved around the sun, astrology could be an elevated enterprise involving staggering erudition. But it could also be practiced by ignorant and unscrupulous charlatans. Obviously, whether it was effective in either case remains open to question. For all that, someone like Dee was widely sought out by the well-educated elite. For example, the earl of Leicester asked John Dee to consult the stars in order to fix the time of Elizabeth's coronation (Salgado 92).

There were two main branches of astrology. The first was known as *natural* astrology and addressed itself to the influences of the planets on

---

[1] For more information about the debate about astrology, see Allen.

[2] Bacon was a statesman who served as solicitor general, attorney general, and later lord chancellor. He was also a philosopher and essayist who wrote extensively about scientific theory.

agriculture and medicine. The second, *judicial* astrology, was the attempt to interpret these influences in order to make predictions and give advice. As Bernard Capp points out: "General predictions for a city or country showed the likelihood of war, disease, or famine in the year or years ahead. The destiny of an individual could be predicted by drawing up the client's nativity, a calculation of the state of the heavens at his birth" (Capp 16). Within the

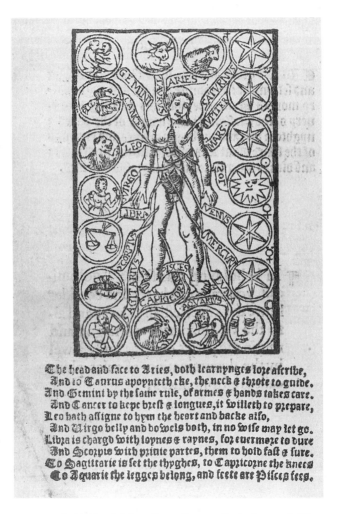

FIGURE 26 *Zodiacal Man, from Thomas Buckminster,* A New Almanac *(1571).*

branch of judicial astrology there were what was known as *elections*, that is the calculation of the most propitious moment for a given enterprise, and *horary* questions "when the astrologer resolved personal problems (medical, moral, and very often matrimonial) according to the state of the heavens when the question was posed" (Capp 16). There was a popular interest in astrology and its predictions and almanacs were widely available (even Bottom has one in *A Midsummer Night's Dream*), predicting harvests, diseases, and wars. These had a standard form with the first section containing a calendar of planetary motions and conjunctions, then a table showing legal terms, followed by what was known as the "Anatomy" or "zodiacal man" depicting the parts and organs of the body controlled by the various signs of the zodiac (Capp 30).

Funerals and Monuments

→ # The Order for the Burial of the Dead   *1559*

In the reign of Edward VI (Elizabeth I's half-brother who died in early adolescence) and under the leadership of Archbishop Cranmer, there was an effort to translate and abbreviate medieval Latin services. The *First Prayer Book of Edward VI* was published in 1548 and its use was enforced by the Act of Uniformity 1549. It was revised in 1552, repealed during the reign of Mary Tudor, and then revived as the *Elizabethan Book of Common Prayer* in 1559. Everyone in England would have been familiar with the funeral service contained in the *Prayer Book,* which in a sense represents the culture's negotiation between life and death.

The priest meeting the corpse at the church stile,[1] shall say: Or else the priests and clerks shall sing, and so go either unto the church, or towards the grave.

I am the resurrection and the life (saith the Lord): he that believeth in me, yea, though he were dead, yet shall he live. And whosoever liveth and believeth in me, shall not die for ever.

---

[1] **stile:** step over a wall or fence.

Book of Common Prayer (1559), from *Liturgical Services, Liturgies and Occasional Forms of Prayer Set forth in the Reign of Queen Elizabeth,* ed. William Keating Clay (Cambridge, 1847), 233–38.

I know that my Redeemer liveth, and that I shall rise out of the earth in the last day, and shall be covered again with my skin, and shall see God in my flesh: yea, and I myself shall behold him, not with other, but with these same eyes.

We brought nothing into this world, neither may we carry any thing out of this world. The Lord giveth, and the Lord taketh away. Even as it hath pleased the Lord, so cometh things to pass: blessed be the name of the Lord.

When they come at the grave, whiles the corpse is made ready to be laid into the earth, the priest shall say, or the priest and clerks shall sing.

Man that is born of a woman hath but a short time to live, and is full of misery: he cometh up, and is cut down like a flower; he flieth as it were a shadow, and never continueth in one stay. In the midst of life we be in death: of whom may we seek for succour, but of thee, O Lord, which for our sins justly are displeased? Yet, O Lord God most holy, O Lord most mighty, O holy and most merciful Saviour, deliver us not into the bitter pains of eternal death. Thou knowest, Lord, the secrets of our hearts, shut not up thy merciful eyes to our prayers: But spare us, Lord most holy, O God most mighty, O holy and merciful Saviour, thou most worthy judge eternal, suffer us not at our last hour for any pains of death to fall from thee.

Then while the earth shall be cast upon the body by some standing by, the priest shall say.

Forasmuch as it hath pleased almighty God of his great mercy to take unto himself the soul of our dear brother here departed: we therefore commit his body to the ground, earth to earth, ashes to ashes, dust to dust, in sure and certain hope of resurrection to eternal life, through our Lord Jesus Christ: who shall change our vile body that it may be like to his glorious body, according to the mighty working, whereby he is able to subdue all things to himself.

Then shall be said, or sung,

I heard a voice from heaven saying unto me: Write from henceforth blessed are the dead which die in the Lord. Even so saith the Spirit, that they rest from their labours.

Then shall follow this lesson, taken out of the xv Chapter to the Corinthians[2] the first Epistle.

Christ is risen from the dead, and become the first-fruits[3] of them that slept. For by a man came death, and by a man came the resurrection of the dead. For as by Adam all die, even so by Christ shall all be made alive: but every man in his own order. The first is Christ, then they that are Christ's at his coming. Then cometh the end, when he hath delivered up the kingdom to God the Father, when he hath put down all rule and all authority and power. For he must reign till he have put all his enemies under his feet. The last enemy that shall be destroyed, is death. For he hath put all things under his feet. But when he saith, all things are put under him, it is manifest that he is excepted, which did put all things under him. When all things are subdued unto him, then shall the Son also him self be subject unto him that put all things under him, that God may be all in all. Else what do they which are Baptized over the dead, if the dead rise not at all? Why are they then Baptized over them? yea, and why stand we alway then in jeopardy? By our rejoicing which I have in Christ Jesus our Lord, I die daily. That I have fought with beasts at Ephesus,[4] after the manner of men, what avantageth it me, if the dead rise not again? Let us eat and drink, for tomorrow we shall die. Be not ye deceived, evil words corrupt good manners. Awake truly out of sleep, and sin not. For some have not the knowledge of God. I speak this to your shame. But some man will say: How arise the dead? with what body shall they come? Thou fool, that which thou sowest is not quickened except it die. And what sowest thou? thou sowest not that body that shall be, but bare corn, as of wheat or some other: but God giveth it a body at his pleasure, to every seed his own body. All flesh is not one manner of flesh: but there is one manner of flesh of men, and other manner of flesh of beasts, and other of fishes, another of birds. There are also celestial bodies, and there are bodies terrestrial. But the glory of the celestial is one, and the glory of the terrestrial is another. There is one manner glory of the Sun, and another glory of the Moon, and another glory of the stars. For one star differeth from another in glory. So is the resurrection of the dead. It is sown in corruption, it riseth again in incorruption. It is sown in dishonour, it riseth again in honour. It is sown in weakness, it riseth again in power. It is sown a natural body, it riseth again a spiritual body. There is a natural body, and there is a spiritual body, as it is also written: the first man Adam was made a

---

[2] **Chapter to the Corinthians:** St. Paul's letters to the Corinthians.   [3] **first-fruits:** offspring or results. In other words, Christ is the life bearer whereas Adam was the death bringer.   [4] **fought . . . Ephesus:** St. Paul refers to the dangers he has encountered on his travels.

living soul, and the last Adam was made a quickening spirit. Howbeit, that is not first which is spiritual, but what which is natural, and then that which is spiritual. The first man is of the earth, earthy. The second man is the Lord from heaven, heavenly. As is the earthy, such are they that be earthy. And as is the heavenly, such are they that are heavenly. And as we have borne the image of the earthy, so shall we bear the image of the heavenly. This say I, brethren, that flesh and blood cannot inherit the kingdom of God, neither doth corruption inherit uncorruption. Behold, I shew you a mystery. We shall not all sleep: but we shall all be changed, and that in a moment, in the twinkling of an eye by the last trump. For the trump shall blow, and the dead shall rise incorruptible, and we shall be changed. For this corruptible must put on incorruption, and this mortal must put on immortality. When this corruptible hath put on incorruption, and this mortal hath put on immortality: then shall be brought to pass the saying that is written, Death is swallowed up in victory. Death, where is thy sting? Hell, where is thy victory? The sting of death is sin, and the strength of sin is the law. But thanks be unto God, which hath given us victory, through our Lord Jesus Christ. Therefore, my dear brethren, be ye steadfast and unmovable, always rich in the work of the Lord, forasmuch as ye know how that your labour is not in vain in the Lord.

The Lesson ended, the Priest shall say,

Lord, have mercy upon us.
Christ, have mercy upon us.
Lord, have mercy upon us.
Our Father which art in heaven. &c.
And lead us not into temptation.
ANSWER. But deliver us from evil. Amen.

The Priest.

Almighty God, with whom do live the spirits of them that depart hence in the Lord, and in whom the souls of them that be elected, after they be delivered from the burden of the flesh, be in joy and felicity: We give thee hearty thanks, for that it hath pleased thee to deliver this N our brother, out of the miseries of this sinful world: beseeching thee, that it may please thee of thy gracious goodness, shortly to accomplish the number of thine elect, and to haste thy kingdom, that we with this our brother, and all other departed in

FIGURE 27 *Everyone living shall die presently, from Richard Day,* A Book of Christian Prayers *(1590). The hope, of course, was to be resurrected on the "last day" to celebrate eternal life with the heavenly host. See longer discussion on pp. 400 and 442.*

the true faith of thy holy name, may have our perfect consummation and bliss, both in body and soul, in thy eternal and everlasting glory. Amen.

The Collect.

O merciful God, the Father of our Lord Jesus Christ, who is the resurrection and the life, in whom whosoever believeth shall live, though he die, and whosoever liveth, and believeth in him, shall not die eternally: who also taught us (by his holy apostle Paul) not to be sorry, as men without hope, for them that sleep in him: We meekly beseech thee (O Father) to raise us from the death of sin unto the life of righteousness, that, when we shall depart this life, we may rest in him, as our hope is this our brother doth: and that at the general resurrection in the last day, we may be found acceptable in thy sight, and receive that blessing which thy wellbeloved Son shall then pronounce to all that love and fear thee, saying, "Come ye blessed children of my Father, receive the kingdom prepared for you from the beginning of the world." Grant this, we beseech thee, O merciful Father, through Jesus Christ, our mediator and redeemer. Amen.

Statue in pure gold   (5.3.299)

> There never was the like number of beautiful and costly monuments
> erected in sundry churches in honorable memory of the dead.
>   —Francis Bacon, *Observations on a Libel,* 1592.

In pre-Reformation Catholicism, it was crucial to observe the memory
of the dead whose soul was thought to be in purgatory, that limbo state
between hell and heaven, where it must be purged before it could pass on to
celestial bliss. For this purpose, chantry chapels were erected throughout
the middle ages so that priests could say and sing masses for the souls of the
departed. The Reformation brought such practices to an end, and where the
chantries survived, they became family mortuaries. The Capulet monument
is the

> [A]ncient receptacle,
> Where for this many hundred years the bones
> Of all my buried ancestors are packed;   (4.3.39–41)

Old Capulet's description of the vault as "packed" creates a disturbing image
of overcrowding in the place of annihilation. Further, the description suggests a more conventionally Catholic burial place than that indicated by the
plan for the golden statues Capulet and Montague promise at the end of the
play to erect for their dead children. The latter smacks of a style of conspic-
uous consumption more associated with gentry Protestantism. The statues
in one sense reflect the new, bourgeois desire to defy death, which Juliet
describes as "the terror of the place," with a show of material wealth. As
Michael Neill points out:

> The passive memorialization of inscriptions recording the virtue and
> piety of the deceased replaced the active rites of intercession. Unlike ear-
> lier tombs . . . the great memorials of this period were almost entirely ret-
> rospective in their appeals, wholly bent upon the world, they were
> conspicuously secular substitutes for the liturgical *memento* of the Mass.
> The more splendid their marble sculpture, the richer their gilding and
> painting, the more superb their heraldic ornamentation, the more elo-
> quently these shrines of memory spoke of the longing for a species of
> immortality which, in spite of everything, it might remain in the power of
> the living to confer.   (Neill 40–41)

In other words, monuments seem oddly and mistakenly defiant in the face
of death; what lasted "forever" was a marble or gilt monument. Golden statues also potentially connote the idolatry that Protestants were so concerned
about, especially the golden calf of the Old Testament, which the Jews were

told to destroy and worship instead the living God who can be neither seen nor represented as an image.

In a startling way, too, the golden statues as a memorial to the dead lovers mark a point where literature departs rather abruptly from life. For Romeo and Juliet were suicides in a society where suicide was regarded as a felony in criminal law — as "self-murder," and as a violation of Christian principles. Surprisingly, in relation to the total population, far greater numbers of adolescents and young people committed suicide than do so today, and they did so in large measure because of the severity of parents (MacDonald 225). Michael MacDonald describes the treatment of suicides as follows:

> Suicides were tried posthumously by a coroner's jury, and if they were convicted as self-murderers, they and their heirs were savagely punished. Their moveable goods, including tools, household items, money, debts owed to them, and even leases on the land that they had warded were forfeited to the crown or to the holder of a royal patent who possessed the right to such windfalls in a particular place. Self-murderers were denied Christian burials; their bodies were interred profanely, with a macabre ceremony prescribed by popular wisdom. The night following the inquest, officials of the parish, the church wardens and their helpers, carried the corpse to the crossroads and threw it naked into a pit. A wooden stake was hammered through the body, pinioning it in the grave, and the hole was filled in. No prayers for the dead were repeated; the minister did not attend. These rituals were occasionally modified or suspended, but some form of profane burial was routinely ordered in cases of self-murder.
>
> (MacDonald 15)

Perhaps this is why love only uneasily transcends death at the end of the play with the forced rhyme of that famously pedestrian concluding couplet: "Never was a story of more woe / Than this of Juliet and her Romeo" (5.3.309–10).

There are certain other aspects of the ending that make the play's closure potentially uneasy. When Capulet and Montague join hands at the end and agree to build the monument, are they finally cooperating or are they still trying to best one another? It is possible that their feudal antagonisms have now been displaced into a realm more appropriate for bourgeois mercantalism: "But I can give thee more, / For I will raise her statue in pure gold" (5.3.298–99). Romeo's condemnation of gold two scenes earlier in his exchange with the apothecary may also trouble the harmony of the ostensible truce at the play's closing:

> There is thy gold — worse poison to men's souls,
> Doing more murder in this loathsome world
> Than these poor compounds that thou mayst not sell.
> I sell thee poison; thou hast sold me none.   (5.1.80–83).

Of course, Romeo may be, in part, simply exculpating the apothecary for any responsibility about his intended suicide, but the argument that gold is evil, though it is certainly conventional, exceeds this moral purpose. "Gold" in the sense of money and "gold" ornaments or idols were often understood as distinct phenomena. However, they were frequently related nonetheless in the period's discourse of iconoclasm (as they are in John Jewel's homily, p. 439) under the more general rubric of "riches" via the biblical injunction that "Ye cannot serve God and mammon" (Matthew 6:24).

→ QUEEN ELIZABETH I

Proclamation Prohibiting Destruction of Church Monuments
1560

In the following proclamation, authorities confront the fact that the clergy's diatribes against idolatry have inspired the zealous members of their congregations to desecrate church monuments. In other words, this text marks a huge contradiction in Protestant teaching on the status of icons, images, and monuments, because the clergy want to condemn Catholic icons but to leave their own undisturbed.

The text below indicates both the prevalence of anti-iconoclasm in the period and the destruction of images as a popular and apparently widespread practice. Protestant orthodoxy, although it was vehement in its condemnation of the evils of idolatry and of the elaborate ornamentation of churches, did not extend to allowing the destruction of tombs and ornaments without the proper authority. At worst, this proclamation, which is a response to the arbitrary desecration of monuments, shows the establishment hoisted with its own petard when confronted with the contradictions of its own rhetoric. Alternatively, we might argue that church and state authorities simply fell victim to religious extremism, a sort of early modern fundamentalism.

Proclamation 469, "Prohibiting Destruction of Church Monuments" (September 19, 1560), in *Tudor Royal Proclamations, Vol. 2*, ed. James F. Larkin and Paul L. Hughes (New Haven: Yale UP), 146–48.

The Queen's majesty, understanding that by the means of sundry people, partly ignorant, partly malicious, or covetous, there hath been of late years spoiled and broken certain ancient monuments,[1] some of metal, some of stone, which were erected up as well in churches as in other public places within this realm only to show a memory to the posterity of the persons there buried, or that had been benefactors to the buildings or donations of the same churches or public places, and not to nourish any kind of superstition;

By which means not only the churches and places remain at this present day spoiled, broken, and ruinated, to the offense of all noble and gentle hearts and the extinguishing of the honorable and good memory of sundry virtuous and noble persons deceased; but also the true understanding of divers[2] families in this realm (who have descended of the blood of the same persons deceased) is thereby so darkened as the true course of their inheritance may be hereafter interrupted contrary to justice, besides many other offenses that hereof do ensue to the slander of such as either gave or had charge in times past only to deface monuments of idolatry and false feigned images in churches and abbeys; and therefore, although it be very hard to recover things broken and spoiled, yet both to provide that no such barbarous disorder be hereafter used, and to repair as much of the said monuments as conveniently may be:

Her Majesty chargeth and commandeth all manner of persons hereafter to forbear the breaking or defacing of any parcel of any monument, or tomb, or grave, or other inscription and memory of any person deceased being in any manner of place, or to break any image of kings, princes, or noble estates of this realm, or of any other that have been in times past erected and set up for the only memory of them to their posterity in common churches and not for any religious honor, or to break down or deface any image in glass windows in any church without consent of the ordinary.

Upon pain that whosoever shall herein be found to offend to be committed to the next jail, and there to remain without bail or mainprize[3] unto the next coming of the justices for the delivery of the said jail, and then to be further punished by fine or imprisonment (besides the restitution or re-edification of the thing broken) as to the said justices shall seem meet, using

---

[1] [marginal note]: Heylin's description of the defacing of images and windows in churches, breaking down of coats of arms, tearing off brasses from tombs and monuments, and taking away of bells and roof-lead is reprinted in Dodd 2:148.   [2] divers: several.   [3] mainprize: bond.

therein the advice of the ordinary and (if need shall be) the advice also of Her Majesty's council in her Star Chamber.[4]

And for such as be already spoiled in any church or chapel now standing, her majesty chargeth and commandeth all archbishops, bishops, and other ordinaries,[5] or ecclesiastical persons which have authority to visit the same churches or chapels, to inquire by presentments of the curates, church-wardens, and certain of the parishioners what manner of spoils have been made, sithen[6] the beginning of Her Majesty's reign, of such monuments, and by whom, and if the persons be living how able they be to repair and re-edify the same; and thereupon to convent the same persons, and to enjoin them under pain of excommunication, to repair the same by a convenient day; or otherwise, as the cause shall further require, to notify the same to Her Majesty's council in the Star Chamber at Westminster; and if any such shall be found and convicted thereof not able to repair the same, that then they be enjoined to do open penance two or three times in the church as to the quality of the crime and party belongeth, under like pain of excommunication.

And if the party that offended be dead, and the executors of the will left having sufficient in their hands unadministered, and the offense notorious, the ordinary of the place shall also enjoin them to repair or re-edify the same, upon like or any other convenient pain to be devised by the said ordinary. And when the offender cannot be presented, if it be in any cathedral or collegiate church which hath any revenue belonging to it that is not particularly allotted to the sustentation of any person, certain or otherwise, but that it may remain in discretion of the governor thereof to bestow the same upon any other charitable deed, as mending of highways or such like: her majesty enjoineth and straightly chargeth the governors and companies of every such church to employ such parcels of the said sums of money (as any wise may be spared) upon the speedy repair or re-edification of any such monuments so defaced or spoiled, as agreeable to the original as the same conveniently may be.

And where the covetousness of certain persons is such that (as patrons of churches, or owners of the parsonages impropriated, or by some other color or pretense) they do persuade with the parson and parishioners to take or throw down the bells of churches and chapels and the lead of the same, converting the same to their private gain and to the spoils of the said places, and

---

[4] **Star Chamber:** court so named for the star pattern on the ceiling; one of the most important courts of the period. For the Crown, it had the advantage that judges were members of the privy council and no jury was present. Thus, it was one of the favorite courts of the monarchs and one of the most unpopular among the people.   [5] **ordinaries:** clerics with ordinary jurisdiction over a specified territory.   [6] **sithen:** since.

make such like alterations as thereby they seek a slanderous desolation of the places of prayer:

Her Majesty (to whom in the right of the crown by the ordinance of Almighty God and by the laws of this realm the defense and protection of the church of this realm belongeth) doth expressly forbid any manner of person to take away any bells or lead of any church or chapel now used, or that ought to be used, with public and divine service, or otherwise deface any such church or chapel; under pain of imprisonment during Her Majesty's pleasure, and such further fine for the contempt as shall be thought meet.

And Her Majesty chargeth all bishops and ordinaries to inquire of all such contempts done from the beginning of Her Majesty's reign, and to enjoin the persons offending to repair the same within a convenient time, and of their doings in this behalf to certify Her Majesty's Privy Council,[7] or the council in the Star Chamber at Westminster, that order may be taken herein.

[7] **Privy Council:** the Crown's chief advisory council.

→ JOHN JEWEL

From An Homily Against Apparel of Idolatry and Superfluous Decking of Churches *1563*

John Jewel (1522–1571) was bishop of Salisbury and a fellow of Corpus Christi College, Oxford. He fled England for Frankfurt and Zurich during Mary's reign, returning in 1559 after she had died. Although from reading what follows we might expect him to be an out-and-out Puritan, Jewel was not someone of the most radical Protestant stripe, in fact. He had a great deal of influence on the moderate Richard Hooker.

. . . [T]he church, or house of God, is a place appointed by the holy Scriptures, where the lively word of God ought to be read, taught, and heard, the Lord's holy name called upon by public prayer, hearty thanks given to His Majesty, for his infinite and unspeakable benefits bestowed upon us, his holy sacraments duly and reverently ministered, and that therefore all that be

John Jewel, From *The Second Tome of Homilies, of such matters as were promised and Entitled in the former part of Homilies, set out by the authority of the Queen's Majesty: and to be read in every parish church agreeable* (London, 1563), Dd.iii-Z z ii verso.

godly in deed, ought both with diligence at times appointed, to repair together to the said church, and there with all reverence, to use and behave themselves before the Lord. And that the said church thus godly used by the servants of the Lord, in the Lord's true service, for the effectuous presence of God's grace, wherewith he doth by his holy word and promises, endue his people there present and assembled, to the attainment as well of commodities worldly, necessary for us, as also of all heavenly gifts, and life everlasting, is called by the word of God (as it is in deed) the temple of the Lord, and the house of God. And that therefore the due reverence thereof, is stirred up in the hearts of the godly, by the consideration of these true ornaments of the said house of God, and not by any outward ceremonies, or costly and glorious decking of the said house, or temple of the Lord, contrary to which, most manifest doctrine of the Scriptures, and contrary to the usage of the primitive church, which was most pure and uncorrupt, and contrary to the sentences and judgments of the most ancient, learned and godly doctors of the church (as hereafter shall appear) the corruption of these latter days, hath brought into the church, infinite multitudes of images, and the same, with other parts of the temple also, have decked with gold and silver, painted with colors, set them with stone and pearl, clothed them with the silks and precious vestures,[1] fantasizing untruly, that to be the chief decking and adorning of the temple or house of God, and that all people should be the more moved to the due reverence of the same, if all corners thereof were glorious, and glittering with gold and precious stones: where in deed they, by the said images and such glorious decking of the temple, have nothing at all profited such as were wise, and of understanding: but have thereby greatly hurt the simple and unwise, occasioning them thereby to commit most horrible idolatry. And the covetous persons by the same occasion, seeming to worship, and peradventure[2] worshipping in deed, not only the images: but also the matter of them, golden and silver: as that vice is of all others in the Scriptures peculiarly called idolatry or worshipping images. Against the which foul abuses and great enormities,[3] shall be alleged unto you. . . .

But to go to God's word, be not, I pray you, the words of the Scripture plain? Beware lest thou being deceived, make to thy self (to say, to any use of religion) any graven image or any similitude of any thing, etc. And cursed be the man that maketh a graven or molten image, abomination before the Lord etc. Be not our images such? Be not our images of Christ and his saints, either carved, or molten and caste, or similitudes of men and women? . . .

---

[1] **vestures:** coverings. [2] **peradventure:** perhaps. [3] **enormities:** moral outrages.

And it is written in the book of Numbers the xxiii Chapter, that there was no idol in Jacob, nor there was no image seen in Israel, and that the Lord God was with that people, where note, that the true Israelites, that is, the people of God, have no images among them, but that God was with them, and that therefore their enemies can not hurt them, as appeareth in the process of that Chapter. And as concerning images already set up, thus sayeth the Lord in Deuteronomy: Overturn their altars and break them to pieces, cut down their groves, burn their images, for thou art an holy people unto the Lord. And the same is repeated more vehemently again in the xii chapter of the same book. Here note what the people of God ought to do to images where they find them. But lest any private persons upon color of destroying of images, should make any stir or disturbance in the common wealth, it must always be remembered that the redress of such public enormities appertaineth to the magistrates, and such as be in authority only, and not to private persons: and therefore the good kings of Judah . . . are highly commended for the breaking down and destroying of the altars, idols, and images, and the Scriptures declare that they, specially in that point, did that which was right before the Lord. . . . And how he will handle, punish, and destroy the people, that so set up, or suffer such altars, images or idols undestroyed, he denounceth by his Prophet Ezekiel on this manner: I myself (saith the Lord) will bring a sword over you, to destroy your high places, I will cast down your altars, and break down your images. . . .

True religion and pleasing of God, standeth not in making, setting up, painting, gilding, clothing, and decking of dumb and dead images, (which be but great puppets and maumets[4] for old fools in dotage,[5] and wicked idolatry, to dally and play with) nor in kissing of them, capping,[6] kneeling, offering to them, incensing of them[7], setting up of candles, hanging up of legs, arms, or whole bodies of ware[8] before them, or praying and asking of them, or of saints, things belonging only to God to give. But all these things be vain, and abominable, and most damnable before God. Wherefore all such do not only bestow their money and their labor in vain, but with their pains and cost, purchase themselves, God's wrath and utter indignation, and everlasting damnation both of body and soul. For ye have heard it evidently proved in these homilies against idolatry, by God's word, the doctors of the church, ecclesiastical histories, reason and experience, that images have been worshipped, and so idolatry committed to them, by infinite multitudes, to the great offence of God's majesty, and danger of infinite souls: and that

---

[4] **maumets:** idols, dolls. [5] **dotage:** senility. [6] **capping:** doffing the cap. [7] **incensing of them:** putting incense on them. [8] **hanging up of legs . . . of ware:** placing gifts of food, etc., before the statues.

A BOOK OF CHRISTIAN PRAYERS

Richard Day, *A Book of Christian Prayers* (London, 1590).

FIGURE 28 (top) *The Maid: Fresh, gallant, and gay: All must with me away.*

FIGURE 29 (bottom) *The Gentleman. Lusty, or sad: Thou must be bad.*

Richard Day's *Book of Christian Prayers* was illustrated with the German painter Hans Holbein's forty-one woodcuts commonly referred to as *The Dance of Death* or the *danse macabre* or *Totentanz* (see Douce). The imagery of the *danse*, which is thought to have "arisen as a homiletic reaction to a peasant custom of dancing in graveyards," (Knowles 85), was to be found everywhere in medieval Europe, including on the walls of Shakespeare's own parish church in Stratford-upon-Avon. The original fifteenth-century poem with accompanying illustrations decorated the walls of the Church of the Holy Innocents in Paris. An English version, translated by John Lydgate, was similarly used with illustrations in St. Paul's Cathedral. In this volume and in the *Book of Common Prayer* (1559), the pictures and verses serve as border illustrations and show, paradoxically, the intense vitality of death and its attendant processes, decay and putrefaction. In many of the pictures, the figure of death is depicted with a musical instrument, just as in a related version, *La Grande Danse Macabre*, there is an orchestra of death (Knowles 83).

The oddly comic scene at the end of act 4, scene 5, with Peter and the musicians originally hired for Juliet's wedding to Paris often bothers modern readers, or seems extraneous. In light of the *danse* tradition, however, these interactions follow an obscure cultural logic that recognized a connection (though not a lock-step causal sequence of events) between the "blind" passion of love at first sight, followed by fatal misfortune, and ultimately the darkness of death. James Black has argued that the scenes depicting the prince with his subjects gathered about him constitute a sort of visual tableau, which becomes progressively tragic, and in the last scene of the play, a pageant of death (Black 250; Knowles 85). From this perspective, the dance of death from the prayer book may serve, in some sense, as a visual analogue to *Romeo and Juliet.*

idolatry can not possibly be separated from images, especially set up in churches and temples, gilded and decked gorgeously: and that therefore our images be in deed very idols, and so all the prohibitions, laws, curses, threats of horrible plagues, as well temporal, as eternal, contained in the holy Scripture, concerning idols, and the makers, maintainers and worshippers of them, appertain also to our images, set up in churches and temples, to the makers, maintainers, and worshippers of them. And all those names of abomination, which God's word in the holy Scripture giveth to the idols of the gentiles, appertain to our images, being idols, like to them, and having the like idolatry committed unto them.

Bibliography

Primary Sources

An Act Concerning Physicians, 1540. In *Statutes of the Realm*, vol. 3, 1509–1541, 793.

Ascham, Roger. *The Schoolmaster: or Plain and Perfect Way of Teaching Children the Latin Tongue.* London, 1570.

Bagot Papers, Folger Shakespeare Library, MSS L.a.67–943.

Bale, John. *The Vocation of John Bale to the Bishopric of Ossory in Ireland His Persecutions in the Same and Final Deliverance.* Rome, 1553.

Bandello, Matteo. *Romeo e Giuletta.* 1554.

Barnfield, Richard. *The Affectionate Shepherd. Containing the Complaint of Daphnis for the Love of Ganymede. Amor Plus Mellis, Quam Fellis Est.* London, 1594.

Bayer, John. *Uranometria.* 1603. n. place.

Belleforest, François. *Histoires Tragiques.* Paris, 1599.

Black, James. "The Visual Artistry of *Romeo and Juliet.*" *Studies in English Literature,* vol. 15, 1975, 245–56.

Brathwaite, Richard. *The English Gentleman.* London, 1633.

Brooke, Arthur. *The Tragical History of Romeus and Juliet.* London, 1562.

Buckminster, Thomas. *A New Almanac and Prognostication.* London, 1571.

Burton, Robert. *The Anatomy of Melancholy.* London, 1621.

———. *The Anatomy of Melancholy.* London, 1632.

Carey, John, ed. *John Donne.* Oxford: Oxford UP, 1990.

Carranza, Jerónimo de. *De la Filosofia de las Armas.* Madrid, 1569.

Caso, Adolph, ed. *Original Text of Masuccio Salernitano, Luigi da Porto, Matteo Bandello and William Shakespeare.* Boston: Dante UP of America, 1992.

Chamberlain, John. *The Chamberlain Letters: A Selection of the Letters of John Chamberlain Concerning Life in England from 1597 to 1626.* Ed. Elizabeth McClure Thompson. London: John Murray, 1965.

Church of England, *Book of Common Prayer* (1559). *Liturgical Services, Liturgies and Occasional Forms of Prayer Set Forth in the Reign of Queen Elizabeth.* Ed. William Keating Clay. Cambridge, 1847.

Clifford, Anne. *The Diary of the Lady Anne Clifford,* with an introductory note by Vita Sackville-West. London: William Heinemann, 1923.

Clinton, Elizabeth Knyvet. *The Countess of Lincoln's Nusery.* Oxford, 1622.

Coryat, Thomas. *Coryat's Crudities Hastily Gobbled Up in Five Months Travels in France, Savoy, Italy, Rhetia Commonly Called Grisons Country, Helvetia alias Switzerland, Some Parts of High Germany, and the Netherlands; Newly Digested in the Hungry Air of Odcombe in the County of Somerset, and Now Dispersed to the Nourishment of the Travelling Members of This Kingdom.* London, 1611.

Cotgrave, Randle. *Dictionary of the French and English Tongues.* London, 1611.

Culpeper, Nicholas. *Pharmacopaeia Londinensis.* London, 1654.

Da Porto, Luigi. *Novella Novamente Ritrouvata d'uno Innamoramento.* Venice, 1535.

Day, Richard. *A Book of Christian Prayers.* London, 1581, 1590.

Di Grassi, Giacomo. *Giacomo di Grassi: His True Art of Defense . . .* London, 1594.

Donne, John. Letter to Sir George More (1601) in *John Donne.* Ed. John Carey. Oxford: Oxford UP, 1990. 86–87.

Eden, Richard, trans. *The Decades of the New World, or West India.* London, 1555.

Ferrand, Jacques. *Erotomania or A Treatise Discoursing of the Essence, Causes, Symptoms, Prognostics, and Cure of Love, or Erotic Melancholy.* Oxford, 1640.

Fleetwood, William. "Report to Lord Burghley" in *Queen Elizabeth and Her Times, A Series of Original Letters Selected from the Unedited Private Correspondence of the Lord Treasurer Burghley, The Earl of Leicester, the Secretaries Walsingham and Smith, and Sir Christopher Hatton.* Ed. Thomas Wright. 2 vols. London, 1838.

Florio, John. *Florio's Second Fruits, to Be Gathered of Twelve Trees, of Divers but Delightsome Tastes to the Tongues of Italians and Englishmen.* London, 1591.

Foxe, John. *Acts and Monuments.* London, 1583.

Franciscus, Andreas. *Itinerarium Britanniae. Two Accounts of Tudor England: A Journey of London in 1497; A Picture of English Life under Queen Mary.* Trans. Cesare V. Malfatti. Barcelona, 1953.

Franco, Giacomo. *Habiti d'huomini et donne Venetiane con la processione della serma Signoria et altri particolari, cioè trionfi feste et cerimonie publiche della città di Venetia.* Venice, 1609.

G. B. A. F. *A Discovery of the Great Subtlety and Wonderful Wisdom of the Italians,*

Whereby They Bear Sway over the Most Part of Christendom, and Cunningly Behave Themselves to Fetch the Quintescence out of the People's Purses . . . London, 1591.

Gibbon, Charles. *A Work Worth the Reading.* London, 1591.

Gouge, William. *Domestical Duties Eight Treatises.* London, 1622.

Great Herbal, The. London, 1529.

Greene, Robert. *The Honorable History of Friar Bacon and Friar Bungay.* London, 1594.

Hakluyt, Richard. *Principal Navigations, Voyages, and Discoveries of the English Nation.* London, 1589.

Hall, Joseph. *Quo Vadis? A Just Censure of Travel as It Is Commonly Undertaken by the Gentlemen of Our Nation.* London, 1617.

Hilder, Thomas. *Conjugal Counsel: or Seasonable Advice, Both to Unmarried, and Married Persons.* London, 1653.

Jewel, John. *The Second Tome of Homilies, of Such Matters as Were Promised and Entitled in the Former Part of Homilies, Set Out by the Authority of the Queen's Majesty, and to Be Read in Every Parish Church Agreeable.* London, 1563.

Joyce, Michael, trans. *Five Dialogues of Plato.* London: J. M. Dent, 1938.

Larkin, James F., and Paul L. Hughes, eds. *Stuart Royal Proclamations. Vol 1: Royal Proclamations of King James I, 1603–1625.* Oxford: Clarendon, 1973.

Lee, Maurice, ed. *Dudley Carleton to John Chamberlain 1603–1624: Jacobean Letters.* New Brunswick, NJ: Rutgers UP, 1972.

McKerrow, Ronald B., ed. *The Works of Thomas Nashe.* 5 vols. London, 1904–10.

Marlowe, Christopher. *The Tragical History of Dr. Faustus.* London, 1604.

Matthey, Cyril G. R. *The Works of George Silver Comprising the "Paradoxes of Defence" [Printed in 1599 and now reprinted] and "Brief Instructions Upon My Pradoxes [sic] of Defence" [printed for the first time from the MS. in the British Museum].* London, 1898.

Moryson, Fynes. *His Ten Years Travel through the Twelve Dominions of Germany, Bohemia, Switzerland, Netherlands, Denmark, Poland, Italy, Turkey, France, England, Scotland, and Ireland.* London, 1611.

Nashe, Thomas. *The Choice of Valentines.* Ed. John Farmer. London, 1899.

———. The *Unfortunate Traveler, or the Life of Jack Wilton.* London, 1594.

Paddy, Sir William et al. *Pharmacopoeia Londinensis of 1618,* reproduced in facsimile, with a historical introduction by George Urdang. Madison: State Historical Society of Wisconsin, 1944.

Painter, William. *The Second Tome of the Palace of Pleasure, Containing Store of Goodly Histories, Tragical Matters, and Other Moral Argument, Very Requisite for Delight and Profit.* London, 1567.

Petrarch, Francesco. *Petrarch: The Canzoniere or Rerum Vulgarium Fragmenta.* Ed. and trans. Mark Musa. Bloomington: Indiana UP, 1996.

Plato. *Five Dialogues of Plato.* Trans. Michael Joyce. London: J. M. Dent, 1938.

Platt, Hugh. *Delights for Ladies, to Adorn Their Persons, Tables, Closets, and Distillatories with Beauties, Banquets, Perfumes & Waters. Read, Practice and*

Censure, with an introduction by G. E. Fussell and Kathleen Rosemary Fussell. London, 1609; repr., 1948.

———. *The Jewel House of Art and Nature. Containing Divers Rare and Profitable Inventions, Together with Sundry New Experiments in the Art of Husbandry, Distillation and Moulding.* London, 1594.

Purchas, Samuel. *Purchas His Pilgramage. Or Relations of the World and the Religions Observed in All Ages and Places Discovered, from the Creation unto the Present.* London, 1613.

Reformatio Legum Ecclesiasticarum, ex authoritate primum Regis Henrici. 8. inchoata: Deinde per Regem Edouardum 6. prouecta, adauctaq; in hunc modum, atq; nunc ad pleniorem ipsarum reformationem in lucem ædita. London, 1571.

Royal College of Physicians of London. *Pharmacopoeia Londinensis of 1618,* reproduced in facsimile, with a historical introduction by George Urdang. Madison: State Historical Society of Wisconsin, 1944.

Rye, William Benchley, ed. *England as Seen by Foreigners in the Days of Elizabeth and James I.* New York: Benjamin Blom, 1967.

St. Bonaventure. *The Life of the Most Holy Father St. Francis . . . Now Lately Translated into Our English Tongue.* Douai, 1635.

Saviolo, Vincentio. *Vincentio Saviolo His Practice. In Two Books. The First Entreating the Use of the Rapier and the Dagger. The Second, of Honor and Honorable Quarrels.* London, 1595.

Segar, William. *The Book of Honor and Arms (1590) and Honor Civil and Military (1602).* Delmar, NY: Scholars Facsimiles and Reprints, 1975.

Shakespeare, William. *Shakespears Sonnets.* London, 1609.

Sidney, Philip. *Astrophil and Stella: Wherein the Excellence of Sweet Poesie Is Concluded.* London, 1591.

Silver, George. *Paradoxes of Defense. Wherein Is Proved the True Grounds of Fight to Be in the Short Ancient Weapons, and That the Short Sword Hath Advantage over the Long Sword or Long Rapier.* London, 1599.

Smith, Henry. *A Preparative to Marriage. The Sum Whereof Was Spoken at a Contract, and Enlarged After.* London, 1591.

Speed, John. *A Prospect of the Most Famous Parts of the World.* London, 1676.

Spenser, Edmund. *Amoretti and Epithalamion.* London, 1595.

Statutes of the Realm. 11 vols. London, 1810–28.

Stockwood, John. *A Bartholomew Fairing for Parents, to Bestow upon Their Sons and Daughters, and for One Friend to Give unto Another; Showing That Children Are Not to Marry without the Consent of Their Parents, in Whose Power and Choice It Lieth to Provide Wives and Husbands for Their Sons and Daughters.* London, 1589.

Stuart Royal Proclamations. Vol. 1: Royal Proclamations of King James I, 1603–1625. Ed. James F. Larkin and Paul L. Hughes. Oxford: Clarendon, 1973.

Swinburne, Henry. *A Treatise of Spousals, or Matrimonial Contracts: Wherein All the Questions Relating to That Subject Are Ingeniously Debated and Resolved. By the Late Famous and Learned Mr. Henry Swinburne, Author of the Treatise of Wills and Testaments.* London, 1686.

Thomas, William. *The History of Italy. A Book Exceedingly Profitable to Be Read Because It Entreateth of the State of Many and Divers Commonweals . . .* London, 1549.

Tudor Royal Proclamations. Ed. James F. Larkin and Paul L. Hughes. 3 vols. New Haven: Yale UP, 1964–69.

Whetstone, George. *An Heptameron of Civil Discourses.* London, 1598.

Secondary Sources

Akrigg, G. P. V. *Jacobean Pageant: or the Court of King James I.* Cambridge: Harvard UP, 1962.

——. *Shakespeare and the Earl of Southampton.* Cambridge: Harvard UP, 1968.

Allen, Don Cameron. *The Star-Crossed Renaissance: The Quarrel about Astrology and Its Influence in England.* New York: Octagon Books, 1973.

Altman, Joel B. *The Tudor Play of Mind: Rhetorical Inquiry and the Development of Elizabethan Drama.* Berkeley: U of California P, 1978.

Andrews, John F., ed. *Romeo and Juliet: Critical Essays.* New York: Garland, 1993.

Anglo, Sydney. *The Martial Arts of Renaissance Europe.* New Haven: Yale UP, 2000.

Appelbaum, Robert. "'Standing to the Wall': The Pressures of Masculinity in Romeo and Juliet." *Shakespeare Quarterly* 48 (1997): 251–72.

Archer, Ian W. *The Pursuit of Stability: Social Relations in Elizabethan London.* Cambridge: Cambridge UP, 1991.

——. "Material Londoners." *Material London ca. 1600.* Ed. Lena Cowen Orlin. Philadelphia: U of Pennsylvania P, 2000. 147–92.

Ariès, Philippe. *The Hour of Our Death.* Trans. Helen Weaver. London: Allen Lane, 1981.

Aylward, J. D. *The English Master of Arms from the Twelfth to the Twentieth Century.* London: Routledge and Kegan Paul, 1956.

Bakhtin, Mikhail. *Rabelais and His World.* Trans. Helene Iswolsky. Bloomington: Indiana UP, 1984.

Bald, R. C. *John Donne: A Life.* Oxford: Clarendon, 1970.

Baskerville, Geoffrey. *English Monks and the Suppression of the Monasteries.* London: Jonathan Cape, 1937.

Belsey, Catherine. "The Name of the Rose in Romeo and Juliet." *Romeo and Juliet: Contemporary Critical Essays.* Ed. R. S. White. New York: Palgrave, 2001. 47–67.

Bergeron, David Moore. *King James and Letters of Homoerotic Desire.* Iowa City: U of Iowa P, 1999.

Berlin, Michael. "Reordering Rituals: Ceremony and the Parish, 1520–1640." *Londinopolis: Essays in the Cultural and Social History of Early Modern London.*

Ed. Paul Griffiths and Mark S. R. Jenner. Manchester: Manchester UP, 2000. 47–60.

Berry, Philippa. "Between Idolatry and Astrology: Modes of Temporal Repetition in Romeo and Juliet." *The Feminist Companion to Shakespeare.* Ed. Dympna Callaghan. Oxford: Blackwell, 2000. 358–72.

——. *Shakespeare's Feminine Endings: Disfiguring Death in the Tragedies.* New York: Routledge, 1999.

Black, James. "The Visual Artistry of Romeo and Juliet." *Studies in English Literature* 15 (1975):245–56.

Bly, Mary. *Queer Virgins and Virgin Queans on the Early Modern Stage.* Oxford: Oxford UP, 2000.

Boose, Lynda. "The Father of the Bride in Shakespeare." *PMLA: Publications of the Modern Language Association of America* 97 (1982): 325–47.

Booth, Stephen, ed. *Shakespeare's Sonnets.* New Haven: Yale UP, 1977.

Borris, Kenneth, and George Klawitter, eds. *The Affectionate Shepherd: Celebrating Richard Barnfield.* Selinsgrove, PA: Susquehanna UP, 2001.

Bowden, Henry Sebastian. *The Religion of Shakespeare.* London: Burns and Oates, 1899.

Bowen, Catherine Drinker. *The Lion and the Throne.* Boston: Little, Brown, 1957.

Bray, Alan. "Homosexuality and the Signs of Male Friendship in Elizabethan England." *Queering the Renaissance.* Ed. Jonathan Goldberg. Durham: Duke UP, 1994.

——. *Homosexuality in Reinassance England.* New York: Columbia UP, 1995.

Bryant, James C. "The Problematic Friar in Romeo and Juliet." *Romeo and Juliet: Critical Essays.* Ed. John F. Andrews. New York: Garland, 1993. 321–36.

Bullough, Geoffrey, ed. *Narrative and Dramatic Sources of Shakespeare.* New York: Columbia UP, 1957.

Calderwood, James L. *Shakespeare and the Denial of Death.* Amherst: U of Massachusetts P, 1987.

Callaghan, Dympna, ed. *The Feminist Companion to Shakespeare.* Oxford: Blackwell, 2000.

——. "The Ideology of Romantic Love: The Case of Romeo and Juliet." *Romeo and Juliet: Contemporary Critical Essays.* Ed. R. S. White. New York: Palgrave, 2001. 85–115.

——. *Shakespeare without Women.* New York: Routledge, 2000.

——. *Woman and Gender in Renaissance Tragedy.* Brighton: Harvester, 1989.

Callaghan, Dympna, Lorraine Helms, and Jyotsna Singh. *The Weyward Sisters: Shakespeare and Feminist Politics.* Oxford: Blackwell, 1994.

Capp, Bernard. *Astrology and the Popular Press, English Almanacs 1599–1800.* Boston: Faber and Faber, 1979.

Carey, John. *John Donne: Life, Mind, and Art.* London: Faber and Faber, 1990.

Charney, Maurice. *Shakespeare on Love and Lust.* New York: Columbia UP, 2000.

Chedgzoy, Kate. *Shakespeare's Queer Children: Sexual Politics and Contemporary Culture*. Manchester: Manchester UP, 1995.

Clifford, David J. H. *Lady Anne Clifford: High Sheriffess*. Wolfeboro Falls, NH: Alan Sutton, 1990.

Cockburn, J. S. "The Nature and Incidence of Crime in England 1559–1625." *Crime in England 1550–1800*. Ed. J. S. Cockburn. London: Methuen, 1977. 49–71.

Cokayne, George Edward. *The Complete Peerage of England, Scotland, Ireland, Great Britain and the United Kingdom: Extant, Extinct, or Dormant*. 13 vols. London: St. Catherine's Press, 1910–59.

Cook, Ann Jenalie. *Making a Match: Courtship in Shakespeare and His Society*. Princeton: Princeton UP, 1991.

Cope, Ester S. *Handmaid of the Holy Spirit: Dame Eleanor Davies, Never Soe Mad a Ladie*. Ann Arbor: U of Michigan P, 1992.

Cressy, David. *Birth, Marriage, and Death: Ritual, Religion, and the Life-Cycle in Tudor and Stuart England*. Oxford: Oxford UP, 1999.

——. *Bonfires and Bells: National Memory and the Protestant Calendar in Elizabethan and Stuart England*. London: Weidenfeld and Nicolson, 1989.

Davies, Kathleen M. "The Sacred Condition of Equality—How Original Were Puritan Doctrines of Marriage?" *Social History* 5 (1977): 563–80.

Dean, David M. *Law-Making and Society in Late Elizabethan England: The Parliament of England. 1584–1601*. Cambridge: Cambridge UP, 1996.

De Rougemont, Denis. *[Amour et l'occident], Passion and Society*. London: Faber and Faber, 1940.

Dickey, Franklin M. "To Love Extreamely, Procureth Eyther Death or Danger." *Romeo and Juliet: Critical Essays*. Ed. John F. Andrews. New York: Garland, 1993. 269–83.

DiGangi, Mario. *The Homoerotics of Early Modern Drama*. Cambridge: Cambridge UP, 1997.

Dodd, Charles. *Dodd's church history of England from the commencement of the sixteenth century to the revolution in 1688. With notes additions, and a continuation by the Rev. M. A. Tierney*. London: C. Dolman, 1839–1843.

Dolan, Frances E. *Dangerous Familiars: Representations of Domestic Crime in England 1550–1700*. Ithaca: Cornell UP, 1994.

——. *Whores of Babylon: Catholicism, Gender and Seventeenth Century Print Culture*. Ithaca: Cornell UP, 1999.

Douce, Francis. *Holbein's Dance of Death*. London: G. Bell & Sons, 1902.

Dubrow, Heather. *Echoes of Desire: English Petrarchism and Its Counter Discourses*. Ithaca: Cornell UP, 1995.

Duffy, Eamon. *The Stripping of the Altars: Traditional Religion in England 1400–1580*. New Haven: Yale UP, 1992.

Duncan-Jones, Katherine, ed. *The Arden Shakespeare: Shakespeare's Sonnets*. London: Thomas Nelson, 1997.

Eade, J. C. *The Forgotten Sky: A Guide to Astrology in English Literature.* Oxford: Clarendon, 1984.

Edelman, Charles. *Brawl Ridiculous: Swordfighting in Shakespeare's Plays.* New York: Manchester UP, 1992.

Enright, J. D., ed. *The Oxford Book of Death.* Oxford: Oxford UP, 1983.

Erickson, Amy Louise. *Women and Property in Early Modern England.* New York: Routledge, 1993.

Evans, G. Blakemore, ed. *Romeo and Juliet.* Cambridge: Cambridge UP, 1984.

Farley-Hills, David. "The Bad Quarto of Romeo and Juliet." *Shakespeare Survey* 49 (1996): 27–44.

Fineman, Joel. *Shakespeare's Perjured Eye: The Invention of Poetic Subjectivity in the Sonnets.* Berkeley: U of California P, 1986.

Fitter, Chris. "Romeo and Juliet: Dearth and the London Riots." *English Literary Review* 30 (2000): 154–83.

Forster, Leonard. *The Icy Fire: Five Studies in European Petrarchism.* New York: Cambridge UP, 1969.

Gibbons, Brian, ed. *The Arden Shakespeare: Romeo and Juliet.* New York: Methuen, 1980.

Gittings, Clare. *Death, Burial and the Individual in Early Modern England.* London: Croom Helm, 1984.

Goldberg, Jonathan. "Romeo and Juliet's Open R's." *Queering the Renaissance.* Ed. Jonathan Goldberg. Durham, NC: Duke UP, 1994. 218–35.

——. "'What? In a Name Names That Which We Call a Rose': The Desired Texts of Romeo and Juliet." *Crisis in Editing: Texts of the English Renaissance.* Ed. Randall McLeod. New York: AMS Press, 1994. 173–202.

Gowing, Laura. *Domestic Dangers: Women, Words, and Sex in Early Modern London.* Oxford: Clarendon, 1998.

——. "'The Freedom of the Streets': Women and Social Space 1560–1640." *Londinopolis: Essays in the Cultural and Social History of Early Modern London.* Ed. Paul Griffiths and Mark S. R. Jenner. Manchester: Manchester UP, 2000. 130–51.

Graves, Michael A. R. *Thomas Norton: The Parliament Man.* Oxford: Blackwell, 1994.

Greene, Roland. *Post-Petrarchism: Origins and Innovations of the Western Lyric Sequence.* Princeton: Princeton UP, 1991.

Greg, W. W. *Introduction to William Shakespeare, Romeo and Juliet, Second Quarto, 1599.* Shakespeare Quarto Facsimiles, No. 6. London: The Shakespeare Association and Sidgwick and Jackson. 1949.

Grier, James. *A History of Pharmacy.* London: Pharmaceutical Press, 1937.

Griffiths, Paul, and Mark S. R. Jenner, eds. *Londinopolis: Essays in the Cultural and Social History of Early Modern London.* Manchester: Manchester UP, 2000.

Hadfield, Andrew. *Amazons, Savages, and Machiavels: Travel and Colonial Writing in English, 1550–1830.* Oxford: Oxford UP, 2001.

———. *Literature, Travel, and Colonial Writing in the English Renaissance, 1545–1625.* Oxford: Clarendon, 1998.

Hager, Alan, ed. *Understanding Romeo and Juliet.* Westport, CT: Greenwood, 1999.

Halio, Jay L. "Handy-Dandy: Q1/Q2 Romeo and Juliet." *Shakespeare's Romeo and Juliet: Texts, Contexts, and Interpretations.* Ed. Jay L. Halio. Newark: U of Delaware P, 1995. 123–50.

———, ed. *Shakespeare's Romeo and Juliet: Texts, Contexts, and Interpretations.* Newark: U of Delaware P, 1995.

Hammond, Paul. *Love Between Men in English Literature.* New York: St. Martin's, 1996.

Henderson, Diana. *Passion Made Public: Elizabethan Lyric, Gender, and Performance.* Urbana and Chicago: U of Illinois P, 1995.

Homer, Joan Ozark. "'Draw If You Be Men': Saviolo's Significance for Romeo and Juliet." *Shakespeare Quarterly* 45 (1994): 163–89.

Honigmann, E. A. J. *Shakespeare: The 'Lost Years.'* Manchester: Manchester UP, 1998.

Hopkins, Lisa. *The Shakespearean Marriage: Merry Wives and Heavy Husbands.* New York: Macmillan, 1998.

Hoppe, H. R. *The Bad Quarto of Romeo and Juliet.* Ithaca: Cornell UP, 1948.

Houlbrooke, Ralph, ed. *Death, Ritual and Bereavement.* London: Routledge, 1989.

Hughes, Philip. *The Reformation in England.* London: Hollis and Carter, 1953.

Hurstfield, Joel. *The Queen's Wards: Wardship and Marriage under Elizabeth I.* New York: Longmans, 1958.

Ingram, Martin. *Church Courts, Sex, and Marriage in England, 1570–1640.* Cambridge: Cambridge UP, 1987; repr. 1990.

Irace, Kathleen. *Reforming the "Bad" Quartos: Performance and Provenance of Six Shakespearean First Editions.* Newark: U of Delaware P, 1994.

James, Max H. *"Our House Is Hell": Shakespeare's Troubled Families.* New York: Greenwood, 1989.

Jones, Ann Rosalind. *The Currency of Eros: Women's Love Lyric in Europe, 1540–1620.* Bloomington: Indiana UP, 1990.

Kahn, Coppélia. *Man's Estate: Masculine Identity and Shakespeare.* Berkeley: U of California P, 1981.

Kennedy, William J. *Authorizing Petrarch.* Ithaca: Cornell UP, 1994.

Kerrigan, John, ed. *The Sonnets and A Lover's Complaint by William Shakespeare.* Harmondsworth: Penguin, 1986.

Kinney, Arthur F., and David W. Swain, eds. *Tudor England: An Encyclopedia.* New York: Garland, 2001.

Klawitter, George. *Richard Barnfield: The Complete Poems.* Selinsgrove, PA: Susquehanna UP, 1990.

Knowles, Ronald. "Carnival and Death in Romeo and Juliet." *Shakespeare Survey* 49 (1996): 69–96.

Lacan, Jacques. *Feminine Sexuality: Jacques Lacan and the École Freudienne.* New York: Pantheon, 1982.

Lake, Peter. "Religious Identities in Shakespeare's England." *A Companion to Shakespeare.* Ed. David Scott Kastan. Oxford: Blackwell, 1999.

Laroque, François. *Shakespeare's Festive World.* Trans. Janet Lloyd. Cambridge: Cambridge UP, 1991.

Lee, Maurice, ed. *Dudley Carleton to John Chamberlain 1603–1624: Jacobean Letters.* New Brunswick, NJ: 1972.

Leinwand, Theodore. "'I Believe We Must Leave the Killing Out': Deference and Accommodation in A Midsummer Night's Dream." *Renaissance Papers* (1986): 11–30.

Levenson, Jill. "'Alla Stoccado Carries It Away': Codes of Violence in Romeo and Juliet." *Shakespeare's Romeo and Juliet: Texts, Contexts, and Interpretations.* Ed. Jay L. Halio. Newark: U of Delaware P, 1995. 83–96.

Liebler, Naomi Conn. *Shakespeare's Festive Tragedy.* London: Routledge, 1995.

Limon, Jerzy. "Rehabilitating Tybalt: A New Interpretation of the Duel Scene in Romeo and Juliet." *Shakespeare's Romeo and Juliet: Texts, Contexts, and Interpretations.* Ed. Jay L. Halio. Newark: U of Delaware P, 1995. 97–106.

Llewellyn, Nigel. *The Art of Death: Visual Culture in the English Death Ritual.* London: Reaktion Books in Association with the Victoria and Albert Museum, 1991.

Locatelli, Angela. "The Fictional World of Romeo and Juliet: Cultural Connotations of an Italian Setting." *Shakespeare's Italy: Functions of Italian Locations in Renaissance Drama.* Ed. Michele Marrapodi et al. New York: Manchester UP, 1997.

Lombardo, Agostino. "The Veneto, Metatheatre, and Shakespeare." *Shakespeare's Italy: Functions of Italian Locations in Renaissance Drama.* Ed. Michele Marrapodi et al. New York: Manchester UP, 1997.

MacDonald, Michael, with Terence R. Murphy. *Sleepless Souls: Suicide in Early Modern England.* Oxford: Oxford UP, 1990.

Maguire, Laurie. *Shakespearean Suspect Texts: The Bad Quartos and Their Contexts.* Cambridge: Cambridge UP, 1996.

Marrapodi, Michele, et al., eds. *Shakespeare's Italy: Functions of Italian Locations in Renaissance Drama.* New York: Manchester UP, 1997.

Masten, Jeffrey. *Textual Intercourse: Collaboration, Authorship, and Sexualities in Renaissance Drama.* Cambridge: Cambridge UP, 1997.

Meader, William G. *Courtship in Shakespeare: Its Relation to the Tradition of Courtly Love.* New York: King's Crown, 1954.

Mendelson, Sara, and Patricia Crawford, eds. *Women in Early Modern England.* Oxford: Oxford UP, 1998.

Milward, Peter. *Shakespeare's Religious Background.* Bloomington: Indiana UP, 1973.

Minta, Stephen. *Petrarch and Petrarchism: The English and French Traditions.* New York: Barnes and Noble, 1980.

Moison, Thomas. "'O Any Thing, of Nothing First Create!': Gender and Patriarchy and *The Tragedy of Romeo and Juliet.*" In *Another Country: Feminist Perspectives on Renaissance Drama.* Ed. Dorathea Kehler and Susan Baker. Metuchen, NJ: Scarecrow, 1991. 113–36.

Morton, E. D. *Martini A–Z of Fencing.* London: Macdonald Queen Anne, 1988.

Musa, Mark, ed. and trans. *Petrarch: The Canzoniere or Rerum Vulgarium Fragmenta.* Bloomington: Indiana UP, 1996.

Neill, Michael. *Issues of Death: Mortality and Identity in English Renaissance Tragedy.* Oxford: Clarendon, 1998.

Norton Shakespeare, The. Ed. Stephen Greenblatt, Walter Cohen, Jean E. Howard, and Katharine Eisaman Maus. New York: Norton, 1997.

Novy, Marianne V. *Love's Argument: Gender Relations in Shakespeare.* Chapel Hill: U of North Carolina P, 1984.

Orlin, Lena Cowen. "Boundary Disputes in Early Modern London." *Material London ca. 1600.* Ed. Lena Cowen Orlin. Philadelphia: U of Pennsylvania P, 2000. 344–76.

Parker, Patricia. *Shakespeare from the Margins: Language, Culture, Context.* Chicago: U of Chicago P, 1996.

Paster, Gail Kern. *The Body Embarrassed: Drama and the Disciplines of Shame in Early Modern England.* Ithaca: Cornell UP, 1993.

Praz, Mario. *The Flaming Heart: Essays on Crashaw, Machiavelli, and Other Studies in the Relations between Italian and English Literature from Chaucer to T. S. Eliot.* New York: Doubleday, 1958.

Porter, Joseph. *Shakespeare's Mercutio: His History and Drama.* Chapel Hill: U of North Carolina P, 1988.

Porter, Roy. "The Prophetic Body: Lady Eleanor Davies and the Meanings of Madness." *Women's Writing* 1 (1994): 51–63.

Prunster, Nicole. *Romeo and Juliet before Shakespeare: Early Stories of Star-Crossed Love.* Toronto: Centre of Reformation & Renaissance Studies, 2000.

Radel, Nicholas F. "Queer Romeo and Juliet: Teaching Early Modern 'Sexuality' in Shakespeare's 'Heterosexual' Tragedy." *Approaches to Teaching Romeo and Juliet.* Ed. Maurice Hunt. New York: Modern Language Association of America, 2000. 991–97.

Roche, Thomas P. *Petrarch and the English Sonnet Sequences.* New York: AMS, 1989.

Rozett, Martha Tuck. "The Comic Structures of Tragic Endings: The Suicide Scenes in *Romeo and Juliet* and *Antony and Cleopatra.*" *Shakespeare Quarterly* 36.2 (1985): 152–64.

Salgado, Gamini. *The Elizabethan Underworld.* London: Wren's Park, 1999.

Schoenbaum, Samuel. *Shakespeare: The Globe and the World.* Washington, D.C.: Folger Shakespeare Library/Oxford UP, 1979.

——. *William Shakespeare: A Documentary Life.* New York: Oxford UP, 1975.

Sedgwick, Eve Kosofsky. "Homophobia, Misogyny, and Capital: The Example of Our Mutual Friend." *Raritan* 2 (1983): 126–51.

Shannon, Laurie. *Sovereign Amity: Figures of Friendship in Shakespearean Contexts.* Chicago: U of Chicago P, 2002.

Sharpe, J. A. *Crime in Early Modern England, 1550–1750.* 2e. New York: Longman, 1984.

Shuger, Debora Kuller. *Habits of Thought in the English Renaissance: Religion, Politics, and the Dominant Culture.* Berkeley: U of California P, 1990.

Sim, Alison. *Food and Feast in Tudor England.* New York: St. Martin's, 1997.

Sinfield, Alan. *Cultural Politics — Queer Reading.* Philadelphia: U of Pennsylvania P, 1994.

Smith, Bruce R. *Homosexual Desire in Shakespeare's England: A Cultural Poetics.* Chicago: U of Chicago P, 1991.

———. *Shakespeare and Masculinity.* Oxford: Oxford UP, 2000.

Soens, Adolph L. "Tybalt's Spanish Fencing in Romeo and Juliet." *Shakespeare Quarterly* 20 (1969): 121–27.

Spence, Richard T. *Lady Anne Clifford: Countess of Pembroke, Dorset and Montgomery (1590–1676).* Stroud: Sutton Publishing, 1997.

Spencer, Theodore. *Death and Elizabethan Tragedy.* Cambridge, MA: Harvard UP, 1936; repr. New York: Pageant Books, 1960.

Stewart, Alan. *Close Readers: Humanism and Sodomy in Early Modern England.* Princeton: Princeton UP, 1997.

Stilling, Roger. *Love and Death in Renaissance Tragedy.* Baton Rouge: U of Louisiana P, 1976.

Stone, Lawrence. *The Crisis of the Aristocracy, 1558–1641.* Oxford: Clarendon, 1965.

———. *The Family, Sex, and Marriage in England, 1500–1800.* New York: Harper, 1977.

———. *The Past and the Present Revisited.* London: Routledge, 1987.

Summers, Claude J. Foreword. *The Affectionate Shepherd: Celebrating Richard Barnfield.* Ed. Kenneth Borris and George Klawitter. Selinsgrove, PA: Susquehanna UP, 2001. 9.

Tester, S. J. *A History of Western Astrology.* New York: Ballantine Books, 1987.

Traister, Barbara Howard. *The Notorious Astrological Physician of London: Works and Days of Simon Forman.* Chicago: U of Chicago P, 2001.

Urkowitz, Steven. *Shakespeare's Revision of King Lear.* Princeton: Princeton UP, 1980.

Vickers, Nancy. "Diana Described: Scattered Woman and Scattered Rhyme." *Writing and Sexual Difference.* Ed. Elizabeth Abel. Chicago: U of Chicago P, 1982.

Wall, Wendy. *The Imprint of Gender: Authorship and Publication in the English Renaissance.* Ithaca: Cornell UP, 1993.

Waller, Gary. *English Poetry of the Sixteenth Century.* New York: Longman, 1986.

Warburton, Charles. *Chief Justice Coke: His Family and Descendants at Holkham.* New York: Scribner, 1929.

Watts, Cedric, ed. *An Excellent Conceited Tragedie of Romeo and Juliet.* New York: Prentice Hall, 1995.

Werstine, Paul. "A Century of 'Bad' Shakespeare Quartos." *Shakespeare Quarterly* 50 (1999): 310–33.

———. "Narratives about Printed Shakespearean Texts: 'Foul Papers' and 'Bad Quartos.'" *Shakespeare Quarterly* 41 (1990): 65–86.

White, R. S., ed. *Romeo and Juliet: Contemporary Critical Essays.* New York: Palgrave, 2001.

Wiesner, Merry E. *Women and Gender in Early Modern Europe.* Cambridge: Cambridge UP, 1993.

Williamson, George C. *Lady Anne Clifford, Countess of Dorset, Pembroke and Montgomery, 1590–1676: Her Life, Letters and Work.* Kendal: Titus Wilson and Son, 1922.

Wilson, Richard. "Shakespeare and the Jesuits." *Times Literary Supplement* 19 December 1997: 11–13.

Worrall, Andrew. "Biographical Introduction: Barnfield's Feast of 'All Varietie.'" *The Affectionate Shepherd: Celebrating Richard Barnfield.* Ed. Kenneth Borris and George Klawitter. Selinsgrove, PA: Susquehanna UP, 2001, 25–38.

Wrottesley, George. *A History of the Family of Bagot of Bagots Bromely and Blithfield, Co. Stafford.* London: William Salt Society, Vol. 11, new series, 1908.

Wymer, Rowland. *Suicide and Despair in Jacobean Tragedy.* New York: St. Martin's, 1986.

Youings, Joyce. "Dissolution of the Monasteries." *Historical Dictionary of Tudor England, 1485–1603.* Ed. Ronald H. Fritze, Geoffrey Elton, and Walter Sutton. New York: Greenwood, 1991.

Acknowledgments

INTRODUCTION

Figure 1. Frontispiece, *Romeo and Juliet* (1597). Reprinted by permission of the Folger Shakespeare Library.

Figure 2. Frontispiece, *Romeo and Juliet* (1599). Reprinted by permission of the Folger Shakespeare Library.

Romeo and Juliet from *The Complete Works of Shakespeare,* 4e. Ed. David Bevington. Copyright © 1997 by Addison-Wesley Educational Publishers, Inc. Reprinted by permission of Pearson Education, Inc.

CHAPTER 1

Figure 3. Frontispiece from Luigi da Porto, *A Newly Discovered Love Story* (1535). Reprinted by permission of the Folger Shakespeare Library.

Figure 4. The City of Verona, from John Speed, *A Prospect of the Most Famous Parts of the World* (1676).

Thomas Nashe, *The Unfortunate Traveler* (1594), from *The Works of Thomas Nashe,* Vol. 2, ed. Ronald B. McKerrow (Oxford: Basil Blackwell, 1958), 281-82; 285-86; 298, 301. Reprinted by permission of Blackwell Publishing.

CHAPTER 2

Figure 5. Two Men Embracing, from Richard Brathwaite, *The English Gentleman* (1633). Reprinted by permission of the Folger Shakespeare Library.

Richard Barnfield, *The Affectionate Shepherd,* from *Richard Barnfield: The Complete Poems,* ed. George Klawitter (Selinsgrove, PA: Susquehanna UP, 1990). Reprinted by permission of Susquehanna University Press.

Figure 6. Medlars, or Open Arses, from *The Great Herbal* (1529). Reprinted by permission of the Folger Shakespeare Library.

Figure 7. Two Men Fencing, from Vincentio Saviolo, *His Practice* (1595). Reprinted by permission of the Folger Shakespeare Library.

Figure 8. Renaissance Weaponry. Photograph by Milan Petricevic. Reprinted by permission of Milan Petricevic.

Figures 9. Posed Swordsman, from George Silver, *Paradoxes of Defense* (1599). Reprinted by permission of the Folger Shakespeare Library.

CHAPTER 3

John Donne, Letter to Sir George More. *John Donne,* ed. John Carey (Oxford: Oxford UP, 1990) 86-87. Reprinted by permission of Oxford University Press.

Francesco Petrarch, *Canzioniere* 3, 11, 12, 13, 17, 169. From *Petrarch: Canzoniere,* ed. Mark Musa (Bloomington: Indiana UP, 1996). Reprinted by permission of Indiana University Press.

Figure 10. Grotesque Parody of Female Beauty, from Charles Sorel, *The Extravagant Shepherd* (1654). Reprinted by permission of the Folger Shakespeare Library.

CHAPTER 4

The Bagot letters appear courtesy of the Folger Shakespeare Library.

Figure 11. Letter of Jane Skipwith to Lewes Bagot, 1610. Reprinted by permission of the Folger Shakespeare Library.

Figure 12. The Nurse, from Richard Day, *A Book of Christian Prayers* (1590). Reprinted by permission of the Folger Shakespeare Library.

Figure 13. The Infant, from Richard Day, *A Book of Christian Prayers* (1590). Reprinted by permission of the Folger Shakespeare Library.

Figure 14. Lady Anne Clifford at Age Thirty. Reprinted courtesy of Skipton Castle, www.skiptoncastle.co.uk.

Figure 15. Sir Richard Sackville, by William Larkin. Reprinted by permission of English Heritage Photographic Library.

Figure 16. Lady Margaret Sackville at Age Four, by Paul Van Somer. Reprinted by permission of a private collection.

Figure 17. Preparing a Feast, by Jan Sadeler. Reprinted by permission of the Folger Shakespeare Library.

Figure 18. Costumes of Venetian Men and Women (*Habiti d'huomeni et donne Venetia*), by Giacomo Franco (1609). Reprinted by permission of the Folger Shakespeare Library.

CHAPTER 5

Figure 19. St. Francis Enraptured, from St. Bonaventure, *The Life of the Most Holy Father St. Francis* (1635). Reprinted by permission of the Folger Shakespeare Library.

CHAPTER 6

Figure 20. The Bones of the Dead Shall Appear above the Sepulchers, from Richard Day, *A Book of Christian Prayers* (1590). Reprinted by permission of the Folger Shakespeare Library.

Figure 21. An Apothecary, from Ambrose Paré, *Works* (1634). Reprinted by permission of the Folger Shakespeare Library.

Figure 22. Canis Major, from John Bayer, *Uranometria* (1603). Reprinted by permission of the Folger Shakespeare Library.

Figure 23. Prognostications, from Thomas Buckminster, *A New Almanac* (1571). Reprinted by permission of the Folger Shakespeare Library.

Figure 24. Table for July, from Thomas Buckminster, *A New Almanac* (1571). Reprinted by permission of the Folger Shakespeare Library.

Figure 25. Table for August, from Thomas Buckminster, *A New Almanac* (1571). Reprinted by permission of the Folger Shakespeare Library.

Figure 26. Zodiacal Man, from Thomas Buckminster, *A New Almanac* (1571). Reprinted by permission of the Folger Shakespeare Library.

Figure 27. Everyone Living Shall Die Presently, from Richard Day, *A Book of Christian Prayers* (1590). Reprinted by permission of the Folger Shakespeare Library.

Figure 28. The Maid, from Richard Day, *A Book of Christian Prayers* (1590). Reprinted by permission of the Folger Shakespeare Library.

Figure 29. The Gentleman, from Richard Day, *A Book of Christian Prayers* (1590). Reprinted by permission of the Folger Shakespeare Library.

Index